Richard Hamilton

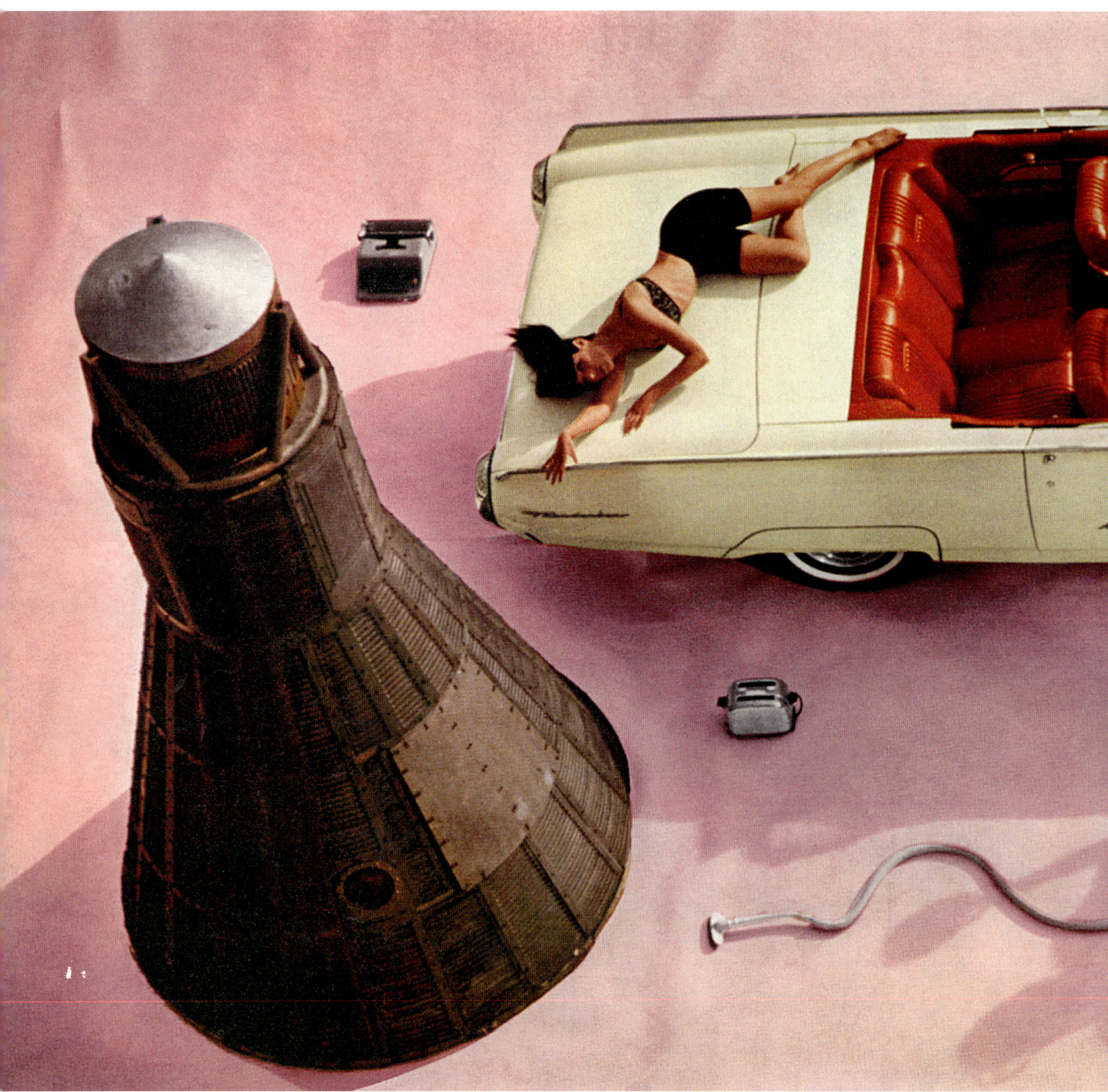

Self-portrait (cover for *Living Arts 2*) 1963 (photograph by Robert Freeman)

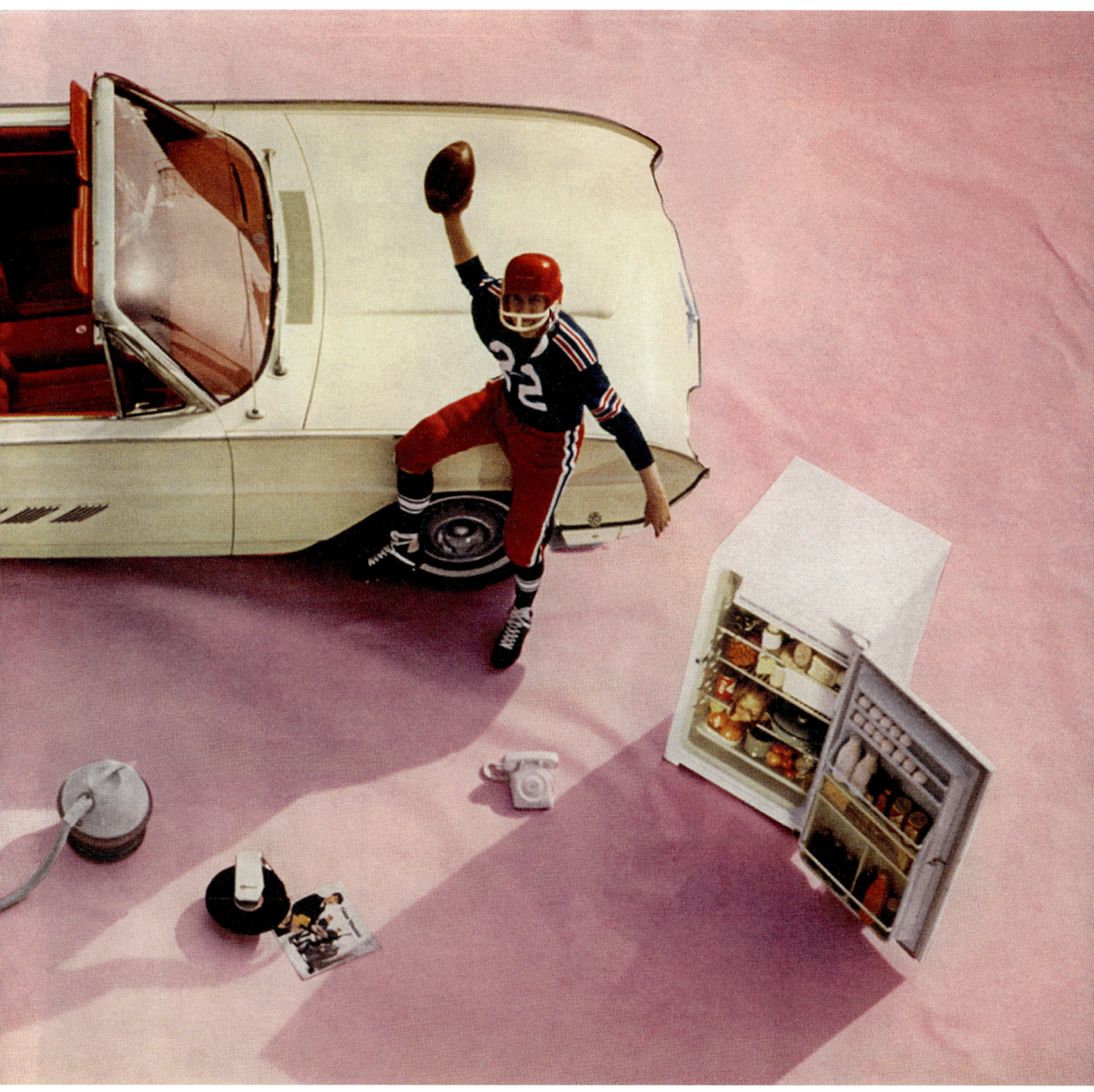

Richard Hamilton

Edited by
Mark Godfrey
Paul Schimmel
Vicente Todolí

Essays by
Benjamin H.D. Buchloh
Hal Foster
Mark Godfrey
Richard Hamilton
Alice Rawsthorn
Paul Schimmel
Fanny Singer
Victoria Walsh

Tate Publishing

This publication was originated by Museo Nacional Centro de Arte Reina Sofía
and TF Editores, Madrid

This edition first published 2014 by order of the Tate Trustees
by Tate Publishing, a division of Tate Enterprises Ltd,
Millbank, London SW1P 4RG
www.tate.org.uk/publishing

on the occasion of the exhibition
Richard Hamilton

Tate Modern, London
13 February – 26 May 2014

Museo Nacional Centro de Arte Reina Sofía, Madrid
24 June – 13 October 2014

Exhibition organised by the Museo Nacional Centro de Arte Reina Sofía
in collaboration with Tate Modern

This catalogue has been generously supported by Keith and Kathy Sachs

A catalogue record for this book is available from the British Library

ISBN 978 1 84976 259 5

Distributed in the United States and Canada by ABRAMS, New York
Library of Congress Control Number applied for

Design: Fernando Gutiérrez
Design assistant: Sergi Pérez and Michael Gibb at Studio Fernando Gutiérrez
Colour reproduction: TF Artes Gráficas
Printed: TF Artes Gráficas

Front cover: Richard Hamilton, *Towards a definitive statement on the coming trends in menswear and accessories (b)* 1962 (detail)
Back cover: Richard Hamilton, *Portrait of the artist by Francis Bacon – study VI* 1970

Table of contents

10 Foreword

12 Curators' Acknowledgements

15 **Introduction**
Paul Schimmel

61 **Seahorses, Grids and Calypso: Richard Hamilton's Exhibition-making in the 1950s**
Victoria Walsh

93 **Among Americans: Richard Hamilton**
Benjamin H.D. Buchloh

125 **Richard Hamilton and Design**
Alice Rawsthorn

169 **The Hamilton Test**
Hal Foster

201 **Talk at the Palais des Beaux-Arts, Brussels, 1971**
Richard Hamilton

235 **Television Delivers People**
Mark Godfrey

267 **Richard Hamilton's "Late" Work**
Fanny Singer

306 Chronology

326 List of Works

334 Bibliography

347 Index

350 Illustration Credits

Foreword

One of the most influential artists of the twentieth century, Richard Hamilton is widely regarded as a founding figure of Pop Art. But Hamilton's importance extends far beyond this paternity. His activity as a painter, teacher, exhibition organiser, political activist, graphic artist, typography-designer, media-experimentalist and champion for other artists continues to speak to new audiences worldwide.

This retrospective, which encompasses the full scope of Hamilton's work from his early exhibition designs of the 1950s to his final paintings of 2011, is the last show made with the artist's participation. Richard died on 13 September 2011. The exhibition *Civil Rights etc.* had just opened at the Hugh Lane Gallery in Dublin, in which Rita Donagh's paintings were hung alongside Hamilton's works. Rita has been a more than generous collaborator on our exhibition in the most difficult of times—a time of immense grief.

The exhibition, conceived by Hamilton for the Museo Nacional Centro de Arte Reina Sofía and organised by this museum in collaboration with Tate Modern, was initiated by Vicente Todolí and Paul Schimmel and came out of many conversations they had with Hamilton before he died. Vicente Todolí, who had worked since a very long time with the artist and developed a deep friendship with Richard, persuaded Hamilton that the show could include the first reconstruction of *Growth and Form*, an exhibition Hamilton devised for the ICA in London in 1951.

The artist visited the Museo Nacional Reina Sofía on several occasions and contributed actively in the selection of works to be showcased in this retrospective, which includes all of Hamilton's main exhibition designs: *Growth and Form* (whose reconstruction also owes much to the research and hard work of Victoria Walsh), *Man Machine and Motion* (which has been recreated by the New Museum of New York), *Fun house*, and *an Exhibit*. In London, *Man, Machine and Motion* and *an Exhibit* will be presented at the ICA, the institution where they were staged in the 1950s when its building was on Dover Street. Mark Godfrey, Curator of International Art and curator of the Hamilton retrospective at Tate, collaborated with the Director of the ICA Gregor Muir and Curator Matt Williams on this joint venture between Tate, ICA and MNCARS.

Hamilton was notable for his engagement with other writers and artists and their works, from James Joyce to Kurt Schwitters to Dieter Roth to Jasper Johns. However it was Marcel Duchamp who was especially important. Hamilton curated the remarkable Duchamp retrospective for the Arts Council in 1966, a show staged in the Tate Gallery. For that occasion Hamilton worked on a reconstruction of Duchamp's *The Bride Stripped Bare by her Bachelors Even (The Large Glass)* which has been part of the Tate's Collection since 1975. In 2009 the artist generously donated his piece *Sieves by Duchamp* to the Museo Nacional Reina Sofía.

This is the fourth exhibition of Richard Hamilton's work at Tate. Following the Arts Council's large survey of Pop Art at the Hayward Gallery in 1969, the Tate Gallery in 1970 organised Hamilton's first museum retrospective, showing 170 works in almost all the media he had then employed, curated by Richard Morphett. Richard Hamilton devised a special wall system and a brilliant—to say the least—sleeve for the catalogue, which reflected again his keen interest in creating exhibitions and book making. In 1983 Tate showed a survey of studies, stage and final proofs for Hamilton's graphic works entitled *Image and Process*. The 1992 exhibition concentrated on "finished" works. Tate director Nicholas Serota wrote in the foreword: "Twenty-two years on from the first show when the emphasis was on Pop it is now possible to see that Pop is simply one aspect, however important, of Hamilton's work..."

Though this is the first major presentation of Hamilton's work at the Museo Nacional Reina Sofía, he had an equally longstanding relationship with Spain. He visited Cadaqués in 1963 on the invitation of Duchamp and at the end of that decade bought a house in the town where he showed his work frequently in the 1970s. Later he would meet the world-renowned Catalan chef Ferran Adriá, and with Todolí, Hamilton edited *Food for Thought, Thought for Food*, a book on elBulli published in 2009. Hamilton reconstructed *an Exhibit* for a show about the Independent Group organised at IVAM in Valencia in 1990, and mounted a retrospective at MACBA in 2003. A year before his death, Hamilton exhibited his prints *Picasso's meninas* at the Museo Nacional del Prado, Madrid, alongside Francisco de Goya's and Pablo Picasso's versions of Diego Velázquez's *Las meninas*.

In this ambitious catalogue, edited by Mark Godfrey, Paul Schimmel and Vicente Todolí, and designed by Fernando Gutiérrez, the authors Victoria Walsh, Benjamin Buchloh, Hal Foster, Alice Rawsthorn, Fanny Singer as well as Schimmel and Godfrey, address many aspects of Hamilton's work from his interest in exhibition design to the relationship of photography and painting in his practice; from his reflections on American art to his political works. The essays cover the full period of Hamilton's practice and demonstrate the astonishing range of his interests.

We want to thank the curators Vicente Todolí, Paul Schimmel and Mark Godfrey. We also would like to acknowledge the work of Rafael García, Coordinator of the Exhibition and Tour, Teresa Velázquez, Head of Exhibitions, Amaia Múgica, Coordinator of the Catalogue, and María Luisa Blanco, Head of Editorial Acitivities. Godfrey has been assisted by Assistant Curator Hannah Dewar and our Head of Exhibition Coordination Helen Sainsbury, by Rachel Kent, Programme Manager, and Wendy Lothian, Registrar. This exhibition and catalogue would not have been possible without the support of many institutions and private collectors. We also want to thank Nigel McKernaghan for his implication and generosity. He has helped us on so many practical issues, especially on many questions of reconstructions. Our special thanks, gratitude and admiration go to Rita Donagh: without her trust and support there would not have been another Richard Hamilton exhibition.

Manuel Borja-Villel
Director
Museo Nacional Centro de Arte Reina Sofía
Madrid

Chris Dercon
Director
Tate Modern
London

Curators' Acknowledgements

It has been an honour to work on this exhibition, and thanks are due to many institutions and individuals. First and foremost we are grateful to Rita Donagh for her extraordinary support in all aspects of the planning and to Nigel McKernaghan, Richard Hamilton's studio assistant for many years, for advice about works and installations and the catalogue.

Hamilton agreed to the reconstruction of *Growth and Form* for this exhibition. This has been a major undertaking led superbly by Victoria Walsh. She has been assisted in her research by Kevin Lotery and Elena Crippa. The fabrication has been overseen by Jeremy Akerman. Specific elements in the reconstruction have been made by Jenny Dunseath. We are also grateful to Roger Hiorns for his advice.

In London, two of Hamilton's early exhibition designs will be staged at the ICA, where they were shown in the 1950s when the institution occupied a building in Dover Street. We would like to thank Gregor Muir for his enthusiasm about collaborating on this project, as well as Katherine Stout, Matt Williams, and Juliette Desorgues for their work on the reconstruction of *Man, Machine and Motion* and Rafael García Horrillo and Sam Martin for their help with *an Exhibit*. Thanks are also due to Massimiliano Gioni, who showed *Man, Machine and Motion* in the New Museum in New York prior to the ICA exhibition.

For this catalogue, a true celebration of Hamilton's career, generously supported by Keith and Kathy Sachs, we thank Victoria Walsh, Benjamin H.D. Buchloh, Alice Rawsthorn, Hal Foster and Fanny Singer for their fascinating contributions. Fanny Singer has also worked tirelessly on a new chronology and on various other elements of research for the catalogue. We are grateful to Jef Cornelis for his willingness to allow us to publish a transcript of Hamilton's talk in Brussels in 1971, and to Mary Nuttall for her help in editing this text. Many individuals have assisted us with images including Rob Airey at the Hatton Gallery, Allison Foster and Adrian Glew in the Tate Archive, Wolfgang Tillmans and Maureen Paley, Paul Graham and staff at Pace, Mark Lancaster, Nayia Yiakoumaki at the Whitechapel Art Gallery Archive, Mark Francis and staff at Gagosian Gallery, Anthony d'Offay, Huc Malla at Galería Cadaqués and Alan Cristea Gallery. Fernando Gutiérrez has designed a beautiful publication, and Sergi Pérez and Michael Gibb have worked indefatigably on all the fine details of the layout. The production of the catalogue has been overseen by Amaia Múgica Achalandabaso and Rafael García Horrillo, Editorial Co-ordinators, Museo Reina Sofía, and we would also like to acknowledge Erica Witschey, Editor; María Luisa Blanco, Head of Editorial Activities, Museo Reina Sofía; Paco Bastida, Editorial Co-ordinator, TF Editores; Gabriela Torres, TF Editores; and Roger Thorp in Tate Publishing.

The research for the catalogue and exhibition was developed in discussion with many individuals and we are grateful to them for sharing their insights with us. Special thanks are owed to Anne Massey who organised two symposia on the Independent Group in the run-up to this exhibition, and Frances Spalding, who orchestrated a conference looking at Hamilton and Victor Pasmore in Newcastle, and Gerard Faggionato. Thanks also to other scholars and Hamilton experts, including Kevin Lotery, Alan Cristea, Andrew Wilson, Matthew Gale, Christopher Riopelle, Gill Hedley, Mark Francis and Nicholas Serota. Richard Morphet, who curated Hamilton's 1970 and 1992 exhibitions at the Tate Gallery, generously shared his memories of working with the artist.

We are extremely grateful to the museums and collectors who have generously lent works to the exhibition. In particular we acknowledge Gary Garrels; Elise S. Haas, Senior Curator of Painting and Sculpture, San Francisco Museum of Modern Art; Simon Martin, Head of Curatorial Services, Pallant House Gallery, Chichester; Philipp Kaiser at the Museum

Ludwig, Cologne; Teresa Millet, Conservator, Institut Valencià d'Art Modern, Valencia; and colleagues at the Art Institute of Chicago; the Arts Council Collection, Southbank Centre, London; Birmingham Museums Trusts; British Council Collection; Collection Ludwig, Ludwig Forum für Internationle Kunst, Aachen; Colección MACBA, Fundación MACBA; Dieter Roth Foundation, Hamburg; Fondazione Marconi, Milan; Kunsthaus Zürich; Kunstmuseum Winterthur; Samsung Museum of Art, Leeum; Louisiana Museum of Modern Art, Humlebæk, Denmark; The Museum of Modern Art, New York; the Philadelphia Museum of Art; the Scottish National Gallery of Modern Art, Edinburgh; the Solomon R. Guggenheim Museum, New York; the Victoria and Albert Museum, London; the Colección Malla i Figueras; Galería Cadaqués; Alan Cristea Gallery, London; Hessisches Landesmuseum Darmstadt, Germany; Museumslandschaft Hessen Kassel, Germany; Ludwig Museum–Museum of Contemporary Art, Budapest. Private lenders to the exhibition include Karin und Uwe Hollweg Stiftung, Bremen; Francesca and Massimo Valsecchi; Frank and Lorna Dunphy; Katherine and Keith Sachs; as well as lenders who have preferred to remain anonymous.

At the Museo Nacional Centro de Arte Reina Sofía, Rafael García Horrillo, Co-ordinator of Temporary Exhibitions, has looked after loan correspondence and has been involved in all aspects of the organisation. We would like to extend our thanks to Manuel Borja-Villel, Director; João Fernandes, Deputy Director; Teresa Velázquez Cortés, Head of Exhibitions; Fernando López García, Touring Exhibitions Manager; Mercedes Roldán Sánchez, Legal Advisor and Natalia Guaza Chamorro, Exhibition Management Co-ordinator. Oiko Arquitectos have supervised all questions relating to installation in Madrid.

At Tate, Hannah Dewar, Assistant Curator, has been involved in all aspects of the exhibition organisation. We would also like to acknowledge the great support we have received from Nicholas Serota, Director; Chris Dercon, Director, Tate Modern; Achim Borchardt-Hume, Head of Exhibitions; Helen Sainsbury, Head of Programme Realisation; and Katy Wan, Administrator, Exhibitions and Displays. Rachel Kent, Programme Manager, and Wendy Lothian, Registrar, have done an amazing job working on the loan contracts and transport arrangements. We have been assisted on conservation questions by Patricia Smithen, Tim Green, Tina Weinder and Marcella Leith, and Phil Monk has overseen all questions relating to installation, assisted by Rhona O'Brien. Glen Williams, Senior Technician, has led a brilliant team installing the show. We have worked on an ambitious series of public events to accompany the exhibition with Marko Daniel, Convenor, Sandra Sykorova, Curator, and Joseph Kendra, Assistant Curator, in the Public Programmes department. At the ICA a complimentary programme has been led by Antonia Blocker.

At Tate, the exhibition has been supported by Tate Patrons and Tate International Council. We are particularly grateful to The Richard Hamilton Exhibition Supporters Group; Alan Cristea Gallery; Veronica and Jeffrey Berman; Johanna and Leslie J. Garfield; Desmond Page; and Karin und Uwe Hollweg Stiftung.

The exhibition at Tate Modern has been made possible by the provision of insurance through the UK Government Indemnity Scheme. On behalf of Tate we would like to thank the Department of Culture, Media and Sport and the Arts Council of England for providing and arranging this indemnity.

Mark Godfrey
Curator
International Art
Tate Modern

Vicente Todolí
Curator

Paul Schimmel
Curator

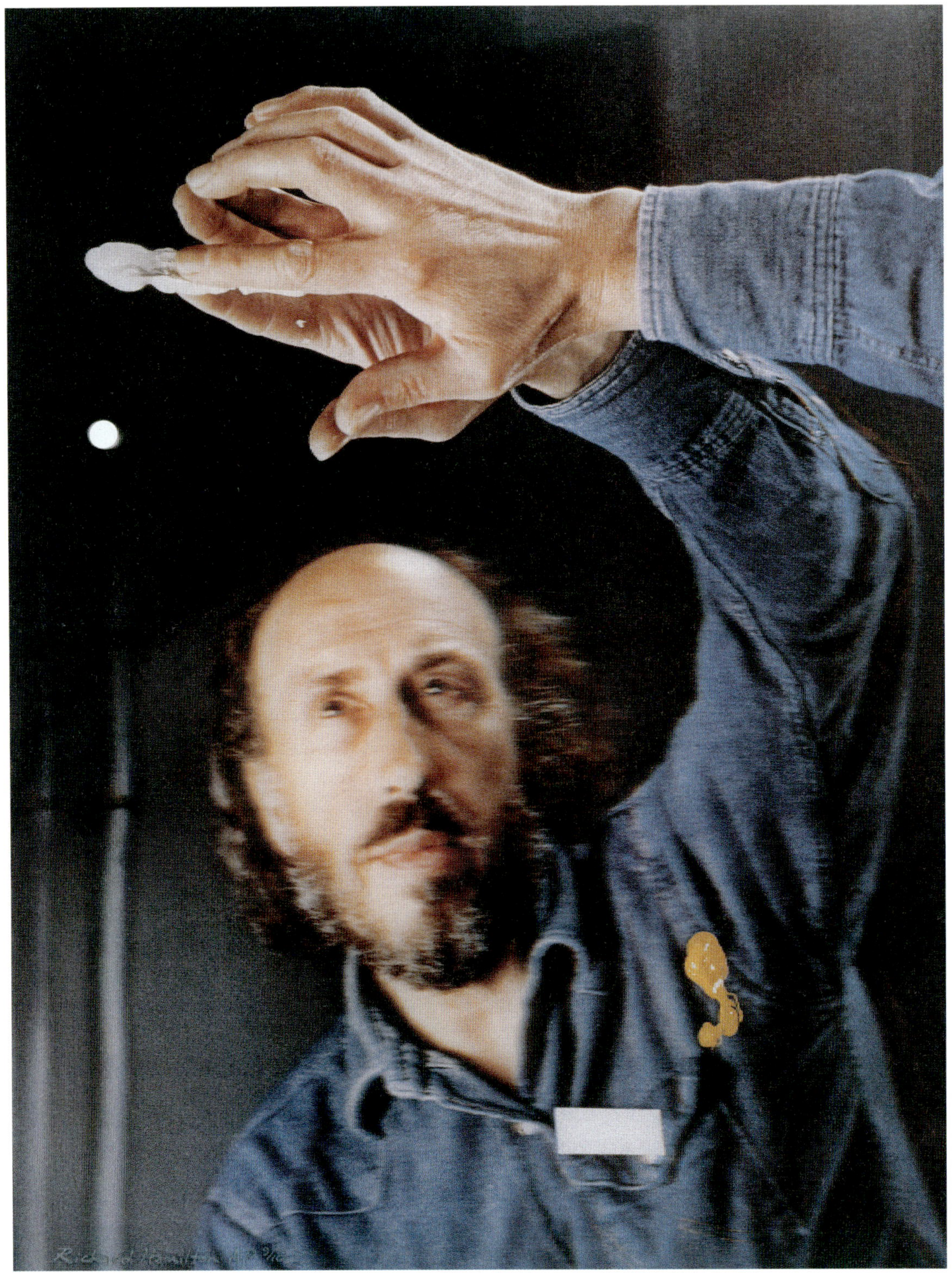

Palindrome 1974

Introduction

Paul Schimmel

This retrospective of Richard Hamilton's work is the last show made with the artist's direct participation. It was realised at a time when he was looking back at his life's work, through the twofold process of thinking about the exhibition itself and writing. The most comprehensive Hamilton retrospective to date, it includes approximately two hundred works produced over the course of six decades. These creations span a diverse range of mediums, including painting, drawing, printmaking and sculpture, as well as re-creations of major early shows that Hamilton organised, designed or contributed to, and installations of complete series of works. Through this selection the exhibition seeks to examine multiple aspects of Hamilton's oeuvre in depth. It aims to convey his far-ranging and continuing relevance, from his international recognition as a proto-Pop artist to his anticipation of appropriation art, installation art and other tendencies explored by subsequent generations of artists up to the present. And it strives to reveal the powerful intellectual, literary and conceptual underpinnings of his groundbreaking work.

The exhibition represents the extraordinary range of mediums and genres that characterised Hamilton's production. It features paintings, prints, drawings, photographs, jet prints, industrial design, graphic design and multiples. Among these works are such genres as still life, portraiture, figuration, landscape, interiors, history painting, political agitprop, religious iconography and appropriation, from both popular culture and the history of art. The sources of these works range from mechanical drawings to popular culture to artists encompassing Old Masters such as Fra Angelico and Giorgione and modernists like Marcel Duchamp.

All of these mediums and genres played important and sometimes groundbreaking roles in Hamilton's coherently diverse oeuvre. This oeuvre is coherent because each work he produced emerged directly from his relentlessly questioning and restless mind. Yet, it is simultaneously diverse because of the sheer variety of these works, which once led him to humorously exclaim to me: "What the hell is going on here?"[1]

As early as 1970, at the time of the Tate Gallery's first major Hamilton retrospective, and just twenty years into what would extend into a sixty-year career, the curator Richard Morphet noted that "the range of [Hamilton's] subject-matter and technique … is unusually wide. Paint is laid down in delicate washes, dripped and smeared with calculated crudity, atomised into minuscule particles and opposed in bold optical contrast."[2] He then enumerated the range of materials, working methods and subjects encompassed in the exhibition—and also recognised the oeuvre's "unity of mood and attitude, and its consistently personal handling of paint."[3] Forty years on, the present exhibition reveals the complete range of Hamilton's practice in even greater breadth as well as how his work as a painter, draughtsman, printmaker, photographer and graphic and industrial designer seamlessly dovetails with his less recognised work as an exhibition designer, curator, art historian and writer.

The retrospective is particularly distinguished by the inclusion of five large-scale installations consisting of re-creations of shows that Hamilton organised, designed or contributed to, including *Growth and Form* (Institute of Contemporary Arts, London, 1951)

1. Conversation with the artist. Subsequent unattributed quotations in the text are also drawn from conversations with the artist.
2. Richard Morphet, "Introduction," in *Richard Hamilton* (London: Tate Gallery, 1970), 7.
3. Ibid.

[pp. 24–31], *Man, Machine and Motion* (Institute of Contemporary Arts, London, 1955) [pp. 46–47], *This is Tomorrow* (Whitechapel Art Gallery, London, 1956) and *an Exhibit* (Hatton Gallery, Newcastle upon Tyne, 1957) [pp. 54–56]. It was a challenge to convince Hamilton that it was worth giving up valuable gallery space that could have been dedicated to his illustrations of James Joyce, his collaborations with Dieter Roth and other significant bodies of work to a full representation of these exhibitions. Initially, critics did not fully appreciate these shows as works of art. At first even Hamilton saw them as separate from, though parallel to, his artistic practice. But with time, other artists, then critics and curators, and finally Hamilton himself came to see them differently: as installations. They precede the Happenings of the late 1950s and early 1960s, and it was only when Hamilton created *an Exhibit* that he began to think of them as "aesthetic experience[s]." They also anticipate a shift in the late twentieth and early twenty-first centuries away from the medium hierarchies that have dominated the history of art and more specifically the growing importance of an international creative sensibility that arose in the 1990s and resulted in the emergence of contemporary installation art. But if the world had not changed around him, it is unlikely that Hamilton would have come to see their full significance.

The diverse range of mediums into which Hamilton inquired posed a related challenge: how to authentically represent an artist who did not privilege one medium over another or even image over word—who deliberately eschewed the notion of style. Hamilton supplanted the commonplace notion of a career united by style, form and technique with a different unifying thread: an investigation into how things work, how they can be deconstructed, and how they can then be reinvented, as well as related explorations of what and how we see. Always believing that only through making something could one really understand it, he launched these probings from a foundation of engineering, science and history, and explored them on planes of pure intuition and imagination. For example, when researching *Reaper* (1949) [pp. 18–21], one of his important early series of works, Hamilton turned away from the history of art and toward a Parisian patent office to create his works directly from original patent drawings (which he had to purchase for five francs each). By appreciating the structure, engineering and functionality of the reaper, he developed a foundation through which to explore it conceptually. In fact, he came to understand this object so completely that he made numerous drawings and even etchings exploring "a variety of techniques, including everything you could do on a copper plate." Working serially allowed him to explore not only the reaper's iconography, but also the great variety of techniques, processes and styles that he could use to bring to fruition a subject that he possessed as if it were his very own.

Hamilton's lack of a consistent style, and his refusal to hierarchically privilege one medium over another, has allowed us to appreciate him as an artist who ultimately may be more recognised for his prophetic relation to postmodernism than for his singular yet much debated status as the first Pop artist. By embracing stylelessness, he became a bridge between the modern and postmodern eras and an important figure for a new generation

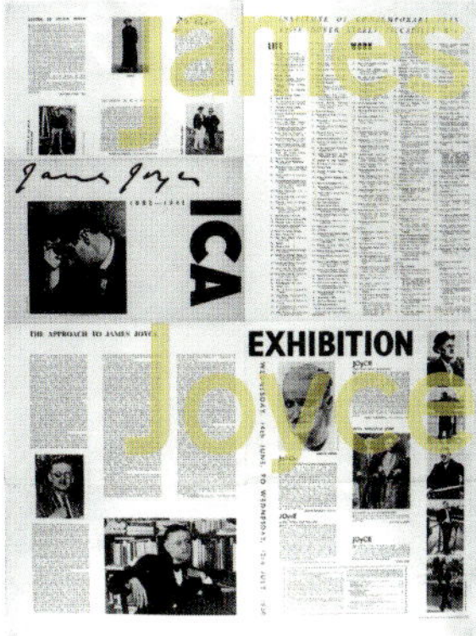

fig. 1
Catalogue/poster designed by Hamilton for the exhibition *James Joyce: His Life and Work*, ICA London, 1950

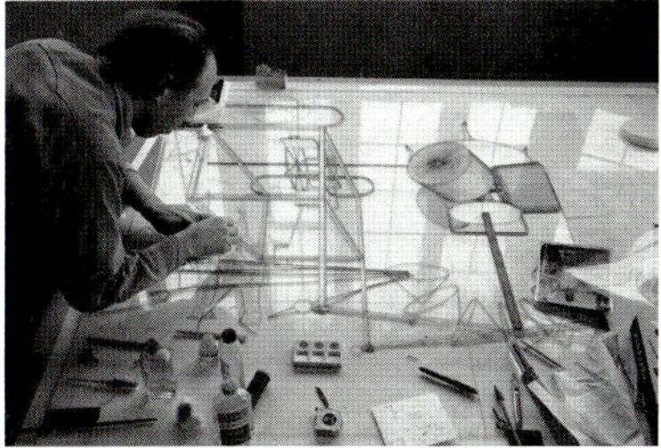

fig. 2
Hamilton reconstructing Duchamp's *Large Glass*, 1965

of conceptually driven artists. The space between the modern and postmodern that he occupies also has parallels in the space between analogue and digital explorations, between handmade and technologically driven production, which the artist also investigated.

In addition, Hamilton's refusal to be defined by a singular style exemplifies the independent spirit that was a feature of his entire career. To be sure, he participated in some of the most significant groups and movements in post-World War II art, and he also worked collectively and collaboratively in an age of heroic individualism. Yet, at the same time he always forged an iconoclastic path, and his independent bent could never allow him to be part of anything for too long. Along these lines, although he studied at the Royal Academy Schools and other institutions, his self-education was just as, if not more, important to his development as an artist. In particular, he learned much from the work of other artists. Early on he absorbed the writings of Joyce [fig. 1] as well as the art and texts of Duchamp—two figures whom he realised shared the same temperament, one that powerfully resonated with his own. Joyce, he remarked, "made me the painter I am, and it was through Marcel that I succeeded to understand that." Through Joyce he came to appreciate that "he did not need a style of working … You do not have to do what most artists do, which is to create a style for yourself." Similarly, he observed that "there was no one to teach me about Duchamp. I had to find out from his writings, which I was bowled over by." And through the elder artist he came to realise that art did not have to be based on the mastery of skills or techniques, but rather that "art was all about thinking."

I suspect that Hamilton found his voice through Duchamp, and that this discovery liberated him from being held captive by the style of his considerable achievements as a proto-Pop artist. In this regard it is significant that in the 1960s, when his peers were honing their styles, Hamilton devoted his time, energy and considerable intellectual prowess to remaking Duchamp's *The Bride Stripped Bare by her Bachelors, Even (The Large Glass)* (1915–23; Hamilton's replica, 1965–66) [fig. 2]. He did not seek to understand Duchamp solely through thinking or writing about him but more directly by (re)making his work. This approach is not uncommon in the history of art (think, for example, of how an artist at his prime such as Fra Filippo Lippi finished paintings begun by Fra Angelico). It is a strategy by which an artist can simultaneously pay homage to and learn from another artist while finding his own voice in the process.

Indeed, underlying Hamilton's work is the persistent search by a man of many minds, who spoke simultaneously in many voices, for a singular voice. The coherence of his diverse oeuvre demonstrates how he successfully and eloquently resolved this apparent paradox. Throughout his life his writings, many of which can be viewed as works of art, played a crucial role in this process. Perhaps this is one of the reasons that Hamilton, forever curious and questioning, once told me that he took great pleasure in "learning from writing, as I try to understand what I did."

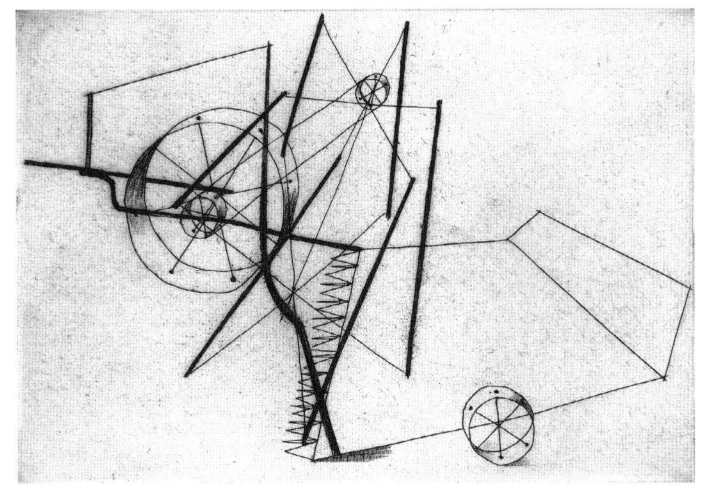

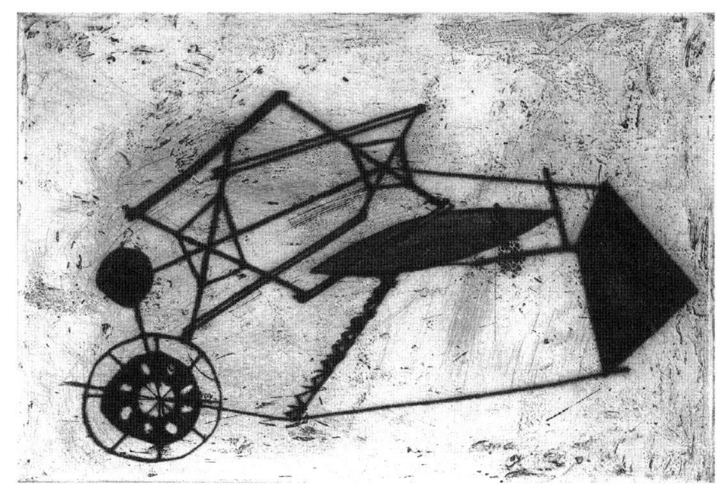

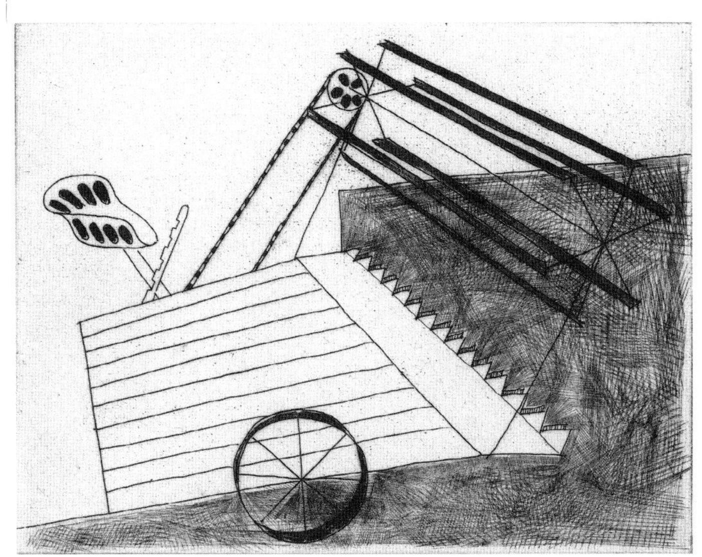

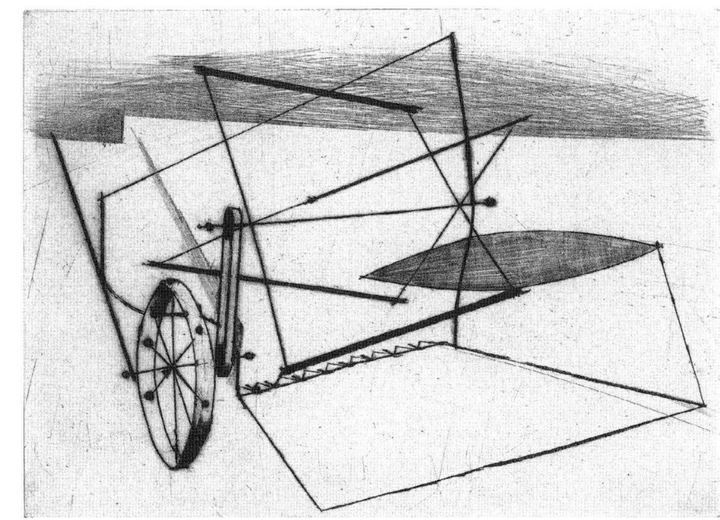

Reaper (a) 1949

Reaper (e) 1949

Reaper (b) 1949

Reaper (f) 1949

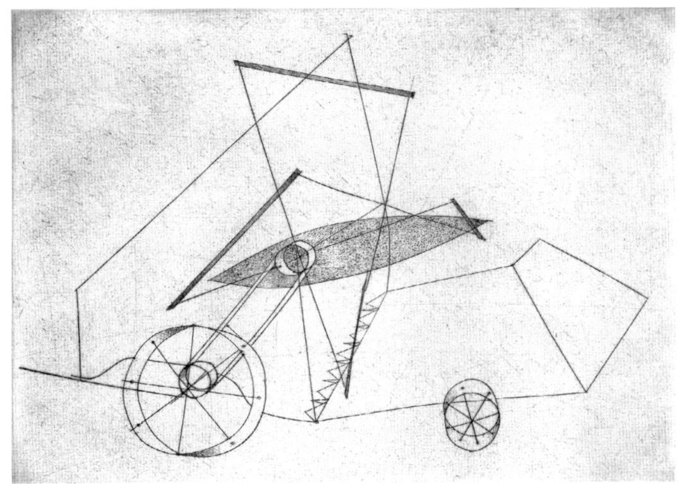

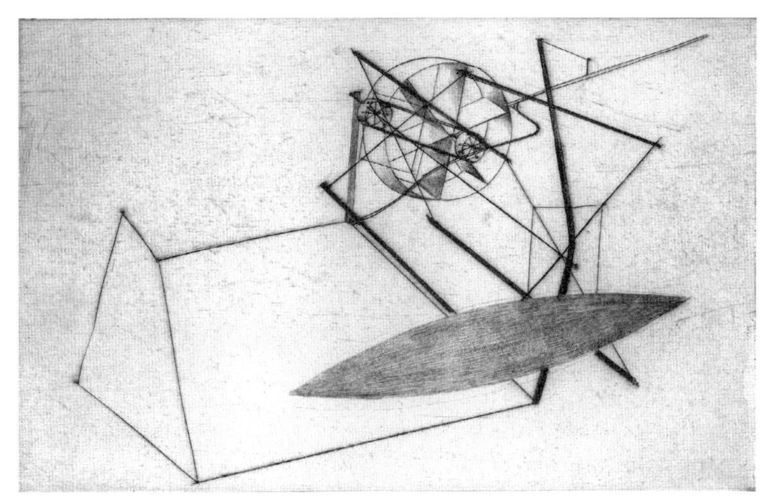

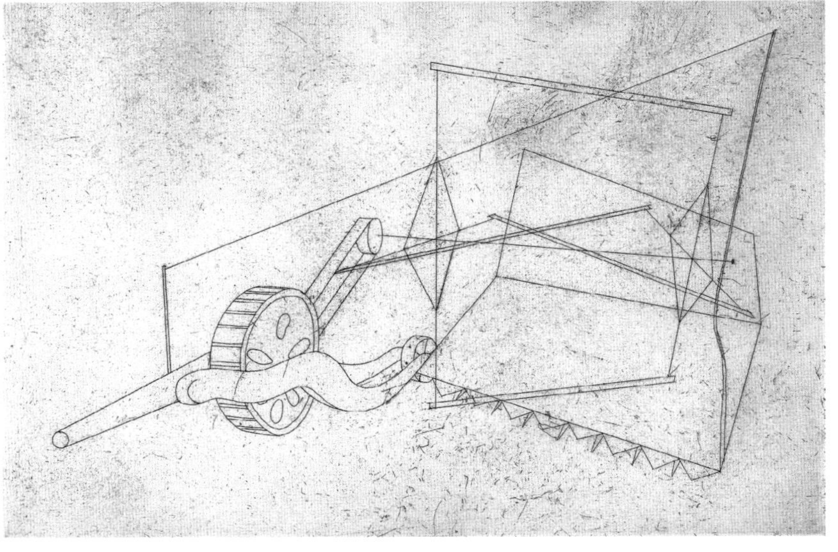

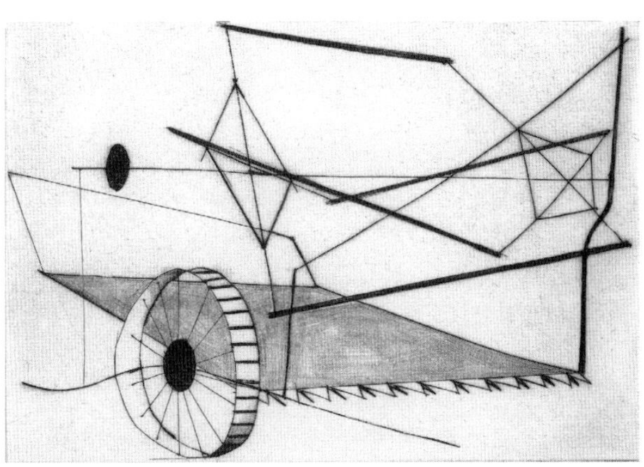

Reaper (c) 1949

Reaper (g) 1949

Reaper (d) 1949

Reaper (h) 1949

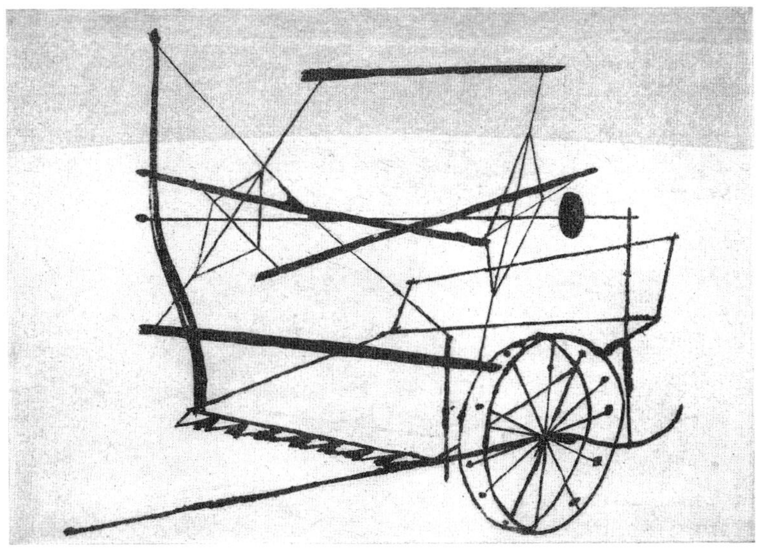

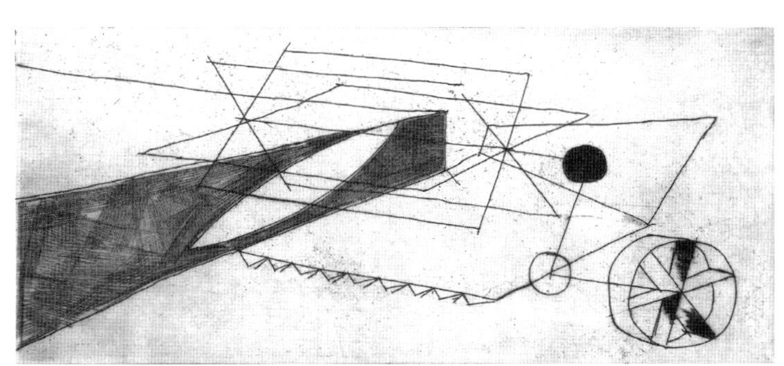

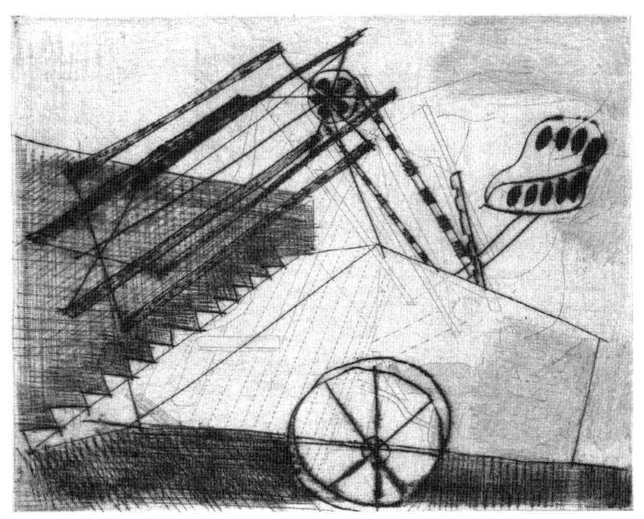

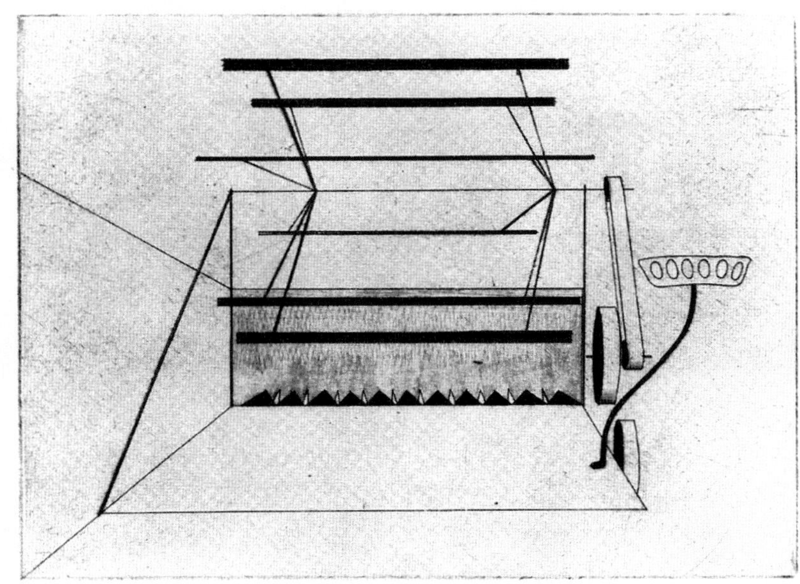

Reaper (i) 1949

Reaper (m) 1949

Reaper (j) 1949

Reaper (n) 1949

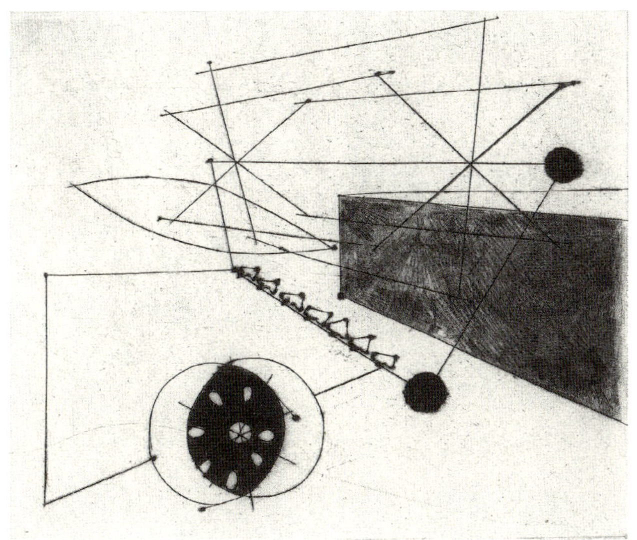

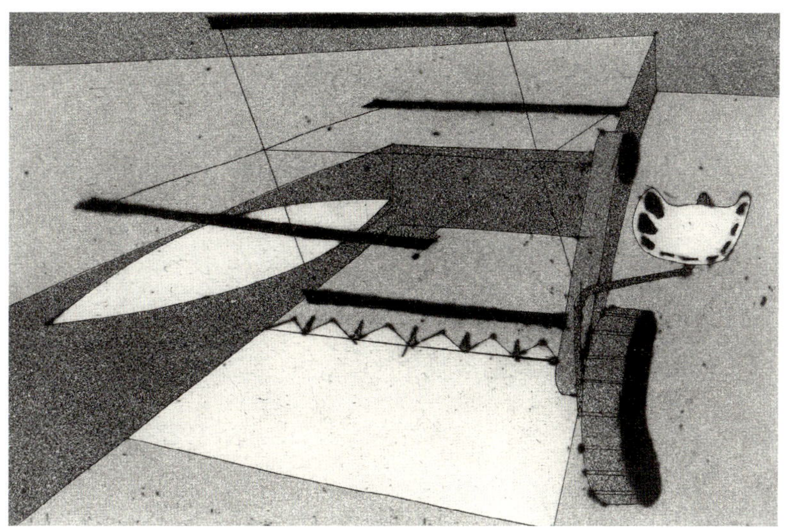

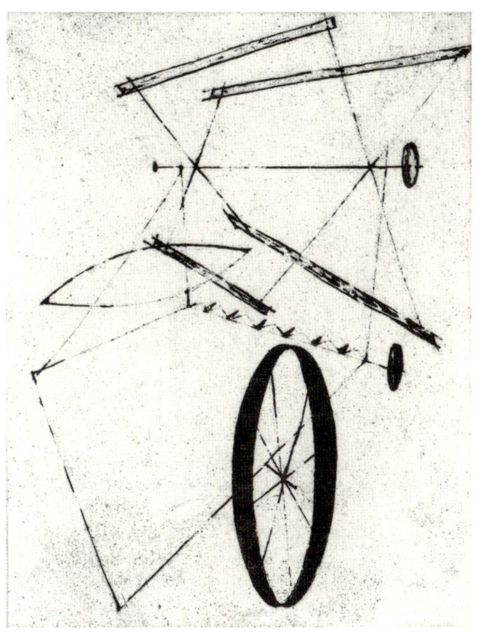

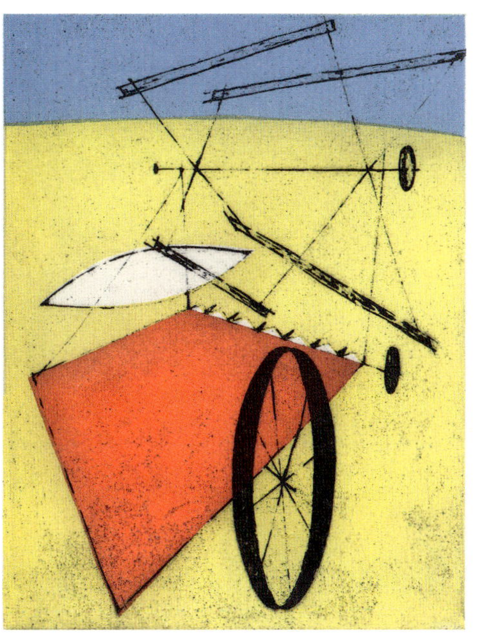

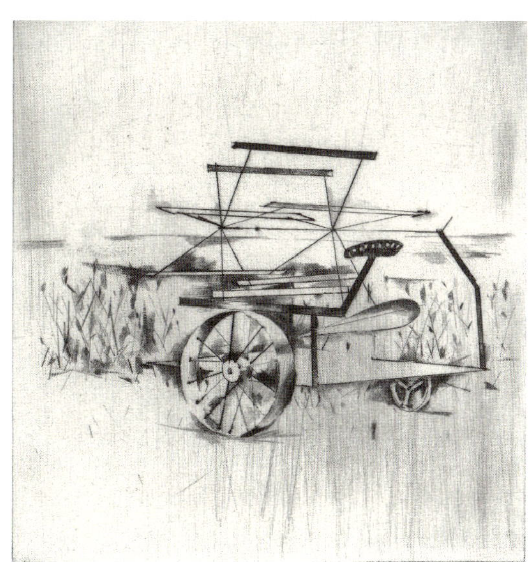

Reaper (k) 1949
Reaper (o) 1949

Reaper (l) 1949
Reaper (o) 1949

Reaper (p) 1949

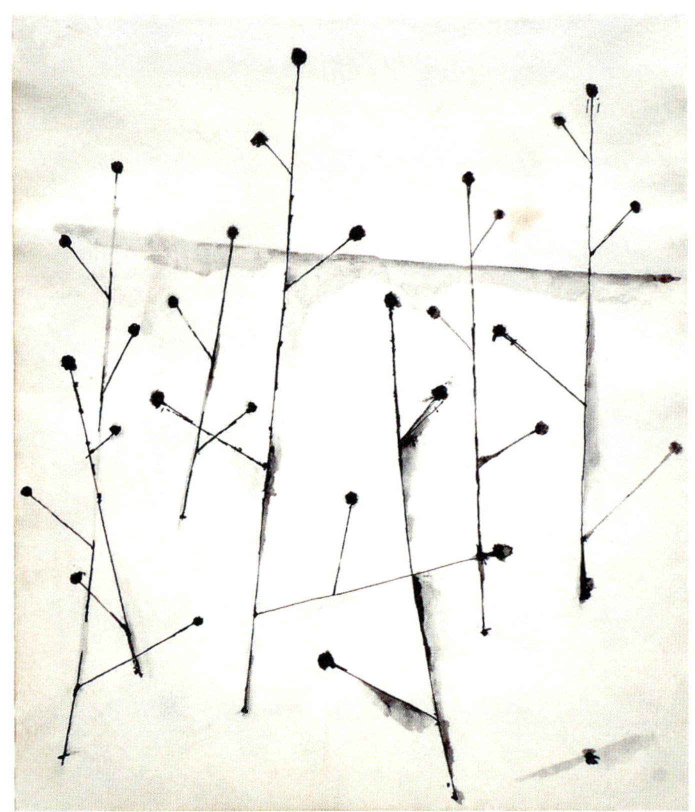

Microcosmos; plant cycle – study 1950

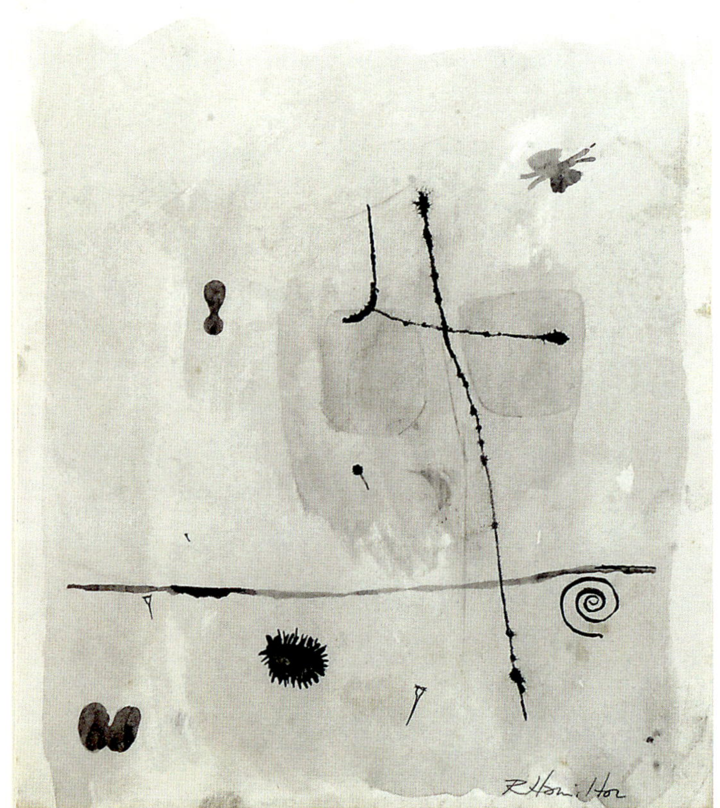

Heteromorphism study 1951

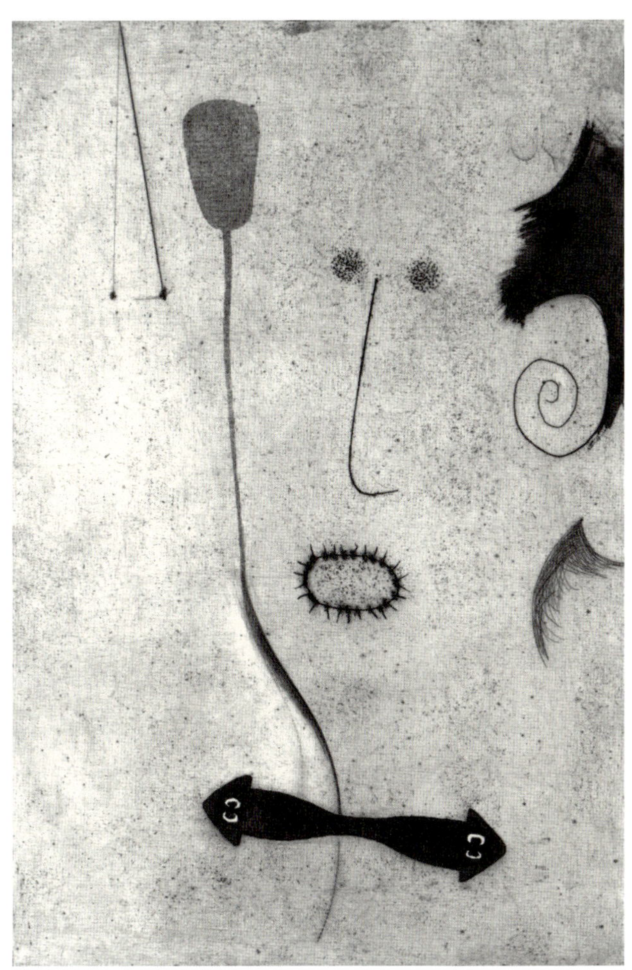

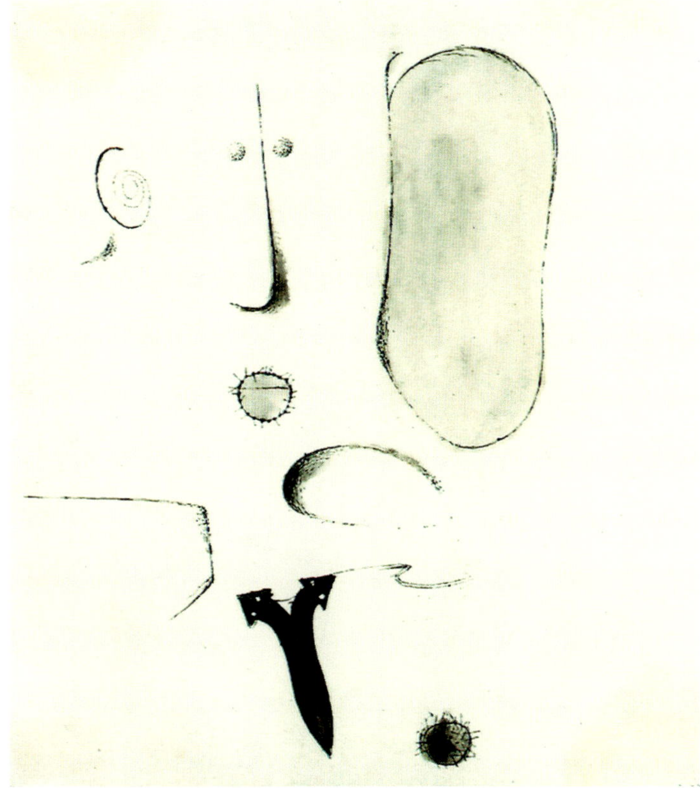

Self-portrait b 1951

Self-portrait – study 1951

Growth and Form ICA, London, 1951

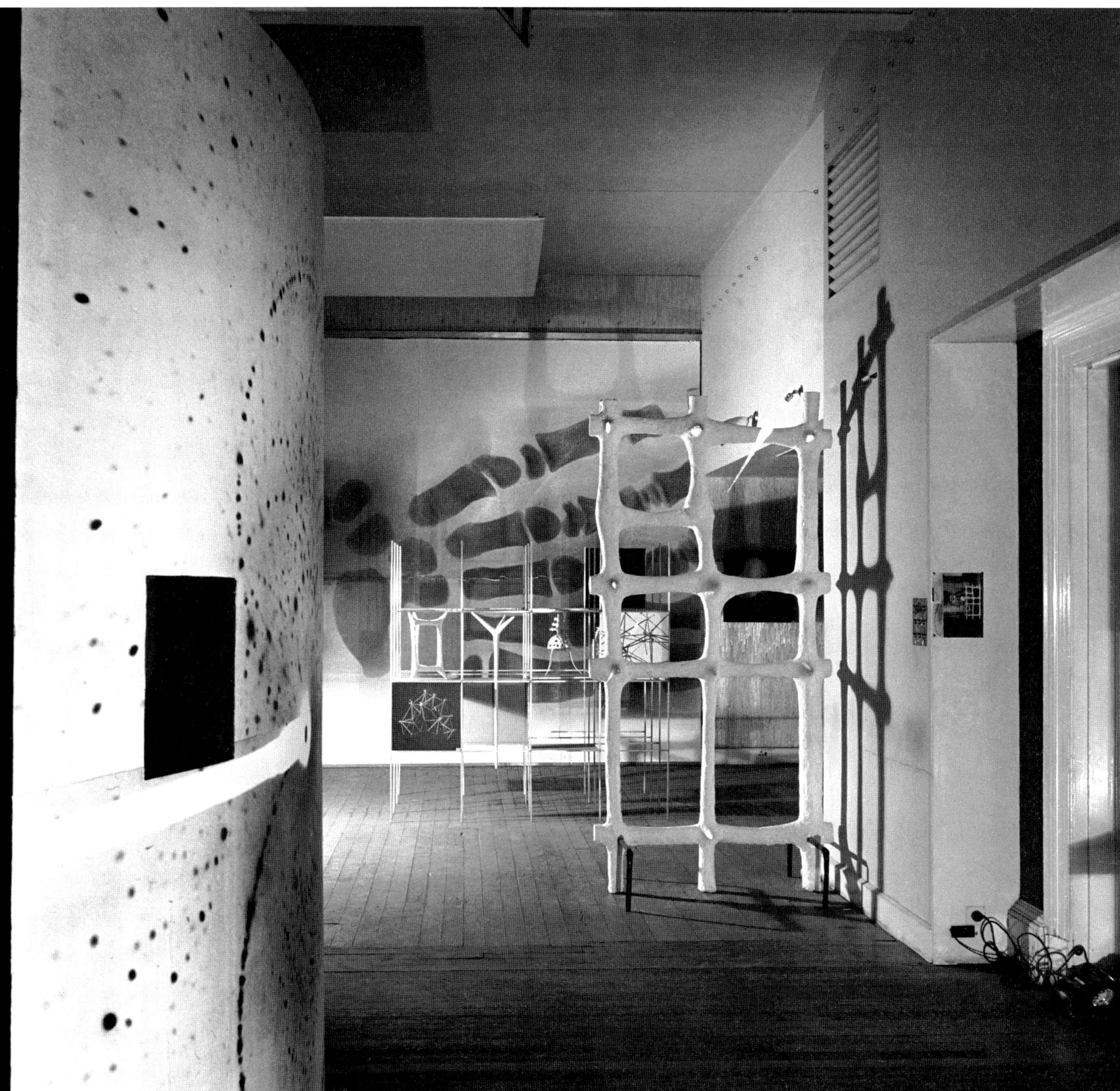

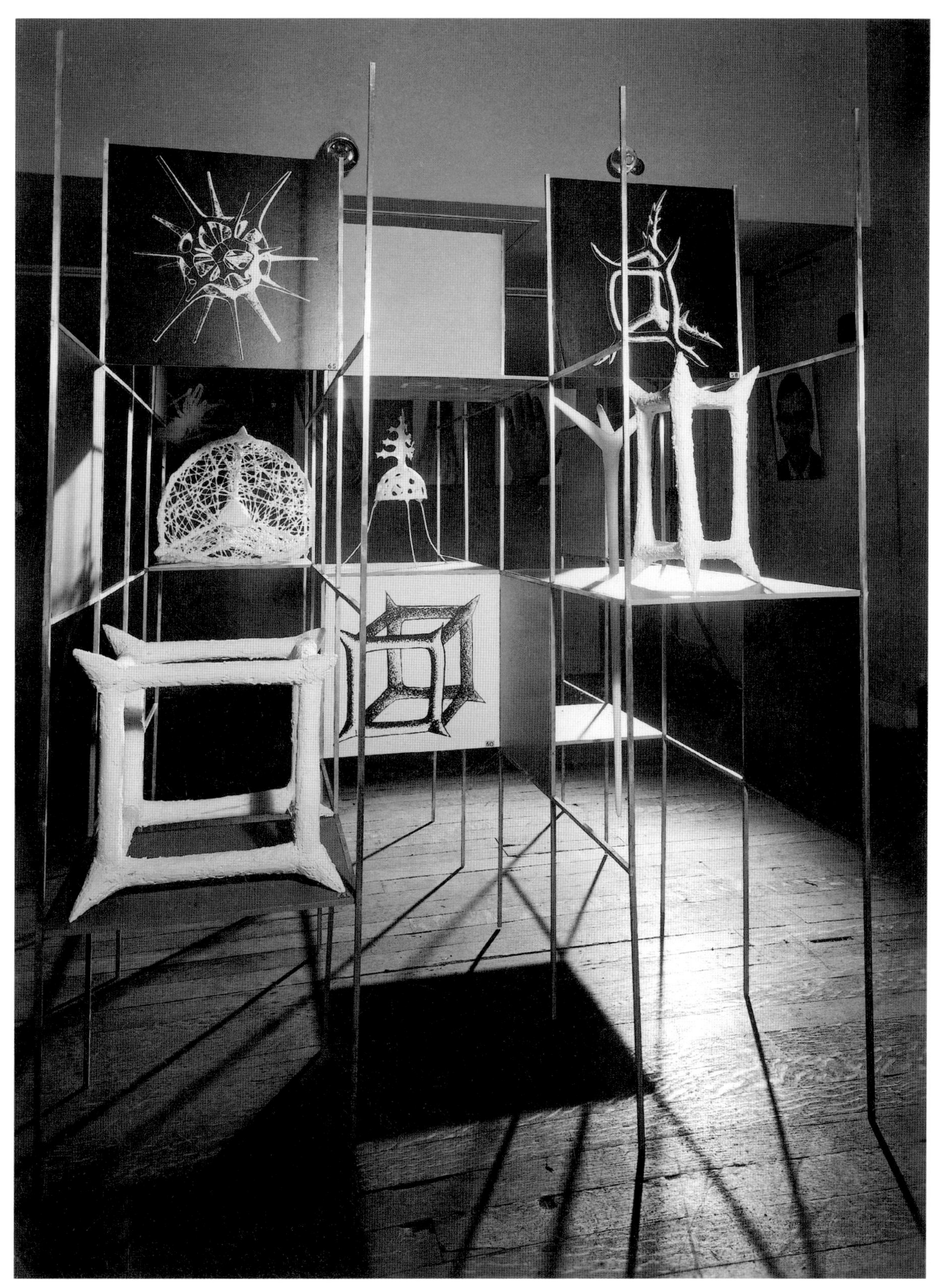

Growth and Form ICA, London, 1951

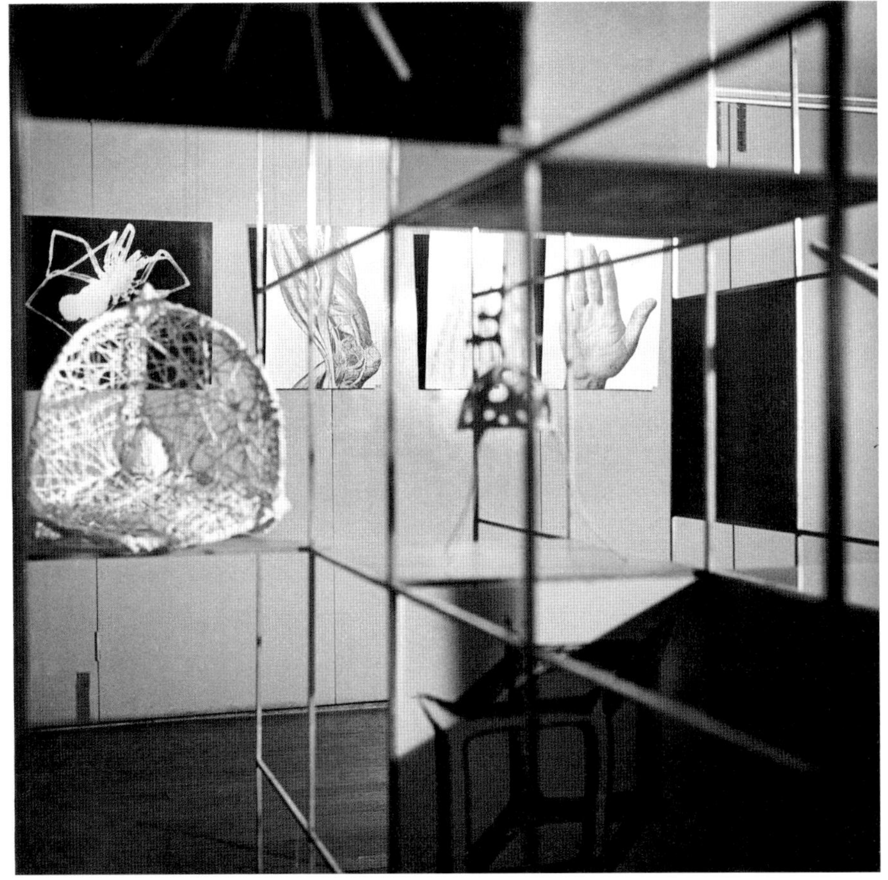

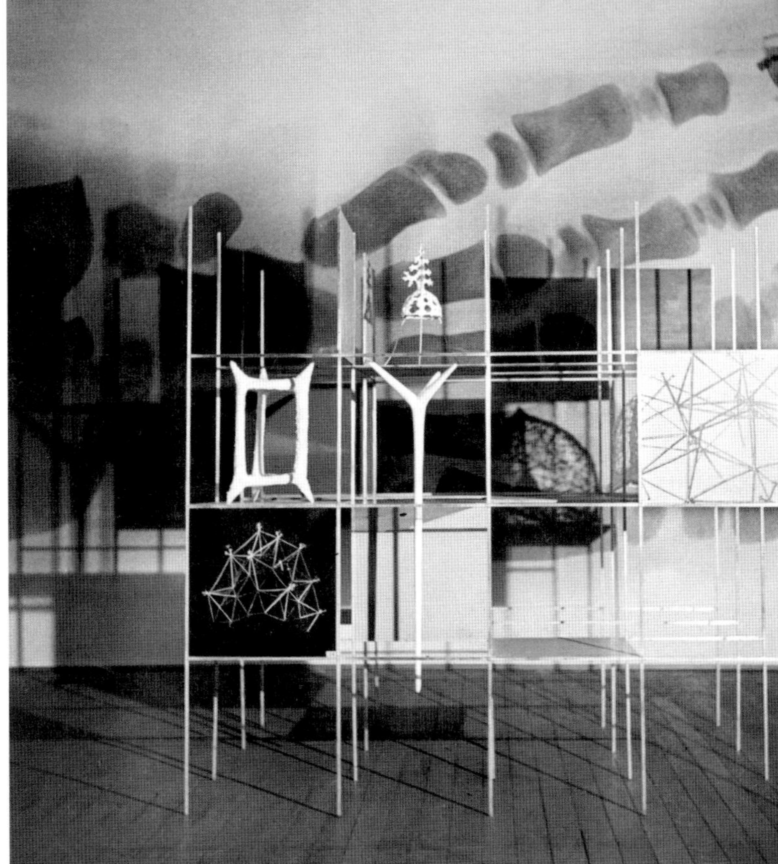

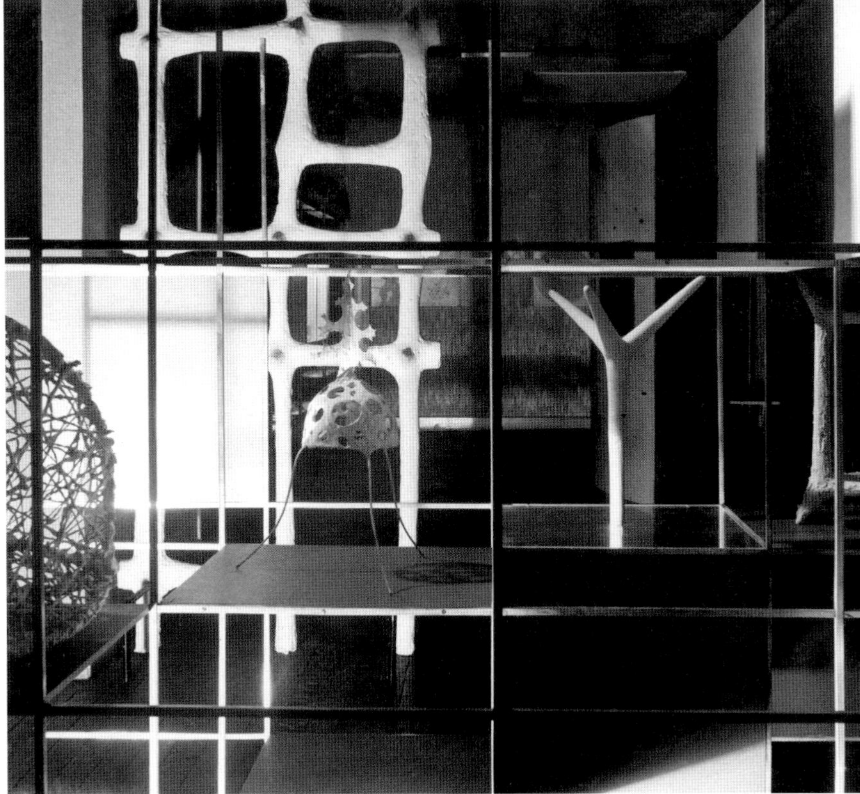

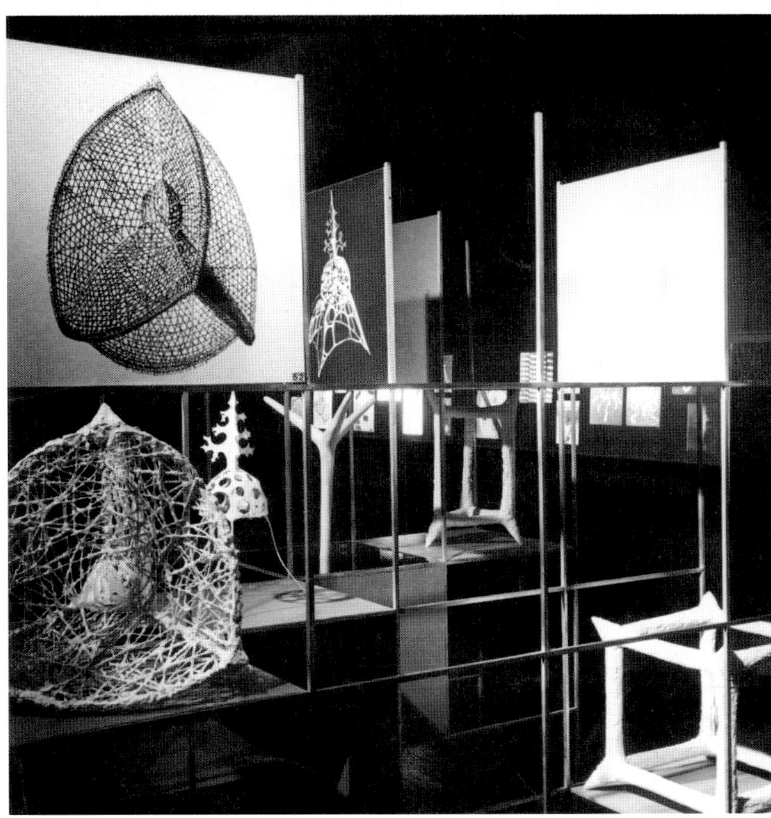

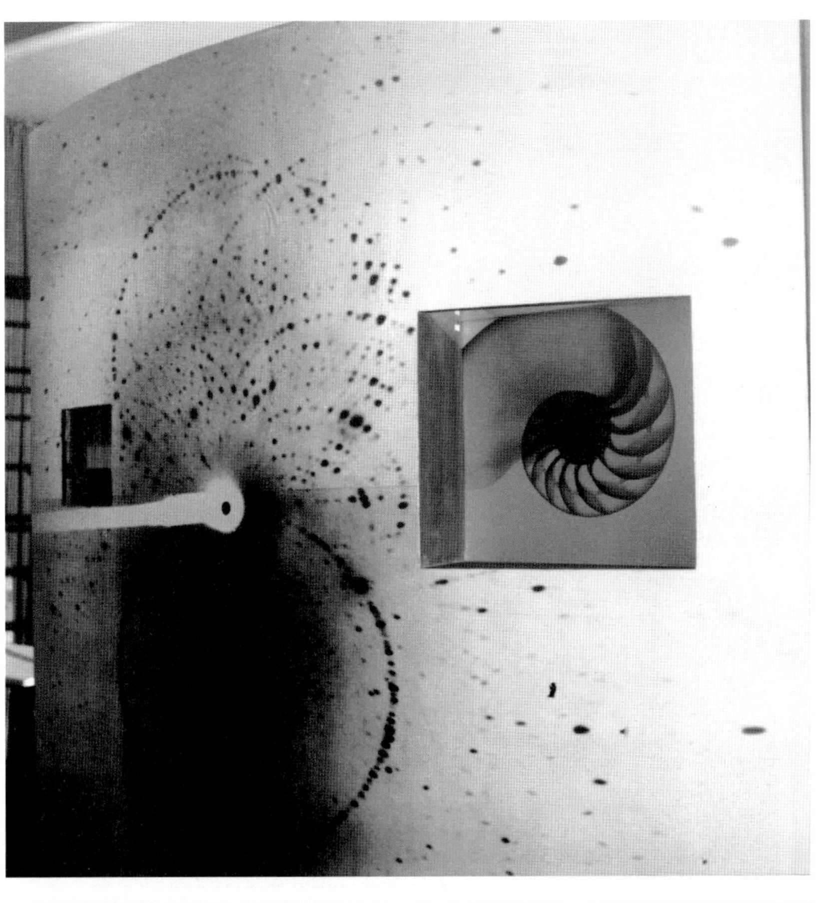

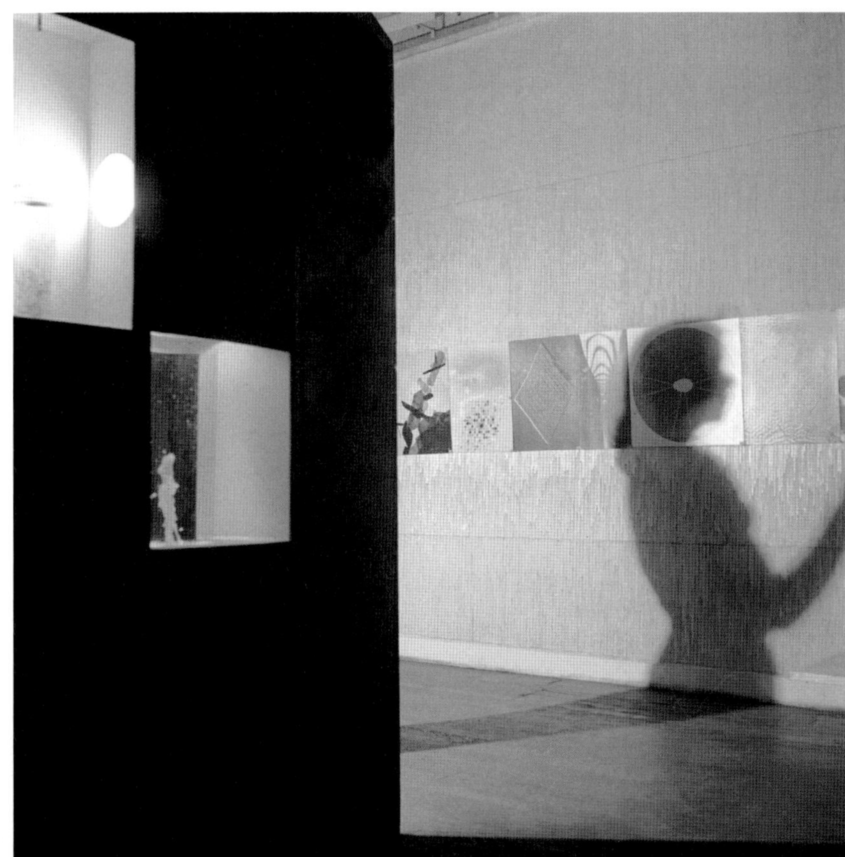

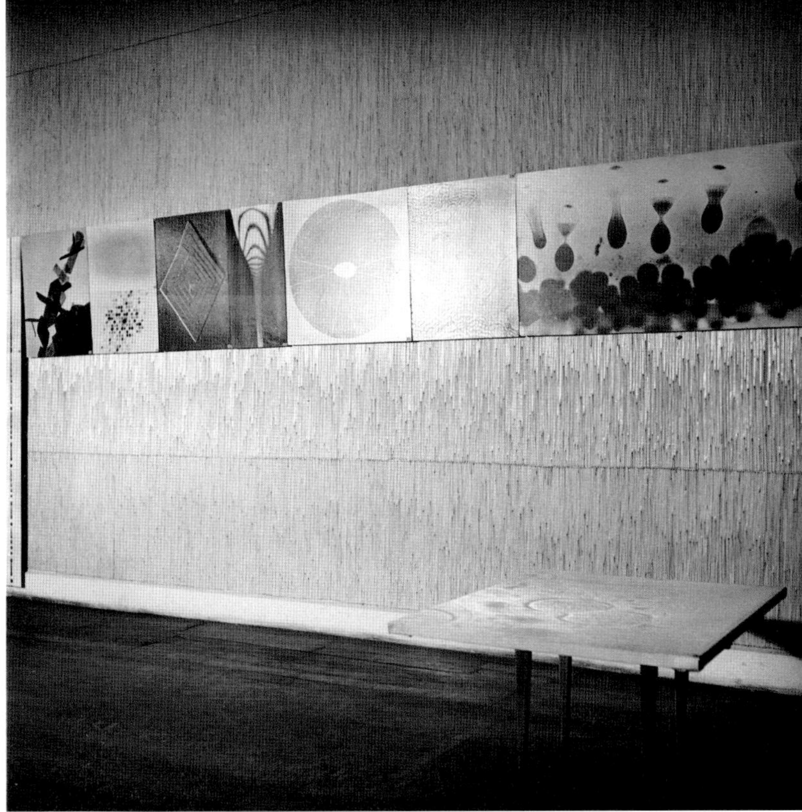

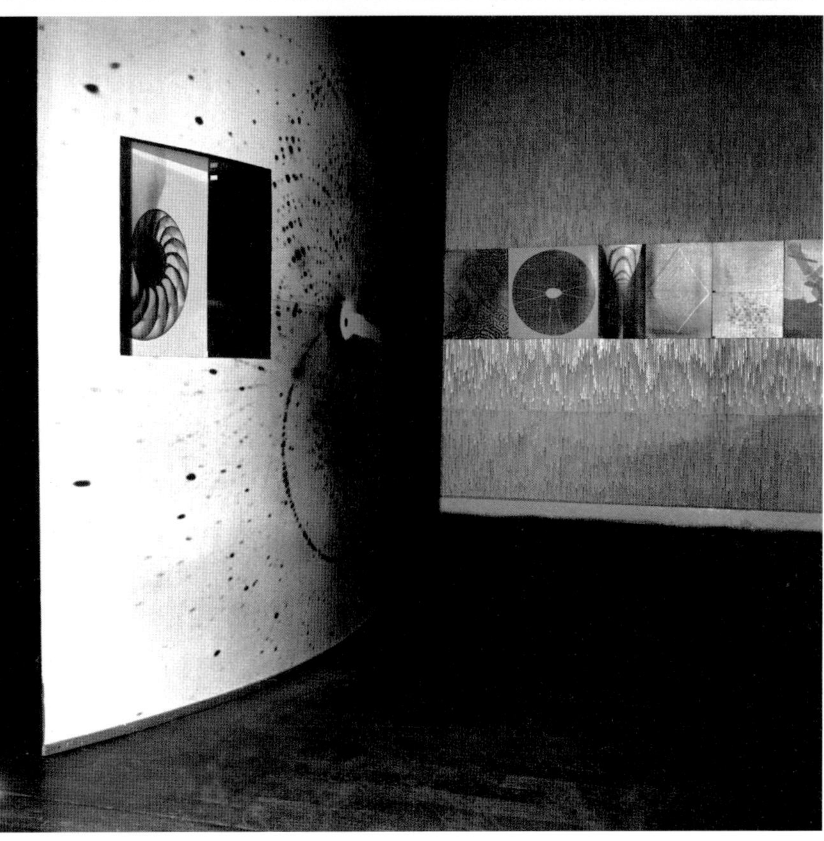

Growth and Form ICA, London, 1951

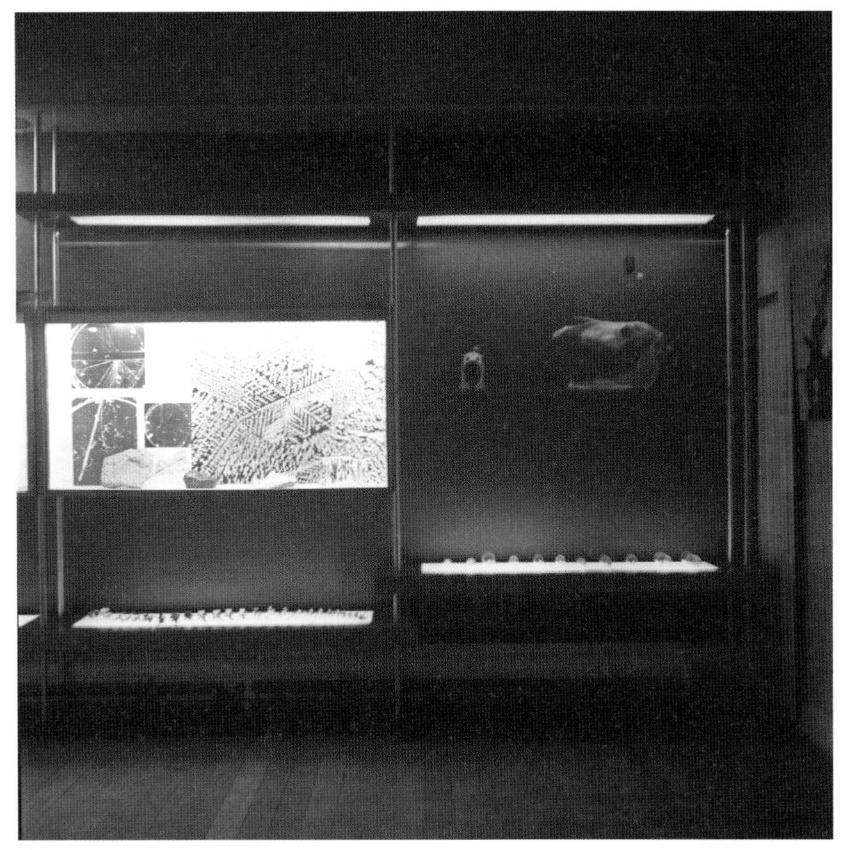

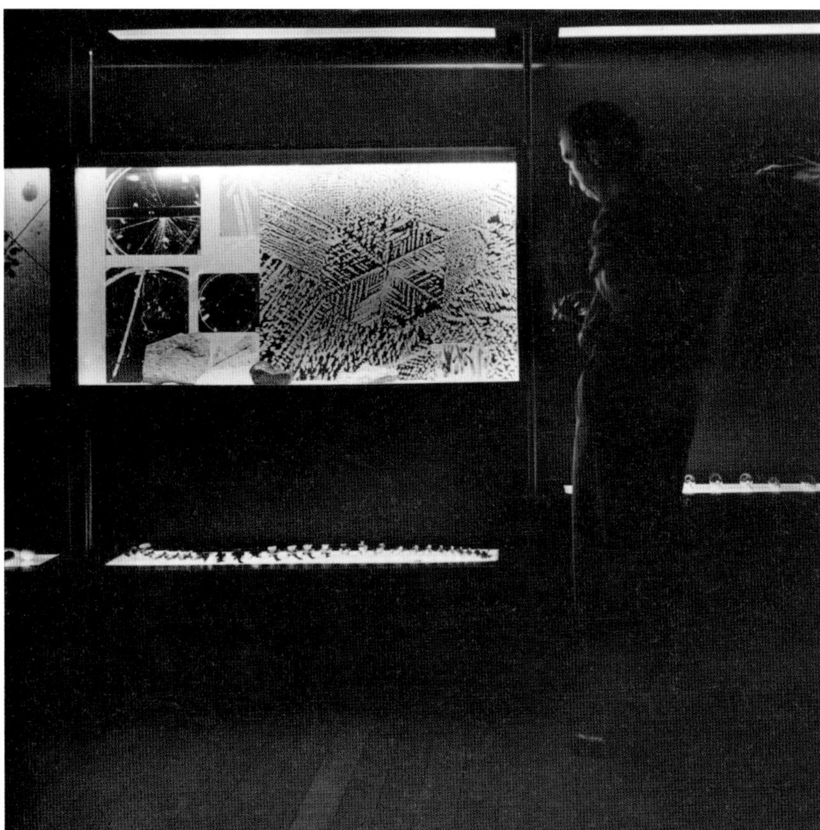

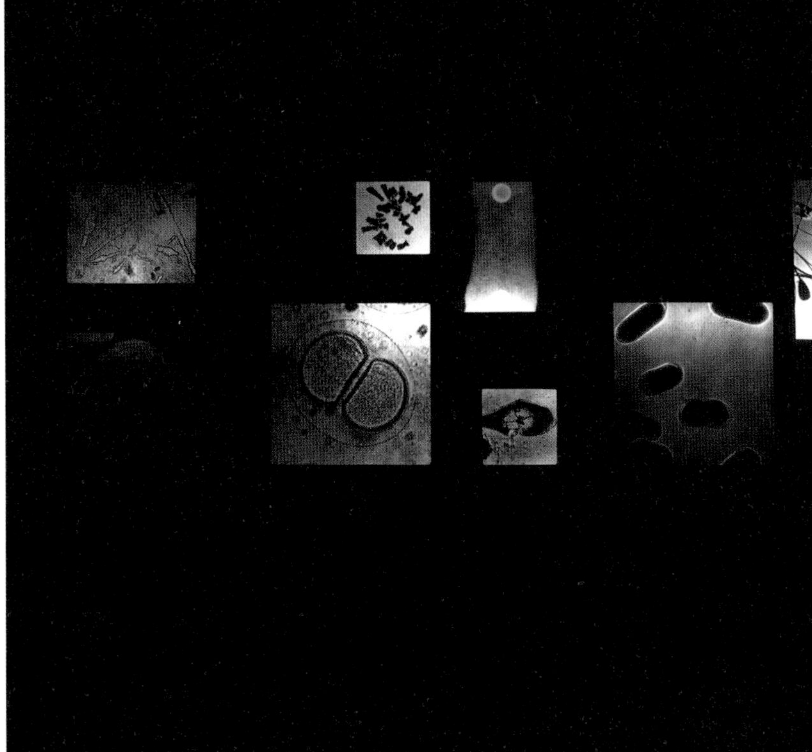

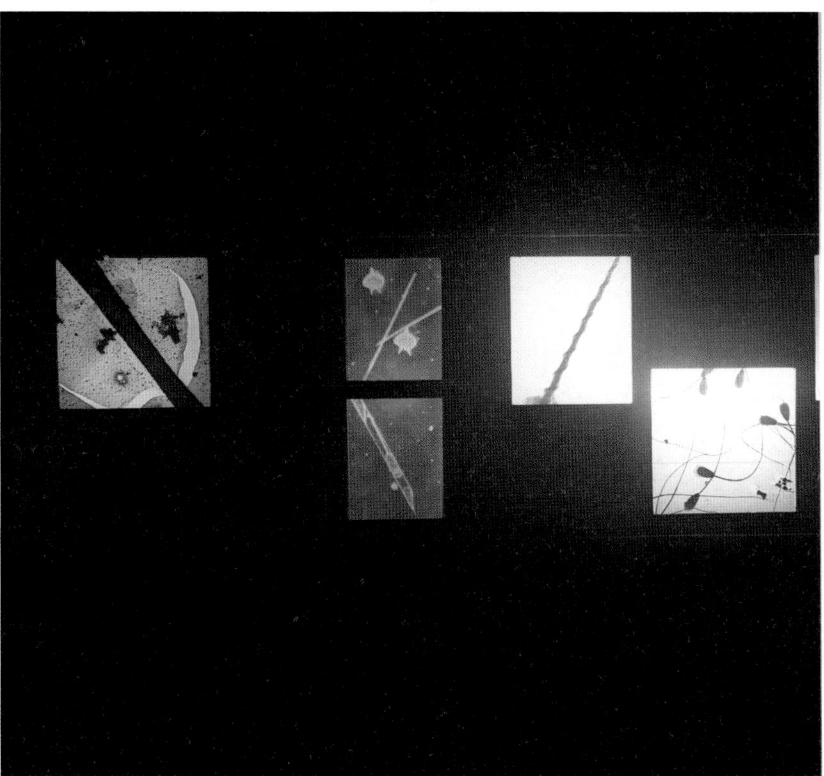

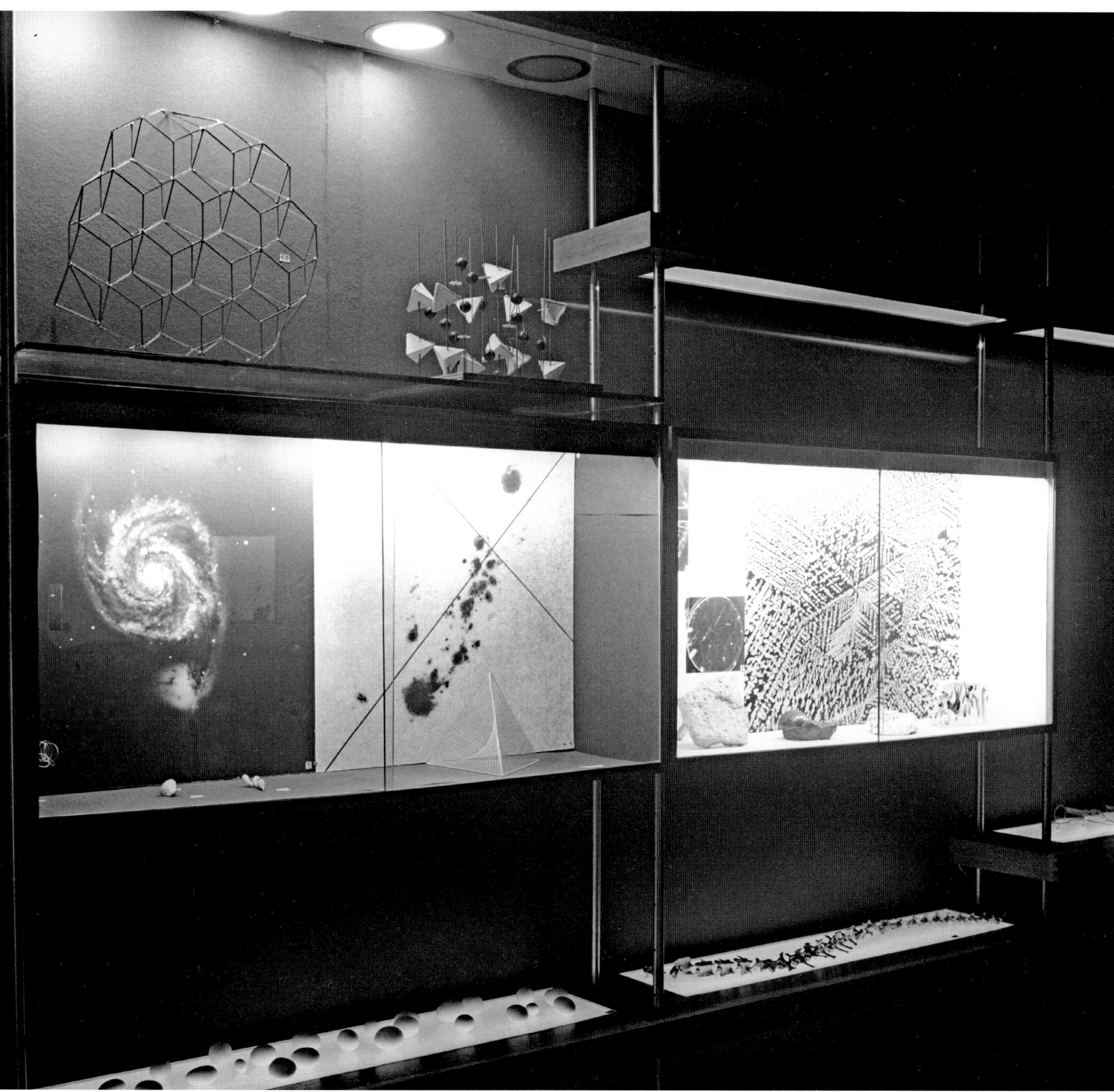

Growth and Form ICA, London, 1951

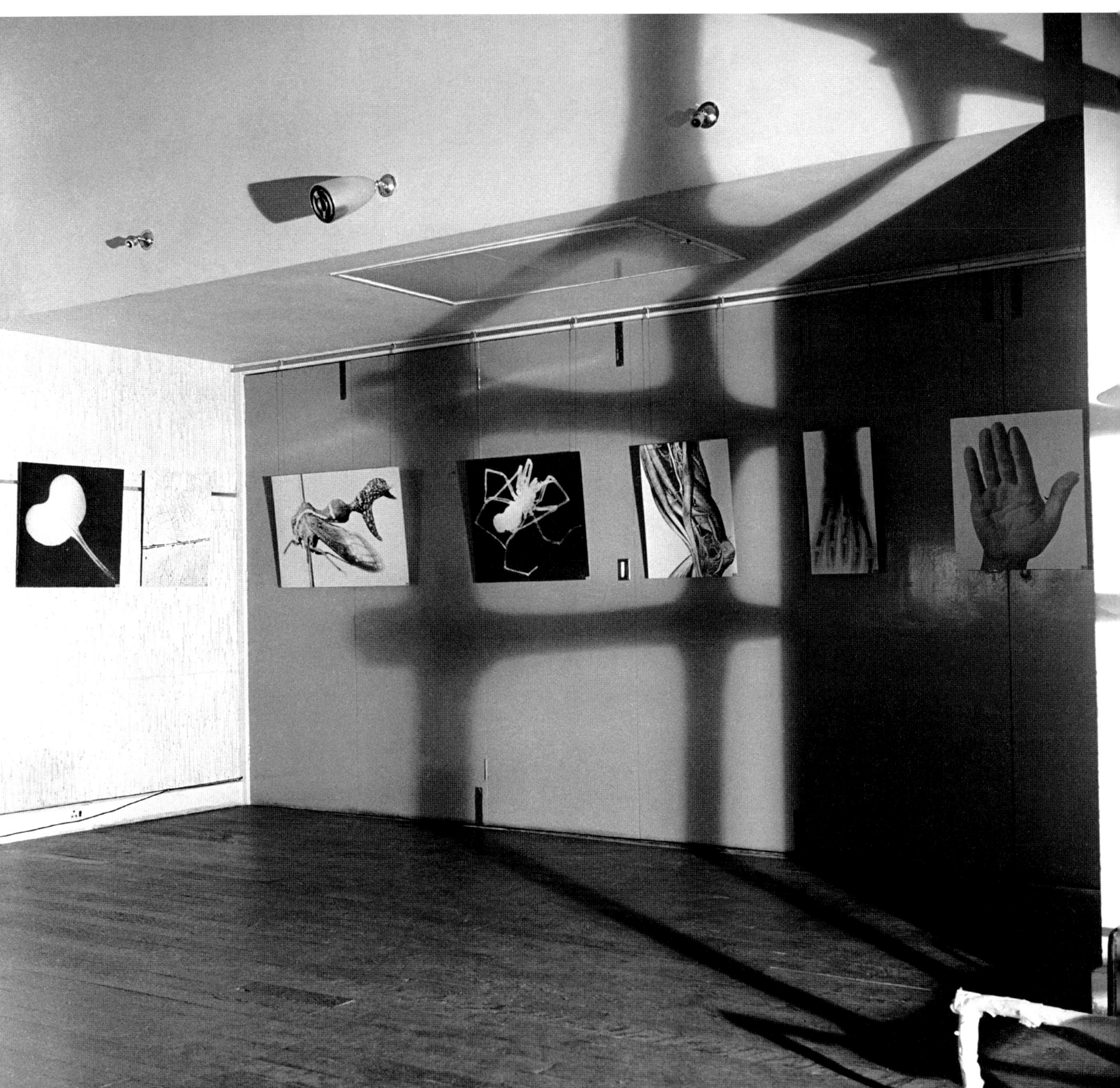

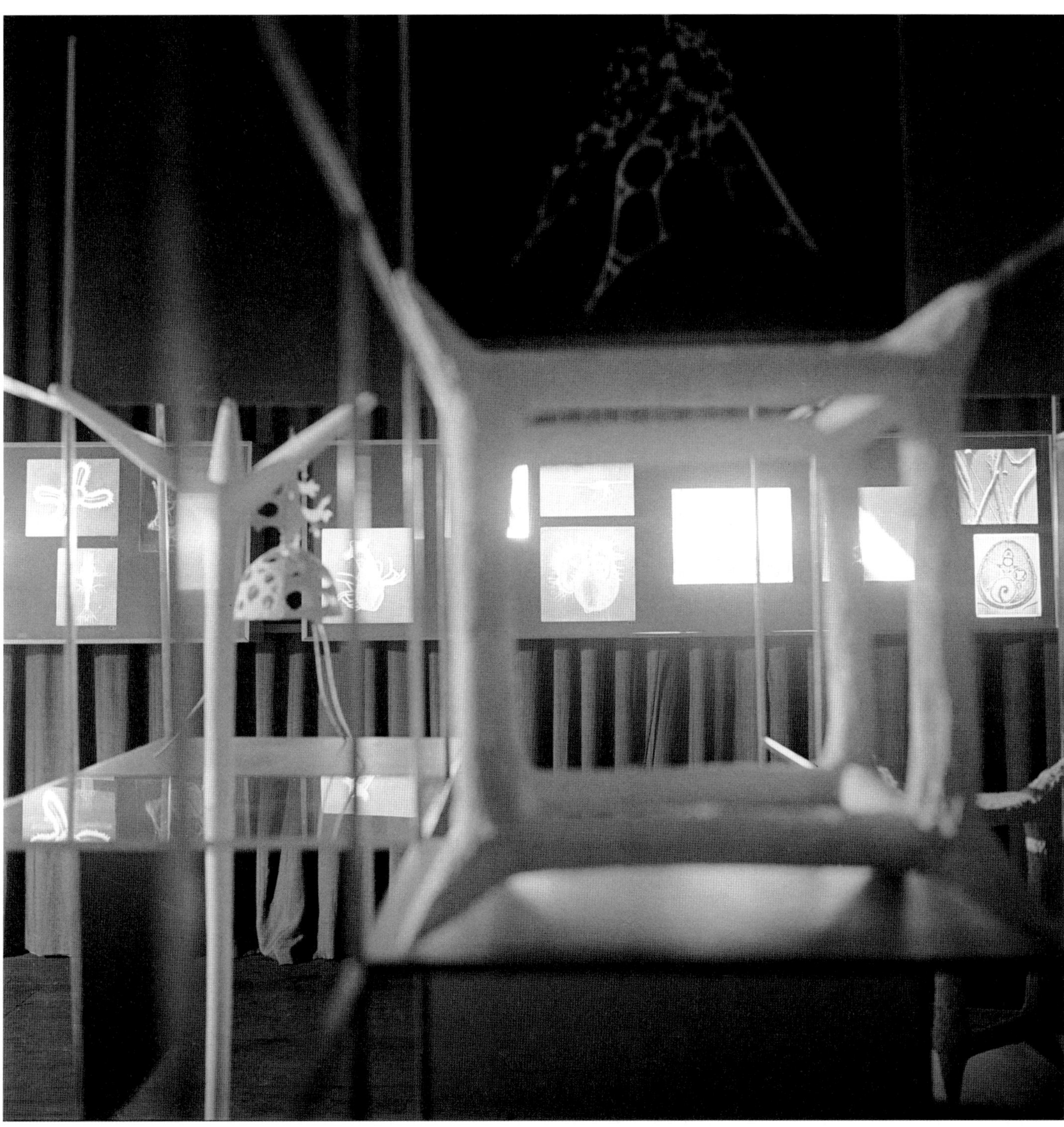

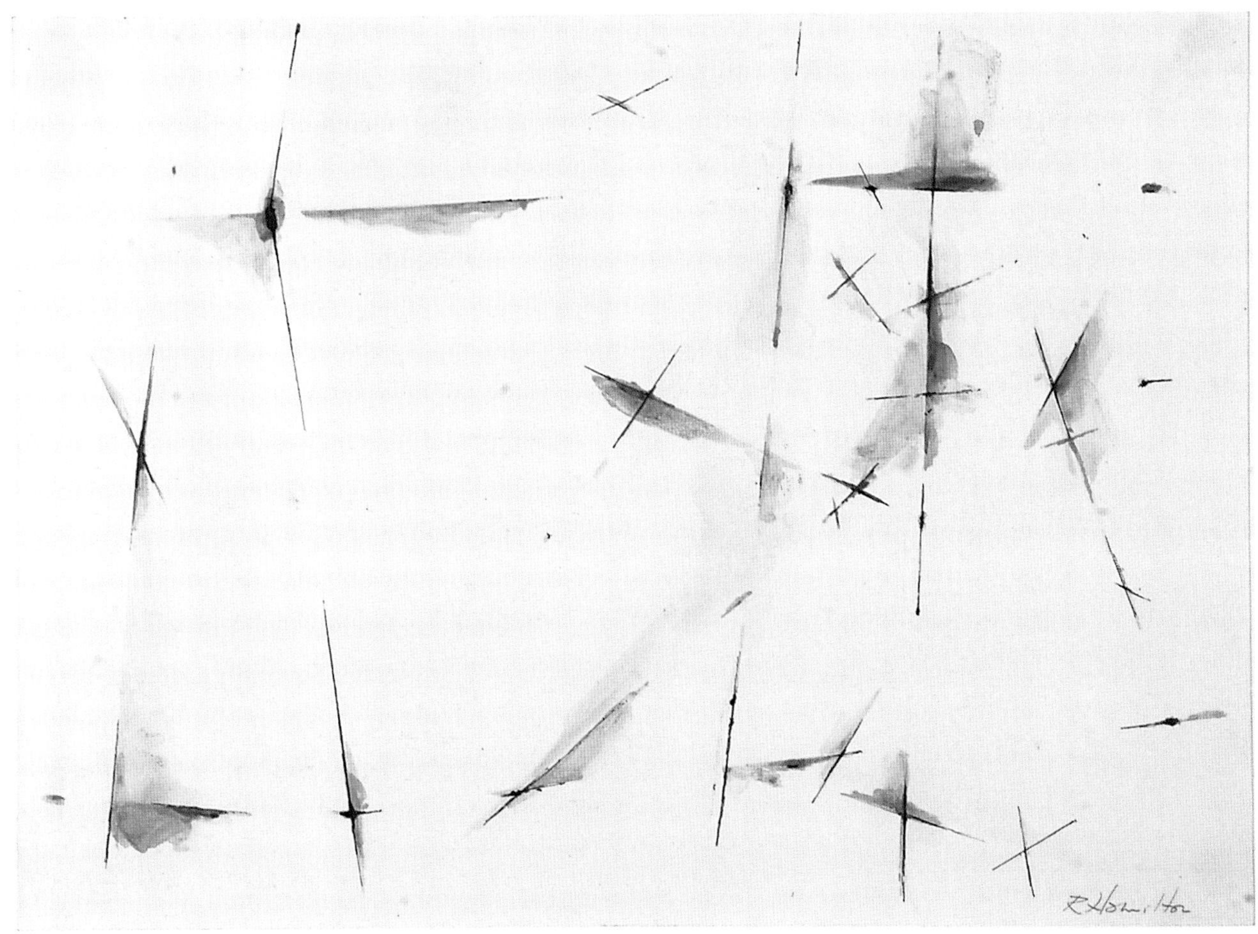

Induction study II 1950

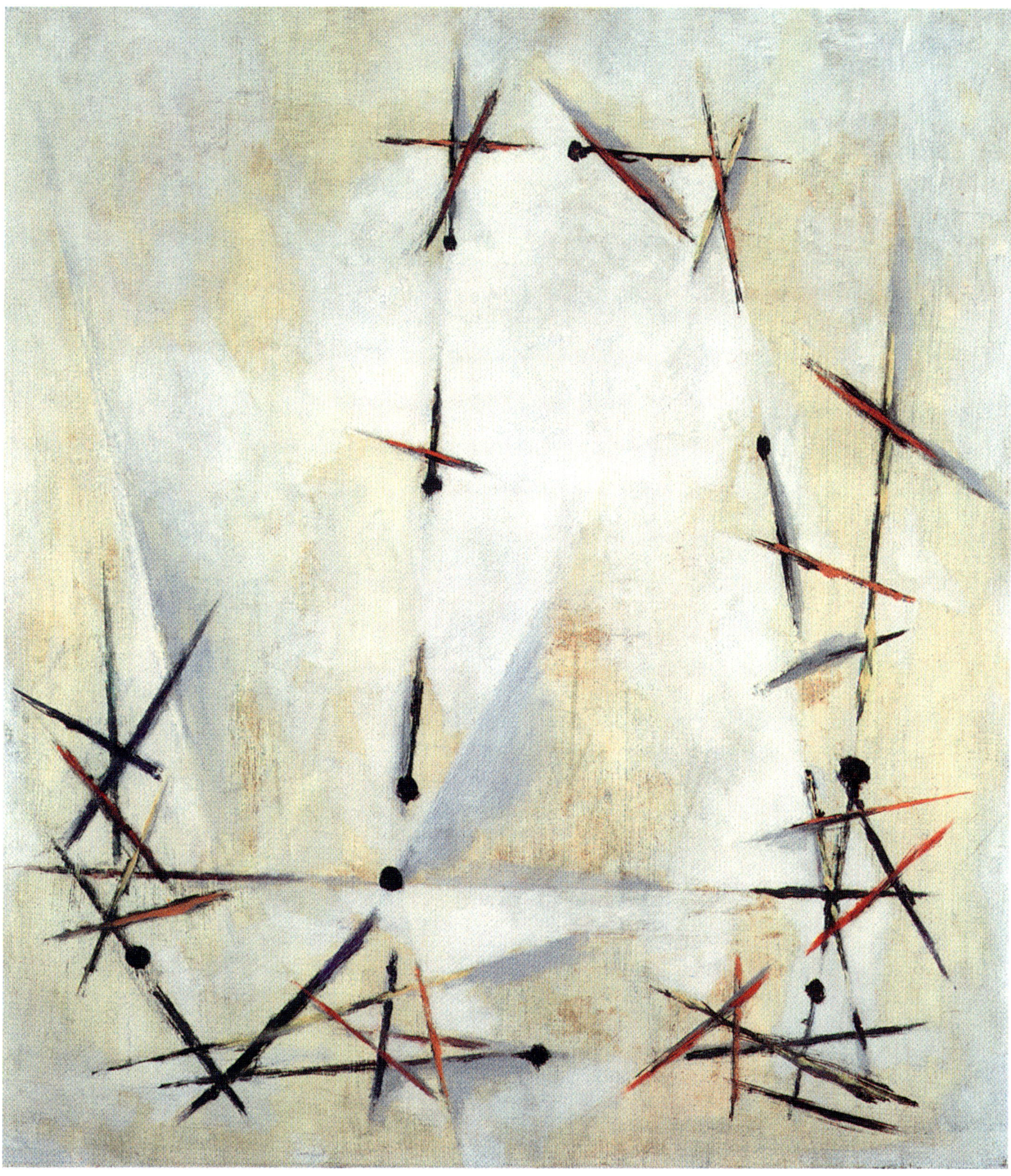

Chromatic spiral 1950

Particular system 1951

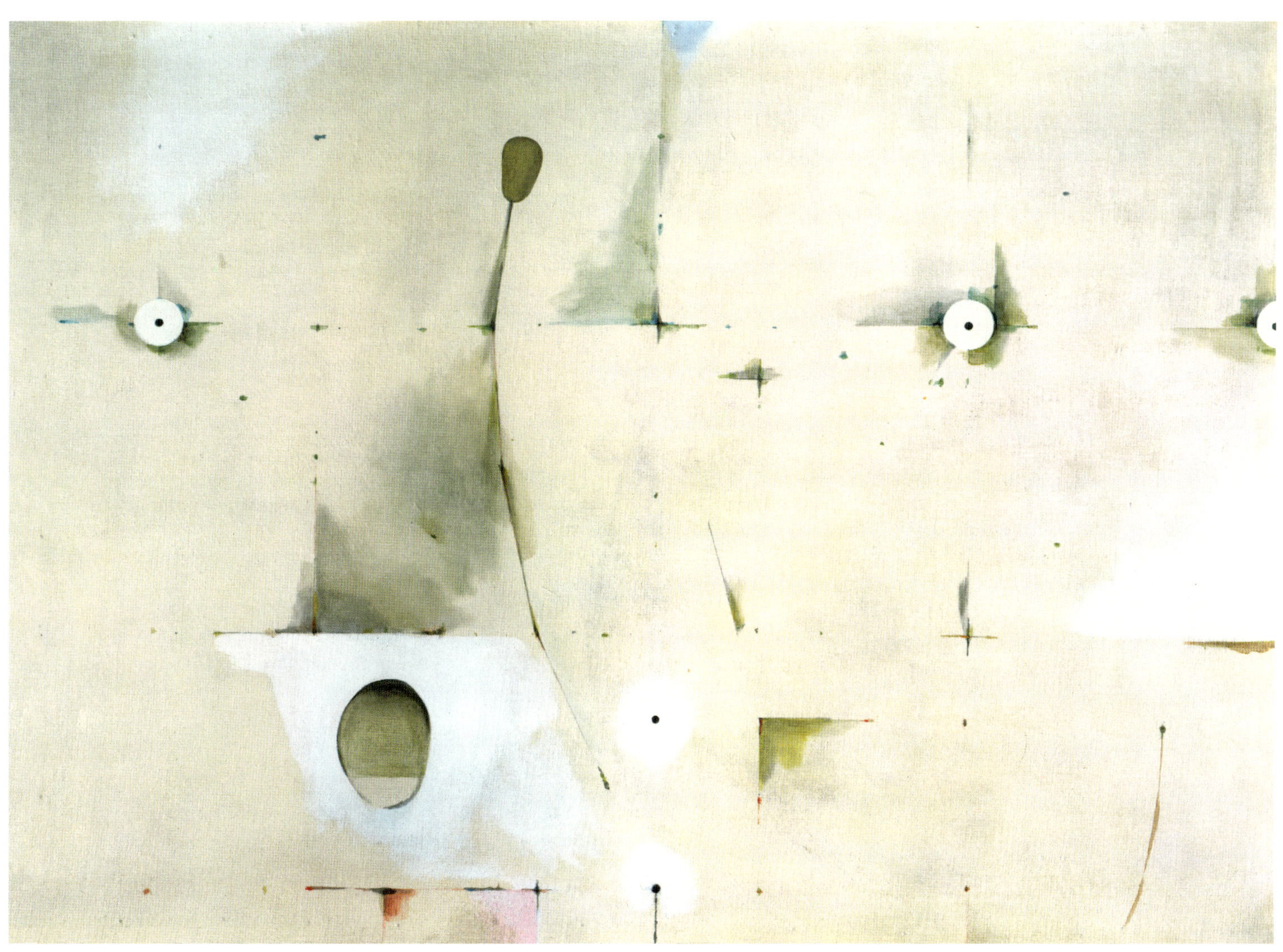

Respective 1951

d'Orientation 1952

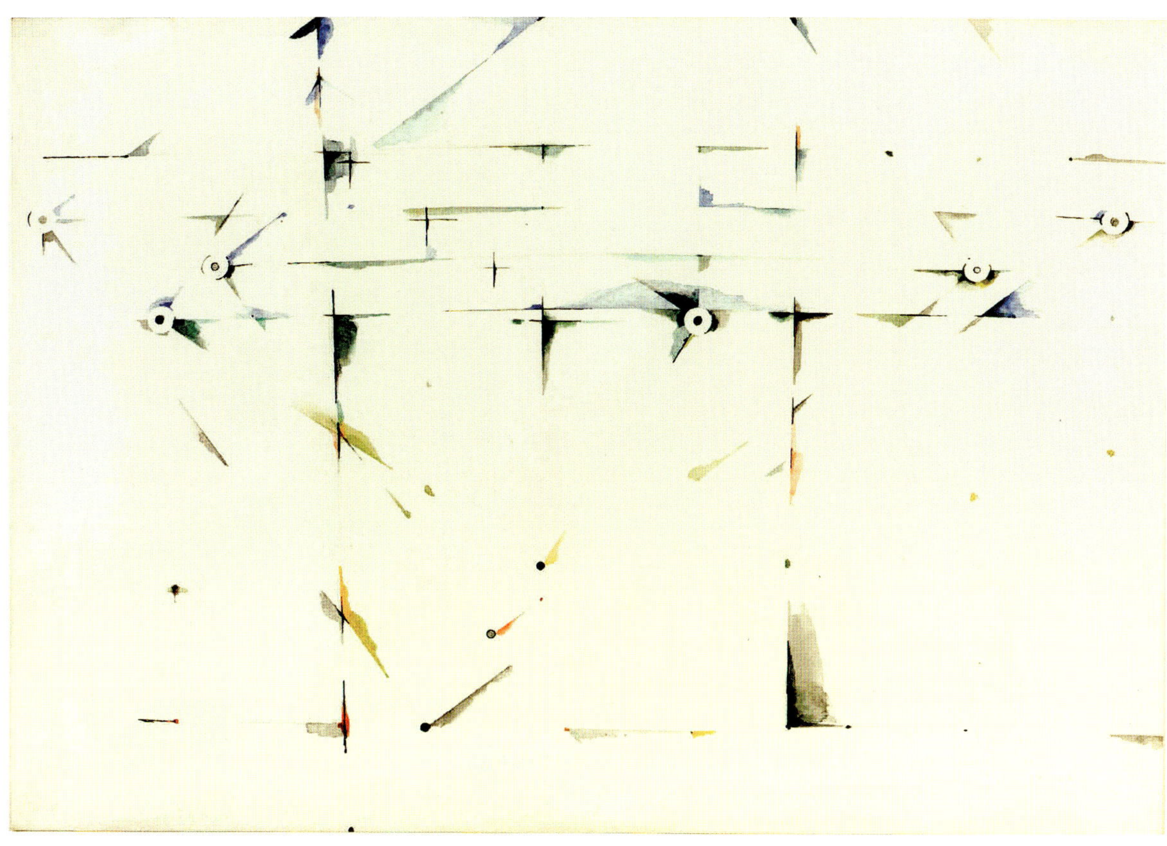

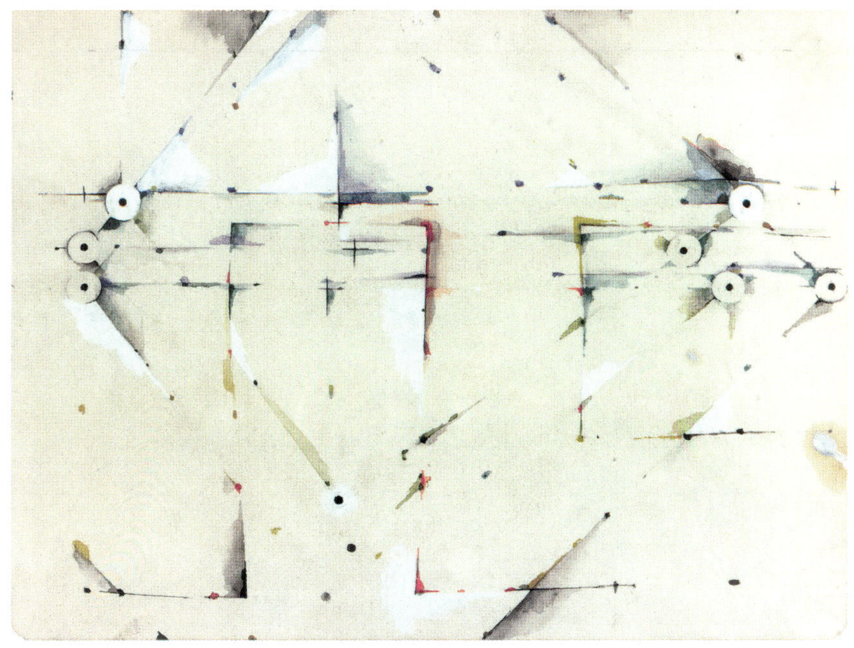

Out and up 1953

Sketch for "Super-Ex-Position" I 1953

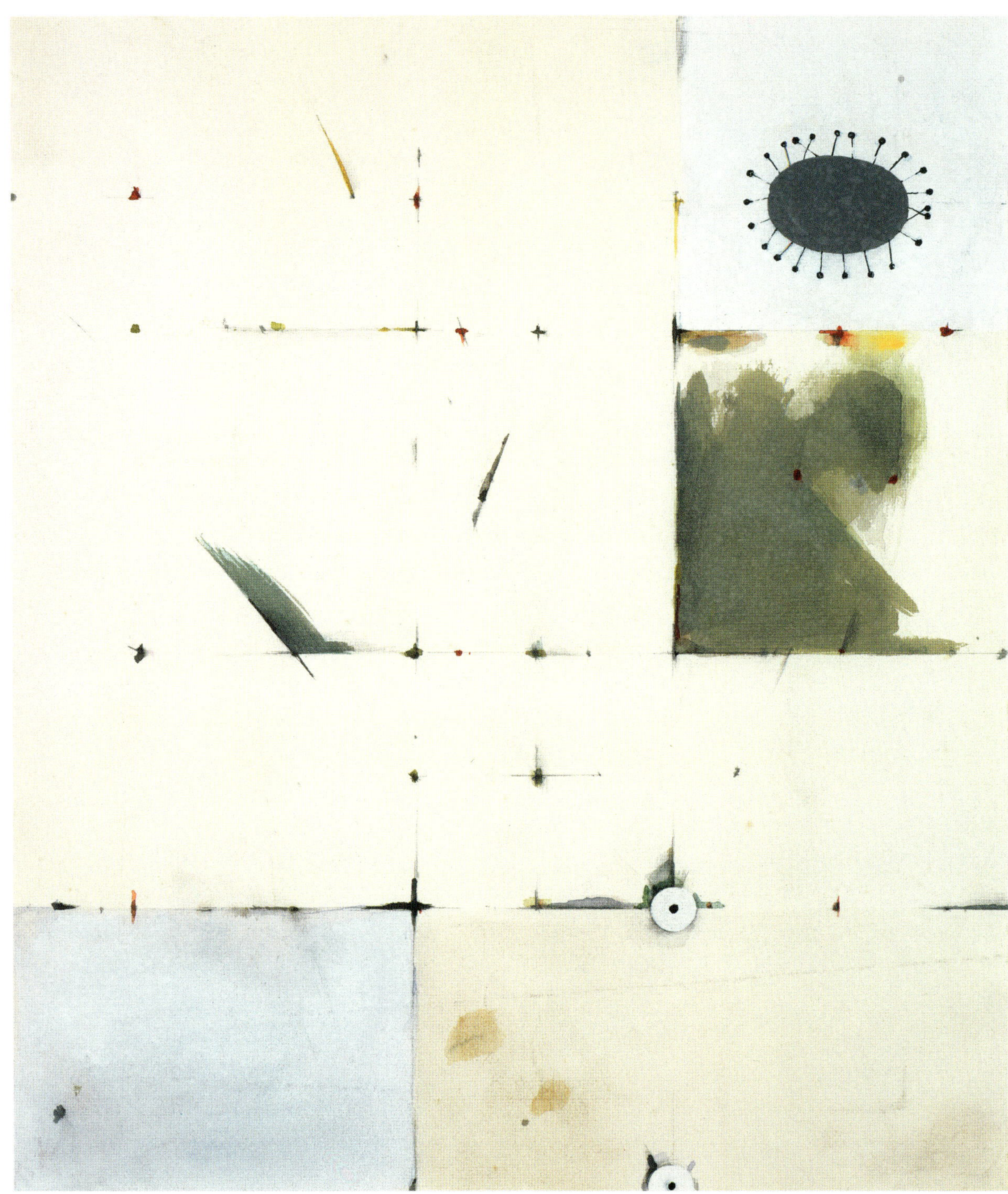

Sketch for "Ex-Position" 1952–53

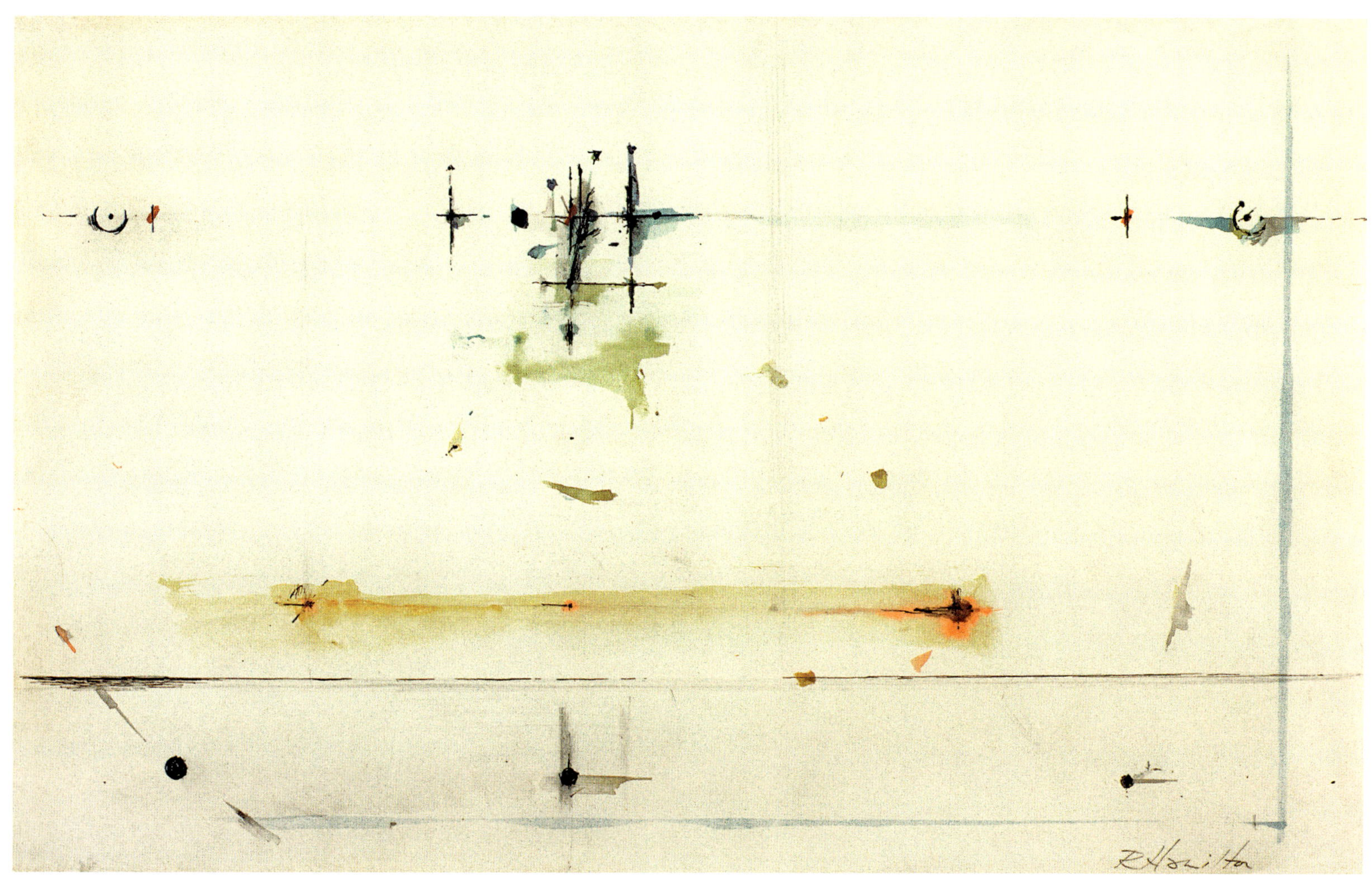

Drawing for "Trainsition" 1954

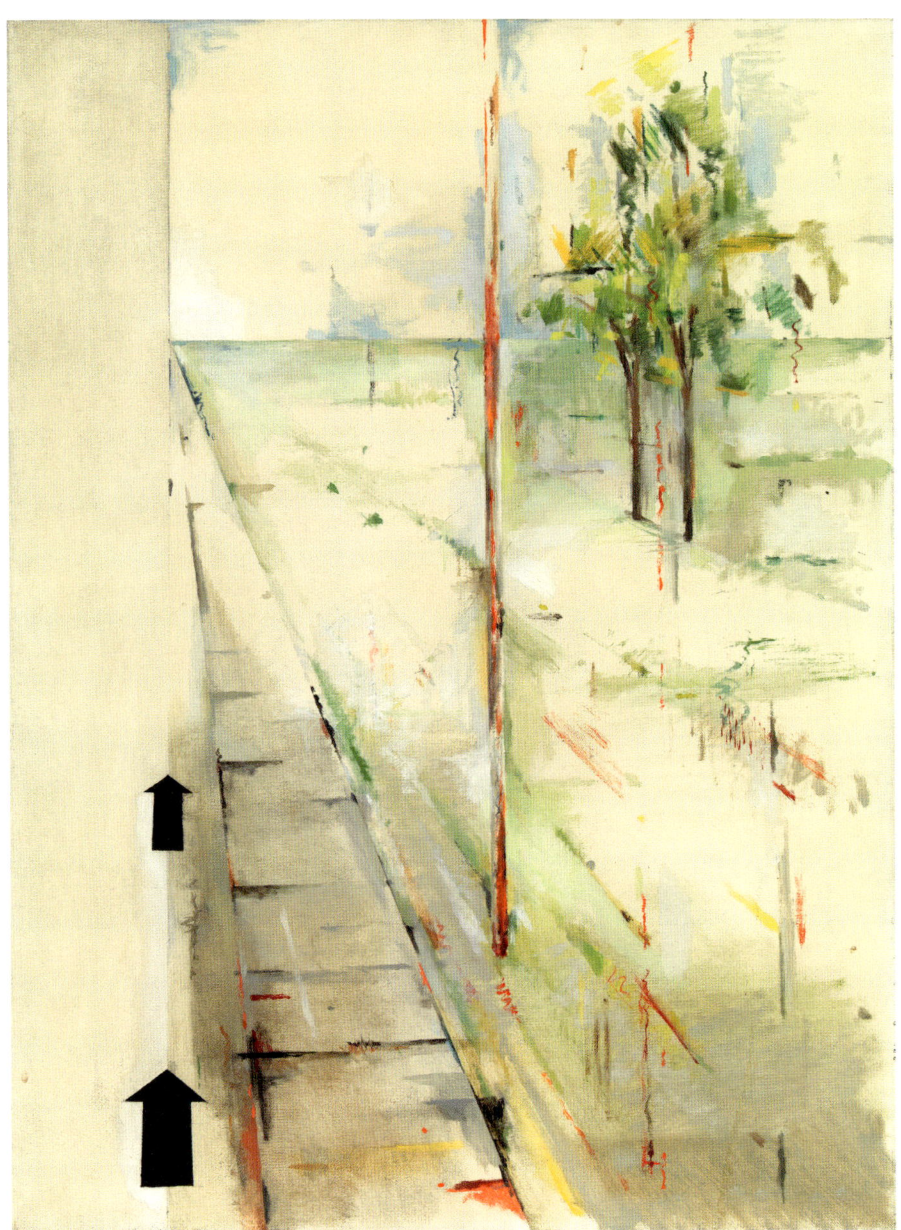

Trainsition III 1954

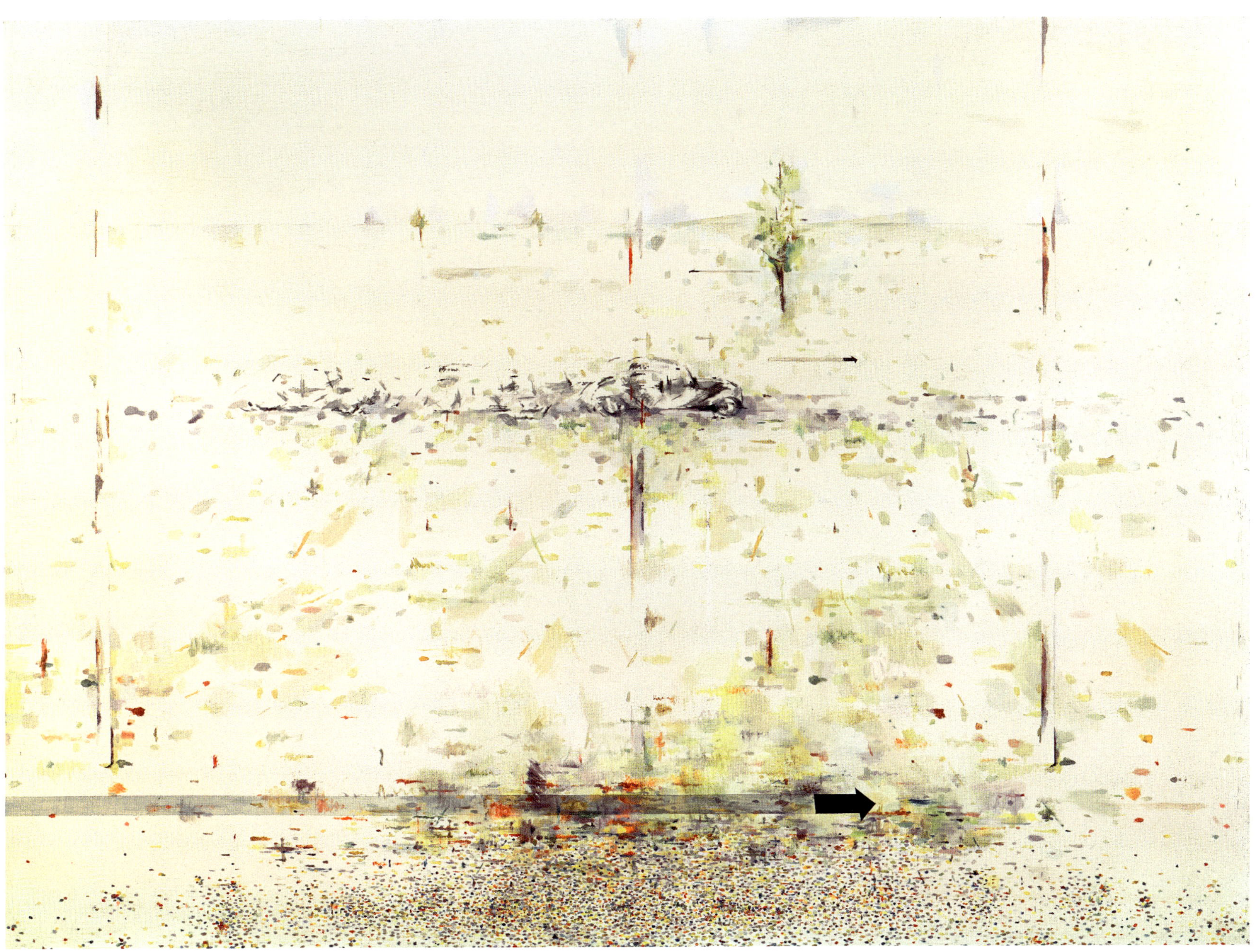

Trainsition IIII 1954

Man, Machine and Motion Hatton Gallery, Newcastle upon Tyne, 1955

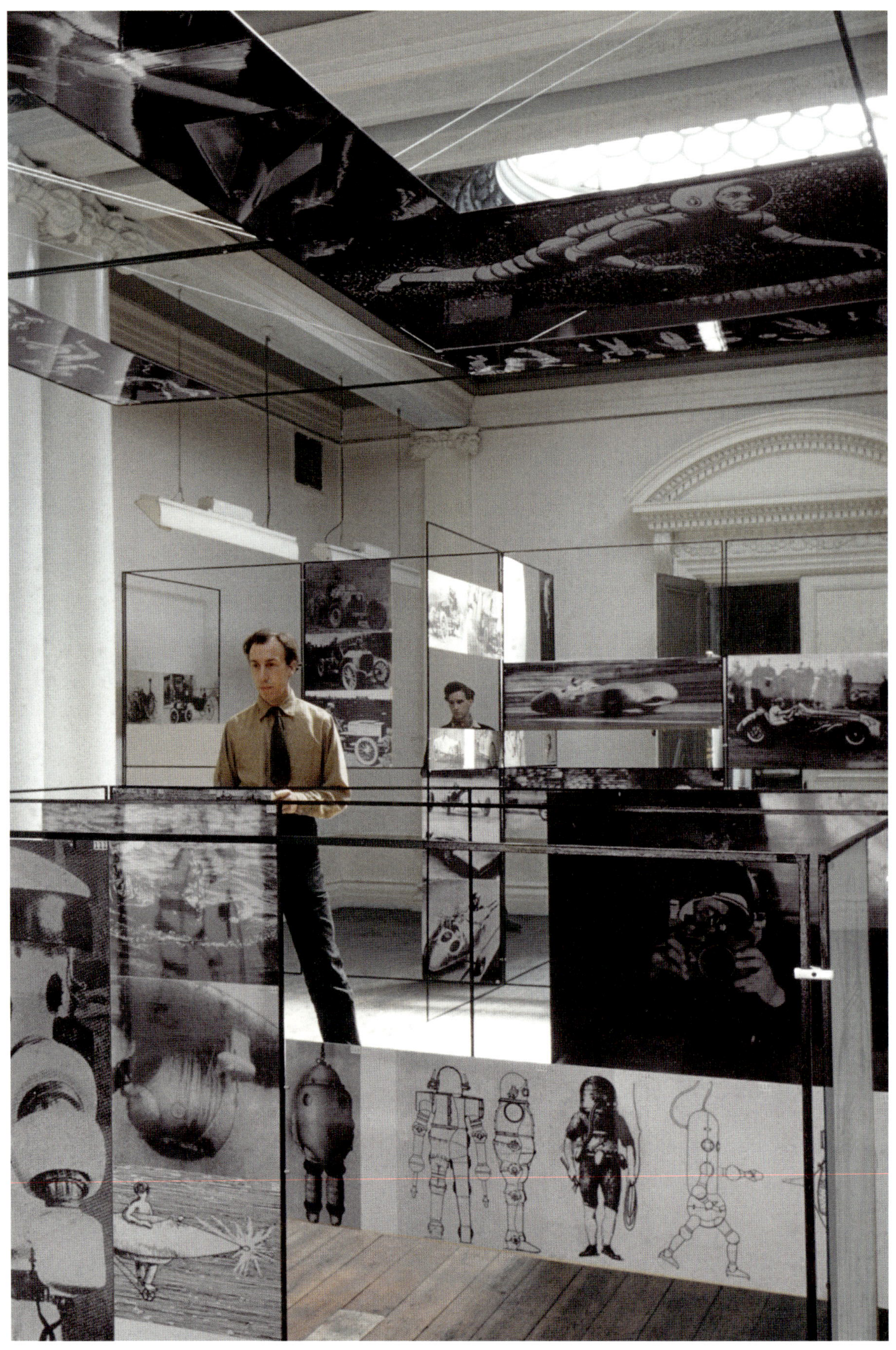

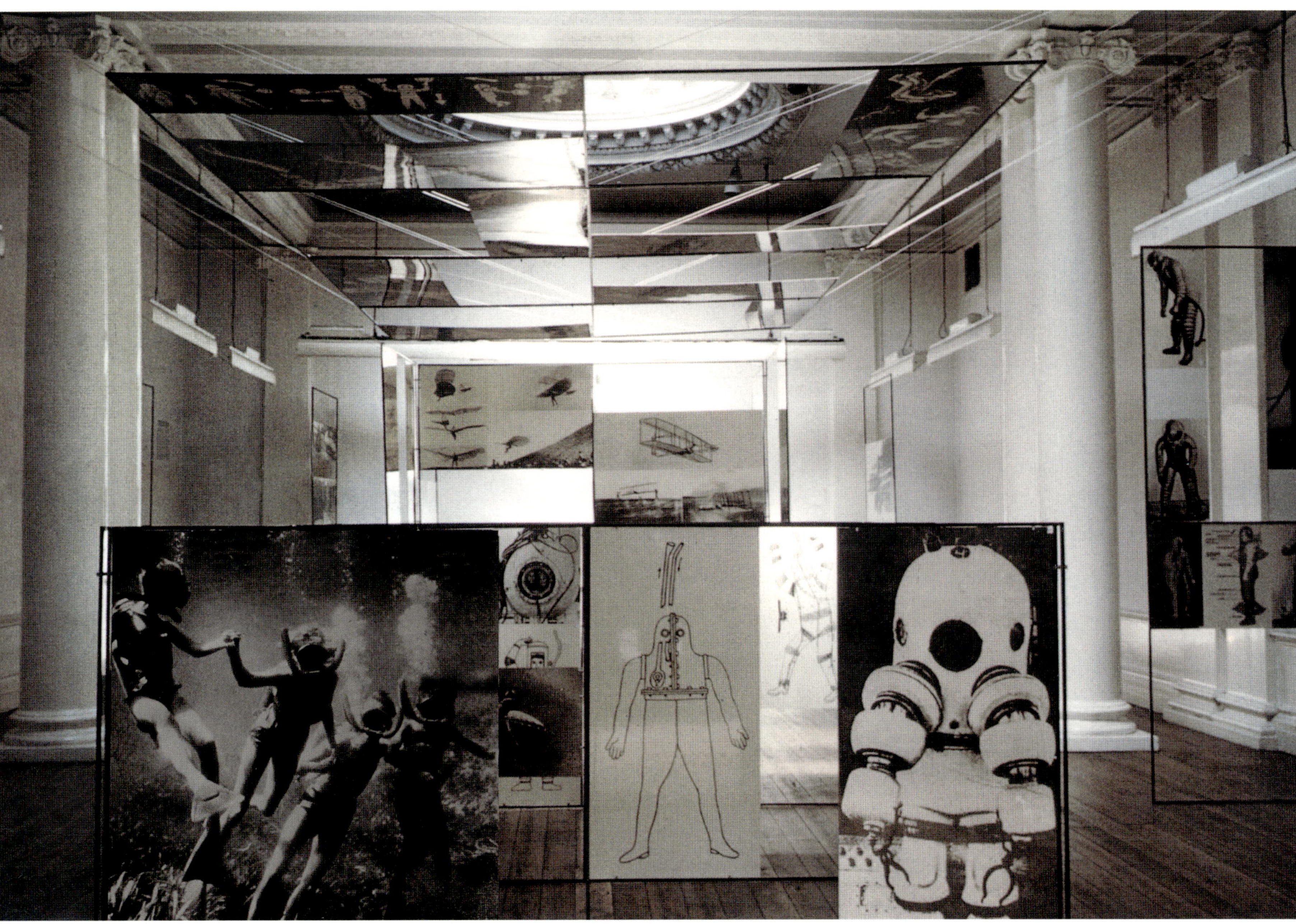

Man, Machine and Motion Hatton Gallery, Newcastle upon Tyne, 1955

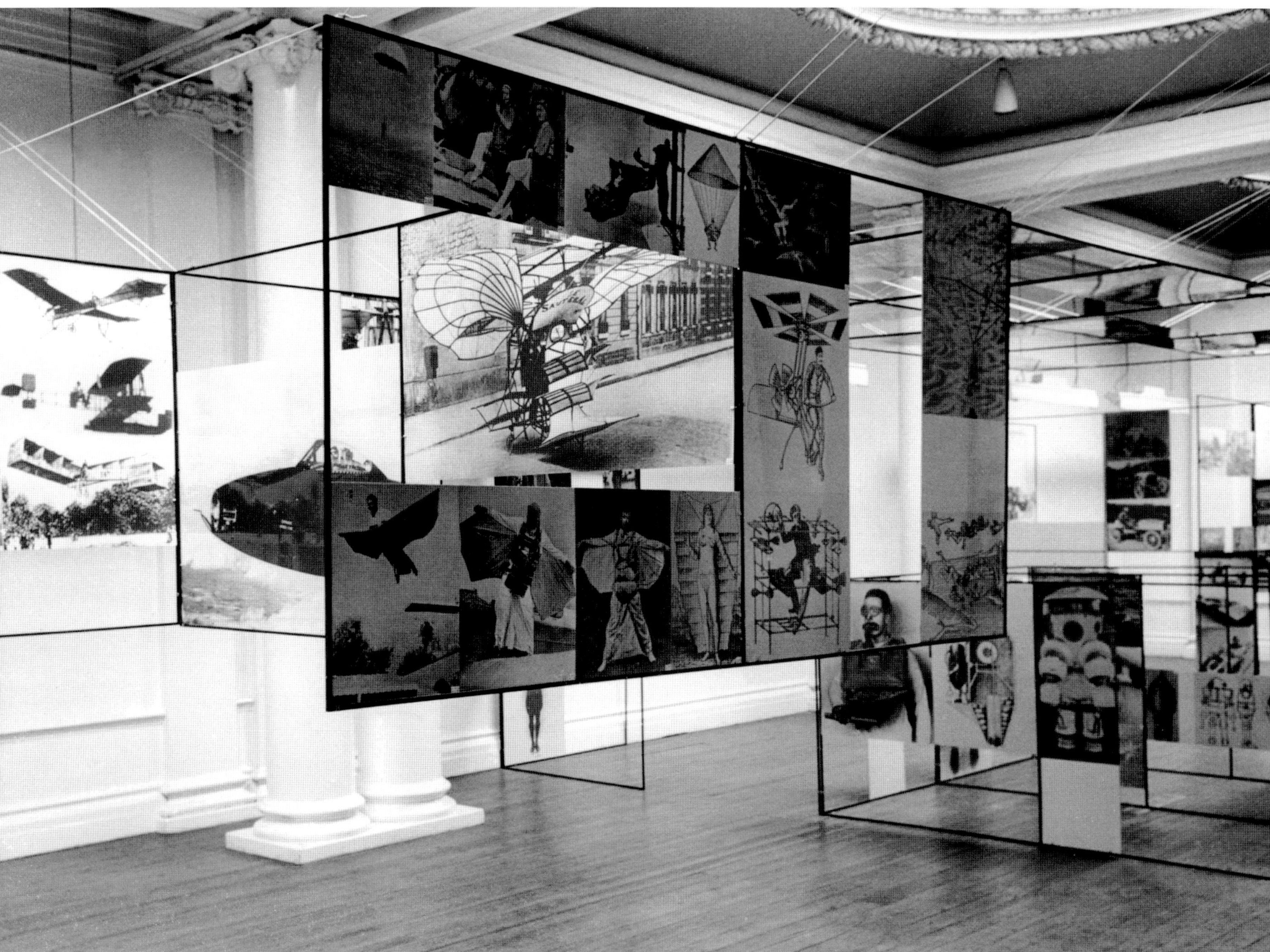

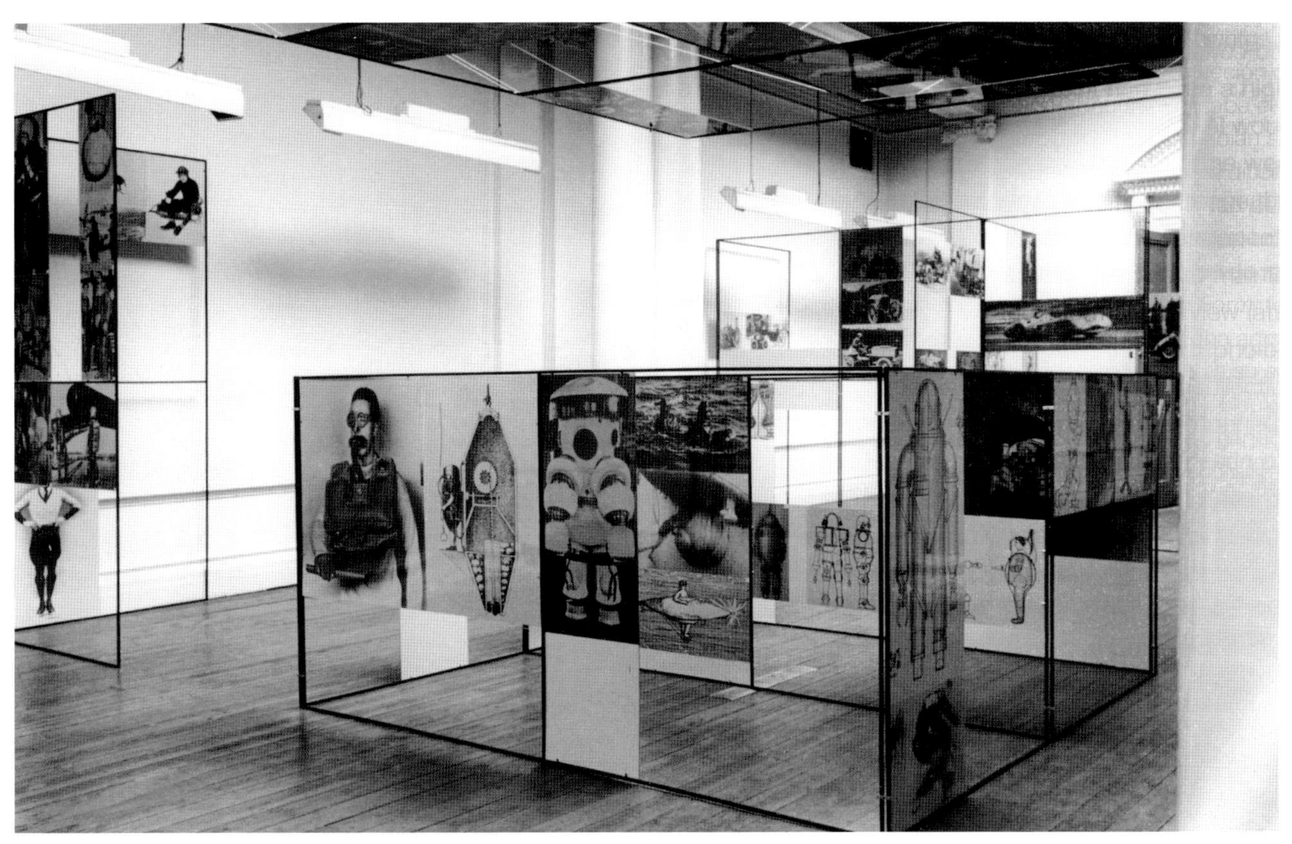

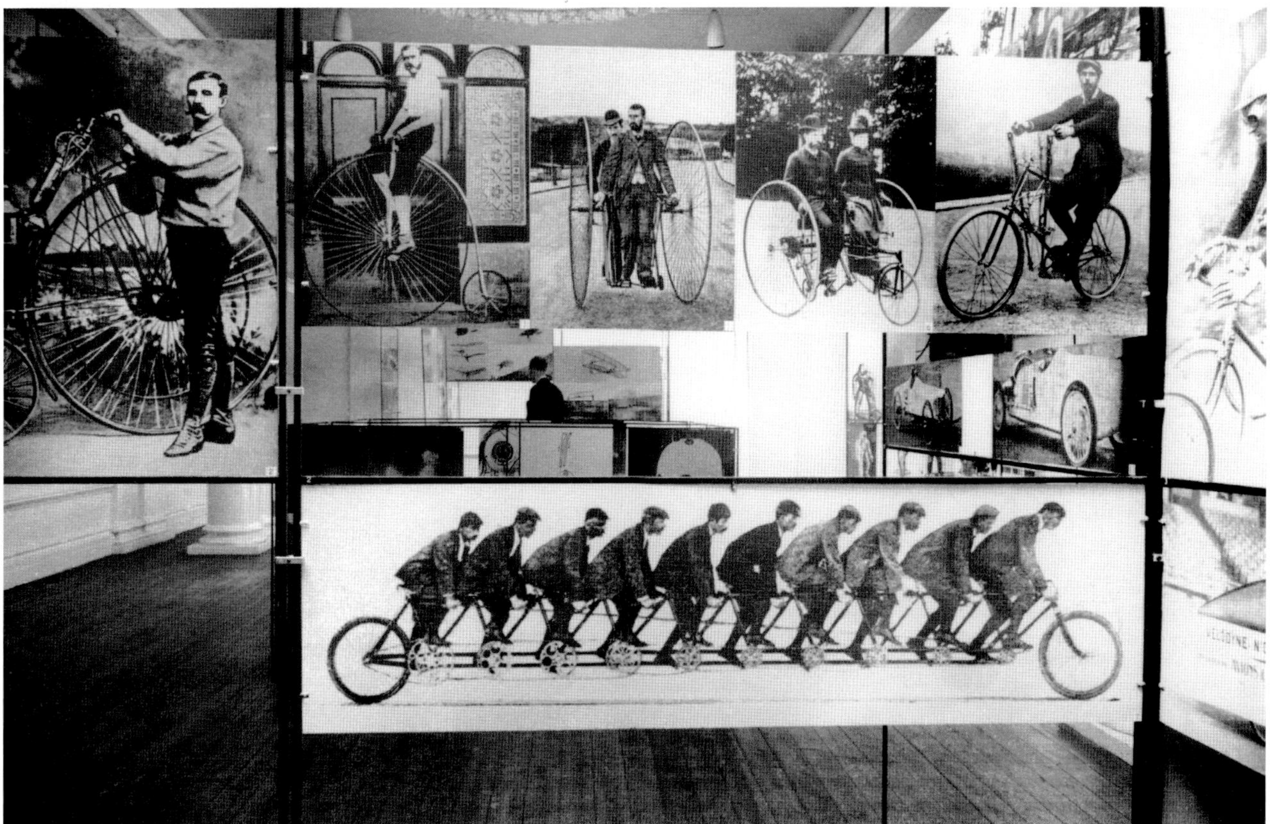

Man, Machine and Motion ICA, London, 1955

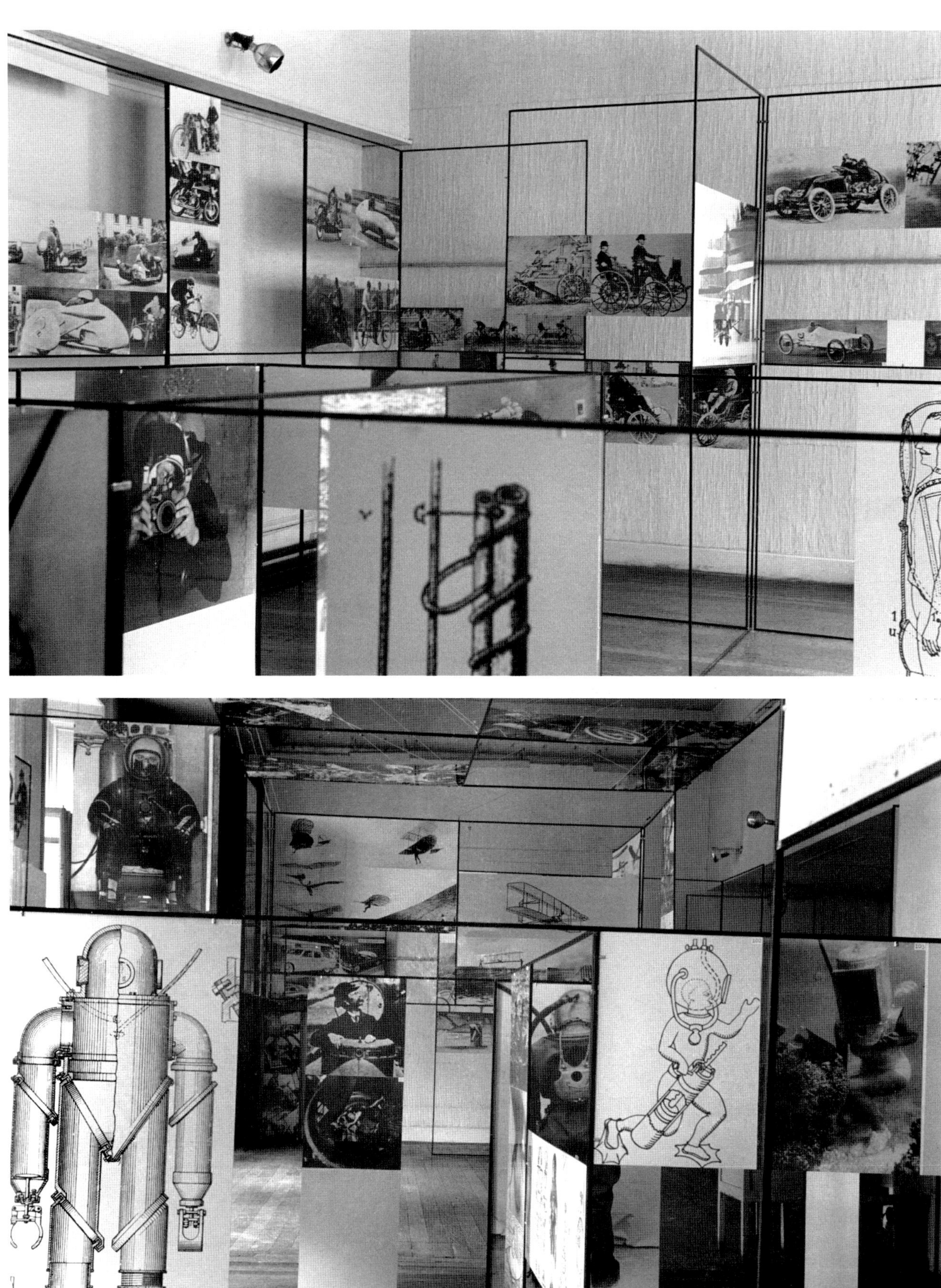

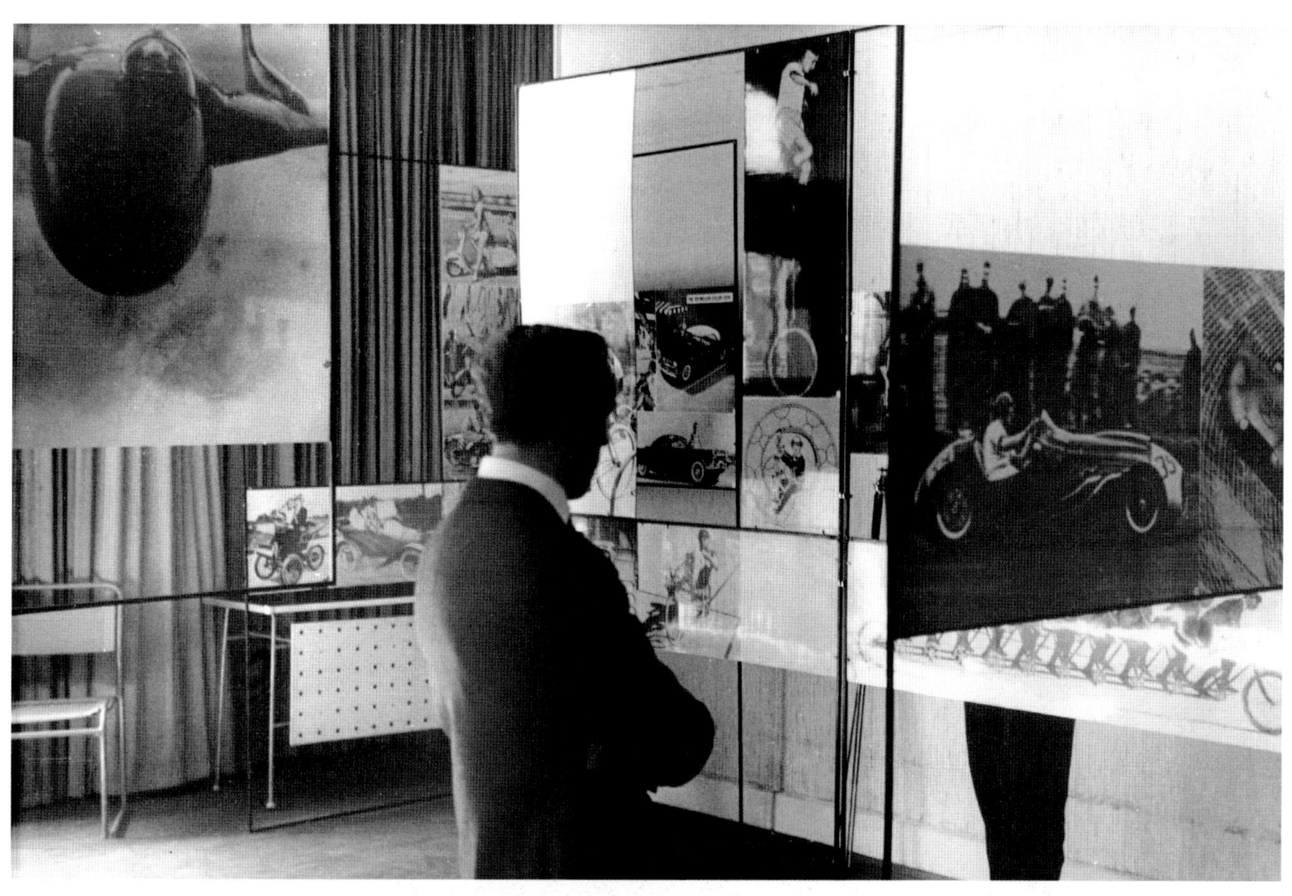

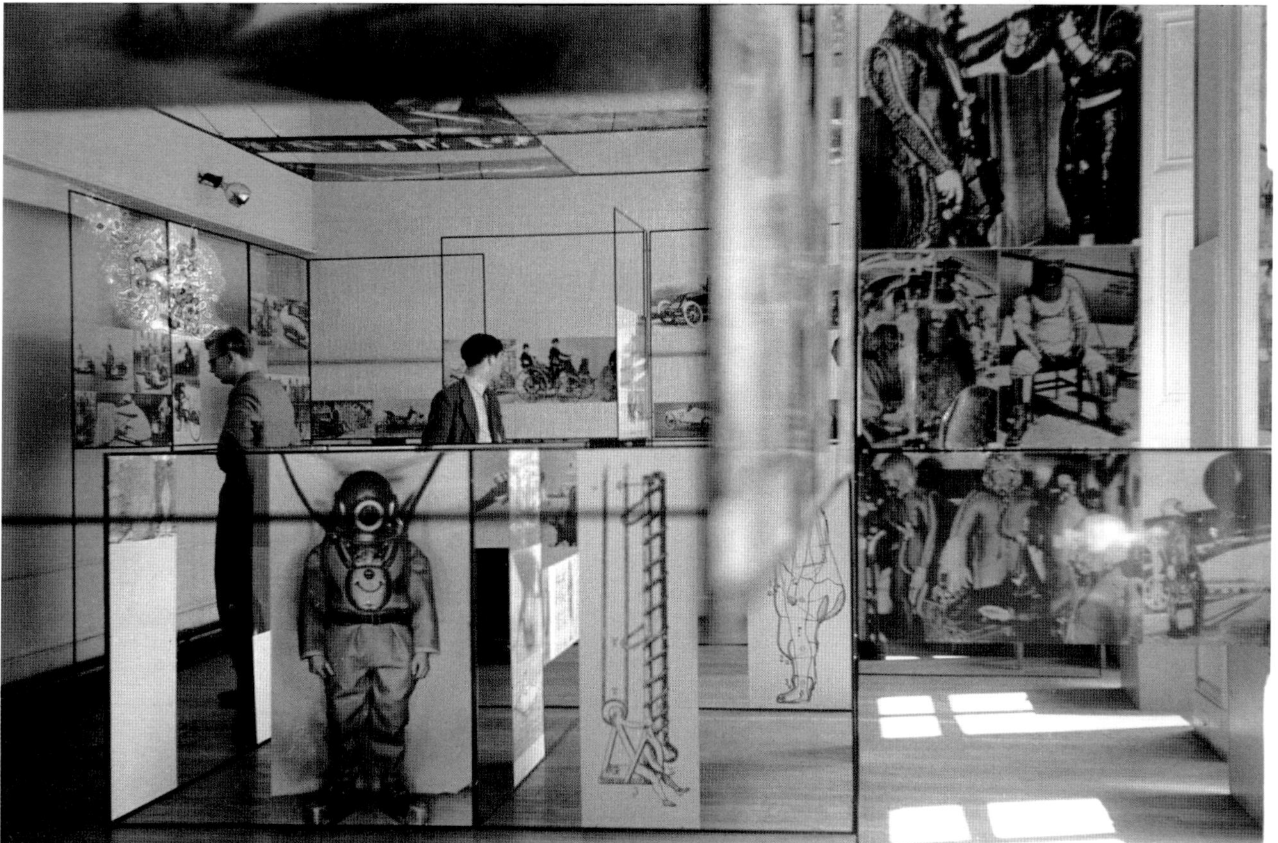

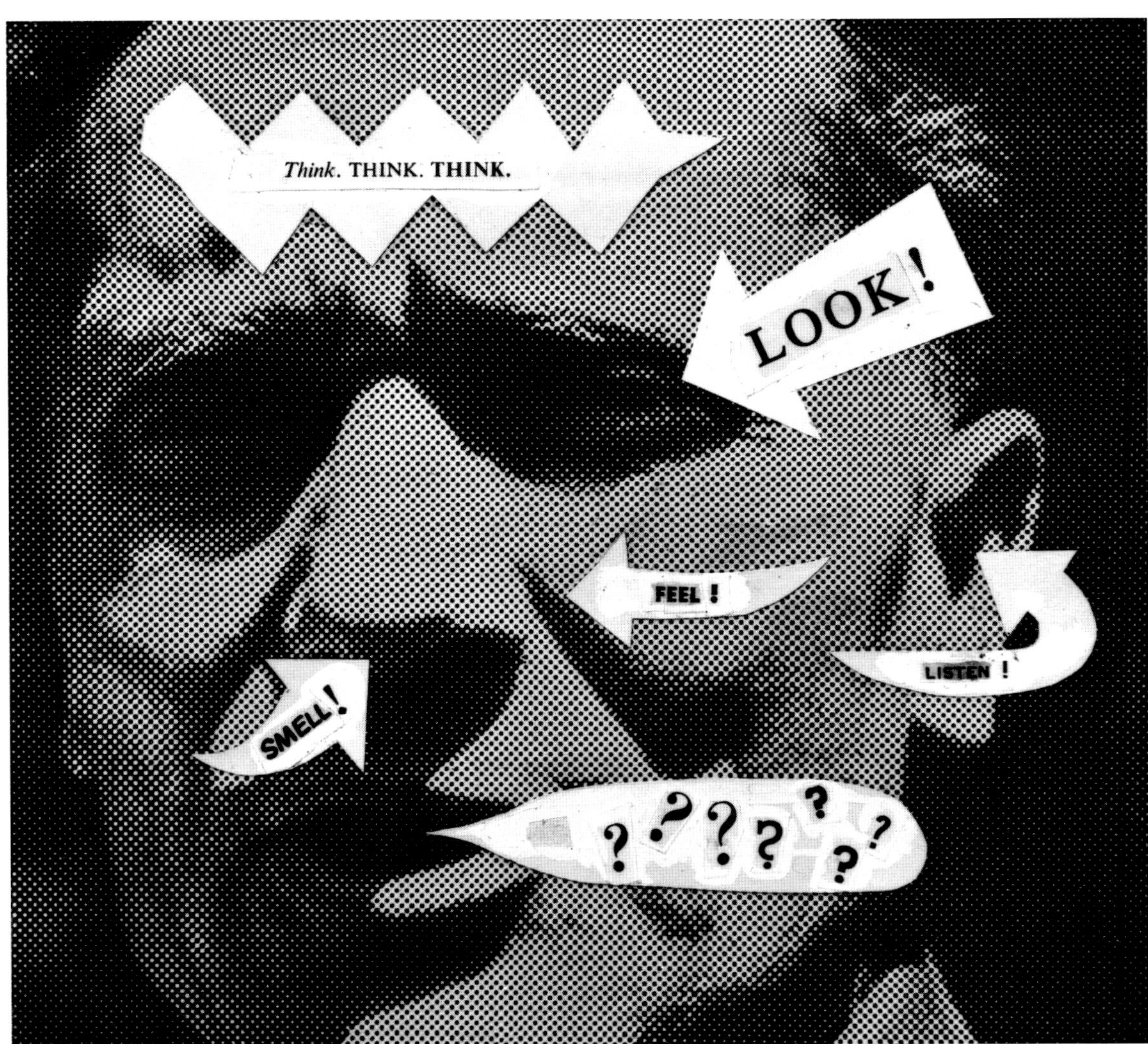

See, hear, smell, touch 1956

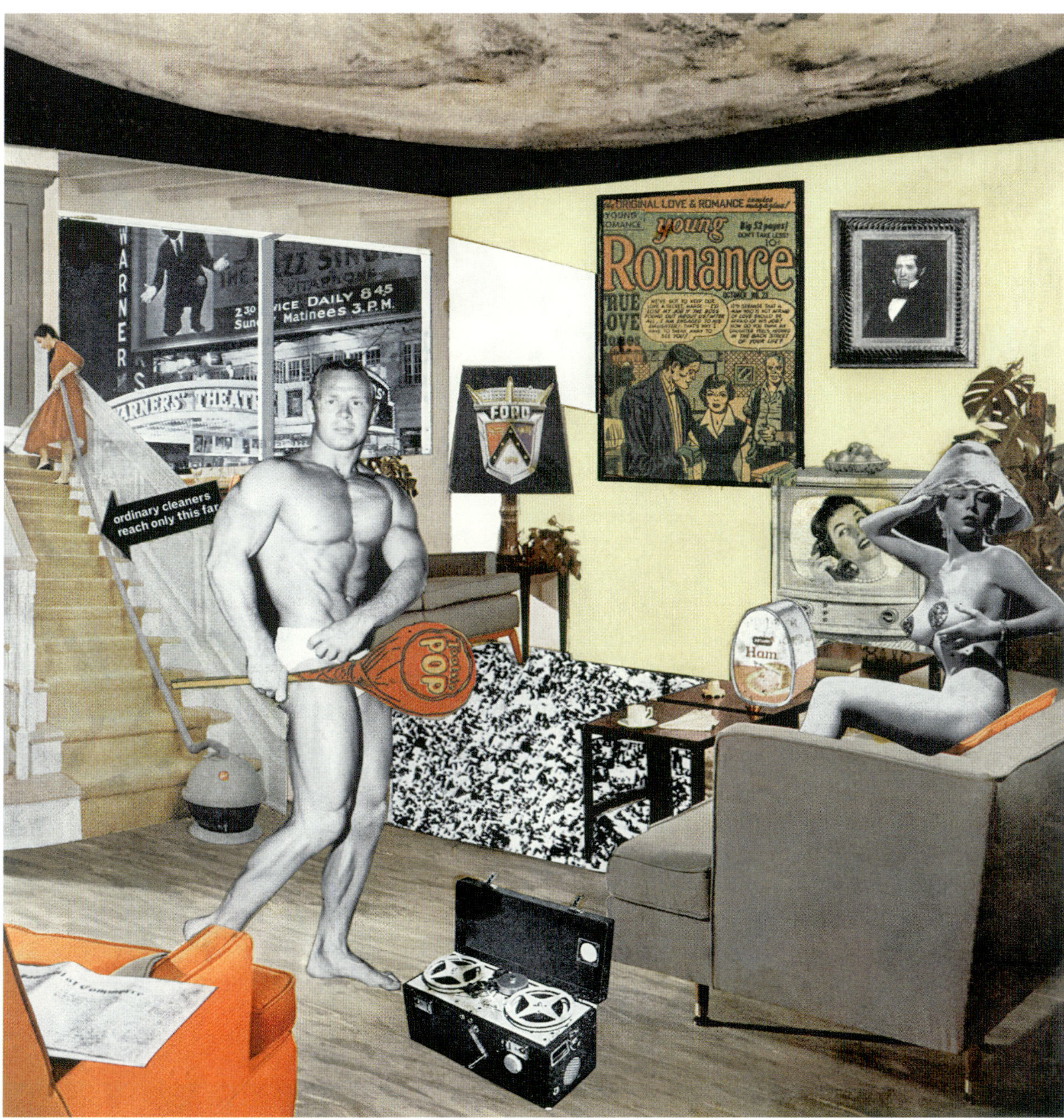

Just what is it that makes today's homes so different, so appealing? 1956

This is Tomorrow, Group 2
(Richard Hamilton, John McHale and John Voelcker) Whitechapel Art Gallery, London, 1956

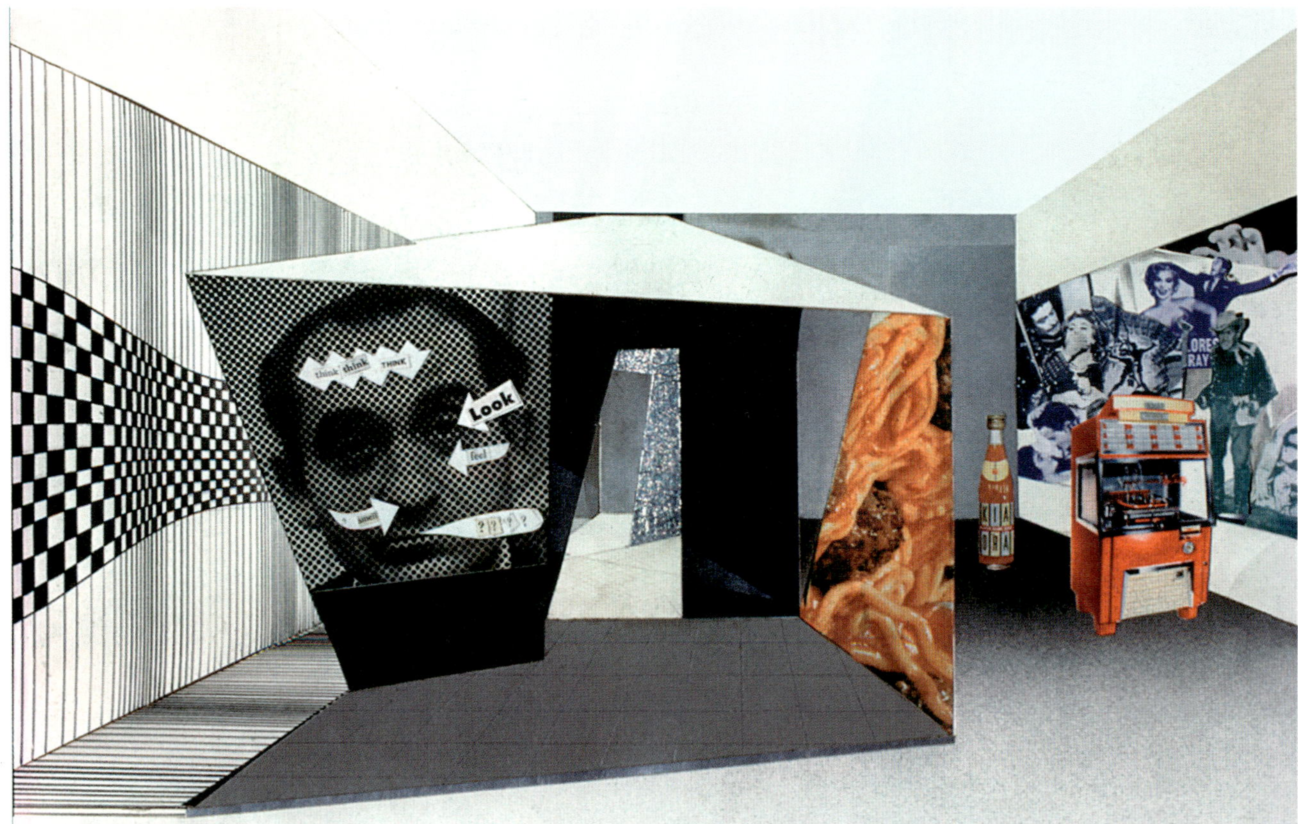

This is Tomorrow, perspective of exhibit 1956

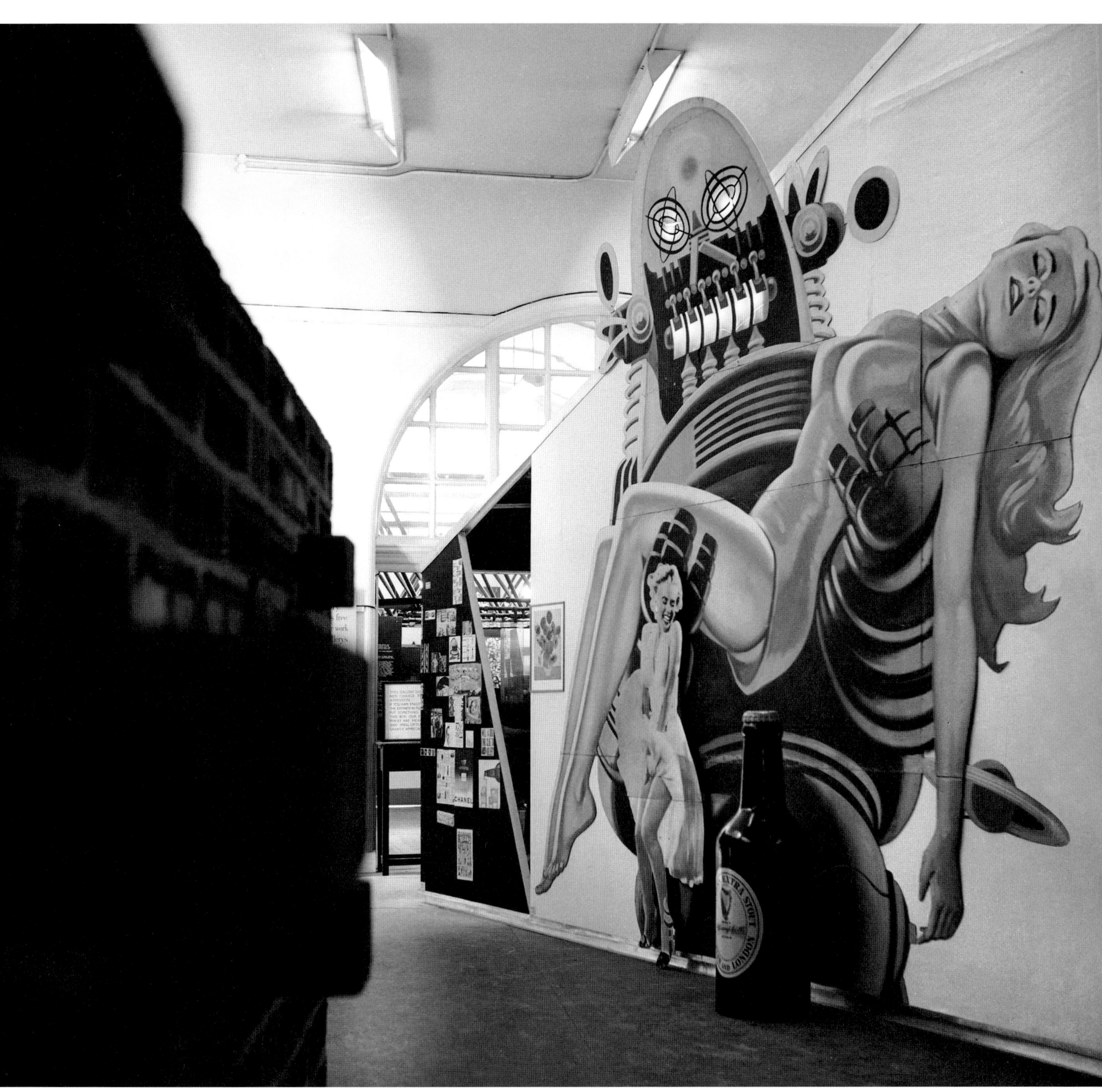
CHANEL
EXTRA STOUT
AND LONDON

This is Tomorrow, Group 2
(Richard Hamilton, John McHale and John Voelcker) Whitechapel Art Gallery, London, 1956

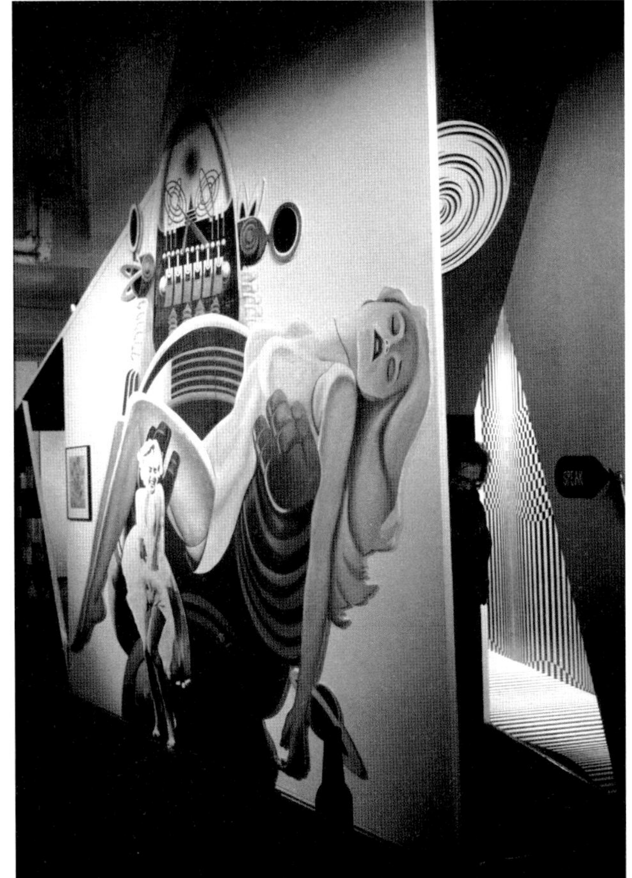

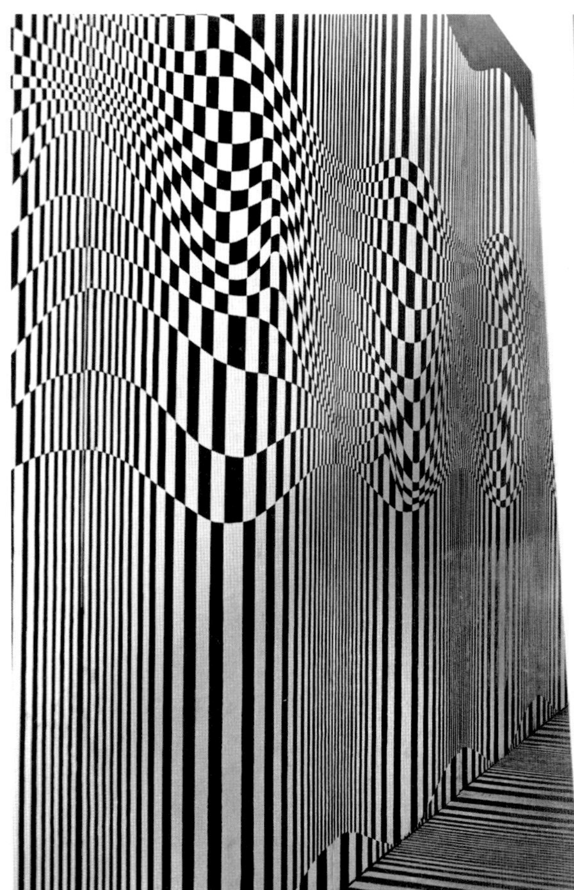

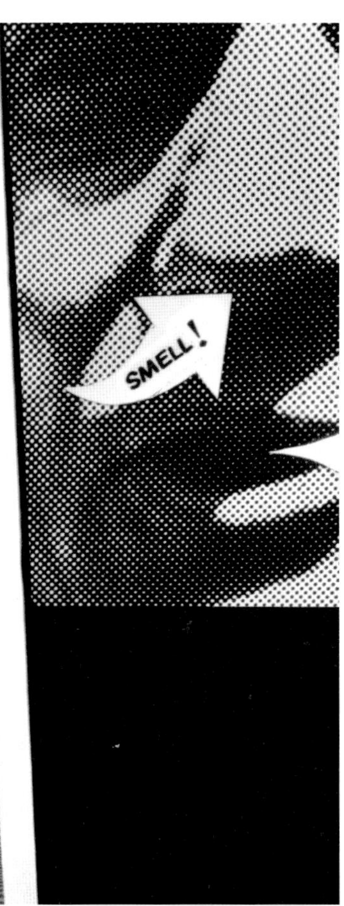

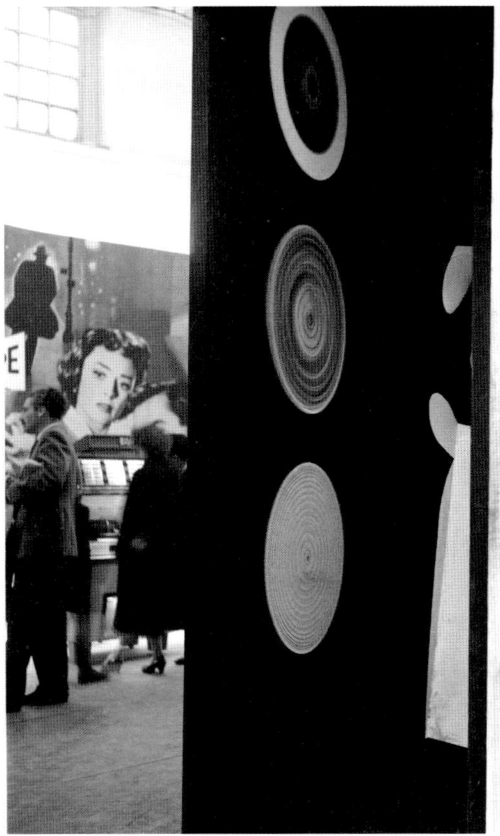

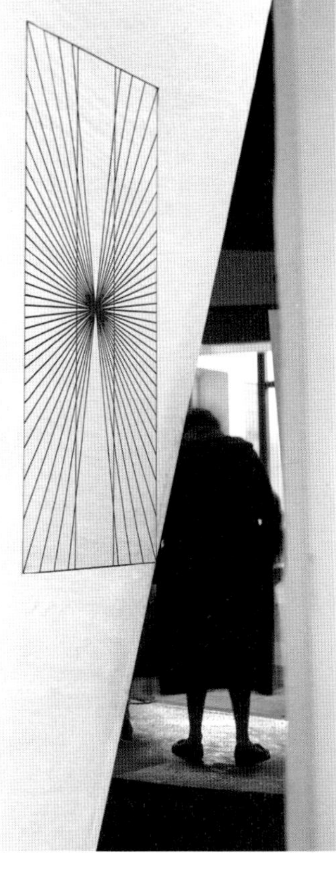

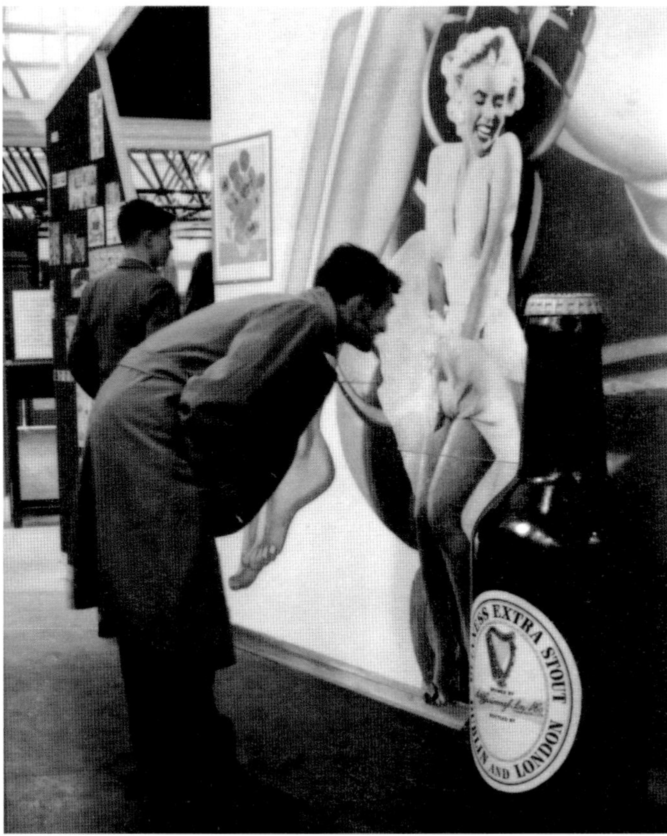

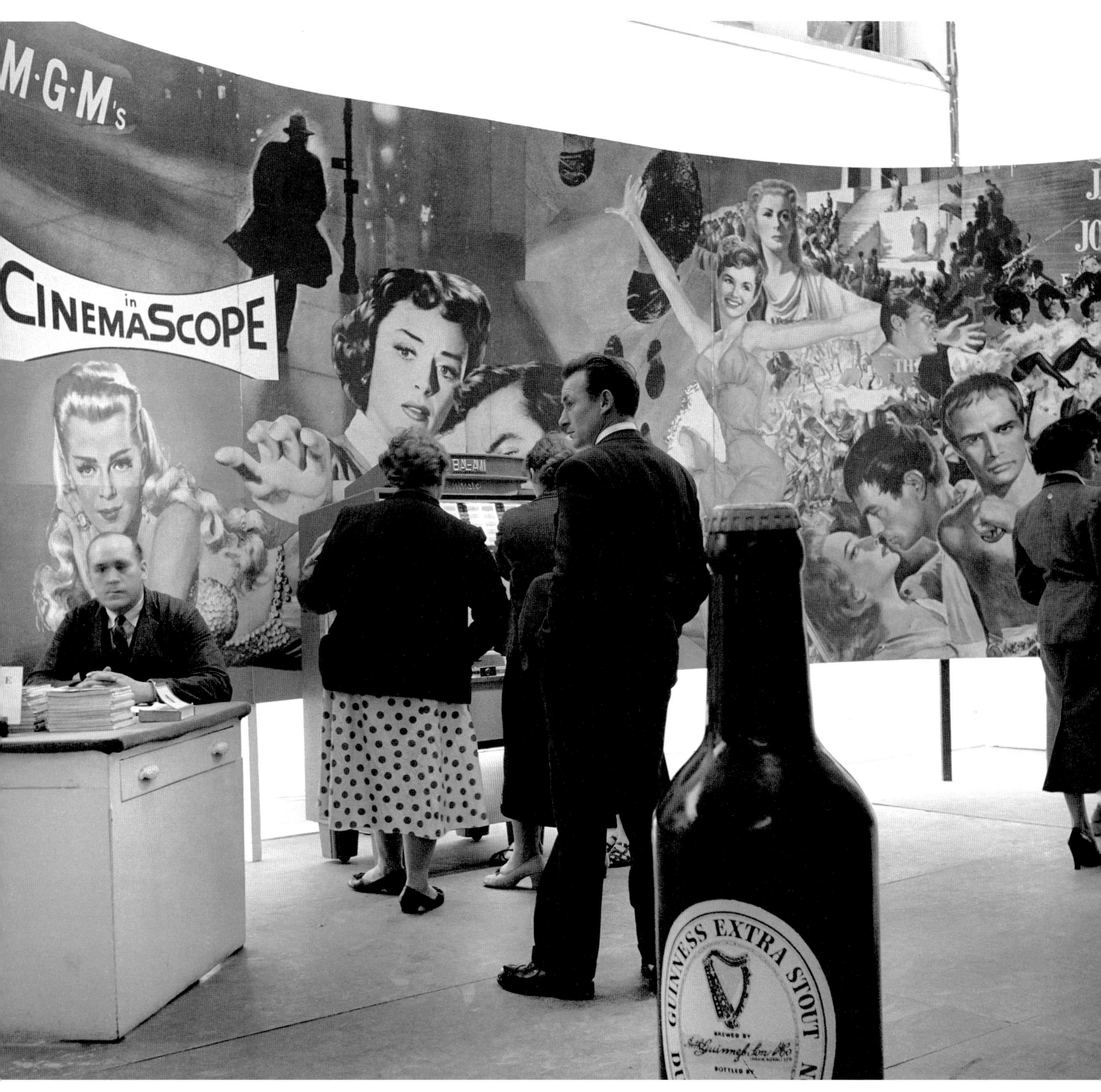
M·G·M's
in
CINEMASCOPE
GUINNESS EXTRA STOUT
BREWED BY
BOTTLED BY

an Exhibit (with Victor Pasmore and Lawrence Alloway) Hatton Gallery, Newcastle upon Tyne, 1957

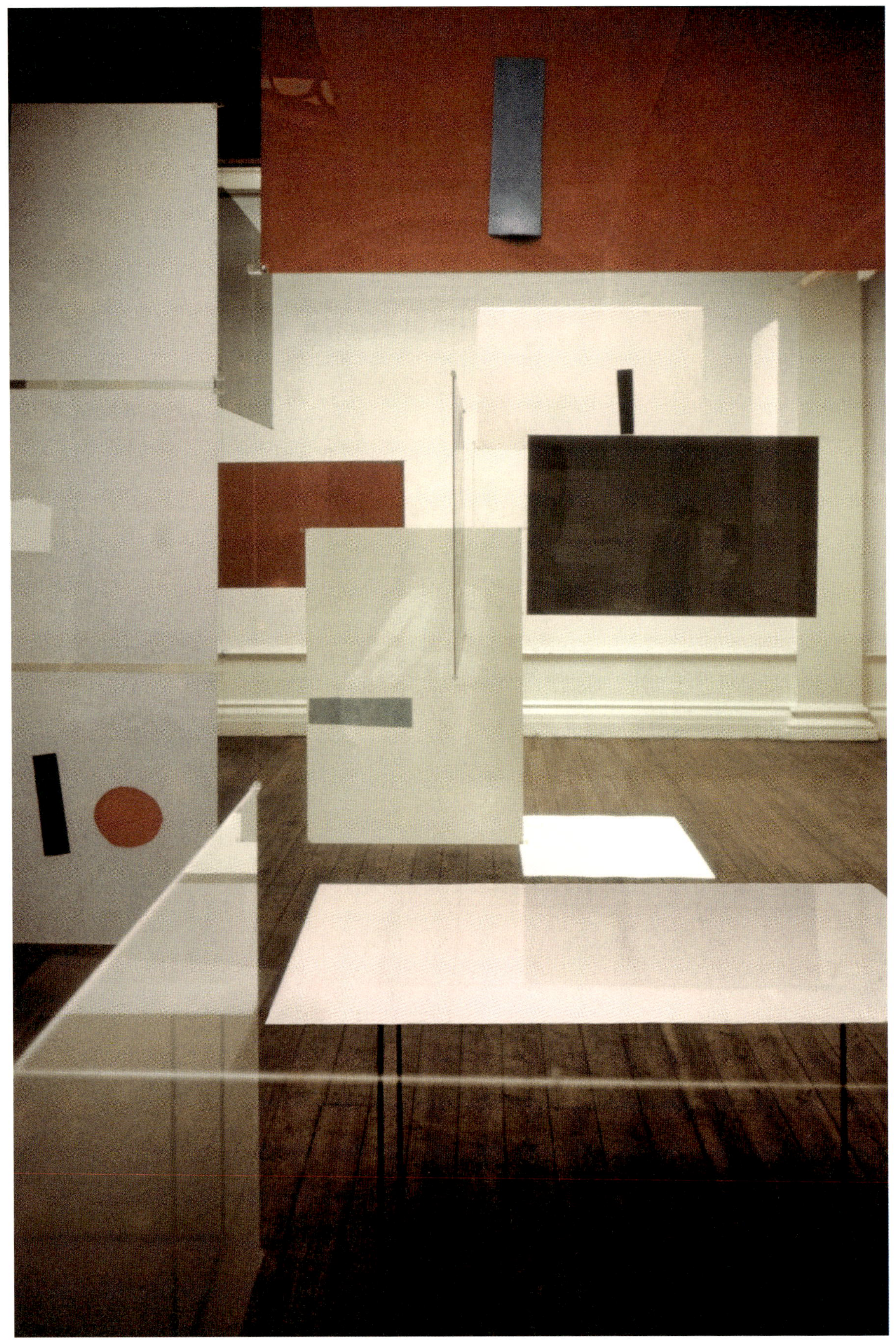

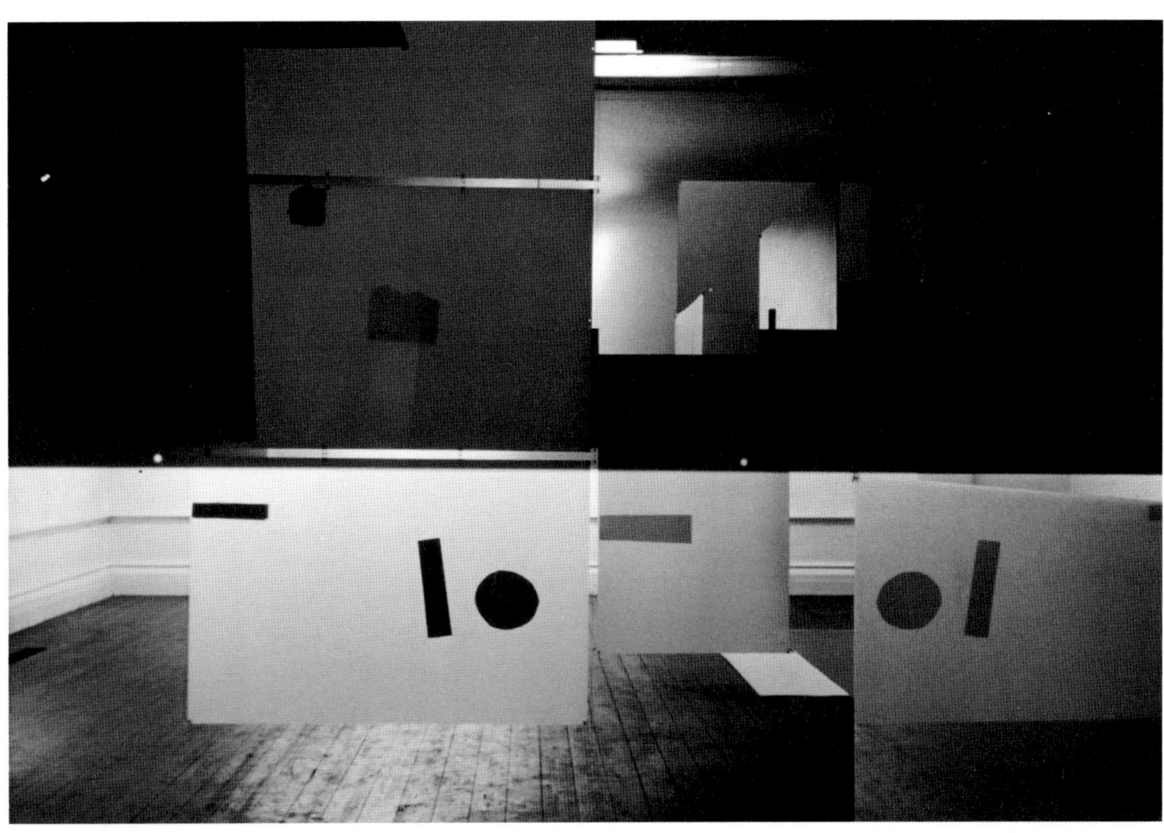

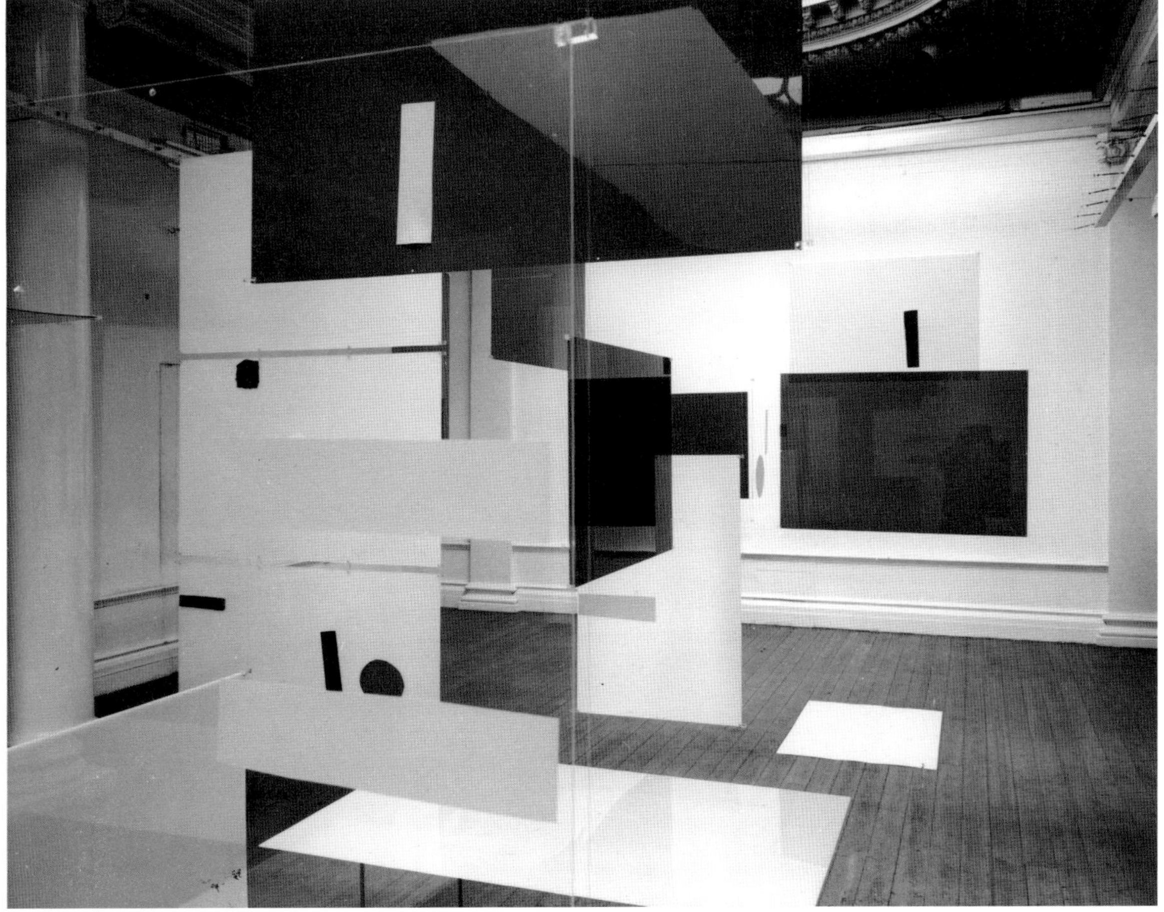

an Exhibit (with Victor Pasmore and Lawrence Alloway) Hatton Gallery, Newcastle upon Tyne, 1957

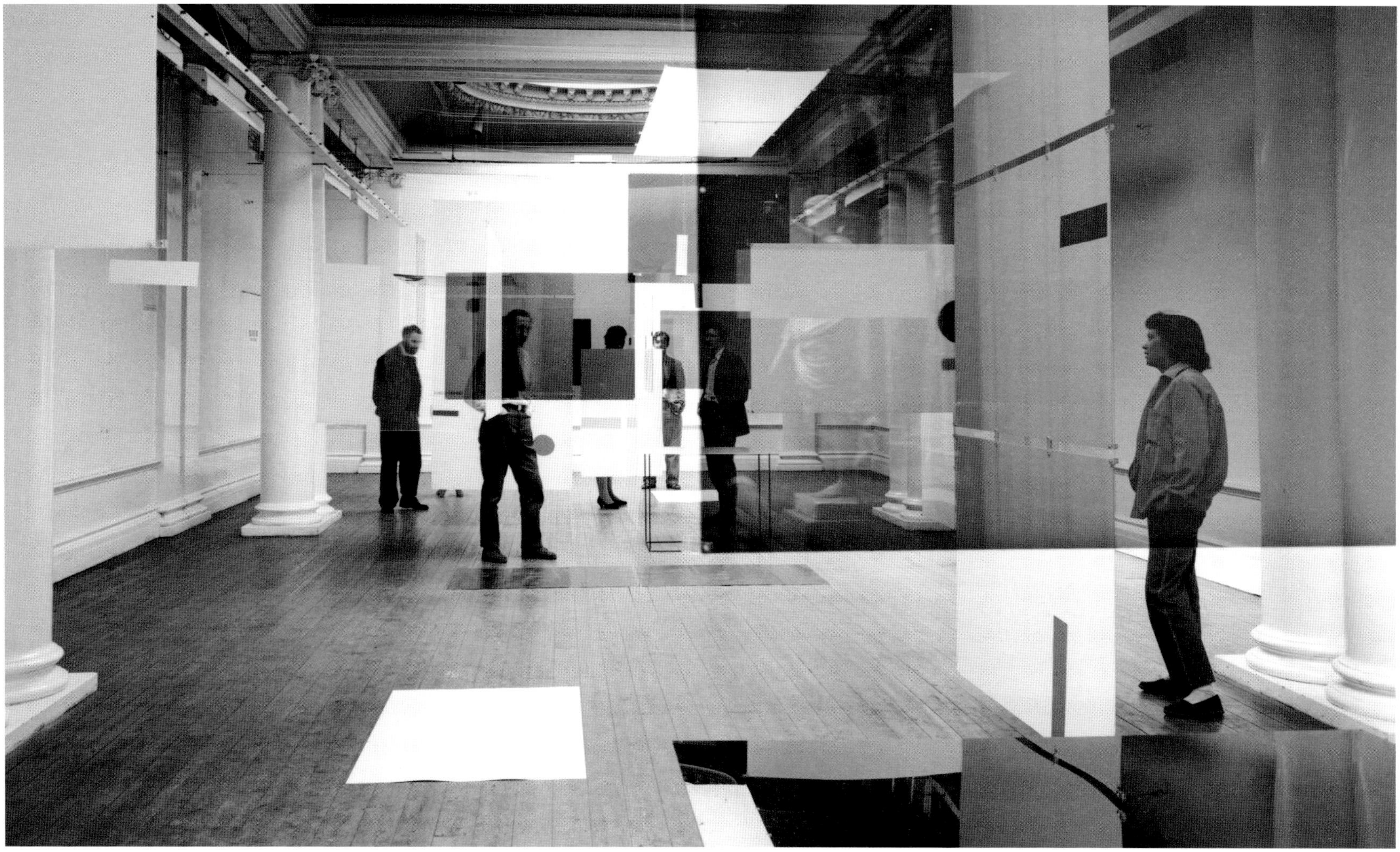

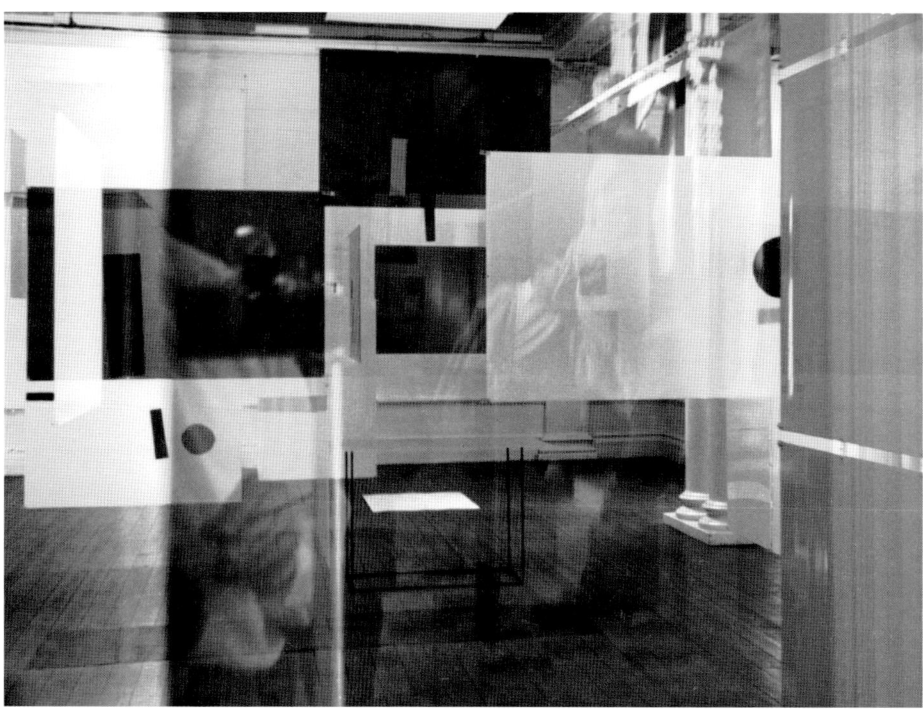

an Exhibit (with Victor Pasmore and Lawrence Alloway) ICA, London, 1957

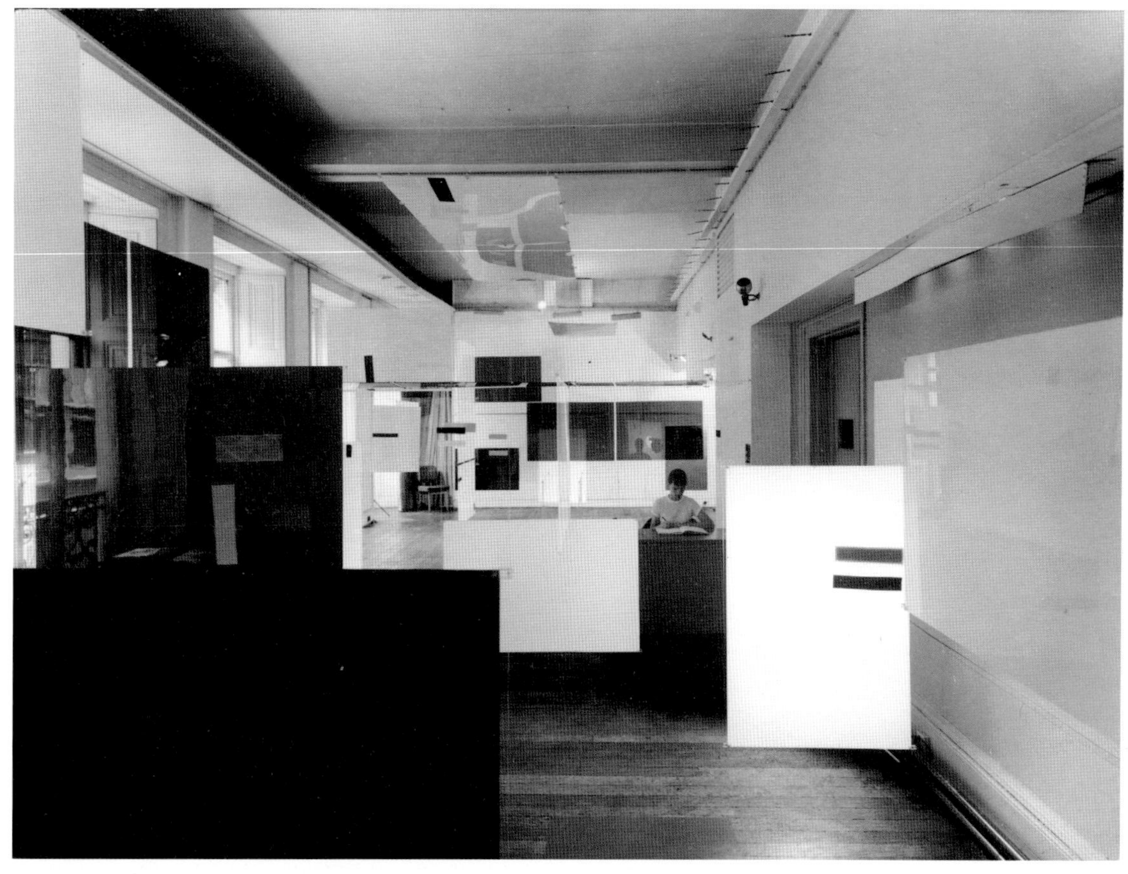

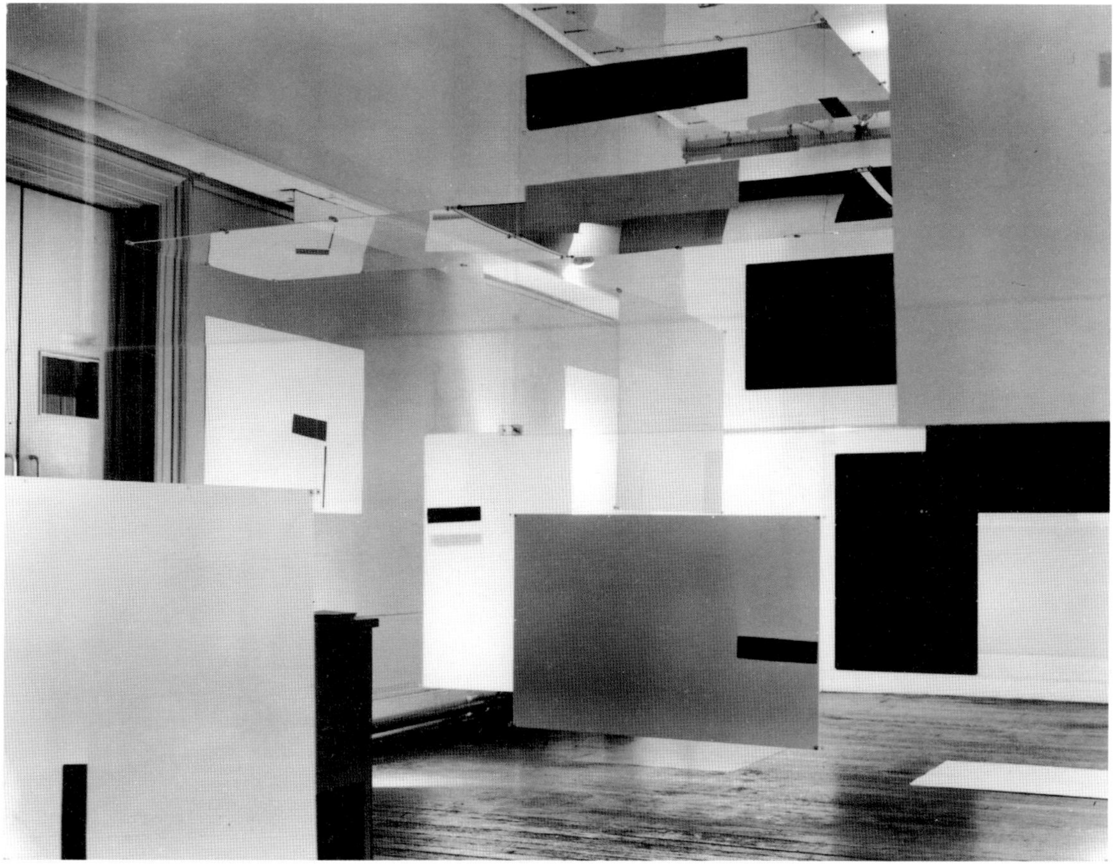

an Exhibit (with Victor Pasmore and Lawrence Alloway) ICA, London, 1957

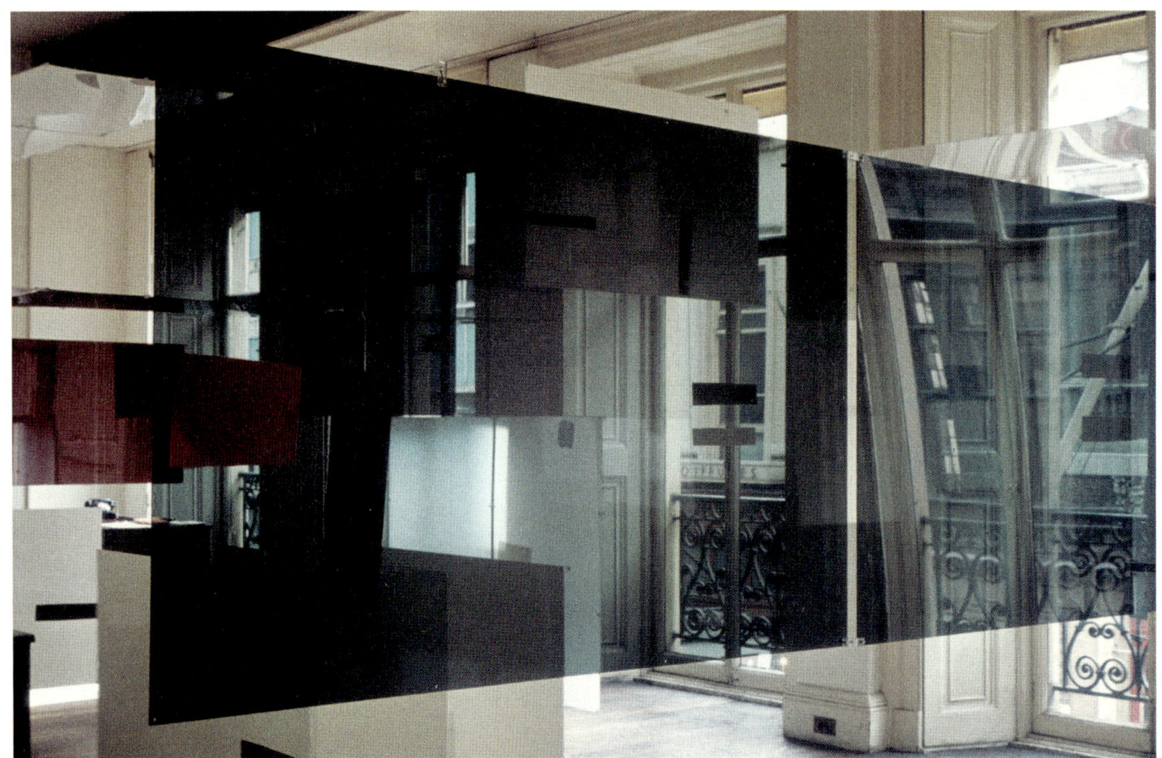

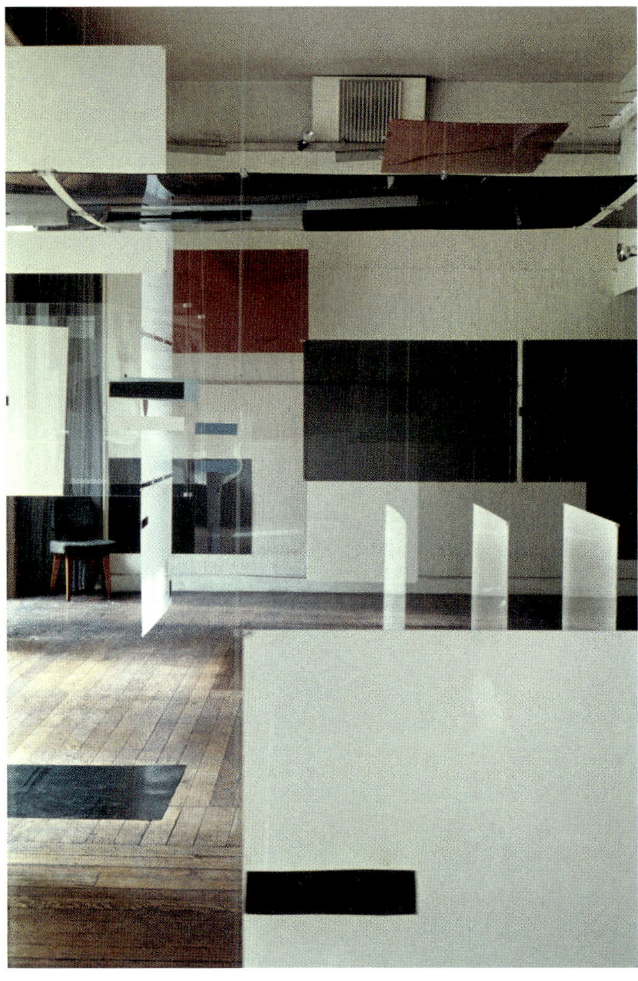

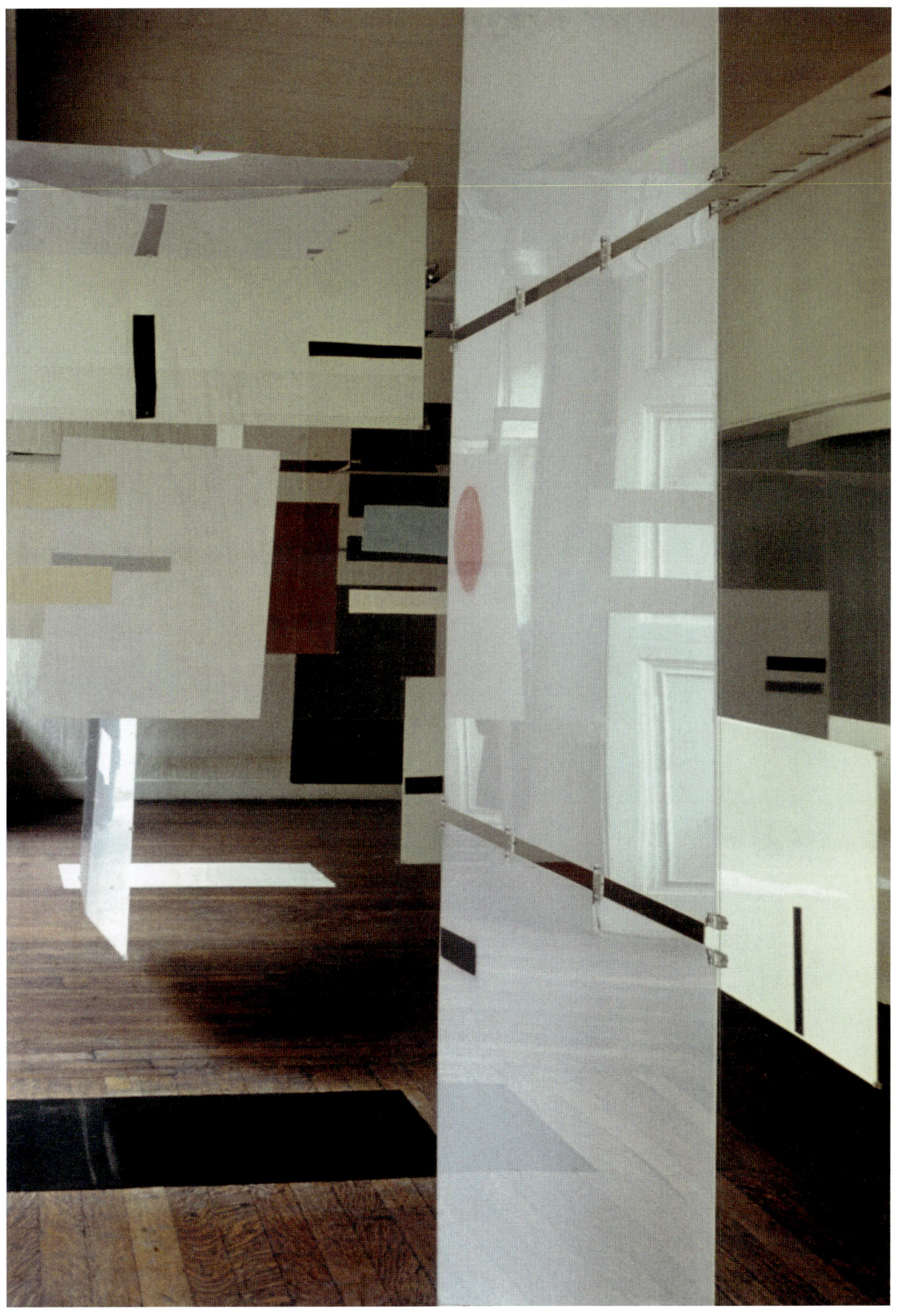

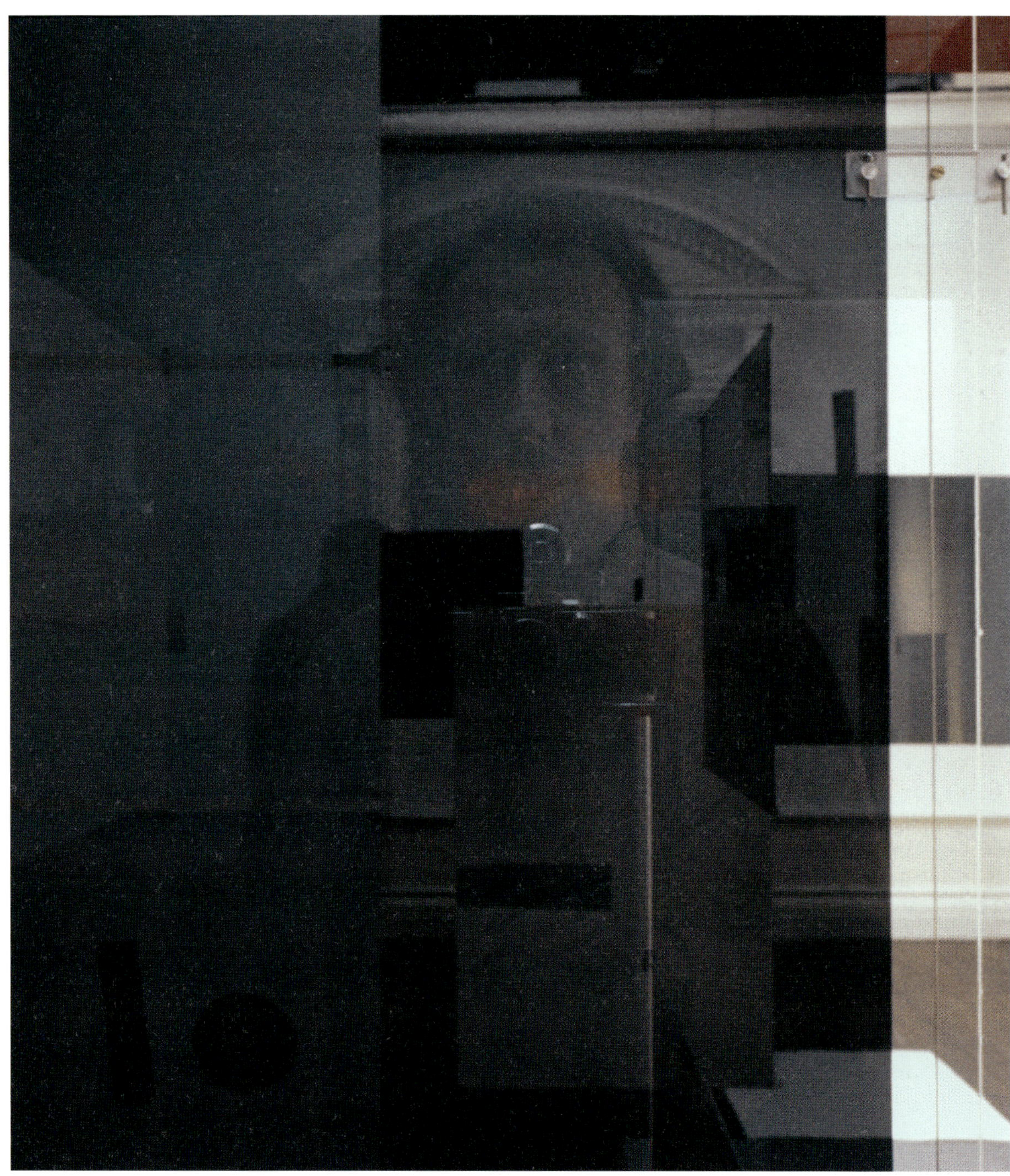

Hamilton in *an Exhibit*, Hatton Gallery, Newcastle upon Tyne 1957

Seahorses, Grids and Calypso: Richard Hamilton's Exhibition-making in the 1950s

Victoria Walsh

As interest in Richard Hamilton's exhibition-making of the 1950s developed in recent years, not least through full or partial reconstructions, Hamilton himself was prompted to offer up more observations and footnotes to their receding histories.[1] Despite repeated approaches, the only show that eluded reconstruction was *Growth and Form* [pp. 24–31], for, as Hamilton maintained, it was an impossible venture: it had been a highly complex research and production project back in 1951, and the source material would be more than difficult to retrace. Renowned for his assiduous archiving, and given the wealth of original material held on the other exhibitions from this period, it seemed strange that *Growth and Form* had eluded Hamilton's collection.[2] In 2011, as plans for this retrospective unfolded and discussions around *Growth and Form* resumed, Hamilton seemed to maintain this position until, at the end of a convivial day of conversation and informal interview (and following a brief reflection about his friend and one-time collaborator, the artist-photographer Nigel Henderson), Hamilton casually disappeared and reappeared with a collection of old and variously sized manila envelopes and packets. As each packet was opened it became apparent that what was being revealed was a substantial array of unseen original installation photographs of *Growth and Form,* along with glass negatives of individual images used in the exhibition and other archival documentation. In addition to this collection of material, two metal canisters were placed down on the table containing 16mm films, two of which were the originals projected in the 1951 exhibition, and another recording a walk through the 1957 show *an Exhibit* in its first installation at the Hatton Gallery in Newcastle [pp. 54–56]. The opportunity to continue the conversations of this day was sadly curtailed by Hamilton's untimely death.

The extraordinary range of material in Hamilton's archive all provides an insight into his approach to exhibition-making, although an explanation of Hamilton's method was in fact partially laid out in a letter he wrote to his friends, the architects Alison and Peter Smithson in January 1957. This aspect of the letter has, however, been entirely over-shadowed by the more notorious list of pithy adjectives that Hamilton put forward in it to define what "Pop Art" is; a list that has marked the letter out as a key moment in the more celebrated history of Pop Art.[3] Starting his letter with the opening gambit that there is a problem, an issue to be addressed, Hamilton acknowledges the writing of his missive as a form of analytical and positional thinking ("as much to sort it out for myself as to put a point of view to you"), continuing: "There have been a number of manifestations in the post-war years in London which I would select as important and which have a bearing on what I take to be an objective…" Within this specific list of seven "manifestations," all of which now fall under the aegis of the Independent Group that gathered at the ICA from 1952–55, Hamilton identifies four exhibitions: *Parallel of Life and Art* (1953), *Man, Machine and Motion* (1955), *House of the Future* (1956) and *This is Tomorrow* (1956).[4] It comes as no surprise that, continuing his pragmatic manner of observation and analysis, he would go on to propose work on another collaborative exhibition:

1. Hans Ulrich Obrist, "Pop Daddy: The Great Richard Hamilton on his Early Exhibitions," *Tate Etc.* 4 (April 2003), http:www.tate.org.uk/context-comment/articles/pop-daddy-richard-hamilton-early-exhibition.
2. In addition to the material Hamilton made available in 2011, this essay is based on two extended conversations with the artist: one in 2000 in relation to the artist Nigel Henderson, and again in 2011. I am also indebted to Rita Donagh and Nigel McKernaghan for being so generous with their time and support. Thanks also go to Mary Banham, Soraya Smithson, Brian Dillon, Anne Massey, Anna Gruetzner Robins, Beth Williamson, Elena Crippa and Andrew Dewdney. The essay also owes much to many earlier conversations with Peter Smithson.
3. Richard Hamilton, "Letter to Peter and Alison Smithson," 16 January 1957, reproduced in Kristine Stiles and Peter Selz (eds.), *Theories and Documents of Contemporary Art* (Berkeley, Los Angeles, London: University of California Press, 1996), 296. The list ran "Popular (designed for a mass audience), Transient (short-term solution), Expendable (easily forgotten), Low cost, Mass produced, Young (aimed at youth), Witty, Sexy, Gimmicky, Glamorous, Big business."
4. For more on these exhibitions and a history of the Independent Group, see Anne Massey, *The Independent Group: Modernism and Mass Culture in Britain, 1945–59* (Manchester: Manchester University Press, 1995) and David Robbins, *The Independent Group: Postwar Britain and the Aesthetics of Plenty* (Cambridge, MA: MIT, 1990).

> My view is that another show should be as highly disciplined and unified in conception as that one [*This is Tomorrow*] was chaotic … Suppose we were to start with the objective of providing a unique solution to the specific requirement of a domestic environment … This solution could then be formulated and rated on the basis of compliance with a table of characteristics of Pop Art … Perhaps the first part of our task is the analysis of Pop Art and the production of a table … Maybe we have to sub-divide Pop Art into its various categories and decide into which category each of the subdivisions of our project fits…

This conceptualisation of exhibition-making as "propositional"—a practice based on the identification of an object of enquiry (problem), contextualised through tabulated analysis (research), visualised though display (method), tested through spatio-temporal experience (exhibition as experiment), and reported and analysed through visual and textual documentation (photograph as evidence)—is, as will be seen, rooted in the work and teaching tradition of the Bauhaus. But, in reassembling the process and development of *Growth and Form,* which clearly became a paradigmatic model of exhibition-making for Hamilton, it also becomes apparent to what extent he drew on the sensibility and tactics of Surrealism and Dada, the literary themes and techniques of Joyce's writing and the example of Duchamp in developing his exhibition idiom.

In unlocking this history and the design process of *Growth and Form* it also becomes clear to what degree Hamilton was testing and developing his own curatorial and conceptual toolbox to establish an inter-relation and dialogue between specific ideas through the mutation of motifs across the shows he organised. Within the scope of this essay three specific and intertwined concept-tools of Hamilton's exhibition-making practice are considered for the way in which he employed and deployed them at both the material and conceptual level: the grid, collage and the photograph. Within the dense network of visual relations and conceptual allusions which Hamilton establishes through their interplay, something of the artist's joy in creating ambiguity, provoking curiosity and frustrating the reductive and literal forces of representational image-reading surfaces.

***Growth and Form* (1951)**

Growth and Form [figs. 1 & 2] originated out of the chance encounter in 1948 when Richard Hamilton met Nigel Henderson at an exhibition. Henderson was enrolled at the Slade School of Art and Hamilton at the Royal Academy Schools. Both were bored and frustrated by the "polite society" of teaching that still revolved around nineteenth-century life-drawing classes and a curriculum that failed to register a changed world post-war. Within a few months Hamilton had transferred to the Slade too, and, according to Henderson, turned up one day, asking him, "why don't we do an exhibition together?" As Henderson remembered, "This

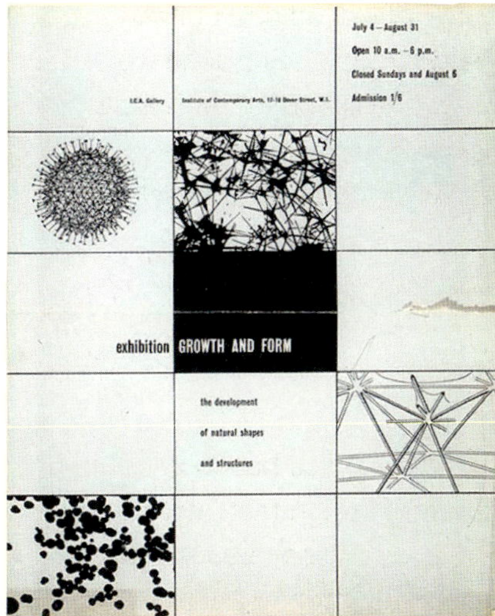

fig. 1
Poster for *Growth and Form*
ICA, London, 1951

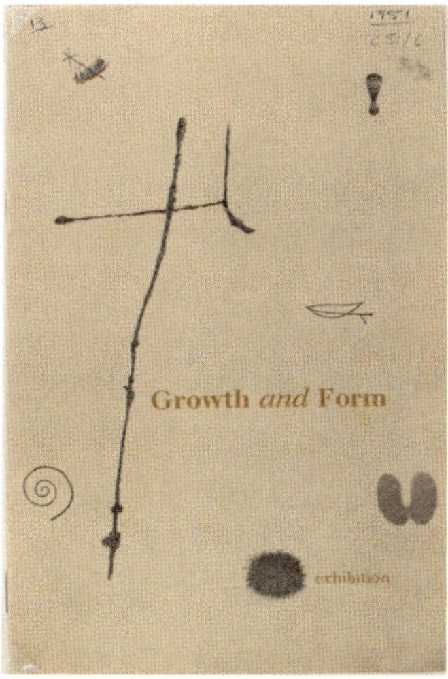

fig. 2
Catalogue cover for *Growth and Form*,
ICA, London, 1951

was quite a shock as I realised quite quickly what he meant by an exhibition and these were not terms in which I had previously thought."[5]

Like many of their contemporaries in the art school, Henderson and Hamilton found a world of visual excitement and intellectual stimulus in the work of three major writers of the moment: György Kepes' *Language of Vision* (1944), Moholy-Nagy's *Vision in Motion* (1947), and Sigfried Giedion's *Mechanization Takes Command* (1948), on which Hamilton directly drew for his series of diagrammatic *Reaper* etchings in 1949 [pp. 18–21]. While invariably cited as profoundly influential works in terms of presenting images of the new visual and scientific order that technology was creating, these books also carried clarion calls for the integration of theory and practice towards rebuilding a broken present and securing a better future. As Giedion would assert in the concluding section of his book, "Man in Equipoise," the future demanded recognition that "Faith in progress lies on the scrap heap" and that what was needed were new balances "between the individual and collective spheres … between the spheres of knowledge … between the human body and cosmic forces … It is time that we became human again and let the human scale rule over all our ventures."[6] By contrast, Moholy-Nagy's call to arms was much more instrumental: what was needed, claimed the Hungarian, was a revitalised function of art in society based on a "socio-biological synthesis," the coming together of art and science, the intellect and the emotions. But this came with the repeated warning throughout his book that "without experimentation there can be no discoveries and without discoveries no regeneration. Although the 'research work' of the artist is rarely as 'systematic' as that of the scientist they both may deal with the whole of life, in terms of relationships, not details."[7]

Moholy-Nagy's philosophy throughout *Vision in Motion* would have perfectly resonated with Hamilton on two accounts. Firstly, at the age of fifteen he had enjoyed privileged access to the Reimann School when it moved to London from Germany in 1937. The Reimann School, while not a direct offshoot of the Bauhaus, shared some of the latter's key teaching principles and curriculum design, but with greater emphasis on practice across disciplines rather than theoretical reflection.[8] Here, Hamilton would have become familiar with the idea of exhibition-making through the principles of "display" and witnessed first-hand new international and experimental work incorporating contemporary technologies and techniques of communication and commercial design. Secondly, building on his exposure to the innovative practices of the School, Hamilton inadvertently found himself developing his technical design sensibility when in 1940, too young to join the army when war broke out, he spent nine months in a Government Training Centre learning technical engineering drawing, which would subsequently provide the key idiom of his exhibition plans. From 1941–42, he was also employed as a "jig and tool" draughtsman at the Design Unit Group; a technical skill based on the replication of tools through template designs, a process that conceptually also resonated with Hamilton's practice.

As Hamilton openly acknowledged on a number of occasions, Henderson played a key role in his life during this period, forging contacts with other artists, opening up

5. Letter from Nigel Henderson to Frank Whitford, 12 October 1971, courtesy of Frank Whitford.
6. Sigfried Giedion, *Mechanization Takes Command* (New York: Oxford University Press, 1948), 714–23.
7. László Moholy-Nagy, *Vision in Motion* (Chicago: Paul Theobald, 1947), 31.
8. See Yasuko Suga, "Modernism, Commercialism and Display Design in Britain: The Reimann School and Studios of Industrial and Commercial Art," *Journal of Design History* 19, 2 (Summer 2006), 137–54.

new cultural vistas and bringing new sources of art and ideas to his attention.[9] In 1948 Henderson introduced Hamilton to the Surrealist collector and co-founder of the Institute of Contemporary Arts, Roland Penrose, along with his wife, the photographer Lee Miller. It was during this visit to the Penroses in their London Hampstead home that Henderson took the opportunity to show Hamilton a copy of Duchamp's *Green Box* (1934) which Penrose owned, and with which Henderson was familiar from his own direct encounters with Duchamp in the 1930s.[10] It is with this combination of a technically trained mind, informed by the socio-aesthetic and socio-biological manifestos of Giedion, Kepes and Moholy-Nagy, and a shared interest in Surrealism and Duchamp, that Hamilton set about developing with Henderson an idea for an exhibition.

As is now well documented, *Growth and Form* was subsequently conceived after Henderson showed Hamilton a copy of D'Arcy Wentworth Thompson's thousand-page tome *On Growth and Form,* originally published in 1917. According to Henderson, in Hamilton's inimitable style, he did "an extraordinarily quick and able gutting of the book," producing a "working script" within a day that was then proposed to Penrose.[11] While the initial close collaboration between Henderson and Hamilton did not last, the proposal clearly benefitted from Henderson's pre-war studies in Biology and his personal connections to leading scientists such as John Desmond Bernal.[12] Drawing on Thompson's description and analysis of morphological development, but not exclusively defined by it, Hamilton's proposal sought to demonstrate the implications that the scientific study of form and structure held for both artists *and* designers in considering the relationship between form and function. As an ICA internal memo highlighted:

> Modern science has made available a rich world of new forms and opened up a new source of inspiration to artists and industrial designers. Owing to the cleavage between science and art this material, potentially revolutionary in its significance for modern design, has not yet been sufficiently noticed. By making available material hitherto difficult to access, such an exhibition may have a profound influence on the trend of design.[13]

To enable access to the most important scientists and innovative laboratories, Penrose appointed an exhibition advisory committee of scientific specialists to support Hamilton in his research. As the planning developed, Hamilton produced two types of information. The first, a narrative script and proposal to the committee alluded to the correlations between Thompson's thesis of morphological development and ideas of "periodicity" which echoed "Joycean philosophy"; the relation of mathematical beauty and the "harmony of the world"; and ideas of transformation—transformation being a prerequisite of regeneration for both Thompson and Moholy-Nagy. Throughout the text, Hamilton spoke of adopting "procedures" from Thompson, of demonstrating temporal processes within the exhibition, and generally outlined how the show would animate the ideas being put forward.[14] The second script,

9. As Hamilton recalled Henderson introducing him to Duchamp's *Green Box*, "this is something that will interest you … he often said that to me and they were usually very important moments in my life," from "Duchamp's Legacy: Richard Hamilton and Sarat Maharaj," Tate Online (7 May 2003), http://www.tate.org.uk/context-comment/video/duchamps-legacy-richard-hamilton-and-sarat-maharaj.
10. See Victoria Walsh, *Nigel Henderson: Parallel of Life and Art* (London: Thames and Hudson, 2001), 14–16. The ICA during this period was also saturated with the Surrealist legacy through the interests of other ICA co-founders including Herbert Read and E.L.T. Mesens, all of whom had been close friends with key Surrealist artists and had formed part of the organising committee of the *International Surrealist Exhibition* in London in 1936.
11. See Walsh, *Nigel Henderson*, 27.
12. Ibid., 14–15.

defined by scientific technical language and description, was a table of information listing the proposed exhibits in relation to their purpose and method of display.[15] As the correspondence shows, however, conflict broke out during the exhibition planning and a corrosive divide emerged between Hamilton and certain members of the committee who wished for a more didactic and straight scientific display. A stand-off between Hamilton and one of the advisors, Lancelot Law Whyte, led to internal arguments at the ICA. As Hamilton later reflected, "Whyte was a dead loss as far as I was concerned," concluding many years later that in the end the exhibition brought him little of interest.[16]

As the proposal noted, the emphasis was on the visual experience of the exhibition: "The painter and sculptor have much to gain from the enlargement of their world of experience by an appreciation of the forms in nature beyond their immediate visual environment. It is the enlarged environment opened by scientific studies that we would reveal for its visual qualities." Conceived as a single mixed-media installation, the show consisted of three sculptural items: a large lens-like structure with recesses (containing in one instance mirrors to demonstrate the curve of refraction); a grid with objects translating drawings of morphological development from Thompson's book into three-dimensions, and image panels on display; and a free-standing cellular structure. Existing display cabinets presented various objects and models including a horse's skull, goat's vertebrae, and eggs. On one wall a large X-ray of a seal flipper was pasted from floor to ceiling; on another, a row of illuminated glass negatives, photomicrographs, electron-micrographs, radiographs and photograms. There were two films, one depicting crystal formation projected onto the ceiling and another of the cell growth of a sea urchin projected onto a table surface. There were also mechanically moving models illustrating mathematical form and another illustrating the changes of shape in a falling drop of blue-coloured water. Electronic flash equipment was also used to reveal the form of a splash.

Despite Hamilton's casual dismissal of the value of *Growth and Form* to him, looking at the previously unseen collection of installation shots it is now clear that Hamilton did in fact get much out of organising the exhibition and that it was in fact both a conceptual and aesthetic triumph in the artist's terms. These terms, defined by the principles of the difference between appearance and reality and Duchamp's strategy of "affirmative irony," enabled Hamilton to create a double narrative to the exhibition: one explicit, the other encoded. To arrive at this point of analysis through the exhibition photographs, the need to be alive to Hamilton's use of photography and collage as conceptual tools is paramount. As Hamilton wrote about photography in 1969:

> Photography is a medium with its own conventions though we treat its product as a truth less flexible than hand-done art … I would like to think I am questioning reality … Assimilating photography into the domain of paradox, incorporating it into the philosophical contradictions of art is as much my concern as embracing its alluring potential as a medium.[17]

13. "Growth and Form Exhibition," *ICA Bulletin*, 28 December 1949, 3–4 (Tate Gallery Archive, TV.955.14.1).
14. Richard Hamilton and Nigel Henderson, "Growth and Form Exhibition: First Draft Schedule," 20 December 1949, ICA Archive, Tate.
15. "General Description / Technical Description" (Table), *Growth and Form*, Tate Gallery Archive.
16. The fallout led to an independent publication of scientific and theoretical papers under the title *Aspects of Form* (London: Lund Humphries, 1951), of which Lancelot Law Whyte appointed himself as editor. Rejecting Hamilton from inclusion in the book, Whyte wrote a stinging preface: "There can be dangers in the collaboration of scientist and artist, for superficial analogies between science and art are harmful to both," noting that no artist was included in the publication because "there was no contemporary Aristotle, Leonardo or Goethe to whom the ICA could turn."
17. Richard Hamilton, "Notes on Photographs," in *Collected Words 1953–1982* (London: Thames & Hudson, 1982), 64–68.

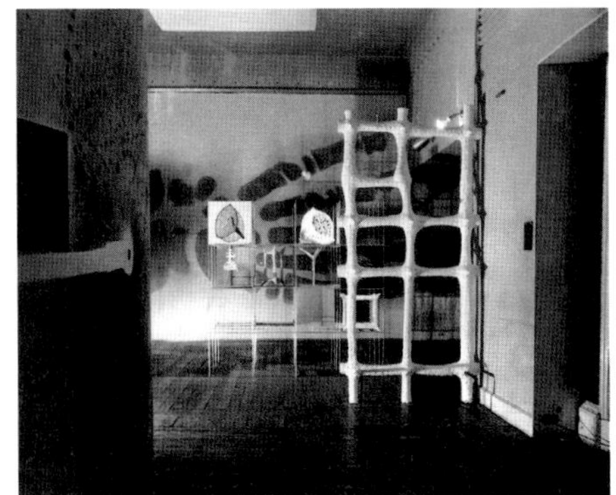

fig. 3
Growth and Form, 1951. Installation view by Nigel Henderson, published in *Architectural Review,* October 1951

In holding back all other perspectives of the exhibition to focus exclusive attention on the iconic photograph of *Growth and Form* [fig. 3] (taken by Nigel Henderson and published in *Architectural Review*), the question arises: what was Hamilton directing the viewer to look at in the image of the cellular structure located in front of the grid display unit, which in turn was placed in front of the enlarged X-ray apparently of a seal flipper? Looking beyond the assumed documentary character of the photograph what we see, however, is the photographic flattening and conflation of these three structures; a re-rendering of their spatial relations into the new planar relation of the photographic print itself, consequently creating a paradoxical visual relation between the geometric grid and the biomorphic form of the cellular structure. For the invested audience of Hamilton's peers, both within the show itself in 1951 and through the printed image in *Architectural Review,* it would have been clear that what this configuration of structures and the organisation of this image created was a visual punning intent on teasing out one of the most topical and contested debates of the late 1940s and early 1950s in design and architecture circles: the conflict between the theoretical tenets of Functionalism represented by Corbusier and those of his detractors, first represented by New Humanism which argued for a more organic and picturesque architecture. The latter was subsequently taken up and recast by the principles of New Brutalism, of which the Smithsons became the key exponents in England, arguing in favour of urban planning that followed "patterns of human association" rather than Corbusier's dictate of "zoned" grid-planning for city centres. For in the flattening of the photographic image, the purity of the geometrical functional grid structure is clearly compromised and complicated both by the superimposed irregular and biomorphic shapes of the cellular structure in front and the skeletal shadow of the X-ray behind, creating more organic and complex inter-relations of form and space than the mathematically determined ones defined by the grid unit alone.

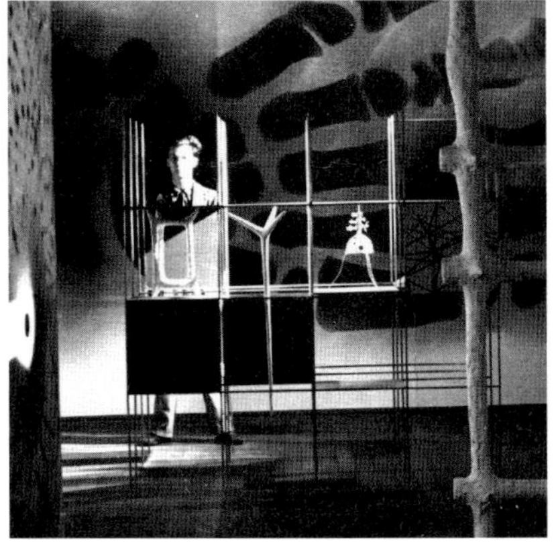

fig. 4
Growth and Form, 1951

At the core of this debate was Corbusier's vision to rebuild post-war Europe and the cities of the future on the principles of the grid and geometrical harmony which he had outlined in his 1929 treatise *The City of To-morrow and Its Planning,* and resurrected in 1949 for the international architecture conference CIAM. Corbusier converted his theory into a visual argument which he articulated through the vehicle of the grid and advocated the design principle of standardised geometrical repetition as the most harmonious and efficient paradigm for urban centres. By contrast, peripheral areas, the suburbs, should, he argued, be populated with homes based on a "cellular system." In addition, Corbusier had also published in 1948 his treatise on the "modulor system," his model of what the ideal scale of architectural proportion should be. By 1949 the language of the grid had accumulated immense significance as Rudolf Wittkower published his *Architectural Principles in the Age of Humanism,* the same year he was appointed Professor at the Slade School of Fine Art where Hamilton and Henderson were studying. Further installation shots reveal a more direct reference to this context: one photograph presents a man posing in one of the modulor positions to demonstrate proportion [fig. 4], while another includes an exact copy of the photo itself pinned on the wall, repeating the perspective and creating a visual double of the image and a further visual pun on Corbusier's principle of repetition. That the exhibition design of these elements spoke as much to the international discussion on Functionalism and New Humanism as it did to the British urban project of New Town Development in England, with which Hamilton's exhibition design collaborator Ronald Avery was involved, was highlighted by the invitation to Corbusier to open the exhibition at the ICA on 10 July 1951, in addition to opening the architectural displays of the Festival of Britain.

Amongst the exhibition scientific committee Hamilton did find a useful ally in the intellectual polymath Jacob Bronowski, who was both a well-respected and established scientist and an informed art writer who had published translations of several of Duchamp's documents in the *Green Box.* In a lecture at the ICA to accompany *Growth and Form,* Bronowski sought to highlight the mutual benefits of art and science coming together and ventured on a detailed analysis of a range of materials and objects whose molecular and atomic structures were revealed under the microscope to be counter-intuitive in shape to their external form. This elegant account, which diffused and blended the distinction between the art form and the natural form, essentially spoke of the difference between appearance and reality, continuously returning to one central theme: the inter-relation of part to whole, or as Bronowski put it echoing the position of New Humanism, "a science that consists of relationships not facts or objects, but of the relationship between them."[18] As a total text Bronowski seemed to infer that despite the apparent disparity between forms in the exhibition there was a common linkage. In many respects this echoed the visual impression of the show as a collaged set of elements which reflect Hamilton's later descriptions of collage as a conceptual tool in which "a variety of techniques … are used to keep the elements separate and retain their individual character," enabling the "making of a new unity of unlikely parts from different sources."[19]

It is now clear, however, in viewing the two original films that were projected in the show and from identifying one specific anomalous exhibit that we now see from the exhibition photographs, that through the conceptual armature of collage, Hamilton had actually created a total coherent environment—an installation in the art historical sense. For on viewing the gentle and bemusing film of sea urchin cells—dividing, connecting, gently jostling and oscillating indecisively in space—the sense of a more poetic, playful and choreographed environment begins to emerge. This is reinforced by the film of crystal formation that was projected on the ceiling and which, in the surrealist tradition established by René Clair in *Entr'acte* (1924), was, it seems, either by chance or design, shown in reverse, producing both a comical effect of de-growth by visual subtraction while also alluding to the mark-making of Klee. This pervasive sense of comic charm was noted by one critic:

> These lofty speculations come curiously and sometimes comically to earth … an octopus sits enthroned upon the sofa of its own coils; skeletal structures are perched amongst the equipment of a diminutive gymnasium and such is

18. Jacob Bronowski, "The Shape of Science in the Arts," 2 August 1951, ICA Archive, Tate.
19. Hamilton, *Collected Words,* 85–86.

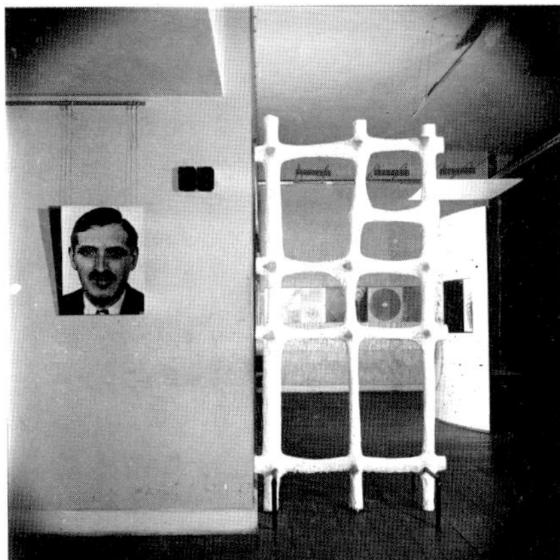

fig. 5
Growth and Form, 1951, view showing exhibit "no. 85 – Head"

> the artful power of science that we leave convinced that we have seen infinity in the Medusa of a jellyfish and eternity in the power of a goat.[20]

The intimation of another narrative running through the exhibition was signalled by the anomalous and discreet inclusion of the only non-scientific image within the show, an imposing photographic portrait of a suited man [fig. 5]. Listed as "no. 85 – Head," the final entry of the exhibition catalogue, the credit line carried the attribution (and conceptual prompt) "By Courtesy of Jean Painlevé." As research suggests, the photograph is of Painlevé's father, Paul Painlevé, but the association to be made is clearly to Jean Painlevé (1902–1989) both through the design of the immersive and aquarium-like environment of the show itself and the surrealist play of fantastical imagery. Painlevé enjoyed immense popularity in the 1940s and early 1950s as a pioneering and experimental filmmaker of underwater science movies and, as a Surrealist collaborator, his films were often described as poetic-lyrical dramas and comedies, characterised by the beguiling anthropomorphic performances of various sea-creatures (most famously the seahorse), which intimated the drama of the human lifecycle—birth, death, love, conflict and separation.[21]

Hamilton's invocation of the enigmatic world of Painlevé's films, combined with the interplay of scale to produce visual ambiguity and the diffusion of wit and humour, directly played off against the depersonalised scientific language of the catalogue, the anonymous nature of the exhibits and the primacy of abstract theory symbolised by the grid, and effectively allowed the exhibition to assume both a sensual and cerebral value. Through the composition of this playful environment, which displayed a more intellectual curiosity and imaginative relation between the worlds of art and science, Hamilton deftly avoided the reductive and rhetorical language of academic, institutionalised science while simultaneously enjoying an encoded private joke at its very expense. It is hard not to speculate that the largest visual image in the show is also the largest visual conceit: for behind the grid is a catalogued X-ray of a seal flipper printed to photomural scale. As an exhibition dedicated to scientific innovation it would not have escaped Hamilton that the first X-ray of the human body was apparently discovered by chance when Wilhelm Röntgen caught his wife's hand under cathode rays in 1895.

Man, Machine and Motion **(1955)**[22]

It was during *Growth and Form* that Hamilton met the architecture critic and historian Reyner Banham, with whom he struck up a strong friendship based on their mutual interest in the history of technology and the "machine aesthetic" which Sigfried Giedion had addressed in both his publications *Space, Time and Architecture* (1941) and *Mechanization Takes Command* (1948). During the following year, 1952, Hamilton secured some teaching at the Central School of Arts and Crafts in London which was developing a new Bauhaus-inspired curriculum under the directorship of William Johnstone and, as Hamilton recalled, this allowed him to draw on the practice of *Growth and Form* as part of his teaching process

20. John Russell, "Formal Intimations," *Sunday Times,* 15 July 1951.
21. This allusion to Painlevé would not have been lost on Hamilton's peers, nor on a visiting public, for in 1948 he had come to fame through a notorious live scientific broadcast on the BBC, "Under the Microscope." See Andy Masaki Bellows, Marina McDougall and Brigitte Berg, *Science is Fiction: The Films of Jean Painlevé* (Cambridge, MA: MIT/Brico Press, 2000).
22. The exhibition opened at the Hatton Gallery in Newcastle in May 1955 and at the ICA in July that year.

in Basic Design.[23] Henderson was also teaching at Central at this time, along with Eduardo Paolozzi, William Turnbull and Peter Smithson. Regular attendees at the ICA, they collectively began to meet to debate topical issues in contemporary aesthetics and culture and within a year had become a more organised meeting group with formal recognition by the ICA management and with Banham as convenor.[24] In 1953 Hamilton was appointed Lecturer in Design at King's College, University of Durham, and immediately began research towards his next exhibition, *Man, Machine and Motion* [pp. 42–47], although his connection with the ICA continued without change, as he remained living in London and organised his teaching to ensure he never missed Banham's programme.

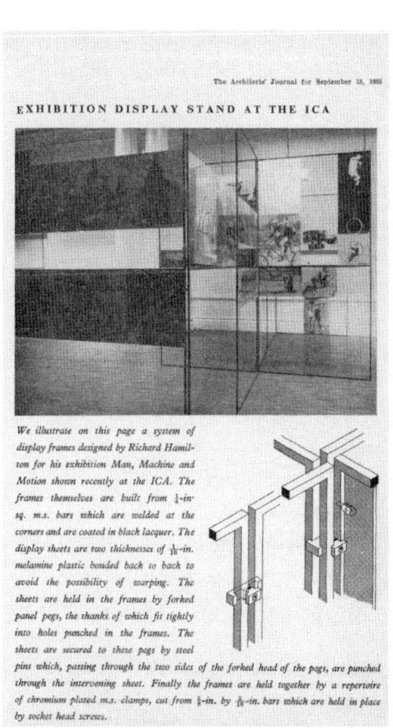
The Architects' Journal for September 15, 1955

EXHIBITION DISPLAY STAND AT THE ICA

We illustrate on this page a system of display frames designed by Richard Hamilton for his exhibition Man, Machine and Motion shown recently at the ICA. The frames themselves are built from $\frac{1}{4}$-in sq. m.s. bars which are welded at the corners and are coated in black lacquer. The display sheets are two thicknesses of $\frac{1}{16}$-in. melamine plastic bonded back to back to avoid the possibility of warping. The sheets are held in the frames by forked panel pegs, the shanks of which fit tightly into holes punched in the frames. The sheets are secured to these pegs by steel pins which, passing through the two sides of the forked head of the pegs, are punched through the intervening sheet. Finally the frames are held together by a repertoire of chromium plated m.s. clamps, cut from $\frac{3}{8}$-in. by $\frac{1}{16}$-in. bars which are held in place by socket head screws.

fig. 6
Display frames designed by Hamilton reviewed in *Architects' Journal,* 15 September 1955

As the touring information for *Man, Machine and Motion* outlined, the exhibition consisted of approximately 200 photographs and photographic copies of drawings mounted in Formica sheets which were then fixed intermittently—with clips designed by Hamilton—across thirty open grid frames made of steel [fig. 6]. Hamilton devised a 4' (1.2 m) modular system: each frame measured 4' x 8' (1.2 x 2.4 m) and the frames abutted each other, or met at a right angle, or were distanced from each other at gaps of multiples of 4' (1.2 m). The frames and photographs were assembled in four distinct groups, one for each category of images: Aquatic, Terrestrial, Aerial and Interplanetary.[25] The images were arranged according to their associated location: the sea photographs were placed at floor level, the images of space were suspended above visitors from the ceiling, while land vehicles were at eye level and flying machines just above. Designed to reiterate the typographic grid of Bauhaus design, the exhibition catalogue described the show as "devoted to machines which extend the powers of the human body in a special way, the machines which increase a man's capacity for mechanical movement" and also emphasised that, "in particular, the exhibition is concerned with the documents, largely photographic, which record these machines in use."

Although the extensive catalogue notes on the exhibits, written by Banham, anticipated the debates around photography and "pop" culture, *Man, Machine and Motion* was in fact still responding to on-going debates about the "grid" which had expanded well beyond architectural discourse and taken on a new urgency in the aftermath of the Milan Triennale of 1951: an event Hamilton would often refer to in passing, while dropping in the name of the architect Francesco Gnecchi Ruscone [fig. 7]. Indeed, Hamilton's own grid design directly drew on the "display frame" grid that Ruscone had designed specifically for the Milan Triennale in 1951 when he created a small bibliographic exhibition based on the most important historical and contemporary studies and treatises on "proportion". The show was carefully designed by Ruscone as an open grid structure that itself reflected on the theme of architectural order and "proportion."[26] Ruscone's design aimed to avoid a linear chronological narrative of "proportion" and, in addition to the books on display, was illustrated by photographic panels mounted across the grid structure. As momentum gathered around the exhibition it became clear that there was a growing international move to determine a common language of architectural proportion and,

23. See Richard Yeomans, "Basic Design and the Pedagogy of Richard Hamilton," in Mervyn Romans, *Histories of Art and Design Education: Collected Essays* (Bristol: Intellect, 2005), and Elena Crippa and Beth Williamson, *Basic Design* [exh. cat.] (London: Tate, 2013).
24. Collectively and now historically known as the "Independent Group," see Robbins and Massey references in n. 4 above.
25. Richard Hamilton, "Man, Machine and Motion," in *Collected Words,* 20.
26. Anna Chiara Cimoli & Fulvio Irace, "Triennial 1951: Post-War Reconstruction and 'Divine Proportion'," *Nexus Network Journal* 15, 1 (Spring 2013), 3–14.

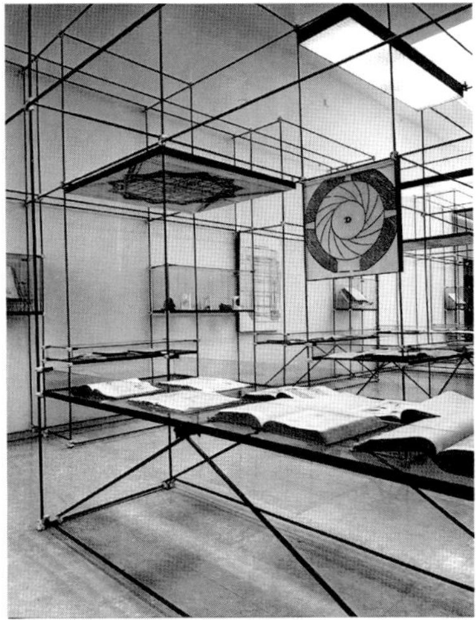

fig. 7
Mostra di Studi sulle Proporzioni
IX Triennale di Milano, 1951
Layout by architect Francesco Gnecchi-Ruscone
Courtesy Archivio Fotografico

given the serious implications this held for the re-development of post-war Europe, architects, designers, artists, engineers, historians and theorists urgently gathered in Milan (including Corbusier, Wittowker, Giedion and Max Bill) for a major conference to debate the subject. The seriousness of the Triennale resonated throughout Europe in the pages of art and architectural magazines and newspapers, and in 1955 Corbusier published his response in the form of his *Modulor 2.*

Ruscone's grid design clearly had an impact on Hamilton's thinking as he began to plan *Man, Machine and Motion* in 1953, and was no doubt stimulated by Independent Group debates at the ICA on these issues, including the architect Colin St John Wilson's talk in November 1953 on "Proportion and Symmetry" which assessed Corbusier's *Modulor.* By March 1955 Banham had begun to think through and assess the limitations of Corbusier's Functionalist theory as it applied to car styling, giving a lecture at the ICA titled "Metal in Motion." The next month Banham published the article "Machine Aesthetic" in *Architectural Review,* in which he developed a comprehensive argument against Corbusier's Functional design theory, highlighting its seductive theoretical quality in writing but its failure at the level of application in the processes of mass production or in relation to its actual applied use. The critical thrust of Banham's article and position against Corbusier, which Hamilton took up directly, fed not only into the selection of photographic images displayed in *Man, Machine and Motion,* but was also conceptually mediated through the grid structure. Banham's thesis was translated and made visible through the paradoxical relation of the rational order of the grid and the bizarre photographs it supported showing machines in actual use [fig. 8], reinforcing the historical and absurd disjuncture between form and function. As the catalogue introduction stated:

> A photograph of an early aeroplane standing unattended has a distinct and separate beauty: the elaborate geometry of it engages the eye. But when a man gets into the machine it gives it quite another meaning. The look of it excites us in a different way, both more intimate, less abstract, and more unexpected. The conventional aesthetic appreciation of machines, the view that the beauty of the machine lies in its harmonious fitness for its function—does not prepare us for this excitement.[27]

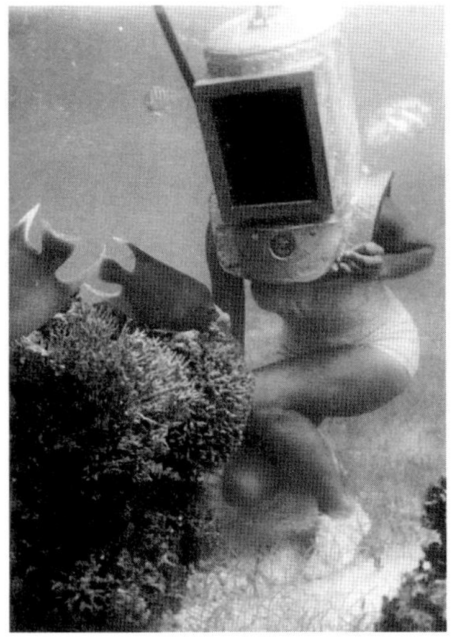

fig. 8
Photograph from the aquatic section of *Man, Machine and Motion,* 1955

What the visitor to the exhibition might also not have been prepared for, and indeed the reader of today, is the surreal humour and sardonic wit of Banham's catalogue text entries, as when discussing "a rocket-propelled sled … the fastest terrestrial transport ever built," noting of the pilot-driver, "Though subject to a force of over 35g … Dr John Stapp, protected by a g-suit, suffered only black eyes caused by his eyeballs trying to leave their sockets."[28]

27. Richard Hamilton (with Reyner Banham and Lawrence Gowing), "Introduction," in *Man, Machine and Motion* [exh. cat.] (Newcastle: Hatton Gallery; London: ICA, 1955).
28. Hamilton, Banham and Gowing, *Man, Machine and Motion,* 19.

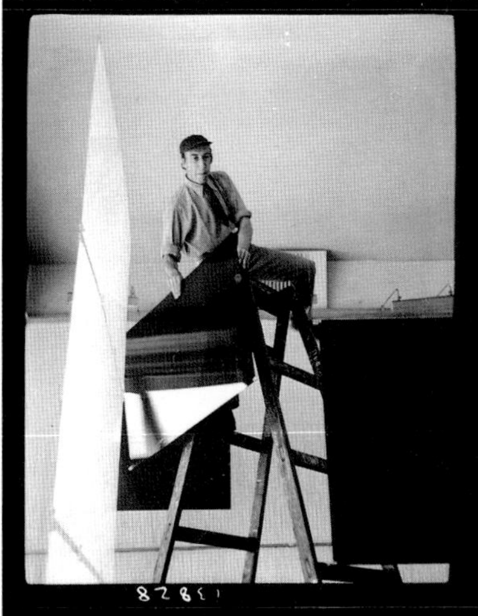

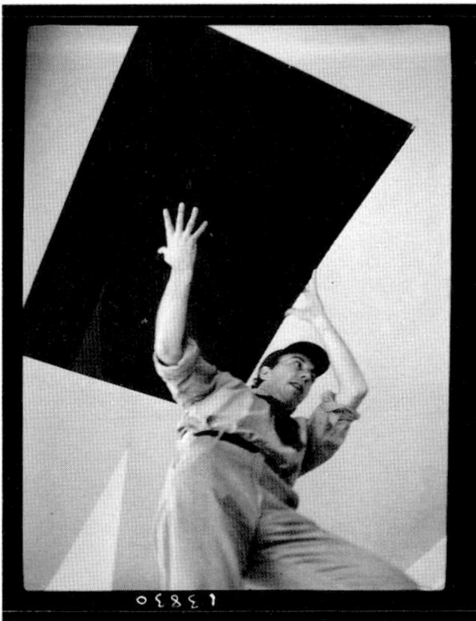

fig. 9
Hamilton installing *an Exhibit* at the Hatton Gallery, Newcastle upon Tyne, 1957

an Exhibit (1957)[29]

While *an Exhibit* [pp. 54–59], perhaps the least well-known of Hamilton's exhibitions, appears as an evacuation of content in terms of its abandonment of the use of ready-made imagery in favour of abstraction, it is in many respects a concise manifestation, or pure distillation, of the aesthetic and conceptual concerns and methodological approach that characterised Hamilton's exhibition-making practice in both *Growth and Form* and *Man, Machine and Motion.* Collaborating with the artist Victor Pasmore and the writer-critic Lawrence Alloway, *an Exhibit* was conceived as "a game / an artwork / an environment," and was comprised of thin acrylic panels (each 4' x 2'8" / 120 x 85 cm) with varying degrees of transparency which were suspended by Nylon thread within a notional 16" (40 cm) rectangular grid at varying heights. Hamilton used the commercially available colours of grey, black and white acrylic as well as transparent sheets. There were also occasional sheets of Indian red acrylic, a colour Pasmore used in his work. Since there were no pre-set plans, the position of each panel was determined by Hamilton and Pasmore during installation [fig. 9]. Hamilton's role was to design the grid and components; Pasmore produced cut-out shapes in coloured paper to attach to the blank panels; and Alloway was to explain and write the instructions for visitors to navigate through it. From the gridded design layout of the invitation, announcing in tabulated form the show's rationale, to the exhibition "manual" poster-guide printed to the same grid aesthetic and colours, and finally to the exhibition-plan itself, the grid was clearly no longer functioning at an indexical or symbolic level, but was to be materialised, inhabited and explored through the embodied and spatial interaction of the actual spectator. As the tabulated invitation highlighted, however, while for Hamilton the exhibition was designed as a spatio-temporal proposition, "a game – pre-planned" to be "played," for the artist Victor Pasmore it was an "artwork" to be "viewed," and for the critic Lawrence Alloway "an environment" to be "populated."

The research for this exhibition had a long history of enquiry in Hamilton's investigation of the relation between vision and motion, particularly seen in the artist's show of paintings at the Hanover Gallery in London in 1955. As Alloway had noted in his review of this exhibition, Hamilton's absorption of Moholy-Nagy's *Vision in Motion* was more than evident. As Moholy-Nagy had written: "Vision in motion is simultaneous grasp. Simultaneous grasp is creative performance—seeing, feeling, and thinking in relationship and not as a series of isolated phenomena. It instantaneously integrates and transmutes single elements into a coherent whole. This is valid for physical vision as well as for the abstract."[30] Notably, in this teaching context that Hamilton was operating in at Newcastle, Moholy-Nagy had also placed particular emphasis on teaching exercises that would foster the idea of the "quality of relationships," and "complex relationships" at that, on which good design was based.[31] In concluding his description of such exercises, Moholy-Nagy proclaimed: "If the same methodology were used generally in all fields we would have the key to our age—seeing everything in relationship."[32] "Seeing everything in relationship" was the ultimate antidote to seeing everything in Corbusier's units.

29. The exhibition opened at the Hatton Gallery, Newcastle, in July 1957 and was re-installed at the ICA in London the following month.
30. Moholy-Nagy, *Vision in Motion,* 143.
31. Ibid., 42.
32. Ibid., 68.

In Hamilton's installation photographs of this gridded configuration, in the absence of any figurative references and through the flattening effect of the printed image, what emerges is a pattern of visual relationships and repetition that creates a new mediated form of visual communication (considerably less evident to the embodied eye in the gallery space). This prefigures the dematerialisation of communication to cybernetic systems and the binary language of noughts and ones. Hamilton's interest in these photographic images as visual "fields" of communication undoubtedly built on the discourse of pattern-formation and pattern-recognition that Herbert Read had spoken of in his preface to *Aspects of Form* in 1951, along with other essays in the volume, which related gestalt theories of perception to painting, sculpture, photography and television.[33] Indeed, when viewing Hamilton's newly disclosed cine film of walking through *an Exhibit* it becomes clear to what extent the artist was interested in the level of visual ambiguity and spatial indeterminacy that emerged on film, particularly recalling one essay in *Aspects of Form* which discussed "the transformation from spatial to temporal co-ordinates [that] is known to television engineers as 'scanning' and in a transmission system is used for economy."[34]

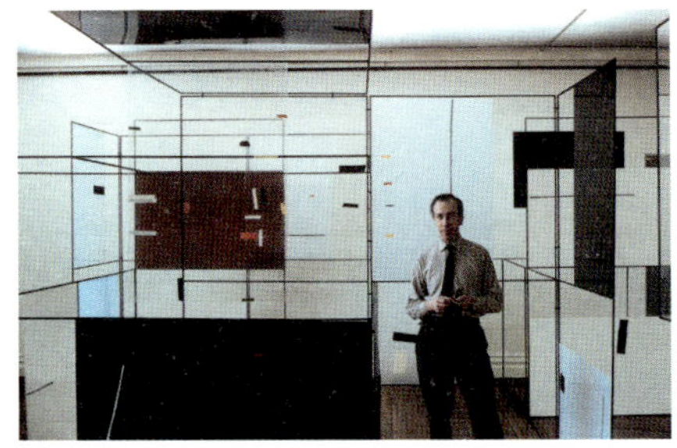

fig. 10
Hamilton within *Exhibit 2*, Hatton Gallery, Newcastle upon Tyne, 1959

Hamilton liked to tell the story that *an Exhibit* came into being after Victor Pasmore told him that *Man, Machine and Motion* "would have been very good if it hadn't been for all those photographs." This anecdote is appealing, but Hamilton was also taking up a challenge posed by the theorist E.J. Meyer who, at an ICA event organised by Alloway in 1955, discussed how the visual arts could not function in the same way as the transmission of information in an electrical network. Like the multiple "mirroring" feature created by the Perspex panels in *an Exhibit,* Hamilton's second version of this installation, *Exhibit 2* [fig. 10], which combined some of the grid structure from *Man, Machine and Motion* with free-standing Perspex panels, clearly tested out cybernetic ideas of the "feedback" principle in the relation between the exhibition and the mobile spectator in space, and between the show and the static viewer of the photographic image.

For all its conceptualisation and apparent abstract qualities, as with the invocation of the world of Painlevé in *Growth and Form* and the Surrealist absurd in *Man, Machine and Motion,* Hamilton took visitors by surprise at the opening preview having scripted and set to Calypso music a song which acted as both an invitation to "play the game" and a bait to test how "maze-dim" or "maze-bright" the visitor was. While Calypso may have seemed obvious given its popularity (Harry Belafonte had just become the first ever record artist to sell over a million copies of his album *Calypso*), it is more than likely that one of the aspects of Calypso music that appealed to Hamilton was the characteristic mixture of improvisation and the "call and response" refrain of the chorus, which paralleled the gestalt "push and pull" analysis of the perception of form in visual communication.

33. Hamilton would also have been aware of Henderson's own photographs of exhibition installations as autonomous visual fields of communication within a paradigm of feedback systems. See Victoria Walsh, "Reordering and Redistributing the Visual: The Expanded 'field' of Pattern-making in 'Parallel of Life and Art' and 'Hammer Prints'," *Journal of Visual Culture* 2 (August 2013).
34. William Grey Walter, "Activity Patterns in the Human Brain," in Whyte, *Aspects of Form,* 183.

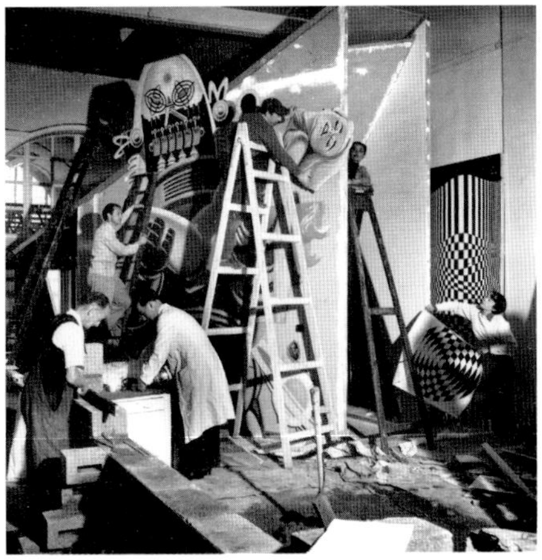

fig. 11
Hamilton, Terry Hamilton, John McHale and Magda Cordell working on the Group 2 installation, 1956
Architectural Press Archive / RIBA Library Photographs Collection

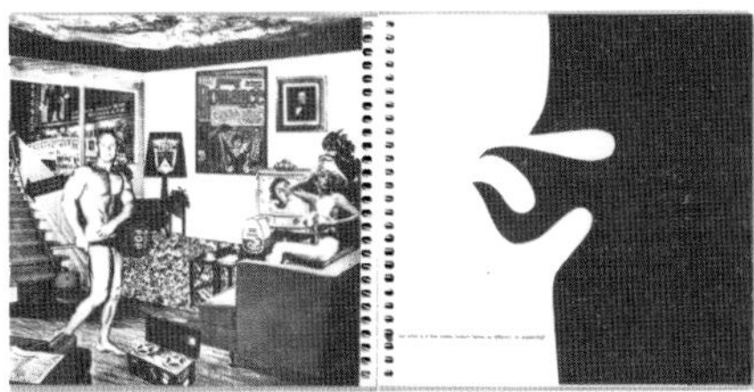

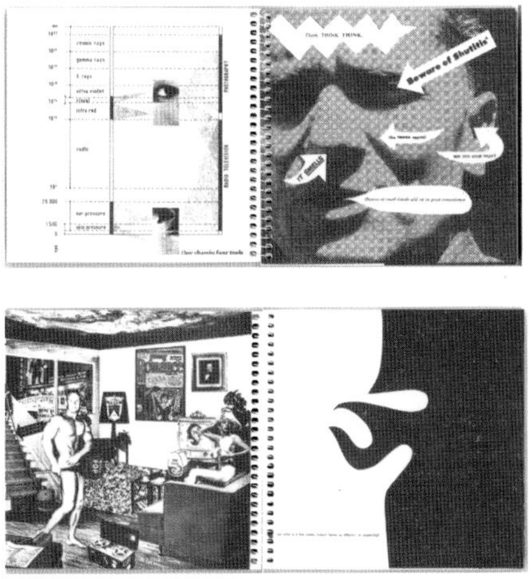

fig. 12
Group 2's spreads from the *This is Tomorrow* catalogue

Group 2 installation – The "Fun house": *This is Tomorrow* (1956)

In 1954 Theo Crosby, editor of *Architectural Design,* invited artists, architects and designers to explore the possibilities of collaboration to address the limits imposed on their fields through specialist practices and to overcome the "purity of media, golden proportions, unambiguous iconologies" that had separated them out.[35] Twelve such groups came together in the exhibition *This is Tomorrow* which attracted just over 19,000 visitors—a notable number in 1956. In Group 2, Hamilton collaborated with the artist John McHale and the architect John Voelcker [fig. 11 and pp. 50–53] Their installation consisted of an a-symmetrical, dramatically angled structure, the "Fun house," covered with an over-sized image of Marilyn Monroe which, along with a large-scale replica bottle of Guinness, mimicked the monumental scale of city hoarding and cinema advertising, although an aesthetic tension was set up between these mass-culture images and the mass-consumption poster of Van Gogh's *Sunflowers* hung on the wall as a work of art. Next to the "Fun house" structure a jukebox was placed in front of a mural of cinemascope film advertisements, which assumed a particular relevance on the opening night when the makers of the movie *Forbidden Planet* that featured Robby the Robot were persuaded to lend the robot for the evening. McHale's interest in modes of visual perception was also highlighted by the inclusion of Duchamp's rotoreliefs. As Hamilton later recalled, "the exhibition was in two parts; divided by John Voelcker's ingenious structure which not only provided several closed spaces but two interestingly different adjacent spaces"; one led straight through to the main hall of the exhibition and the other to the closed space.[36]

Although Group 2's installation was seen as an anti-art statement, collectively the installation sought to offer a critical commentary on the role of mass media imagery in the formation of popular culture and its impact on contemporary modes of visual perception. Both of these were of particular interest to McHale who, having spent time in America, was keen to introduce this new visual vocabulary into his work. Having designed the ICA exhibition *Collages and Objects* in 1954, McHale wanted to continue this idiom which is clearly reflected in the exterior of the installation, and which employed Hamilton's signature Bauhaus technique of scaling up imagery. As has been well documented, Hamilton also opted to explicitly use collage in the image he compiled for the poster and catalogue [fig. 12]—the now infamous icon of Pop Art, *Just what is it that makes today's homes so different, so appealing?* [p. 49].[37] Like Hamilton's exhibition strategy, the image was compiled from a tabulated list of image requirements and, although appearing somewhat incongruous with previous work, the poster continued to represent a direct engagement with the architecture and design debate on Corbusier's Functionalism. As Group 2's statement declared in the catalogue, "We reject the notion that 'tomorrow' can be expressed through the presentation of rigid formal concepts." Indeed, Voelcker himself had been part of the Milan Triennale conference on "Divine Proportion" in 1951.

35. Lawrence Alloway, "Introduction," in *This is Tomorrow* [exh. cat.] (London: Whitechapel Gallery, 1956).
36. See Hamilton, *Collected Words,* 22.
37. See *This is Tomorrow* [exh. cat.] (London: Whitechapel Gallery, 1956).

As with each and every inclusion of an anomalous image in Hamilton's work, awareness of the multi-levels at which the poster image functions is clearly signalled by various elements of the collage. On closer analysis, it becomes clear that with characteristic wit (both Surrealist and Duchampian) Hamilton was continuing to toy with Corbusier through the tabulated domestic interior by playing out, both illusionistically and symbolically, the principles of architectural order and proportion that he, Wittowker, Ruscone, the Smithsons and Banham were all tallying with in and through the grid following the 1951 Milan Triennale. Paradoxically, as this image unpredictably and rapidly gained iconic status through reproduction and entered the domestic and private interiors of numerous homes by way of posters and postcards, Hamilton must have enjoyed the irony that such a cast of characters as he had included—Corbusier and Banham amongst them—would be forever memorialised through the conditions of mass culture in so many anonymous environments. As Banham knowingly noted in his own review of the exhibition, Group 2's installation contained "images that can carry the mass of tradition and association, or the energy of novelty and technology, but resist classification by the geometrical disciplines…" In 1957, having sent his letter to the Smithsons and apparently receiving no reply, Hamilton conceived his next installation and first major interior for the *Ideal Home Exhibition,* which he titled *Gallery for a Collector of Brutalist and Tachiste Art.*[38]

The tricks of today are the truths of tomorrow[39]

As noted at the outset, Nigel Henderson introduced Hamilton to Duchamp's *Green Box* in 1948 at Roland Penrose's, and in 1955 Henderson lent Hamilton his own copy of the *Green Box.* Intrigued and enthralled by Duchamp's deft manipulation of symbols and meaning, Hamilton's own repertoire of visual devices and conceptual strategies clearly informed his approach to exhibition-making and the complex conceptual relation between the grid, collage and the photograph that ensued. In 1956 Hamilton gave a talk on Duchamp at the ICA, and by 1957 he had "a rough draft of a literal translation of all the papers in the *Green Box.*"[40] In 1982, reflecting on his reconstruction of Duchamp's *The Large Glass* (Tate), Hamilton noted:

> To work from photographs isn't satisfactory because much information, even at the straightforward level of fabrication, is lost. The alternative method, that of using the detailed documentation of the *Green Box* to cover the ground again—to reconstruct procedures rather than imitate the effects of action—was the one adopted.[41]

Hamilton's description of the approach taken as procedural rather than duplicative renders by implication his own archive of photographic installation shots, diagrammatic plans and other material on *Growth and Form* comparable material status to Duchamp's *Green Box.*

38. See Ben Highmore, "Richard Hamilton at the Ideal Home Exhibition of 1958: Gallery for a Collector of Brutalist and Tachiste Art," *Art History* 30, 5 (November 2007), 712–36.
39. Man Ray, "Painting of the Future and the Future of Painting," ICA talk, 27 October 1954.
40. I am indebted to Anna Gruetzner Robins whose paper "'It's Later Than You Think': Richard Hamilton's Remaking of Marcel Duchamp's 'The Large Glass'," was presented at the Pasmore/Hamilton conference in Newcastle, 3–4 May 2013.
41. Hamilton, *Collected Words,* 212.

Like Duchamp's *Green Box,* Hamilton's archive provides little empirical value or practical guidance in terms of reproducing the exhibition. Like Duchamp, Hamilton refused to advise directly on the reconstruction. What he did authorise and set in motion before his untimely death, however, was the means by which, through tabulated research, analysis and assemblage of ideas, information, data and metadata, the procedures of *Growth and Form* could be retrieved and worked from. This essay is a first working script of that process.

The "anomalous entry" in Hamilton's exhibitions—the portrait of Paul Painlevé, the form of Calypso, the portrait in *Just what is it…*—all testify to Hamilton's commitment in keeping the relationship between art and culture, individual and society, and art, technology and science, intellectually and creatively dynamic to sustain conditions of transformation rather than stasis. Publicly identifying himself as early as 1951 as an "intellectual artist" at an ICA debate, Hamilton's synthesis of theory and practice, and his rejection of theory over practice, reveals itself as much in his staging of the spectator in his exhibitions as in the orchestration of practical experiments as part of his teaching practice. As Lawrence Alloway noted in his review of Hamilton's 1955 exhibition of paintings, "Anyone who saw—and to see was to become involved—Hamilton's *Growth and Form* … will remember his Bauhaus display tactics."[42] But as Banham also observed in his review of the same show, while all the paintings presented appeared as highly technical and conceptual investigations into vision and movement based on grid analysis, "Each picture requires a close and imaginative attention for these are genuinely intellectual paintings" accompanied by "punning Joycean titles"—provocatively concluding, "one should always remember Hamilton is an illusionist."[43]

In 1951 Hamilton produced a collage etching and aquatint on paper titled *Self-portrait* (Tate) [p. 23]. Historically, due to its date, this image has been aligned with the biological image-world of *Growth and Form* associated with D'Arcy Wentworth Thompson. On closer inspection, however, shapes and forms appear and disappear, through the push/pull motion of gestalt perception, and we begin to discern that the image speaks more to the underwater world of acrobatic sea beasts and metamorphic forms, summoning up Jean Painlevé's eulogy to the seahorse:

> Everything about this animal, a victim of contradictory forces, suggests that it has disguised itself to escape, and in warding off the fiercest fates, it carries away the most diverse and unexpected possibilities.[44]

42. Lawrence Alloway, "Re Vision," *Art News and Review* 6 (January 1955).
43. Reyner Banham, "Vision in Motion," *Art*, 5 January 1955. It is not insignificant that between 1942 and 1945 Hamilton worked for the English Military Intelligence and in 1947 he completed an army-training course in camouflage.
44. See Bellows, McDougall and Berg, *Science is Fiction,* xvii.

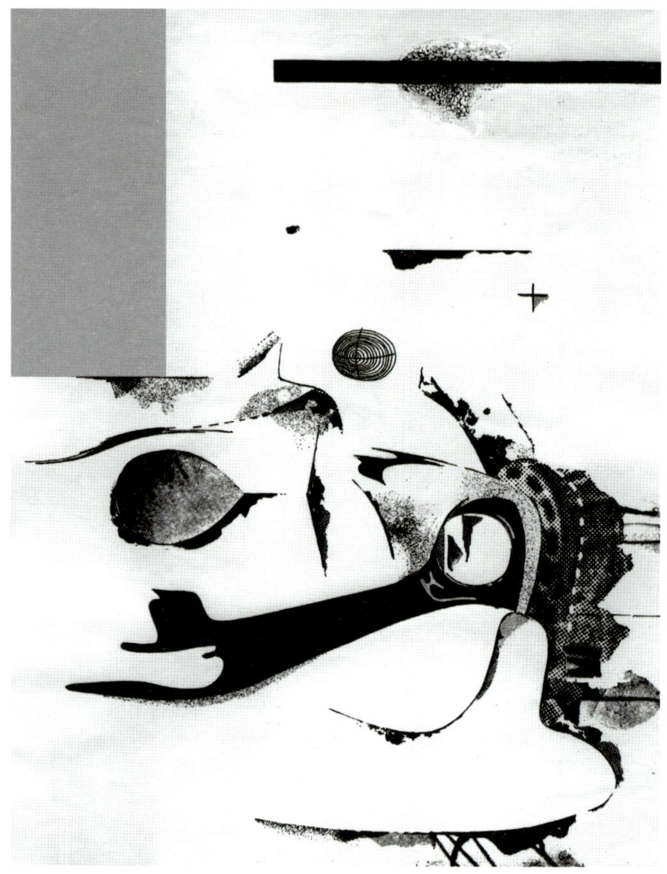

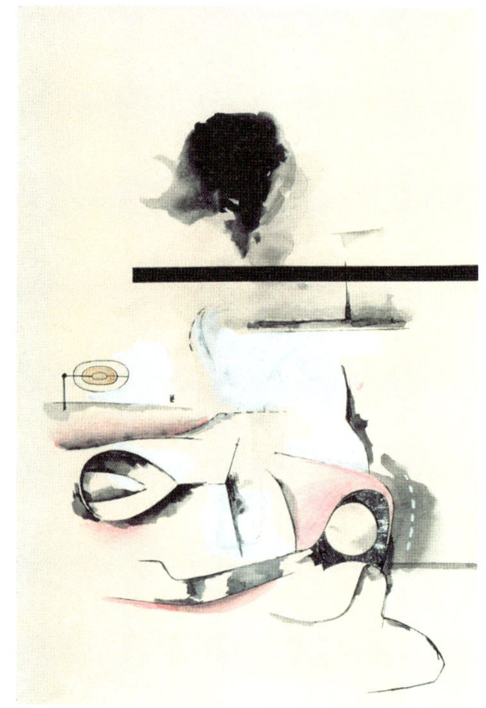

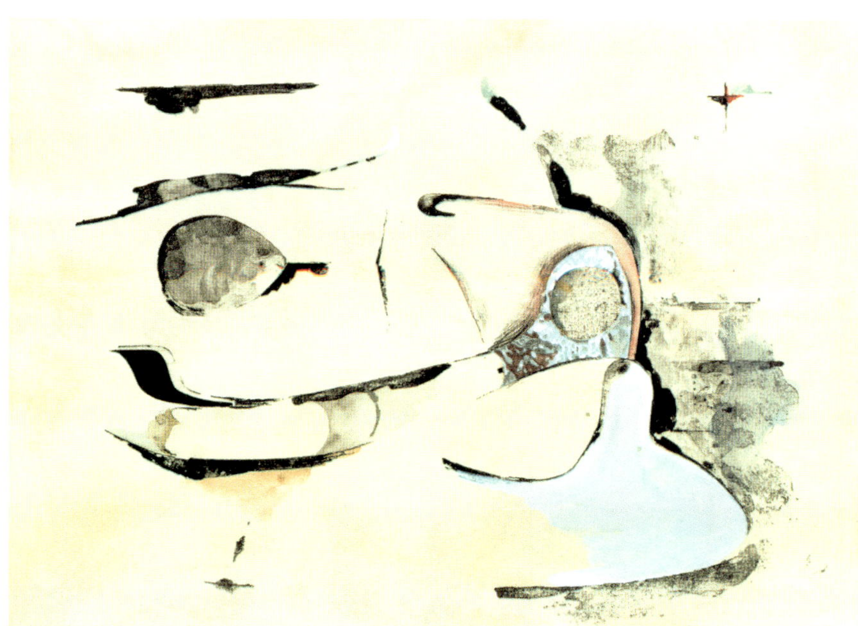

Hommage à Chrysler Corp. (version for line reproduction) 1958

Hommage à Chrysler Corp. (a) 1957

Study for Hommage à Chrysler Corp. 1957

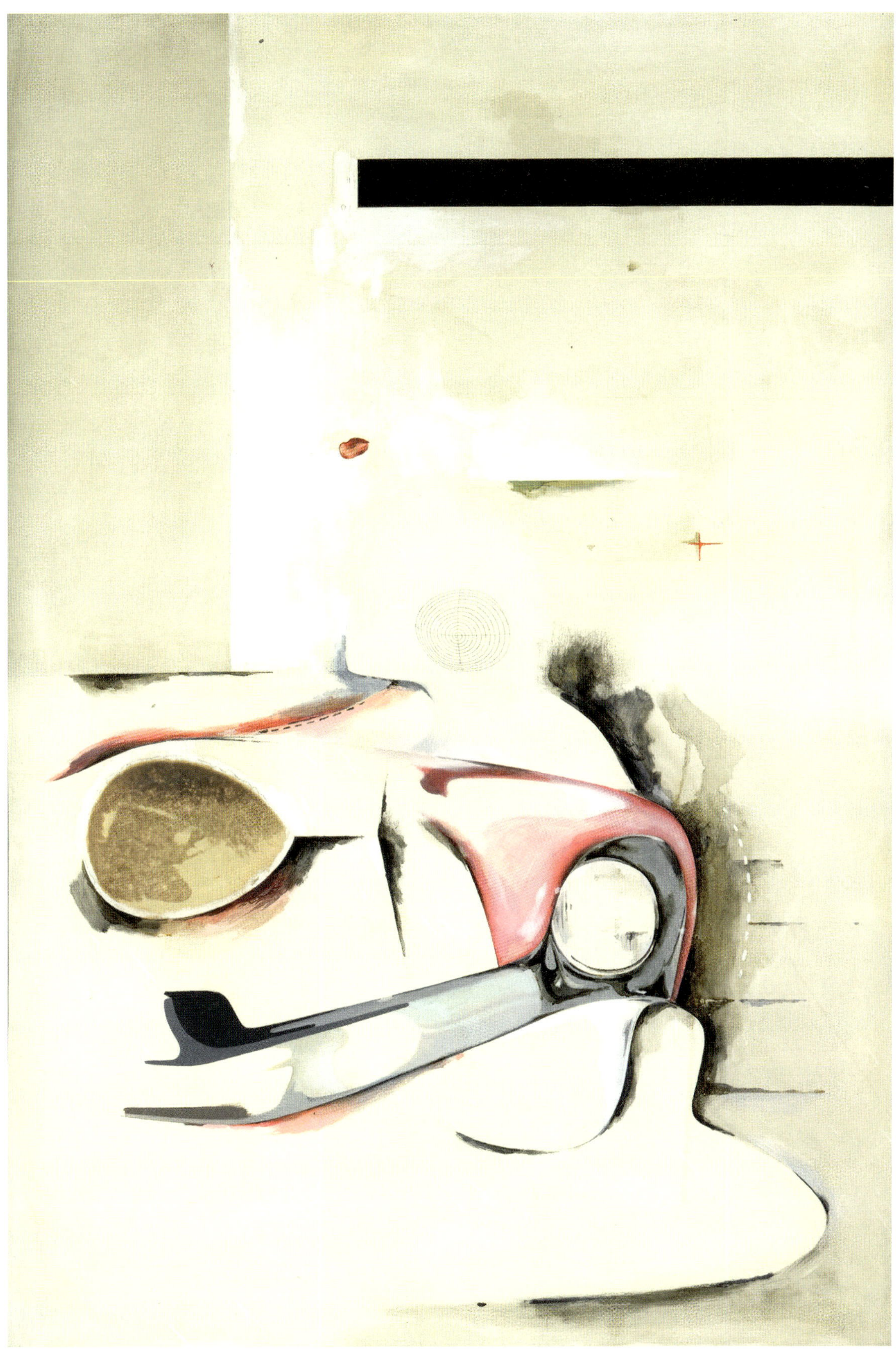

Hommage à Chrysler Corp. 1957

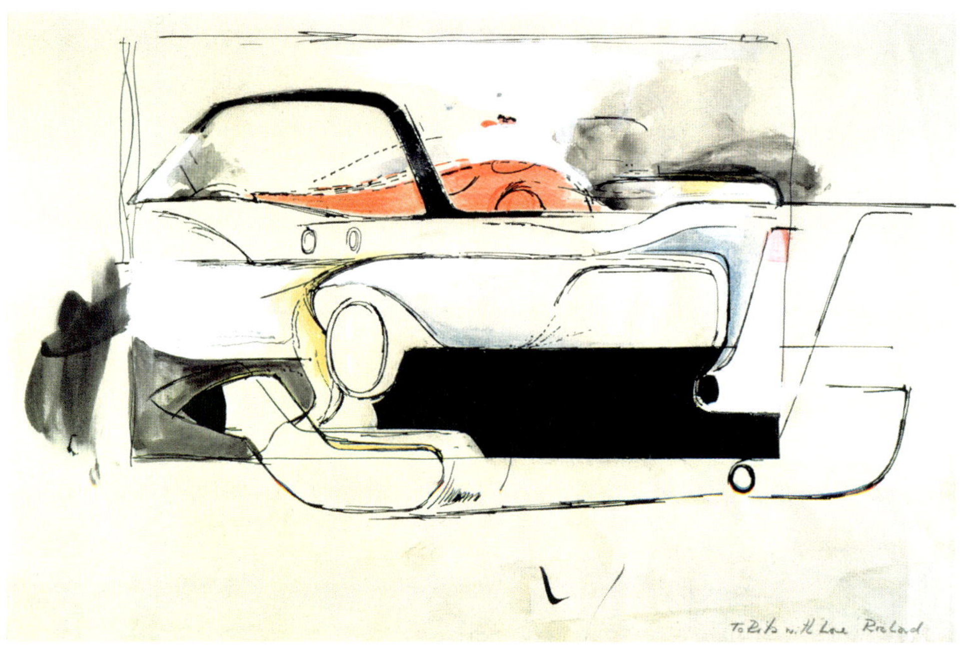

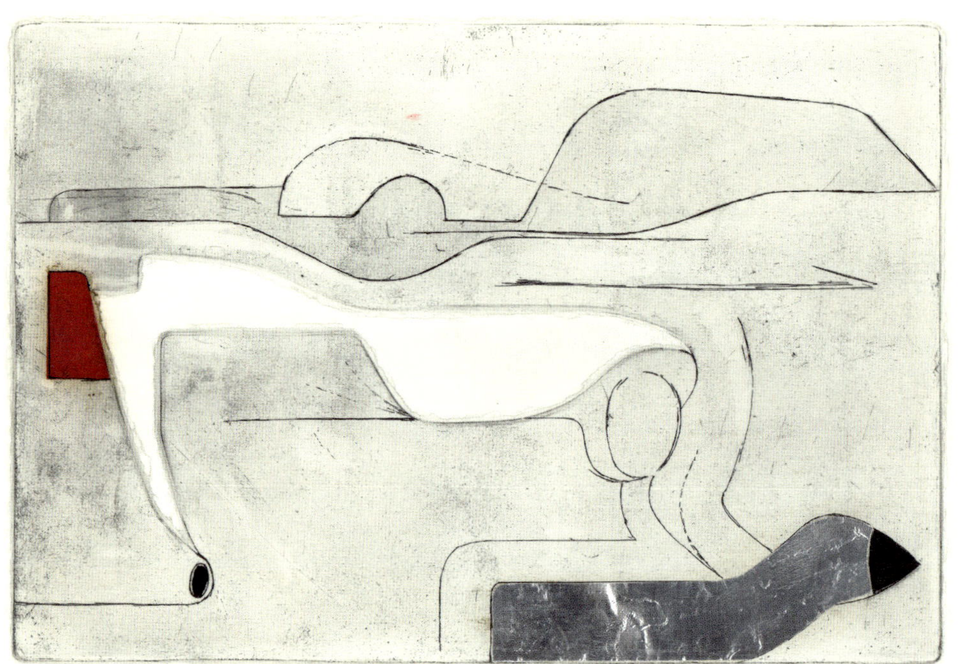

Study for "Hers is a lush situation" 1957

Hers is a lush situation, etching 1958

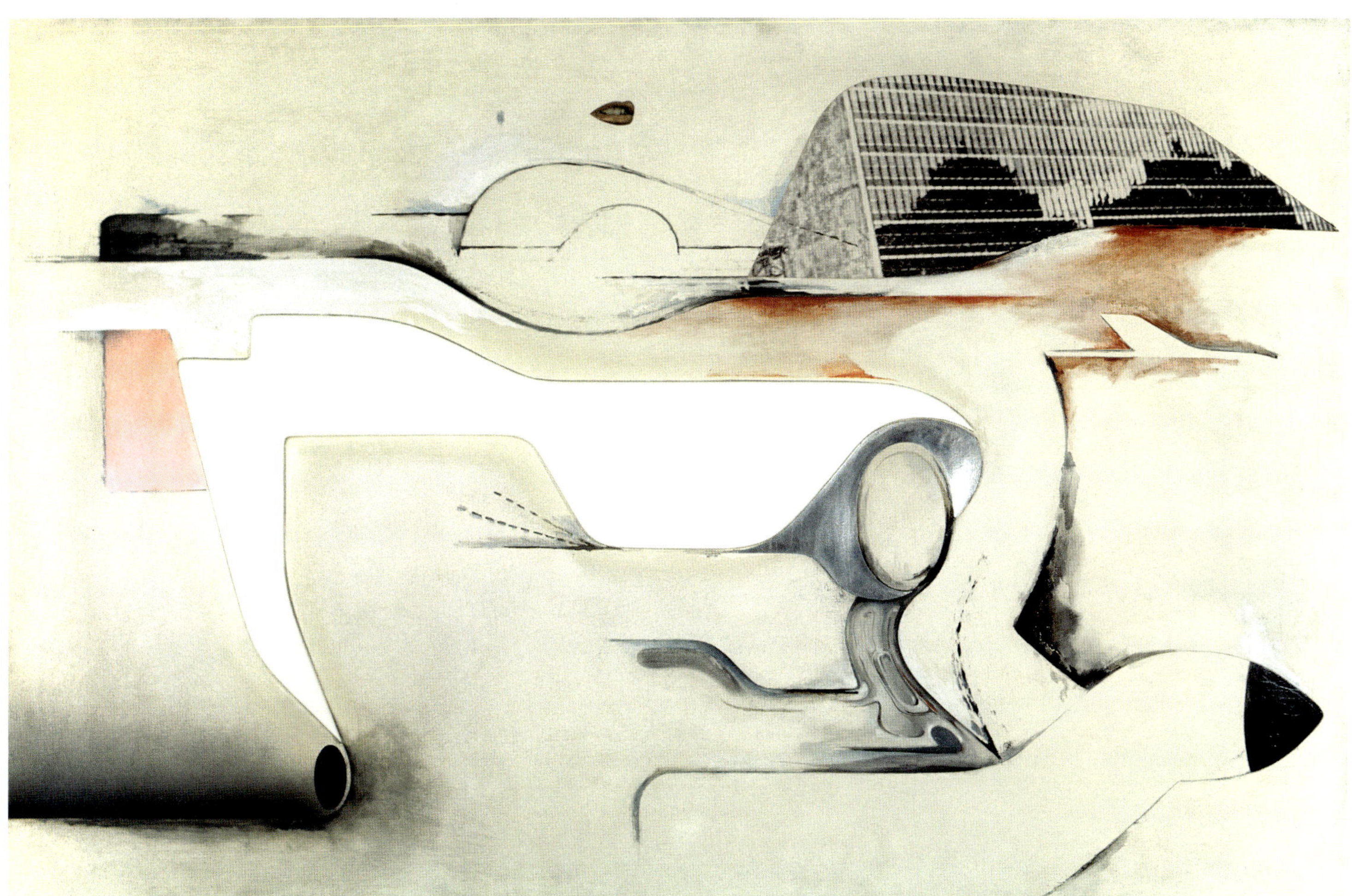

Hers is a lush situation 1958

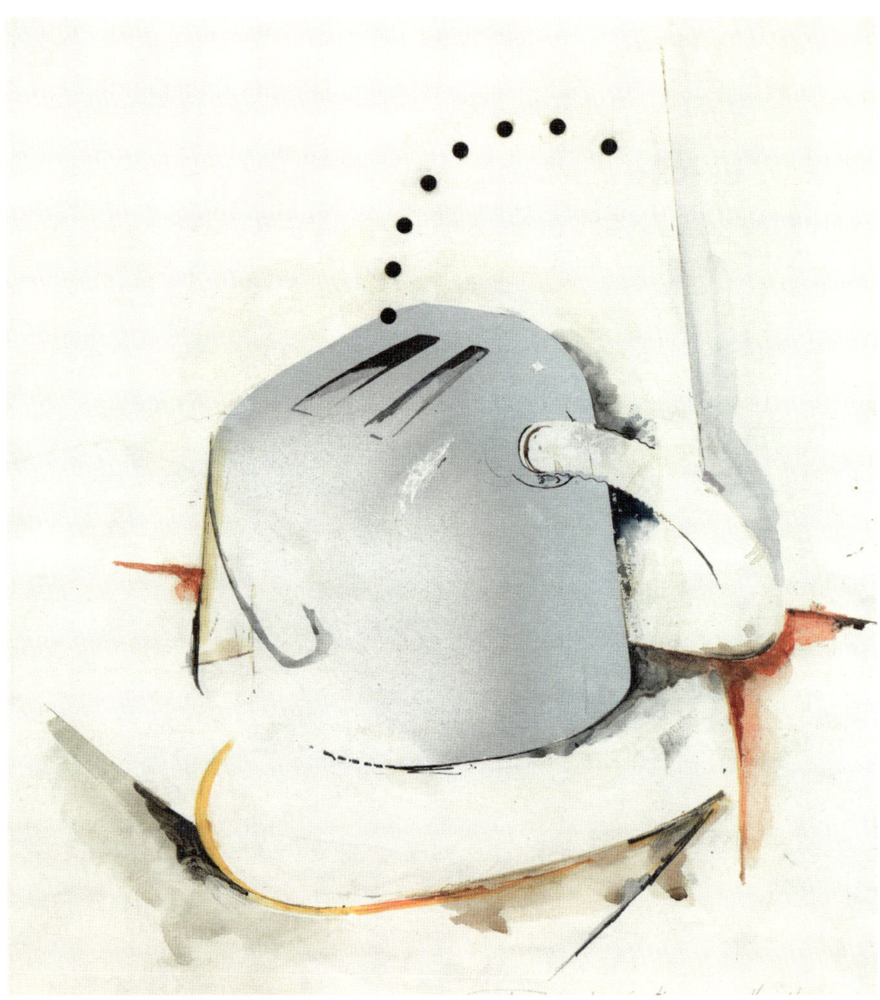

Toastuum 1958

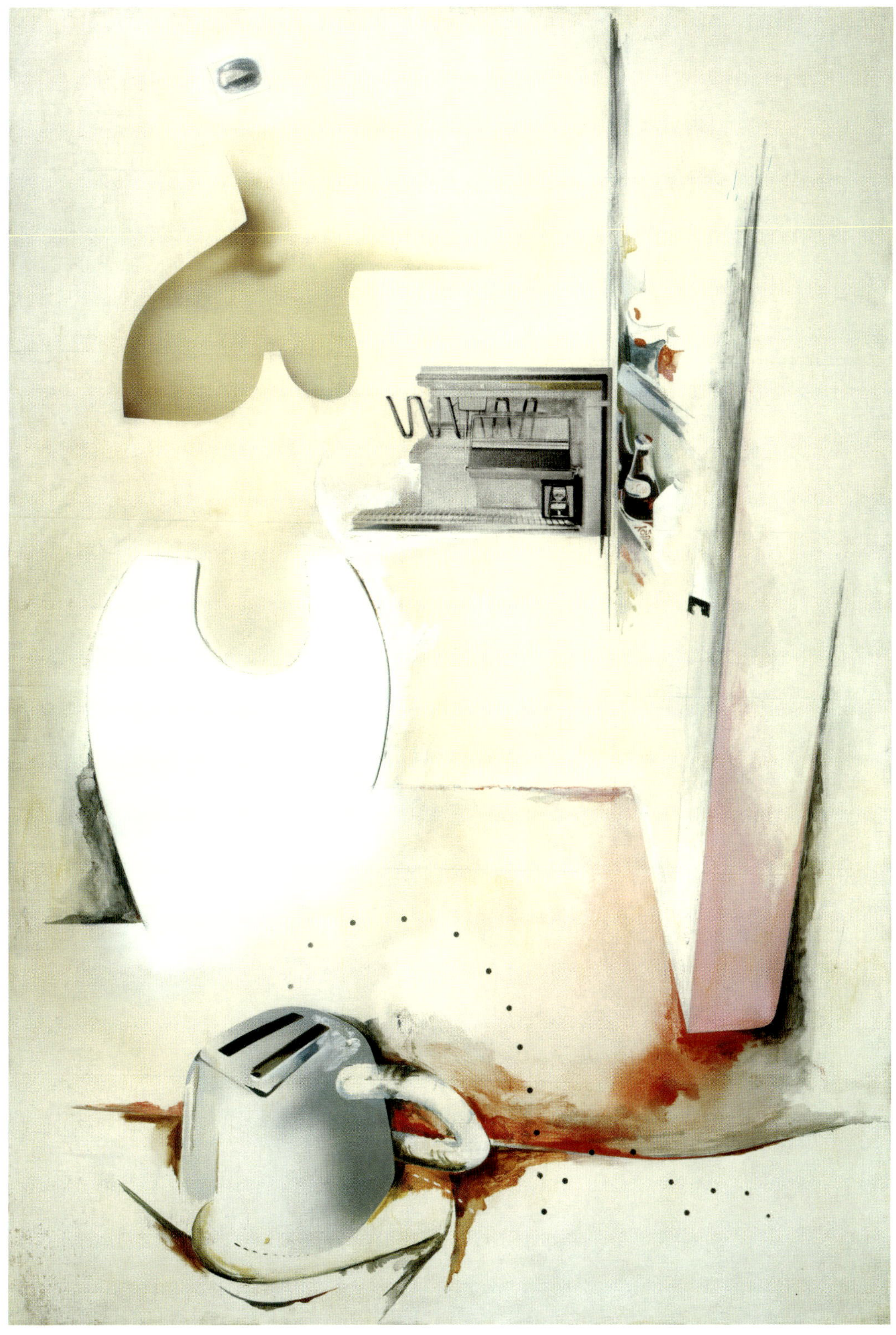

$he 1958–61

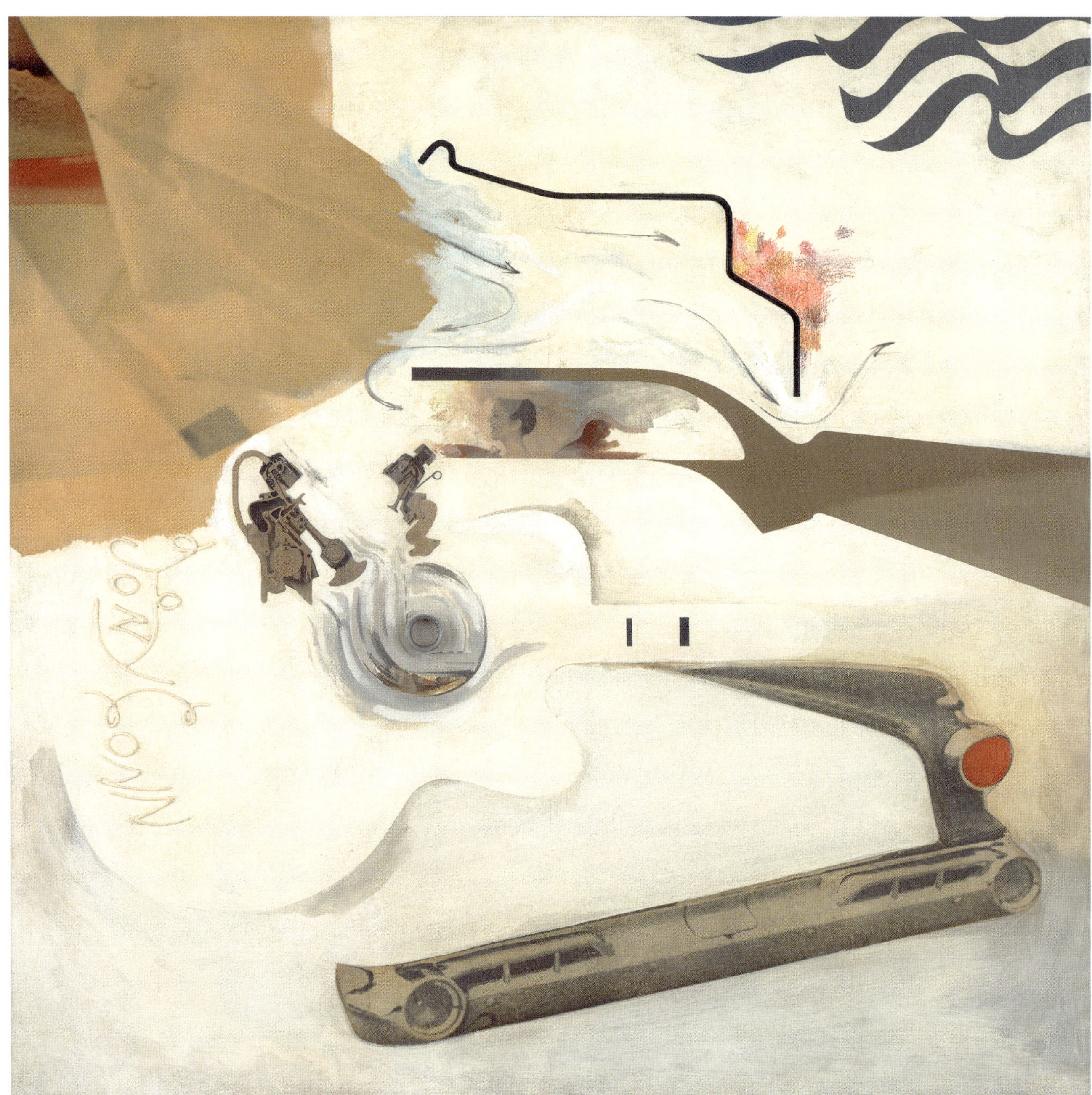

Glorious Techniculture 1961–64

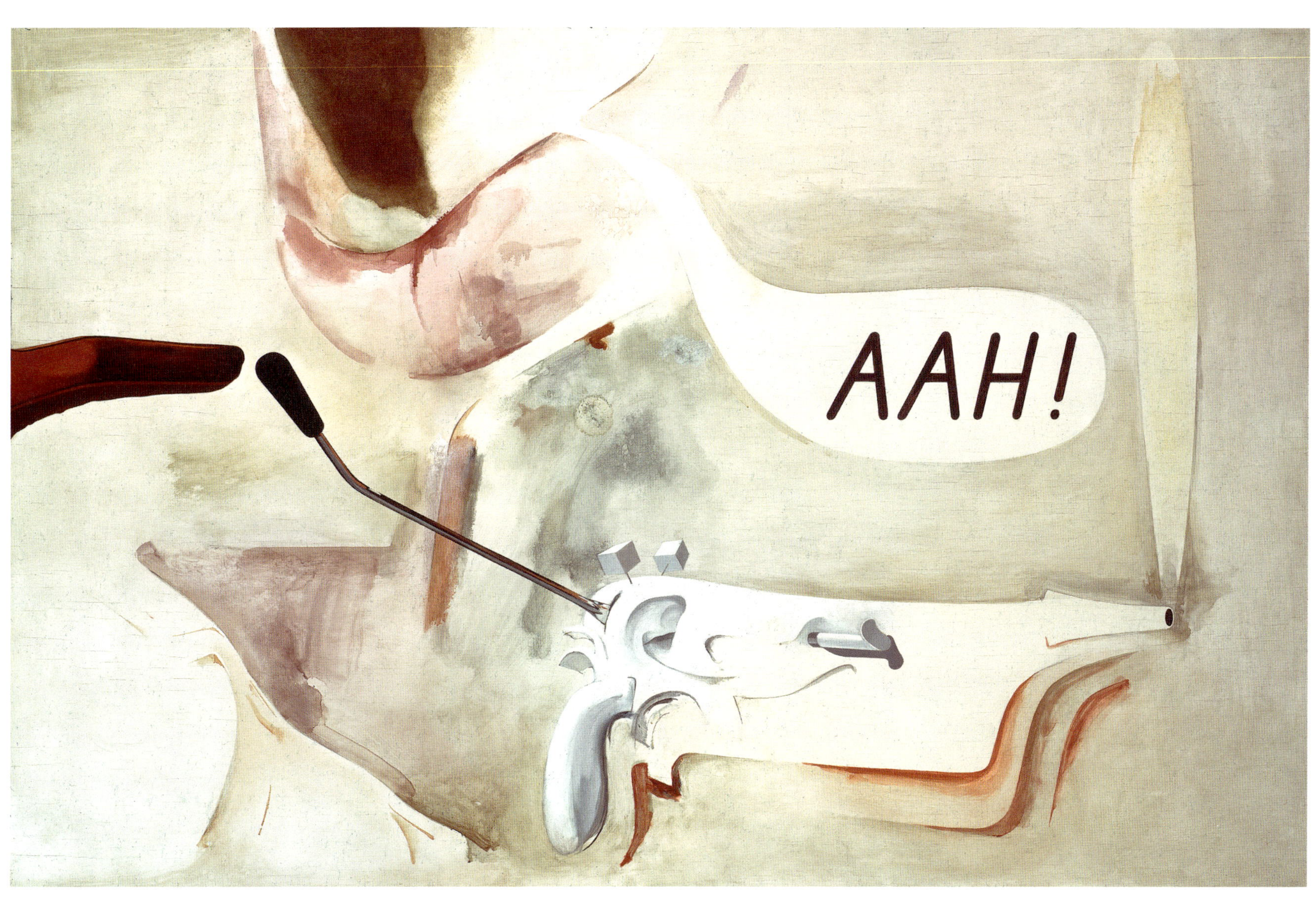

AAH! 1962

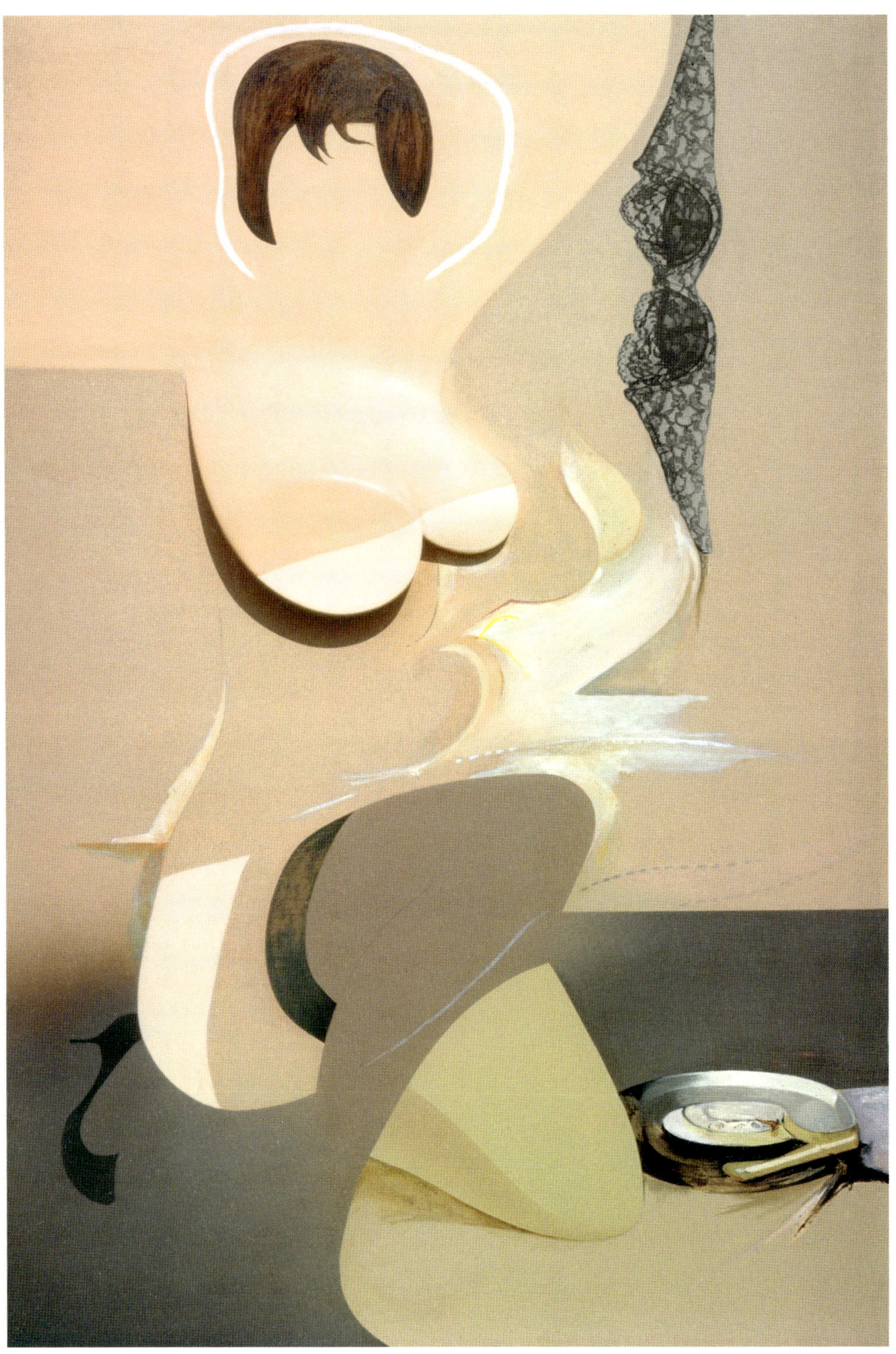

Pin-up 1961

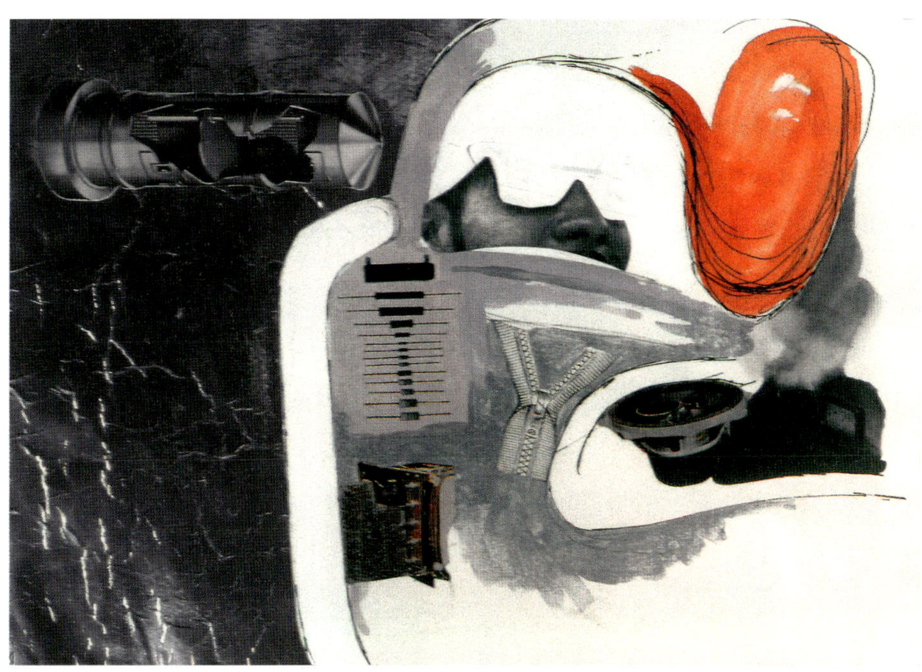

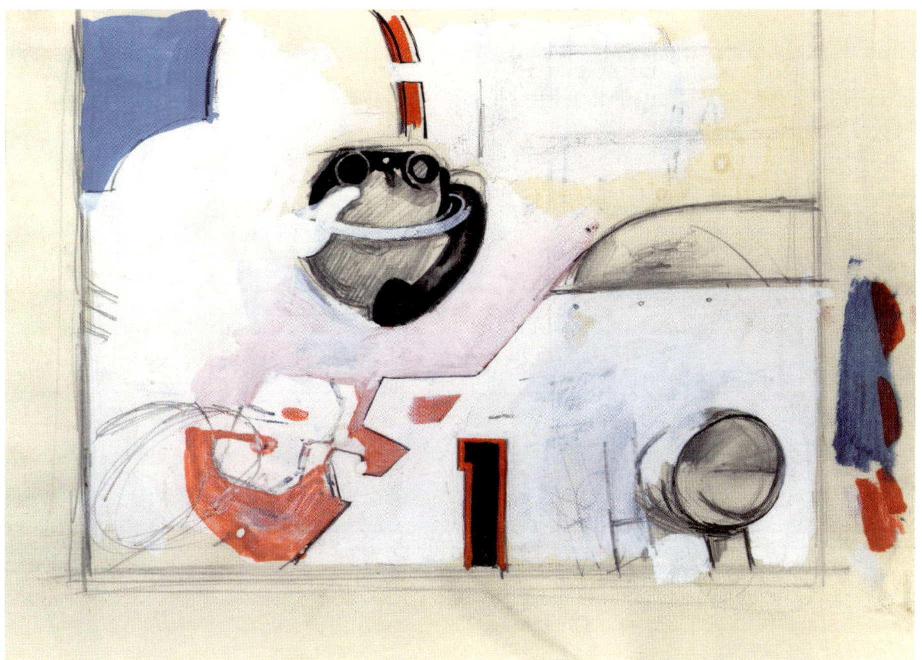

Towards a definitive statement on the coming trends in menswear and accessories (a) sketch II 1962

Towards a definitive statement on the coming trends in menswear and accessories (b) sketch 1962

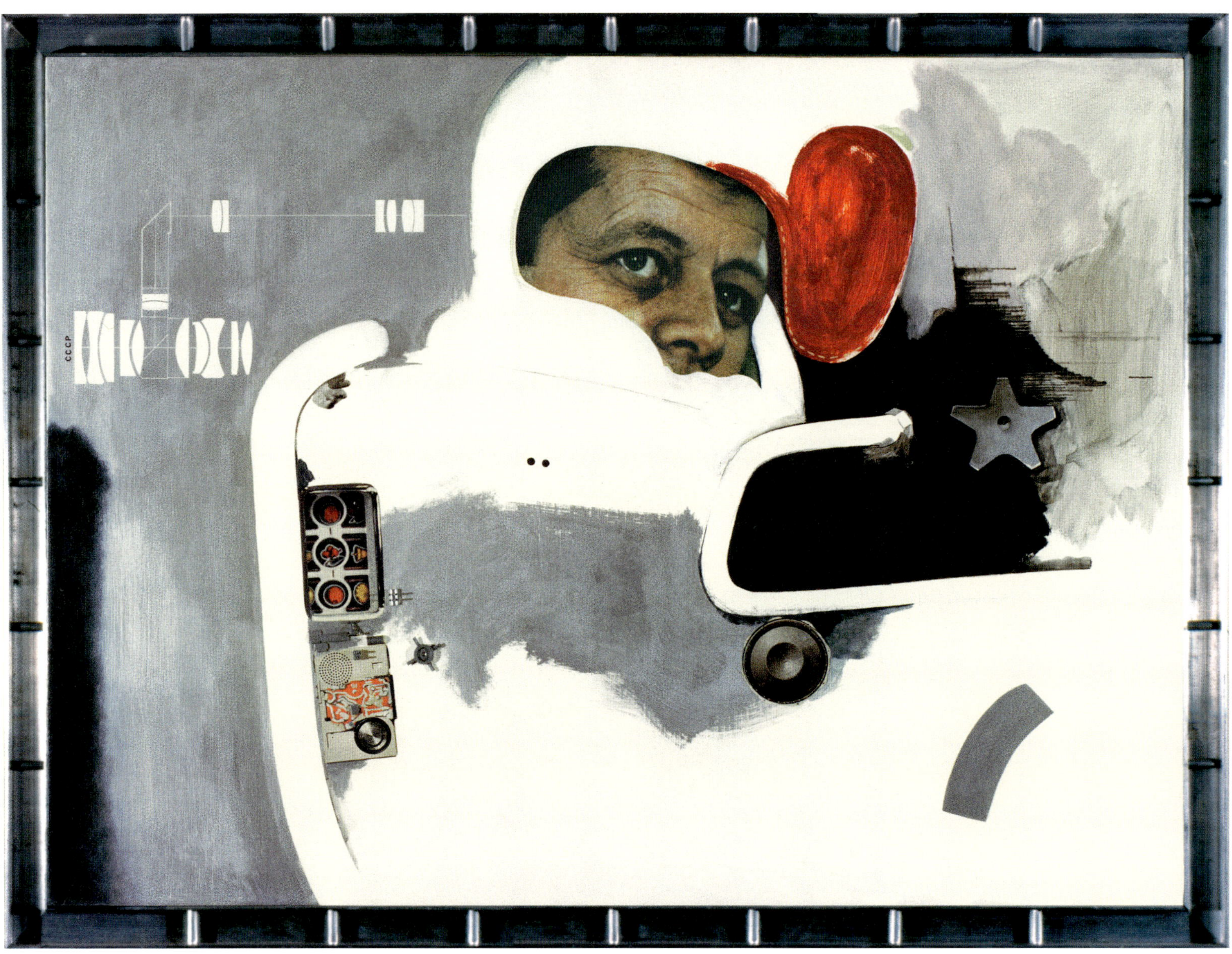

Towards a definitive statement on the coming trends in menswear and accessories (a) "Together let us explore the stars" 1962

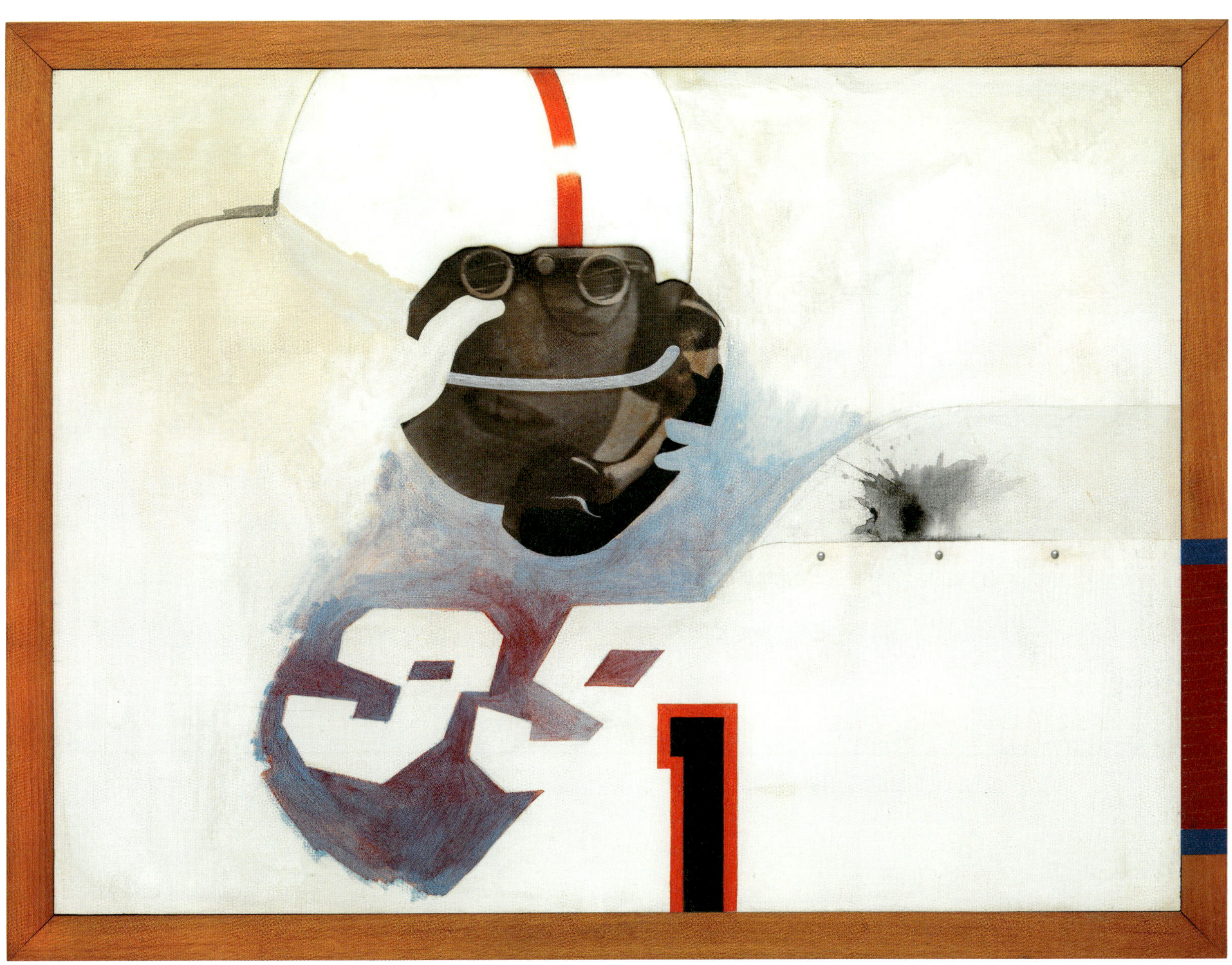

Towards a definitive statement on the coming trends in menswear and accessories (b) 1962

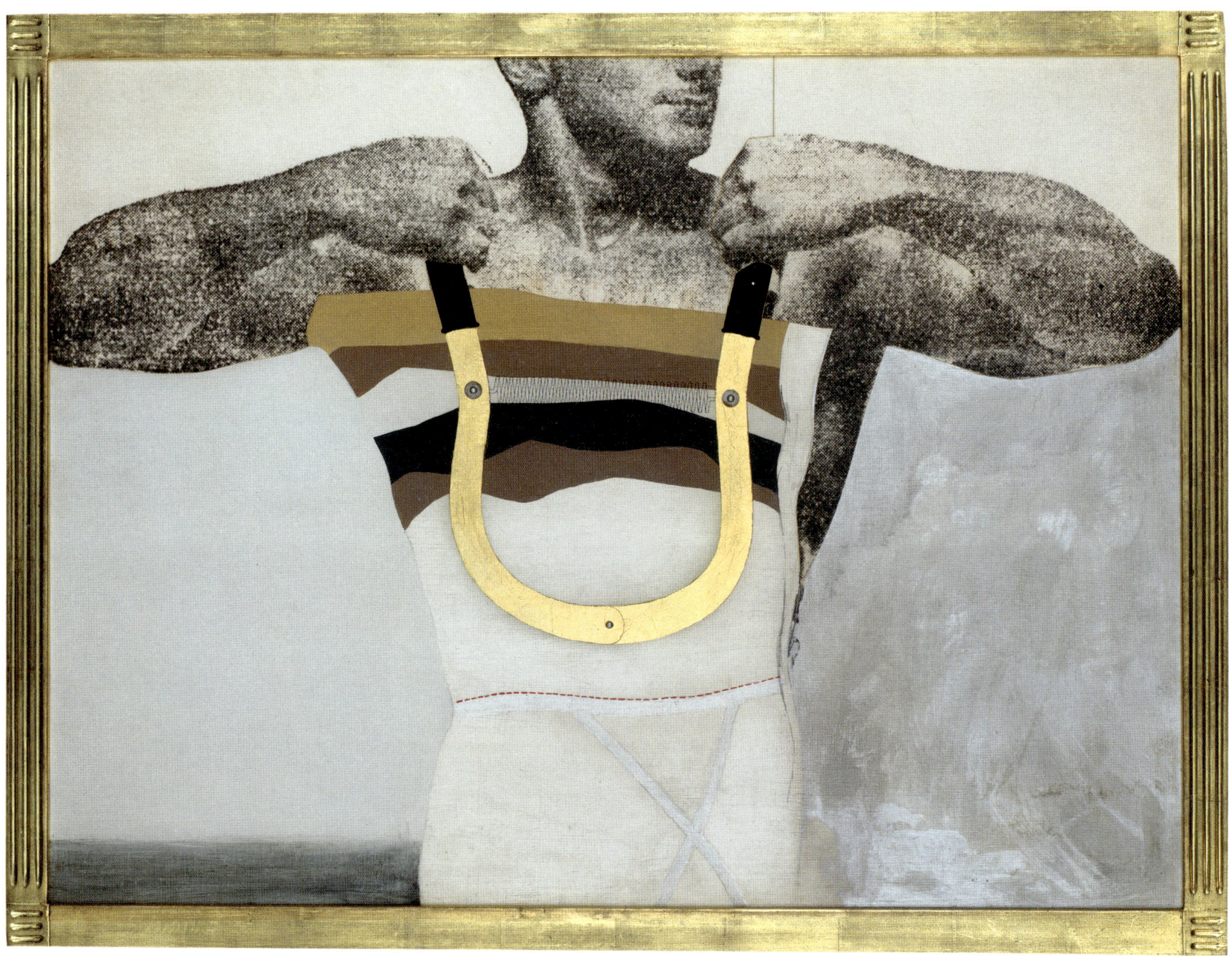

Towards a definitive statement on the coming trends in menswear and accessories (c) Adonis in Y-fronts 1962

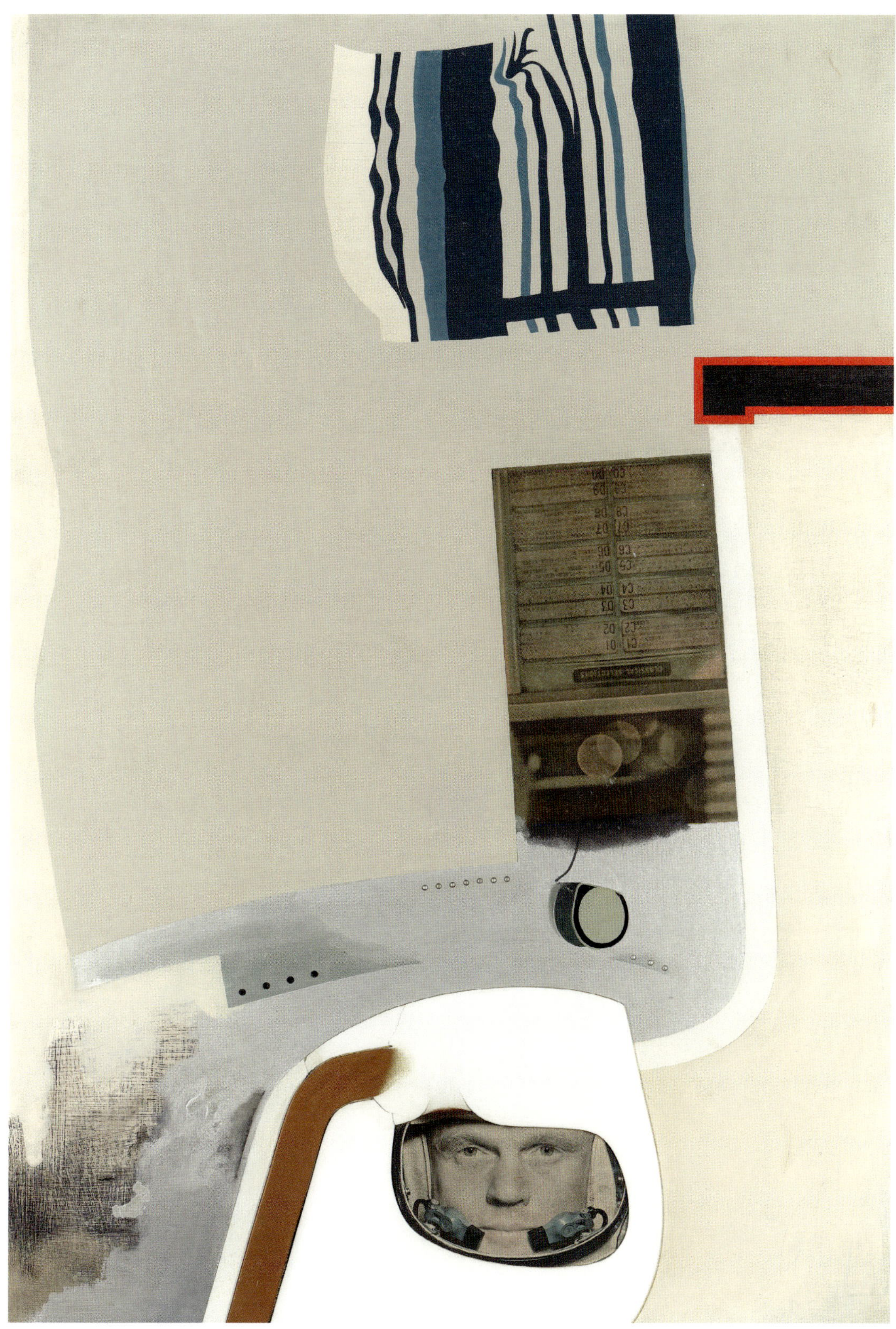

Towards a definitive statement on the coming trends in menswear and accessories (d) 1963

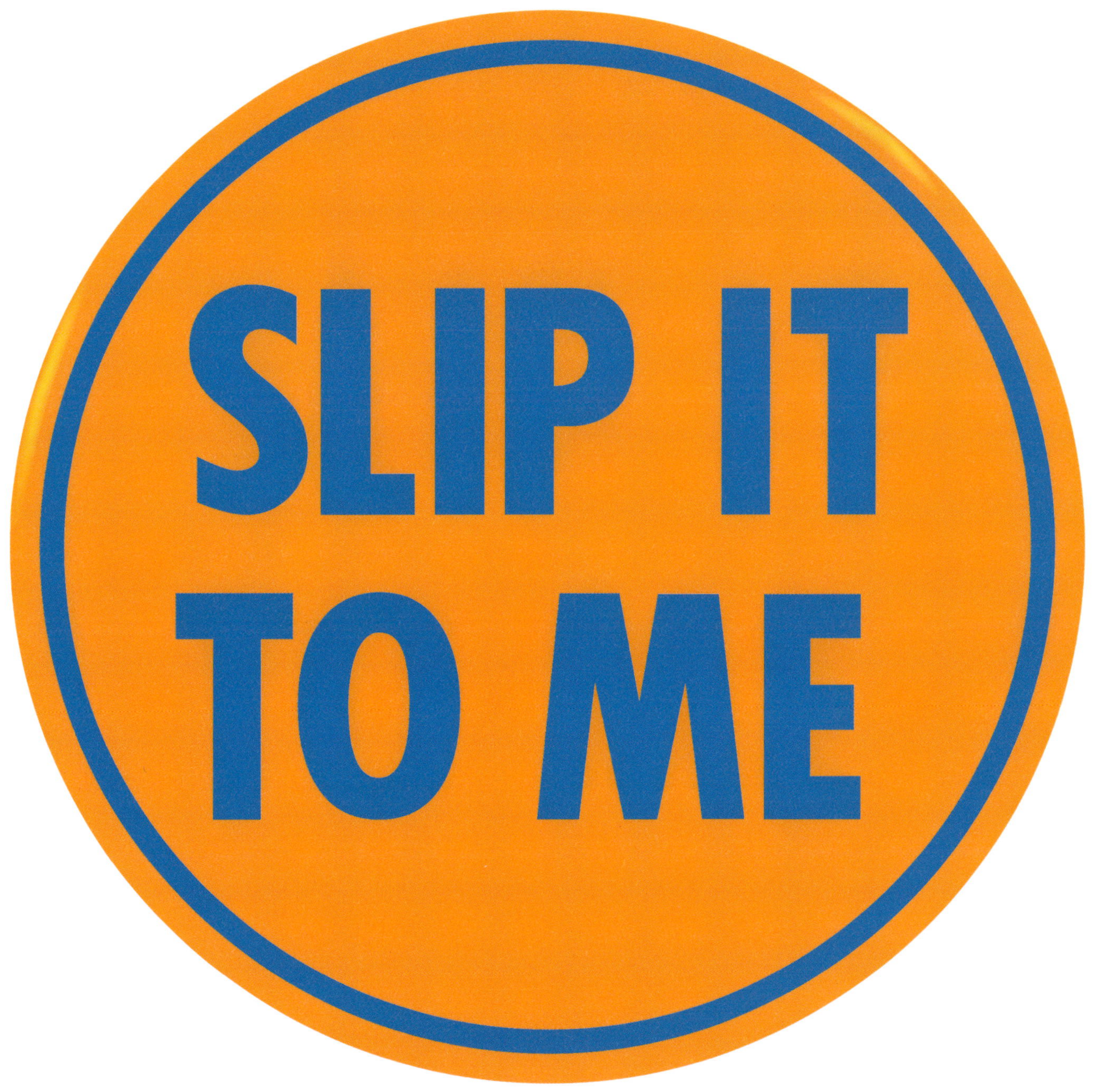

Epiphany 1964

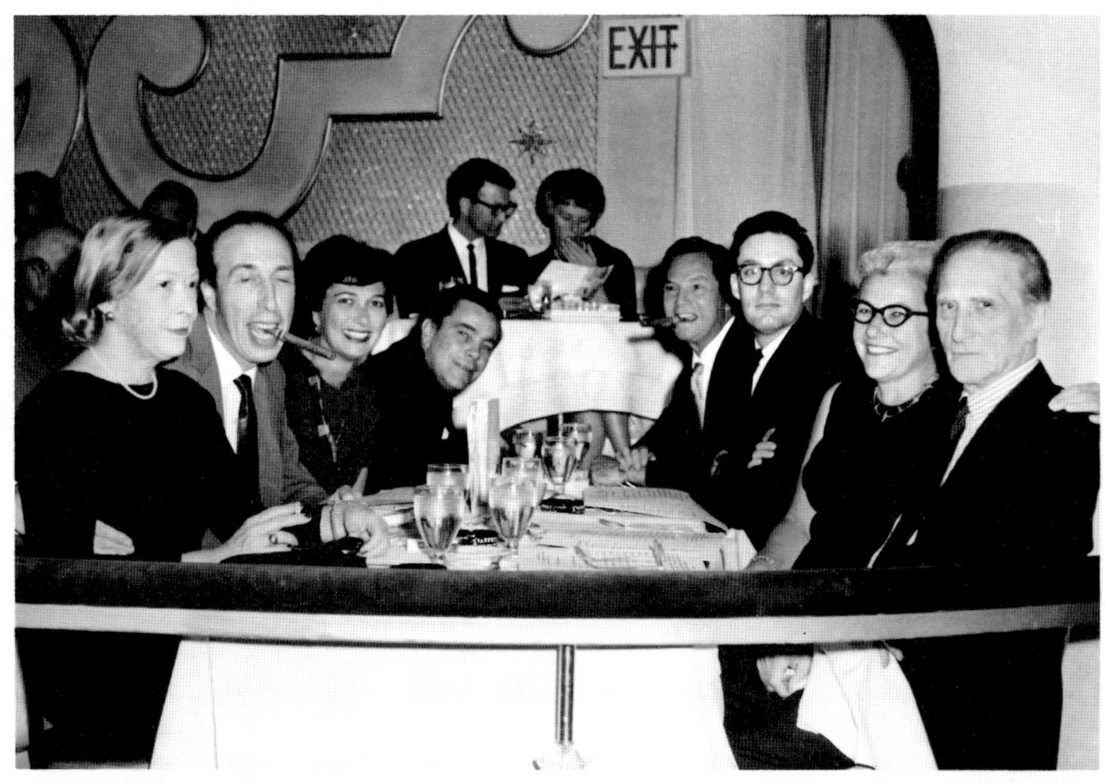

Richard Hamilton (second from left) in Las Vegas with (left to right) Teeny Duchamp, Betty Factor, William N. Copley, Donald Factor, Walter Hopps, Betty Asher and Marcel Duchamp 1963

Among Americans: Richard Hamilton

Benjamin H.D. Buchloh

Industrial design, as a method of organising production more than of configuring objects, did away with the utopian vestiges inherent in the poetics of the avant-garde. Ideology was no longer superimposed on activity—which was now concrete because it was connected to real cycles of production—but was inherent in the activity itself.
Manfredo Tafuri, "The Dialectic of the Avant-Garde," 1973

I find I am not yet sure about the "sincerity" of Pop Art. It is not a characteristic of all but it is of some—at least, pseudo-sincerity is.
Richard Hamilton, letter to Peter and Alison Smithson, 16 January 1957

For quite a long time now, certainly since Anne Massey's groundbreaking and detailed account of the Independent Group in 1995, we have been aware of the impact of American mass culture on the British group and the role it played in its artistic and historical foundations. Whether this embrace responded to a benevolent influx of new goods and information, customised to suit a specifically English variation of post-World War II desires, or whether the inflow was actually experienced as a manipulative invasion, rampant in various guises in post-war Europe from West Germany to Paris, from Amsterdam to Italy, remains subject to critical debate. A theoretical analysis of this history—the first post-war confrontation of the two circles of what formerly had been called avant-garde culture and an utterly unimagined expansion of the sphere of mass culture—has yet to be carried out.

Consequently, some of the more complex details of these exchanges have never been clarified. For example, whether Reyner Banham's early affirmative attitude or Lawrence Alloway's belated euphoria for the compounds of American mass desublimation were in fact shared by the artists in the Independent Group as well. Or whether—as would not be atypical for aesthetic practices in general, and Richard Hamilton in particular—a much deeper ambiguity, if not a sly subversive opposition to the seemingly inevitable extent of cultural Americanisation, might have operated in the work of at least some of the Independent Group's members.[1]

An admittedly much later encounter between Hamilton, the foremost figure of British post-World War II reconstruction culture, and his peers in the recently formed scene of American Pop Art might allow us to shed light on some of these questions. Hamilton met Ed Ruscha, Andy Warhol and Claes Oldenburg, among others, during his visit to Los Angeles in 1963, when he attended the opening of Marcel Duchamp's first retrospective exhibition, organised by Walter Hopps at the Pasadena Art Museum (8 October–3 November). And when he returned to London via New York, Hamilton also encountered Roy Lichtenstein, and possibly Jasper Johns, during his first visit to this city. Thus, on that occasion the Englishman in Hollywood met for the first time not only Duchamp—an artistic father figure

1. A quick glance at a contemporaneous and in many ways comparable movement in a different city, the Nouveau Réalisme of Paris, shows a similar discrepancy between a critic's affirmative and apologetic claims and the actual artists' subversive criticality. If we read the manifestoes and writings of Pierre Restany on the work of this group, we could easily be led to assume that the practices of Arman and Villeglé, of Hains and Dufrêne, were also deeply committed to the celebration of the newly Americanised forms of a culture of totalising consumption, an everyday life devoted to the systematic destruction of the subjects of a social and political public sphere. When we listen to the artists' statements, however, and study their works more carefully than Restany did, we actually discover deep disagreement with and a radical negativity towards those transformations of the public sphere that Americanisation had brought about. In this context, it is not accidental that at least some of these artists were very close to the emerging Internationale Situationniste, a group whose response to these newly instituted realities of the Society of the Spectacle and of totalitarian consumption could hardly have been more antagonistic.

for him since 1952, during the ascendance of Henry Moore and Barbara Hepworth to world fame and local hierarchical power—but also "Duchamp's children," or the "Neo-Dadaists" as some of the key figures in American Pop Art had been baptised recently in certain critical writings, and as he himself would call them shortly thereafter. Although Hamilton talked explicitly on several occasions about this most memorable event and his chance encounters, in the following paragraphs we will trace the more implicit dialogical responses within the work he produced after he returned to London. Starting in 1964 with *Epiphany* [p. 91], the most enigmatic of his post-American objects, these works record the impact and trace the imprints of Hamilton's American discoveries within an amazing range of ambiguous responses.

After Los Angeles, Hamilton had to confront a triadic constellation: first the temptations awaiting an Englishman in Hollywood, a very charged affair since quite a few fellow countrymen (many in Hollywood's culture industry, but for our context most notably Reyner Banham and David Hockney) never really returned from that venture, after having acquired a peculiarly hybrid identity as a result of their fascination with California. Second, there was the intensity of Hamilton's encounter with the retrospective of Duchamp's major works, a pivotal exhibition, ironically assembled in a provincial American museum on the West Coast (an event that Hamilton must have anticipated with impatience, since his aesthetic admiration and scholarly interest had grown continuously since his first encounter with Duchamp's work in 1952). And last, though no less important in this three-point structure, were the actual meetings with a number of artists, some of whom (such as Ed Ruscha) he might never even have heard of before, and others (like Andy Warhol) who had been known to Hamilton before his American visits.[2]

To historicise for a moment: it is obvious that the impact of Hamilton's encounters in 1963 was not comparable to the shock Theodor W. Adorno or Bertolt Brecht experienced when discovering American culture in Los Angeles after their arrival in the late 1930s. After all, the British artist had already traversed the first twenty years of an intense European assimilation of American economic and ideological demands. Nevertheless, there might still have been some bewilderment, however residual and refined by comparison to the European emigrés' sudden estrangement when arriving in California.

In which psychic, cognitive and artistic registers would Hamilton have responded to these new encounters at the very core of the American culture industry? Would he have experienced an exacerbated desire for instant emulation (an option evidently chosen in the work of Hockney or Banham, for example)? Or would initial doubts and an emerging disillusionment have prevailed eventually in Hamilton's responses to the extreme forms of advanced mass-cultural technologies, from photography to film, from industrially produced music to ad campaigns on colour television?

An even more complex question: in which temporality (past or present) would Hamilton now have placed Duchamp's project? Would he have mourned the loss of an esoteric subtlety of artistic thought under advanced conditions of reification at the beginning of

2. Warhol's second exhibition at Irving Blum's Ferus Gallery, after the sensational flop of the *Campbell Soup Cans* in 1962, ran concurrently with the Duchamp retrospective and consisted of individually cut silver silkscreens of *Elvis* from the giant rolls of printed canvas that Warhol had sent to Blum. The *Campbell Soup Cans* could be viewed in Blum's office.

the twentieth century, for which Hamilton had admired Duchamp's work ever since his first discovery? And if Duchamp was the ancestral figure of the most radical modernity for Hamilton, could he still provide the standards against which to judge not only his own projects but also gauge the work of the American Pop artists he now encountered?

A partial answer to these questions can be found when we sketch out a comparative iconography of mass-cultural citations: those that Hamilton discovered during his first visit to the United States (for example, in the work of Jasper Johns, Andy Warhol and Ed Ruscha), and those he would incorporate in his own work after the Los Angeles/New York journey was completed. We could differentiate these citations according to the manifest or latent projective intensity with which artists motivate their iconic choices, or we could presume that these icons have to be the representations of the state and the structures of collective desire at the moment of the pictorial production (in the way that one could argue that Manet's choice of the image of Olympia as a prostitute in 1863 was not all that different from Warhol's choice of Marilyn in 1962, since in each case the actually governing—even if extremely different—conditions of artistic and collective desire appeared as an integral element of the artist's iconic choice).

And even if certain images, such as Warhol's *Elvis*, might have appeared at first as being less erotically charged to Hamilton, they might have triggered both a sudden attraction and a slowly growing sense of unbridgeable difference separating the Englishman in Hollywood from his American pop peers, as we will try to argue.

How would Hamilton possibly have distinguished his citational iconography from that of his American colleagues? First of all, the initially rigorously anti-iconographic concept of Duchamp's ready-made had perhaps, even unknowingly, acquired an additional dimension of historical representation in American hands. In other words, what had once been a mere declaratory nominalist principle had now gained a potentially affirmative or critical dimension—an effect most evident in the (mis)-readings of Jasper Johns' first flags in 1954–56 as either a declaration of loyalty to, or a polemical detachment from the project of a specifically American painting. Obviously, one would never have posed the question whether a bicycle wheel or a bottle dryer were delivering an affirmative or a critical charge in terms of the problems of nation-state culture or ideological inscription. Whereas now, contemplating the *Flag*, and even more so the iconic representations of advanced consumer culture such as *Campbell*, *Elvis* and *Marilyn*, Hamilton had to reflect on the possibly treacherous, if involuntary side effects of the Americanisation of the ready-made concept and its suturing side effects.[3]

Furthermore, these discrepancies would have been all the more evident to Hamilton since he had actually initiated a similar iconography of mass-cultural consumption seven years earlier, beginning with the painting *Hommage à Chrysler Corp.* in 1957 [p. 77]. When we compare his early paintings and those of his American pop peers, however, the profound differences in their respective approach towards painting and the ruling technologies of image production are striking. One of Warhol's gambits, which had shocked a rather naive

3. We could perhaps imagine Hamilton's responses to have been somewhat similar to the extreme ambiguity which Marcel Broodthaers, later a close friend of Hamilton's in London, articulated when confronting the new iconography of advanced forms of consumption for the first time in 1964. Even if the new generation of Pop artists seemed to have embraced this iconography as a sign of an apparently inescapable condition of object experience, to a European eye that embrace would have appeared more likely as a peculiarly masochistic acceptance of an imposed regime from which dissidence and difference were only temporarily unthinkable.

art world at the time, had been his supposedly radical sacrifice of traditional means of painterly production. This rupture became even more pronounced when Warhol abandoned the last remnants of artisanal manufacture by shifting from the matrices of stamped paintings to the apparently anti-artistic operations of a silkscreen studio in which his paintings were produced by a host of anonymous collaborators. In view of what the universe of total advertisement on television already demanded from its purveyors at that time, we can now recognise more easily that Warhol had actually deployed a rather quaint imaging technique that was already arcane even within the field of publicity, its primary application. Yet against painting's claims to sustain a status of the "high" art object, silkscreens were still perceived as subversive and shocking. By contrast, Hamilton, with few exceptions, had always suspended his work between the dialectical challenges of painting and the ready-made (from Cézanne to Cubism and Duchamp). Undoubtedly, Hamilton saw himself as placed within a painterly culture in which the mnemonic resuscitation of painting's past and the presentist confrontation with painting's dire actuality were always to be fully enacted (in this regard, it is not at all surprising that Hamilton recognised a kindred spirit in Jasper Johns, who had been confronting a very similar set of problems since the mid-1950s).

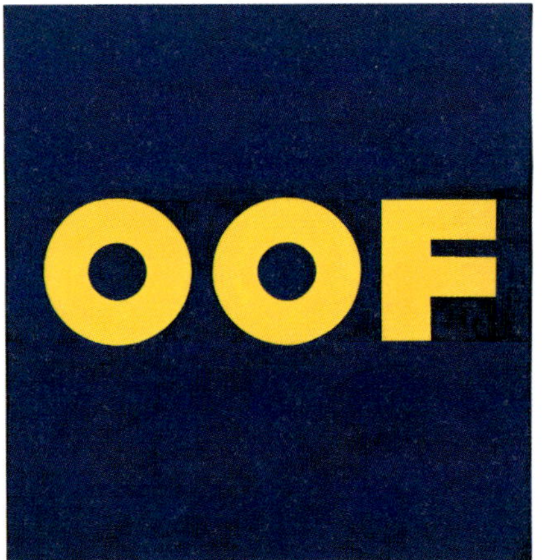

fig. 1
Ed Ruscha
OOF, 1962 (reworked 1963)
Oil on canvas
The Museum of Modern Art, New York

Ready-made excess

In manifest contrast, the approaches to painting Hamilton encountered in Los Angeles, in the work of Ruscha and Warhol in particular, claimed to have resolved these conflicts once and for all by substituting the matrix of the ready-made for any of the traditional pictorial operations. This newfound congruence between ready-made matrix and the dissolution of the painterly process was quite literally consummated first of all on the level of iconography by singularising any depicted object (e.g. Ruscha's single word paintings like *OOF* [fig. 1], in 1962, or substituting a single or a serialised image of a brand (as, of course, in the *Campbell Soups* and ever after in Warhol's oeuvre). In his earlier paintings, Hamilton had refused or failed to follow this elimination of an immanent pictorial syntax (of compositional relations, of illusions of perspectival recession, of volume and depth of modelling, to name but a few), as much as he had retained residual key features of painterly production (such as gesture, facture, tone, chiaroscuro) in all of his work of the late 1950s and the early 1960s. Once in Los Angeles, he would have recognised that his earlier paintings—in spite of their very advanced iconography—had precisely lacked that degree of American resolution.

Not surprisingly, the artist now responded to the discovery of Ruscha's early word paintings with an excessive deployment of the ready-made's typically underhanded, yet subversive resources. If Ruscha had kept the linguistic and phonetic signal in its place in a monochrome pictorial field, Hamilton now substituted a giant simulacrum of a text button—reading SLIP IT TO ME (a typical American cult object to communicate popular opinions, slogans and wisdoms, or more often, the absence thereof)—for the painterly support itself.[4] Thus he dismantled precisely the last remnant of painterly conventions which Ruscha (and Warhol as well, of course) had failed or refused to reflect upon: stretcher frame, canvas and paint application. Furthermore, rather than submitting an inane colloquial phonetic fragment like Ruscha's *OOF*, Hamilton's *Epiphany* offers a textual citation that opens up a much wider spectrum. Ranging from a slightly obscene sexual innuendo to an athletic command, the disc perhaps addresses first of all his pop peers, in an ironical quest for the recognition of his earlier mastery. Ultimately, the command might even disguise any attempt at an artistic communicative act in the aegis of mass-cultural domination. In any case, as Hamilton forces the linguistic citation back onto the button, its original support, and displaces painting's conventional support, his work even manages to exceed the proto-conceptualist and linguistic turn that Ruscha had initiated.

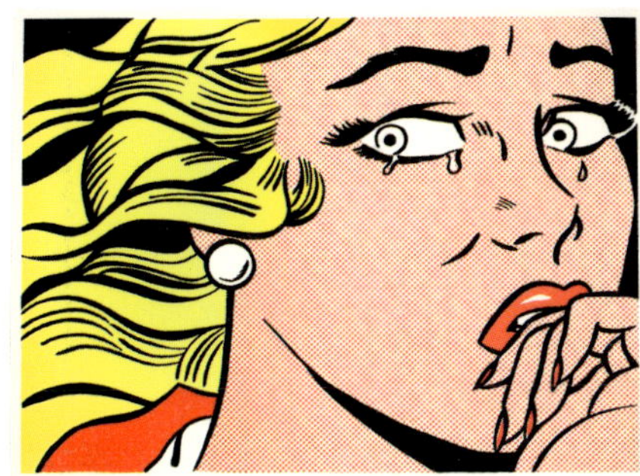

fig. 2
Roy Lichtenstein
Crying Girl, 1963
Offset lithograph
Courtesy Roy Lichtenstein Foundation

A second example which allows us to trace Hamilton's American encounters is entitled *A little bit of Roy Lichtenstein for...* [p. 107], explicitly citing a fragment of Lichtenstein's lithograph *Crying Girl* [fig. 2], which had been published in 1963. Returning from Pasadena via New York, Hamilton had met the artist and discovered the print. As before with *Epiphany,* it appears that Hamilton went to work on this second dialogic response shortly after his return, producing his Lichtenstein paraphrase in 1964. Selecting a metonymic detail from the Pop master's offset lithograph, he subjected the print to the very same principles that Lichtenstein had initially applied to the original comic strip clipping. However, in the process of an allegorical selection, fragmentation and enlargement, Hamilton duplicates and exacerbates the pop icon's innate ready-made structure once again, dissolving now even the seductive power of the Comic citation by reducing it to the mere skeleton of technological reproduction. Thus, in duplicating the procedure of citation, a puzzling set of differences between the two artists emerges. First of all, the detail in Hamilton's print appears as totally abstracted from both its high cultural quotation and its mass cultural source, thereby reversing the very principles that had made American Pop Art an instant sensation: its unleashing, after the drought of abstraction, of what had been variously perceived as a new iconography that was redeemingly legibile, ironically attractive, if not even seductively conciliatory towards mass culture. Hamilton, by contrast, now undoes precisely all of these attractions. First of all, he fragments even further Lichtenstein's humorous citations of the erotic dramas of everyday life and everyman's existence as enacted in Comics. In the second place, Hamilton reconverts the citation back into the very abstract pragmatics of a mere technical production procedure, the Ben-Day dot technology which at that time was about to become Lichtenstein's calling card, guarantee of international branding and name recognition. Thirdly, in the return to a purely technical register of the image and its production procedures, Hamilton's strategy of ascetic negation dismantles Pop Art's perpetual *clin d'oeil* concerning the conciliatory responses to the dialectics of high and low. Exchanging Pop's iconographic pleasures for an exclusive focus on the bare technological conditions of image production with an almost Mallarméan precision, Hamilton's *A little bit...* insists on the fact that signification and reification are jointly embedded first and last in the technical and material structures of production alone.

4. Hamilton bought the button in "a seedy joke shop in Pacific Ocean Park" (*Collected Words*, p. 55). I owe Mark Godfrey thanks for having initially pointed out to me that Hamilton also discovered Ruscha and his so-called word paintings during the visit to Los Angeles. Godfrey has furthermore quite credibly suggested that the title *Epiphany* not only demarcated Hamilton's newly won insight into how American Pop Art differed from his earlier Pop paintings but also made reference to a passage from Joyce's *Ulysses*, as Fanny Singer establishes in the chronology elaborated for this catalogue.

Mourning painting

Thus Hamilton's earliest dialogic responses to American Pop Art seem to operate in two ways: on the one hand, in a set of arcane and arch gestures, he expands the limitations of the Americans' painterly reception of the ready-made, pointing to its historical origins as having been more radical, and to the pervasive epistemological consequences in the present. On the other hand, and in manifest dialectical opposition, the artist retains the horizon of modernist pictorial traditions and aesthetic conventions as an immutable challenge to the apparent simplifications that the pictorialised ready-made had promised.

One of the most important works, if not *the* most important painting that Hamilton produced immediately after his return from the United States, would undoubtedly be his *Interior I* (1964) [p. 108]. At first glance, the painting seems to perform an all-out mnemonic counter-attack against the recently discovered world of American art. Just like *Epiphany*, its strategies are partially citational, yet these citations are certainly not delivered from a perspective of parody, least of all from one of cultural superiority. Even if the work now mobilises multiple references to the history of painting as a vanishing, yet still powerful epistemological horizon, *Interior I* suspends us between a model of painterly mourning on the one hand, and a Duchampian defiance of painting on the other. Constructing a canny enumeration of all the resources to which a painter before Pop, like Picasso, still had been thought to have access to, Hamilton's citations range from Velázquez's *Las meninas,* through Cézanne, once again, to culminate in a grand homage to Cubism, here ranging from the *Demoiselles* to the heights of Synthetic Cubist collage and relief constructions. Furthermore, in terms of its technical construction, the painting shifts perpetually between the eerily outdated performances of painterly craft and collage's mission to deconstruct painting once and for all.

We can begin with the virginal blue curtain on the left side of the painting, the device of pictorial mourning from Manet's *Olympia* to Picasso's *Demoiselles* (mourning, because what is revealed by the theatrical gesture of opening the curtain is nothing less than the actual demise of the very promises of sublime gratification that painting until the beginning of modernity had in fact offered, either by opening the window onto the world, or by removing the curtain to the side).

A second modernist device, equally cited from both *Olympia* and the *Demoiselles*, is the triangular protrusion into the picture plane, which sutures Hamilton's spectator with the uncanny interior of a seemingly soulless realm of reification. Yet to the same extent that Hamilton's triangular wedge operates as a device of phenomenological inscription, it reminds us of the precarious nature of all painterly representations at this time: its almost somatic smudges seem to embody the murky zones of painting's intricate relationship to repression and disavowal, rather than to revelation and representation. Inherited from Francis Bacon, that uncanny fusion of paint and wound, of facture and medical suture, of pigment and somatic excrescence, had of course already been deployed in Hamilton's earlier work, such as *$he* in 1958 [p. 81], where that same mismatch (or mishmash) between smears of red pigment and bodily pain had been one of Hamilton's most startling reflections on the conditions of chroma and painterly facture in the present.

Then there is the spatial construction of *Interior I* as scenario. Beyond the curtain and the triangular wedge, a stage set opens up, defined by two slightly conflicting, yet emphatically perspectival axes, designed with the pedantic pride of an early Renaissance painter who wants to prove that he has mastered the system. Yet Hamilton's discrepant perspectival display originates not only in the recognition that the system has lost its function, but also in the insight that the very experience of spatial and social situations in which the subject could figure itself spatially and could be situated socially by perspectival construction have disappeared. Velázquez's *Las meninas* resounds in the back of Hamilton's painting precisely because it is one of the key works within which a painter's conception of an emerging bourgeois subjectivity (the painter painting) had found an initial and yet already culminating formulation. And it is only logical that the *Demoiselles* and Cubism at large are mobilised by Hamilton in the very same pictorial space as the manifest and inevitable counterforces of those historical promises of Renaissance and Baroque spatial constructions, since they had signalled their historically necessary termination.

Quite plausibly then, the left side of the wall construction refers directly to the undoing of painting in Cubism, from the insertion of an actual mirrored surface (as Juan Gris had done in 1914) to the shadow of the little side table upon which many of the Cubist still lifes had been placed and on which the games of the *double entendre* between table and tableau had been played. Further on, the painting records a resounding, if unmotivated shadow, and continues into a field of painterly sfumato, where light and shade, ambience and atmosphere are subtly delivered once more as though Hamilton wanted to invoke English landscape painting as a counterforce to his own Cubist citations. At the end of that set on the left axis, we enter a slightly disjointed cella, so to speak, crowned by yet another Velázquez citation, an unfathomable and distant painting. Mock Cubist in chromatic terms, and mock Bacon in terms of its facture, it is underlined by a rather disorderly accumulation of small brushstrokes at the bottom of its display wall, deposited as though on an altar to painterly dissolution.

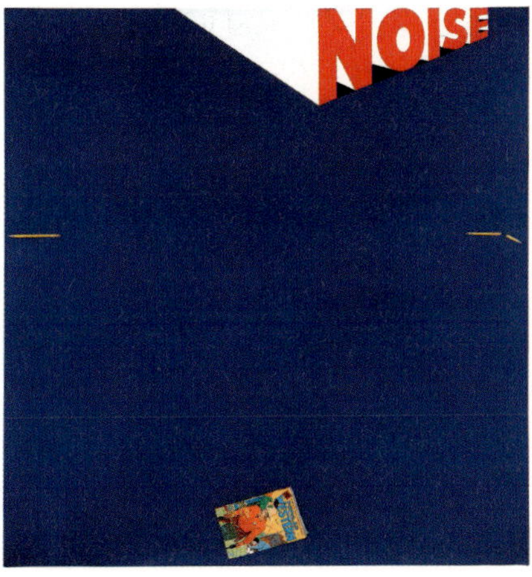

fig. 3
Ed Ruscha
Noise, Pencil, Broken Pencil, Cheap Western, 1963
Oil on canvas
Gagosian Gallery, New York

On the opposite side, the rather grand construction of an utterly banal, almost empty office desk serves as the second perspectival crossing. The *faux bois* of its surfaces, volumes and frames, once again, all explicitly invoke Cubism's disillusioning deconstructions, culminating in the grotesquely open drawer on the lower right corner (quite possibly a homage to Jasper Johns' *Drawer* from 1957). Whereas the pencil on the desk might deliver another trace of Hamilton's encounter with Ruscha's work in Los Angeles (as in *Noise, Pencil, Broken Pencil, Cheap Western*, 1963 [fig. 3]). Yet in a gesture typical of Hamilton's citational excess, his pencil (just like Duchamp's bottlebrush in his *Tu m'* in 1918) is now an actual pencil, displayed in utter solitude on the otherwise bare and blank painted tabletop.[5]

5. Mark Godfrey has quite convincingly pointed out to me that the construction of the tabletop clearly records yet another major discovery that Hamilton had made during his sojourn in Los Angeles, namely Claes Oldenburg's *Bedroom Ensemble* which was exhibited at the gallery of Virginia Dwan at that time. This would then imply one additional reference, namely the craftsmanship that Richard Artschwager had developed in the application of artificial surfaces, such as faux bois and formica, skills which he had provided in the production of Oldenburg's *Bedroom Ensemble*.

As the tabletop recedes further, the two spatial diagonals intersect. The right hand set ends in a wall of collage elements: one a magazine reproduction of a somewhat unfathomable annunciation (possibly by Ghirlandaio), and a black and white photographic reproduction of the very scene of the painting itself (complete, except for the removal of precisely that spatial detail of the wall onto which it is attached). As a startling *mise en abyme*, this photograph of the painting reproduces its most striking element, which we have left for last in our complicated description: the almost centrally positioned photograph of a standing female figure, directly staring out at the spectator (like *Olympia* and the *Demoiselles*, but now in stark black and white, placed between the glued mirror and the sfumato sphere, and clearly announcing itself as the most drastic element of an anti-pictorial montage aesthetic in full mass-cultural dependency).

Depicting the Hollywood actress Patricia Knight, almost totally unknown in the mid-1960s, the image initiates yet another typical Hamilton response after his return from America. It is an effect, as we will argue later in more detail, which will, rather than emphasise the mythical power of the images of industrial culture, as Pop Art generally did, subtly destabilise it. Firstly, by substituting a surrogate figure of minor fame for the most powerful stars (as opposed to Warhol's Marilyn, Elvis or Elizabeth Taylor, for example). And secondly, by emphasising the figure's obsolescence, invoking the principle of passing time as a promise of an imminent delivery from other icons still operative in the present. Thus Hamilton's dual strategy of derivation and obsolescence triggers a sudden and subtle de-cathexis that dissolves the very pathological fixation on fame and celebrity which binds social subjects to the images of the stars.

Rather distinct from his peers in Pop, one could argue that on the level of iconography alone, Hamilton will from now on perform a number of operations that have undoubtedly contributed as much to his recognition as to his relative illegibility. After all, what type of image recognition could he have anticipated by devoting a painting to the representation of Patricia Knight in 1964? Or three years later in 1967, at the height of an emerging Anglo-American English Rock culture, when painting a magisterial portrait of the American crooner Bing Crosby, appearing in the film *White Christmas* (1954), singing an Irving Berlin song from 1942? By that time Crosby had become an utterly obsolete icon of white American middle class comfort, sunken from unfathomable stardom in the 1950s to delivering canned variety shows on television. Especially when compared to Warhol's images of Elvis, the extent to which Hamilton once again performed his dual strategy of substitution and temporal displacement should become all the more apparent. A disturbing dislodgement of the ruling stars by a surrogate image is matched with a provocative outdatedness, undoubtedly only one of the many reasons why Hamilton's paintings acquired an almost sphinx-like status in English and European art of that period.[6]

Perhaps this allows us to pose an additional question, which seems to have motivated all of Hamilton's production during the 1960s and into the 1970s: the desire to understand in what manner and to what extent the Americanisation of British identity was actually

6. This argument seems to be contradicted by the fact that only one year later Hamilton would create the notorious painting *Swingeing London* [p. 163], depicting Mick Jagger and the art dealer Robert Fraser in handcuffs after a drug bust. However, as I have argued in an earlier essay, in this case different strategies achieve a similarly devastating effect of estrangement from the compulsions of mass cultural identification. See my essay "Richard Hamilton: Utopia, Design, Stigma," in Hans Ulrich Obrist (ed.), *Richard Hamilton: Modern Moral Matters* (London: Serpentine Gallery, 2009).

initiated and sustained through the image production of the cultural-industrial complex. More precisely, how these images could have possibly contributed to form actual features of a post-World War II British identity in subsequent decades. In other words, a sartorial and ever so slightly satirical analysis of the mutual assimilation of codes (e.g. the careful depiction of Crosby in his Anglo-American Gentleman's outfit) reverses the historical processes of the coding operations, rewinding the assimilation of what was once perceived as a quintessentially English subject into an American one, and its mass cultural return after the war. While citing the desire to recuperate the losses of its identitarian subjects of the pre-war period, *I'm dreaming of a white Christmas* [p. 115] simultaneously dissects the celebrated American image technologies that had actually assured the dissolution of these subjectivities.

A new aesthetic of production

As *A little bit of Roy Lichtenstein for...*, *Interior I* and *I'm dreaming of a white Christmas* indicate, after his return from America, Hamilton reversed the pop provocations, shifting from simplicity to extreme complexity, from primitive forms of design to the most elaborate processes of painting and printmaking, from simulacral low-tech to the elusive tropes of high art. One could argue that—rather than subverting painterly standards in a mock citation of commodity culture's ready-made designs—Hamilton now aligned the production standards of a work of art with the actually governing finesse of the regimes of advanced image technology.

In earlier moments of the twentieth century, artistic affirmations of new technological horizons of collective production had not only dislodged painting from its privileged seat of superiority, but also disseminated radical ideas of a new collectivity of the production of perception. Hamilton, by contrast, appears to have formulated a rather different production aesthetic, ultimately operating in utter opposition to the progressivist ideas ruling Constructivism and the Bauhaus throughout he 1920s. Leaving behind their ethics of a future collective accessibility and their optimism invested in new distribution forms for the work of art (which still had a faintly mythical, if not comical afterlife even in Warhol's prints and Ruscha's books), Hamilton shifts the making of painting and prints to a fundamentally different ethics and aesthetics of production. It is one in which the actually ruling, extremely complex technical processes of production are manifestly those which are necessary to construct the mythical simplicity with which the images of the culture industry engage the spectator in their infinite operations of seduction and suturing. Thus the endless variations that Hamilton produces in the development of the subsequent print version of *I'm dreaming of a white Christmas*, and its subsequent reversal into an even more hermetic and mysterious image entitled *I'm dreaming of a black Christmas* [p. 114] acquire a sudden and altogether different dimension of historical specificity: precisely an almost allegorical repetition, not of the devalorisation of objects, for which the allegorical has been known ever since Walter Benjamin's extensive discussion of these principles in Baroque and modernist poetics, but as allegories of the production processes of the culture industry itself. In their

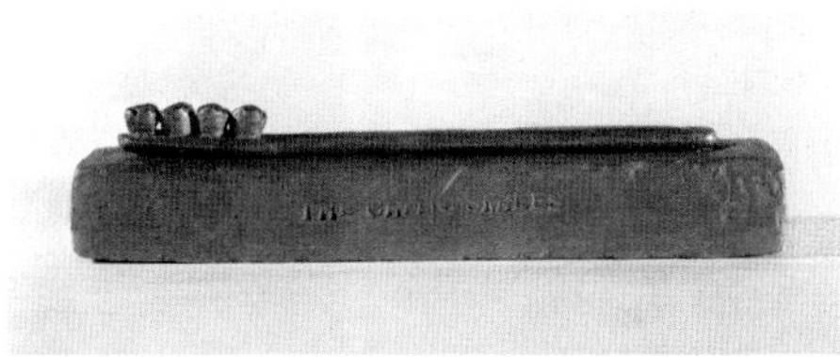

fig. 4
Jasper Johns
The Critic Smiles, 1959
Sculp-metal
Private collection

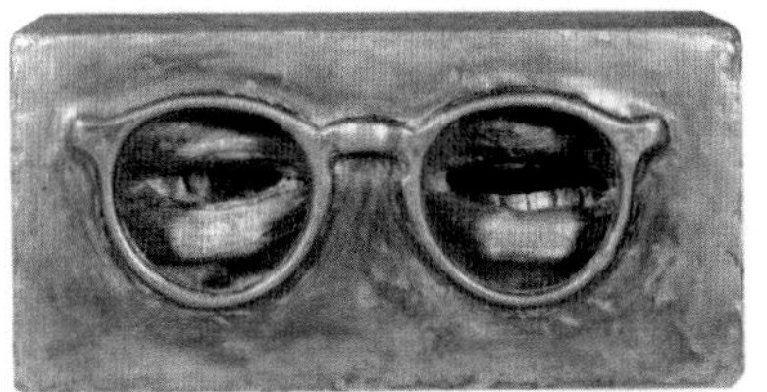

fig. 5
Jasper Johns
The Critic Sees, 1961
Sculp-metal on plaster with glass
Private collection

multifarious complexity they recall the enormous amount of hidden labour and acknowledge the industry's ever expanding ambitions towards technological standards, ruses, ploys and strategies necessary to design the matrices within which American mass culture would conquer the world at large.

Somewhat astonishing perhaps, Hamilton's responses to his American encounters seem to have preoccupied him as late as 1968, when he finally engages in an explicit dialogue with Jasper Johns. That year he made a print based on a photograph of an object assemblage entitled *The critic laughs* [p. 144], later producing a multiple also called *The critic laughs* in 1971–72 [p. 145]. As had been the case in the dialogue with Lichtenstein, these works have obviously been conceived in explicit response to two reliefs by Johns, the first one from 1959, entitled *The Critic Smiles* [fig. 4], and the second one an assemblage relief that Johns had produced in 1961, *The Critic Sees* [fig. 5]. As Hamilton has stated himself (and as scholars have argued extensively since then), one of the primary bonds between Johns and Hamilton had been their shared intense preoccupation with the legacies of Marcel Duchamp. Here is Hamilton's own account: "I was on the edge of things, we all were here. Until 1963 I knew the work of Jasper Johns better than anything else because he was an admirer of Marcel Duchamp: we had something in common."[7]

But when we compare the materials and processes of Johns' travesties on the roles and functions of critics to those deployed by Hamilton, numerous crucial divergences appear once again. These will not only further our comprehension of the variations and differences within European and American Duchamp reception, but they will also clarify Hamilton's fundamentally distinct attitudes regarding the actual epistemological validity of the ready-made in the present.

And if we have tried earlier to clarify these differences with iconographic comparisons, we hope that they will now become equally evident by comparing the different materials deployed by Johns and by Hamilton to produce these hybrids between sculpture and ready-made. Before we even recognise their grotesque and sardonic humour deriding the critic, Johns' two works, from 1959 and 1961 respectively, confront us with a peculiar variety of the achromatic, an almost ill tempered materiality, exuding from the vernacular material of sculp-metal, a widely available hobby- and home-workers' lead surrogate from the 1950s. We could argue that Johns' achromatic leaden material, manifestly banal in its derivation from the amateur's ordinary pleasures, operates as the sculptural counterpart to the artist's rediscovery of encaustic as a hallowed artisanal tradition of painterly execution. Yet, in both practices, Johns' encaustic painting and in his achromatic lead-substitute, the deeply melancholic operation of emptying the painterly and sculptural process of its artisanal dimensions—of colour, of modelling, of mimetic desire—is conjoined with a stubborn insistence to hold on to some of its residual features, and to counteract the epistemological regime of the ready-made.

The differences between Johns' and Hamilton's materials and processes could not be more telling, since the grey sculp-metal's artisanal residues do not seem to appeal to Hamilton at all. Rather, his assemblage embraces the utterly alienated, collectively

7. "Richard Hamilton in Conversation with Michael Craig-Martin" in Hal Foster and Alex Bacon (eds.), *Richard Hamilton*, October Files 10 (Cambridge, MA: MIT Press, 2010), 8.

ruling conditions of common object experience: even his teeth—still carefully modelled in Johns' relief—are now industrially produced (like a cruel variation of Duchamp's industrially produced comical part object when he used a falsie for the cover of the catalogue of the *Exposition Internationale du Surréalisme* in 1947). Hamilton mounts the glistening dentures made from hard plastic—an uncanny *memento mori* icon of a partial skull—on top of one of the triumphs of domestic design and bodily comfort, Braun's recently developed first electric toothbrush.[8] Exceeding once again at the Duchampian game of situating the aesthetic object within those forms most alienated from artistic materials and artisanal manufacture, i.e. in this case the most advanced design of consumer culture, it is only logical that the artist's name has even replaced the imprint of the corporate logo, Braun.

Hamilton's responses to Johns, both in the original 1968 version, and in the subsequent edition in 1971 as an even more provocative ready-made object complete with a piece simulating an actual denture, and the Braun toothbrush's professional case as a presentation device, tilt these dialectics of painterly tradition and Duchampian episteme all the way to the side of the ready-made. In a statement about the laminated offset-litho version of his 1968 print for documenta IV, *The critic laughs*, Hamilton identifies every aspect of the production, design and distribution of the work as integral to its initial conception (confirming our somewhat still speculative ideas about a new type of production aesthetic sketched out above):

> [Lamination is] stylistically, in the nature of promotional material for the product. Multiple editioning of the object is an obvious development. As with all consumer products, packaging and presentation posed subsequent problems … Product, package, and promotional matter is the cycle of the consumer-goods industries. Nothing in my experience and practice suggests that this same cycle does not apply to that category of human activity we label "art."[9]

Thus, Hamilton demands that spectators accept an emphatic identification with the irredeemable condition of an industrially produced object culture as the design standard of all artistic decisions, whether they concern material, production processes, surface, execution, signature, even its proper framing devices. Now, none of these, in Hamilton's hands, allow even for the slightest temptation of lapsing back into a painterly credo, motivated by a residual belief in the continuing credibility of the artisanal modes, melancholic, fetishist or otherwise. Looking back to 1989, Hamilton described these dualities in less dramatic, but no less pertinent terms:

> The series of works inspired by Braun since 1966 attempted to introduce a contradiction into the lexicon of source material of Pop. They posed the question: does the subject matter of most American Pop Art significantly exclude from our examination those products of mass culture which might be the choice of a Museum of Modern Art "good design" committee? Clearly, this research also touched on problems encountered by Marcel Duchamp in

8. Once again, I owe an important detail to Mark Godfrey's generous editorial suggestions when reading my essay, pointing out to me that the 1968 print shows a candy version of edible teeth that Hamilton's son had bought for him in Brighton. In the 1971–72 edition, these sugar teeth had been remade in dental plastic.
9. Hal Foster and Alex Bacon (eds.), *Richard Hamilton*, October Files 10 (Cambridge, MA: MIT Press, 2010), 133–34.

> his invention of the ready-made. The studied neutrality of his solutions in this area could not be repeated, but the instrument of irony he used so effectively in other works could be adopted with advantage. The phrase from his notes for the *Large Glass*, "an irony of affirmation," became a guiding principle in my considerations.[10]

My last example of Hamilton's dialogue with his American encounters is the most complex and, admittedly, my argument, at least for the time being, the most speculative. In 1965–66 Hamilton produced six reliefs called *The Solomon R. Guggenheim* [pp. 151–53], and in 1970 he published a second relief series as an edition of multiples, in reduced format and with the abbreviated titles *Guggenheim (black)*, *Guggenheim (white)* and *Guggenheim (chrome)*. My hypothesis is that this series not only reacts to one of the most remarkable examples of American architecture that Hamilton encountered during his first visit to New York in 1963, and to Richard Artschwager's drawings of multi-storey buildings (Hamilton had been impressed by these works, having been introduced to Artschwager by Lawrence Alloway during the trip), but that it is also yet another, even though a particularly well disguised allegorical response to the challenges presented to him by the production of Andy Warhol, whose work—as we mentioned above—he had encountered at the ICA in London a year prior to his journey to the United States, as Hamilton recalls in a conversation with Michael Craig-Martin: "I saw a Warhol at the ICA, a great Warhol, a great Marilyn, an enormous square with—I don't know how many—forty or fifty Marilyns. That's how I remember it anyway"[11] [fig. 6].

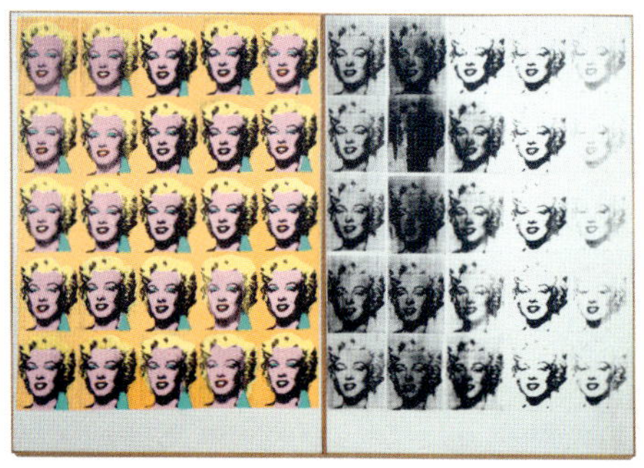

fig. 6
Andy Warhol
Marilyn Diptych, 1962
Acrylic paint on canvas
Tate

A few, merely formal observations will have to sustain my speculative comparison for the time being. First, one might imagine that for Hamilton, the building's "organic" spiral shape would have resonated with the natural morphologies and structures that had been explored by D'Arcy Wentworth Thompson and which had been celebrated in Hamilton's exhibition design for *Growth and Form* in 1951. Yet, in a statement published in 1999, Hamilton compares the spiral of the Guggenheim to the shape of the *Exquisite Form* bra he had featured in his 1957 tabular painting, *Hommage à Chrysler Corp* [p. 77].[12] Like the lingerie manufacturers, Hamilton had translated the organic into an ossified fetish, an inorganic inanimate object. Second, Hamilton positions the relief of the Guggenheim Museum's vast architectural façade within the very narrow confines of a square (four feet by four feet), similar to the awkward tightness with which Warhol had cropped the grand cult icon of the American movie industry within the extremely compressed spatial squares of his paintings and prints. Third, intensifying this impression of confinement even further, the reliefs which were depicting the architectural façade and the sky or spatial ground against which it is placed have been chromatically and materially homogenised by Hamilton in the casting procedure, thereby not only fusing figure and ground but also representation and support in a heretofore unknown synthesis of image and object, if not ultimately articulating the final conflation of subject and object in the condition of specular reification altogether.

10. Ibid., 138–39.
11. Ibid., 7–8. Obviously, there is no square-format painting containing forty or fifty Marilyns in Warhol's oeuvre. But the *Marilyn Diptych* now in the collection of the Tate Gallery was indeed shown at the ICA in London in 1962. And while the first Marilyn painting, *Gold Marilyn Monroe*, was vertical in format, all subsequent paintings of individual Marilyn portraits were contained in a tightly framed square format, as was, most strikingly and sensationally, the portfolio of *Ten Marilyns* that Warhol published in 1967 to great acclaim, and which we would argue contributed to Hamilton's decision to publish the second series of his Guggenheim reliefs as an edition of multiples.
12. Kynaston McShine (ed.), *The Museum as Muse: Artists Reflect* (New York: Museum of Modern Art, 1999), 111.

And lastly, a fourth reason might legitimise our comparison: the fact that Hamilton repeats, or even exceeds the extreme arbitrariness of the gaudy industrial tints and chromatic clashes that had been one of the hallmarks of Warhol's Marilyn portraits since 1962 (culminating of course in the dissonant colour choices for his portfolio *Ten Marilyns* in 1967). The six fibreglass reliefs were cast and painted in the colours gold, black, black and white, spectrum, metal flake and Neapolitan (an unfathomably funny reference to the pink, cream and greenish ice cake traded by that name), and might have even contributed to a reverse inspiration for Warhol's still more synthetic industrialisation of colour in the Marilyn portfolio. Accordingly, these *Solomon R. Guggenheim* reliefs appear as cumbersome, not to say discomforting hybrids of representation, readable neither as paintings nor as sculptural objects or reliefs properly speaking, or as architectural models of an architectural façade, they become pure spectacularised design, part iconic types, part plastic relief, part picture, part branded architecture. Again, the description of the conception and manufacturing process given by Hamilton himself foregrounds these hybrid aspects that would have been rather alien to Frank Lloyd Wright's ambitions (or, for that matter, to any American architect or artist at that time):

> I was thinking of myself … as covering the whole ground from visualisation of the building to the planning to construction and even later to photographing and publicising. It was an attempt to mirror the whole activity of architecture in the confines of a small panel … four feet square."[13]

In a 1952 letter to his patron Solomon R. Guggenheim, Frank Lloyd Wright had stated the principles guiding the conception and execution of the Museum:

> Every building signifies a state of affairs, social, therefore political. This building signifies the sovereignty of the individual: Democratic. Instead of the solidarity of the mass led by one: Fascist. Therefore this building is neither Communist nor Socialist but characteristic of the new aristocracy born of Freedom to maintain it ... The nature of the building design is such as to seem more like a temple in a park on the Avenue than like a mundane business or residential structure.[14]

We cannot address here the architect's slightly hypertrophic demands made for a building design that he had initially conceived for a parking garage, but we can certainly argue that these aristocratic promises for architecture's agency and enactment of a sovereign democratic subjectivity were no longer operative in 1963, when Hamilton discovered the building in New York at the climax of American Pop Art. And these promises for a new, architecturally mediated democratic subjectivity would have been even less plausible to Hamilton reflecting with hindsight on his American discoveries.

13. Richard Hamilton, as cited in Richard Morphet (ed.), *Richard Hamilton* (London: Tate Gallery, 1970), 67.
14. I am grateful to Akili Tommasino Olujimi for having brought this letter and numerous other details about the Guggenheim Museum to my attention in his research paper on Richard Hamilton.

Rather, we would argue, he would have grasped to what extent Wright's initially radical democratic architectural aspirations had been slowly and steadily recoded since 1959, when the building had been inaugurated shortly before the architect's death. Shifted into an altogether different sphere of public experience, the façade of the museum had acquired the features of a designed product, and the branded identity necessary for cultural consumption in the age of total spectacularisation. While these had been of course the very transformations that Warhol had affirmatively, perhaps even inadvertently, signalled, when confounding the iconographies of Hollywood with the iconographic traditions of painterly culture, Hamilton, in dialectical opposition to Warhol's flip inversions in the sphere of high-cultural versus mass-cultural representations, now addresses these changes as they occur in the actuality of social spaces: on the site of the museum as one of the last functioning institutions of the bourgeois public sphere. If Warhol's *Marilyns* had announced the inevitable substitution of the mass-cultural object for the avant-garde traditions of the twentieth century, Hamilton now seems to have initiated a reverse perspective, one in which he anticipated the eventual destiny of the museum itself.

Thus, once again, what distinguishes Hamilton's project from that of his American Pop Art peers is an uncanny anticipation of the double destiny of the work of art. First of all, its epistemic destiny, now to be shifted from an object of enlightenment and radical opposition to one of entertainment and affirmative consumption. Second, and equally important, the *Guggenheim* reliefs reflect on the work's institutional destination as much as on the destiny of the institution. After all, it was precisely at this moment that the museum was beginning its transition from a site within the bourgeois public sphere where democratically formed subjects would encounter and reflect the collective conditions of the experience of the unconscious, to an institutional rallying point where all the forces of contestation and subversion, initially operative in the artistic practices of the avant-garde and the neo-avant-garde, could now be condensed and controlled under the mythical auspices of universal democratic accessibility in the enforced practices of consumption.

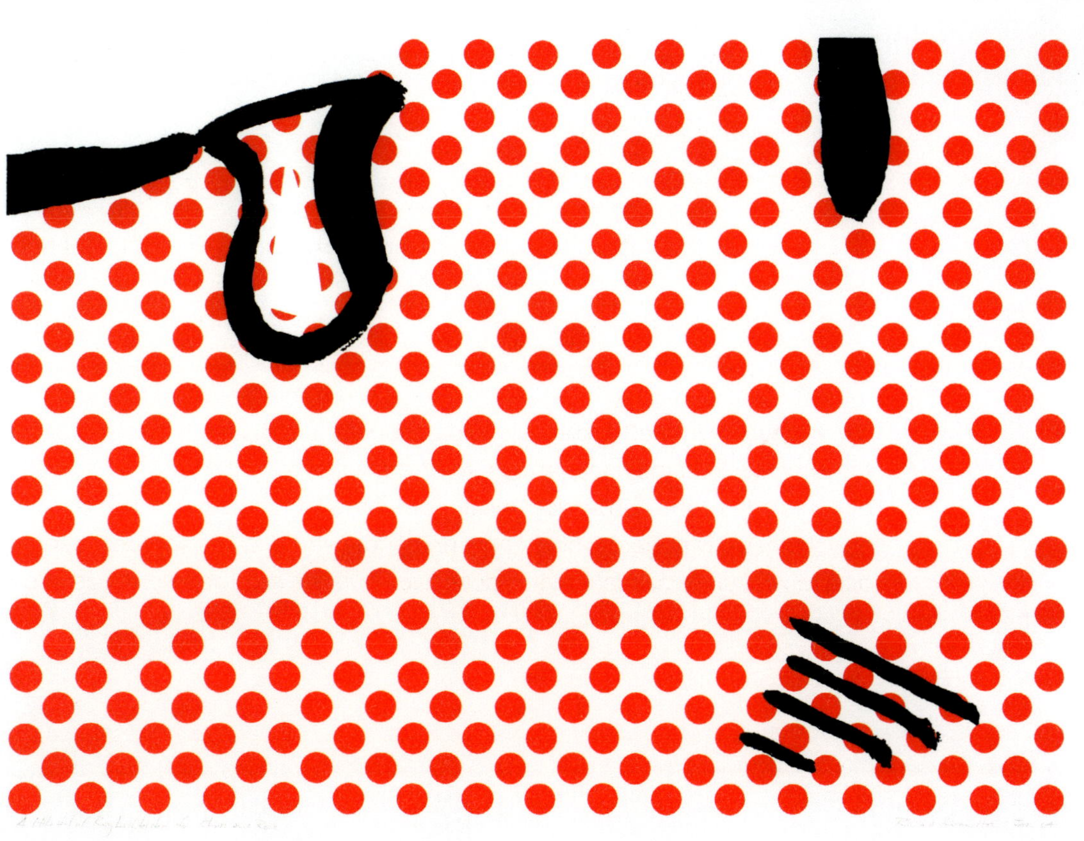

A little bit of Roy Lichtenstein for... 1964

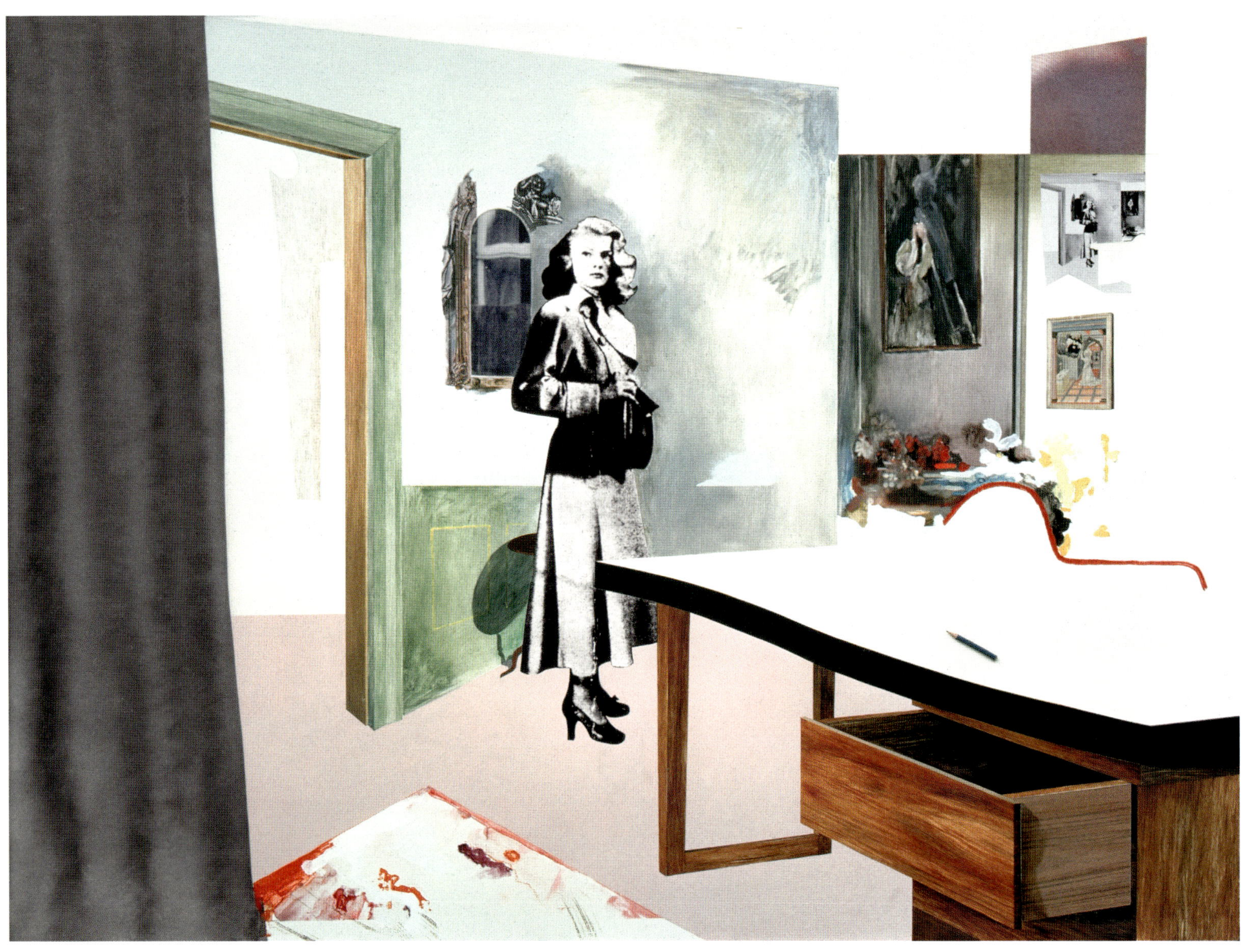

Interior I 1964

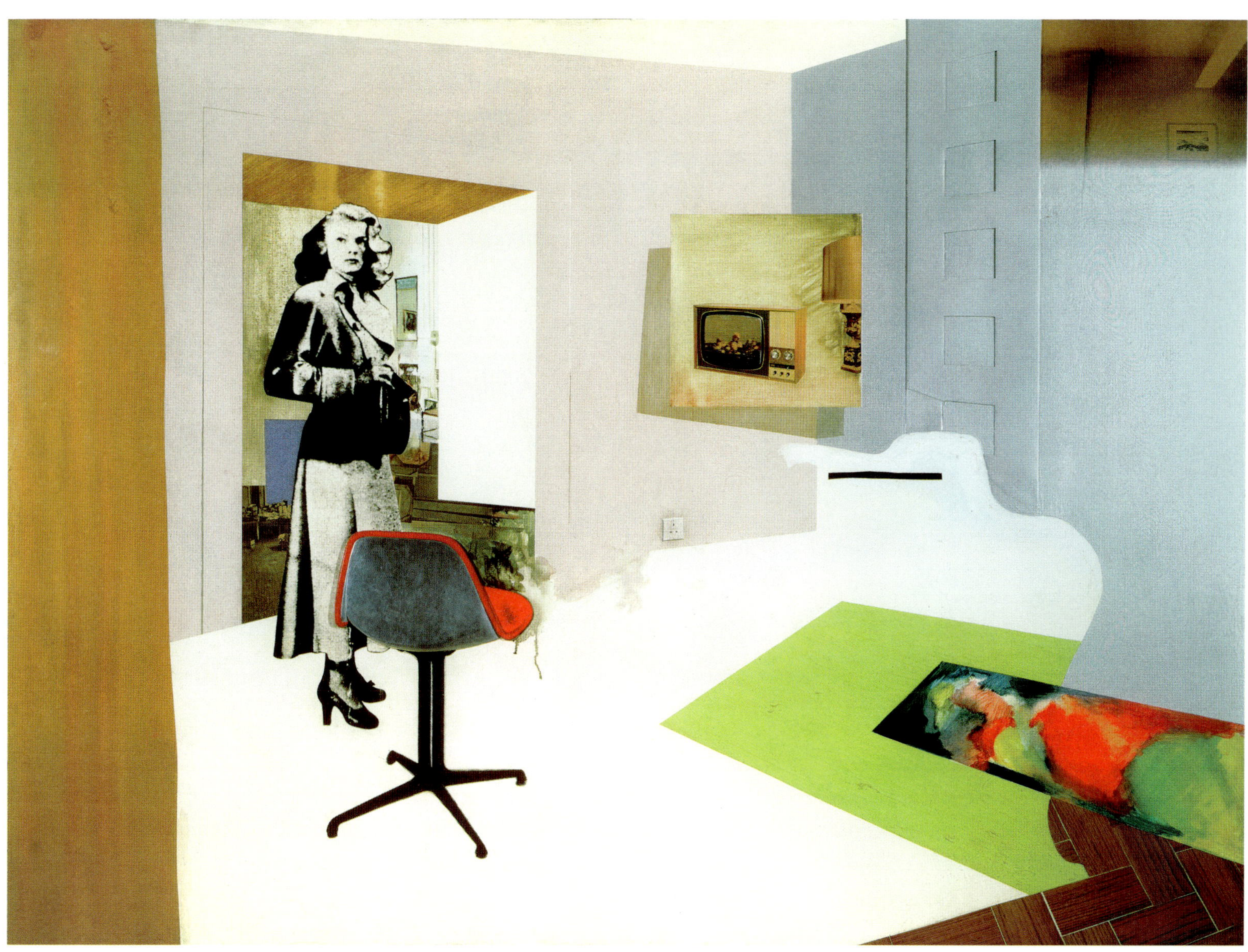

Interior II 1964

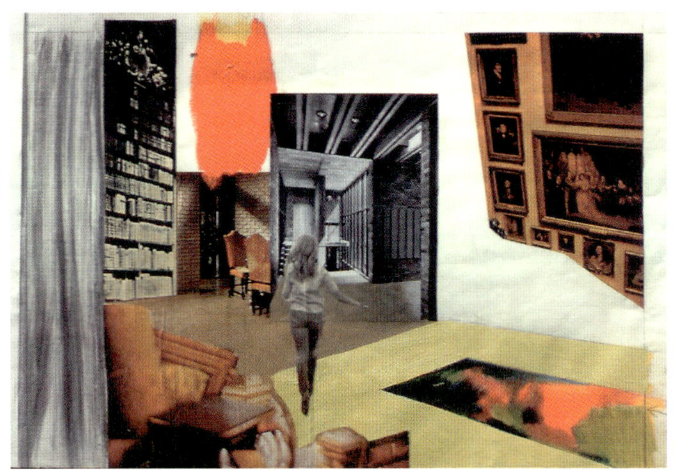

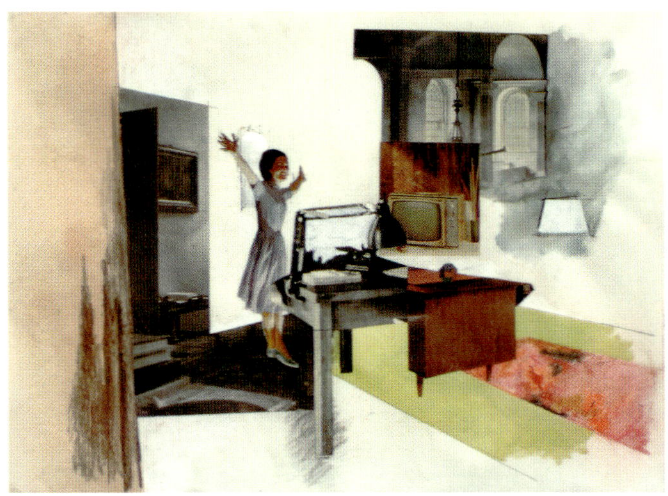

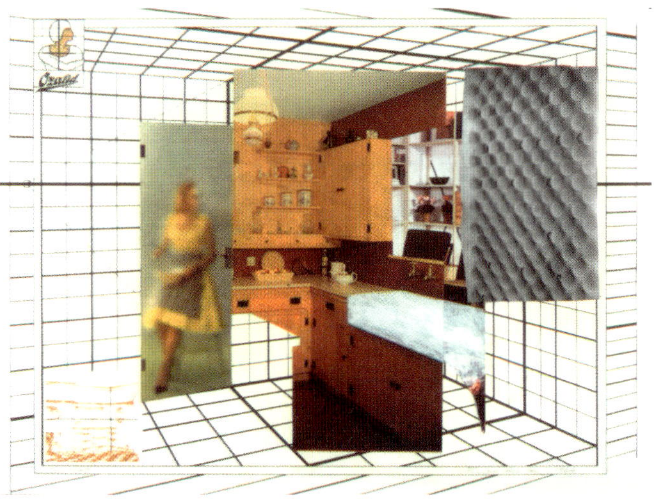

Interior study (c) 1964

Interior study (b) 1964

Magic Carpets 1964

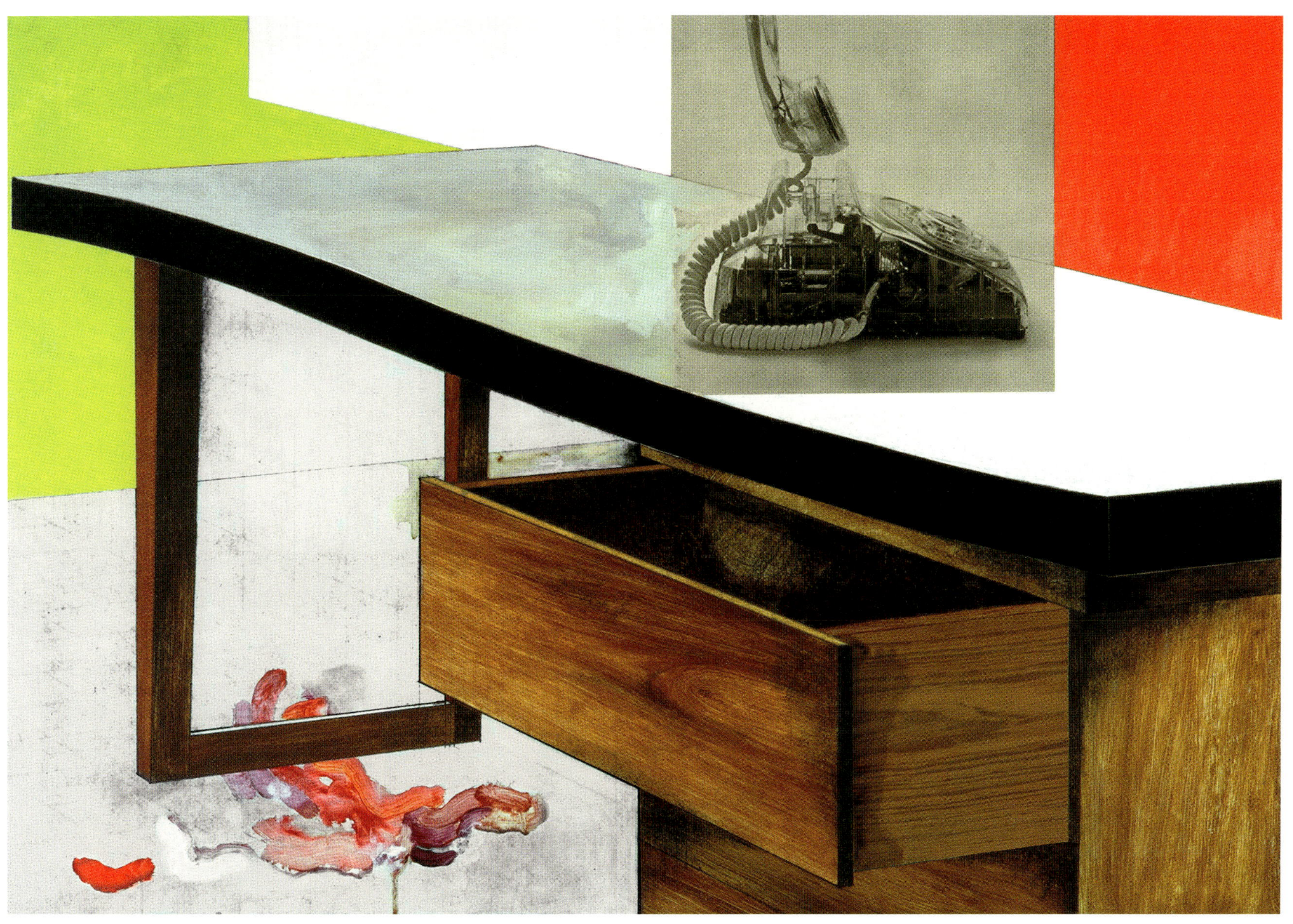

Desk 1964

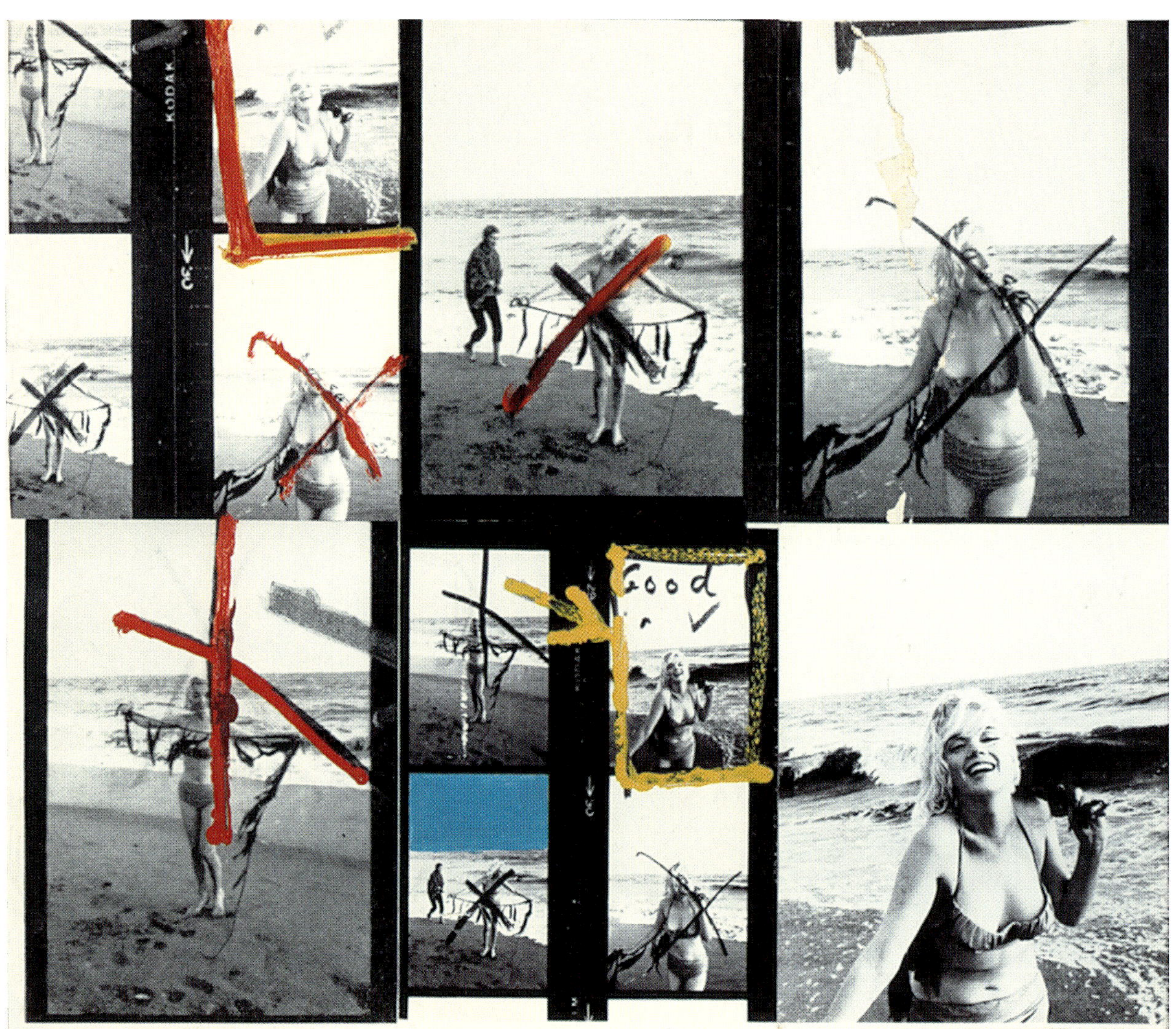

My Marilyn (paste-up) 1964

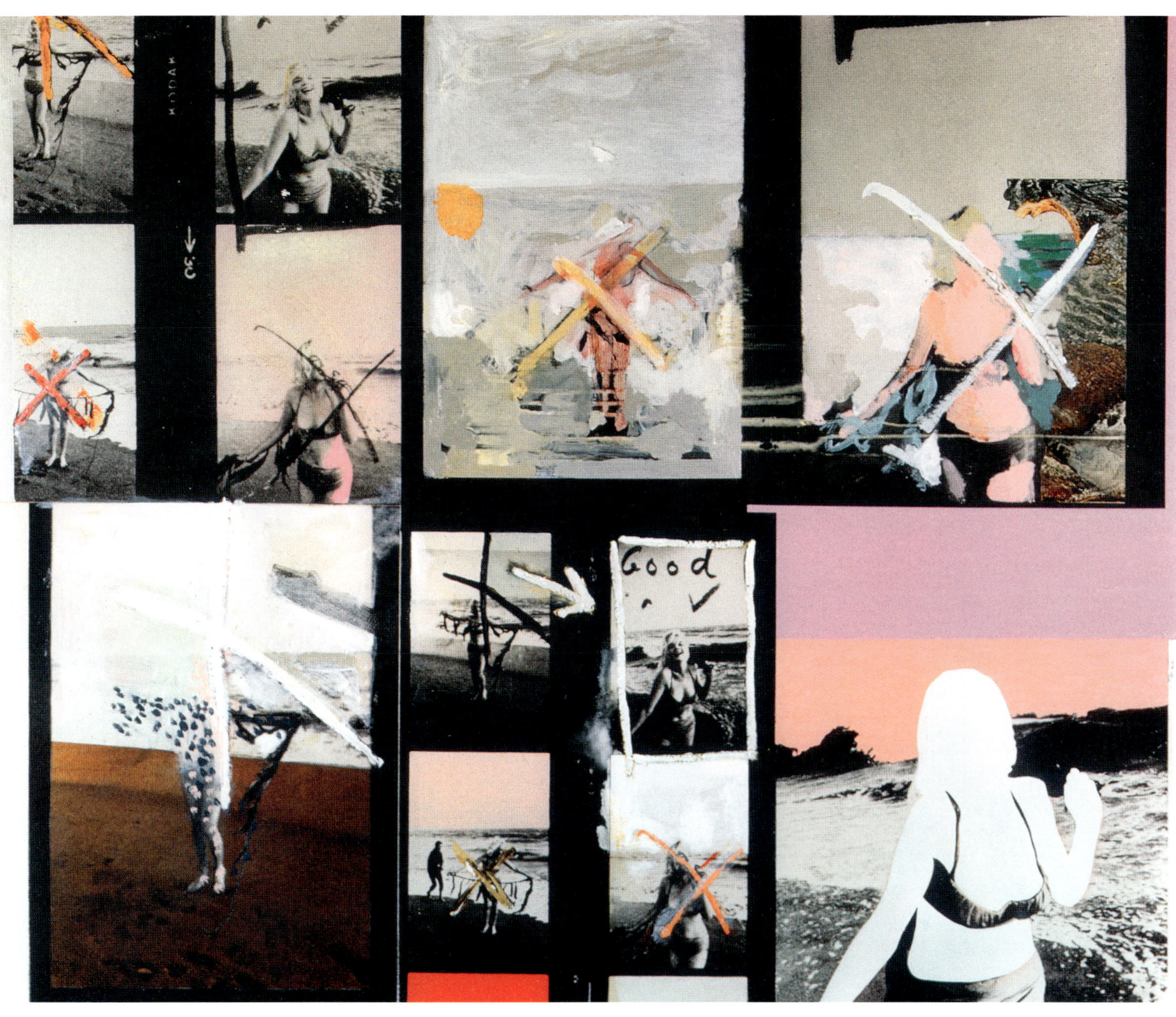

My Marilyn 1965

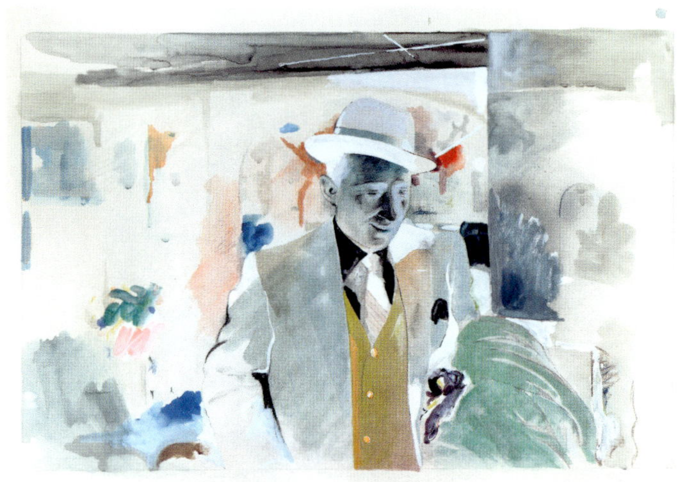

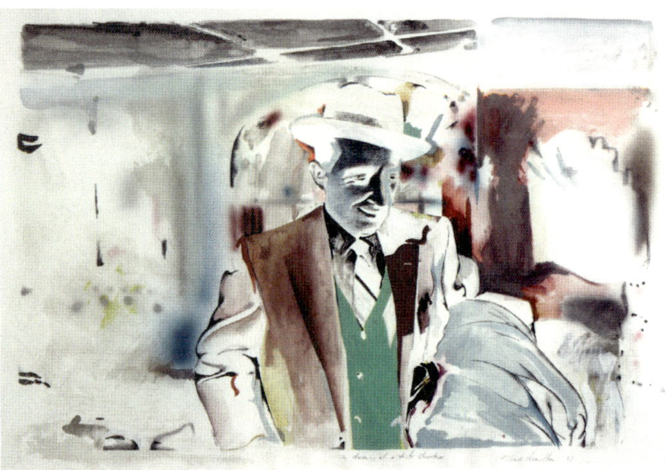

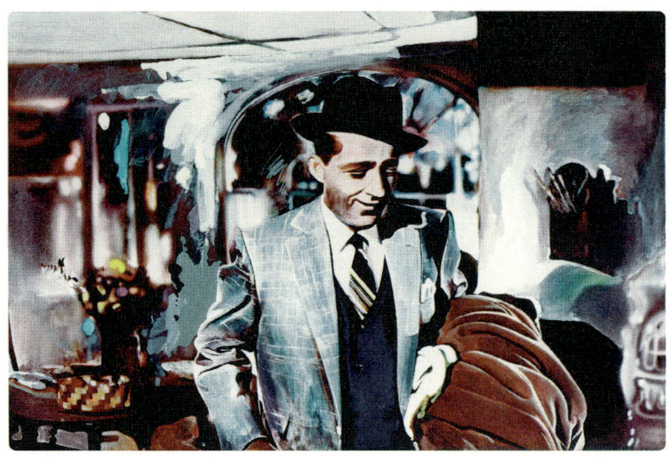

I'm dreaming of a white Christmas – sketch 1967

I'm dreaming of a white Christmas – study 1967

I'm dreaming of a black Christmas 1971

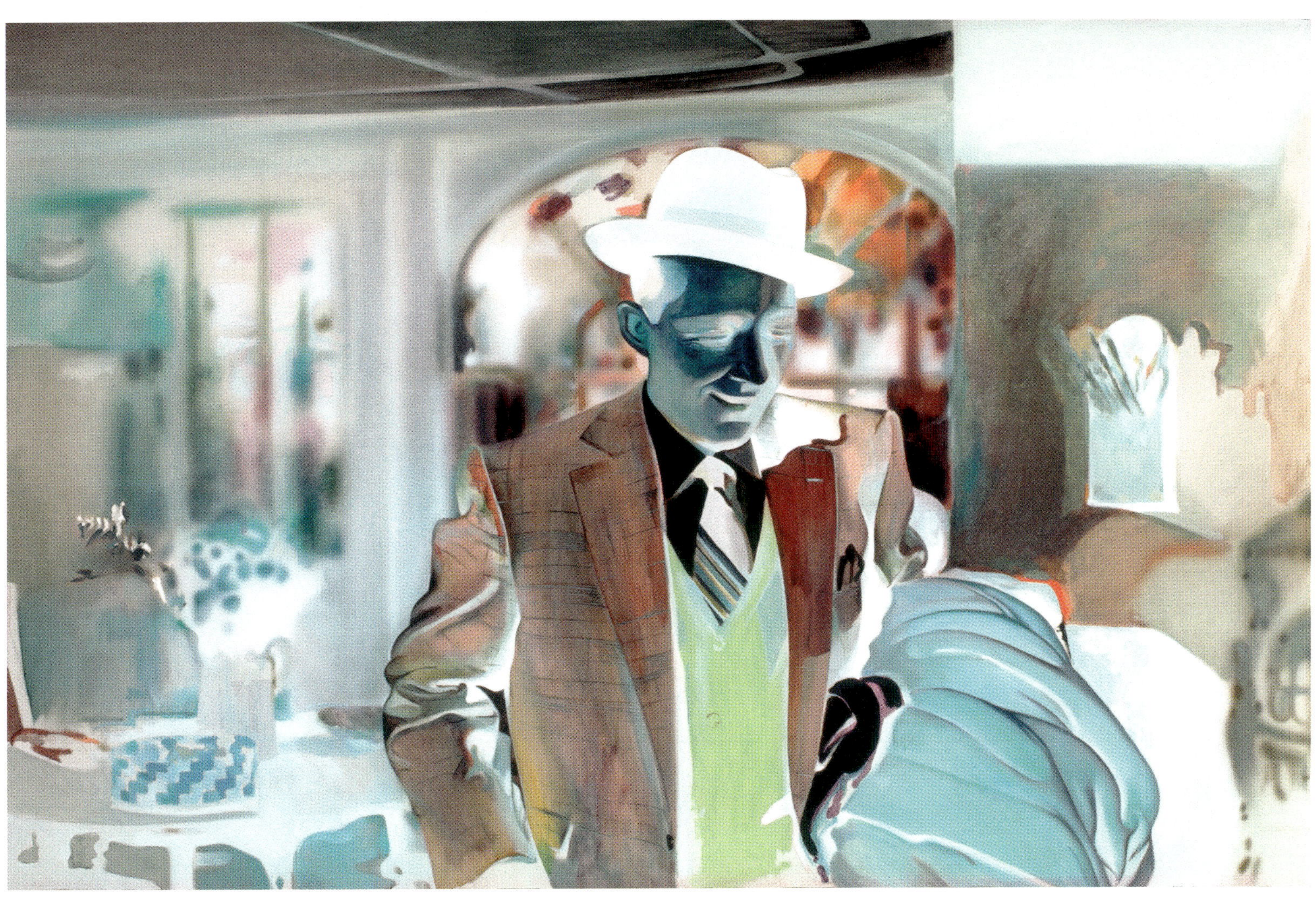

I'm dreaming of a white Christmas 1967–68

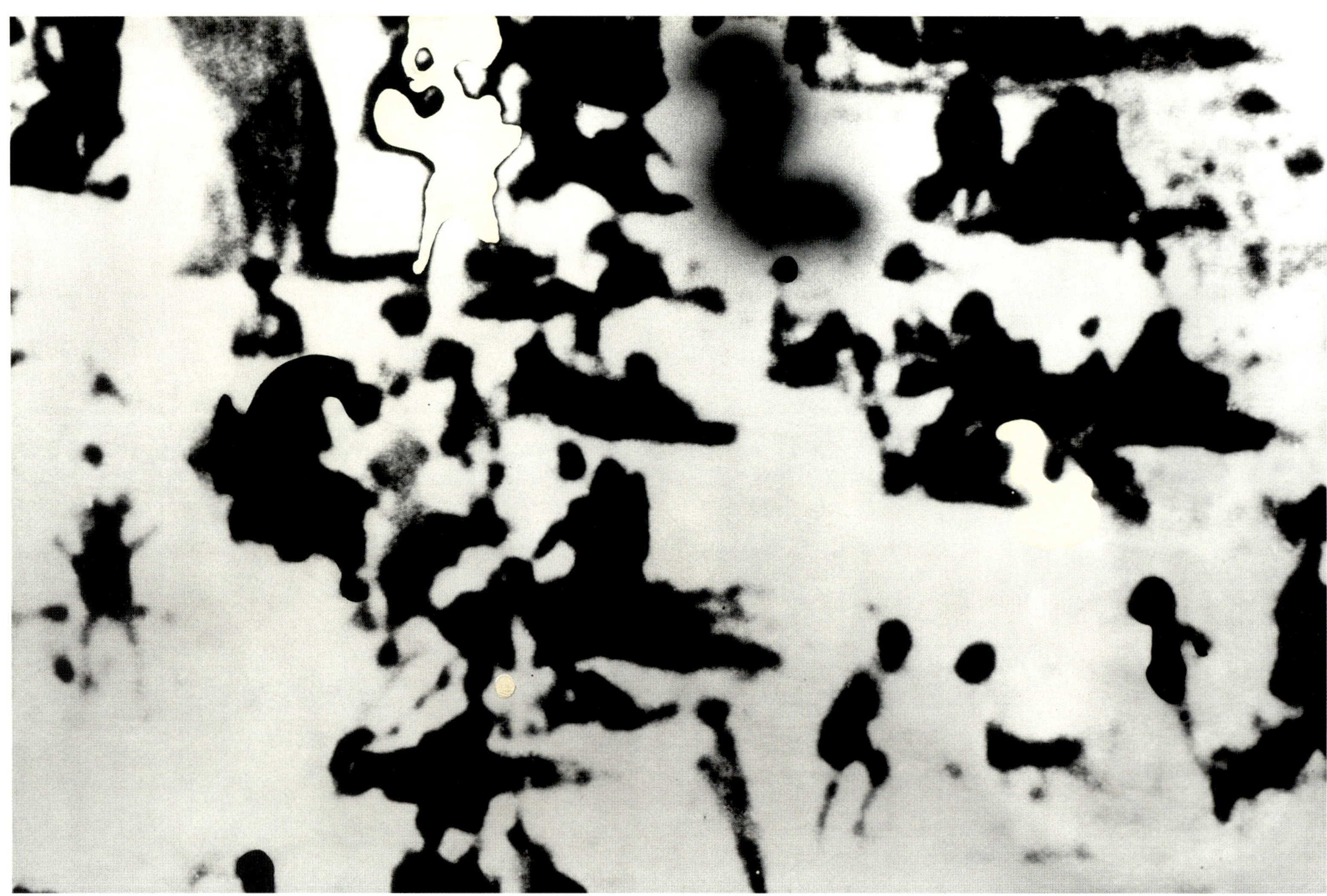

People 1965–66

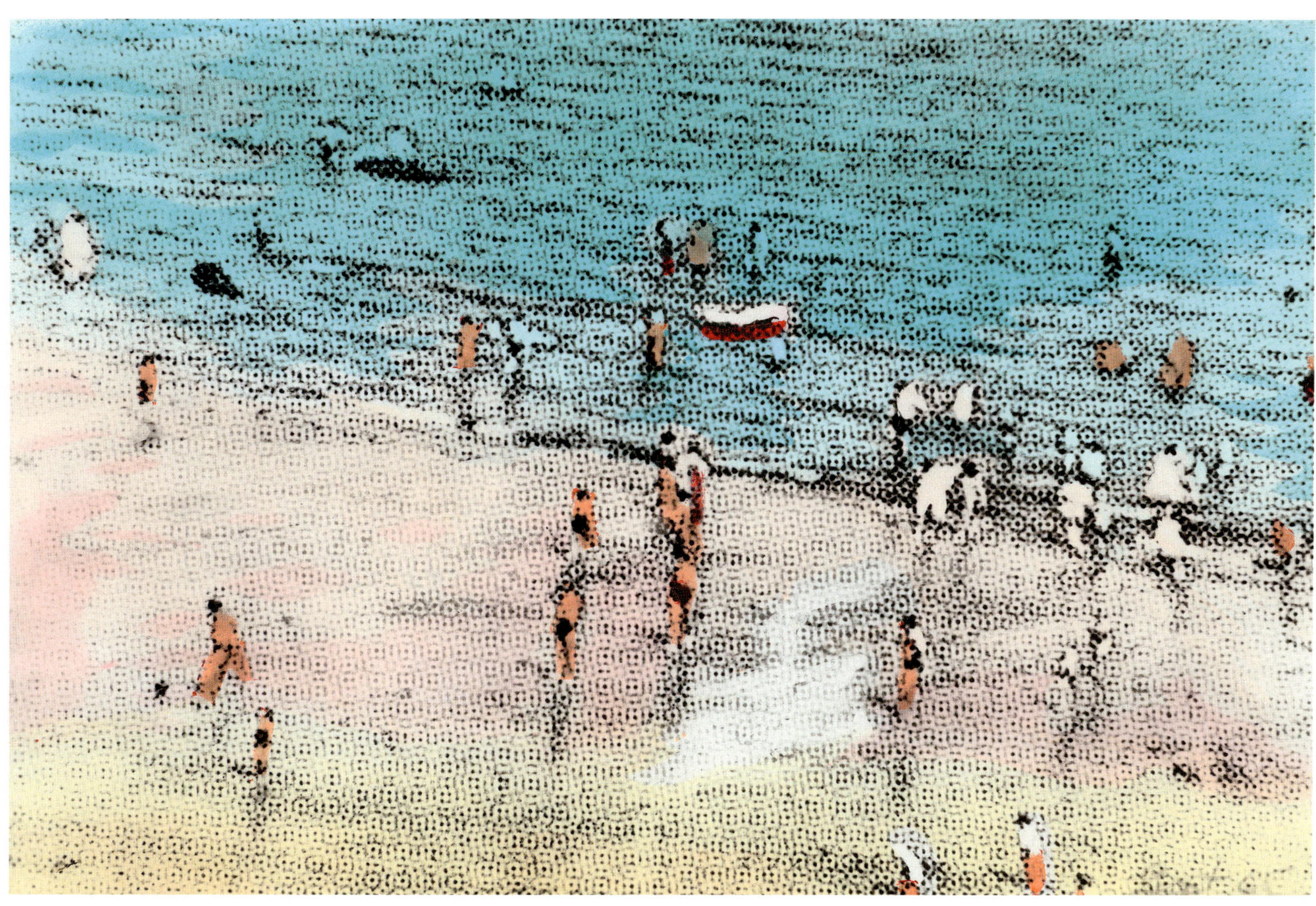

Whitley Bay 1965

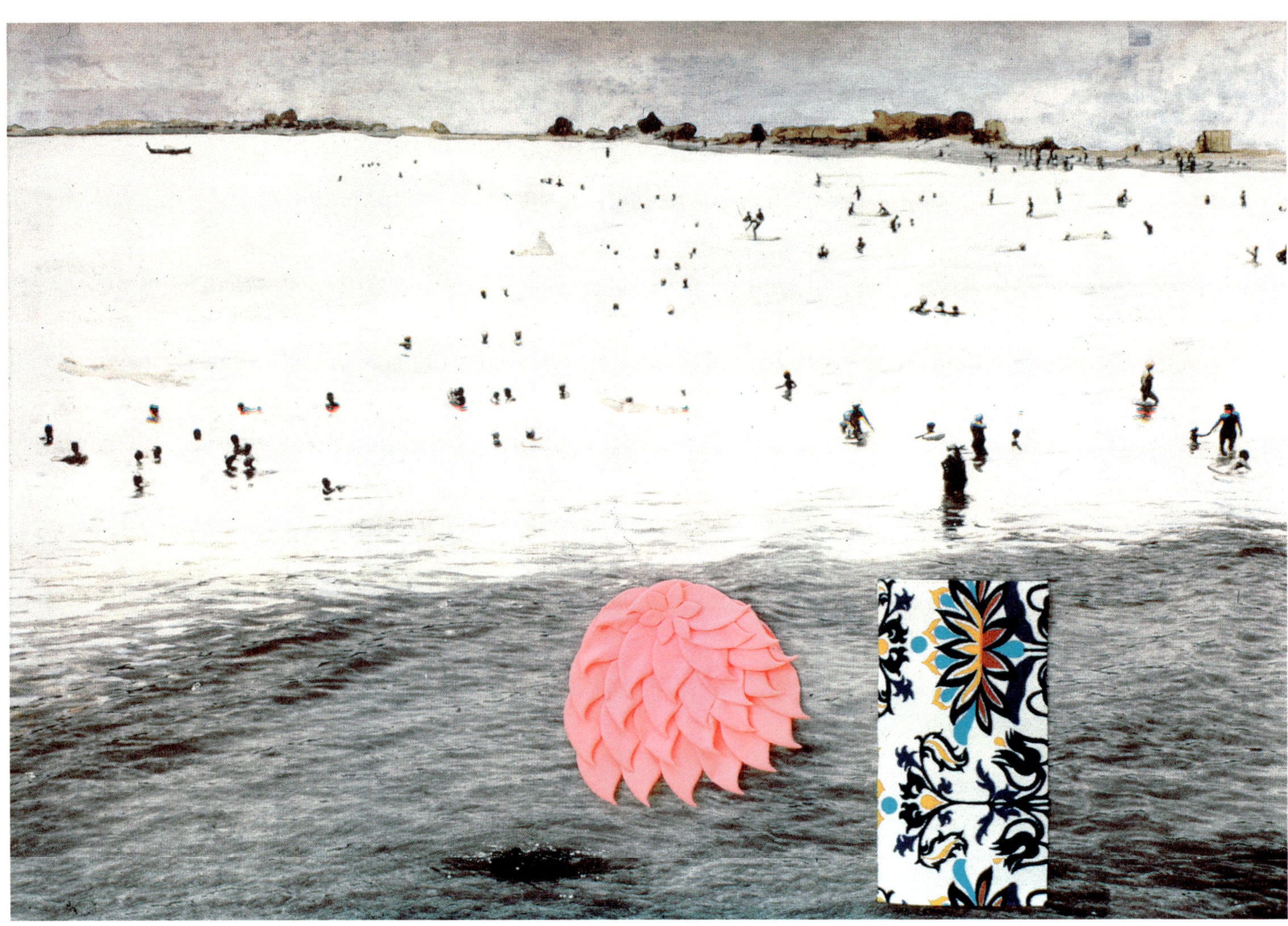

Bathers I 1966–67

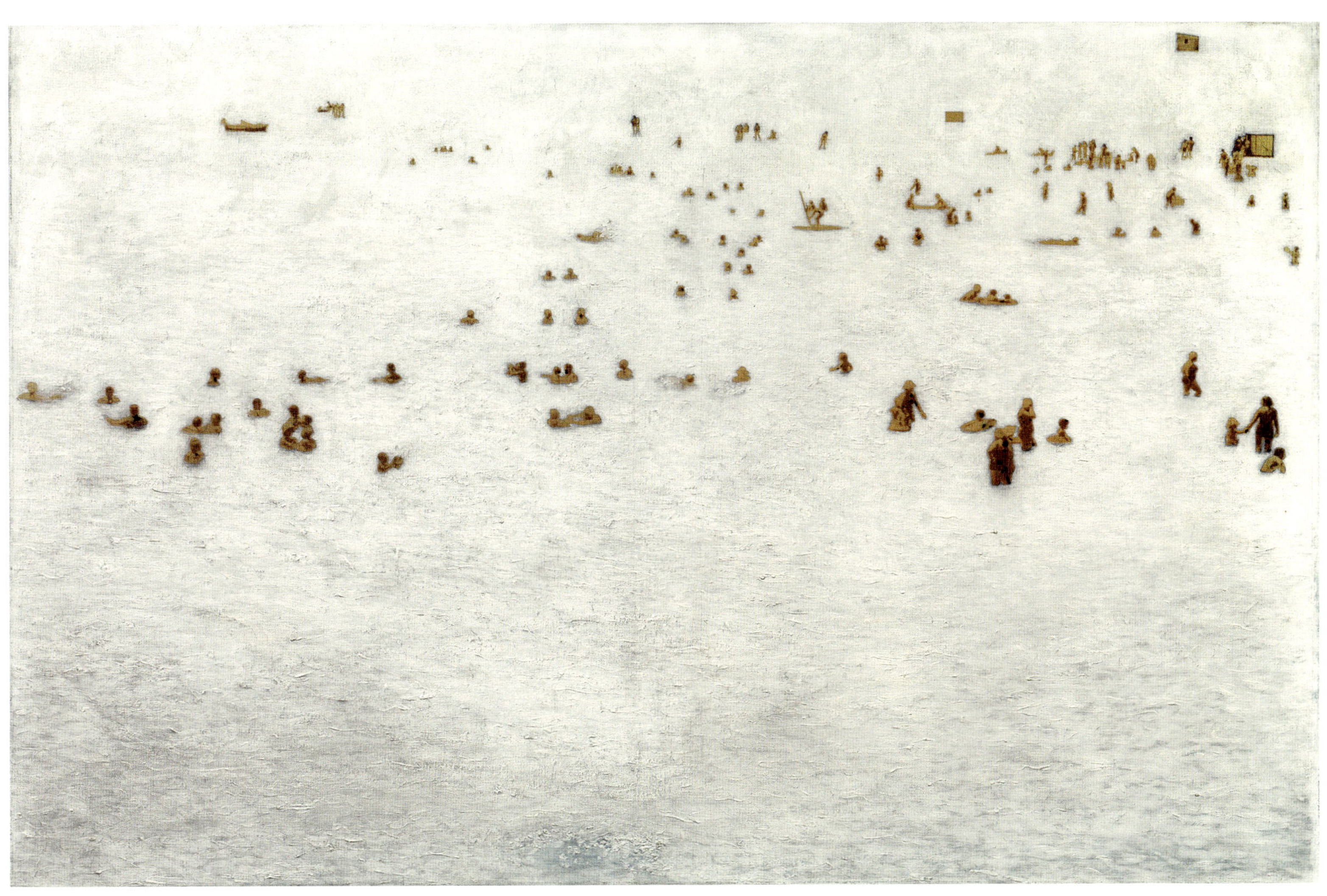

Bathers II 1967

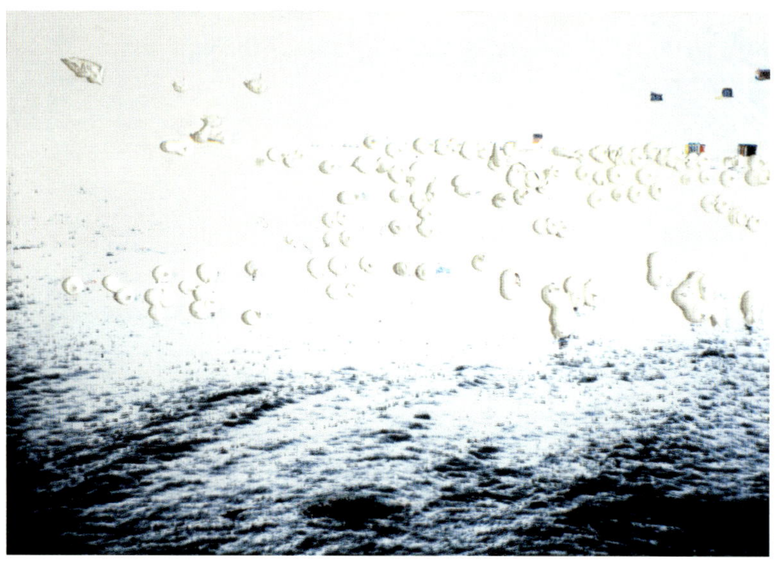

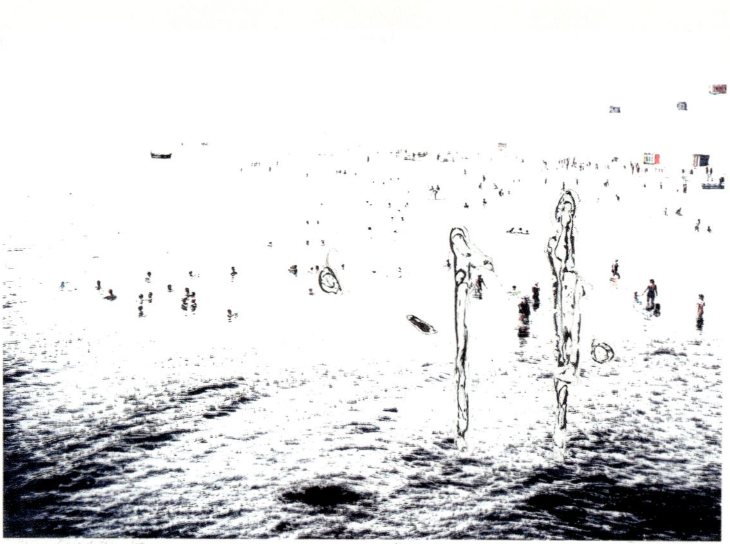

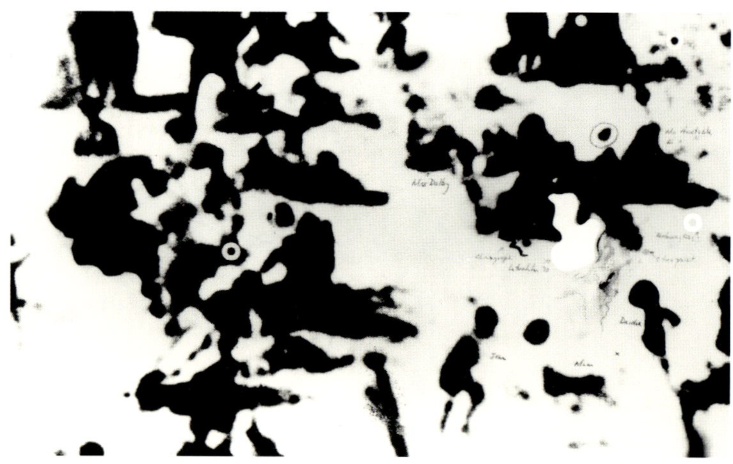

Bei uns (in collaboration with Dieter Roth) 1968-69

People/Popel (in collaboration with Dieter Roth) 1968

Bei ihr (in collaboration with Dieter Roth) 1969

People again 1969

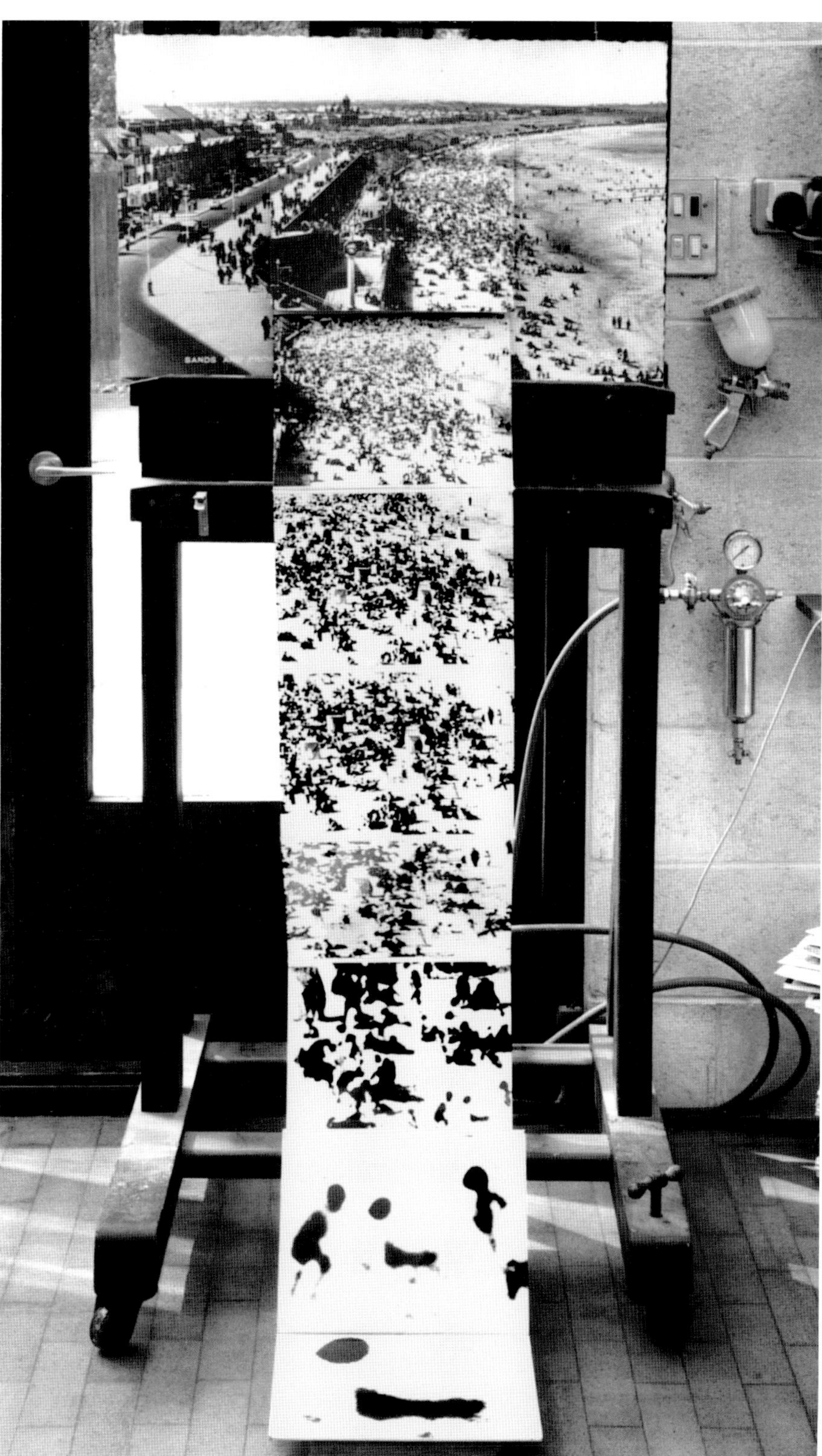

People multiple (1/1) 1968

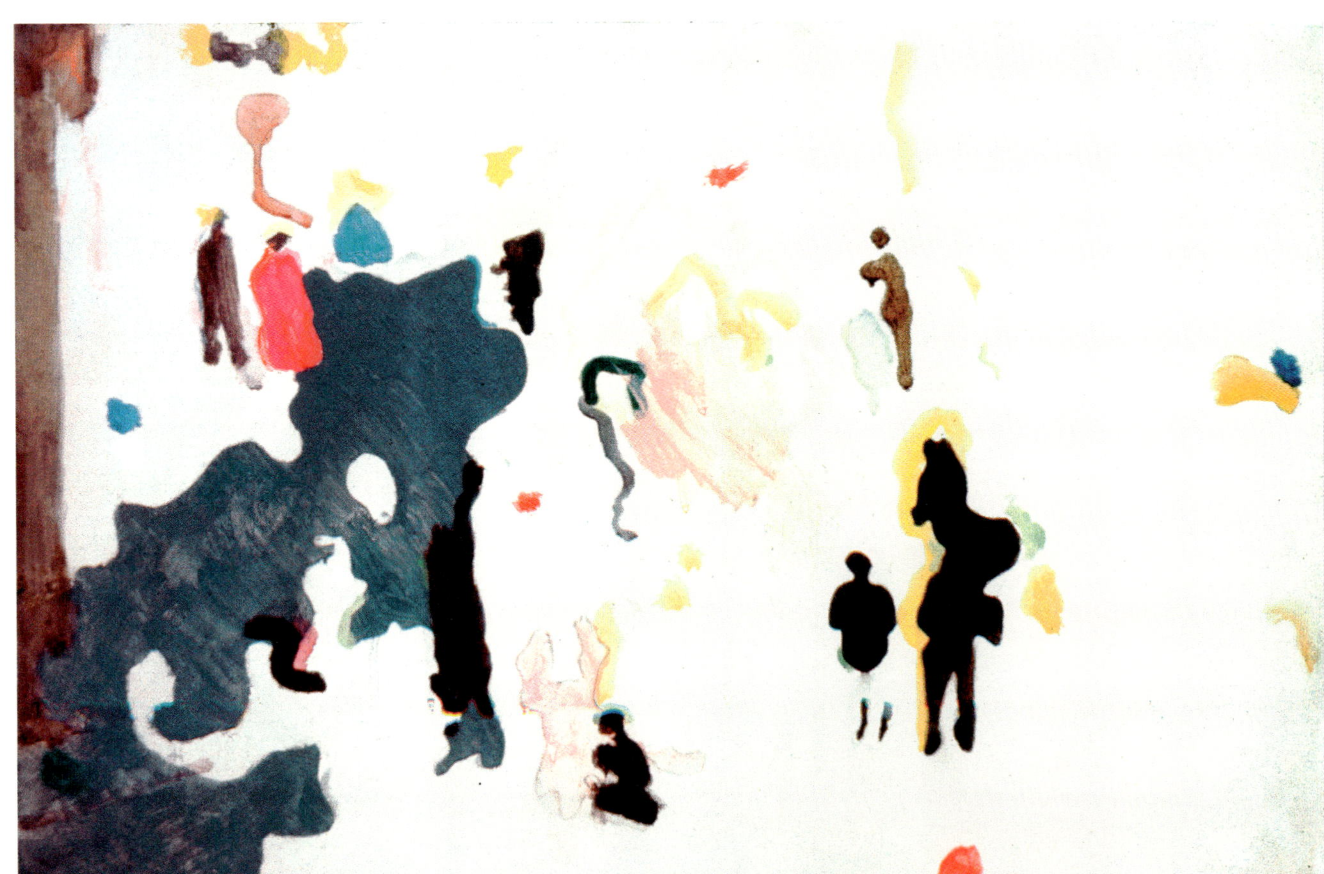

Trafalgar Square study 1965

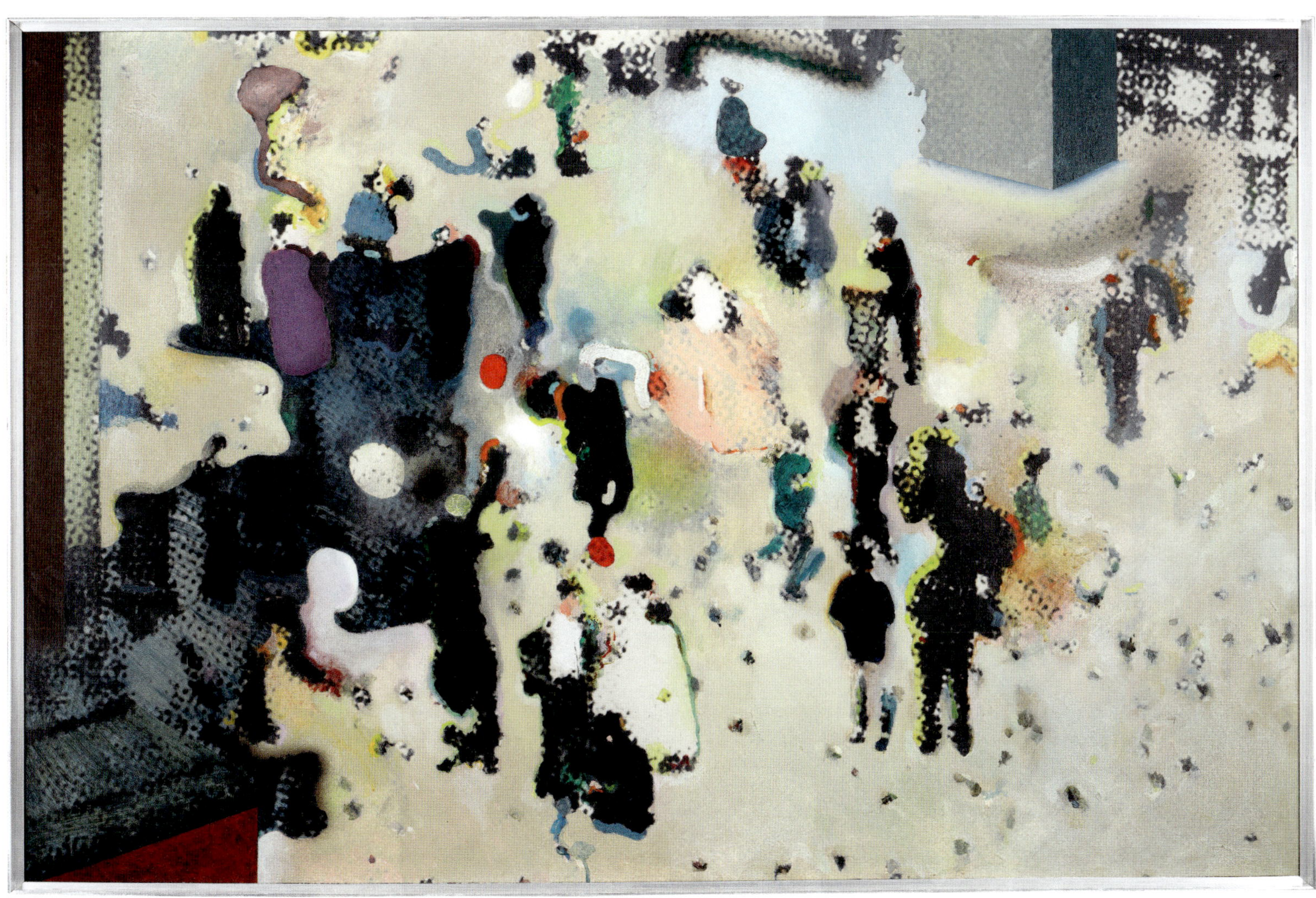

Trafalgar Square 1965–67

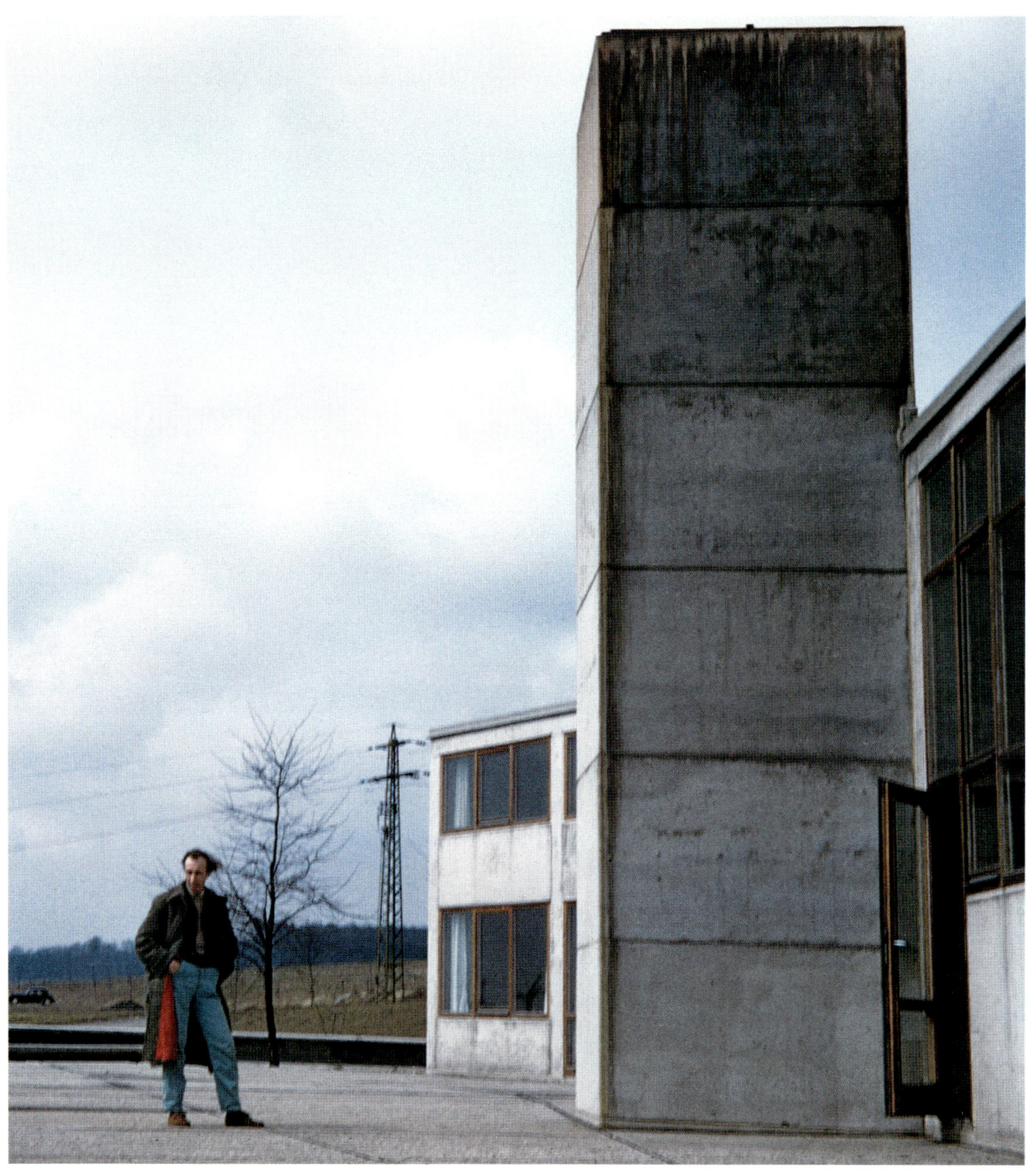

Hamilton outside the Hochschule für Gestaltung, Ulm 1958

Richard Hamilton and Design

Alice Rawsthorn

Once a week during the late 1940s, the art director of British *Vogue,* Alex Kroll, invited a group of young artists and designers who had shown an interest in fashion illustration to studio sessions at the magazine's offices, where he monitored their progress. Among them was Richard Hamilton, then a painting student at the Slade School of Fine Art, who attended these meetings for a few months in 1949 before being informed that his work was "too artistic" for *Vogue.*[1]

"Too artistic" though it may have been for a fashion magazine, Hamilton would be told repeatedly for the next decade that his work was not artistic enough by the custodians of the British art establishment, who suspected that much of it would more accurately have been classified as design than art. The reason is evident in an essay by Hamilton in a 1962 issue of *Architectural Design* magazine. "Contemporary art reacts slowly to the contemporary stylistic scene," he wrote. "How many major works of art have appeared in the twentieth century in which an automobile features at all? How many feature vacuum cleaners?"[2] Very few, was the answer, whereas Hamilton's paintings were filled with them as well as with robots, comic books, Hollywood stars, television sets, billboards, *Playboy* pin-ups and other totems of technology and consumer culture. The titles of his artworks alluded to them too; and his essays were not only rich in references to magazines like *Design, Architectural Design* and *Typographica,* but often published in them.

Hamilton's insistence on exploring design, technology and consumerism with the same passion and intellectual rigour as art history seemed inexplicable to the grandees, who considered such terrain to be tarnished by its association with commerce and industry. When the Arts Council organised a 1964 survey of the most important paintings and sculptures of the last decade, it included some thirty artists, but not Hamilton.[3] Six years later, the curatorial consensus had changed so radically that the Tate devoted a solo show to Hamilton, including many of the paintings it had ignored in 1964 as well as his investigations into the design of cars, kitchen gadgets and fashion imagery.[4] The cover of the catalogue was devoted to *Toaster* [p. 138], a 1967 work inspired by the promotional literature for the Braun HT 2 single-slit toaster.

By then, Hamilton's eclectic vision of contemporary culture was widely accepted within progressive circles, in large part due to his own influence, though also to the writing of his friend and fellow Independent Group member, the design critic Reyner Banham, and the French cultural theorists Roland Barthes and Jean Baudrillard. Hamilton continued to pursue his interest in design and to champion cultural inclusivity for the rest of his life. Fraught and ambivalent though art's relationship to design still is, it would be far more so without him and what the art critic David Sylvester described as "his consuming obsession with the modern—modern living, modern technology, modern equipment, modern communications, modern materials, modern processes, modern attitudes."[5] Given Hamilton's importance in the evolution of British design culture, what role did it play in his development as an artist? And what impact did he have on our understanding of design, and its rapport with art?

1. See Richard Morphet (ed.), *Richard Hamilton* (London: Tate Gallery, 1992), 187.
2. Richard Hamilton, "An Exposition of *$he,*" in *Collected Words 1953–1982* (London: Thames and Hudson, 1982), 12. Originally published in *Architectural Design* 32, no. 10 (October 1962), 485.
3. *Painting and Sculpture of a Decade 1954–64* was held at the Tate Gallery, London, from April to June 1964.
4. *Richard Hamilton* was held at the Tate Gallery, London, from March to April 1970, then toured from May to August to the Stedelijk Van Abbemuseum, Eindhoven, and Kunsthalle, Bern.
5. David Sylvester, *About Modern Art,* as cited in Michael Bracewell, *Re-make/Re-model: Art, Pop, Fashion and the Making of Roxy Music, 1953–1972* (London: Faber and Faber, 2007), 59.

The antipathy towards design in post-war Britain was not confined to the visual arts, but reflected a broader distrust of industrialisation and mechanisation that had emerged among the intelligentsia during the nineteenth century. Britain had led the Industrial Revolution in the late 1700s when, for a brief period, the frenzied mills of pioneering industrialists like the Staffordshire potter Josiah Wedgwood seemed so exhilarating that intellectuals and socialites set off from London on factory tours of Manchester and the Midlands. By the early 1800s, the enthusiasm for industry had faded and the stereotype of the "dark, satanic mill" was born. Factories were seen as dirty and dangerous, their wares as shoddy, their workers as subversive and their owners as vulgar, even by their own children who were mostly educated at private schools where, as the economic historians Correlli Barnett and Martin Wiener have written, they imbibed the values of the landed aristocracy, including a disdain of commerce, industry and science. By the late 1800s, such prejudices were lent intellectual weight by William Morris, John Ruskin and other members of the Arts and Crafts Movement, who advocated a revival of rural craftsmanship. Their beliefs proved pervasive in Britain even during the early twentieth century when the influence of Russian Constructivism transformed perceptions of industrial design elsewhere in Europe, by giving it a moral and political purpose as a means of translating scientific and technological advances into products and services that could help millions of people to become happier, healthier and more productive.

All but a tiny minority of Britons remained inured to the Constructivist zest for modernity until the 1930s, when the modern movement gained momentum as *émigré* artists, architects, designers and intellectuals sought refuge in Britain from the Nazis' growing power in Europe, but its popularity proved short-lived. As World War II loomed, many of the *émigrés* left for safer havens, including Walter Gropius, László Moholy-Nagy and other former teachers at the Bauhaus art and design school in Germany, who settled in the United States. After the war, the British public associated technology with the horror and destruction caused by the Blitz and the atom bomb, rather than with social and political progress. The late 1940s and 1950s were golden years for science, when many of the innovations developed for military use during wartime were translated into technologies that transformed daily life. Most of those breakthroughs were made in the secrecy of scientific research centres, like Bell Laboratories in New Jersey, where the transistor was invented in 1947, and the electrical engineering department of the University of Manchester, which staged a demonstration of the first stored memory computer the following year. Thrilling though those innovations now seem, few people outside scientific circles were aware of them at the time. The flurry of interest in design and technology in British cultural circles during the pre-war era had been replaced by indifference, if not hostility.[6]

Not for Hamilton. Born into a working class family in London in the early 1920s, his formative influences were very different to those of the typically privileged, privately educated establishment grandees who had been, as Banham put it, "isolated from humanity by the Humanities."[7] Conversely, he and Hamilton, like several other members of the Independent

6. The cultural historian Richard Hoggart summarised the British establishment's view of consumerism and popular culture in his 1957 book *The Uses of Literacy* by describing the US mass media as being "full of a corrupt brightness, of improper appeals and moral evasions." Richard Hoggart, *The Uses of Literacy: Aspects of Working Class Life* (London: Chatto & Windus, 1957), 340.
7. Reyner Banham, "Pop and the Body Critical," *New Society* (16 December 1965), 25.
8. Reyner Banham, "Who is this 'Pop'?," *Motif* 10 (Winter 1962/63).

Group, shared childhood memories of enjoying Hollywood Westerns at the local cinema and devouring comic books and popular music. "There is one very good reason why the IG was with it so long before anyone else," wrote Banham. "The key figures … were all brought up in the Pop belt somewhere. American films and magazines were the only live culture we knew as kids."[8]

As well as deriving great pleasure from popular culture, Hamilton was highly knowledgeable about its production, in particular about design's role in the process, thanks to the succession of jobs he took on to make ends meet while studying painting and establishing himself as an artist. After leaving school at fourteen, he had to wait two years before starting a course at the Royal Academy Schools. He worked as an office boy in the advertising department of an electrical engineering firm, then joined the display team of the Reimann School, which was founded in 1937 as Britain's first commercial art school by two Jewish *émigrés* from Germany, Albert and Klara Reimann. Hamilton's job there was to build sets for exhibitions of work by the teachers and students, but he was allowed to attend life-drawing classes in his free time. Working at the school introduced him to typography, art direction, photography, fashion, set design and other aspects of "commercial art," as well as the modernist thinking of the Reimanns and the *émigré* artists and designers they employed as teachers, Alex Kroll among them.[9]

During the war, Hamilton received a similarly impromptu yet thorough grounding in technology when the Royal Academy Schools closed and he was sent to a Government Training Centre to study engineering draughtsmanship. He was then employed as a "jig and tool" draughtsman at the Design Unit Group, a ramshackle operation run by the bandleader Jack Jackson, for Electrical & Musical Industries, which owned various engineering firms and the record company EMI. Jackson and his team were intended to deploy their engineering skills to help the war effort, but Hamilton spent much of his time organising lunchtime concerts of recordings he found in the archives. Even so, he had a zest for engineering, possibly inherited from his father, who had worked as a driver and shared his love of cars with him, and fell in with a group of acoustical engineers who devoted their spare time to constructing sound equipment. After the war, he returned to the Royal Academy Schools and later enrolled at the Slade, but his wartime work at EMI, followed by a stint of National Service with the Royal Engineers, imbued him with a nuanced understanding of the engineering side of design, and its relationship to science and technology, that complemented his knowledge of commercial art.

When Hamilton left art school, that combination of skills enabled him to earn a living while starting his career as an artist. He considered working in fashion illustration, hence his interest in Kroll's "studio sessions" at *Vogue,* and took on other commercial projects, including designing corporate logos for both Churchill Gear Machines and Granada Television. His experience of set building at the Reimann School served him well when curating exhibitions, like *Growth and Form* (1951) [pp. 24–31] and *Man, Machine and Motion* (1955) [pp. 42–47], and his first teaching assignments were in the design departments of art

9. "I learned how to do a lot of things, such as cut lettering for exhibition stands, but the main quality of the place was that I met people who were exceptionally talented in their field," Richard Hamilton said of the Reimann School to the curator Hans Ulrich Obrist in 2003. "I was given great encouragement for a while by a stage designer called 'Professor' Haas-Heye. On one occasion, he gave me a shilling and said go and see the Picasso show at the Burlington Gallery, behind the Royal Academy—the *Guernica* exhibition, a life-time experience." Hans Ulrich Obrist, "Pop Daddy: The Great Richard Hamilton on his Early Exhibitions," *Tate Magazine* 4 (March/April 2003).

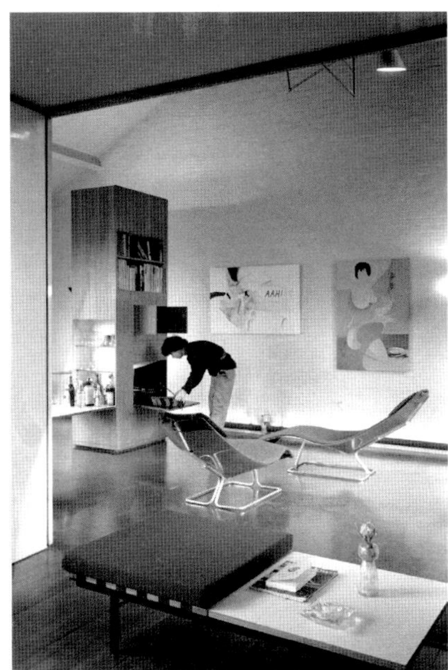

fig. 1
Terry Hamilton inside the Highgate house, 1962

schools. Hamilton taught typography and industrial design at the Central School of Arts and Crafts, before joining the Fine Art Department of the University of Newcastle in 1953 as a Lecturer in Design where he ran a Basic Form course.[10] Victor Pasmore had taught furniture design at the Central School before setting up the Basic Design course with Hamilton in Newcastle. At the time, so few professional designers were able or willing to teach design that young artists were often pressed into doing so. Hamilton was unusual in being better equipped for the role than many of his peers, but it would be foolish to romanticise his commitment to design teaching. He saw the Basic Design course as a means to an end, having taken it on in the hope of being allowed to teach art too, and of eventually stopping teaching as soon as he could support himself and his family as an artist.

Nonetheless he made the most of the design resources available to him at Newcastle, drawing on the university's printing equipment and photography department, hitherto used mostly for medical research, for the exhibitions he curated at the Hatton Gallery, and their accompanying posters and catalogues. One of his students, Mark Lancaster, recalls Hamilton's enthusiasm for the university's photocopier, an early version of the machine. When Hamilton returned to London, he would post material to Lancaster in Newcastle asking him to photocopy it and send the copies to him by mail.[11] Hamilton enjoyed the sybaritic side of Pop culture in Newcastle, going to lunchtime dances at the Majestic Ballroom and Rock and Roll concerts at City Hall, and was fascinated by fashion, unusually so for an Englishman of his generation. Marcus Price, who ran Newcastle's most fashionable menswear shop, told the cultural historian Michael Bracewell how Hamilton would drop in with his own discoveries, including original Wrangler cowboy shirts from the US with enormous cuffs and mother-of-pearl studs.[12] Encouraged by Banham, Hamilton sustained his interest in international developments in design and technology, reading the latest periodicals and writing for several of them, particularly those edited by another IG colleague, Theo Crosby, such as *Living Arts and Architectural Design.*

Hamilton's concept of design, which he elaborated in "Persuading Image," a 1960 essay for *Design* magazine, was thoughtful and open-minded, but neither original nor iconoclastic.[13] He accepted the orthodox definition of design as a commercial force, rather than seeing it as a more fluid instinctive process, "not a profession but an attitude," as Moholy-Nagy had phrased it in his 1947 book *Vision in Motion*.[14] Nor did he share the political ambitions for design championed by the Italian artist and design theorist Bruno Munari during the 1950s and 1960s.[15] The publication of "Persuading Image" prompted a feisty debate among designers, but the controversy reflected the conservatism of British design culture, rather than any radicalism on Hamilton's part. Yet his design judgments were generally astute. Hamilton was equally adept at identifying excellence, being among the first to appreciate the growing importance of the new design school at Ulm in West Germany during the 1950s,[16] and at spotting mediocrity, especially in what were popularly considered to be sacred cows, like the whimsical "festival style" inspired by the Festival of Britain[17] and the showmanship of the French-born doyen of American commercial design, Raymond

10. When Hamilton was first employed in Newcastle upon Tyne, it was in the Fine Art Department of King's College, University of Durham, which was later renamed the University of Newcastle upon Tyne.
11. Author's interview with Mark Lancaster, January 2013.
12. Bracewell, *Re-make/Re-model: Art, Pop, Fashion and the Making of Roxy Music,* 42.
13. Richard Hamilton, "Persuading Image," *Design* 134 (February 1960), 28–32.
14. László Moholy-Nagy, *Vision in Motion* (Chicago: Paul Theobald & Co., 1947), 42.
15. Bruno Munari's thinking on design was articulated in the collection of his columns for the Italian daily newspaper *Il Giorno,* published as the 1966 book *Design as Art*. See Bruno Munari, *Design as Art* (London: Penguin Books, 2008).

Loewy.[18] Often, his judgments were rooted in his technical knowledge, as illustrated by "Glorious Technicolor, Breathtaking Cinemascope and Stereophonic Sound," a lecture he gave in Newcastle and London in 1959, which included an inspired analysis of the cultural impact of technological change on cinema, television and photography.[19]

Critically, Hamilton drew repeatedly on his interest in design and technology in his work as an artist. In his 1956 *Just what is it that makes today's homes so different, so appealing?* [p. 49] he critiqued consumer culture by collaging images of aspirational objects and phenomena of the era: among them, a tape recorder, tinned ham, a male bodybuilder and topless female model, a poster for a pulp novel and the blazing neon lights of a cinema. For his 1957 *Hommage à Chrysler Corp.* [p. 77] and the following year's *Hers is a lush situation* [p. 79], he explored the role of sexuality in the design of the most fetishised consumer products of the time, American cars.

Other artists occupied similar terrain, including Andy Warhol and Roy Lichtenstein in the United States, and Eduardo Paolozzi and Peter Blake in Britain, but tended to be jolly and celebratory. Hamilton's approach was more diagnostic, though not cynically so. It is evident from his work that he recognised—and enjoyed—the sybaritic nature of his subjects, but his choices and mode of analysis were more precise and sophisticated than those of his contemporaries. Both *Hommage* and *Hers* were based on Banham's research into the strategic use of design by the US automotive industry. The former juxtaposes elements of the cars featured in Chrysler and General Motors' advertisements with particular parts of a woman's body to illustrate how, say, the curves of the headlamps mimic the lines of her breasts. The contrast between the first two words of the title "Hommage à", which allude to the "high art" of Cubism in early twentieth century Paris, and the American corporate jargon of "Chrysler Corp" signals the satirical sub-text, while "Corp" serves as a *double entendre* by alluding to *corps,* the French word for "body." Hers portrays the lips of the movie star Sophia Loren hovering above various emblems of automotive styling, including chrome tail fins and a wraparound windscreen through which the driver can see flashes of the towering United Nations headquarters in New York. Hamilton found the title in the closing words of a review of a 1955 Buick in the US magazine *Industrial Design:* "The driver sits at the dead calm centre of all this motion, hers is a lush situation."[20] Not that he had spotted those words at random, the review was written by Deborah Allen, a talented young American design critic who he and Banham admired greatly.

He returned to those themes in *$he* [p. 81], an oil painting and collage completed in 1961 in which he explored the sexualised imagery of domestic appliance advertising. "The worst thing that can happen to a girl, according to the ads, is that she should fail to be exquisitely at ease in her appliance setting," Hamilton explained in an essay for *Architectural Design.* "Sex is everywhere, symbolised in the glamour of mass-produced luxury—the interplay of fleshy plastic and smooth, fleshier metal. This relationship of woman and appliance is a fundamental theme of our culture; as obsessive and archetypal as the Western movie gun duel."[21] By then, Hamilton had also begun an analysis of male narcissism

16. Richard Hamilton, "Ulm," *Design* 126 (June 1959), 53–57.
17. Richard Hamilton, "Inquest on the Festival of Britain," in *Collected Words,* 147–49.
18. Richard Hamilton discussed Raymond Loewy in his 1959 lecture "Persuading Image," in *Collected Words,* 135.
19. "Glorious Technicolor, Breathtaking Cinemascope and Stereophonic Sound" was a lecture given by Hamilton in 1959. The unpublished typescript was eventually published in *Collected Words,* 113–31.
20. Deborah Allen, "Guide for Carwatchers," *Industrial Design* (January 1955), 89.
21. Richard Hamilton, "An Exposition of *$he,*" *Architectural Design* 32, no. 10 (October 1962).

in advertising by collaging stereotypically "manly" images of the space race, a transistor radio, stock market listings, motor racing, classical archetypes of male beauty and the face of President John F. Kennedy in *Towards a definitive statement on the coming trends in menswear and accessories* (1962–63) [pp. 85–89], whose subtitles included "Together let us explore the stars" (a quote from one of Kennedy's speeches) [p. 86] and "Adonis in Y fronts" [p. 88]. The title came from an annual feature on male fashion in *Playboy* magazine to which Hamilton added the conditional first word, "Towards," arguing that fashion was too fluid a field for any prediction to be "definitive." He later deconstructed fashion photography in his 1969 *Fashion-plates* [pp. 168, 180–83], in which the facial features of different women, including Jane Holzer's hair and Verushka's lips, were collaged into new "faces." The collages reveal the intensity of Hamilton's interest in fashion, including glimpses of the black models who were then becoming popular with designers like Yves Saint Laurent. They were also eerily accurate in anticipating the way that contemporary art directors digitally enhance their subjects by erasing anomalies to create "flawless" representations of female beauty.

By the mid-1960s, the representation of design in Hamilton's work had changed radically. He continued to depict the outcome of the industrial design process through the marketing imagery with which it was presented to the public, but was focusing on mass-manufactured products of exceptional quality and portraying them as "high design," the industrial equivalent of "high art." Rather than poking fun at consumer culture as he had once done, or revelling in its sexiness, kitsch and jollity like fellow Pop artists, Hamilton depicted the industrial artefacts that he considered worthy of thoughtful consideration with a seriousness that was markedly more subversive than his earlier satire, beginning with the Braun electric grill in his 1965 *Still-life* [pp. 136–37].

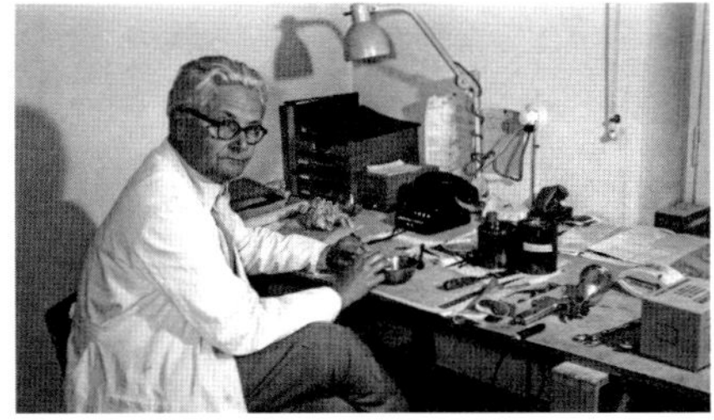

fig. 2
Wilhelm Wagenfeld, c. 1956

Hamilton had become aware of Braun's electronic products during the late 1950s, possibly because of his interest in the Ulm School of Design, which he had visited in 1958. Founded five years before with the aim of perpetuating the spirit and values of the Bauhaus, the Hochschule für Gestaltung (HfG) swiftly developed a singular approach to design education, specifically with regard to industrial design, which was grounded in rigorous research into the materials, finishes and processes used to manufacture a product, and its subsequent performance and durability. Several of Ulm's teachers, including Hans Gugelot and Wilhelm Wagenfeld [fig. 2], a student of Moholy-Nagy's at the Bauhaus, acted as consultants to the brothers Artur and Erwin Braun, who had inherited the Braun electronics company after their father's death in 1951. By the mid-1950s, the Brauns were putting HfG's industrial design principles into practice by applying the transistor and other wartime technologies to audio products, like radios and gramophones, and working with Gugelot and other designers to define a restrained visual language, distinguished by its use of carefully chosen modern materials in clean shapes and subtle, carefully coded colours. Among those designers was a young architect, Dieter Rams [fig. 3], who would later become head of design at Braun.

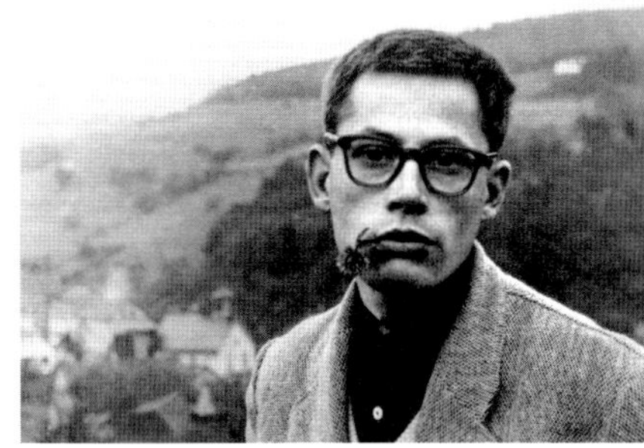

fig. 3
Dieter Rams, 1957

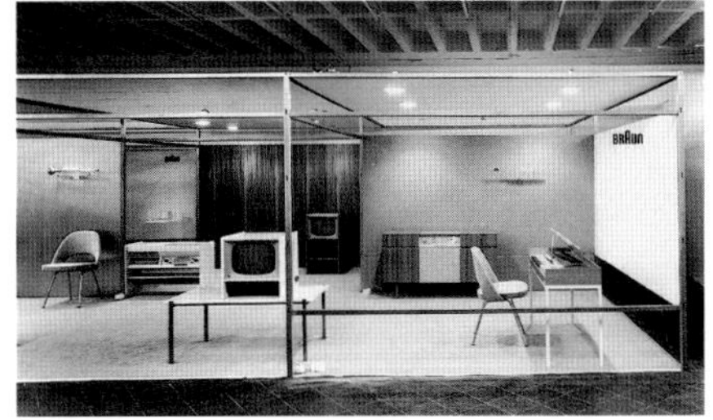

fig. 4
A mockup of the D 55 Braun pavilion at Ulm, 1955

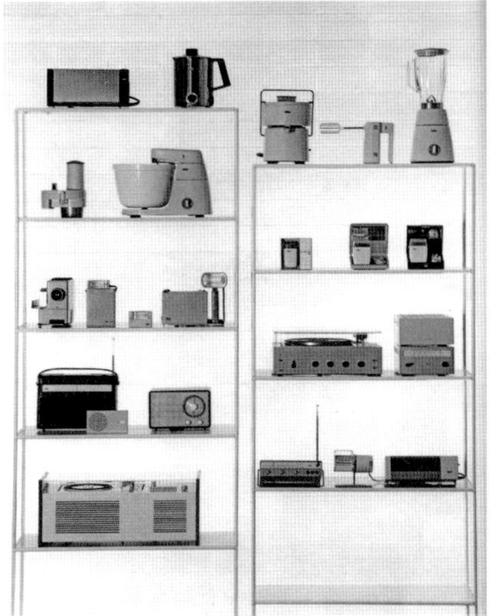

fig. 5
Braun product range, c. 1963

During the 1960s and 1970s, Braun was feted as the apogee of industrial design [fig. 4 & 5], playing a similar role in consumer culture as Apple has done in recent years. Thoughtful, disciplined and unobtrusive, its design aesthetic was the opposite of the flamboyantly styled American cars and electrical gizmos in Hamilton's earlier work. The company's marketing material was designed in the same quietly imposing style as its products. When Hamilton used a promotional image of the electric grill in *Still-life* the effect was respectful, almost reverential; so much so that his playful decision to replace the brand name "Braun" with its English equivalent "Brown" in identical typography seemed to signal his qualms about tinkering with something so impeccable, rather than presenting it as a jocular parody.

He adopted a similar approach in the *Toaster* series [pp. 138–43], beginning by using chromed steel and Perspex to reconstruct one of the HT 2's panels, and supplanting Braun's brand name with his surname (a device he would repeat in his 1975 *Advertisement* by replacing "Ricard," the trademark of the French *pastis,* with "Richard" [p. 146]). Hamilton's decision to use metal and Perspex in the original *Toaster* [p. 141] has been read as an attempt to replicate the experience of encountering an industrial object, as has the contrast between the mirrored surface of the steel and the fuzziness of the unfocused background. But when the piece was damaged while being shipped back to Hamilton's studio from an exhibition in Germany, the insurance company refused to pay up, arguing that the shards of metal and plastic could not belong to a work of art. Eventually, the insurer backed down, and Hamilton remade the work.[22] When he was asked, several years later, to comment on Rams' achievements for an exhibition of his products in Berlin, Hamilton stated: "My admiration for the work of Dieter Rams is intense and I have for many years been uniquely attracted towards his design sensibility; so much so that his consumer products have come to occupy a place in my heart and consciousness that Mont Sainte-Victoire did in Cézanne's."[23] The allusion evoked the Cubist "high art" reference in the first two words of *Hommage à Chrysler Corp.*

Towards the end of his career, Hamilton revisited his preoccupation with Braun by making a new edition of *Toaster* for a 2009 exhibition at the Gagosian Gallery in London, but his most compelling tribute to the company's design purism could very easily have debunked it. *The critic laughs* [pp. 144–45] was a series of ready-made objects he produced in the late 1960s and early 1970s, inspired by an impromptu decision to attach the giant sugar teeth, which his son had brought back from holiday as a souvenir, to the top of his own Braun electric toothbrush, rebranded as "Hamilton" (1968). Ghoulish though the results look, the tacky fake teeth enhance the refinement of Braun's beautifully resolved device.[24]

A similar sense of reverence is apparent in Hamilton's other mid-1960s studies of design aesthetics: a series of fibreglass and cellulose reliefs mimicking the spiralling form of the Guggenheim Museum in New York and an intriguing failure, his unsuccessful attempt to replicate the patterns of the treads of five car tyres manufactured in different periods. Hamilton abandoned his first effort when the geometry proved too complex to be reproduced

22. See Morphet (ed.), *Richard Hamilton,* 164.
23. Ibid. Braun's lead designer for the HT 2 single-slit toaster was not Dieter Rams, but his colleague Reinhold Weiss. However, Rams was in charge of the Braun design team during its development.
24. The original sugar false teeth were later replaced by a specially commissioned replica made from a dental acrylate compound.

in a perspective drawing, but the choice of subject matter illustrates the sophistication of his design knowledge as adroitly as his early interest in Braun. Mundane though car tyres may seem, they are examples of mass-manufactured products which are made in such huge quantities that their manufacturers can justify using advanced materials and highly complex aesthetic effects. Hamilton was unusually perceptive in recognising this, and his initial failure to replicate the treads justified his choice by demonstrating their intricacy. By contrast, Lichtenstein had depicted a tyre in a far simpler style in his 1962 oil painting *Tire,* ignoring the complexity that so intrigued Hamilton, but initially eluded him.

Eventually, Hamilton succeeded in producing an accurate rendering of the tyres by collaborating with a computer programmer at the Massachusetts Institute of Technology, who wrote a programme to illustrate the treads based on his calculations in 1971 [pp. 158–59]. At the time, computers seemed like the stuff of science fiction to most people. They were so expensive that only the largest companies or universities could afford them, and so enormous that they occupied entire rooms, where they were operated by specially trained technicians. Everyone else was banned from entry. A number of artists, including Gustav Metzger and Bruce Lacey, were experimenting with them, and the Institute of Contemporary Arts in London had presented an exhibition of their work, *Cybernetic Serendipity,* in 1968. Many of the artists in the show were interested in exploring what type of imagery a machine would produce when left to its own devices but, as always, Hamilton was focused not on the imagery itself, but its impact on other people, what Gilles Deleuze described as its affect.

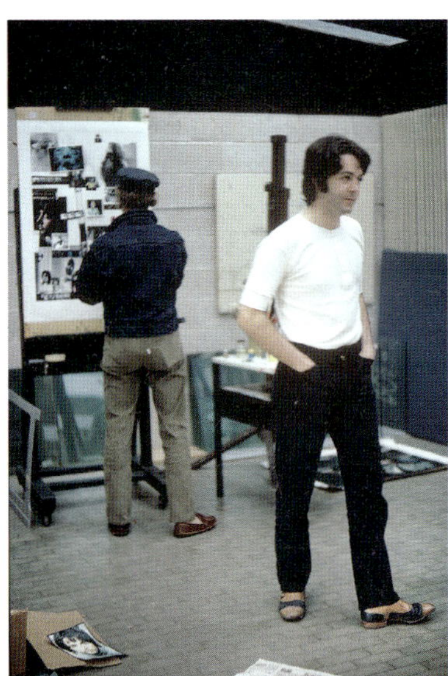

fig. 6
Hamilton and Paul McCartney in Highgate studio working on insert for *The Beatles,* 1968

The design projects he undertook from the mid-1960s onwards had the same goal. His treatment of the most famous one, the double album released by the Beatles in 1968, officially named *The Beatles* but commonly known as "The White Album," was complicated by the intensity of the band's fame and Hamilton's ambivalence towards it [p. 161]. Tempting though it is to interpret his decision to make the cover a blank white canvas as an inspired exercise in popularising conceptualism, the truth is more prosaic. The Beatles had planned to call it *A Doll's House* after the eponymous Ibsen play, only for another British band, Family, to release a debut album entitled *Music in a Doll's House.* Unable to think of a more distinctive title, the Beatles decided to name the record after themselves.[25] Hamilton was suggested as a possible sleeve designer by his then-gallerist Robert Fraser, who was friendly with John Lennon and Paul McCartney, and was summoned to the Beatles' offices to discuss the project [fig. 6]. "I was sitting waiting in an outer office watching beautiful girls in mini skirts taking dogs out for a walk, things like that," he told Bracewell. "The whole thing was so artificial and so silly… Then I was allowed into the presence of Paul, and by that time I was bad-tempered. So when he said that they wanted me to do the cover … I said 'Why don't you do it yourself?' … Then Paul said: 'Come on, haven't you got any ideas?' and I said, 'Well, my best idea is to leave a white cover'—and it went on from there."[26] Hamilton was convinced that EMI would veto the idea of releasing a record with an empty cover, but the Beatles were so powerful that they forced it to proceed, even with his insistence that each of the millions of albums should be individually numbered. Haphazard though

25. See Ian MacDonald, *Revolution in the Head: The Beatles' Records and the Sixties* (London: Random House, 1995), 262.
26. Bracewell, *Re-make/Re-model: Art, Pop, Fashion and the Making of Roxy Music,* 149–50.

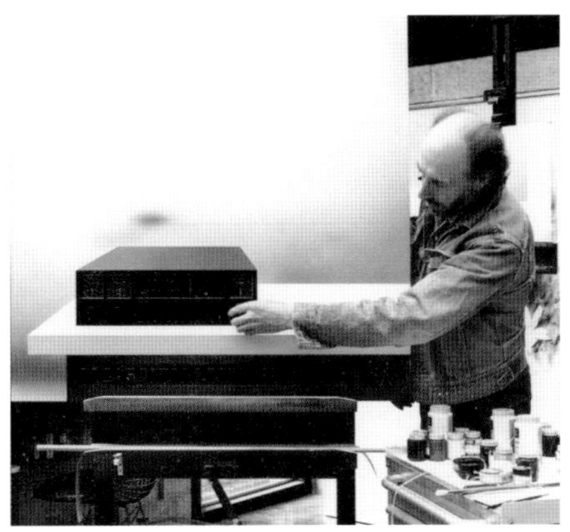

fig. 7
Hamilton with *Lux 50 – functioning prototype*, 1979

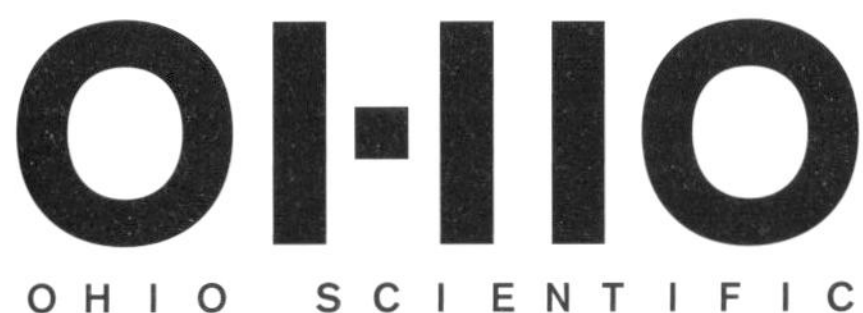

fig. 8
Logo for OHIO Scientific, 1986

the design process was, the outcome was an eloquent protest against the hysteria of Beatleseque celebrity and consumerism, which remains potent today, not least because of the extremity of Hamilton's concept. Only one album can ever make such a strong impact by adopting a blank white cover: just as only one brand can do so by choosing a blank white label, as Martin Margiela's fashion house did, or by dispensing with visible branding, like the Muji homeware stores, whose name means "no name" in Japanese.

Hamilton was free to pursue his own agenda in subsequent design exercises, starting with one for Lux Corporation, a Japanese electronics manufacturer that invited him to develop an artwork based on its audio equipment to mark its fiftieth anniversary. Conceived as an amplifier, which would be flat and light enough to hang on a wall like a painting, the Lux 50 was completed in 1979 [fig. 7 and p. 149]. An image of the amplifier is painted on to an aluminium panel covering the machine itself. Hamilton described it as "a two-dimensional representation of a piece of equipment which also performs the functions expected of the object portrayed."[27] Robert Rauschenberg had deployed a similar strategy to dramatically different effect in 1959 by submerging three radios in the paint and plaster of *Broadcast.* A decade after completing the Lux project, Hamilton worked with OHIO Scientific [fig. 8], a computer company owned by the Swedish group Isotron, on the development of a mini-computer, which he named—and branded—the 01–110. The project proved to be unexpectedly complicated, not least because Isotron was taken over by the Diab Data group in 1986, but the 01–110 was finished in time for an exhibition at Moderna Museet in Stockholm [p. 148]. Hamilton insisted that it was operative throughout the show, as he would in later exhibitions, presumably to demonstrate that it was capable of executing a practical function alongside its role as an artwork.

Neither work would be deemed remarkable if judged solely on its design merits, though nor were Hamilton's commercial design projects, like his corporate logos for Churchill and Granada. Conceptually, the Lux 50 is the more original of the two, but not when compared to other technological concepts of the era. Stylistically, both products aspire to Braun's subtlety and discipline, but lack its finesse. Like Donald Judd's furniture, Hamilton's amplifier and computer are interesting not in terms of their design, but for what their ambiguity tell us about his evolution as an artist. The Lux 50 and 01–011 were intended as provocations to the stereotypical distinctions between both disciplines. As they fulfil one essential requirement of industrial design by executing their practical functions as an amplifier and computer respectively, why should they also be deemed to be artworks? Because someone calling himself an artist conceived them? Because they were exhibited in an art gallery? Or because, as works of art, they were free from the threat of obsolescence that haunts conventional versions of the same products, once their technology was superseded? Hamilton treated both projects as research exercises through which he could study their respective industries, just as today's "speculative designers" like Daniel van der Velden and Vinca Kruk of the Dutch design group Metahaven use the design process as a medium of intellectual enquiry to slake their curiosity about political phenomena. But his chief

27. Richard Hamilton, "conceptltechnology>artwork," in *Richard Hamilton: teknologi <ide> konstverk,* ed. Bo Nilsson (Stockholm: Moderna Museet, 1989), 22–23.

preoccupation was, once again, to analyse their affects; this time in terms of how the objects were perceived typologically as examples of art and design.

The legacy of Hamilton's fascination with design as an artist, teacher, lecturer, essayist and occasional designer still resonates in the work of other artists of his generation, like Ed Ruscha, Franz West and Isa Genzken, and younger ones such as Dominique Gonzalez-Foerster, Christoph Büchel, Nairy Baghramian, Mark Leckey and Helen Marten. His influence is equally evident on the emerging genre of conceptual designers, including Julia Lohmann, Christien Meindertsma and Dunne & Raby, who, like Metahaven, use the design process as a medium of research, often into the affects of design culture, and produce work whose principal function is to enable them to conduct such investigations. Resonant though Hamilton's reappraisal of the relationship between design and art has proved to be, the spirit with which he conducted it has been equally valuable: thoughtful, empathic, passionate, rigorous and, above all, optimistic.

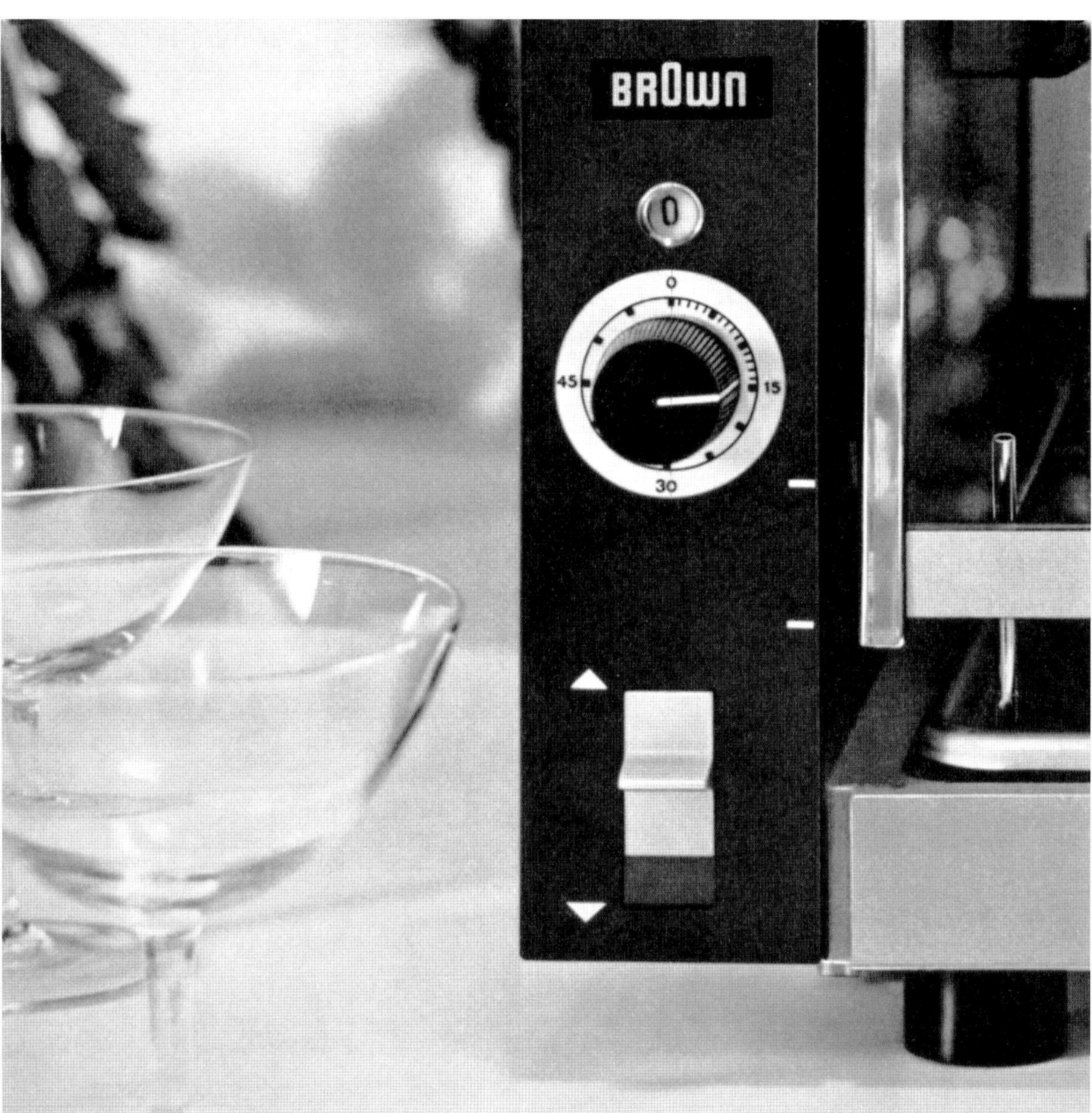

Still-life – study 1965

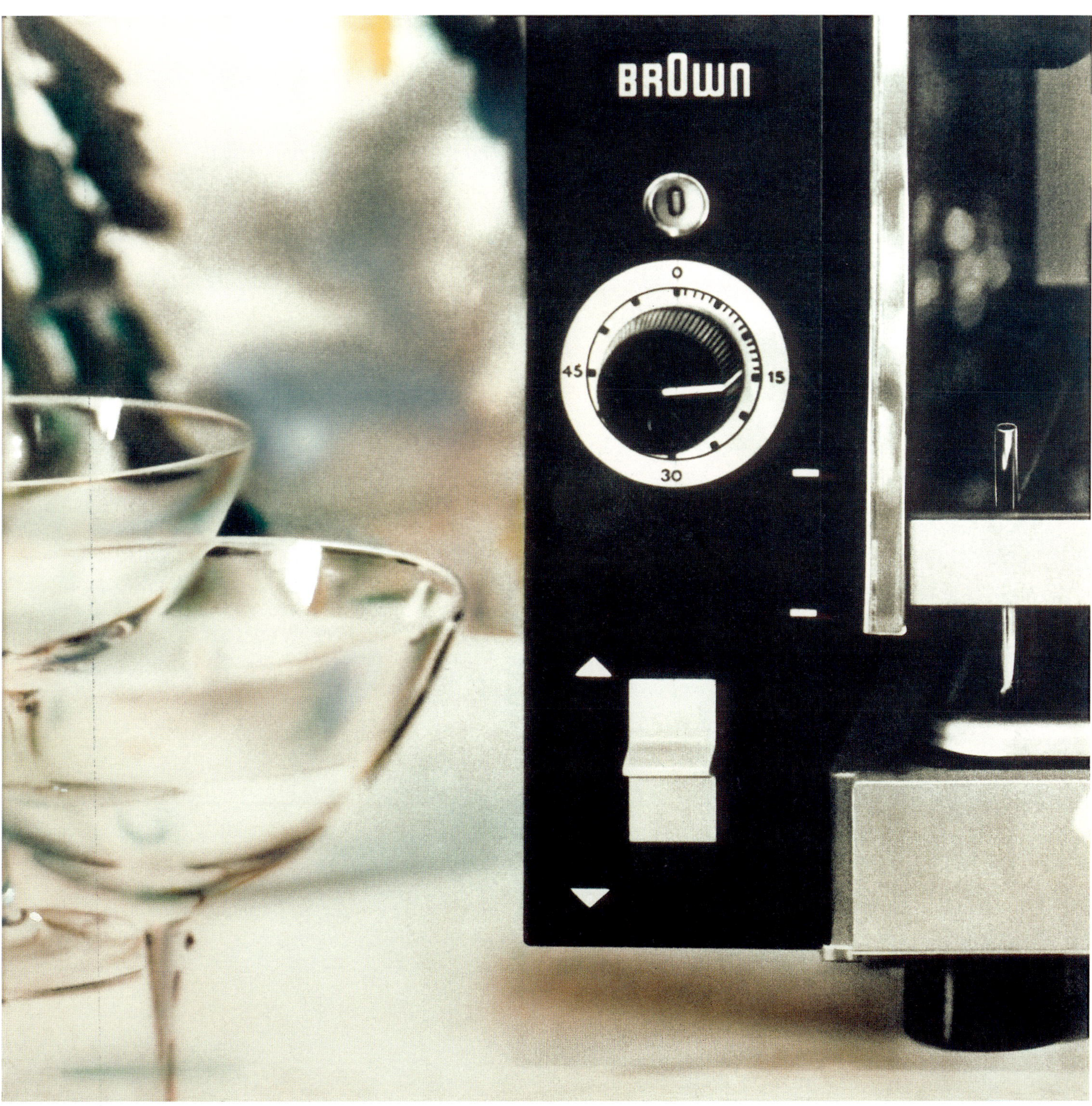

Still-life 1965

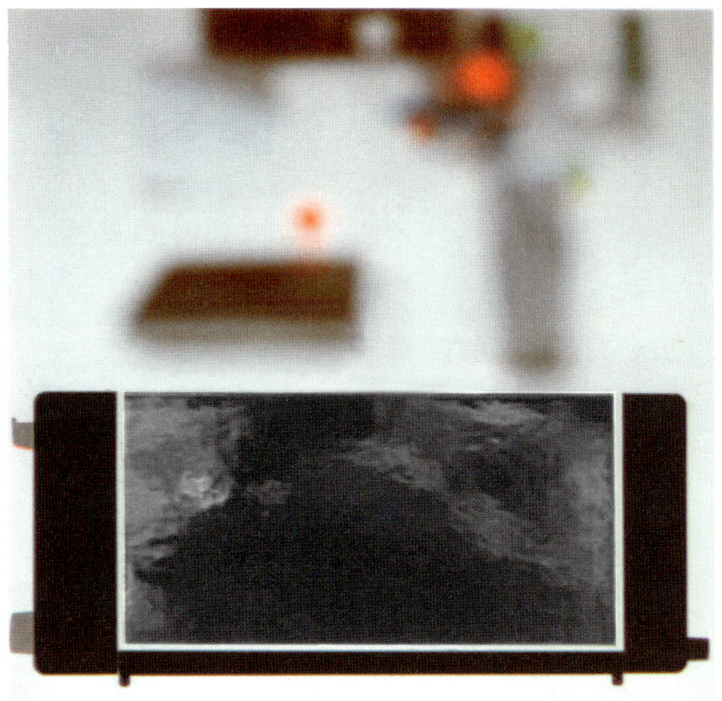

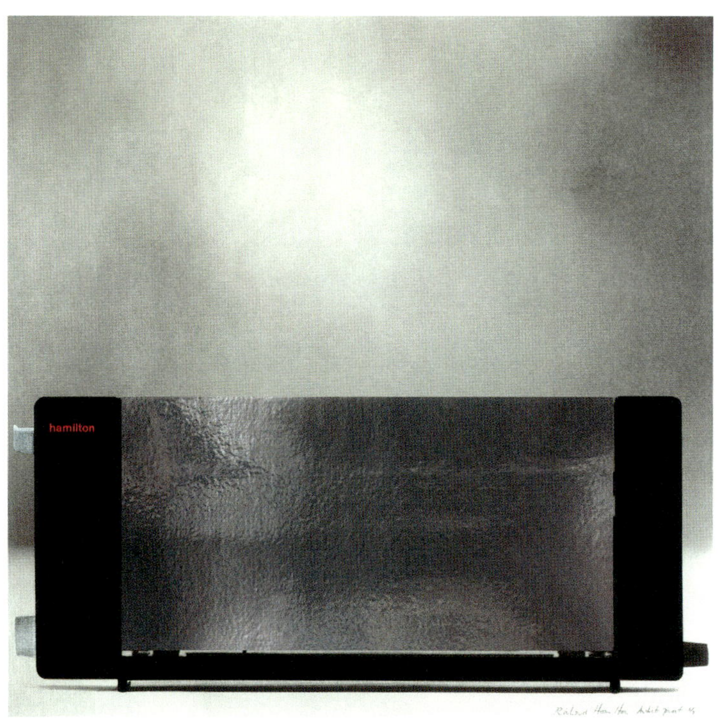

Toaster

New, practical, outstanding, this print was made possible by a number of fresh ideas. The proof of the excellence of the toaster that inspired this work of art has been supplied by the results of severe endurance tests recently performed. The appliance was kept working for a total of 1458.3 hours (not counting brief periods for cooling). This was the time taken to toast 50 000 slices of bread. That is a pile of bread well over a quarter of a mile high.
Just how outstanding the design is can be proved by the fact that it has been included among the most attractive objects for everyday use exhibited at the New York Museum of Modern Art – the only automatic toaster in the world to achieve this honour.
White bread, black bread or even rye bread? Ask your friends and neighbours and they will tell you that toast is a first-class delicacy. It tastes good and has never been the cause of anyone losing their driving licence. It keeps you fit and your body needs it.

Printed on Saunders plain mould special printing s/o demi 80.5 lb/500 (complete with Marlerfilm and Marlerflex ink and applied metalized silver polyester) in an edition of 75.
Dimensions 25" wide, 35" high, image area 23" square.

Toaster study I 1969

Toaster – lithograph 1967

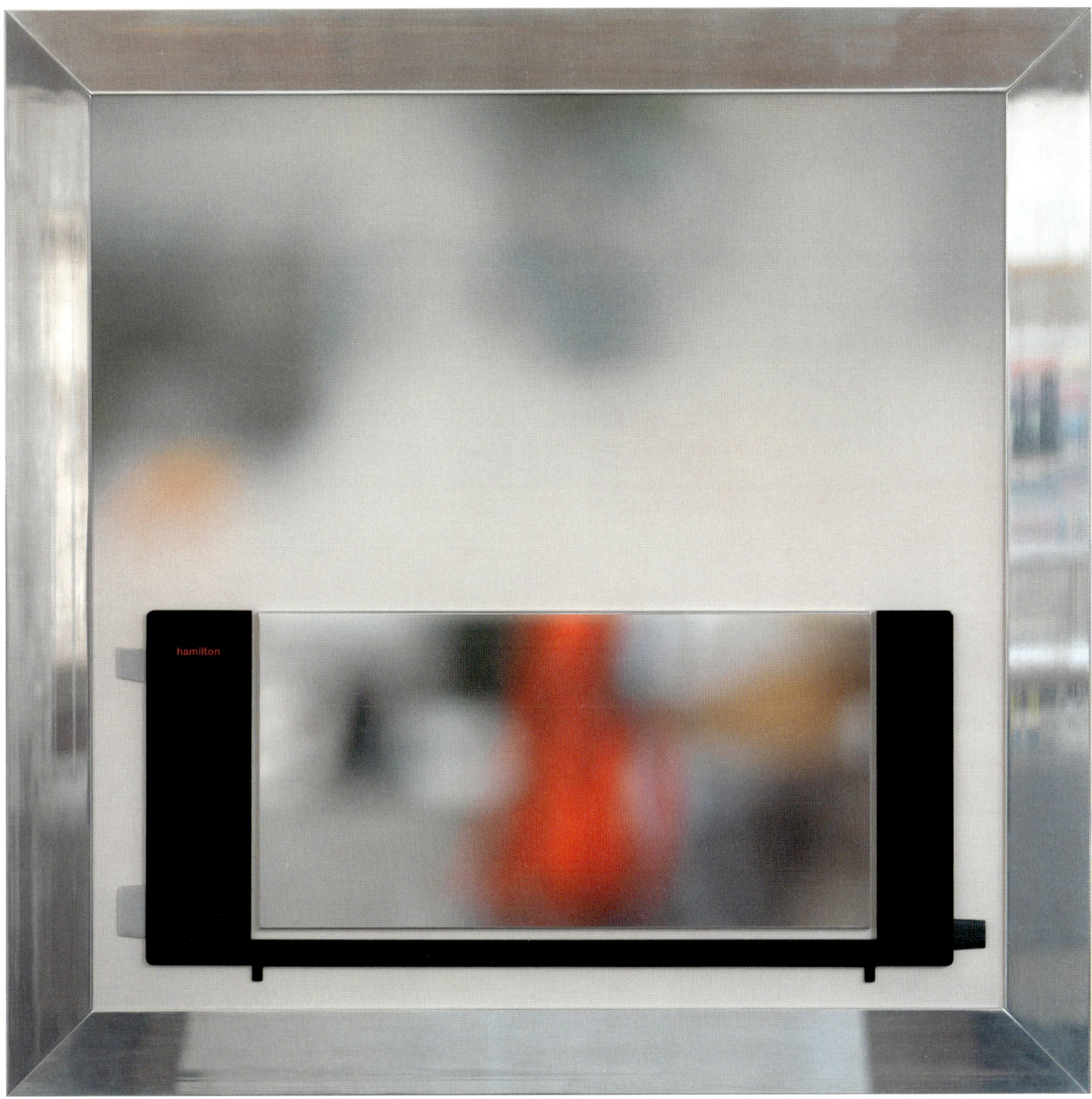

Toaster 1966–67

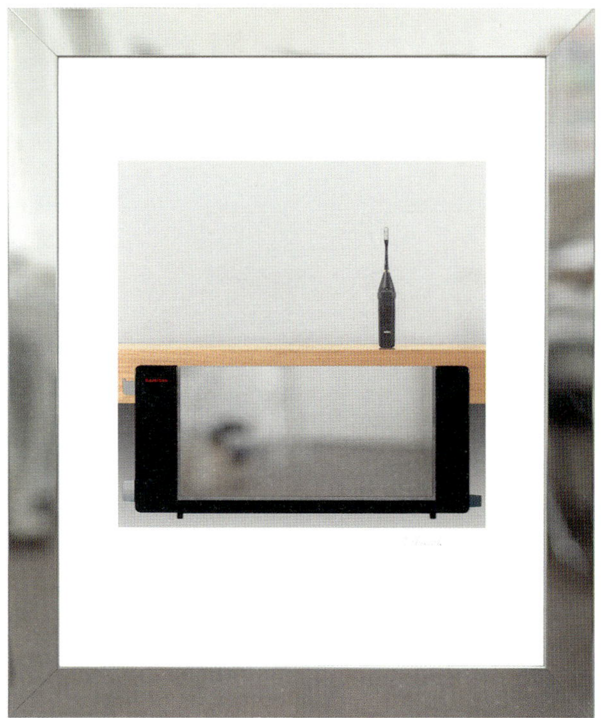

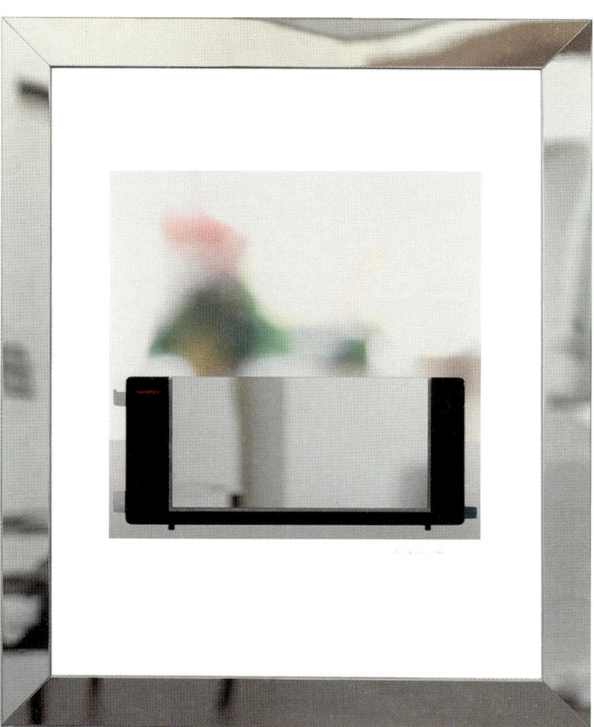

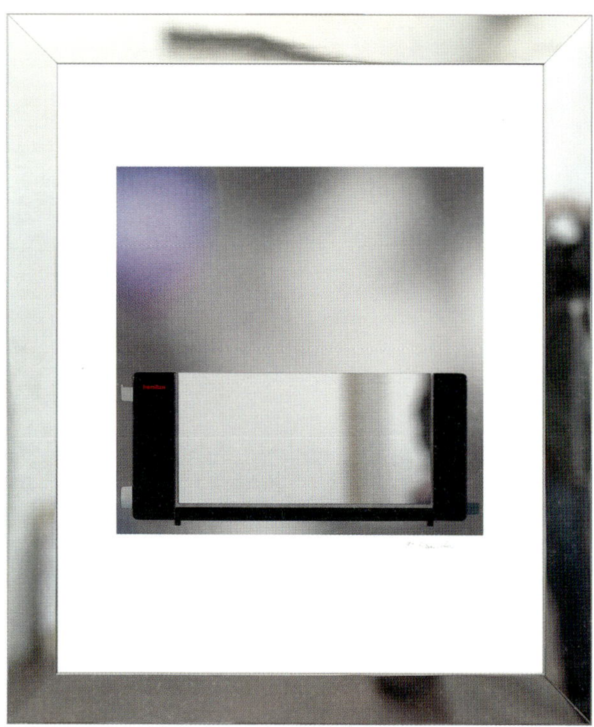

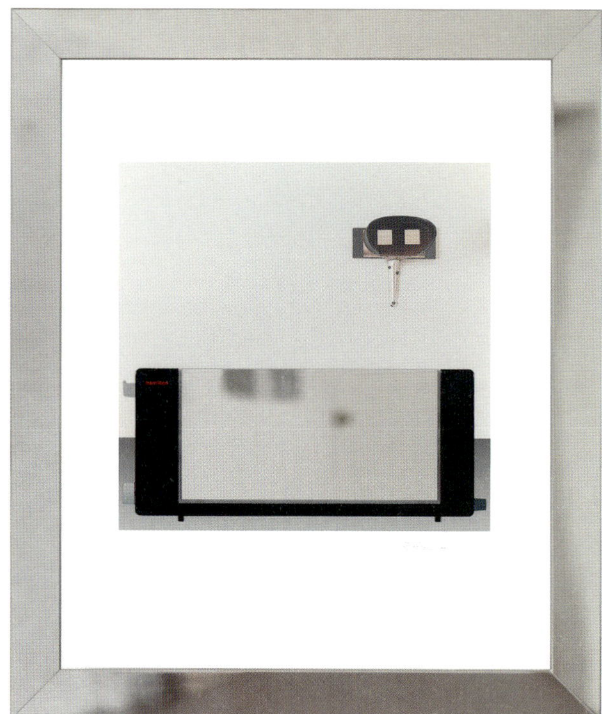

Toaster deluxe 1 2008
Toaster deluxe 5 2008

Toaster deluxe 2 2008
Toaster deluxe 6 2008

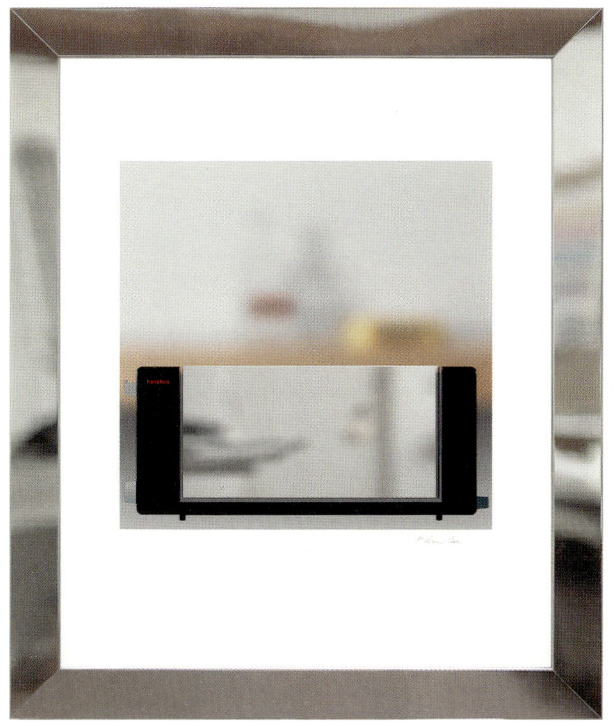

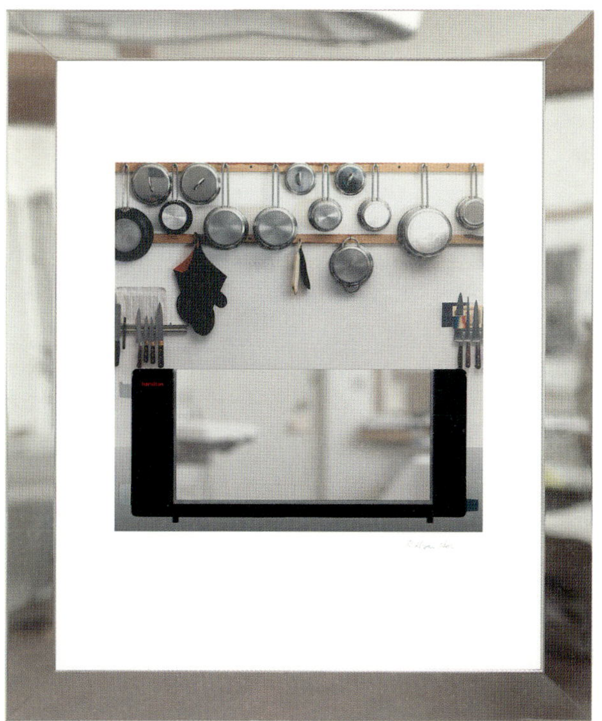

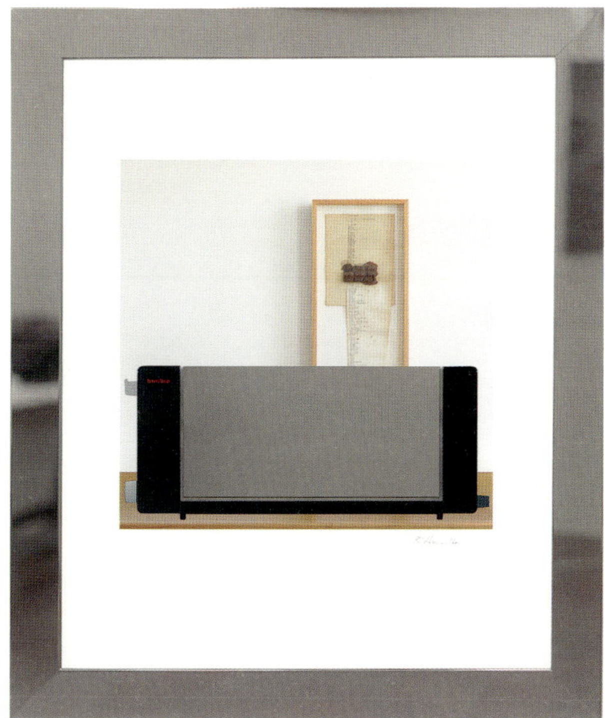

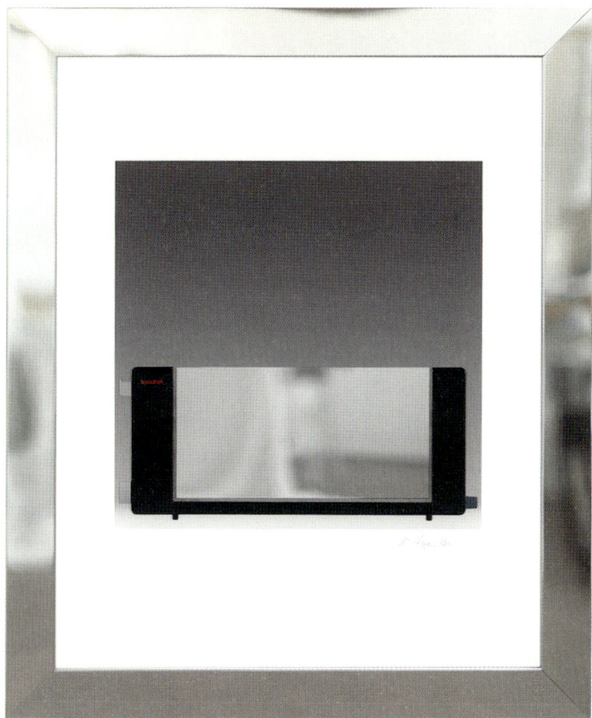

Toaster deluxe 7 2008

Toaster deluxe 9 2008

Toaster deluxe 8 2008

Toaster deluxe 10 2008

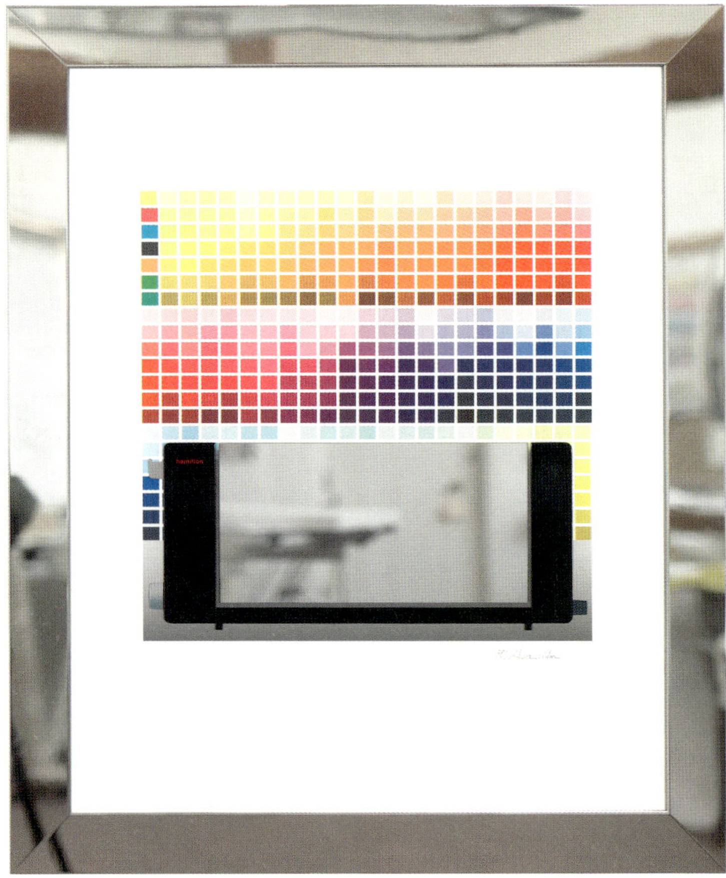

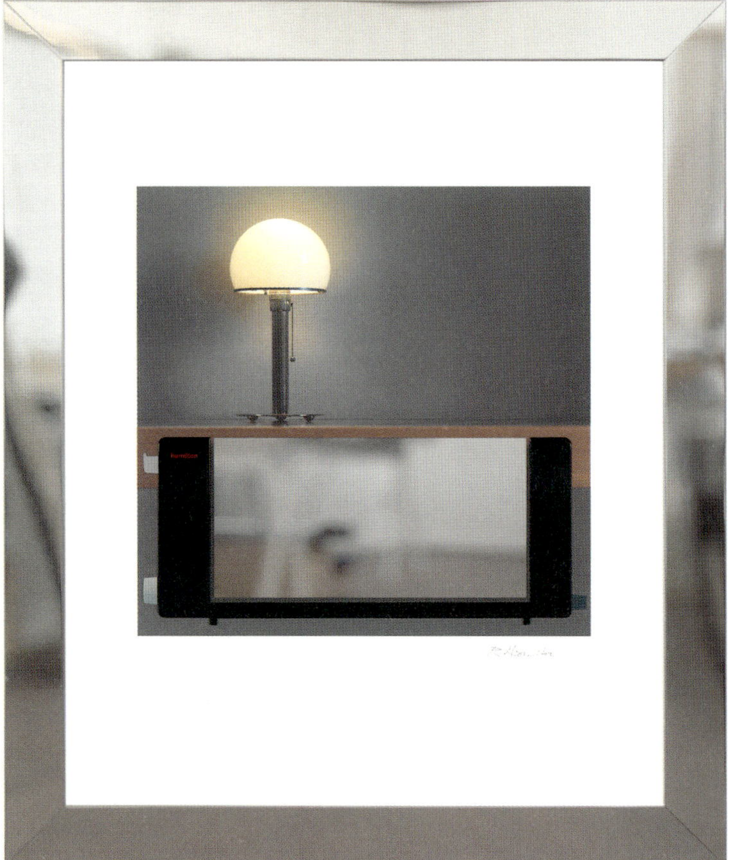

Toaster deluxe AP 1 2008

Toaster deluxe AP 2 2008

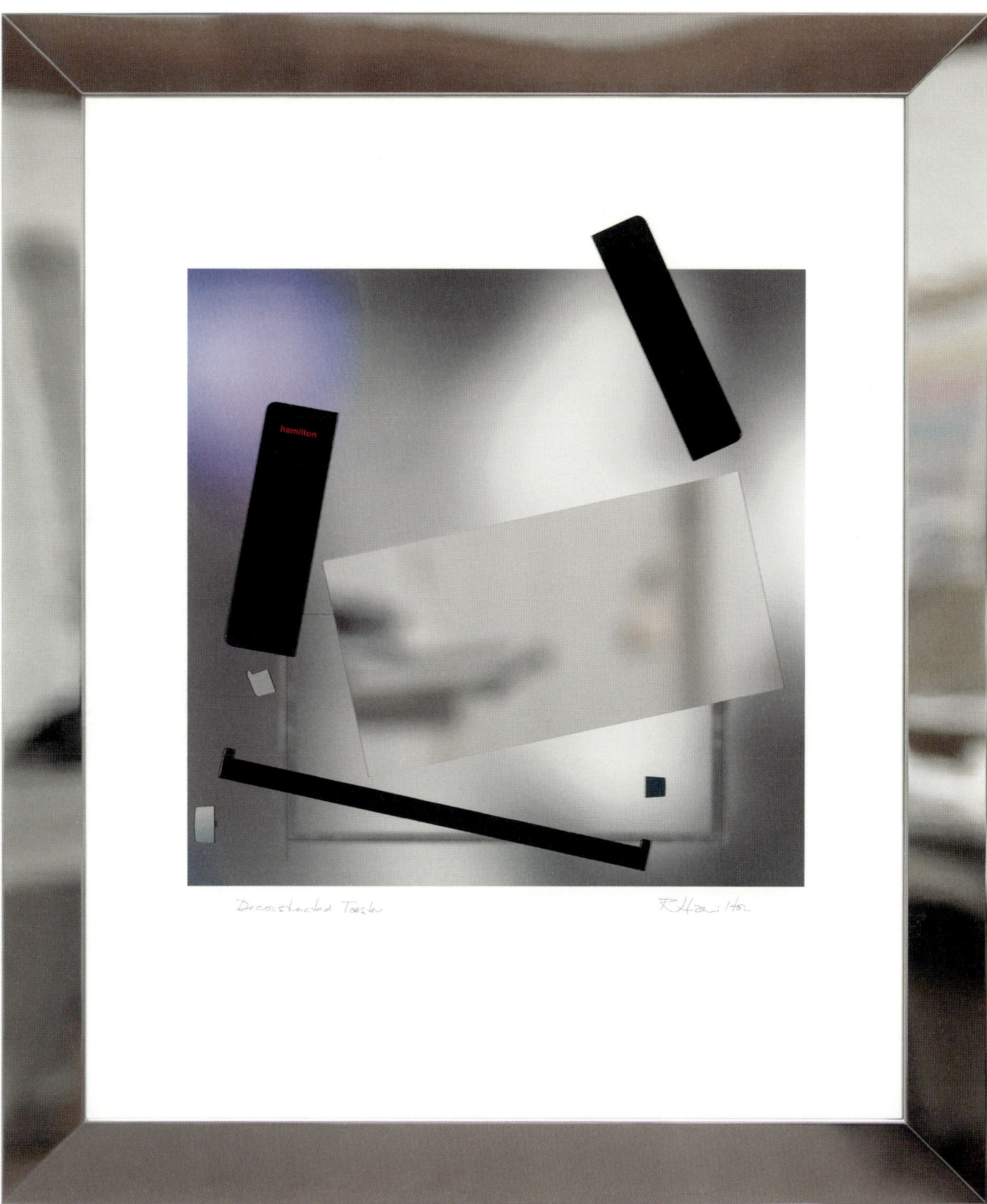

Toaster deluxe deconstructed 2008

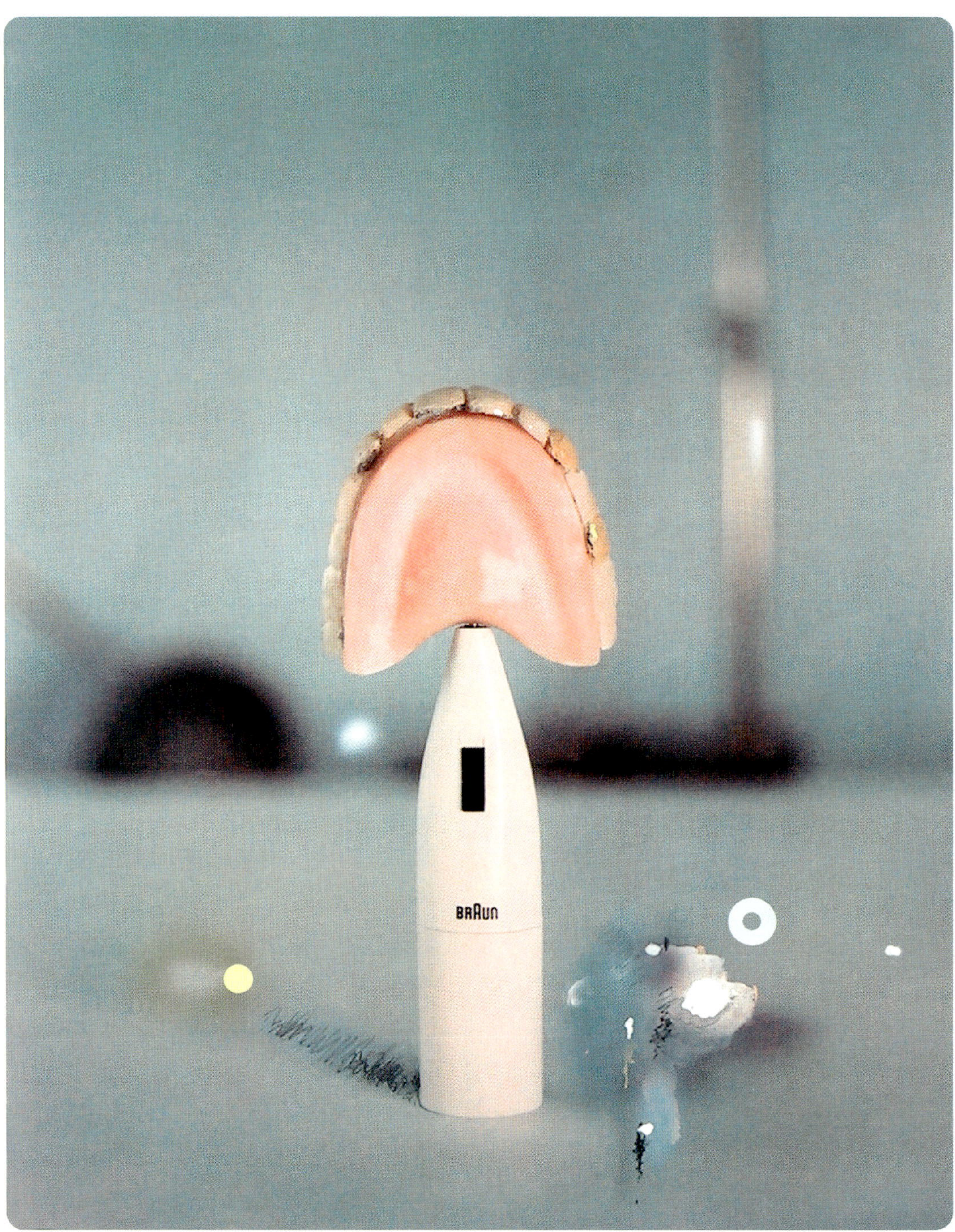

The critic laughs 1968

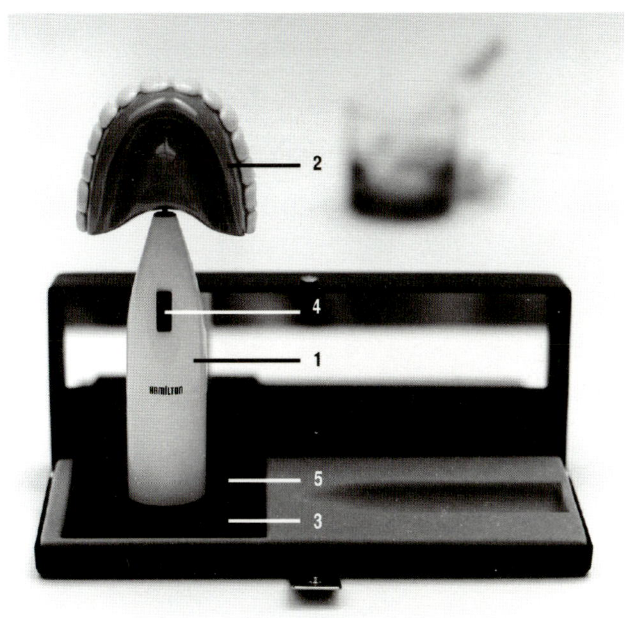

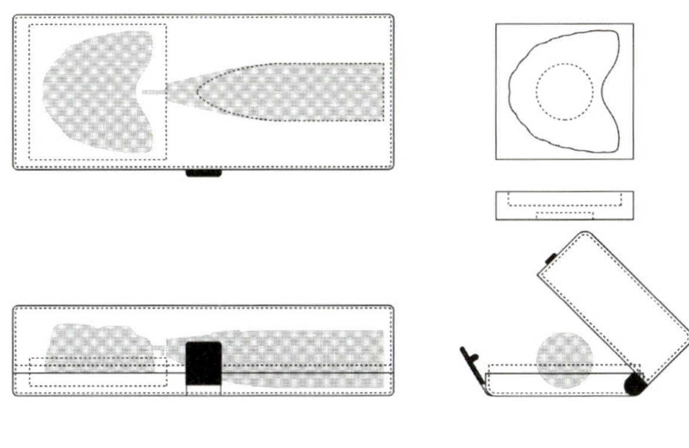

The critic laughs – illustration 1972

The critic laughs – case 1971

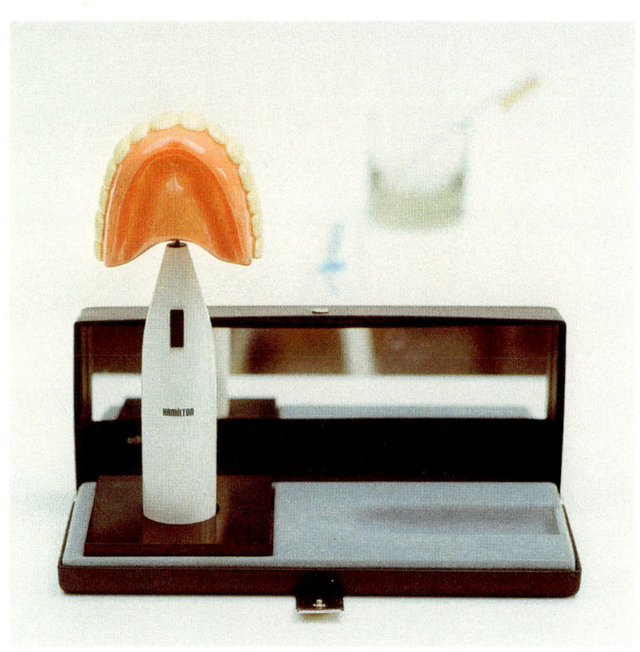

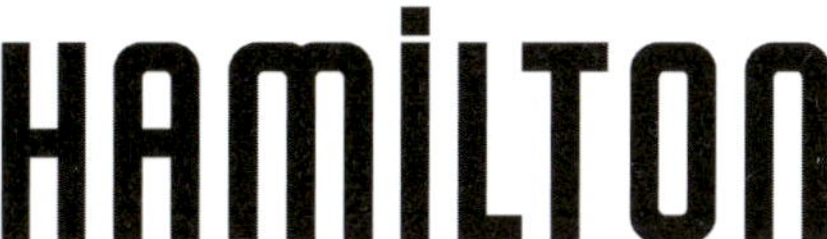

The critic laughs 1971–72

Trade mark 1972

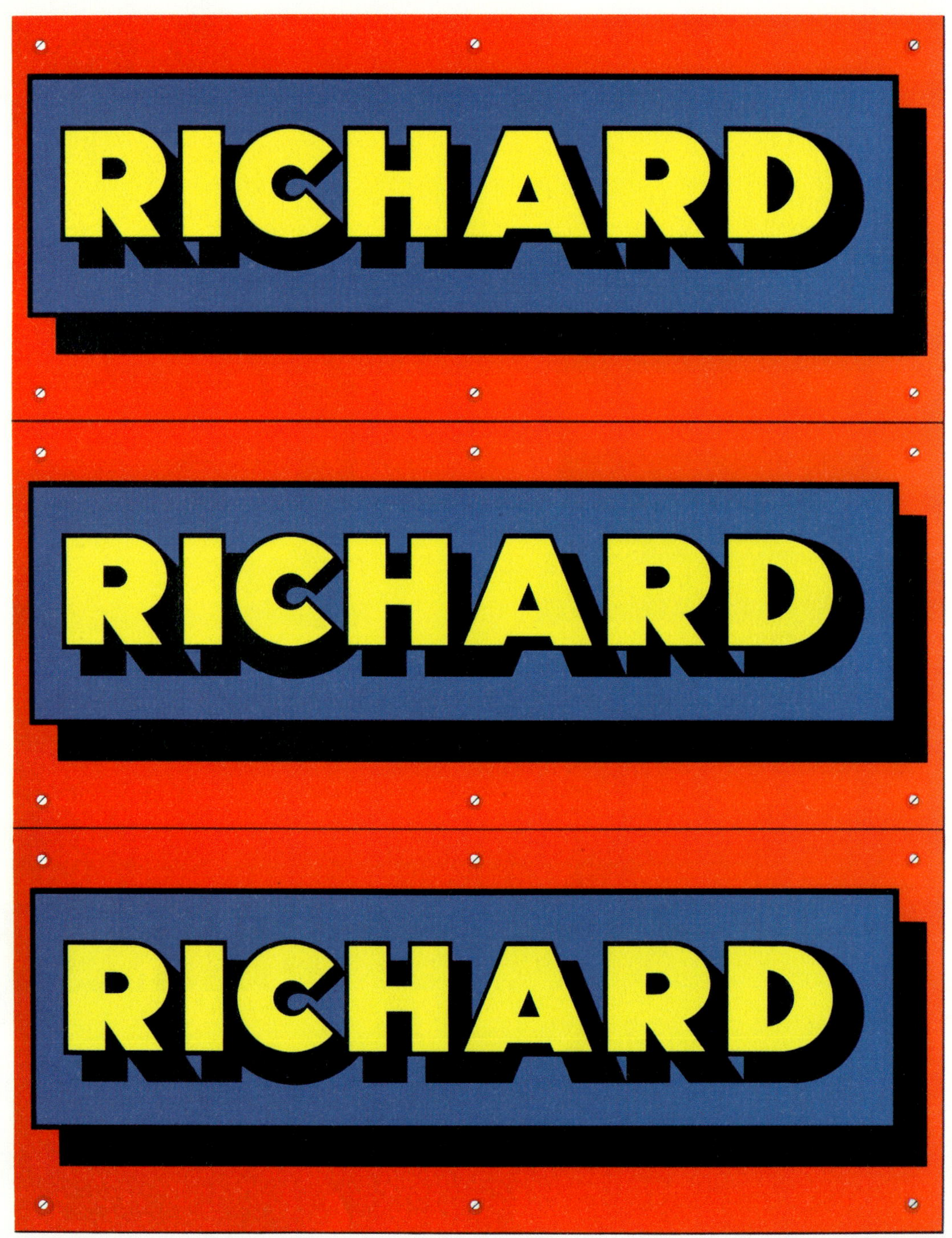

Advertisement 1975

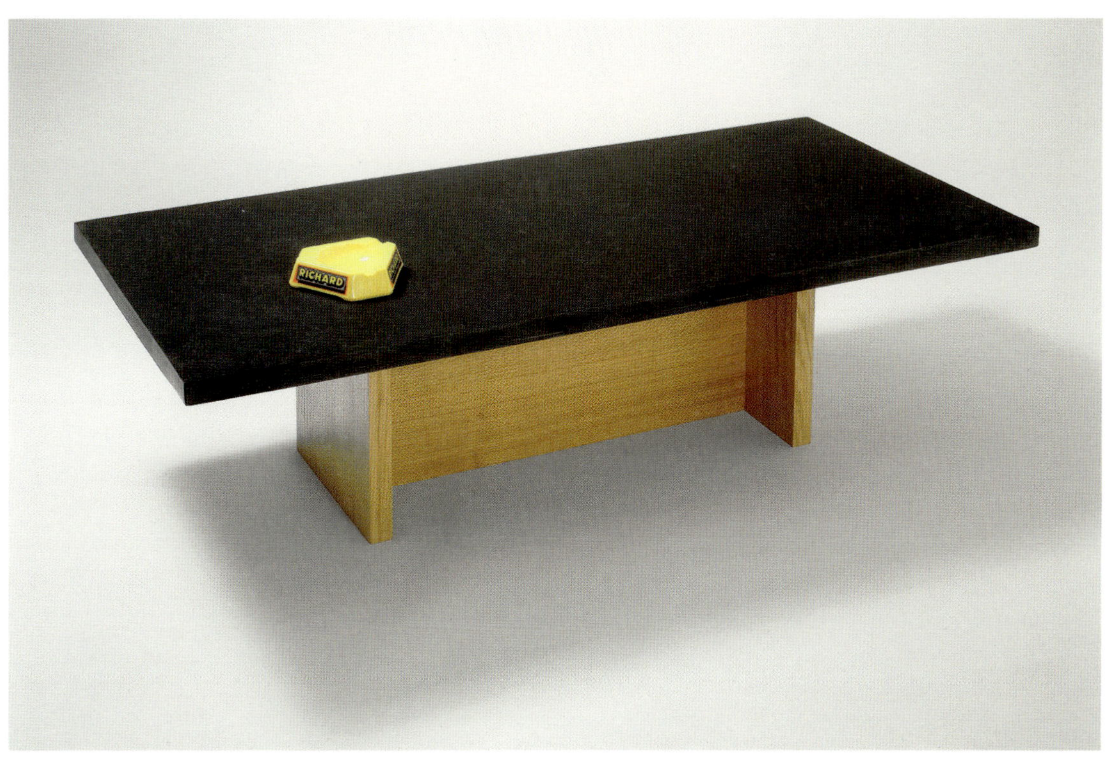

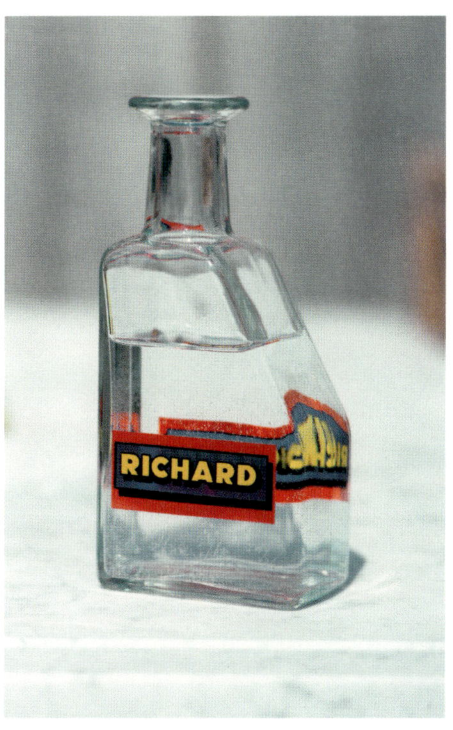

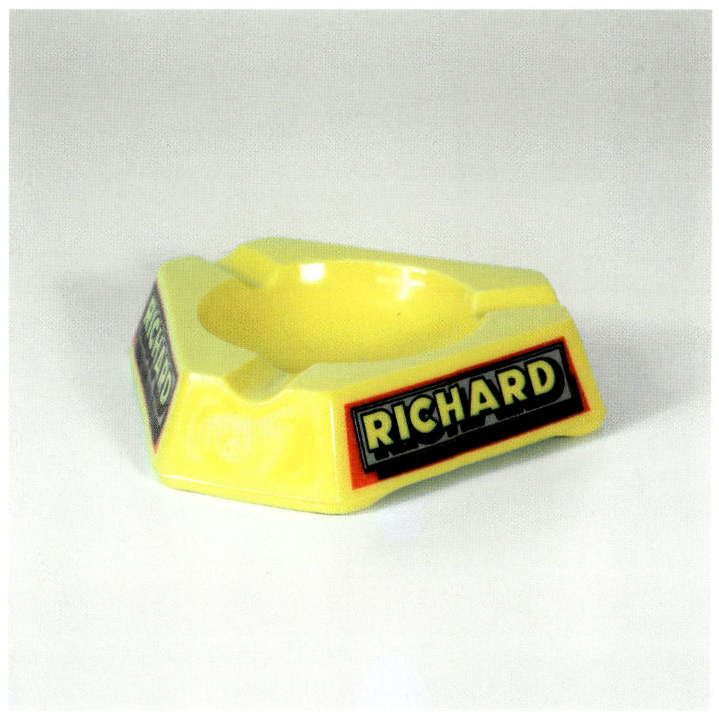

Table with ashtray 2002

Carafe 1978

Ashtray 1979

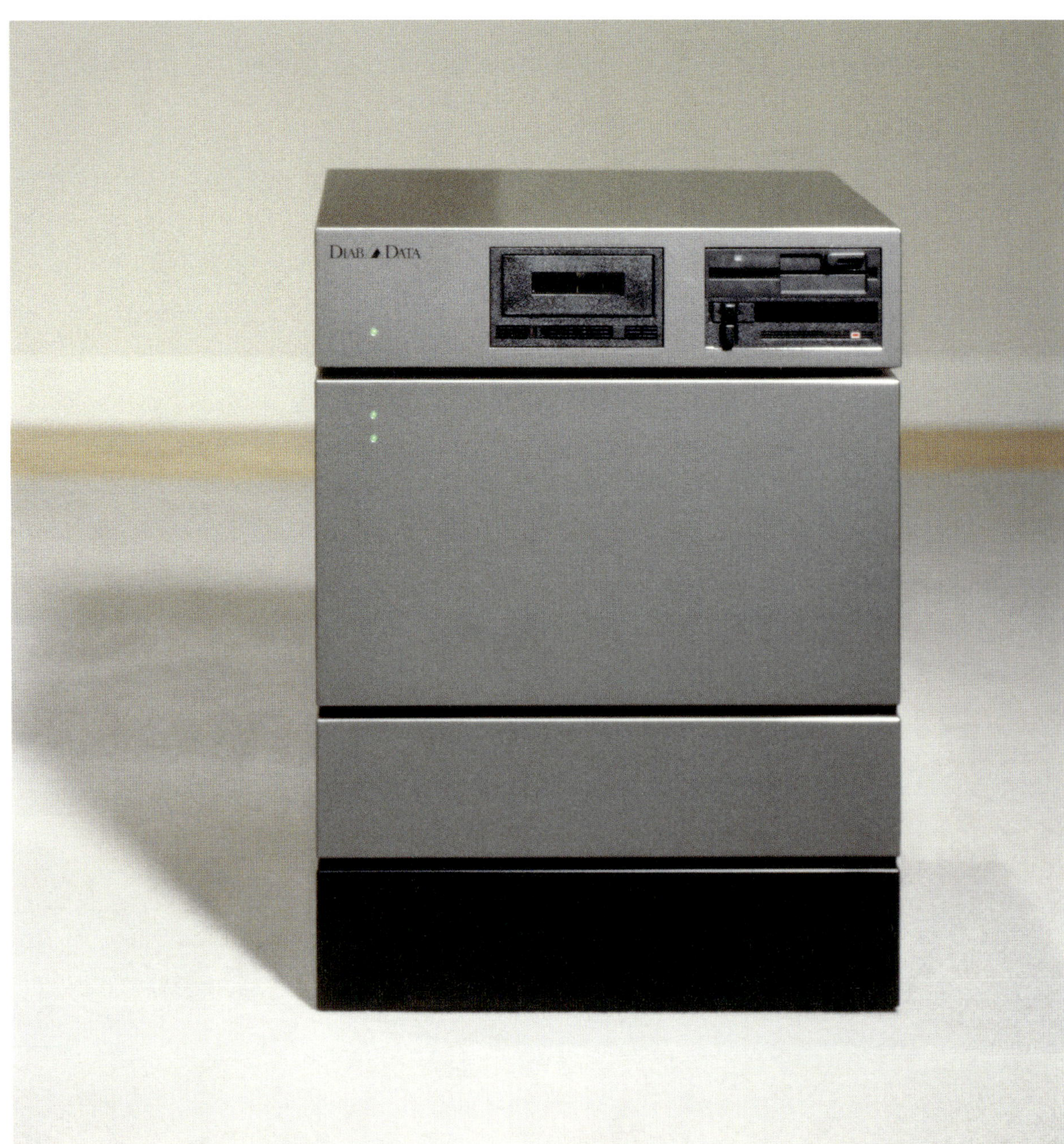

Diab DS-101 computer 1985–89

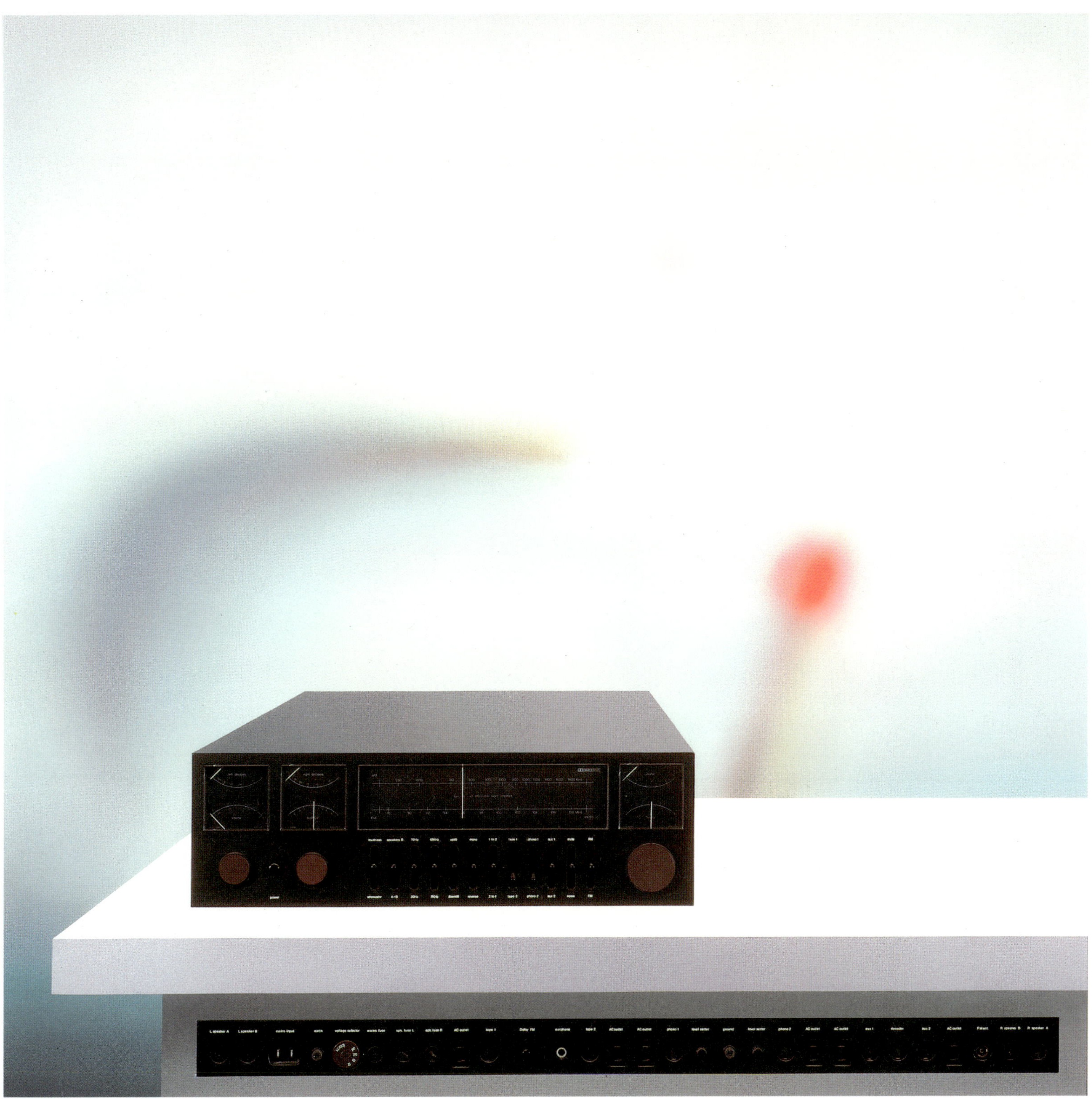

Lux 50 – functioning prototype 1979

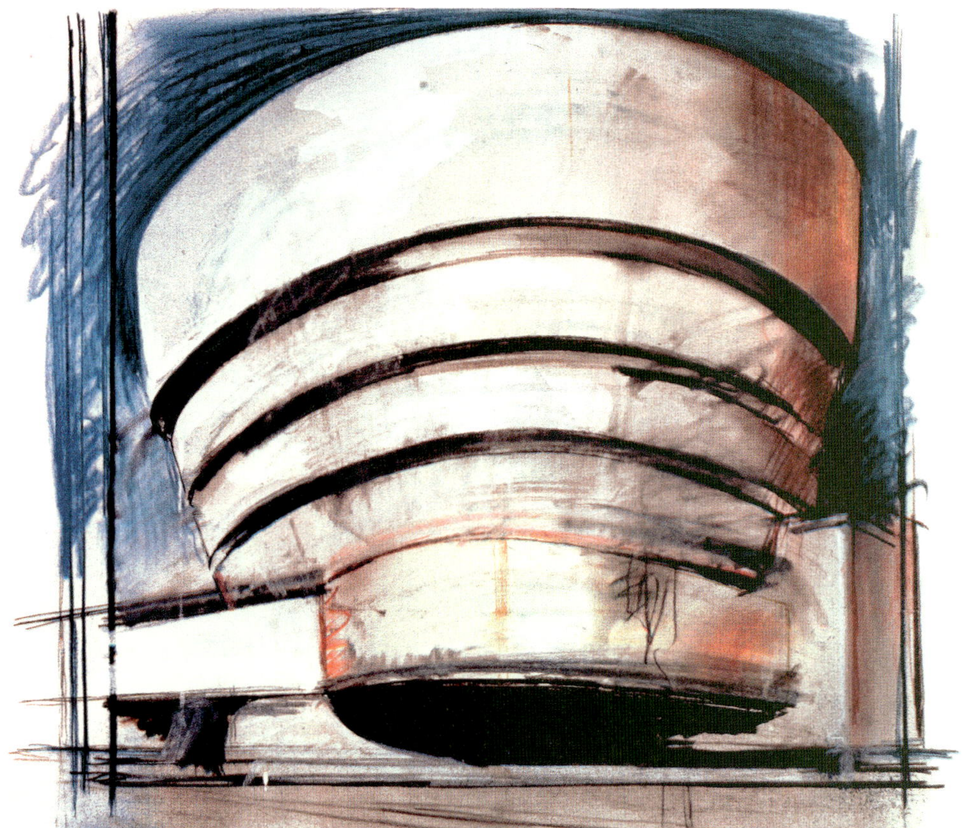

The Solomon R. Guggenheim – architect's visual 1965

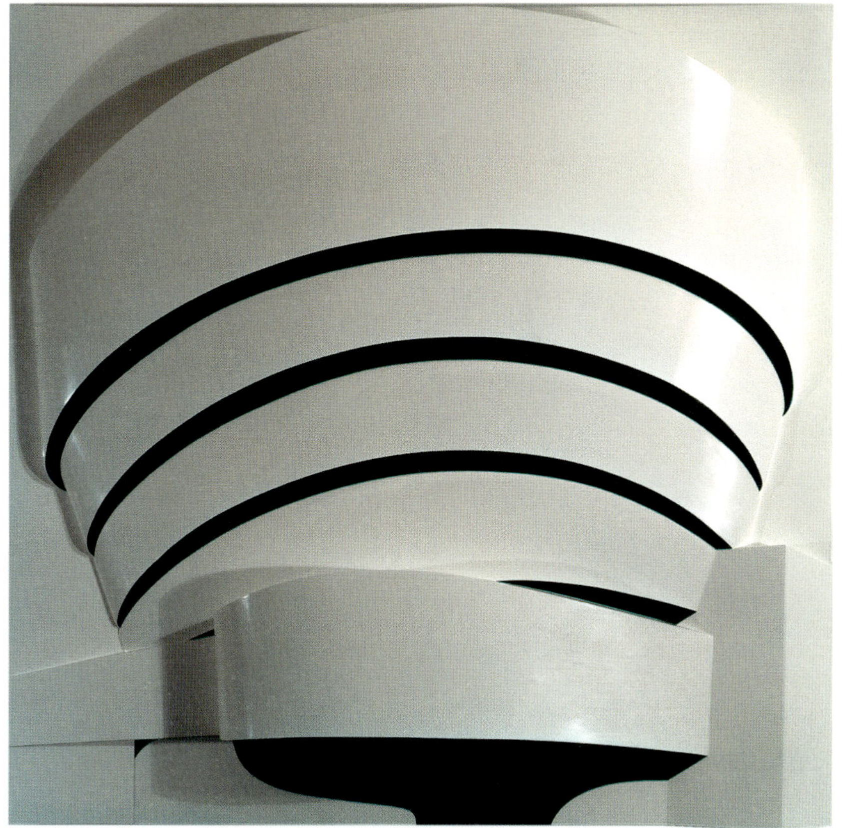

The Solomon R. Guggenheim (Black and White) 1965–66

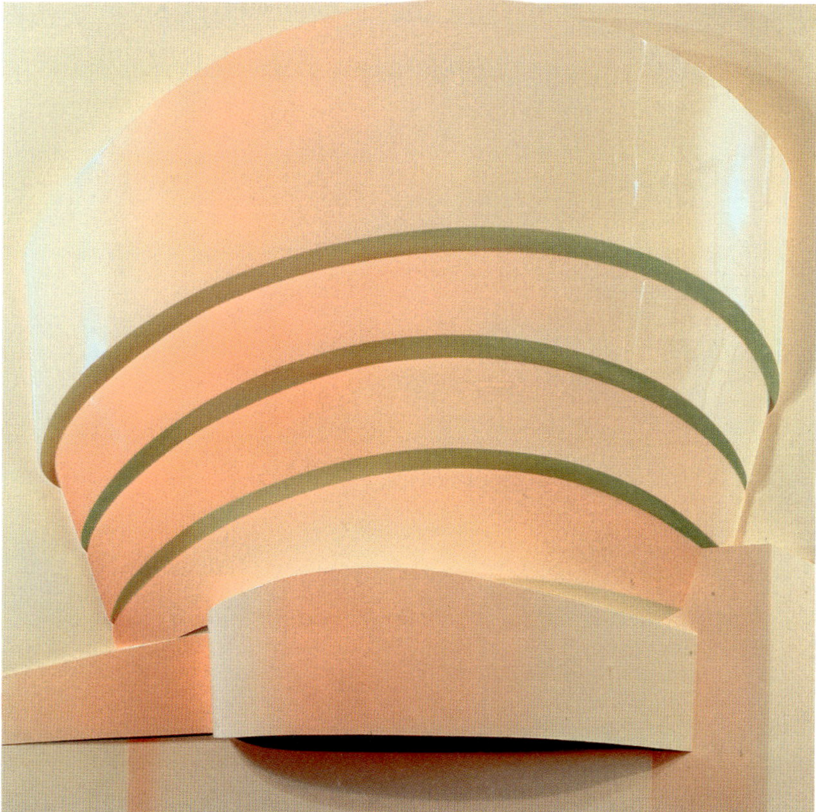

The Solomon R. Guggenheim (Neapolitan) 1965–66

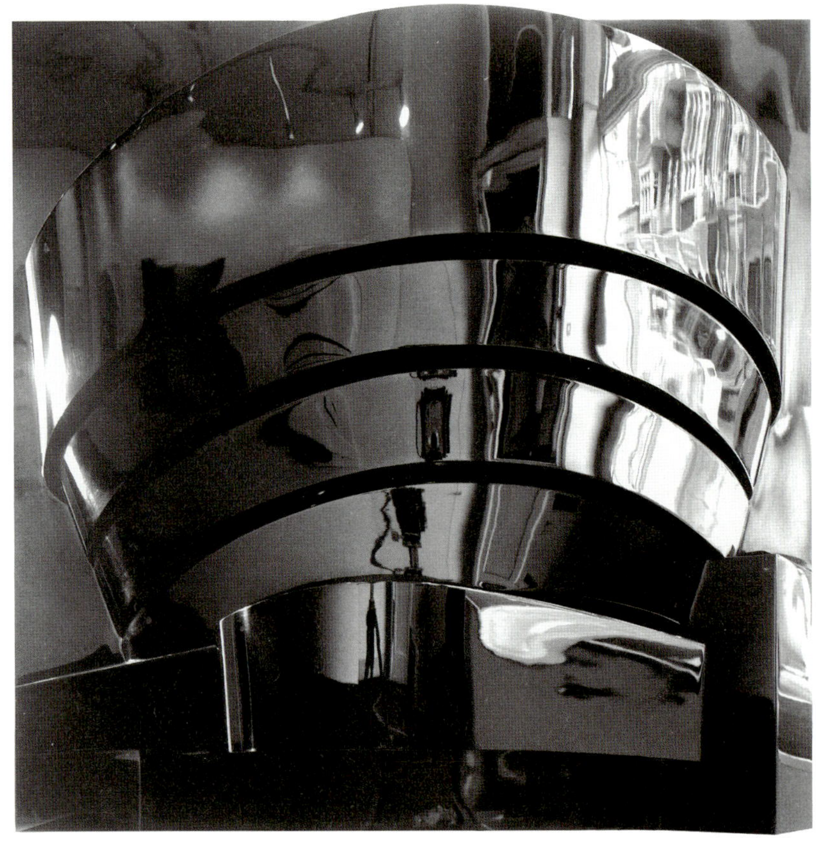

The Solomon R. Guggenheim (Black) 1965–66

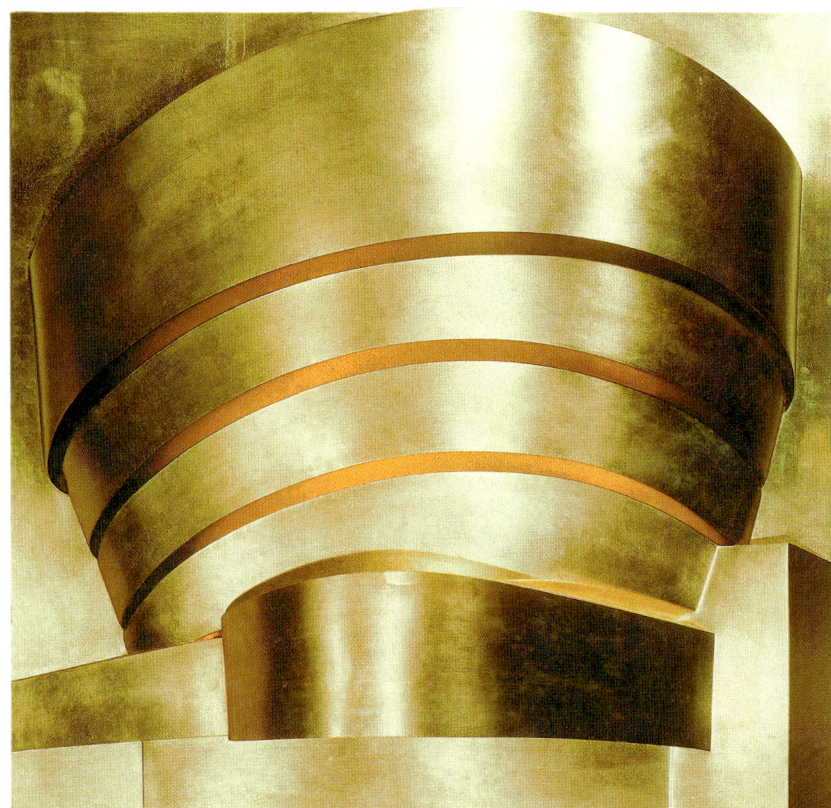

The Solomon R. Guggenheim (Gold) 1965–66

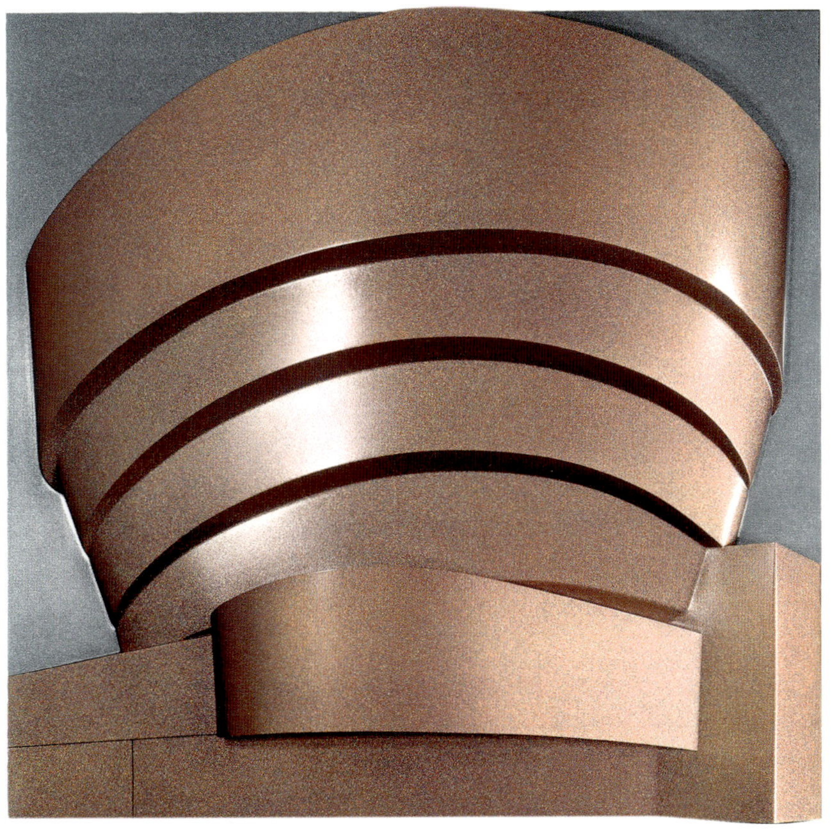

The Solomon R. Guggenheim (Metalflake) 1965–66

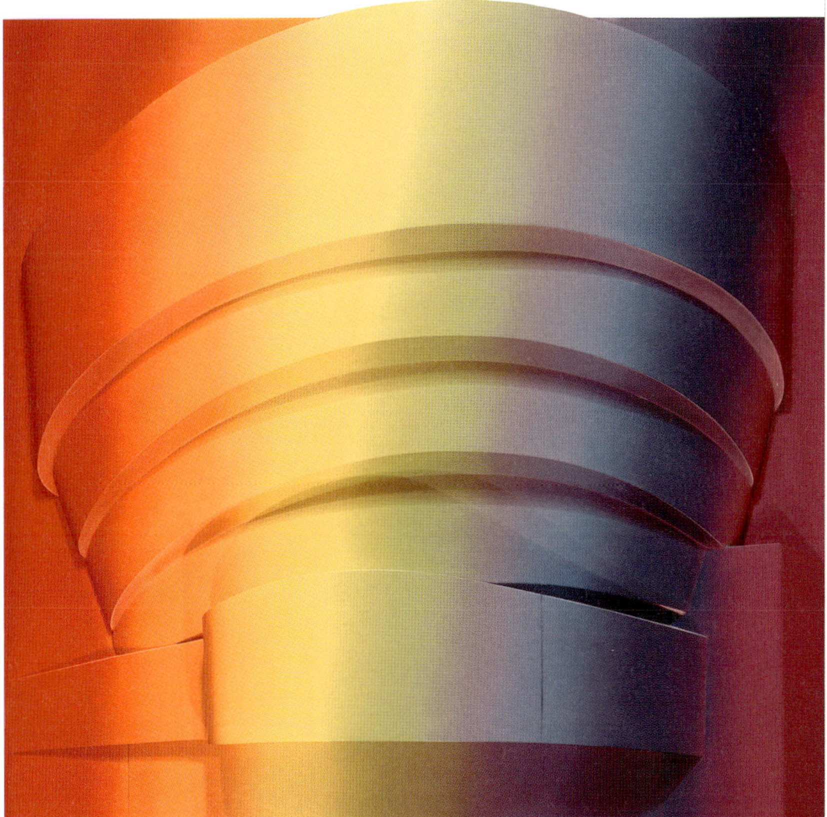

The Solomon R. Guggenheim (Spectrum) 1965–66

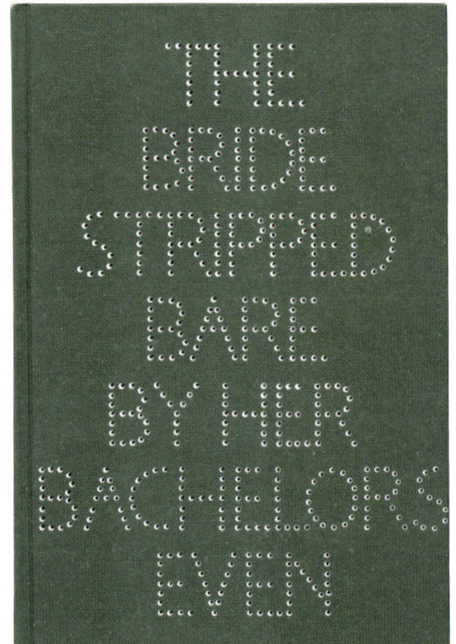

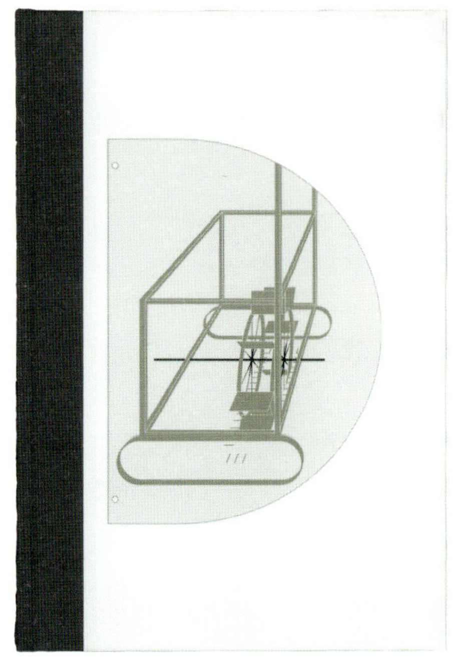

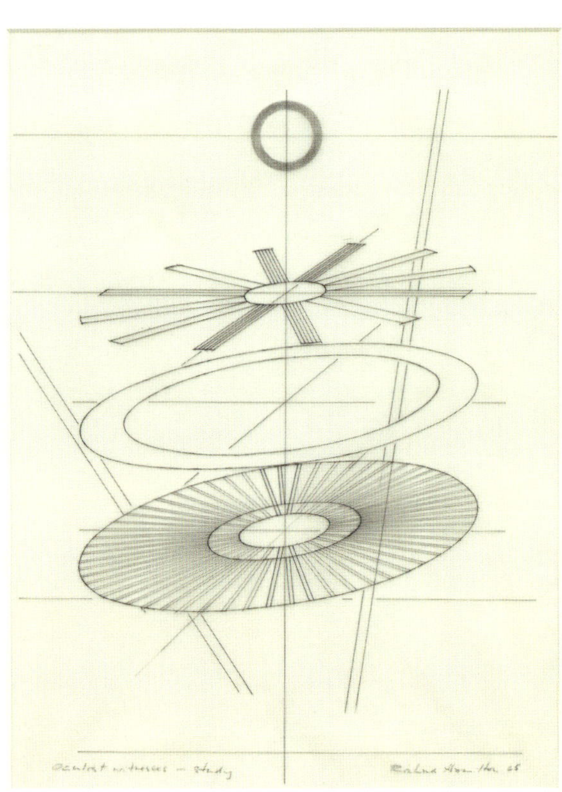

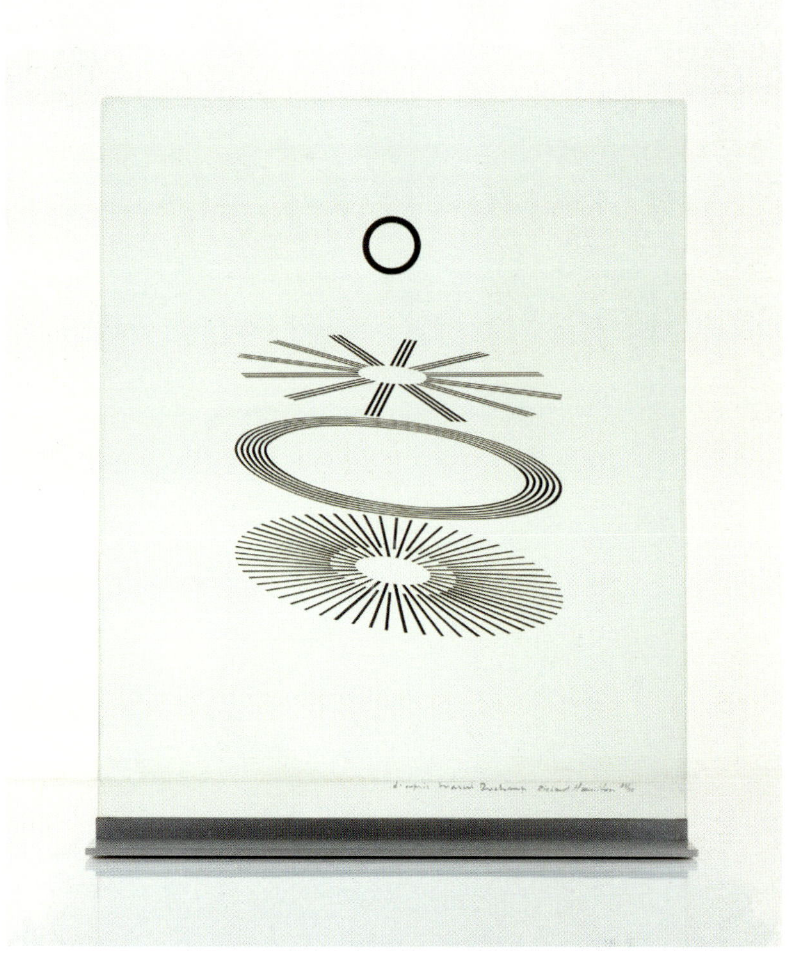

The bride stripped bare by her bachelors, even 1960

Oculist witnesses – study 1965

à l'infinitif 1999

Oculist wltnesses with Marcel Duchamp 1968

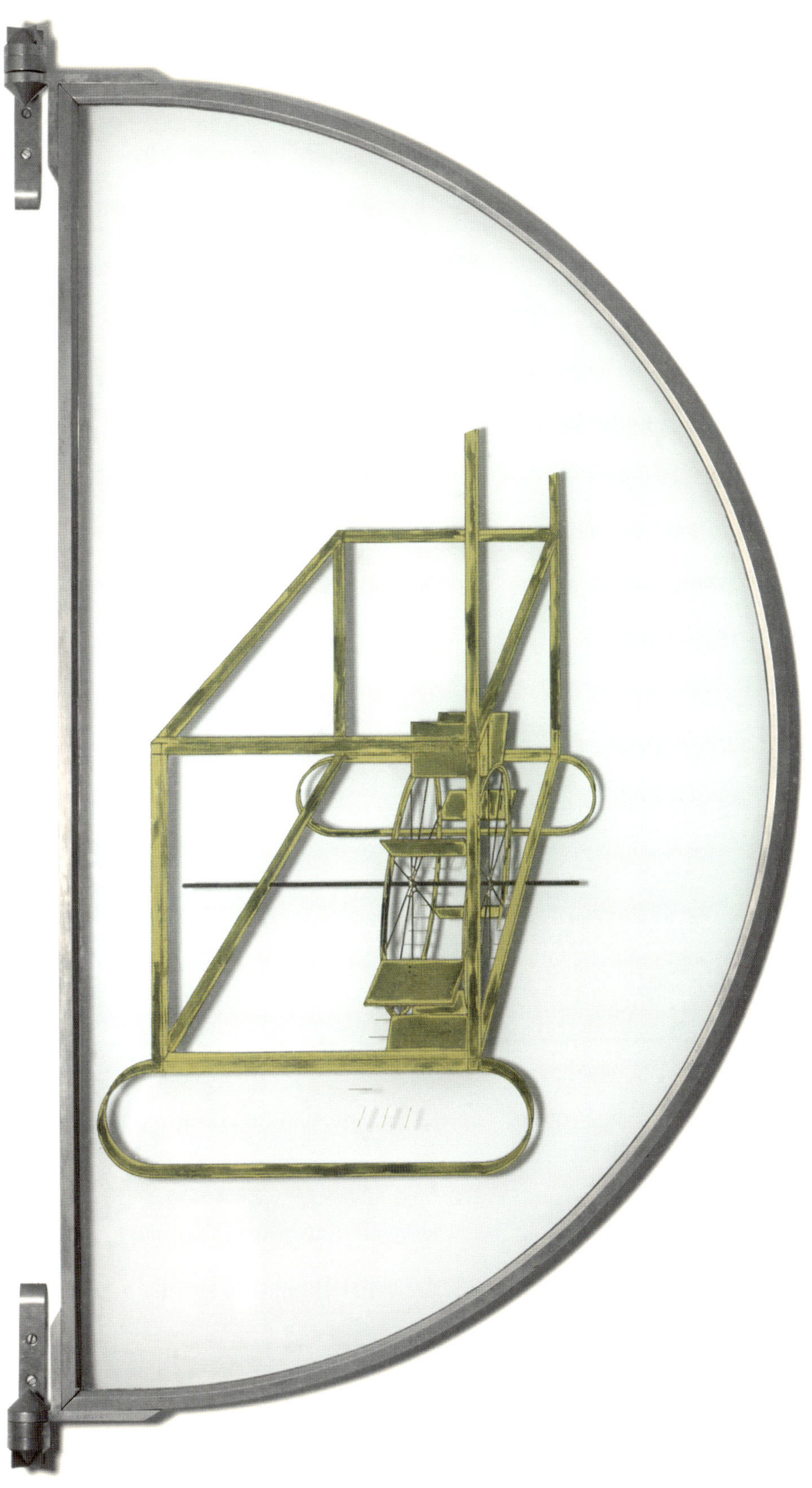

Marcel Duchamp **Glider containing a water mill (in neighbouring metals)**
1913–15, reconstruction by Richard Hamilton 1966

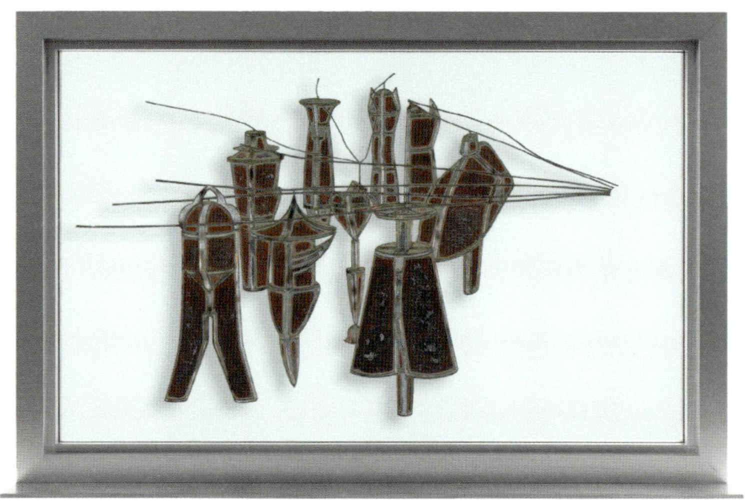

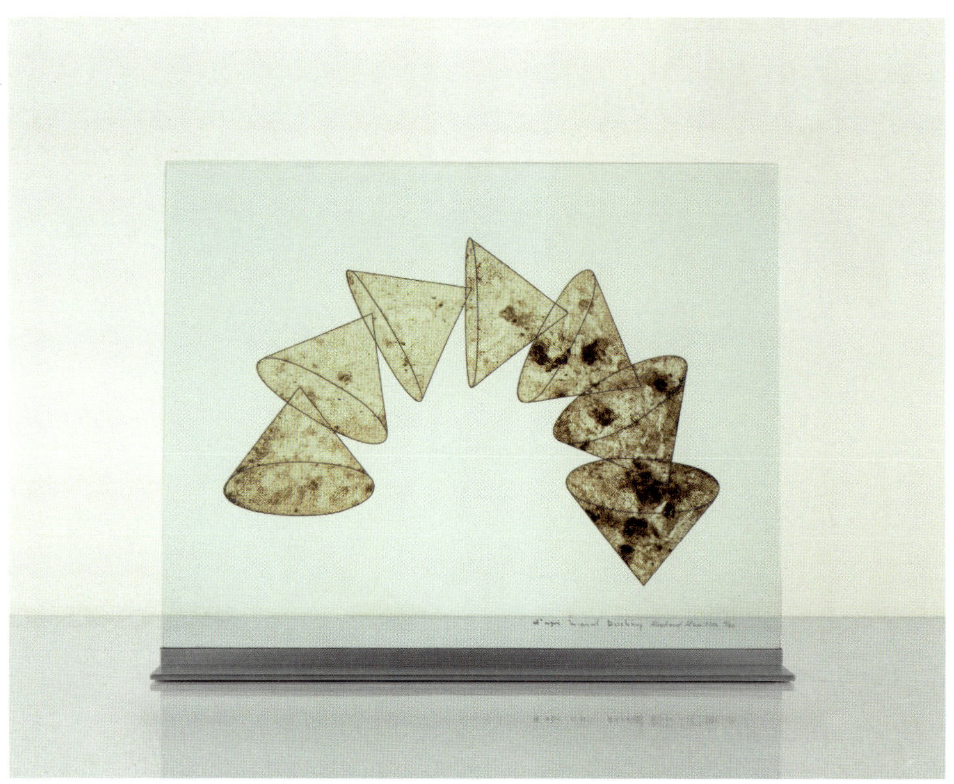

Marcel Duchamp **Nine malic moulds**
1914–15, reconstruction by Richard Hamilton 1965

Sieves with Marcel Duchamp 1971

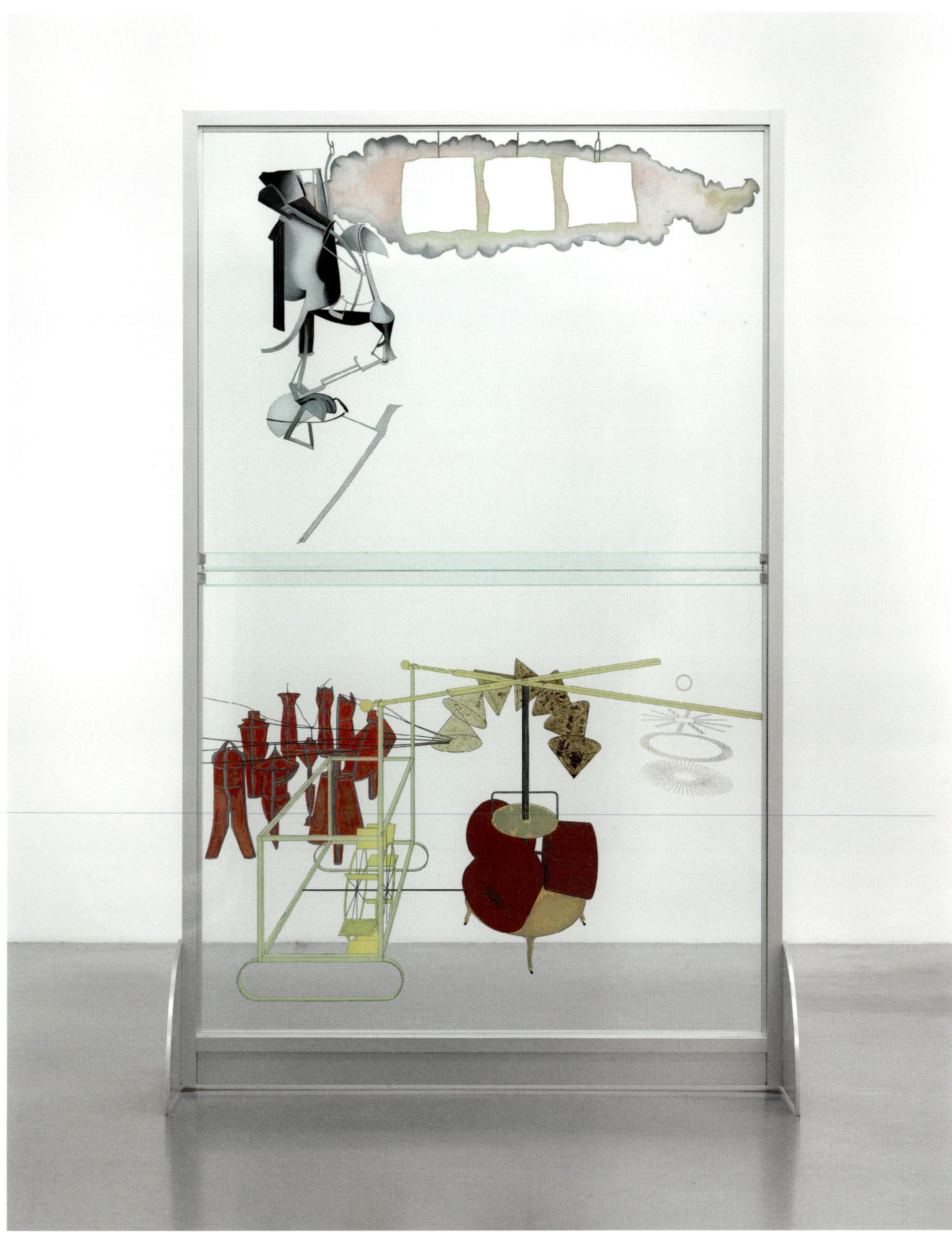

Marcel Duchamp **La Mariée mise à nu par ses célibataires, même** [The Bride Stripped Bare by her Bachelors, Even (The Large Glass)] 1915–23, reconstruction by Richard Hamilton 1965–66, lower panel remade 1985

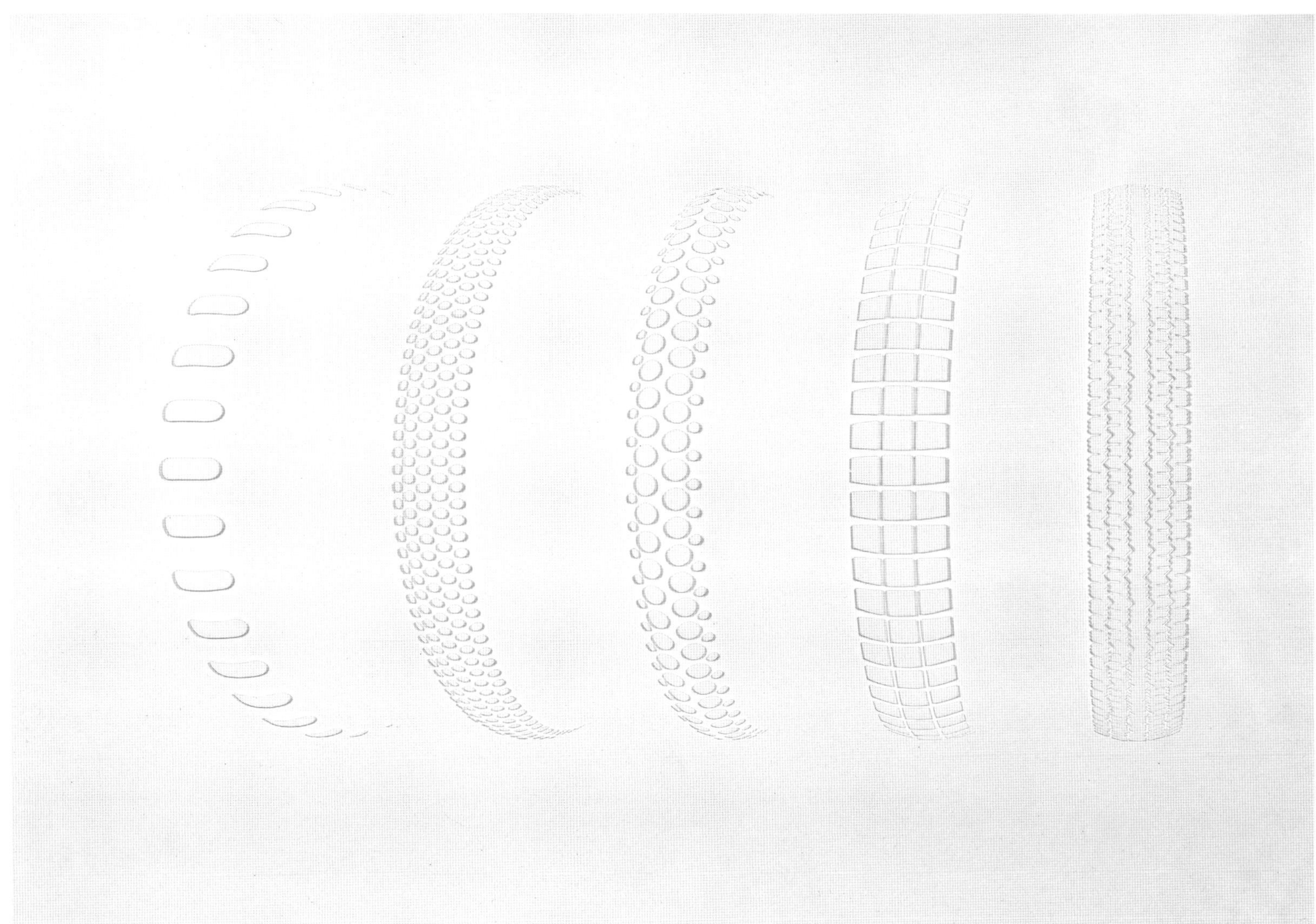

Five Tyres remoulded (relief cast in white silicone elastomer) 1971

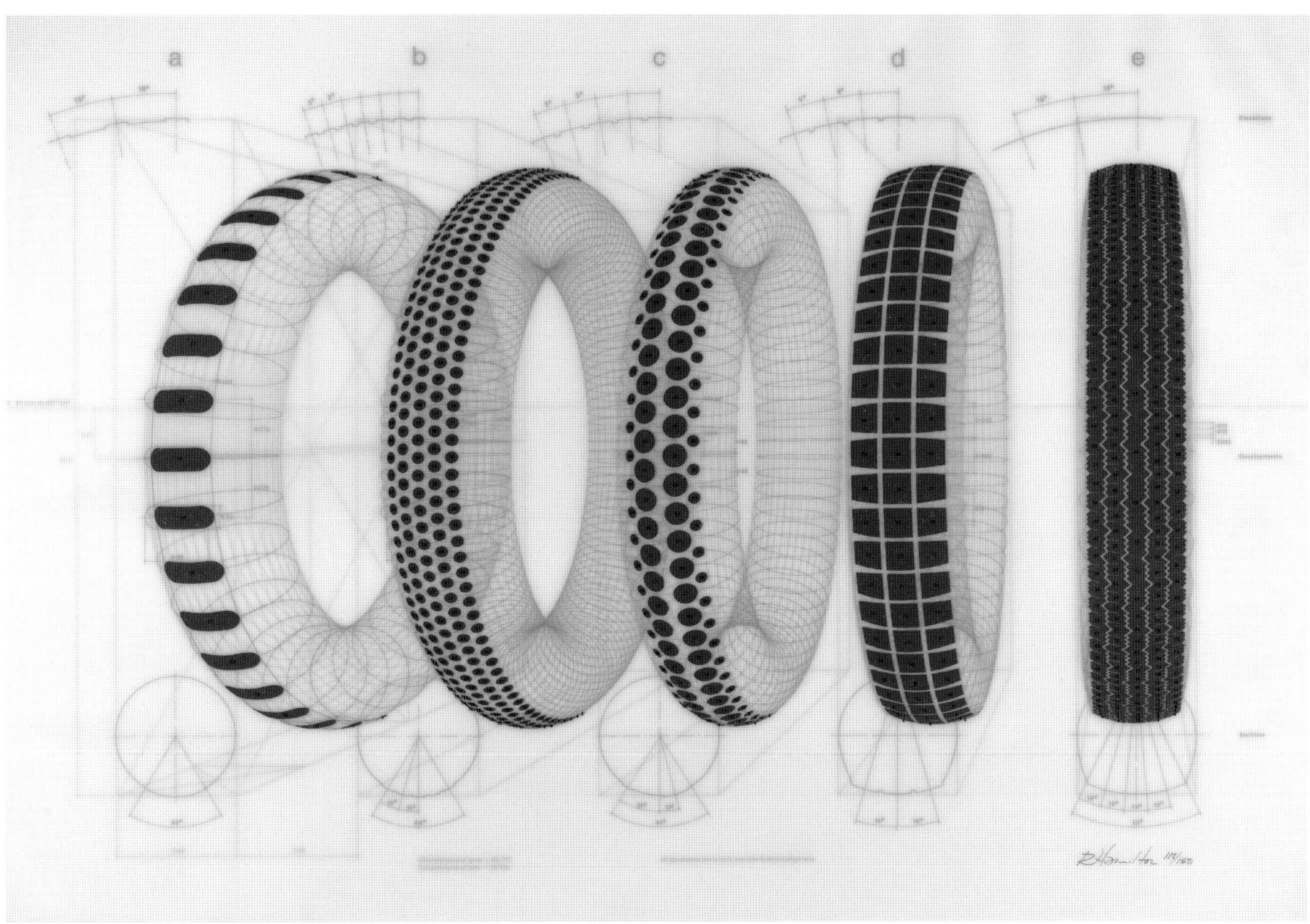

Five Tyres remoulded (porfolio) 1971

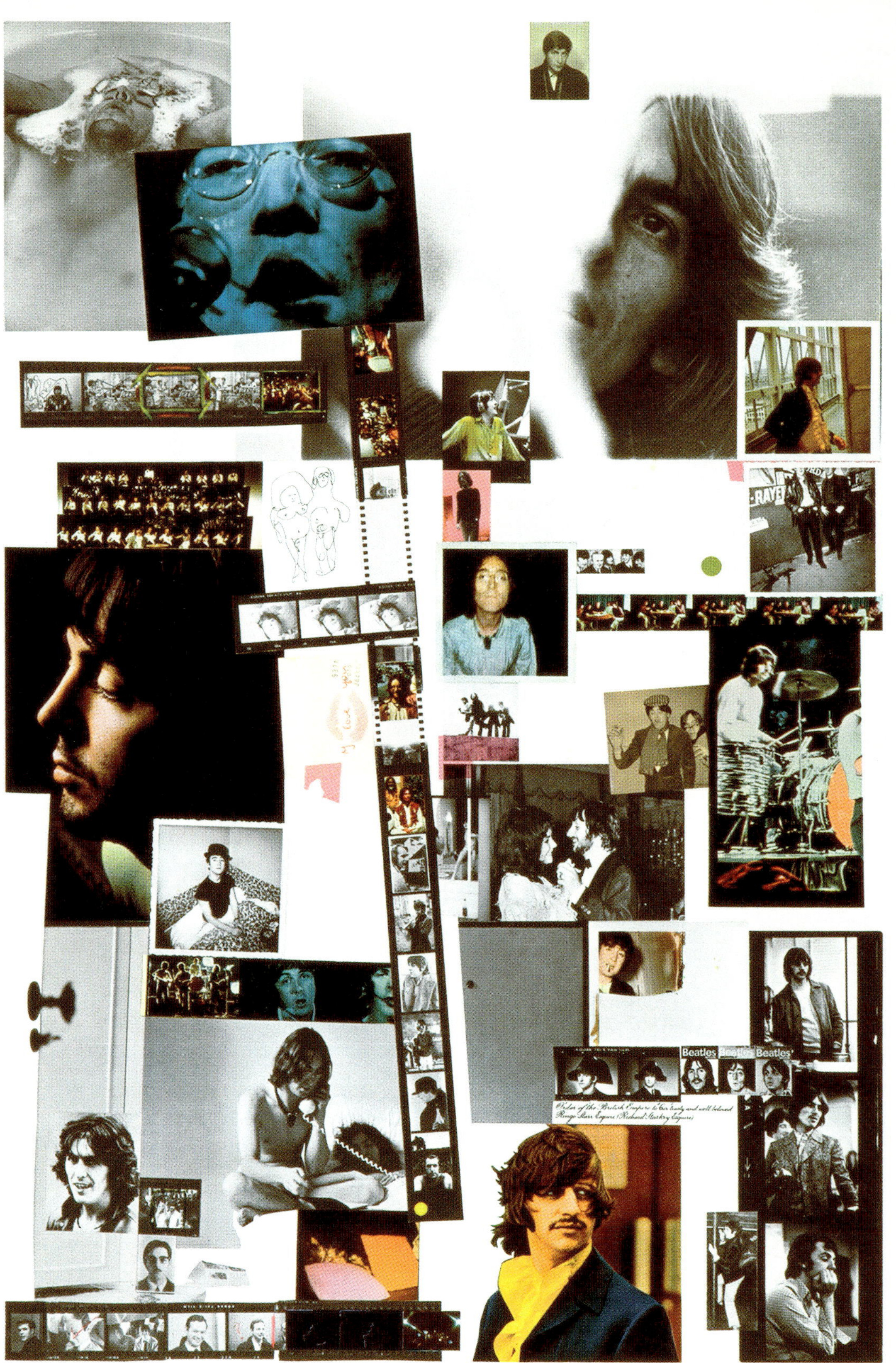

The Beatles 1968

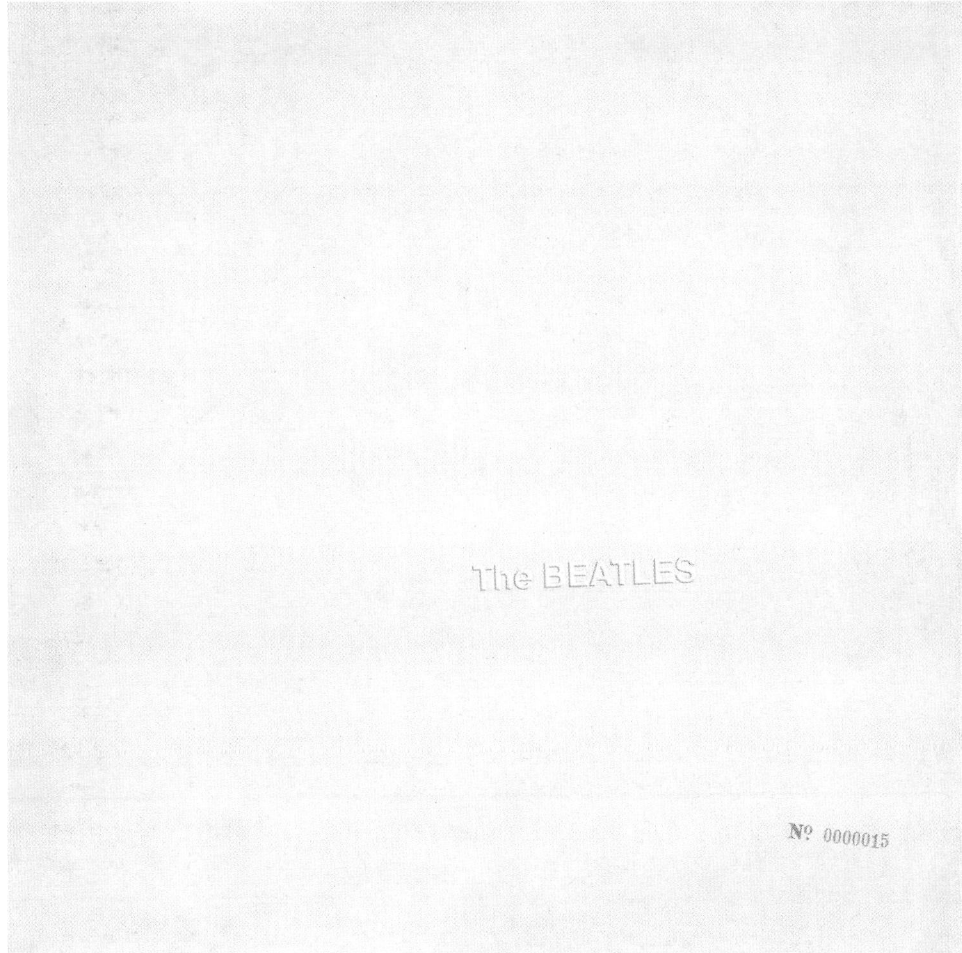

The Beatles 1968

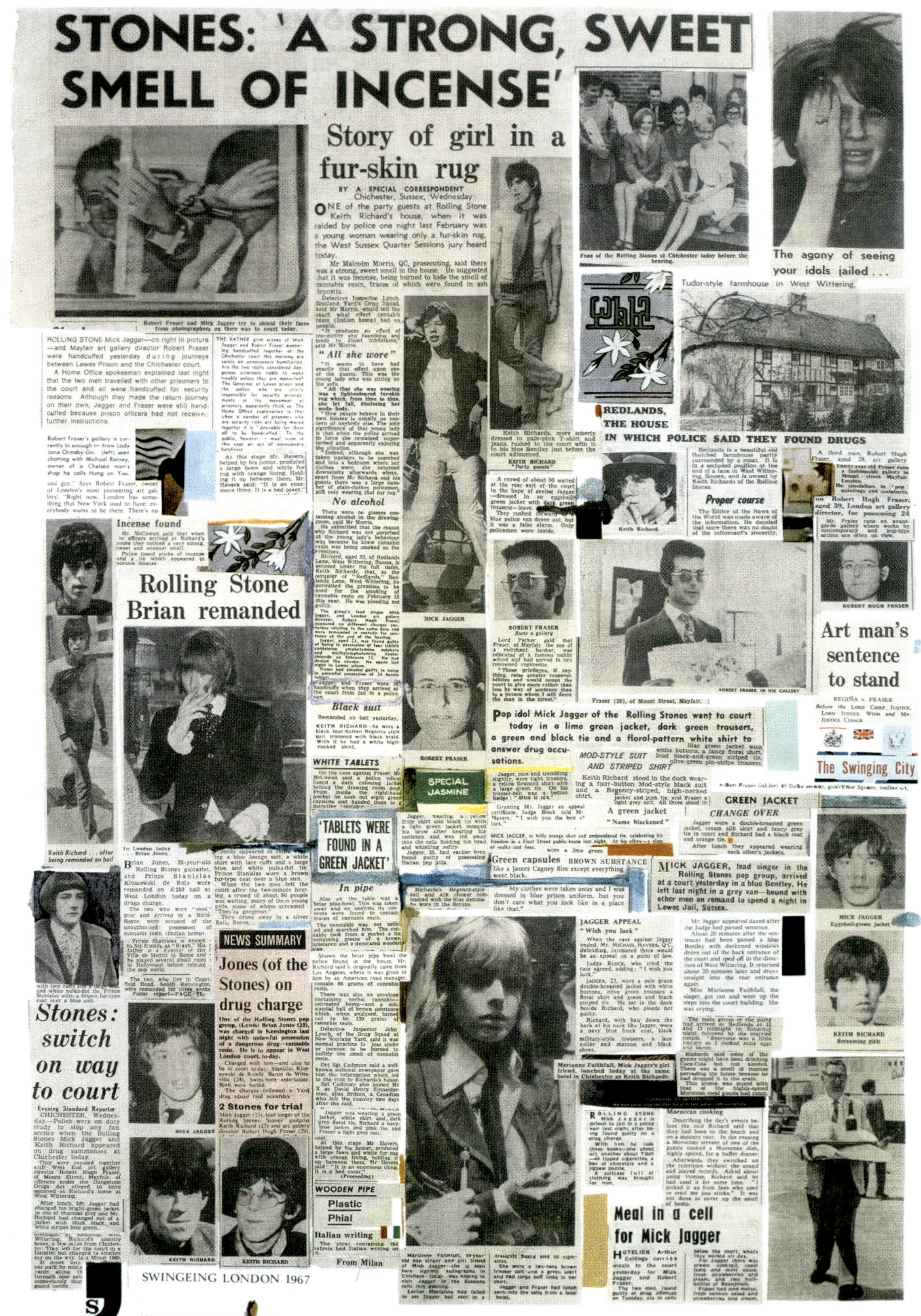

Swingeing London 67 – poster 1968

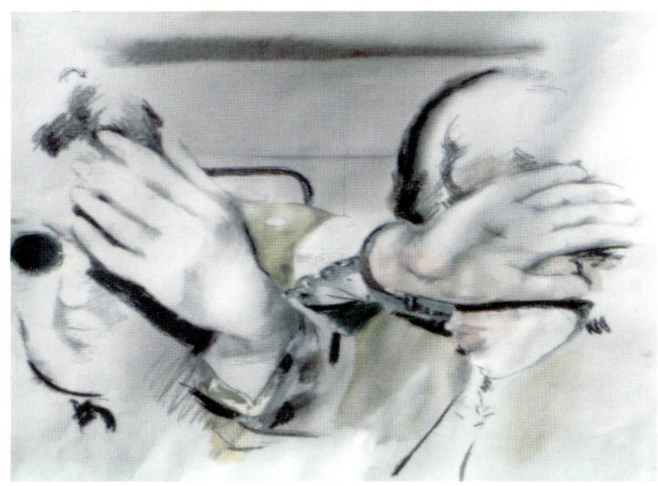

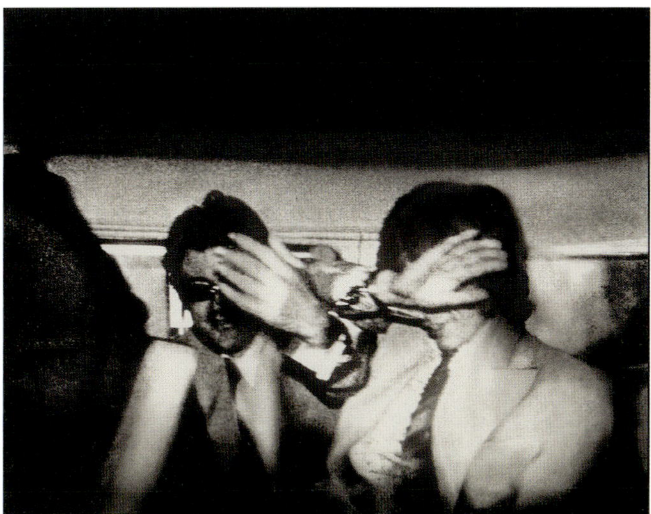

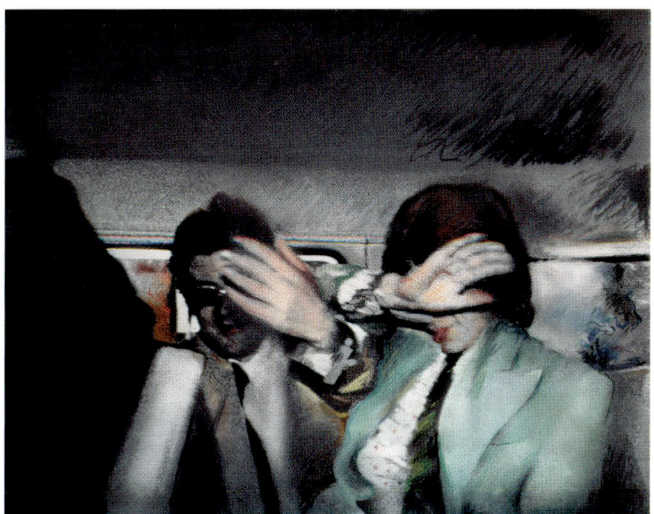

Swingeing London 67 – sketch 1968

Swingeing London 67 – working drawing 1968

Swingeing London 67 – screen print 1969

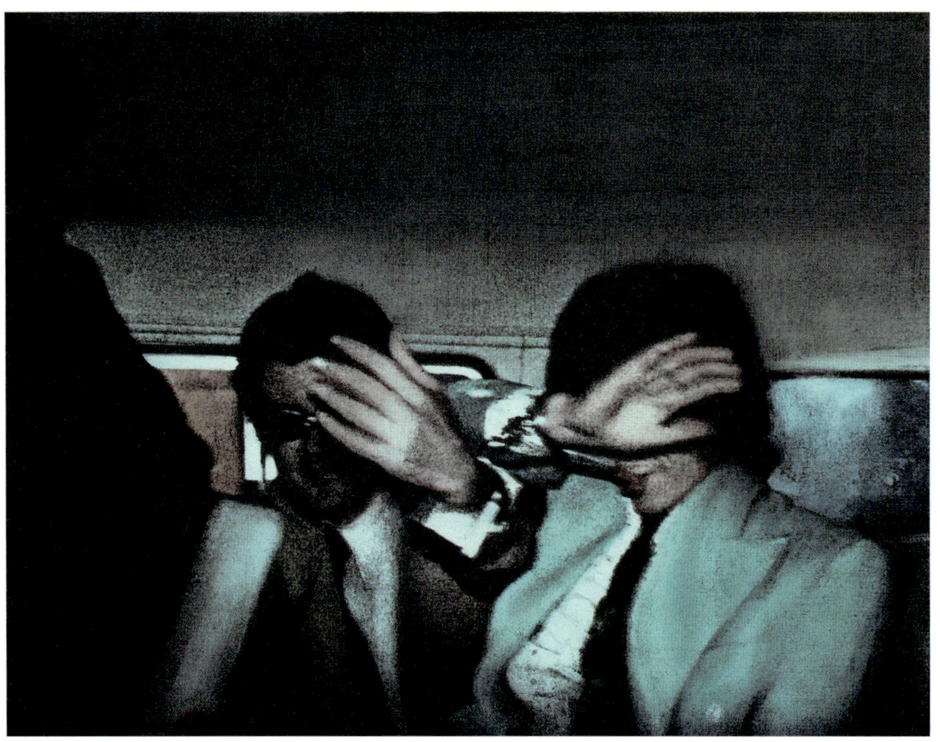

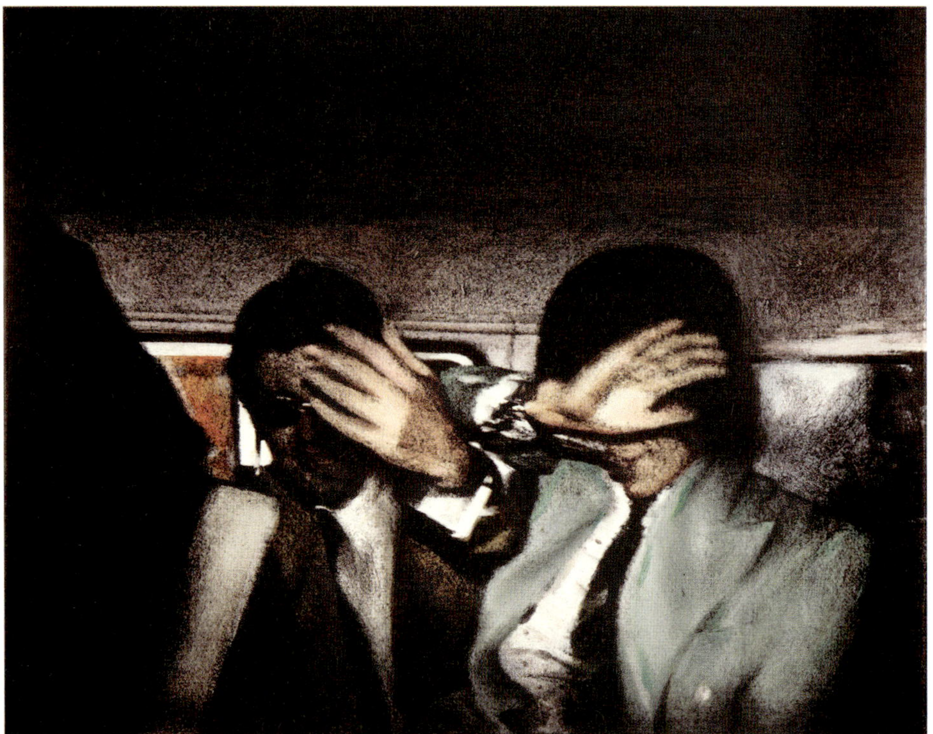

Swingeing London 67 (a) 1968–69
Swingeing London 67 (b) 1968–69

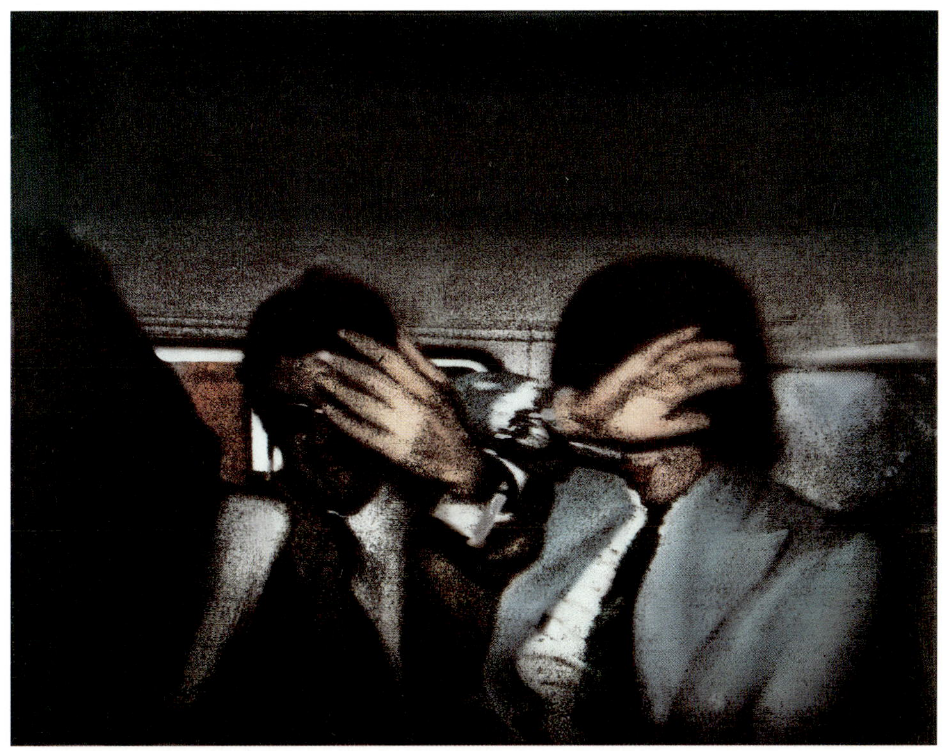

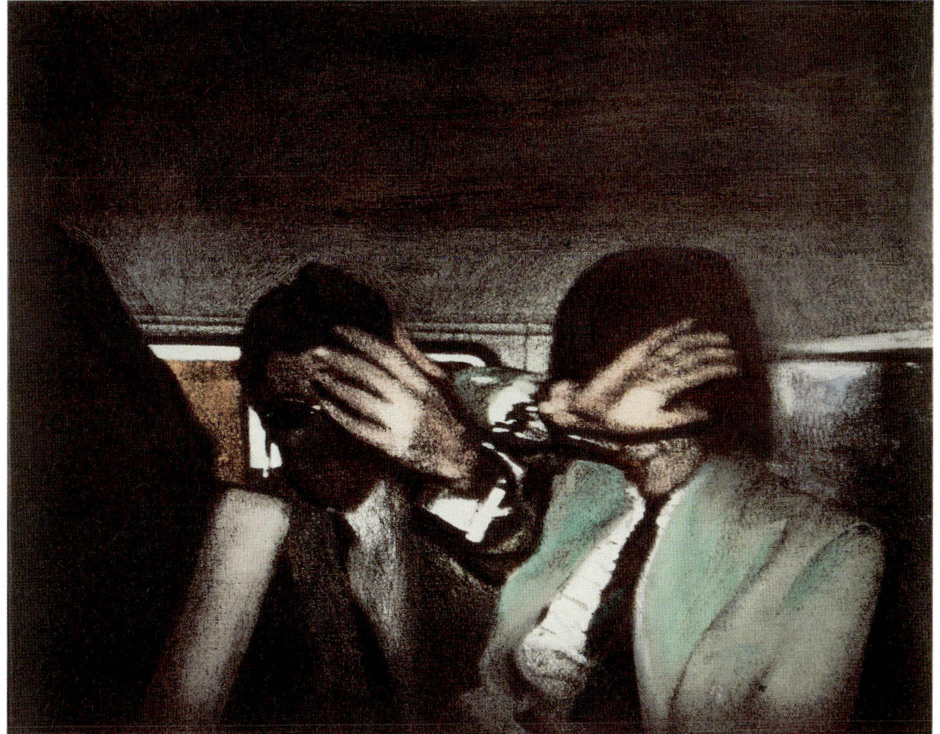

Swingeing London 67 (c) 1968–69
Swingeing London 67 (d) 1968–69

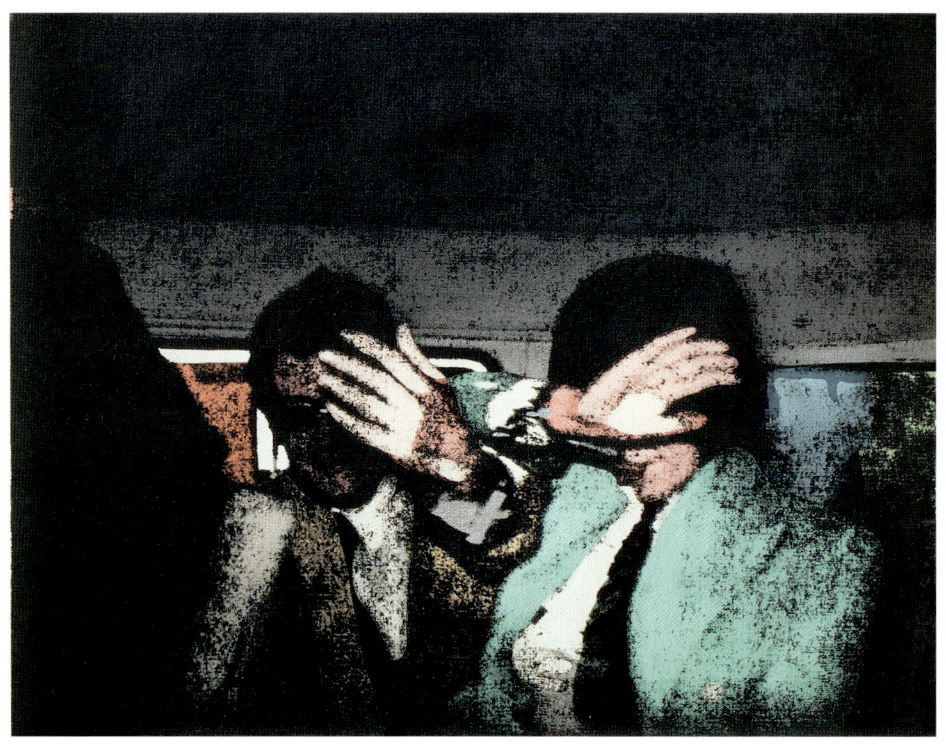

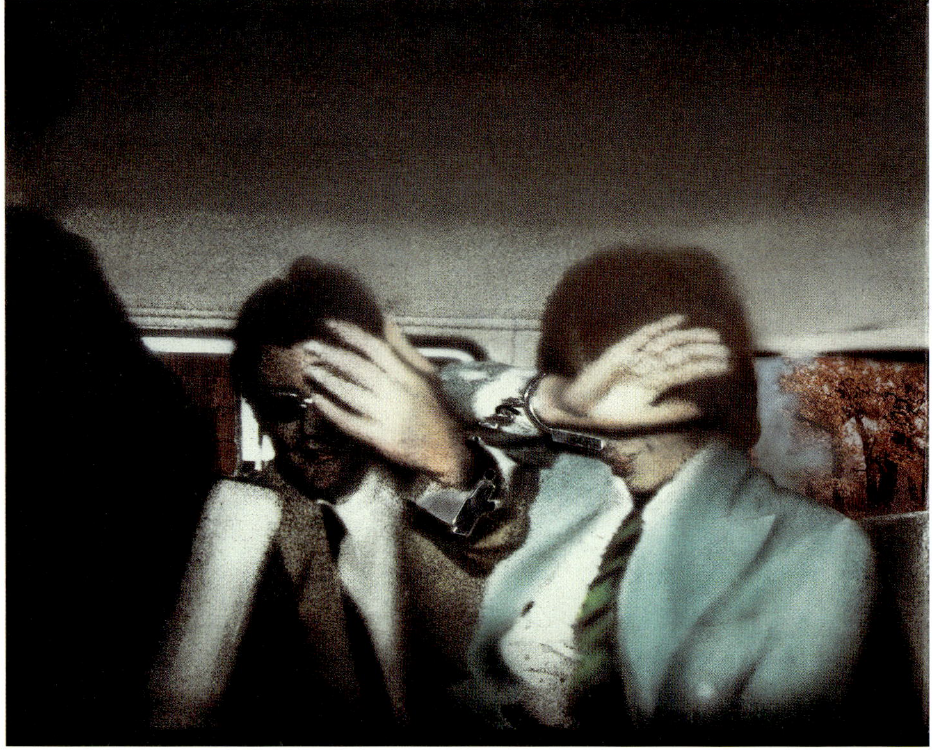

Swingeing London 67 (e) 1968–69

Swingeing London 67 (f) 1968–69

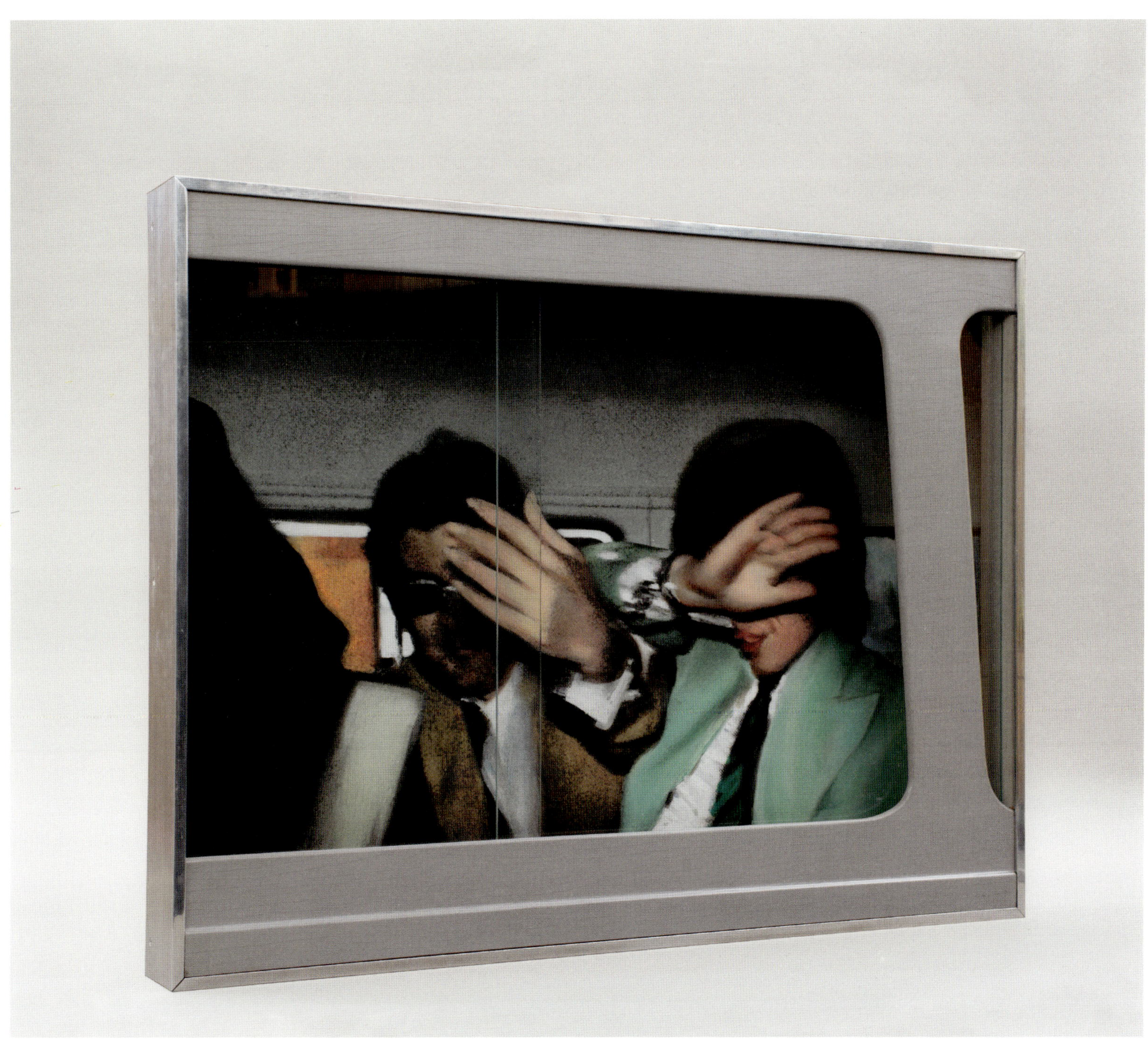

Swingeing London 67 1968

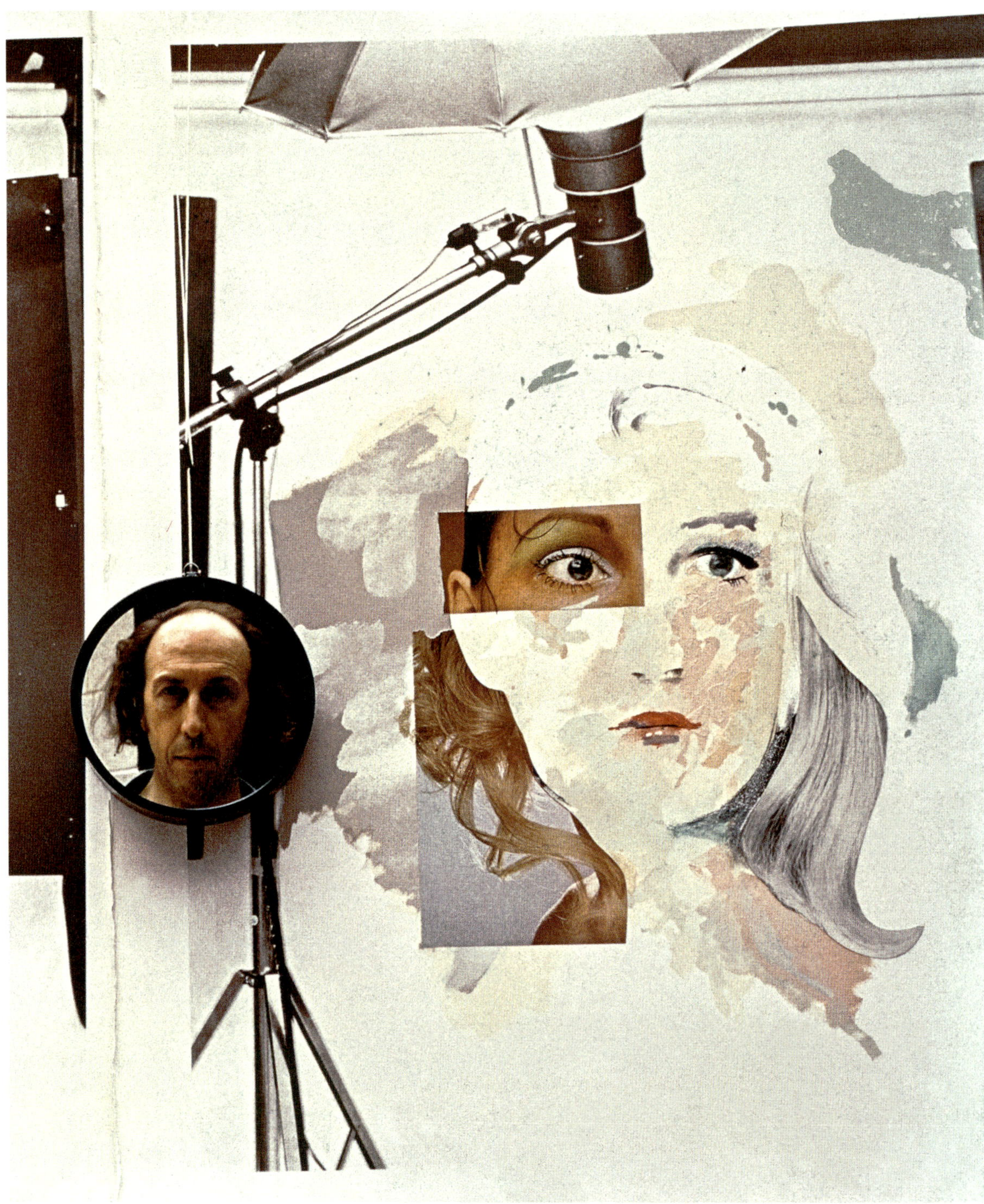

Hamilton with *Fashion-plate (cosmetic study II)* 1969

The Hamilton Test

Hal Foster

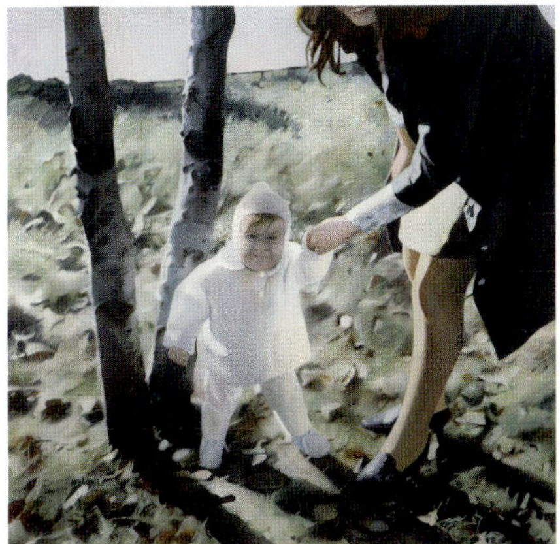

fig. 1
Mother and child, 1984
Oil on canvas
Private collection

Richard Hamilton based *Mother and child* (1984–85) [fig. 1] on a photograph given to him by a young printer in Milan in 1969. Due to the language barrier, the two men found it difficult to communicate until the Italian showed the Englishman a snapshot of his wife and child in a park, a quintessential image of the nuclear family, with the father implied in the scene as photographer. For reasons not clear to Hamilton, he kept the photo in his studio for fifteen years, "until it began to assume its place among the genres as a 'Mother and child'," at which point he adapted it as a painting.[1] Bending over, the mother supports her child by the hand (its gender is not definite, but it seems to be a boy). Bundled up in white, the boy smiles up at his father, who, focused down on his son, lops off the top of his wife. It is a happy scene nonetheless: the upright son is triumphal, perhaps on the verge of his first step; though sidelined, the mother beams too; and the proud father captures the moment with his camera.

I begin this essay on the rapport between painting and photography in Hamilton with this work because it is especially telling of this aspect of his practice. A lowly snapshot "assumes its place among the genres" of high art, but retains its photographic quality as it does so: the spontaneity of the snap is preserved, and even the painterly brushiness of the high grass mottled by the harsh light of the brisk day can be read as photographic overexposure. By this point in his career Hamilton had already produced, out of ephemeral images like this one, portraits, landscapes, still lifes and interiors, among other genres. On this score, of course, "mother and child" is a central category of art history as well as family albums: here Hamilton calls up Impressionist predecessors such as Mary Cassatt and Berthe Morisot, who featured intimate scenes of domestic life, and the sacred type of Madonna and Child is distantly evoked too. On the one hand, then, Hamilton seizes on a transitory scene, and so observes a primary criterion for Pop sources as presented in his famous letter of 1957 to the architects Alison and Peter Smithson.[2] On the other hand, he transforms this mundane moment into a mnemonic image, even an iconic one, with its own art-historical resonance.

In this double move Hamilton is also true to the great formula concerning the relation of modern art to modern life articulated by Baudelaire in 1863: "By 'modernity'," the poet wrote, "I mean the ephemeral, the fugitive, the contingent, the half of art whose other half is the eternal and the immutable."[3] "I would like to think of my purpose," Hamilton stated a century later in an echo of Baudelaire, "as a search for what is epic in everyday objects and everyday attitudes."[4] Obviously, the terms of this modern dialectic of art and life had changed in the interim, especially with new developments in media technology, and Hamilton was very alert to these shifts in techniques of representation. Such techniques of representation are also techniques of subject-formation, and he was always guided by the insight, shared by his Pop colleagues, that our acculturation in a consumerist society operates through mass images more than any other form. At the same time *Mother and child* evokes a stage in subject-formation that is not culturally specific, at least according to Lacanian psychoanalysis, and that is the fabled "mirror stage" in which the infant, supported by the

1. Richard Morphet (ed.), *Richard Hamilton* (London: Tate Gallery, 1992), 178. Hamilton had a strong hand in the writing of these catalogue notes for the 1992 retrospective at the Tate.
2. "Pop Art is: Popular (designed for a mass audience), Transient (short-term solution), Expendable (easily forgotten)…" See Richard Hamilton, *Collected Words 1953–1982* (London: Thames and Hudson, 1982), 28.
3. Charles Baudelaire, "The Painter of Modern Life," in *The Painter of Modern Life and Other Essays,* trans. and ed. Jonathan Mayne (London: Phaidon Press, 1964).
4. Hamilton, *Collected Words,* 37.

mother, first delights in the imagistic coherence of its upright body. Importantly, however, the painting suggests that this stage occurs in the interest of the father: the boy looks not at his reflection, much less at his mother (who functions only as a prop), but at the *pater familias* with the camera (might the child already imagine his reflection there?). And in turn the father exchanges the photo of this male encounter, the token of this patriarchal initiation, with another man, Hamilton, who refashions it in painting for our analysis. For all the happy smiles in the snapshot, then, and for all the sensuous plenitude of the infantile world conveyed by the painting, there is also a suggestion of loss or at least of separation here. As imaged in the parted tree behind the boy, this is a scene of splitting too, as the infant, now gendered as a boy, is passed from the hand of the mother to the world of the father, from her bodily intimacy to his visual control.[5]

Here as elsewhere, Hamilton challenges our common views of the painting-photo rapport, both past and present. Almost since its emergence in the 1830s, photography was pitted against painting, with the former taken to trump the latter in the artistic task of accurate representation. At the same time photography was seen as mechanical in operation, that is, as not a proper art at all, and in this regard photography and painting came to be opposed ontologically as well: the former was understood as an automatic impression of the world—"a message without a code," as Roland Barthes would phrase it—whereas the latter was still credited with the auratic touch of the artist.[6] On the same grounds the two were soon contrasted as mediums, with photography regarded as multiple in production and painting as unique, an opposition that Walter Benjamin turned to the advantage of photography, which he took to challenge both the originality associated with painting and the authority associated with its tradition.[7]

In his practice Hamilton disputed most of these arguments point by point. In his view photography was implicated in painting from the beginning (Courbet, Manet, Degas...), and fundamental to his work is the exploration of this continued implication, which he undertook in many prints as well. Thus, over his long career, Hamilton worked through a great variety of photographic formats as either source or structure of his pictures: the magazine advertisement, the publicity still, the fashion shoot, the postcard and so on.[8] At the same time he often found painterly effects already present in these photographic formats: "a distinction between camera work and painting hardly operates in a good deal of photographic magazine and advertising material."[9] As is evident in his "tabular pictures" from the late 1950s to the middle 1960s, Hamilton was especially drawn to seductive passages in photographic sources that move from focus to blur, from finish to facture, and back again. He mimicked this "marriage of brush and lens" in order to complicate the opposition not only between photography and painting but also between sight and touch, and he employed collage to this end as well.[10] Although conceptually the optical and the haptic are often held apart (it is a binary that structures many classic texts in

5. In this light the child assumes his place in the social order as the photo "assumes its place among the genres." Might Hamilton suggest that both gains come at a cost? *Mother and child* follows not only *Treatment room* (1983–84), an installation that reflects on the clinical discipline of the Thatcher government, but also *The citizen* (1982–83), a painting of an Irish hunger striker that is the first of three on the Troubles in Northern Ireland, the others being *The subject* (1988–90) and *The state* (1993). During these years, then, Hamilton was concerned with how we are positioned politically, or (to use the Althusserian idiom) how we are interpellated by ideological state apparatuses such as the family, the hospital, the military, etc.
6. See Roland Barthes, "Rhetoric of the Image" (1964), in *Image Music Text,* trans. and ed. Stephen Heath (New York: Hill and Wang, 1977), 32–51.
7. See Walter Benjamin, "The Work of Art in the Age of its Technical Reproducibility" (1936), in Michael Jennings et al. (ed.), *Selected Writings, Volume 3: 1935–1938* (Cambridge, MA: Harvard University Press, 2002), 101–33.

Western art history), Hamilton suggests that our senses are never so distinct, and that they become more confused as media technologies become more invasive. Also central to his work, then, is the tracking of this increased mediation, not only of the visual arts but of our very sensorium.

Nevertheless, one might still wish to associate painting with the unique and photography with the multiple, and yet here again Hamilton delighted in exceptions. Sometimes, for example, he repeated a painting with variations, as in *Interior I* and *II* (1964) [pp. 108–9] and *Chicago project I* and *II* (1969) [fig. 2], and thus, in a way reminiscent of Robert Rauschenberg in *Factum I* and *II* (1957), qualified the absolute singularity of painting. Often, too, Hamilton added a rote patch of squiggly colours with no apparent purpose other than to stand as a quasi-photographic sign of painterliness, and thus, in a way reminiscent of Roy Lichtenstein with his cliché brushstrokes, complicated the autographic character of painting. On the other side Hamilton also troubled the association of the photograph with the multiple, usually through painterly marks that align repetition with difference as much as sameness: as is evident in his prints too, he was fascinated by the mutability that arises from multiplicity.

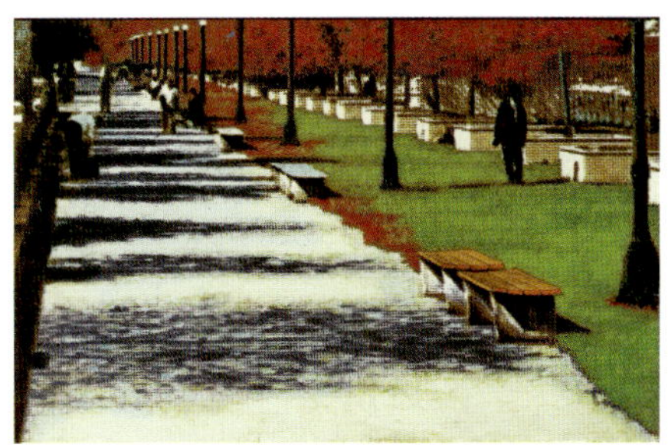

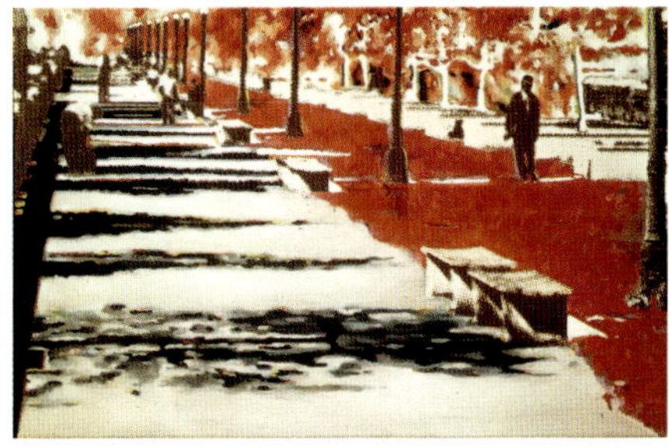

fig. 2
Chicago project I, 1969
Acrylic on photograph on board
The British Council

Chicago project II, 1969
Oil on photograph on canvas
The British Council

Recently a new wrinkle has appeared in the painting-photo rapport, and Hamilton can be taken to question it as well. I mean the argument that photography, refashioned as an electronic medium, has permitted a range of contemporary artists to recover the essential attributes of modern painting, even to recentre the tradition of the tableau, after its apparent displacement by a whole host of post-studio practices in the postwar period. In this view digital technology has rendered the photographic surface less an indexical imprint of the world than a compositional screen for the artist to manipulate at will. It has also allowed a shift in scale to large formats intended first for the gallery wall (not the book page), with the pictures to be beheld as though they were paintings (the market incentive here is not irrelevant). Michael Fried, a critic-historian deeply invested in the tableau tradition, has put this argument most boldly. For Fried such artists as Jeff Wall, Thomas Struth and Andreas Gursky have reclaimed the pictoriality of painting by means of digital photography, and have thus moved to restore the tradition of the tableau, with its values of compositional unity and instantaneous effect, to its rightful pre-eminence in visual art.[11]

Hamilton begs to differ, at least in part. Despite his commitment to the work of Duchamp—who, from *Nude Descending a Staircase, No. 1* (1911) through *Boîte-en-valise* (1934–41), also played with the painting-photo rapport—Hamilton regarded the tableau as central. So, too, he viewed his photographic formats (again, understood broadly as the advertisement, the postcard and so on) as a means not to recover the displaced tradition of painting but rather to test its continued validity. In order for this art to remain pertinent in a consumerist world of mass images, Hamilton believed that it must be pressured by new media. Thus, when faced with a novel version of the photographic, his question was

8. These are only the formats I touch on below. Others adapted by Hamilton include the product catalogue in *Still-life* (1965) and *Toaster* (1966–67), the soft-porn centrefold in *Pin-up* (1961), the contact sheet in *My Marilyn* (1965), the tabloid photo in *Swingeing London 67* (1968–69) and *Unorthodox rendition* (2009–10), and the snapshot in his Polaroid portraits and self-portraits—and this list is merely a beginning. Even before his tabular pictures, for example, Hamilton was interested in the chronophotography of Marey and Muybridge (which he approached via the Futurists and Duchamp), as is evident in his exploration of the capture of movement in the *Trainsition* paintings and *re Nude* (all 1954).
9. Hamilton, *Collected Words,* 64–65.
10. Ibid., 65.
11. Michael Fried, *Why Photography Matters as Art as Never Before* (New Haven and London: Yale University Press, 2008). More precisely, for Fried these artists have restarted the dialectic of "absorption and theatricality" *vis-à-vis* the beholder that he has long seen as the dynamic of advanced painting from Diderot to Manet and beyond. For more on the place of the tableau in Hamilton, see my *The First Pop Age: Painting and Subjectivity in the Art of Hamilton, Lichtenstein, Warhol, Richter, and Ruscha* (Princeton: Princeton University Press, 2012).

always: "Can it be assimilated into the fine-art consciousness?"[12] And by "assimilated" he meant not only at the level of content (that was easy enough) but in terms of facture, form and effect. That is, could painting absorb different kinds of surfaces, including those that were printed and electronic (or, as Hamilton called them, "screened" and "scanned")?[13] Could it adapt different sorts of structure, such as those introduced by collage? Could it coordinate different ways of looking and reading, such as those implied by all these heterogeneous materials and media?[14] The results of these tests were never known beforehand—Hamilton worked in his studio not unlike a scientist in his laboratory—but if painting could assimilate these various modalities, then not only might its traditional genres be retained (again, the portrait, the landscape and so on), but also its "ancient purpose" might be preserved (again, the holding together of the ephemeral and the eternal, the everyday and the epic)—preserved precisely because renovated.[15] Put to the test by photographic media, the art of painting would persist through this testing. However, for Hamilton it was not a question of survival alone: far from an outmoded form, he regarded painting as a meta-medium well positioned to reflect on technological transformations in society at large (here he saw its relative slowness as an advantage, not the opposite). Indeed, Hamilton put digital means to painterly ends as soon as they became available to him; they are featured in his later work, especially his final pictures, which, based on the Balzac novella *Le Chef-d'oeuvre inconnu* (2011), portray or otherwise cite such masters as Titian, Poussin, Courbet and Manet.[16]

A few examples might help to clarify the Hamilton test of painting. Although his tabular pictures are more familiar than his other works, they are too important in this context not to consider here. Hamilton initiated this suite of paintings soon after the dispersal of the Independent Group in the wake of *This is Tomorrow* [pp. 50–53], the landmark exhibition at the Whitechapel Gallery in 1956. It was for the catalogue of this show that Hamilton produced his famous collage, *Just what is it that makes today's homes so different, so appealing?* [p. 49]. Made up of snippets of advertisements from American magazines (even the title was found in this way), this tiny work is a puzzle of pieces fitted into the semi-coherent space of a semi-futuristic interior. With the tabular pictures Hamilton transferred this practice of collage to the medium of painting, and thereby set up the generative tension that runs throughout the suite: the fragmentary motif derived from photography versus the integrated composition of painting, the tabular part versus the tableau whole. Each work was conceived not only as "a compilation of themes derived from the glossies," as Hamilton commented of *Hommage à Chrysler Corp.* (1957) [p. 77], but also as "an anthology of presentation techniques" found there.[17] In this way each painting is mediated a few times over: "a sieved reflection of the ad man's paraphrase of the consumer's dream," as he remarked of *$he* (1958–61) [p. 81].[18] Pastiche was thus "a keystone of the approach," and yet, for all the "different plastic dialects" voiced in the tabular pictures, they are still resolved as paintings. Moreover, for all that pastiche mitigates against style (inasmuch as the citationality of the one is at odds with the singularity of the other), the paintings are distinctively Hamiltonian.[19]

12. Hamilton, *Collected Words,* 35.
13. Ibid., 52.
14. The various formats elaborated by Hamilton do imply various modalities of reception, some more contemplative, others more distractive, some more private, others more public and so on.
15. Hamilton, *Collected Words,* 42.

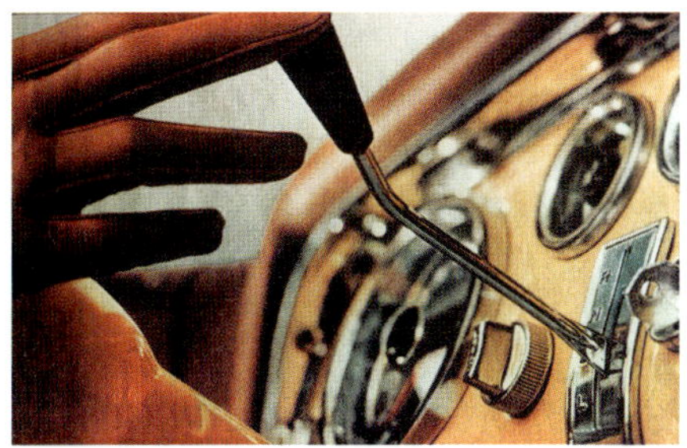

fig. 3
Advert for the 1955 Plymouth in *Life*, 11 April 1955

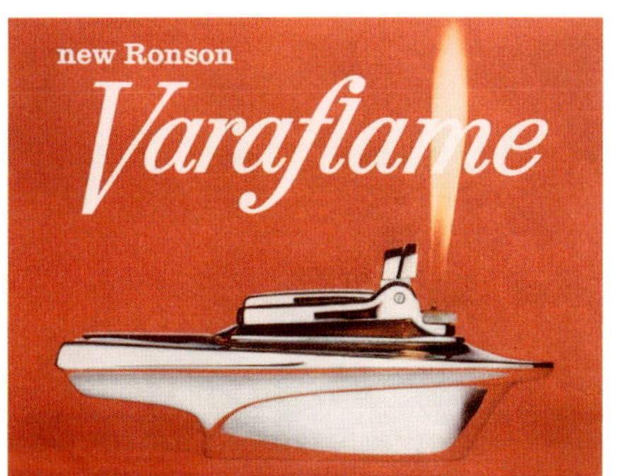

fig. 4
Advert accompanying Hamilton's text "Urbane Image," *Living Arts* 2, 1963

And what are the effects? In a text related to *AAH!* (1962) [p. 83], a lush painting based on a car advertisement that pictures an elegant finger about to touch a gear knob in an otherwise surreal interior, Hamilton anticipates the response of the viewer: "Definition swings in and out along a lip length. A world of fantasy with unique erotic overtones. Intimacy, trespass, yet on a purely visual plane. Sensuality beyond the simple act of penetration—a dizzy drop into swoonlike coloured fuzz, clicked, detached and still, for appreciative analysis."[20] Here the confusion of the optical and the haptic is explicitly erotic (a visual plane invites a fantasy of penetration), and this sensuality seems real enough. At the same time we know that the effect is contrived, and in fact it is not the viewer that Hamilton ventriloquises here but "the ad man's paraphrase of the consumer's dream." Both sensuous and manipulative, the advertisement-turned-painting offers phenomenological intensity and commercial interpellation at once—indeed, almost as the same thing. In a consumerist world where sexual fetishism and commodity fetishism redouble one another, Hamilton implies, the two experiences are difficult to distinguish: "a dizzy drop into swoonlike coloured fuzz" is the look and feel of ecstasy and reification alike [fig. 3]. The purpose of the picture, then, is to rehearse these effects for our "appreciative analysis"; importantly with Hamilton one can have both the aesthetic and the critical—the two need not be opposed [fig. 4].

In the end the tabular picture is an answer to questions such as these: How many "disparate conventions" can a painting assimilate and still function as a picture? How many different affects can a viewer absorb and process? In particular, can the fetishistic involvement solicited by a commodity-image be reconciled with the sublimatory distance associated with the work of art? Rather than compromise sublimation, might fetishisation recharge it, and might aesthetic experience be remotivated as a result?

Another example of the Hamilton test of painting. Soon after the tabular pictures, he turned to another sort of photographic source, the publicity still. Constructed less for commodity appeal than for narrative intrigue, this format invites a spectatorial involvement that is less fetishistic than voyeuristic. *Interior I* and *II* are based on the same still for *Shockproof* (1948) [fig. 5], *a film noir* directed by Douglas Sirk, who was known for his lavish style. The still shows a *femme fatale*, played by Patricia Knight, in a tense pose in an ambiguous interior; a dramatic event is about to happen or has recently occurred, and in fact at this moment in the movie the woman has just shot a man. Hamilton does not picture the fallen body, however, and this absence renders the *mise en scène* of the paintings all the more enigmatic.

In *Interiors* Hamilton is interested in how the publicity still suggests a situation by visual means alone, and how painting might exploit these means to its own ends. Hamilton exaggerates the false perspective of the film set; in fact he underscores the constructed nature of the space here at every turn. *Shockproof* was already dated by 1964—not only the *femme fatale* but *film noir* was outmoded in the bright world of Pop—and this makes the still seem even more pictorial as a fragment of the past. To this framed past Hamilton then adds contemporary images of his own, with each painting fitted with a prime example of

16. The representation of Titian is based on his self-portrait (c. 1562) at the Prado, which bears a resemblance to the elderly Hamilton. Titian died in his late 80s; Hamilton died at 89 in 2011.
17. Hamilton, *Collected Words*, 31.
18. Ibid., 36.
19. Ibid., 31–38.
20. Ibid., 50.

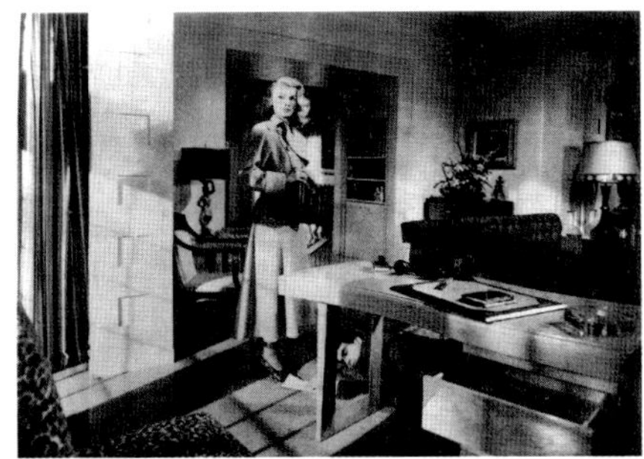

fig. 5
Still showing Patricia Knight from *Shockproof,* 1948, directed by Douglas Sirk

modern design: in *Interior I* [p. 108] this is a sleek desk contrived by the artist (it is featured in *Desk* also from 1964), and in *Interior II* [p. 109] a La Fonda chair produced by Charles and Ray Eames in 1961. These objects come from a time other to the period of the film, and this is not the only alien temporality in these pictures. "Any interior is a set of anachronisms, a museum," Hamilton wrote apropos of the *Interiors,* and one of his concerns here is to see how painting might assimilate not only different images but also different times.[21] In this regard Hamilton suggests an analogy between the film set and the artist studio as a place of both composition and exhibition: a plane of colours like a palette appears at lower left in *Interior I* and at lower right in *Interior II,* and several pictures float on the nominal walls in each painting. In *Interior I* a photo of a prior stage of the painting appears to the right, which condenses a complicated relay of representations—from publicity still to silkscreened image, to photograph, to painting. Near this picture is a larger one based on a magazine spread that shows the daughter of Berthe Morisot posed in front of a painting by Morisot, which suggests another circuit of images, another chain of temporalities (in this process even more visual information is lost). In *Interior II* the relay between representations becomes one between media too; in addition to a blue rectangle behind the woman meant to stand for an Yves Klein monochrome, there is a photo-collage of contemporary television fitted with a picture of the recent assassination of John F. Kennedy. Again various times are held in suspension.

The *Interiors* call up more than the modern studio painting à la Matisse; they also invoke Dutch and Spanish interiors à la Vermeer and Velázquez, that is, Baroque "meta-paintings" that, as arrangements of other pictures, reflect on picturing as such.[22] Both *Interiors* include different surfaces that suggest different models of representation—the window, the mirror (a real one is collaged behind the woman in *Interior I*), the abstract plane and the photographic print, and thus different modes of signification—perspectival representation, realist depiction, non-objective painting and mechanical reproduction. Two points should be underscored here. First, as with the tabular pictures, the viewer is asked to negotiate between fragment and whole, the tabular and the tableau, with the latter term in each pair privileged. With the *Interiors* this operation is complicated further by the various space-times introduced by the internal pictures, not to mention by the basic tension between the duration of the implied film and the instantaneity of the actual painting. Yet this tension is also resolved in favour of pictorial unity ("the dangerous moment" in the *film noir,* we might say, is made to support "the pregnant moment" of the tableau tradition), and "attempts to read the pictures are forced back to an acceptance of their totality."[23] The second point should be obvious by now: here again a lowly photo, a publicity still, is the basis for a sophisticated reflection on the art of painting.

From the tabular pictures to the *Interiors* Hamilton shifts from scenes of delight, in which the woman is presented as an attractive commodity among others, to scenarios of danger, in which the woman is caught in a narrative construction. In *My Marilyn* (1965) [p. 115], his next major work, Hamilton presents femininity *per se* as a construction: in this

21. Ibid., 62.
22. I borrow this term from Victor Stoichita, *The Self-Aware Image: An Insight into Early Modern Meta-Painting* (Cambridge: Cambridge University Press, 1996).
23. Morphet (ed.), *Richard Hamilton,* 178. The phrase "pregnant moment" derives from *Laocoön: An Essay on the Limits of Painting and Poetry* (1766) by Gotthold Lessing.

oil and collage on photograph, which is based on a contact sheet of publicity photos of Marilyn Monroe on a Los Angeles beach, being is almost one with imaging. And yet, though Marilyn is the object of this operation, she is also its subject, that is, she is the primary author of her own iconicity (Hamilton goes so far as to transcribe her markings on the contact sheet to the surface of his painting). Moreover, though *My Marilyn* is no more feminist than are the *Interiors,* all three images ask us to reflect on "the visual pleasure" afforded to "the male gaze" by classic Hollywood cinema a decade before Laura Mulvey published her influential essay on this topic.[24]

A related instance of the constructed photo, in which feminine identity is again put together, is the fashion shoot, which Hamilton took up in his "cosmetic studies" titled *Fashion-plate* (1969) [pp. 168, 180–83]. Here the initial idea was to reflect on a central genre of the tableau tradition, the figure painting, yet, as sometimes happened to Hamilton, the collage studies displaced the final work. The *Fashion-plates* are based on a type of model photography, the full-page headshot, that is common in cosmetics advertisements in such magazines as *Vogue* (which is one source of the photographic material here). This type focuses on three parts above all—eyes, lips and hair—and Hamilton does the same; in fact he turns these parts into artificial signs that are connected only enough to signify "head." In doing so, Hamilton stresses the constructed aspect of his models to the point where they become ambivalent assemblages, part fetish, part monster: the eyes are utterly denatured, the lips often labial and the hair almost Medusan. This move to break down the fetish is a characteristic one in Hamilton, and here he includes the photographic set-up as well: the components of the fashion shoot—lights, reflectors and paper backdrops—are rendered as part of the image, and they too appear fragile.

Once again Hamilton makes a photographic source resonate with art-historical associations. He applies actual bits of make-up to his fictive models, and this move again conjures up "the painting of modern life" championed by Baudelaire. However, Baudelaire wrote "in praise of cosmetics" in his celebrated essay—he saw them as the ultimate in artifice—and in this respect Hamilton might be closer to Manet, whose paintings often suggest an ambivalence about *maquillage*: on the one hand, Manet delighted in the modern analogy between painted canvas and painted face as well as in the frank flatness of both; on the other hand, this very flatness sometimes registers the deleterious effects of urban shock on his female subjects.[25] At the same time the fragmentation of the Hamilton models also evokes the fracturing in Cubist portraits (which, like the cosmetic studies, signify "head" more than they depict it) and, even more perhaps, the fracturing in Dadaist anti-portraits. Indeed, like Hannah Höch in her photo-collages of "the new women" of the 1920s, Hamilton in his photo-collages of the new models of the 1960s renders them as fetish-monsters, glamorous and grotesque in equal parts, constructed and deconstructed at once. In this regard the cosmetic studies also count as a riposte to the celebration of sheer surface in Warhol, Lichtenstein and other Pop artists who often equated the superficialities of the Pop face and the Pop image; again Hamilton breaks down the fetish in a way that his American peers tend not to do.[26]

24. See Laura Mulvey, "Visual Pleasure and Narrative Cinema," *Screen* 16, 3 (Autumn 1975), 6–18. With his title Hamilton appears to distinguish his version of Monroe from prior versions by de Kooning, Warhol and other American artists, in which Marilyn is not authorised in this way (on the contrary).
25. Baudelaire, "The Painter of Modern Life," 34. On *maquillage* in Manet, see Jean Clay, "Ointments, Makeup, Pollen," trans. John Shepley, *October* 27 (Winter 1983), 3–44.
26. The *Fashion-plates* also anticipate work by feminist artists (such as Silvia Kolbowski) that analyses the construction of the model in an explicit critique.

A final example of the Hamilton test of painting. In 1963, on his first visit to the United States, Hamilton met Warhol and others involved in Pop. After this encounter he often worked up his compositions from one image, or even one part of one image, as the Americans were wont to do. Such was his approach in several pictures based on found postcards, most involving beach leisure and urban tourism, such as *Whitley Bay* (1965), *Trafalgar Square* (1965–67) and *People* (1965–66), all of which are oil on photograph on panel. In each instance a photographic detail is enlarged to the point that its character *qua* detail—its ability to deliver information about a referent—is all but lost.

In *Whitley Bay* [p. 117] Hamilton began with a black-and-white blow-up of a part of a postcard, in this case of the beach at this seaside town in north-eastern England (which is not far from Newcastle where Hamilton taught from 1953 to 1966); he then applied washes of colour dye by hand. Greatly enlarged, the half-tone dots of the postcard undercut rather than support the illusion of the scene, and though the added colours—irregular bands of yellow, pink and turquoise—evoke the sand and the sea in a warm sun, the bathers, scattered on the beach and in the water, appear as little more than pale verticals dotted with black points to which white patches of paint are sometimes attached. In effect, these photographic details become painterly blurs, which is to say they become the opposite of details. *Trafalgar Square* [p. 123] applies much the same method to an urban scene. Here, however, the added colours are denser, and the printed dots of the postcard and the pointillist touches of the artist are difficult to distinguish. Like Lichtenstein, Hamilton thus folds photography and painting into one another, but to very different effect, for here distinct figures become amorphous shapes (with the American it is the other way around). Finally, *People* [p. 116] is also derived from a Whitley Bay postcard, another picture of random bathers on the beach, but, since the source was not a half-tone reproduction it could be subjected to more enlargements than the ones in *Whitley Bay* and *Trafalgar Square.* Hamilton first made a 35-millimetre negative of a part of the image, enlarged the print, and then repeated the process to the point where the forms become *informe.*

And here again added patches of black and white paint only further obscuring the referent.

With the postcard paintings Hamilton is concerned with locating the line between information and noise in the image (one could count on this artist to be involved with the cybernetic discourse of the period); at the same time these pictures bear on a primary topos in modernist art, the threshold between representation and abstraction. Typically, though, Hamilton works to complicate the inherited terms of this relationship. The photograph is associated with representation, of course, yet here its enlargement erodes rather than enhances the definition of the referent—"a search for this moment of loss," Hamilton tells us, "became the real subject of the series"—and so photography comes to fall on the side of abstraction.[27] In this respect these pictures anticipate *Blow-Up* (1966), the signal film by Michelangelo Antonioni in which a forensic search for a clue to a murder in an enlarged photograph ends in utter uncertainty. Yet whereas Antonioni seems to regard this

27. Hamilton, *Collected Words,* 68.
28. In the early Brian de Palma film *Greetings* (1968), Hamilton appears in one scene where he explains, to a stranger in a park, a postcard piece, closely related to *People,* in which his various enlargements of the beach image unfold in accordion fashion. The stranger associates it with *Blow-Up;* Hamilton responds, modestly, that he made the piece before the appearance of the movie. He also indicates that the figures in the lower right of *People,* now formless, are a mother and a son, the iconic constellation to which he returns in *Mother and child.* (Thanks to Mark Godfrey for this reference.)

uncertainty as a release from constraint—he concludes his film with an unexpected scene of antic mimes in a London park—Hamilton holds us to the epistemological ambiguity of his pictures. In fact the technical limits of photography staged here might prompt us to consider the ideological limits of any representation.[28]

When painters of modern life such as Manet and Seurat treated subjects of leisure, they focused on groupings of class: it was as if its existence were too blatant, too intractable, for it not to be represented, however difficult it might be to define. However, in the postcard paintings of Hamilton "the figure" of class comes to be lost in "the ground" of the crowd. One of the great questions for early twentieth century modernists on the left was how to represent the masses (this was the first age not only of mass media but also of mass parties); under the different circumstances of full spectacle this became a Pop question too. For his part Warhol responded with silkscreened images of mass icons, usually in the form of commodities and celebrities. Hamilton is more specific than Warhol—at least in title and theme his *Trafalgar Square* and *Whitley Bay* are not unlike Manet's *Music in the Tuileries Gardens* (1862) [fig. 6], say, and Seurat's *A Sunday Afternoon on the Island of La Grande Jatte* (1884). At the same time he is also more general, for his subject is generic "people," and he views this "anonymous humanity" in almost statistical terms as so many "endless patterns of group relationships."[29] On the modern task of mass representation, then, painting, even painting aided by photography, fails; for all his commitment to the medium, Hamilton also acknowledges its limits.

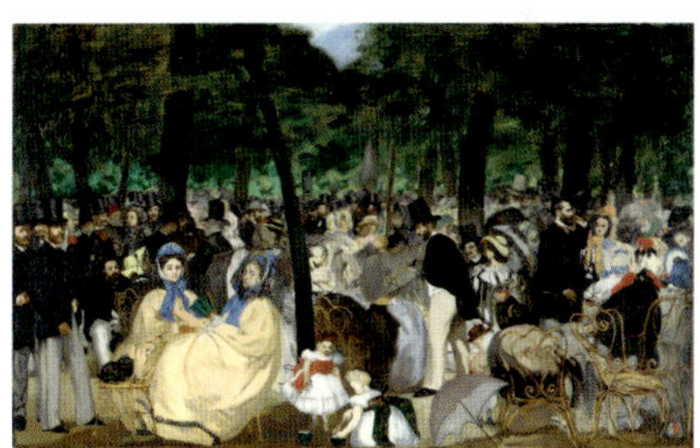

fig. 6
Edouard Manet
Music in the Tuileries Gardens, 1862
Oil on canvas
National Gallery, London
Sir Hugh Lane Bequest, 1917

"In the '50s," Hamilton wrote in retrospect from the late 1960s, "we became aware of the possibility of seeing the whole world at once, through the great visual matrix that surrounds us; a synthetic, 'instant' view. Cinema, television, magazines, newspapers immersed the artist in a total environment and this new visual ambience was photographic."[30] This is a telling statement in several respects. It captures the full emergence of capitalist spectacle, of an immersive space of mediated perception, and it is this photographic matrix that Hamilton worked to engage in his painting. The statement also suggests that, in his own way, Hamilton was no less a media theorist than Moholy-Nagy or Marshall McLuhan, but one that was never so affirmative or technophilic. For Hamilton there was no telos to the history of media—no dialectical sublation of one form by the next as projected by Moholy, no functional absorption of one technology by the next as proposed by McLuhan. For Hamilton the task of the artist-critic was different: to set various "presentation techniques" in conversation, with painting positioned as the mediator, the medium that might anthologise the forms, and archivise the effects, of the others. As opposed to the levelling often associated with Pop, then, Hamilton sought to differentiate experience, and this is why he retained the old medium of painting, but also why he worked to renovate it. His statement on "the great visual matrix" also allows us to clarify the two different ideas of "the instant" in his art: the "synthetic" view of mass media in a "total environment" on the one hand, and the "epiphanic" view of painting "experienced as a totality" on the other.[31] "It is an epiphany," Hamilton wrote of *The Arnolfini Portrait* (1434) by Jan van Eyck [fig. 7], a painting that is

29. Hamilton, *Collected Words,* 68. In distribution Hamilton sometimes sought to be as mass as possible; for example, the *White Album* he designed for the Beatles in 1968 was billed as "a limited edition" of five million.
30. Hamilton, *Collected Words,* 64.
31. Ibid., 104. For more on this point see Foster, *The First Pop Age,* 52–58.

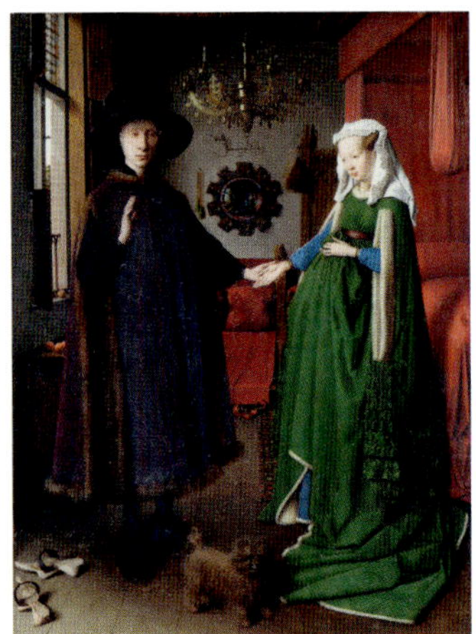

fig. 7
Jan van Eyck
The Arnolfini Portrait, 1434
Oil on oak
National Gallery, London

sometimes placed at the head of the tableau tradition, "a crystallisation of thought that gives us an instant awareness of life's meaning. No other art has the capacity to be entirely there, totally existent like a phenomenon of nature."[32] Again and again Hamilton sought to reconcile, not to conflate, these two kinds of instant, to intensify the one with the other.[33]

To what end? In another celebrated phrase Baudelaire once defined art as "the mnemotechny of the beautiful."[34] If the gruesome history of the twentieth century dashed that particular promise of aesthetic happiness, Hamilton still believed in the mnemonic power of painting, and a key question posed by his art is what makes an image iconic. Might art-historical allusions deepen the cultural effectivity of photo-based representations, and vice versa? For me the answer lies in the way that, when I think of the Swinging Sixties in London, I see *Swingeing London 67* (1968–69) [p. 163], and yet I also see an archetypal gesture of embarrassment inscribed in our cultural memory (namely, *Expulsion from the Garden of Eden* [c. 1424] by Masaccio). Or when I think of American students abused by state police during the same period, I see *Kent State* (1970) [p. 252], and yet I also see an archetypal figure of death to be found in that same image-repertoire (namely, *The Body of the Dead Christ in the Tomb* [1521–22] by Hans Holbein). Sometimes, too, when I think of the imagistic complexities of the family drama, I see *Mother and child*.

32. Ibid., 264.
33. Another project in which these two ideas of the instant are brought together is his series of portraits based on Polaroids which, initiated in 1968 as pictures of Hamilton by other artists and acquaintances, also developed into self-portraits. In the portraits we watch as Hamilton and friends come to terms with the new language of the Polaroid technology with its immediate prints: its fun, its informality, its intimacy, the camera handed between familiars to play with, with a status somewhere between a curiosity and an instrument, and so on. In these displaced portraits Hamilton complicates authorship, as he does in his *Portrait of the artist by Francis Bacon* (1970), an oil on collotype done in the style of Bacon. With colours that are often saturated, these portraits are also almost automatically Pop. Yet in the self-portraits, in which his face appears at different distances behind a glass plane marked with bright squiggles of oil paint (as if to evoke the emulsion of a Polaroid print), we see Hamilton force this most casual and spontaneous of photographic devices into dialogue with the most reflexive and studied of painting genres—the self-portrait.
34. Charles Baudelaire, "The Salon of 1846," in Jonathan Mayne (ed.), *The Mirror of Art: Critical Studies of Charles Baudelaire* (Garden City, NY: Doubleday Anchor Books, 1956), 83.

Fashion-plate study (a) self-portrait 1969

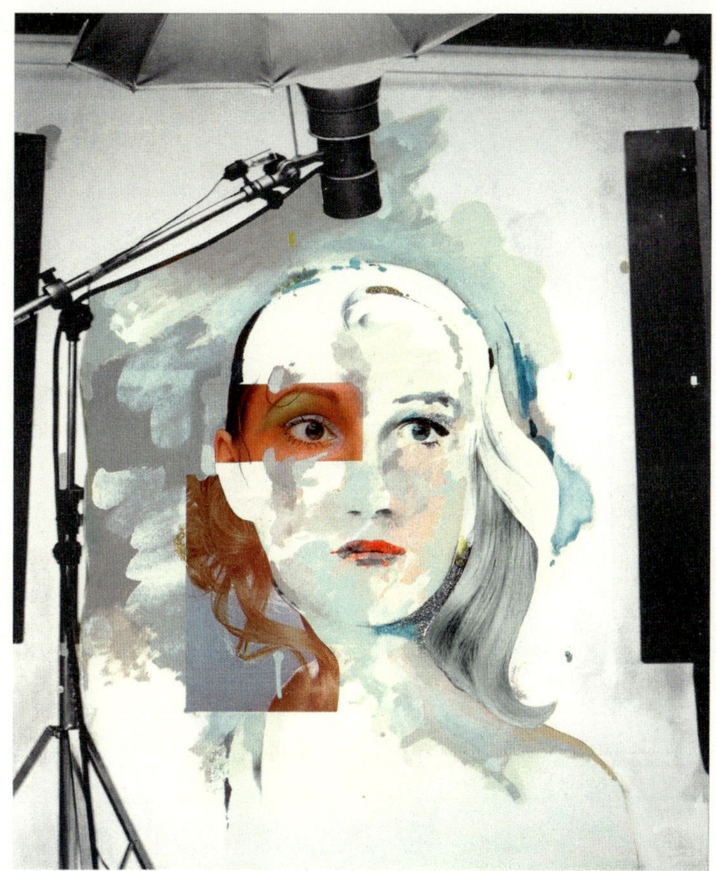

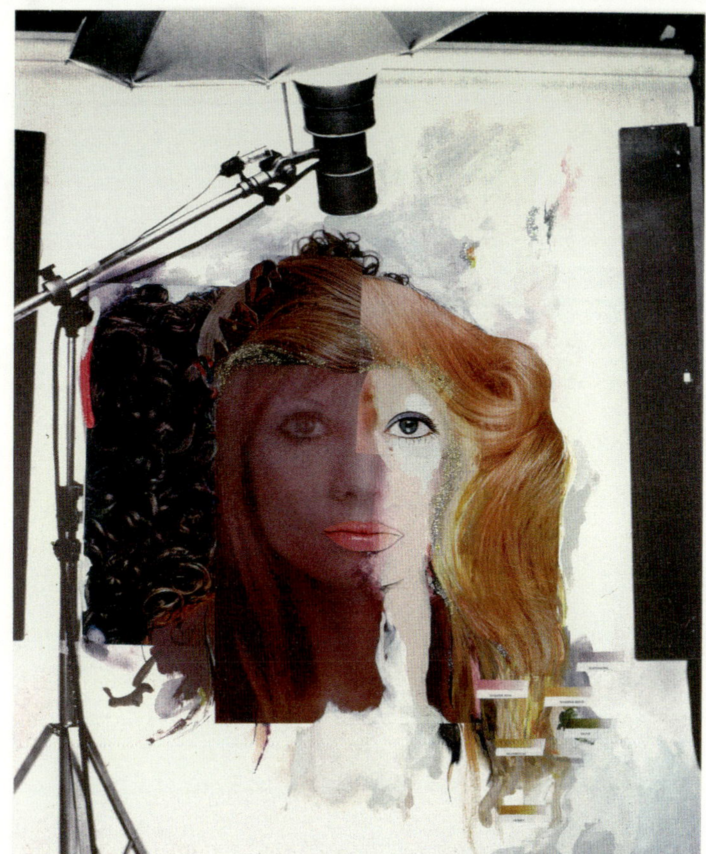

Fashion-plate (cosmetic study II) 1969

Fashion-plate (cosmetic study III) 1969

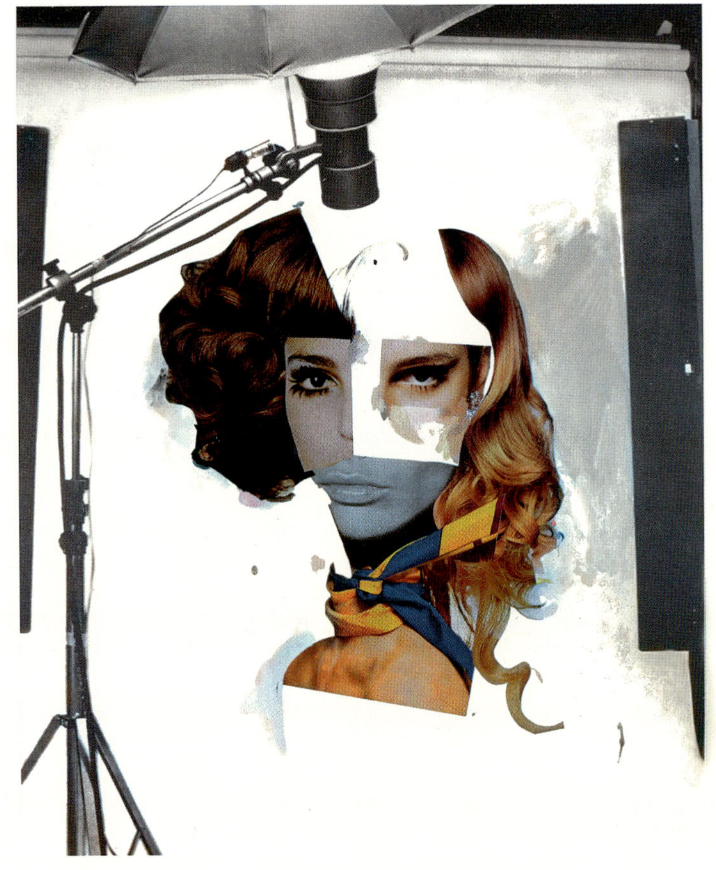

Fashion-plate (cosmetic study V) 1969

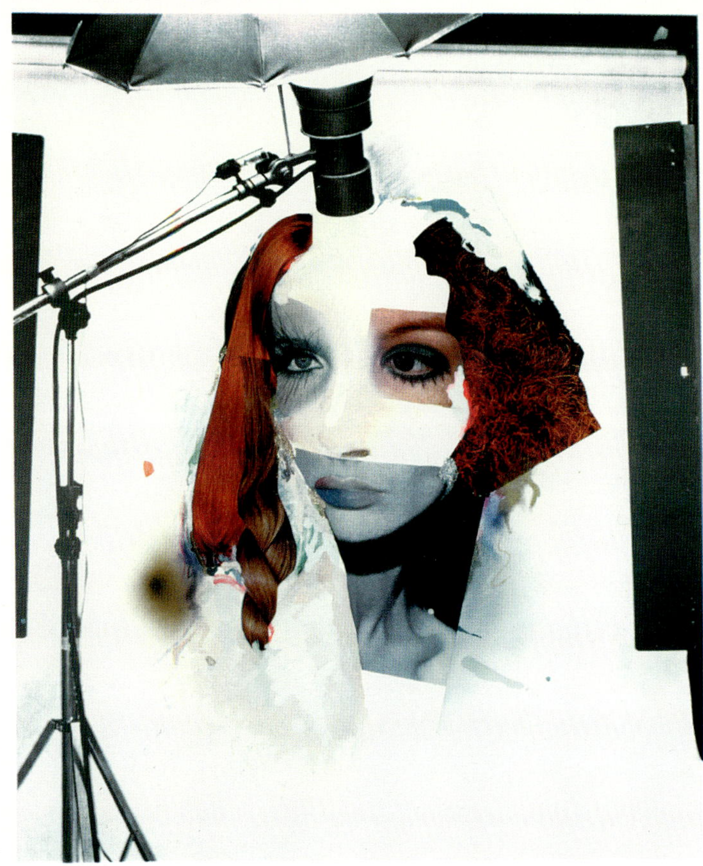

Fashion-plate (cosmetic study VI) 1969

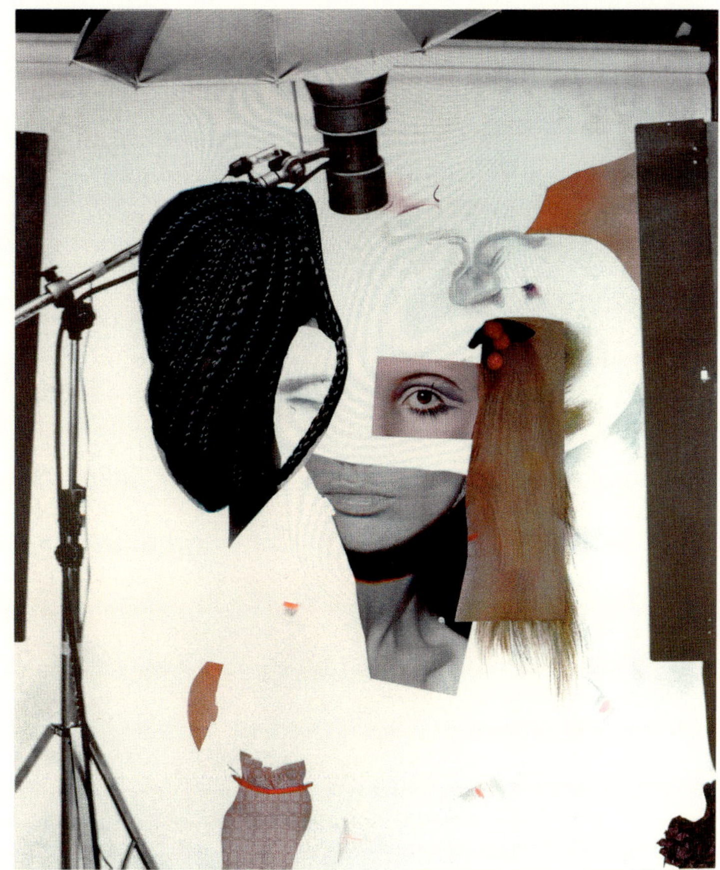

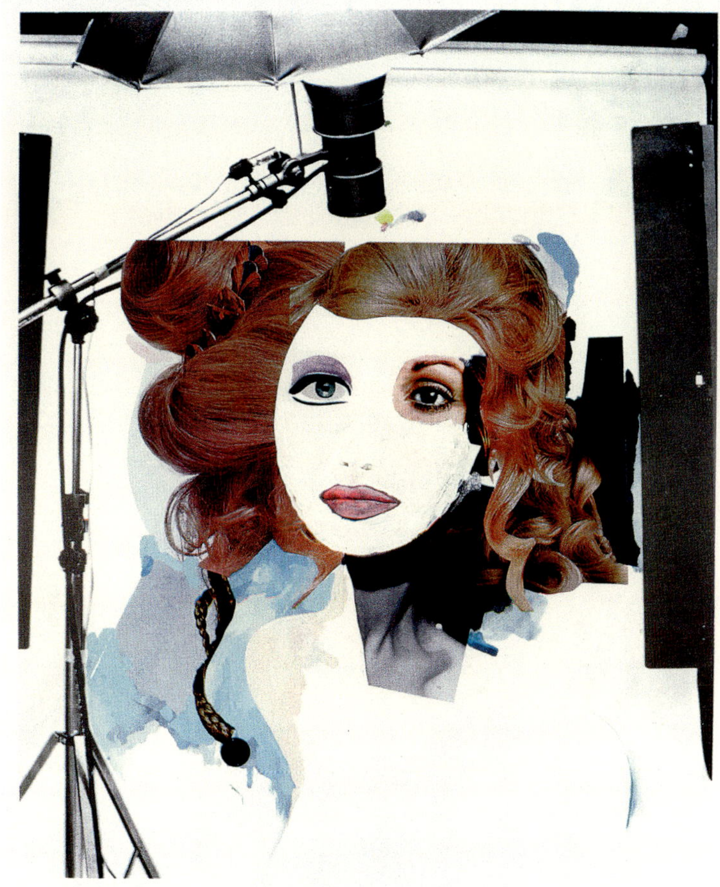

Fashion-plate (cosmetic study VII) 1969

Fashion-plate (cosmetic study VIII) 1969

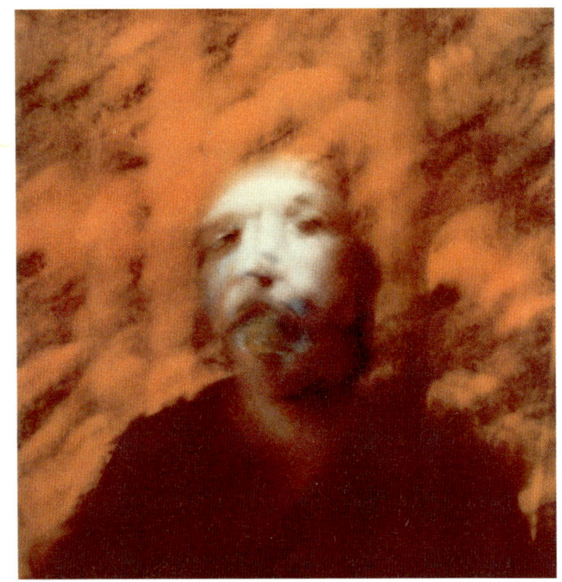

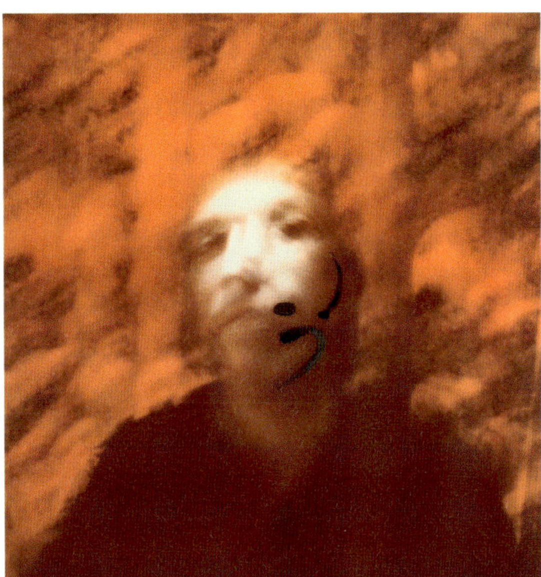

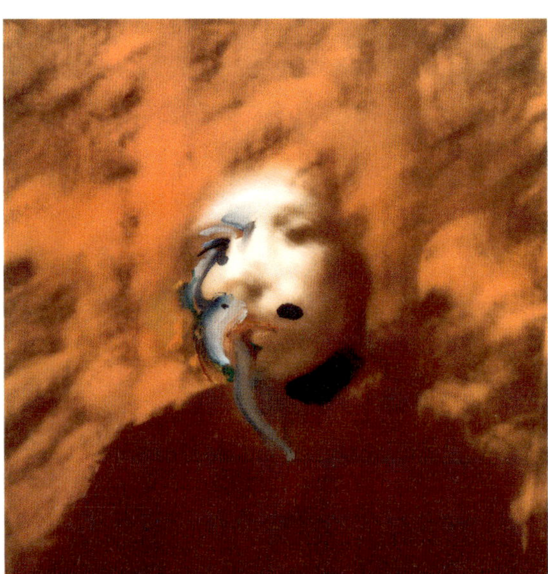

Portrait of the artist by Francis Bacon – studies I–VI 1970

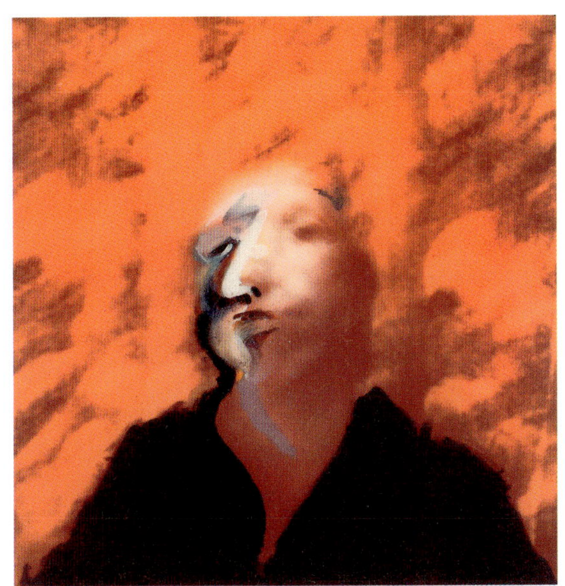

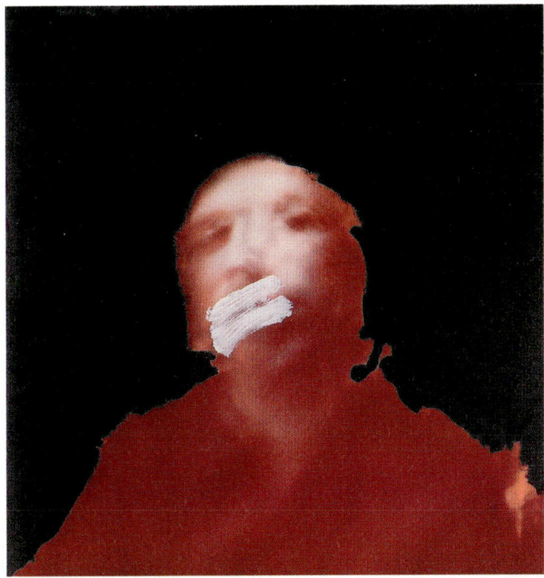

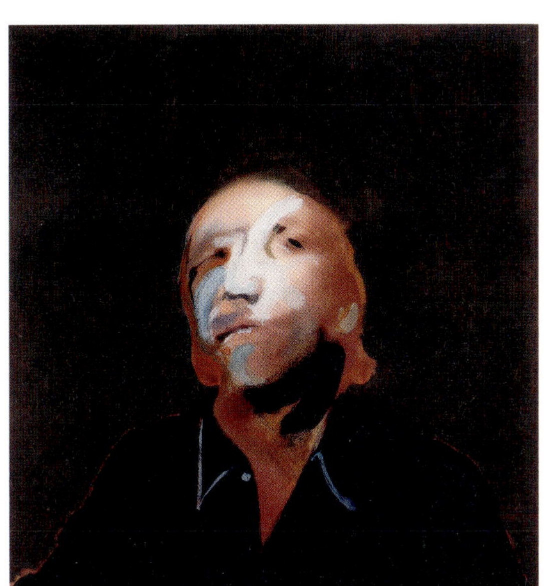

Polaroid Portraits Vol. 1

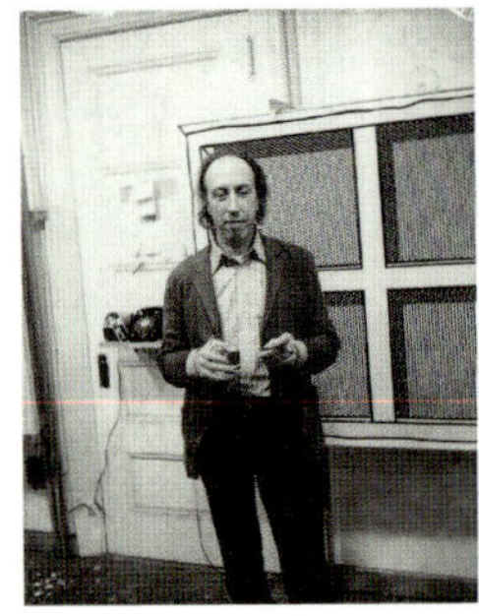
Roy Lichtenstein 16.3.68

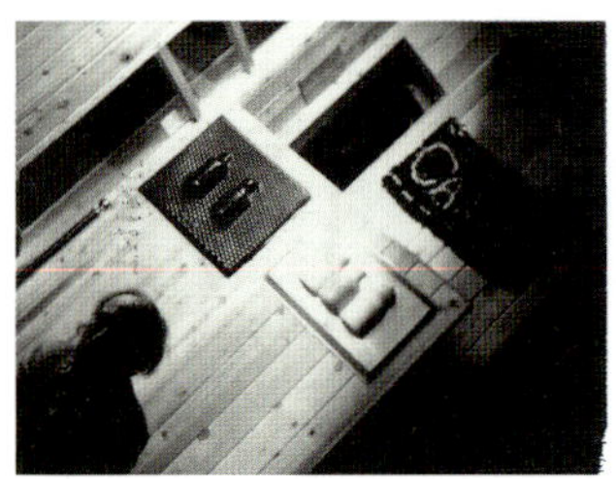
N E Thing Co Ltd 25.9.68

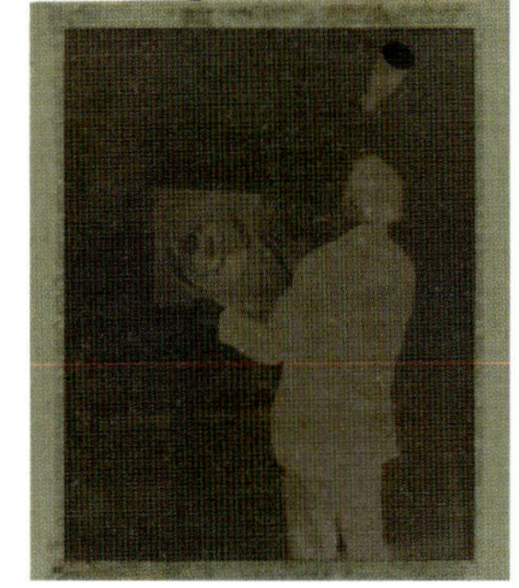
Dieter Rot 23.12.68

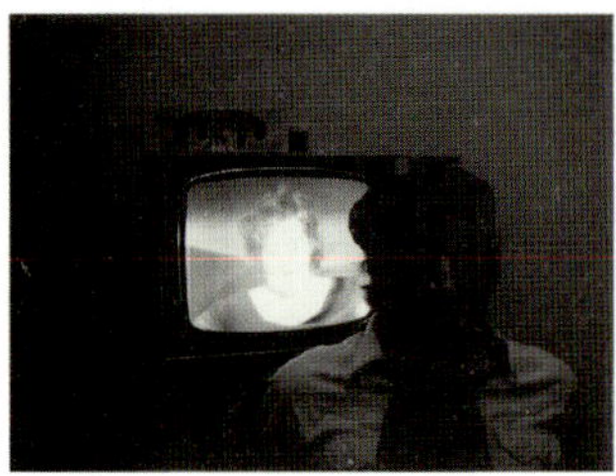
George Brecht 23.12.68

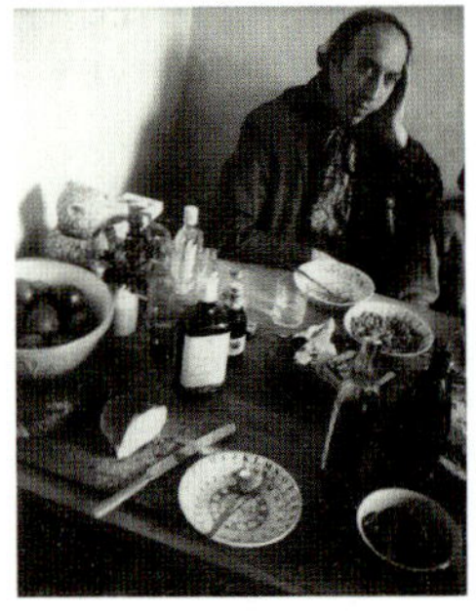
Barry Flanagan 26.12.68

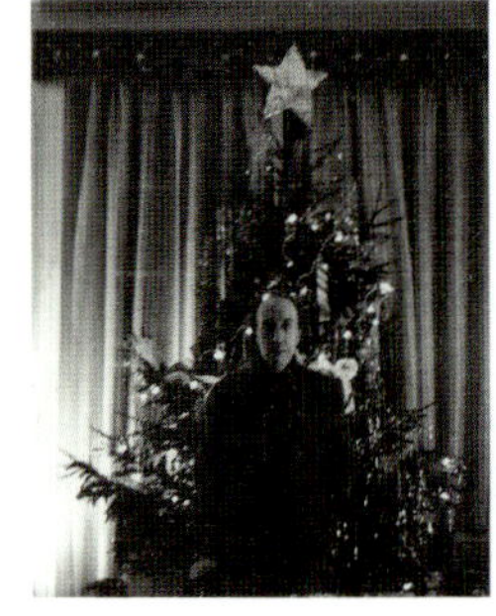
Jim Dine 27.12.68

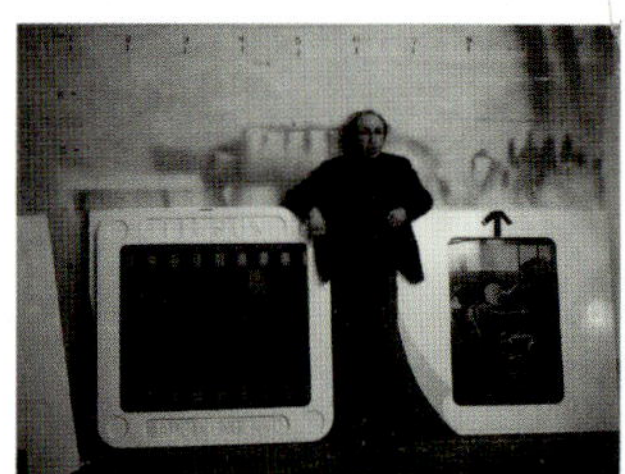
Joe Tilson 27.12.68

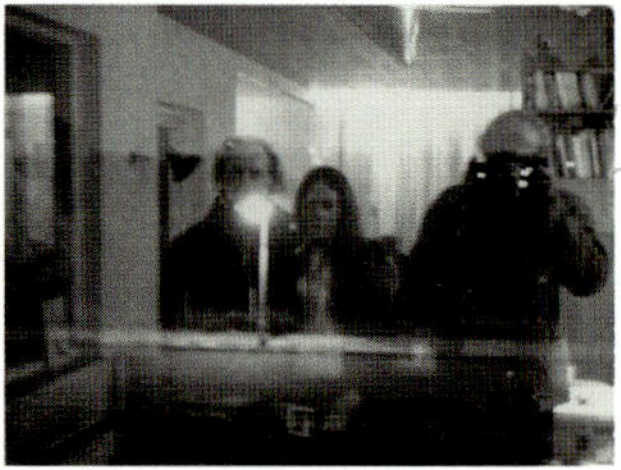
Jim Rosenquist 9.7.69

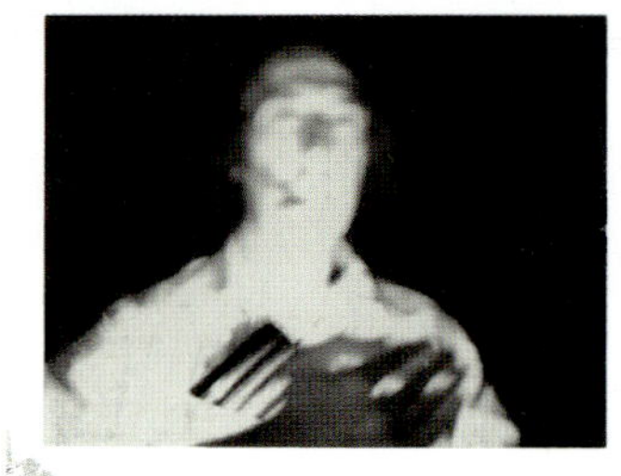
Claes Oldenburg 12.7.69

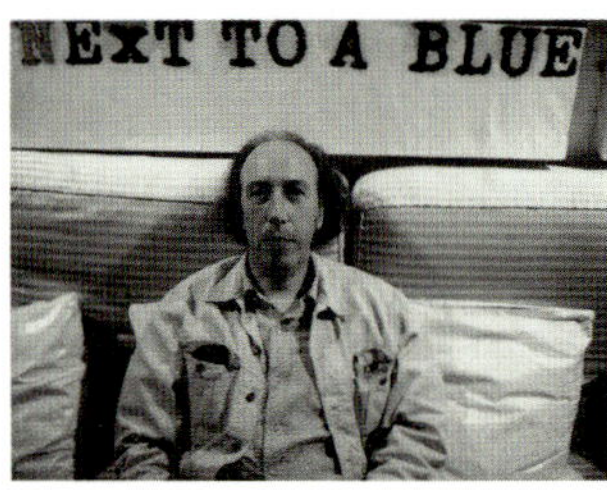

Robert Creeley 12.7.69

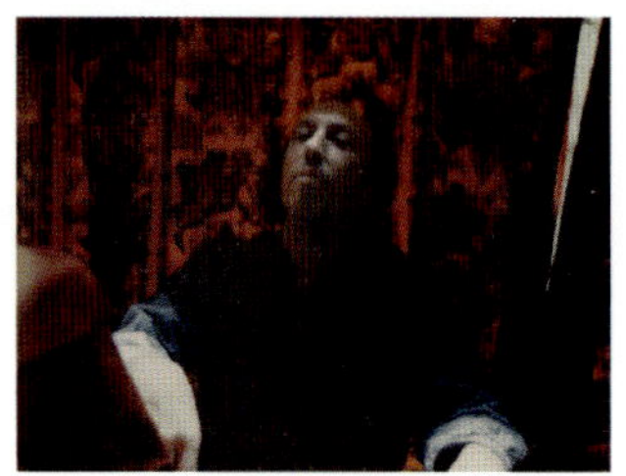
Francis Bacon 14.7.69

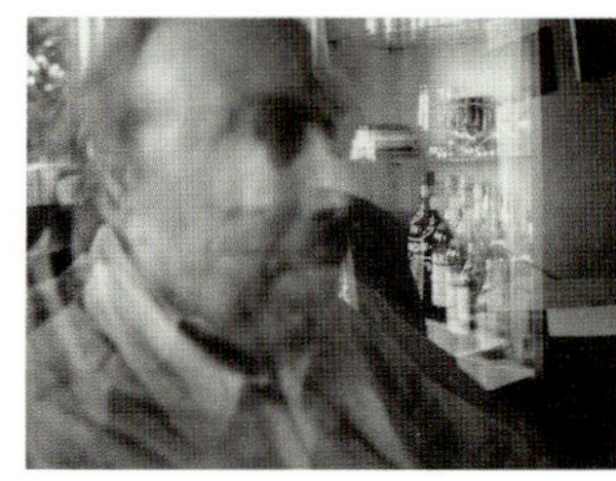
Wolf Vostell 19.7.69

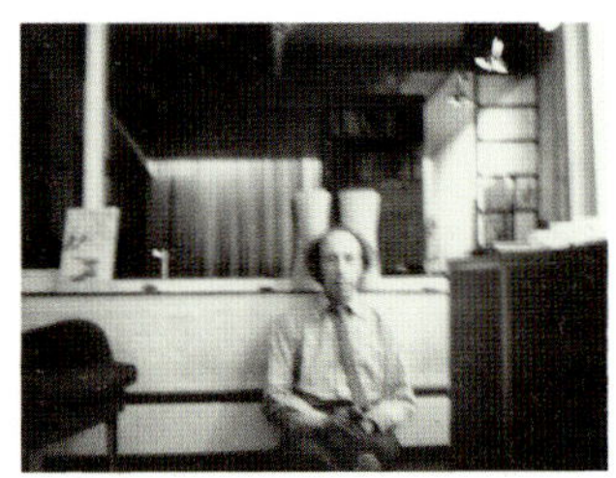
Bill Copley 28.7.69

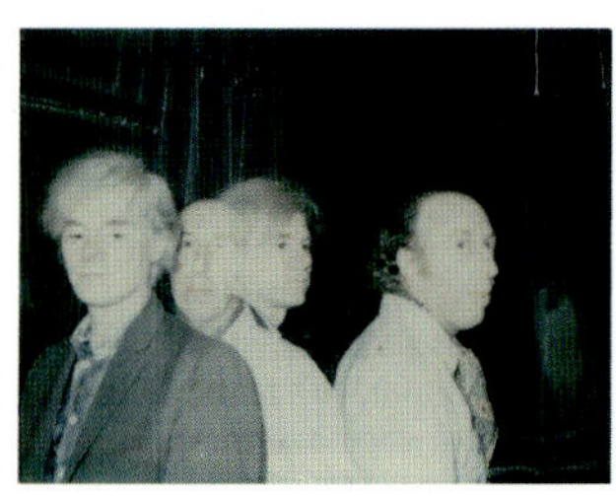
Brigid Polk 16.9.69

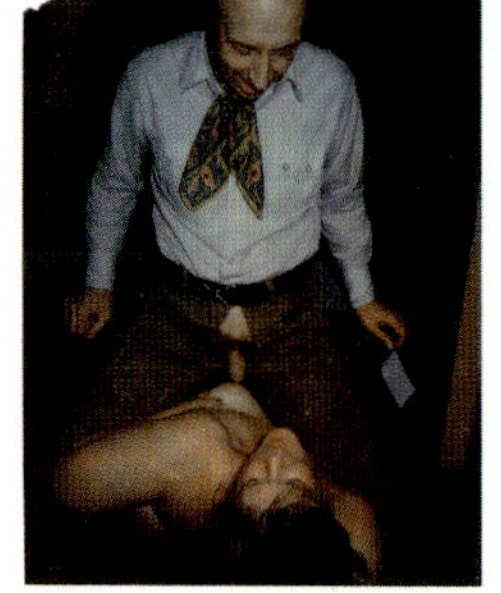
Andy Warhol 16.9.69

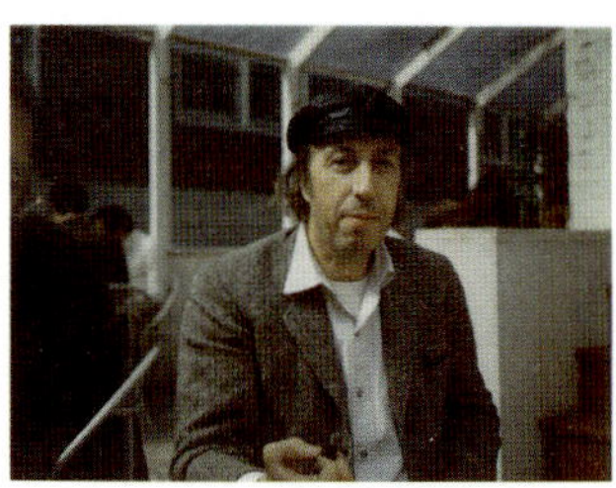
Robert Morris 16.9.69

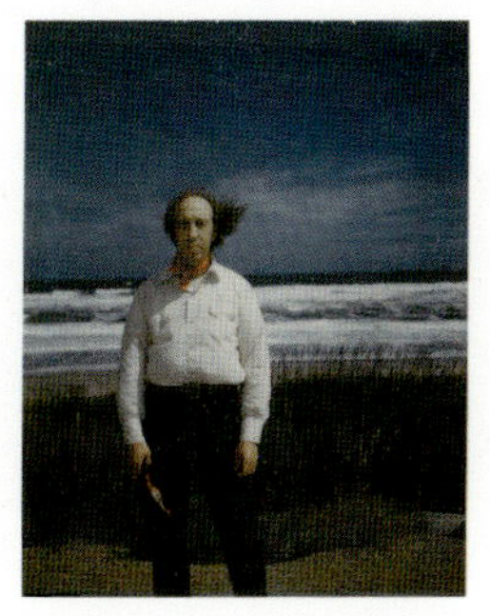
Jasper Johns 21.9.69

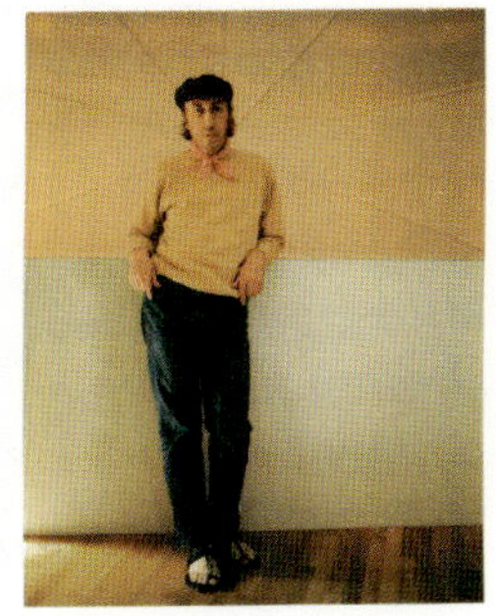
Bob Benson 21.9.69

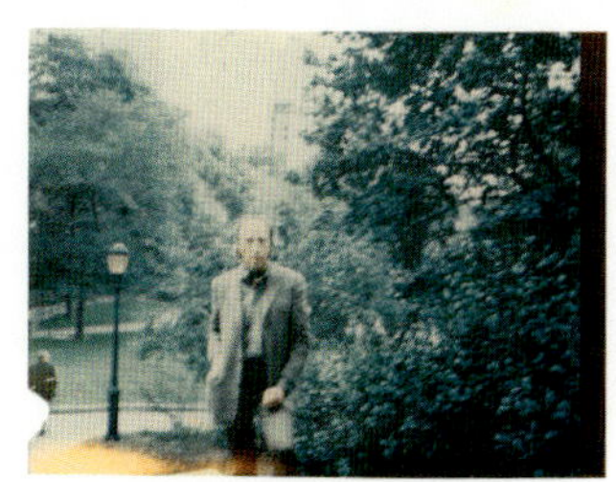
La Monte Young 25.9.69

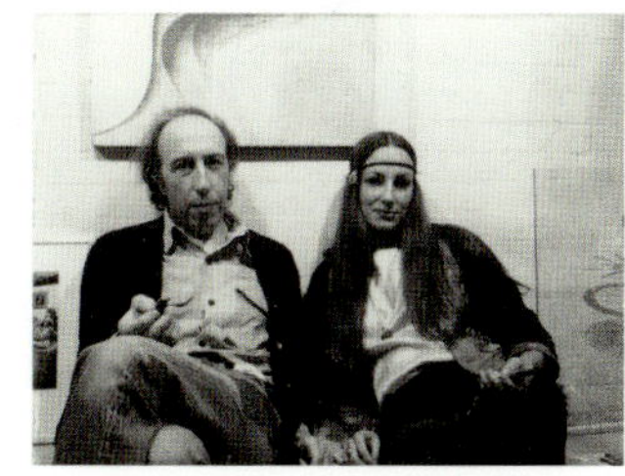
Ron Kitaj 29.10.69

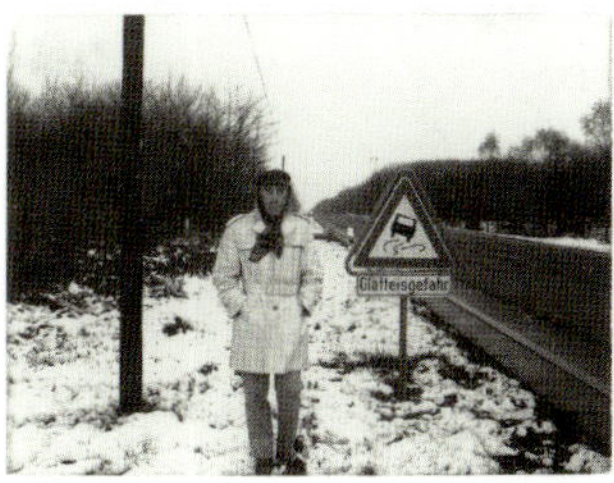
Christo 29.11.69

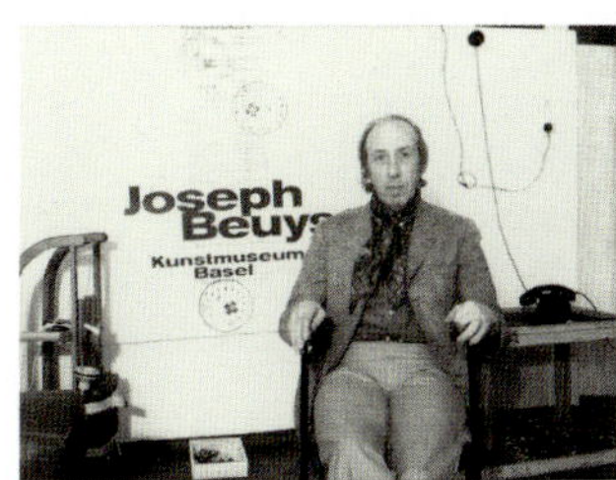

Joseph Beuys 30.11.69

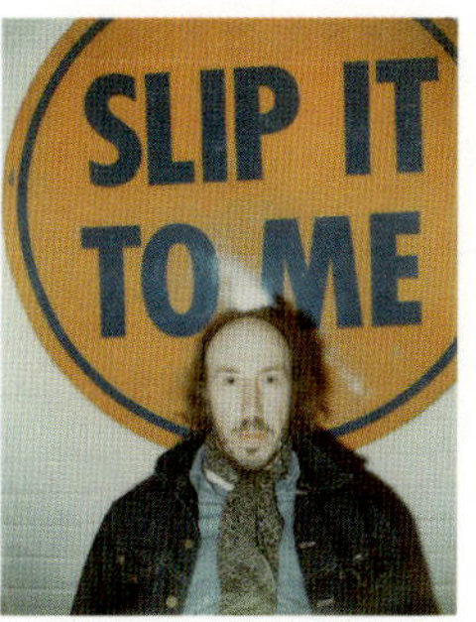

David Hockney 28.1.70

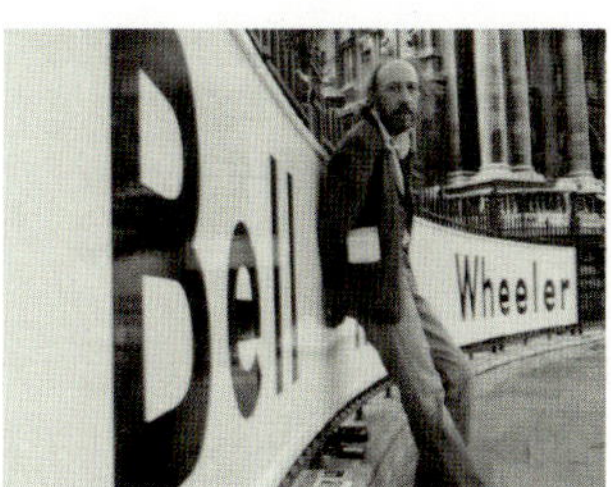

Larry Bell 4.5.70

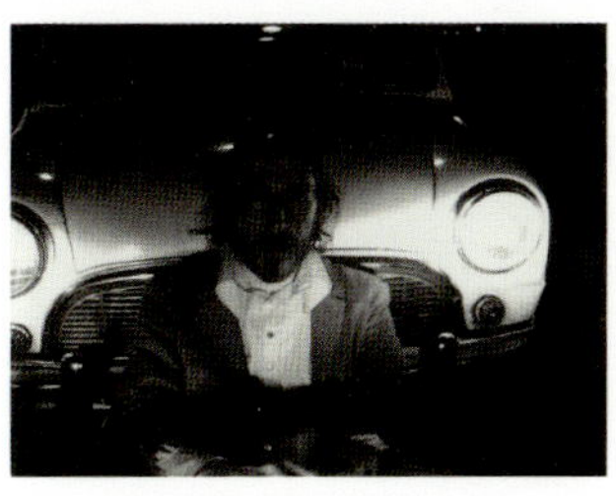
Bob Irwin 4.5.70

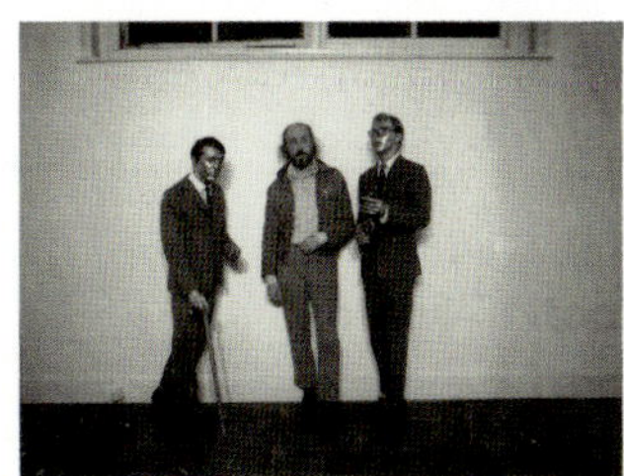
Gilbert and George 12.11.70

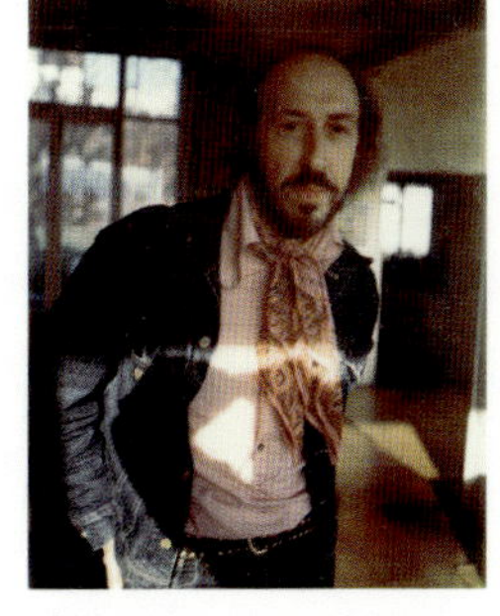
Henri Cartier-Bresson 10.1.71

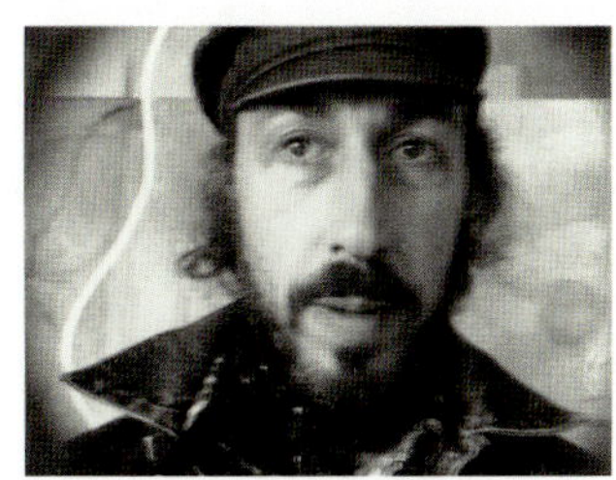
Rita Donagh 23.3.71

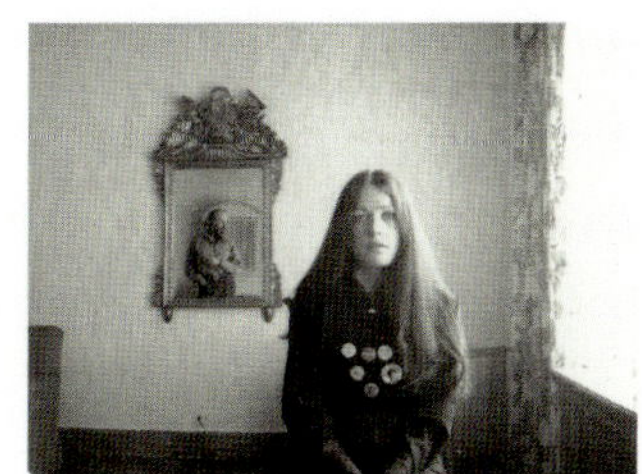
William Katz 20.7.71

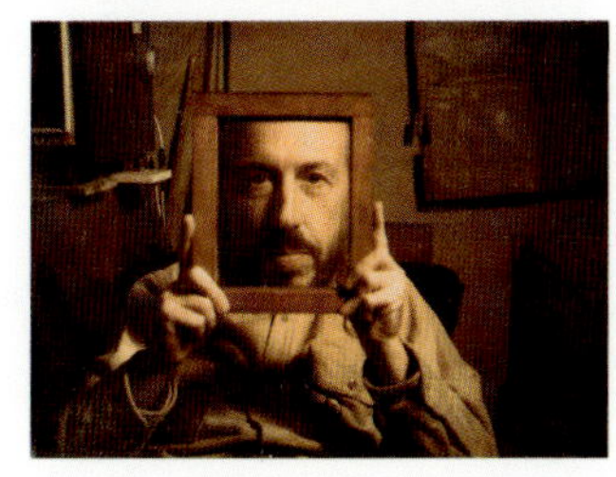
Man Ray 27.10.71

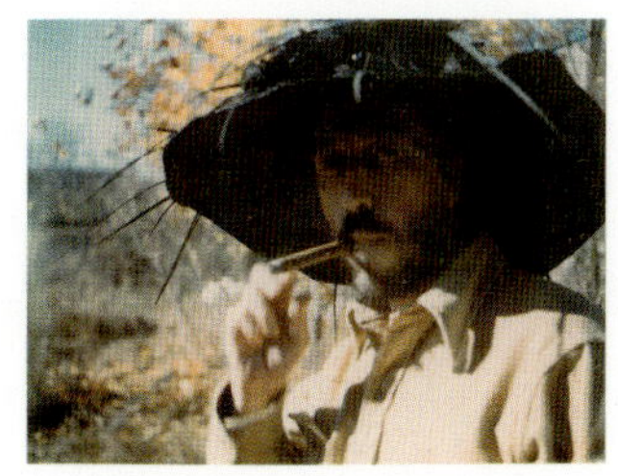
Jean Tinguely 28.10.71

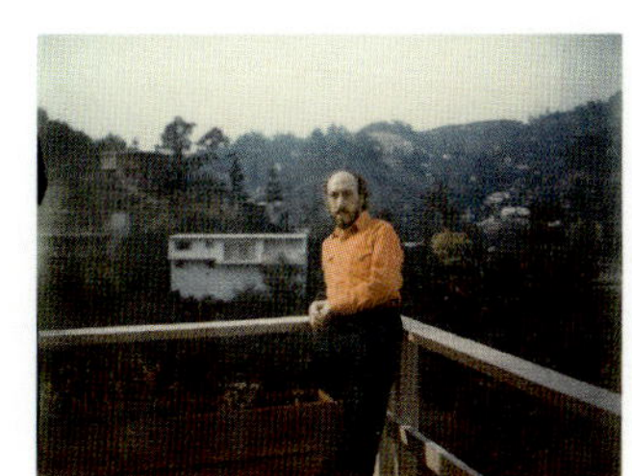
Emmett Williams 11.11.71

Polaroid Portraits Vol. 2

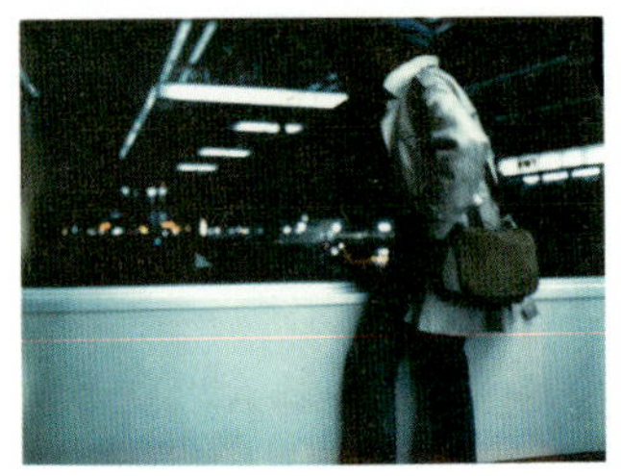
Bruce Conner 14.11.71

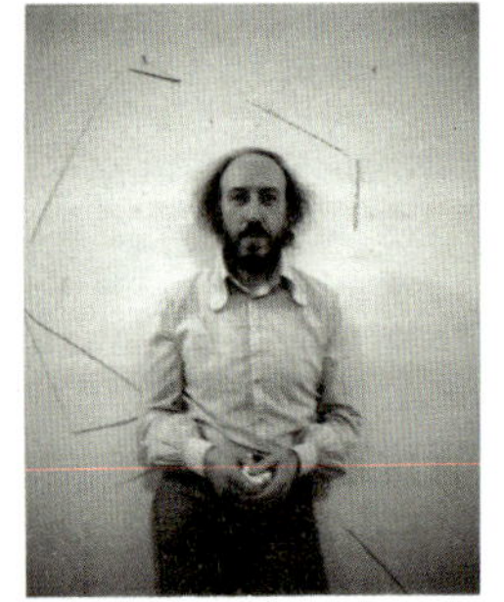
Yoko Ono 25.11.71

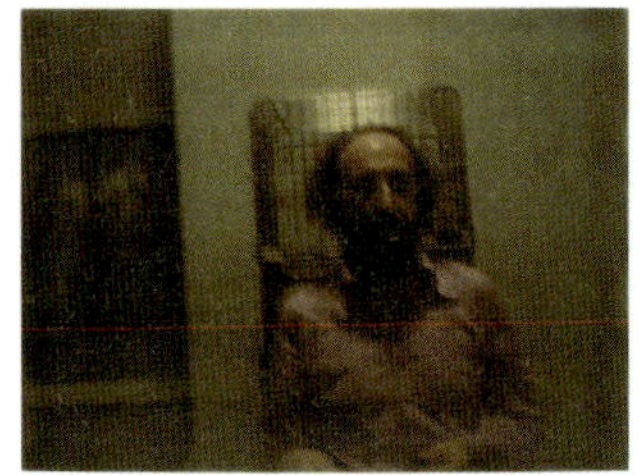
Louise Nevelson 25.11.71

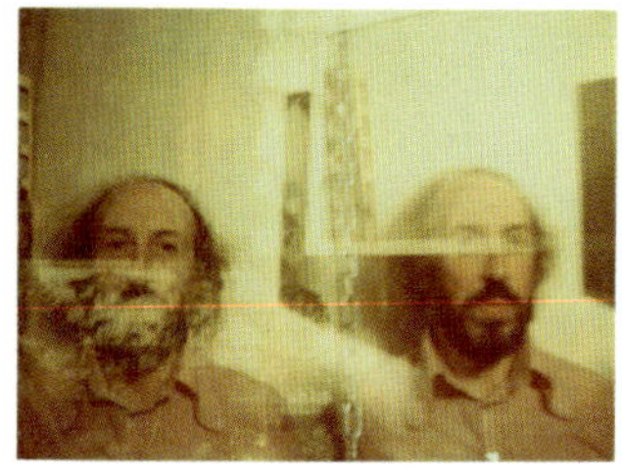
John Lennon 25.11.71

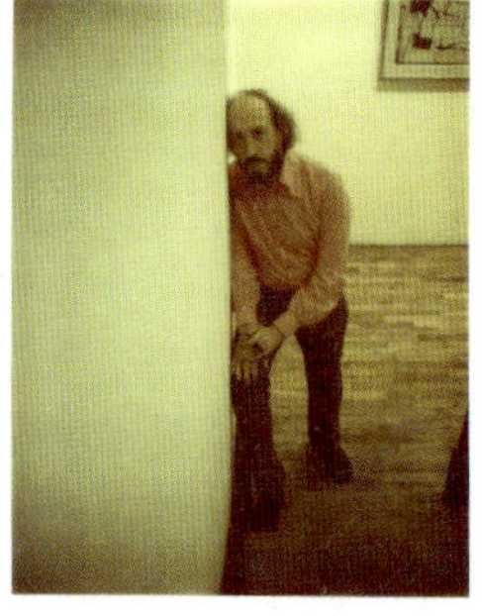
Tadanori Yokoo 25.11.71

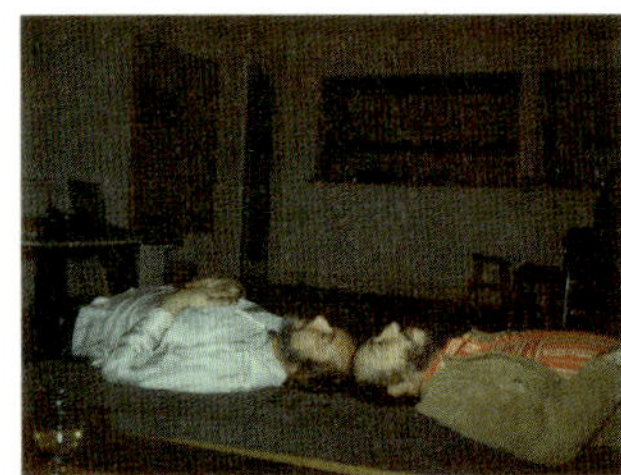
John Cage 27.11.71

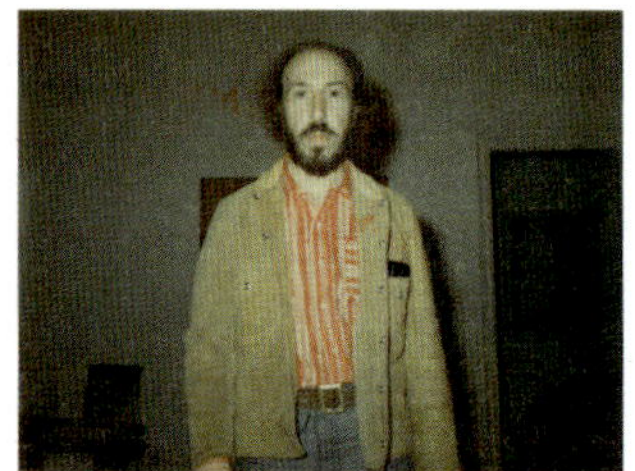
Merce Cunningham 27.11.71

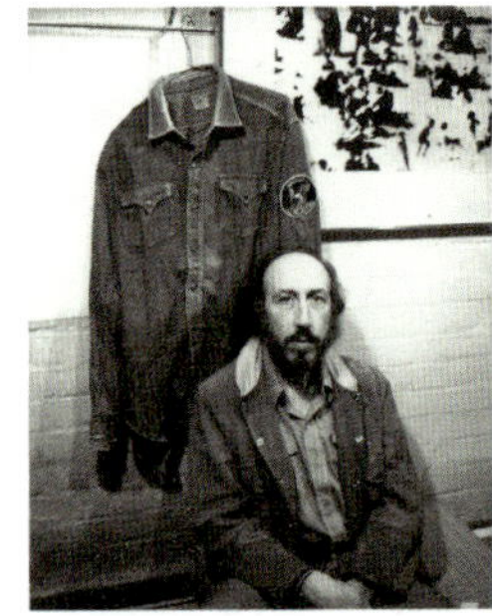
Marcel Broodthaers 15.3.72

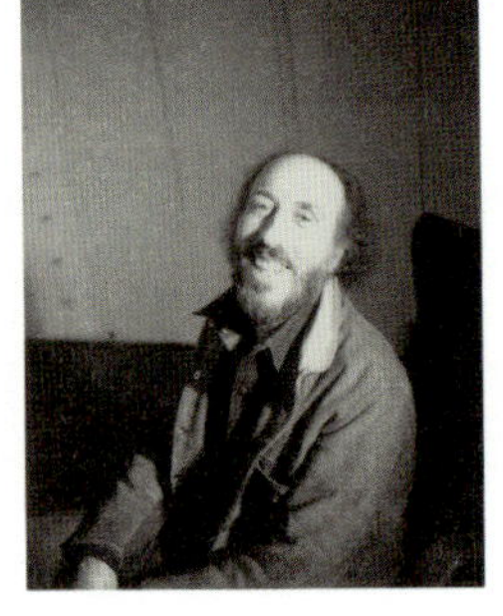
Ugo Mulas 7.12.72

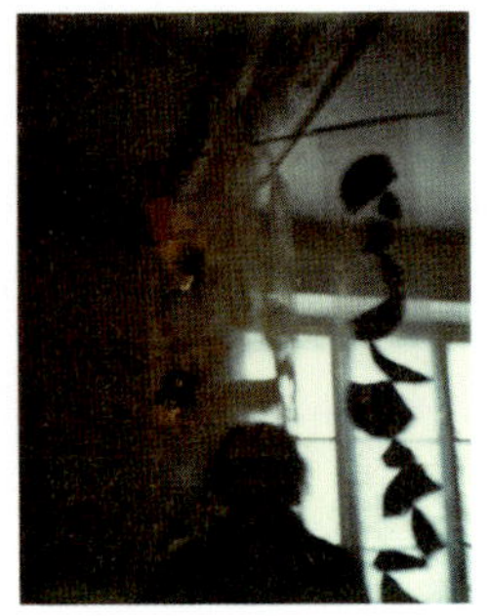
Max Ernst 18.3.73

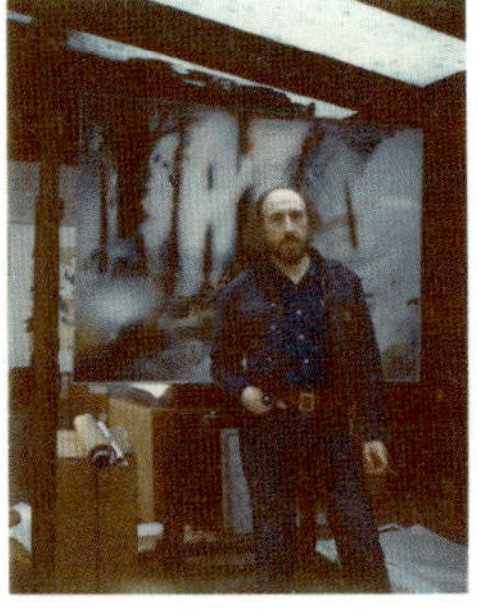
Barry McCallion 10.4.73

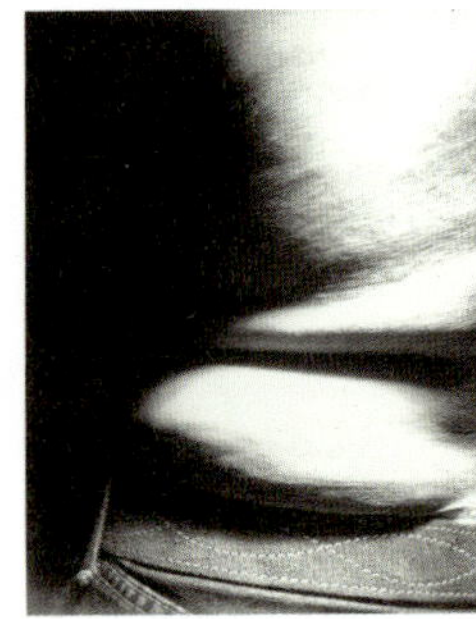
Mark Boyle 11.4.73

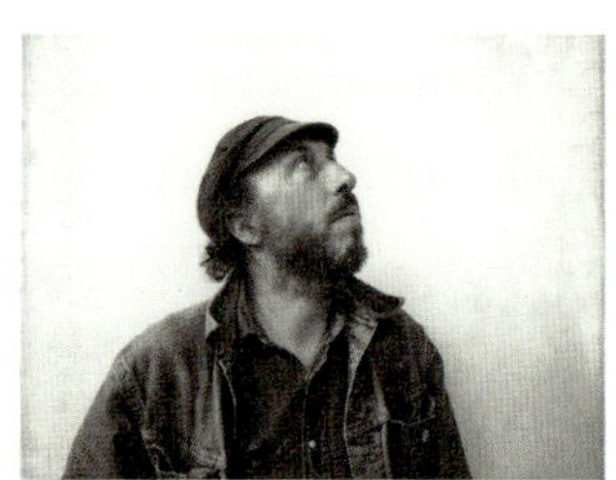
Edward Ruscha 10.5.73

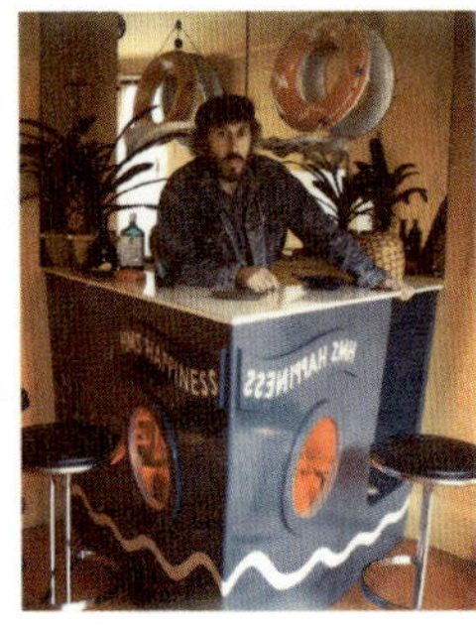
Patrick Hughes 10.6.73

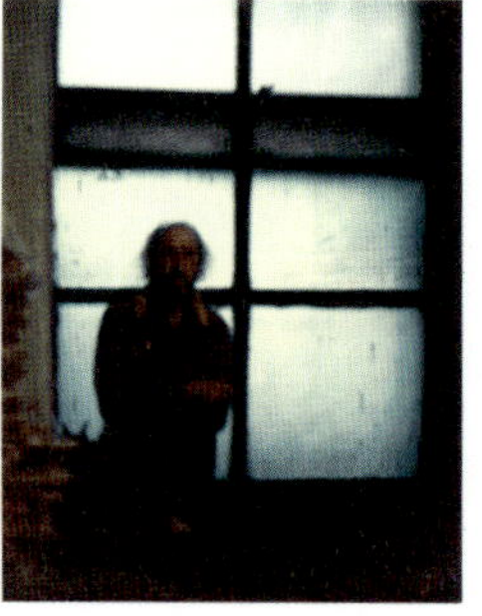
George Segal 15.9.73

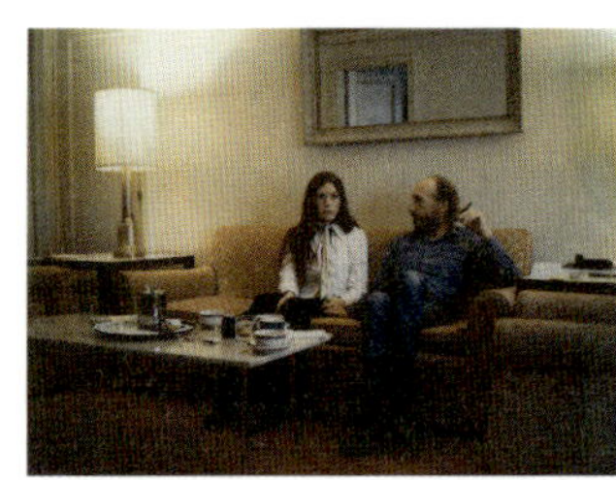
Gerhard Richter 16.9.73

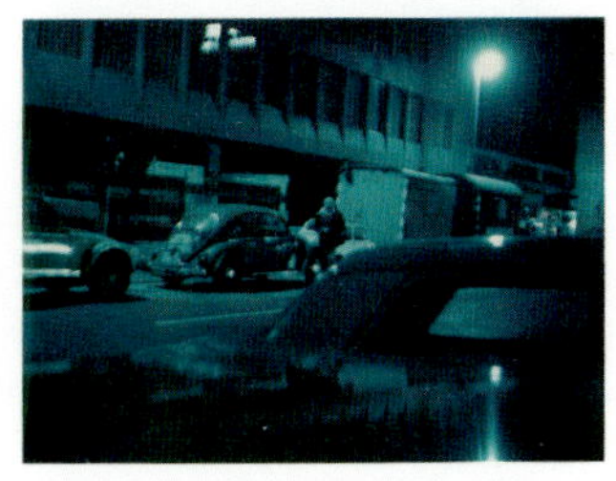
Oswald Wiener 10.10.73

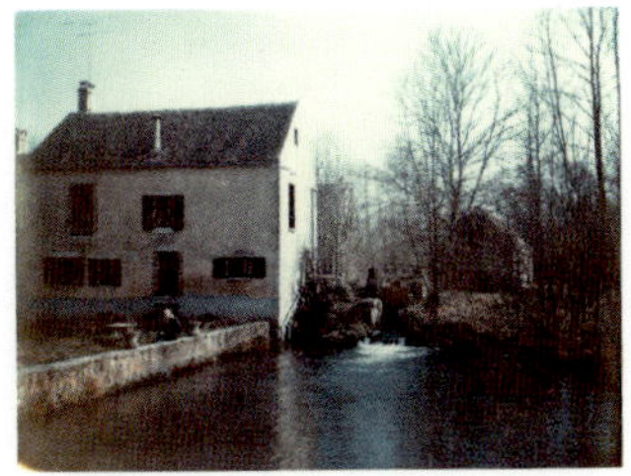
Daniel Spoerri 24.2.74

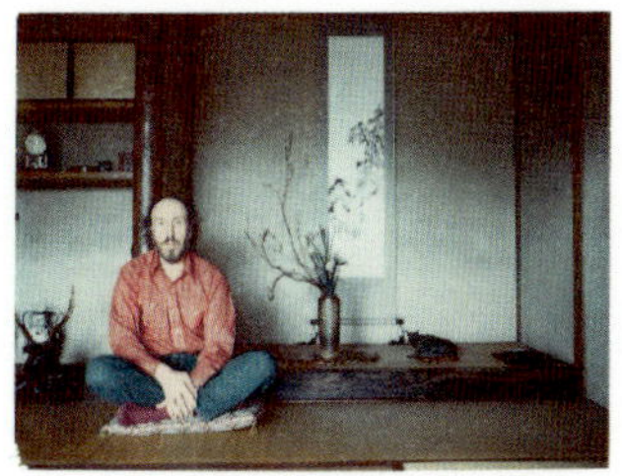
Mieko Shiomi 21.3.74

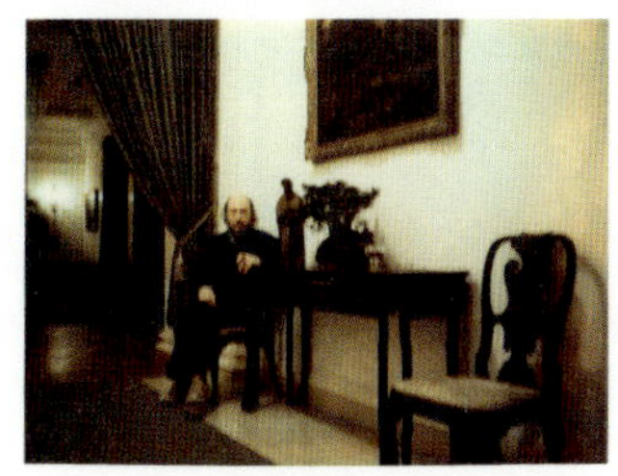
Ay-O 25.3.74

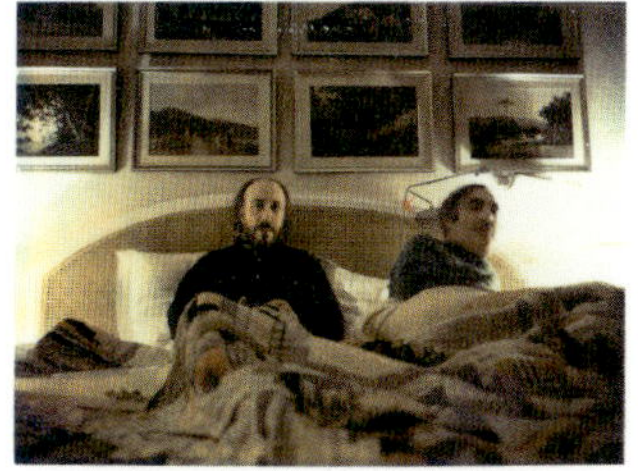
Sam Francis 25.3.74

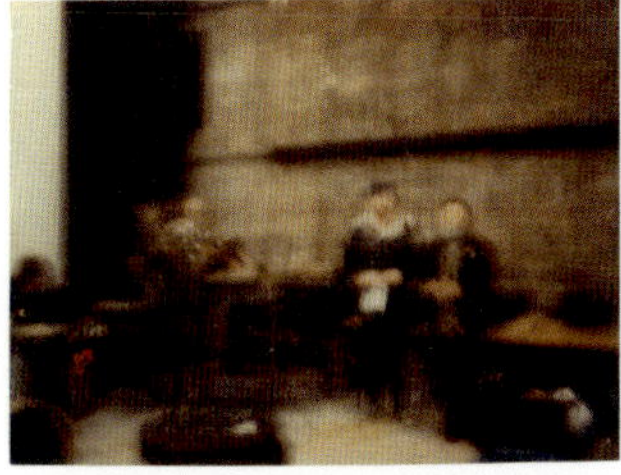
Nam June Paik 26.1.75

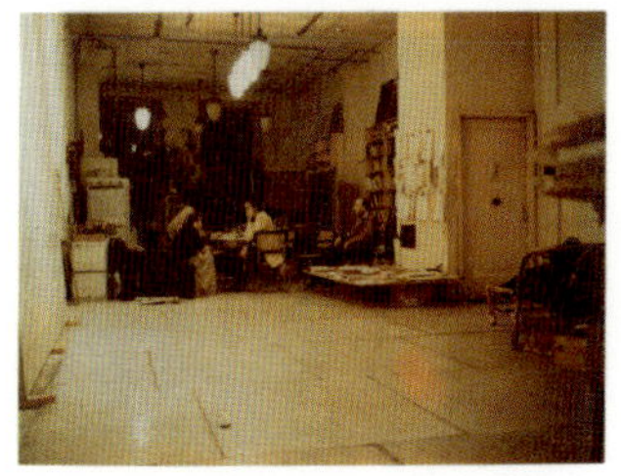
Arakawa 27.1.75

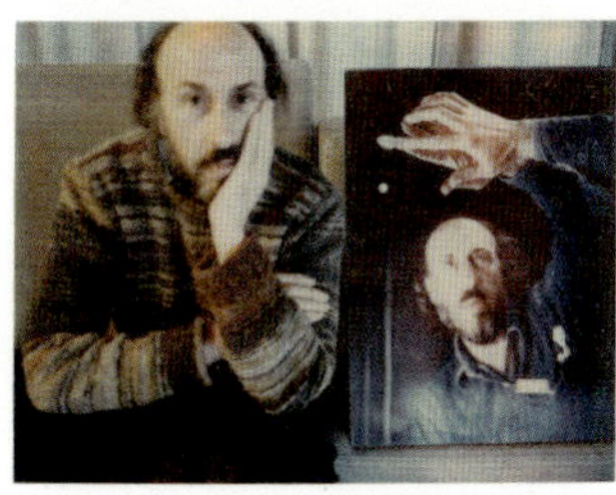
Dorothy Iannone 15.2.75

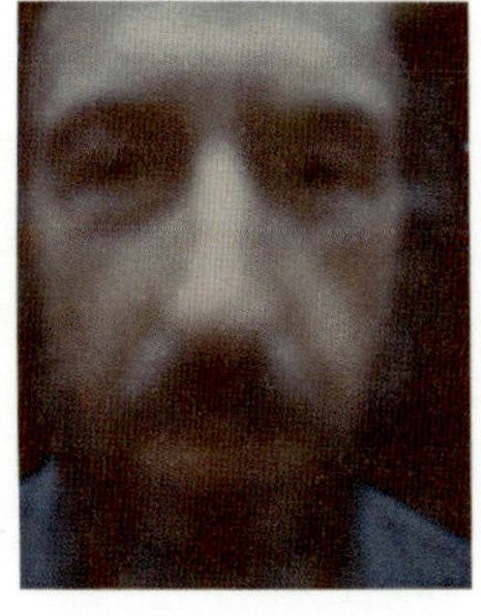
Ellsworth Kelly 6.6.75

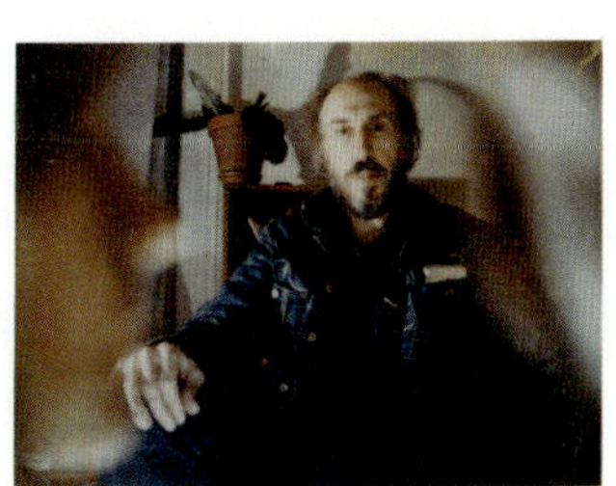
John Latham 5.11.75

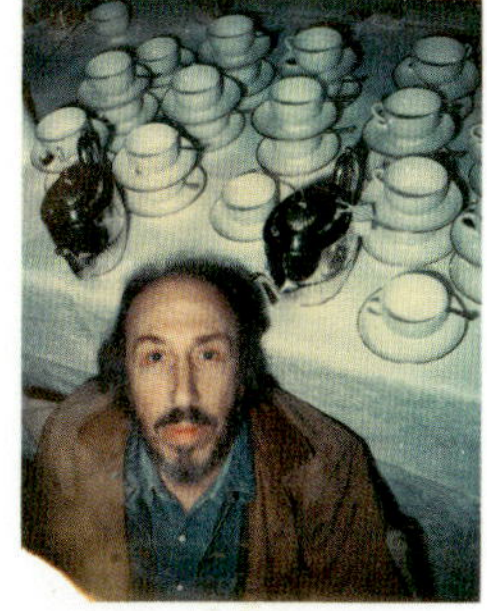
Buckminster Fuller 1.4.76

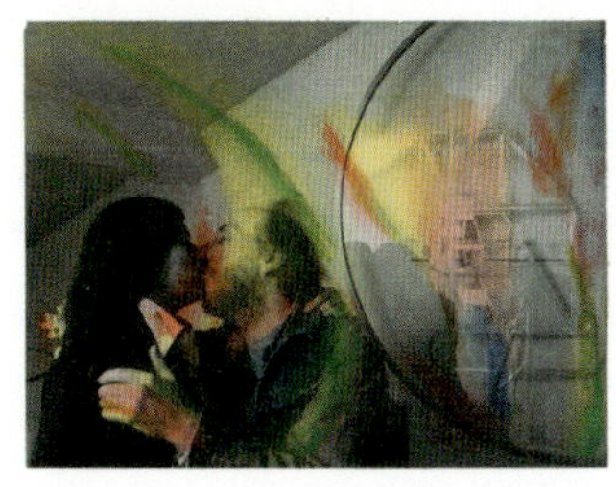
Marc Camille Chaimowicz 9.4.76

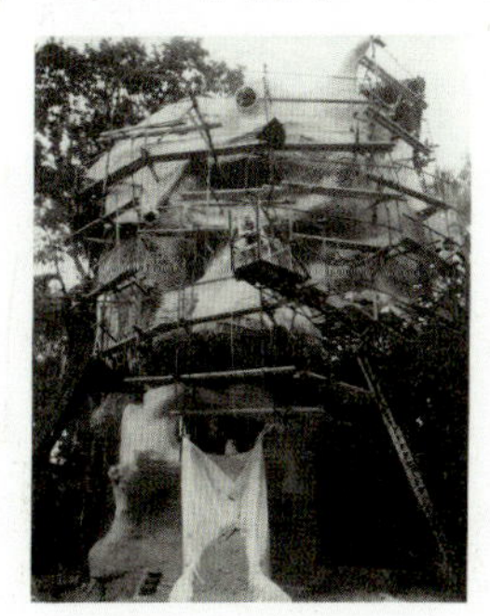
Niki de St Phalle 8.8.76

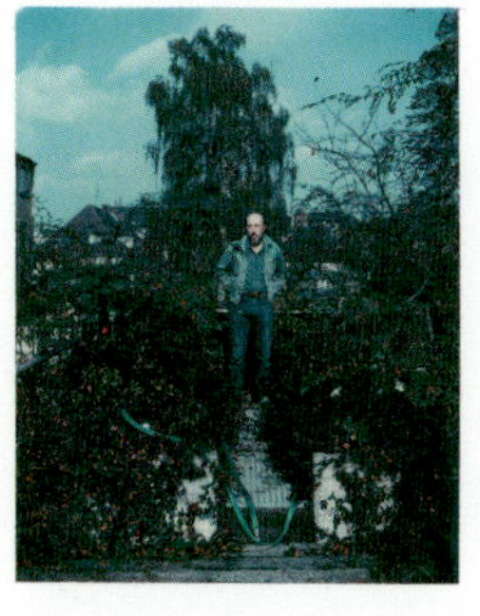
Hermann Nitsch 21.10.76

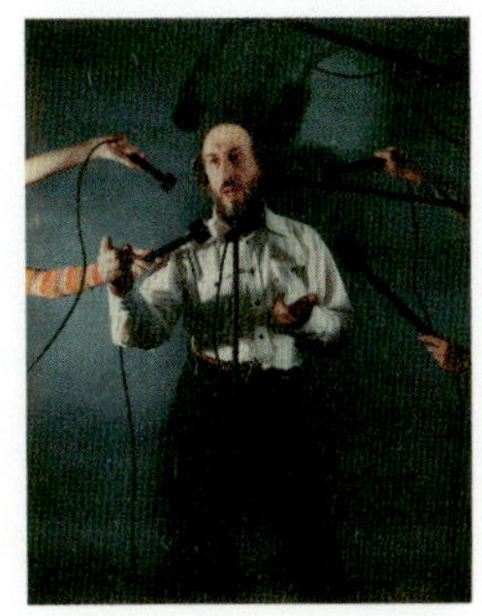
General Idea 19.11.76

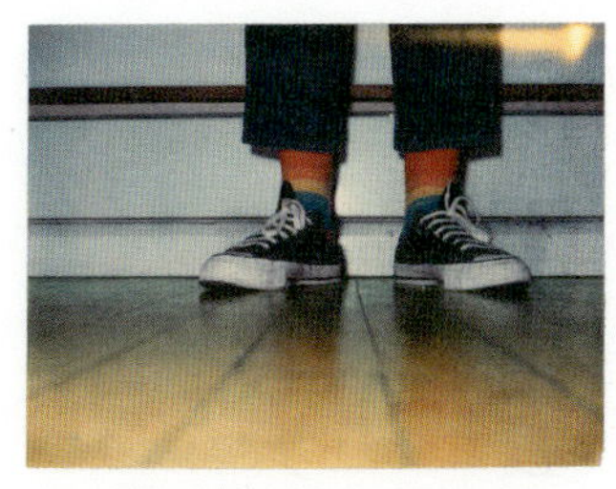
Greg Curnoe 27.11.76

Polaroid Portraits Vol. 3

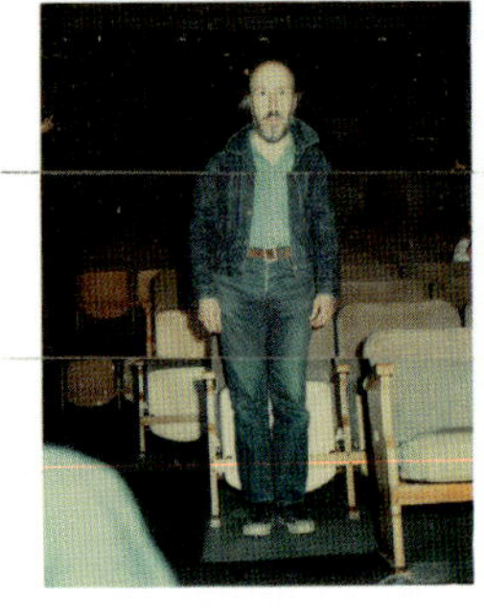

André Thomkins 01.7.77

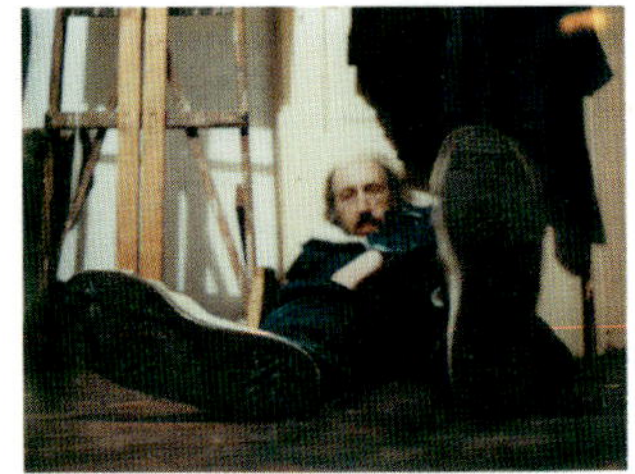

Timm Ulrichs 2.4.78

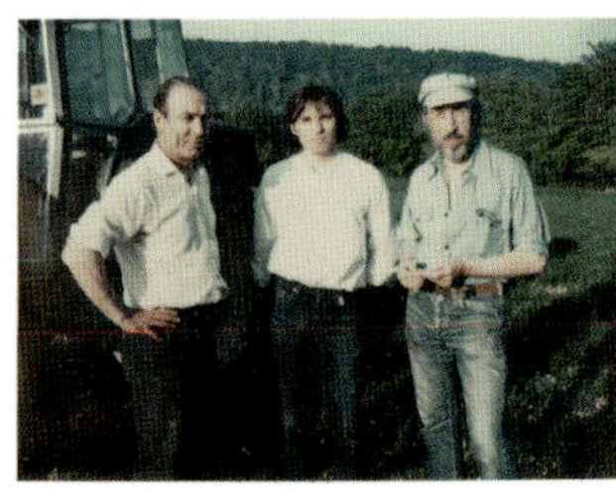

Braco Dimitrijevic 27.5.78

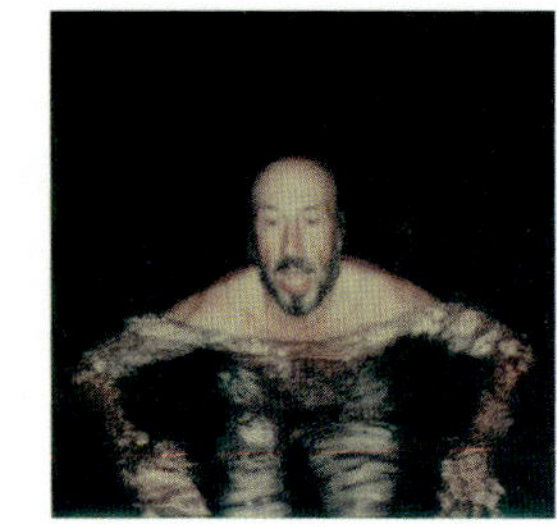

Eduardo Arranz-Bravo 18.7.78

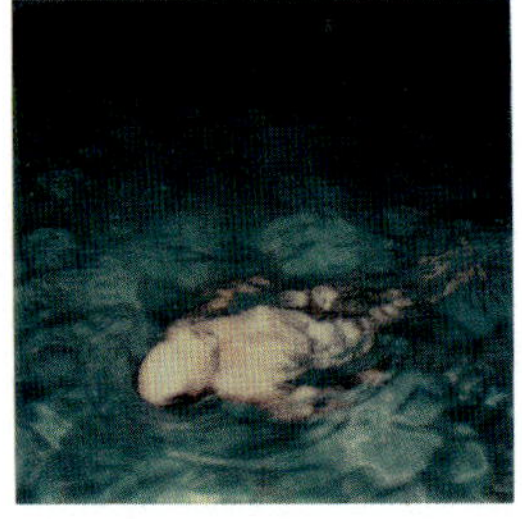

Rafael Bartolozzi 18.7.78

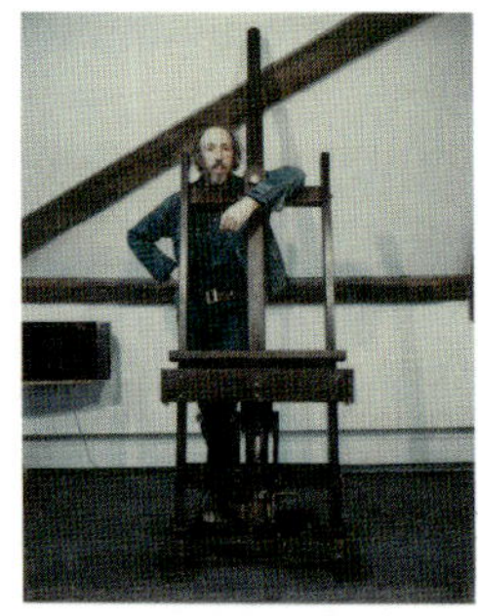

Carl Fredrik Reutersward 14.10.78

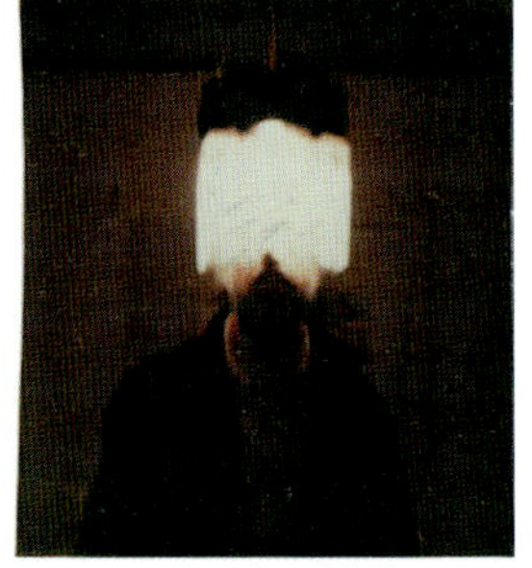

Ed Kienholz 9.3.79

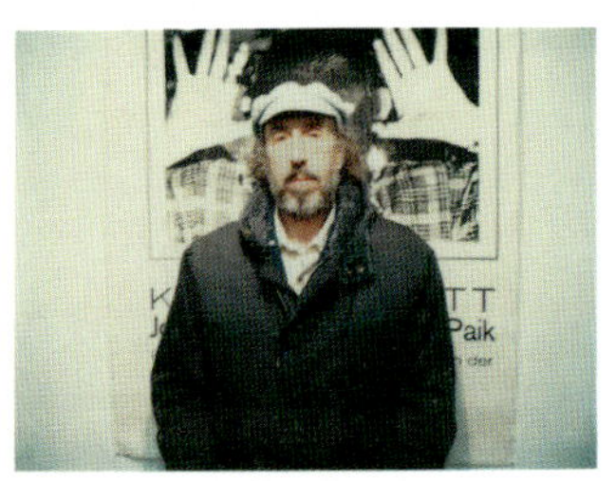

K P Brehmer 10.3.79

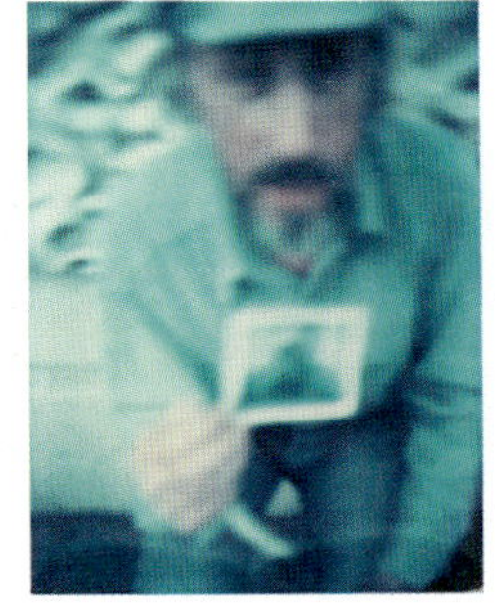

Carolee Schneemann 19.6.79

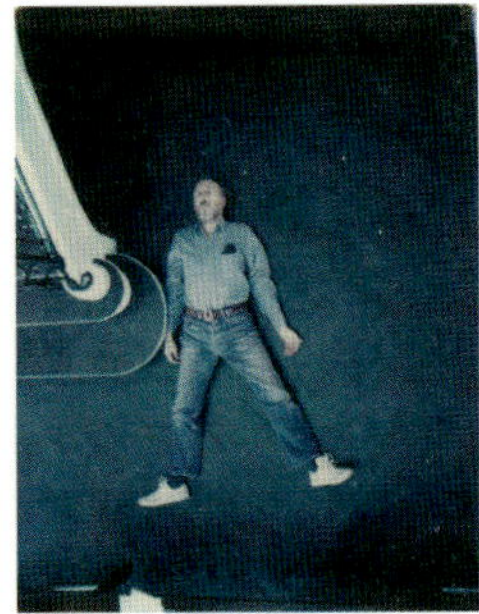

Valerio Adami 5.10.79

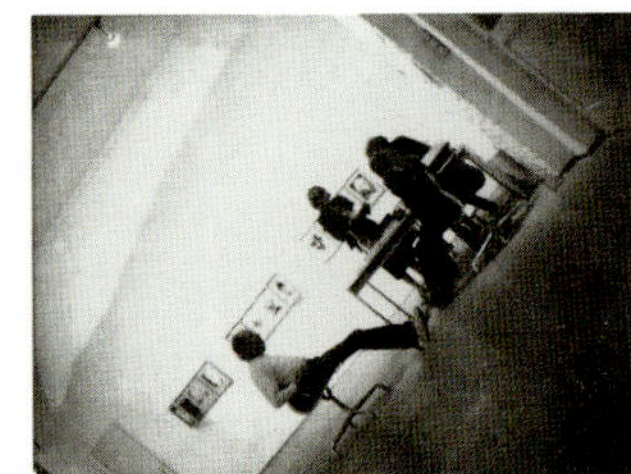

Stefan Wewerka 22.11.79

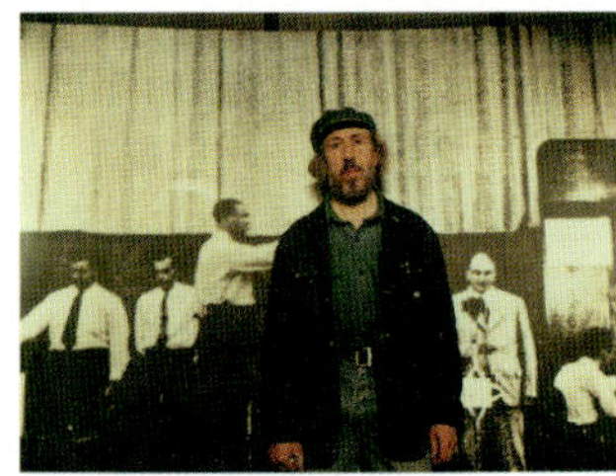

Takis 18.1.80

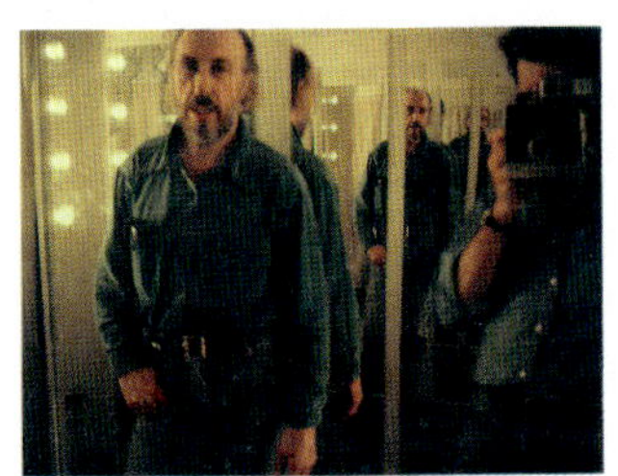

Allan Kaprow 18.1.80

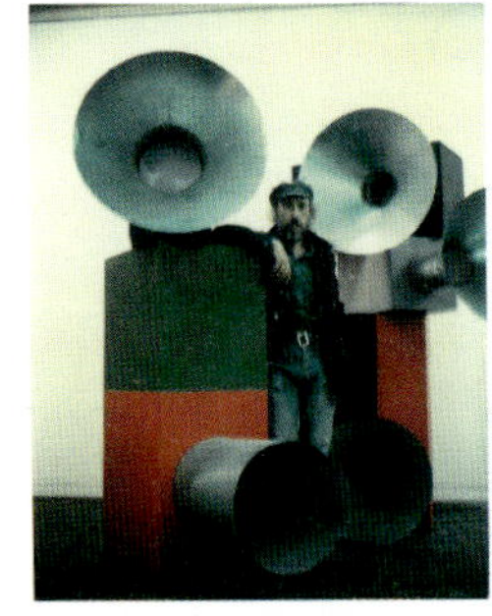

Bob Watts 18.1.80

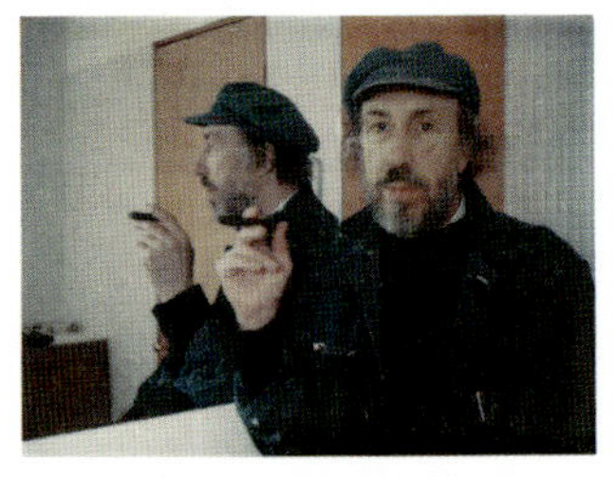

Anthony Caro 23.2.80

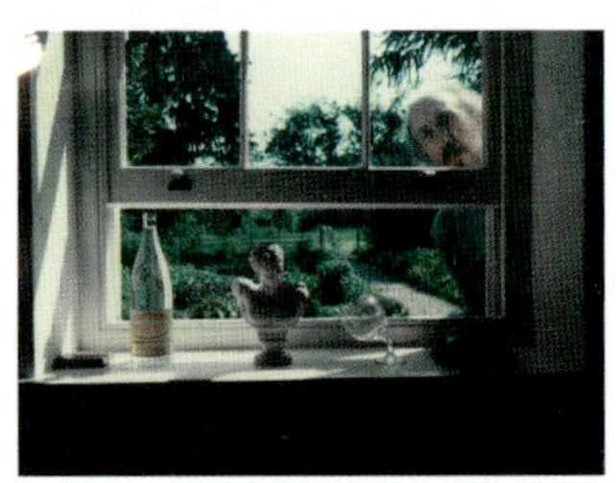

Günter Brus 4.6.80

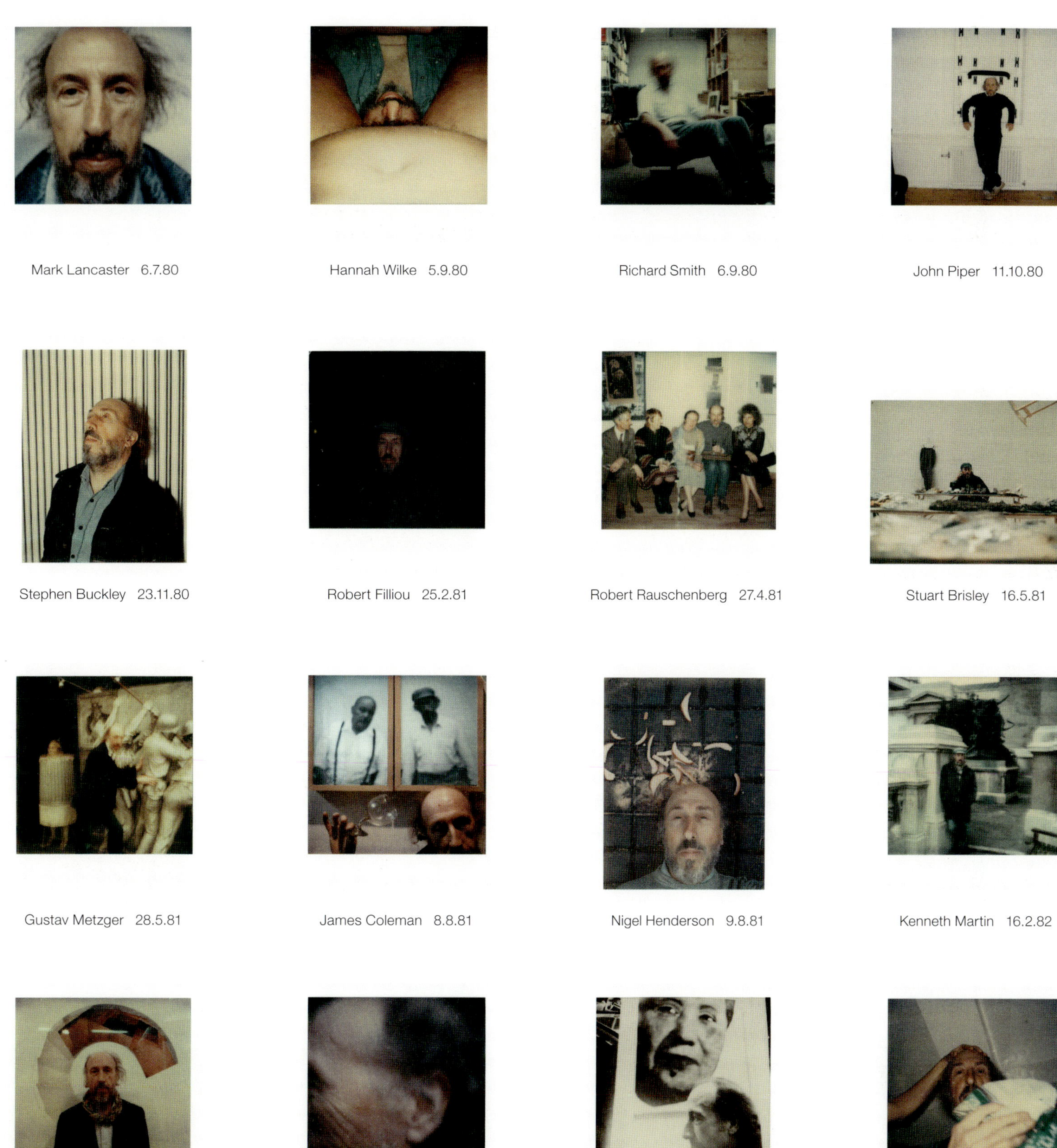

Mark Lancaster 6.7.80

Hannah Wilke 5.9.80

Richard Smith 6.9.80

John Piper 11.10.80

Stephen Buckley 23.11.80

Robert Filliou 25.2.81

Robert Rauschenberg 27.4.81

Stuart Brisley 16.5.81

Gustav Metzger 28.5.81

James Coleman 8.8.81

Nigel Henderson 9.8.81

Kenneth Martin 16.2.82

Jan Dibbets 16.2.82

Dieter Rams 29.6.82

Linda McCartney 23.6.82

Paul McCartney 23.9.82

Polaroid Portraits Vol. 4

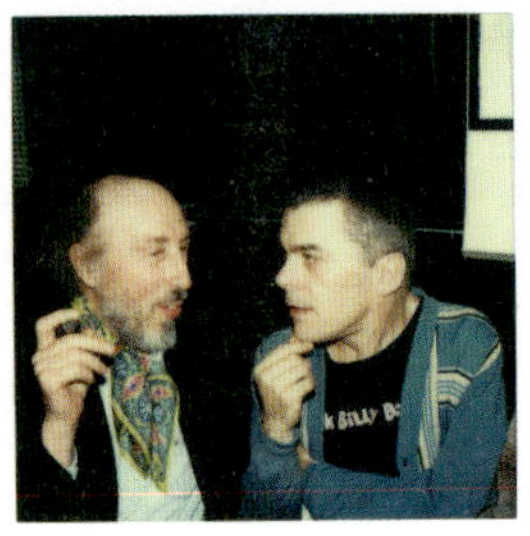

Peter Blake 10.2.83

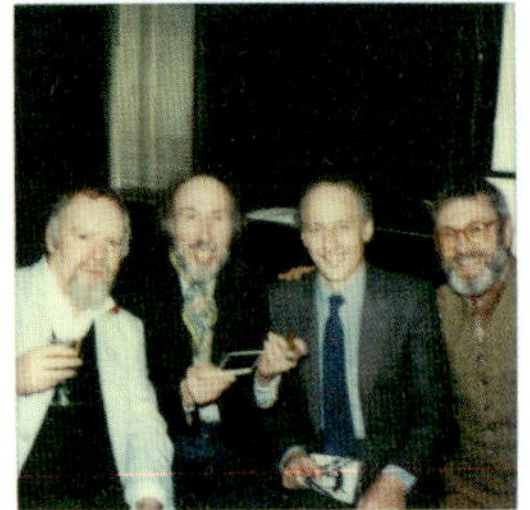

Ian Dury 10.2.83

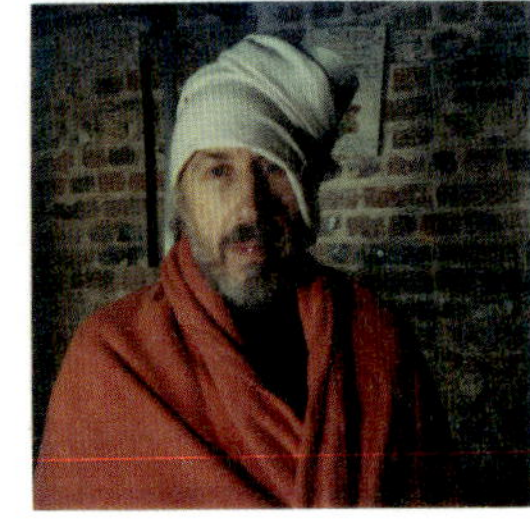

Basil Bunting 27.2.83

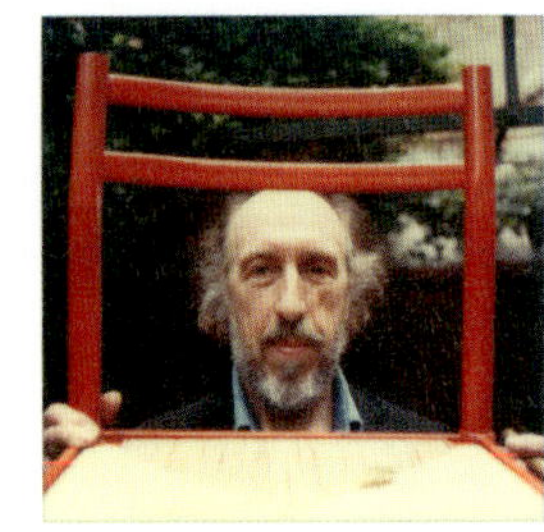

Max Bill 10.4.83

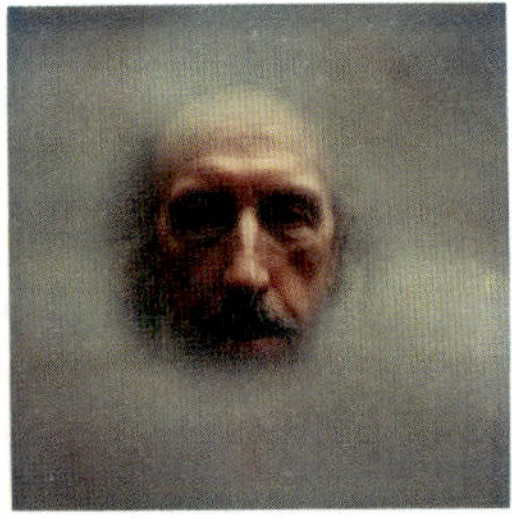

Louis le Brocquy 10.4.83

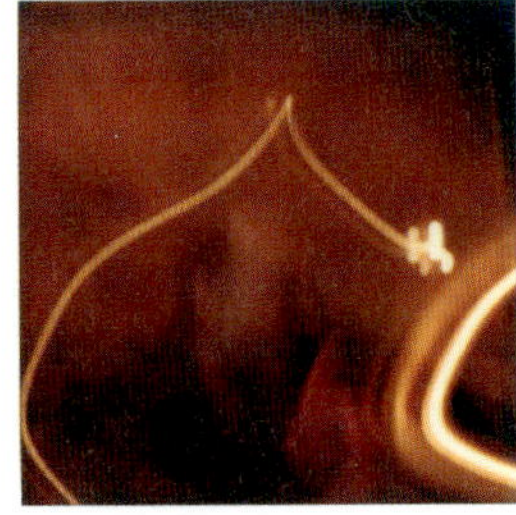

Arnulf Rainer 10.4.83

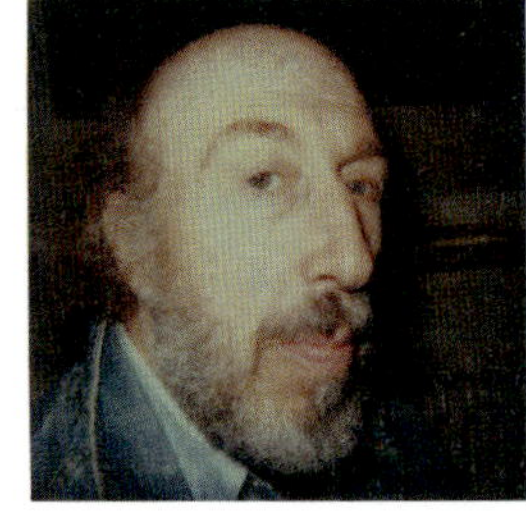

Klaus Staeck 30.9.84

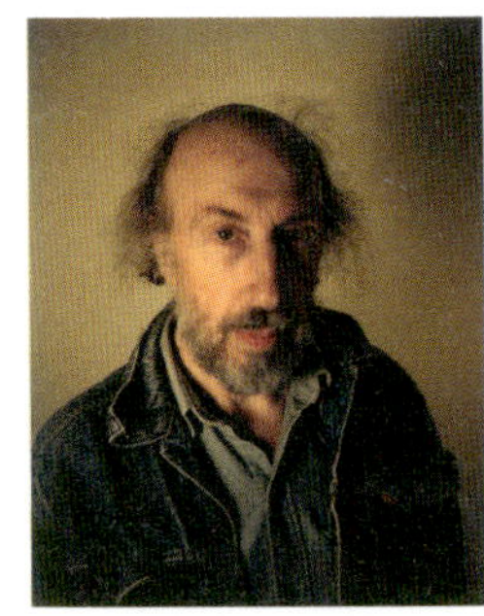

Bryan Ferry 24.8.85

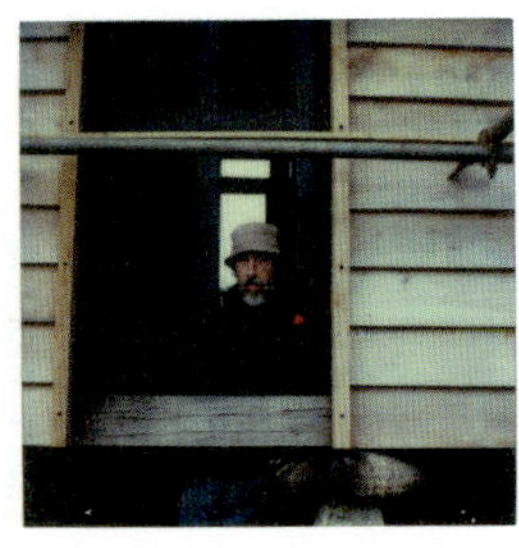

Cedric Price 6.7.86

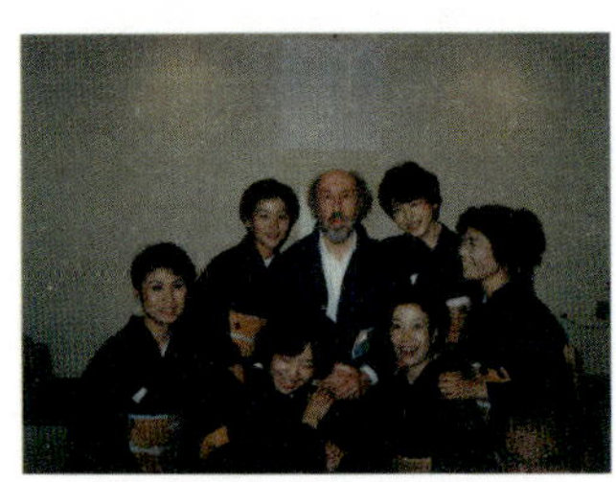

Shigeo Fukuda 17.10.86

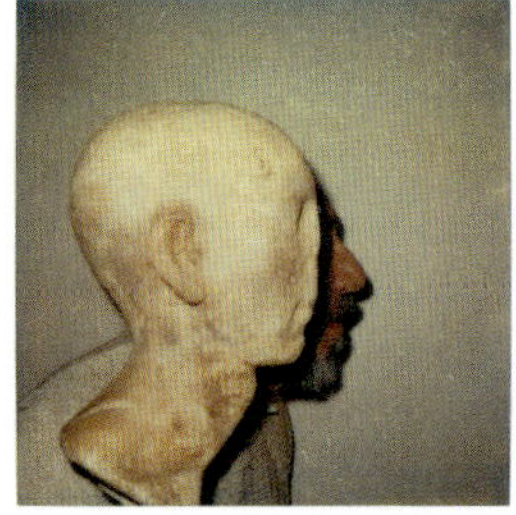

Pol Bury 24.3.88

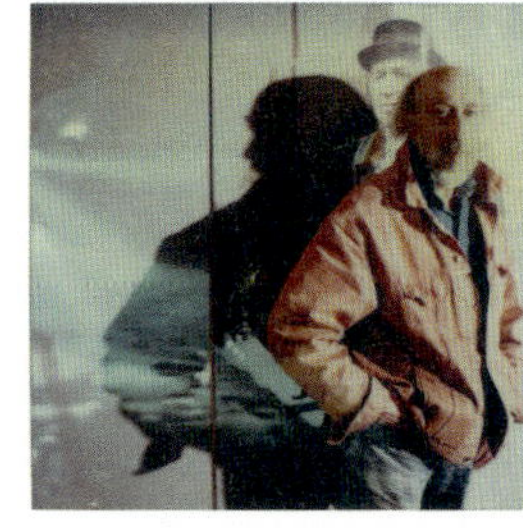

Tim Head 6.11.88

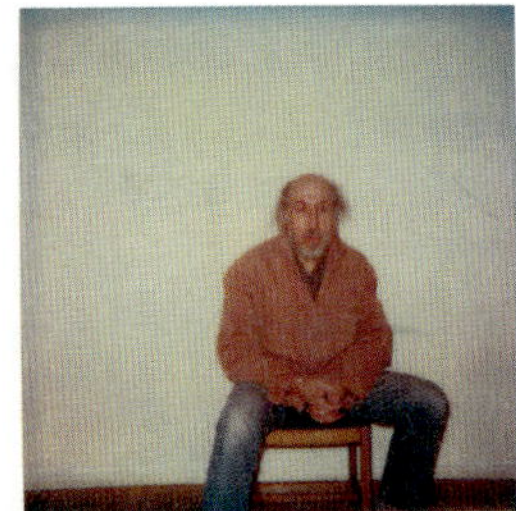

Walter de Maria 8.3.89

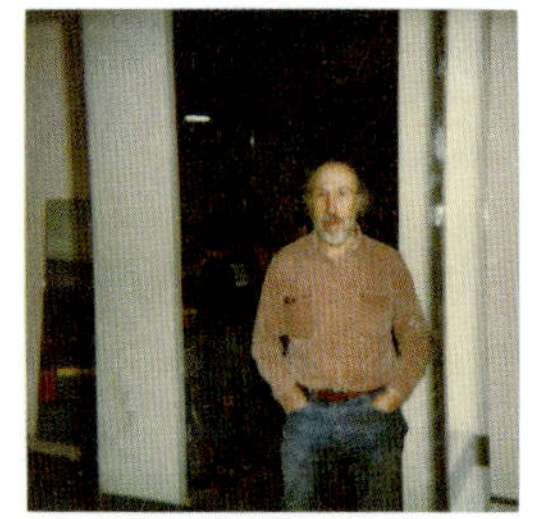

Richard Wilson 10.10.89

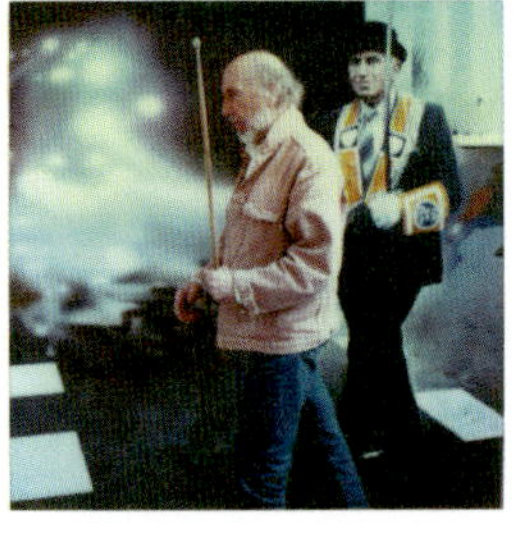

Derek Boshier 12.6.90

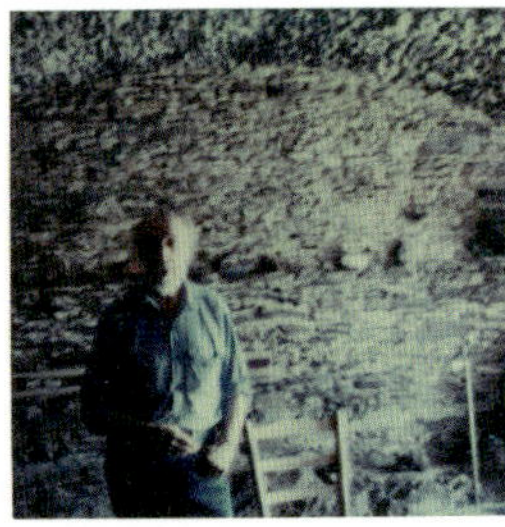

Mario Merz 20.7.90

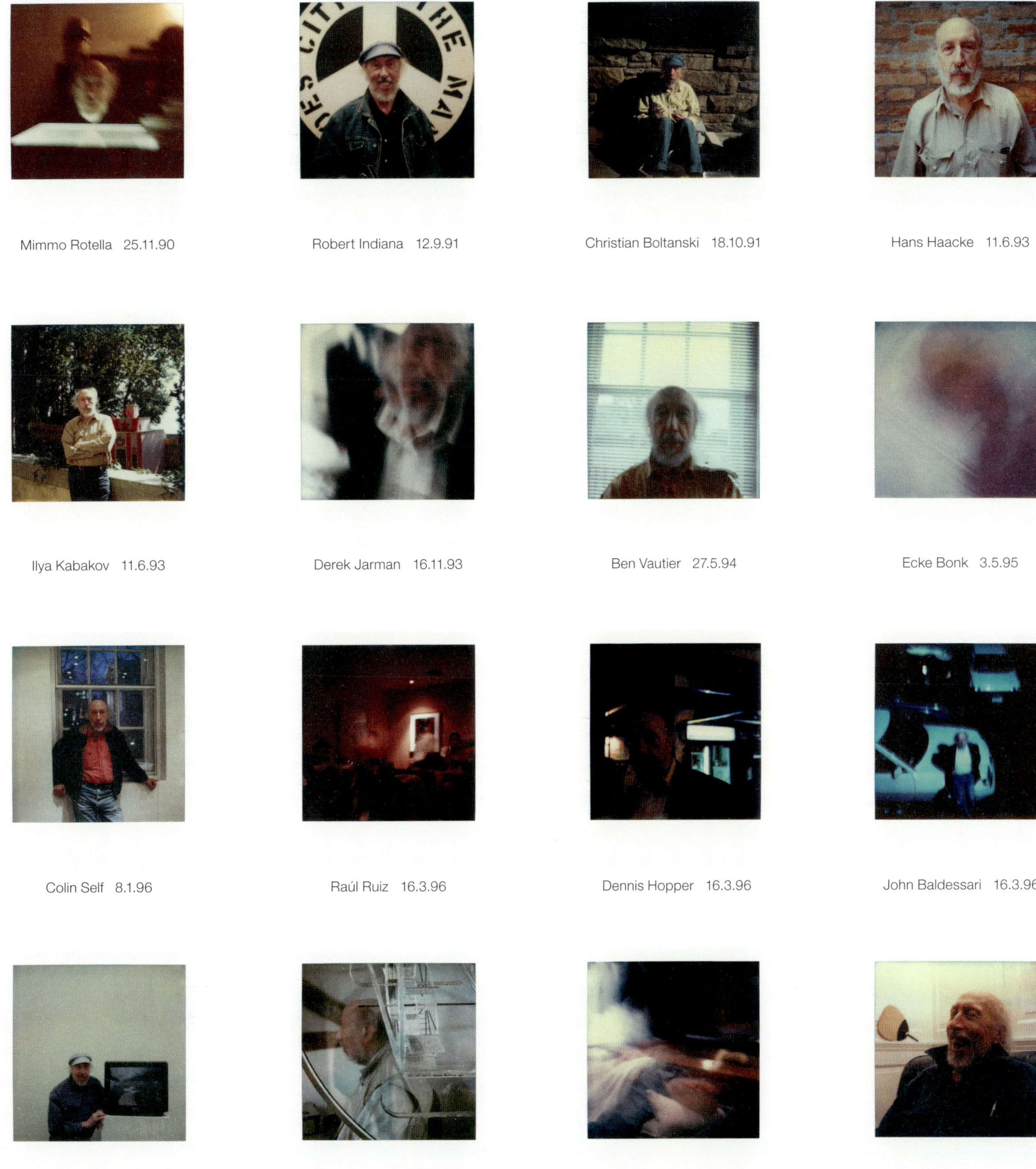

Mimmo Rotella 25.11.90

Robert Indiana 12.9.91

Christian Boltanski 18.10.91

Hans Haacke 11.6.93

Ilya Kabakov 11.6.93

Derek Jarman 16.11.93

Ben Vautier 27.5.94

Ecke Bonk 3.5.95

Colin Self 8.1.96

Raúl Ruiz 16.3.96

Dennis Hopper 16.3.96

John Baldessari 16.3.96

Michelangelo Pistoletto 19.4.97

Jean Sabrier 3.8.98

Ferran Adrià 25.9.99

Bruce Mau 25.11.00

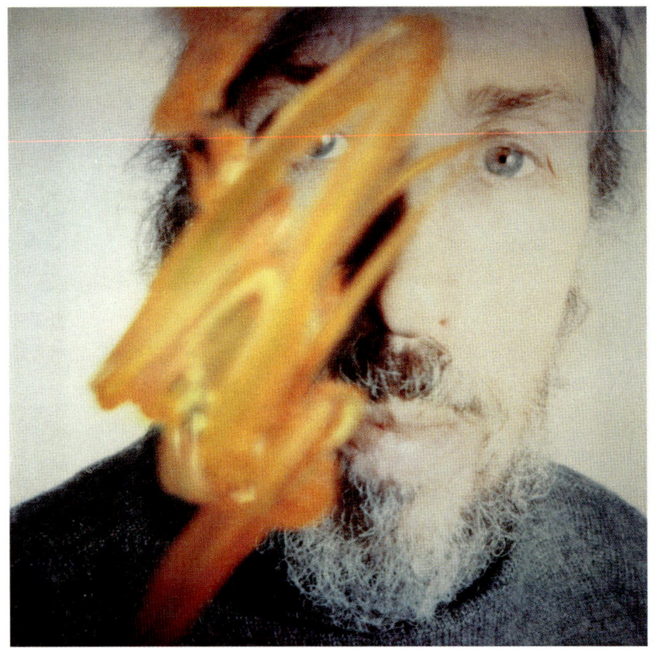

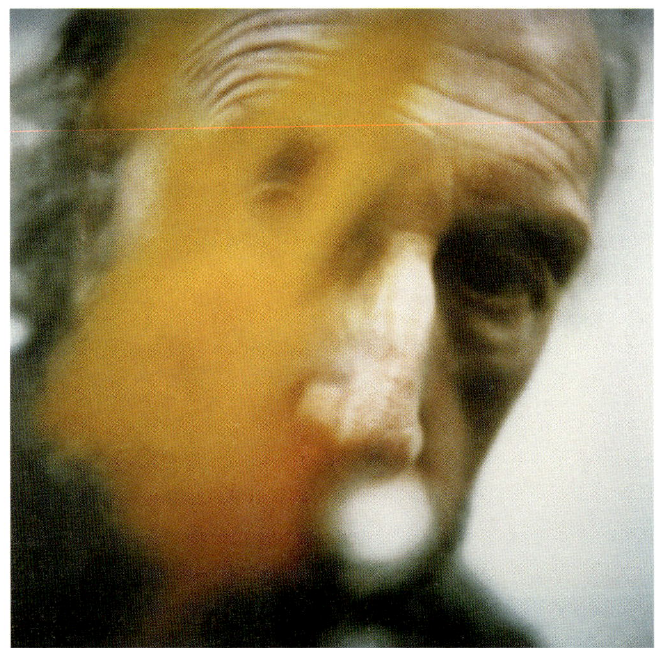

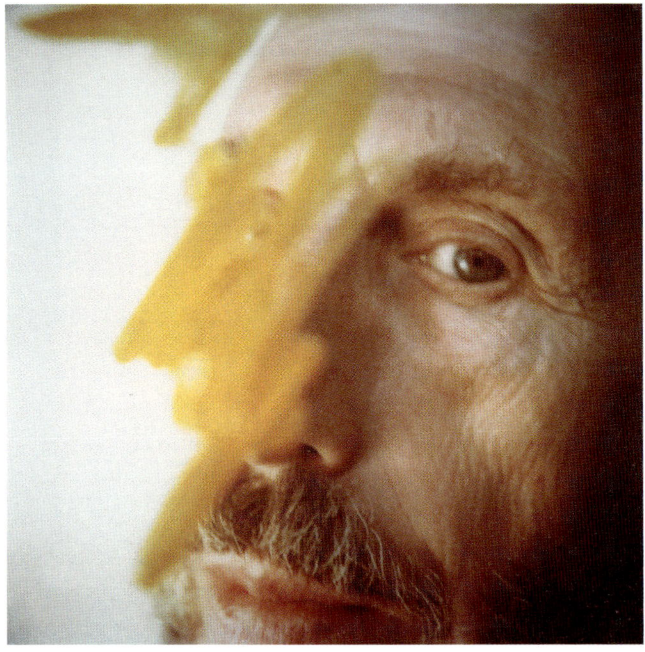

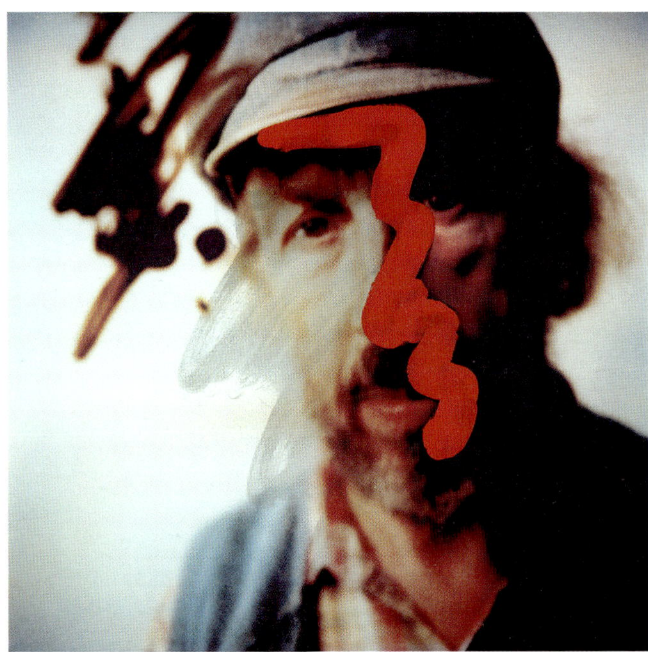

Self-portrait 05.3.81 a 1990

Self-portrait 05.3.81 c 1990

Self-portrait 12.7.80 a 1990

Self-portrait 13.7.80 a 1990

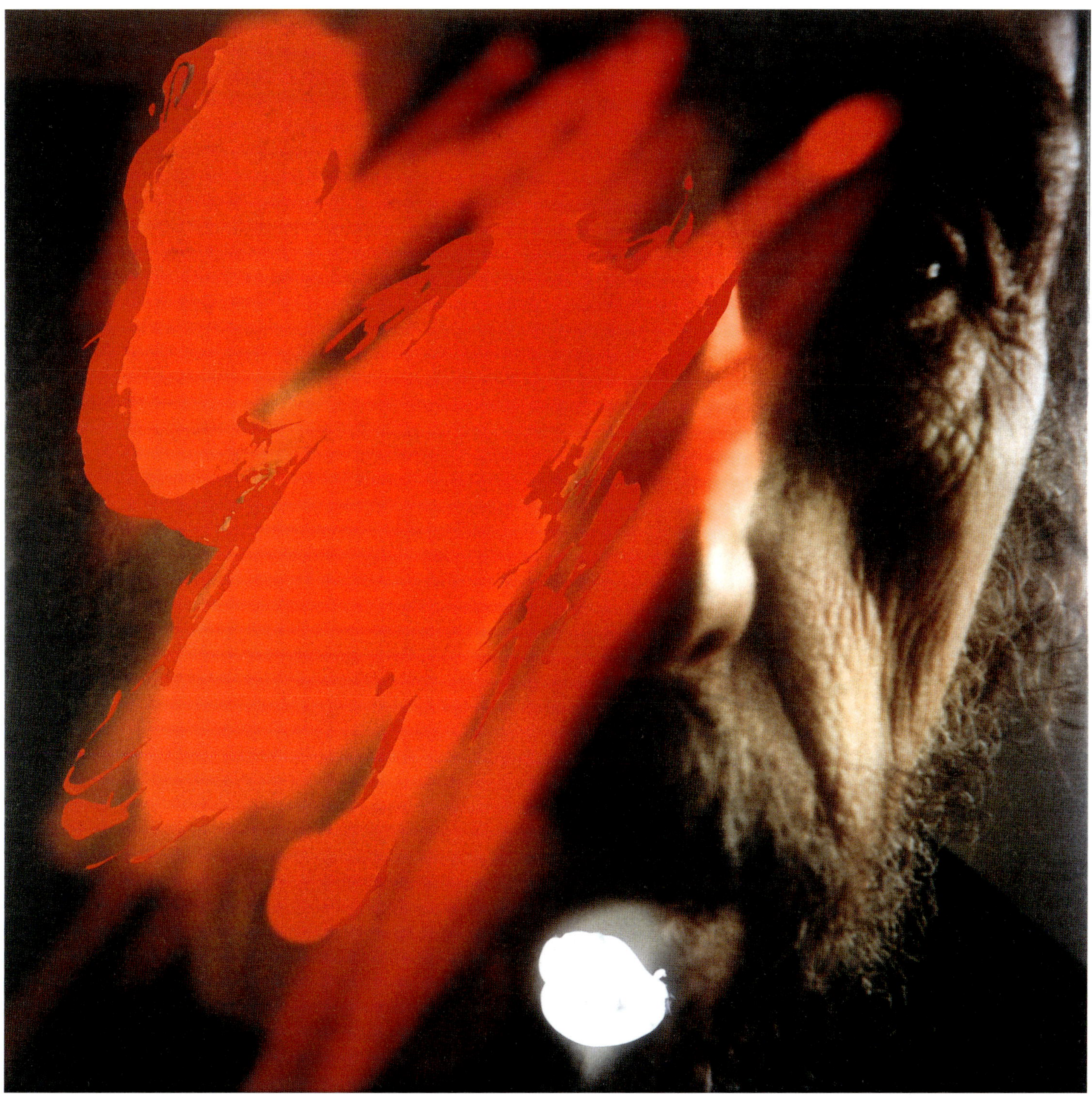

Self-portrait 04.3.81 b 1990

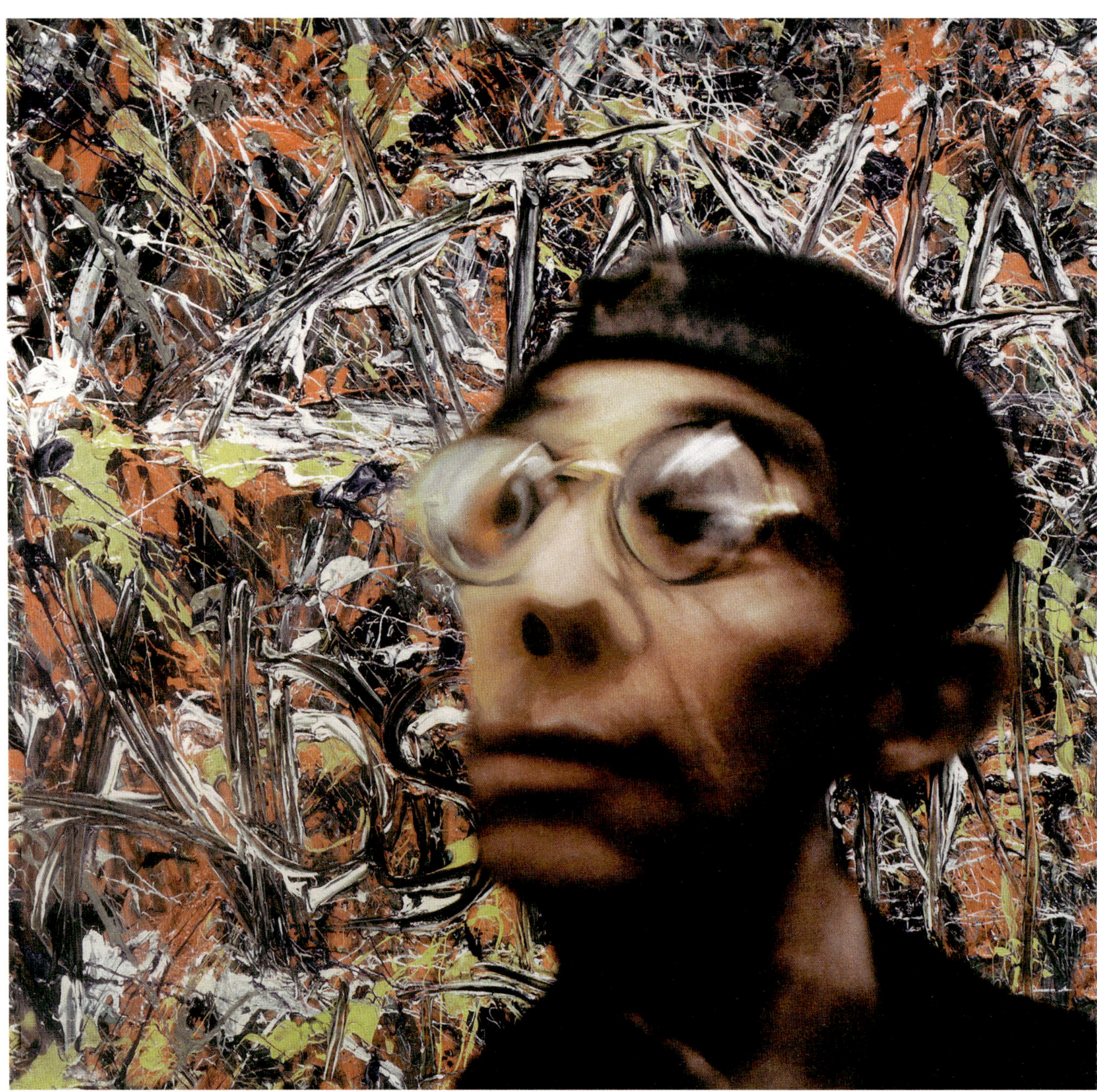

Derek Jarman 1994

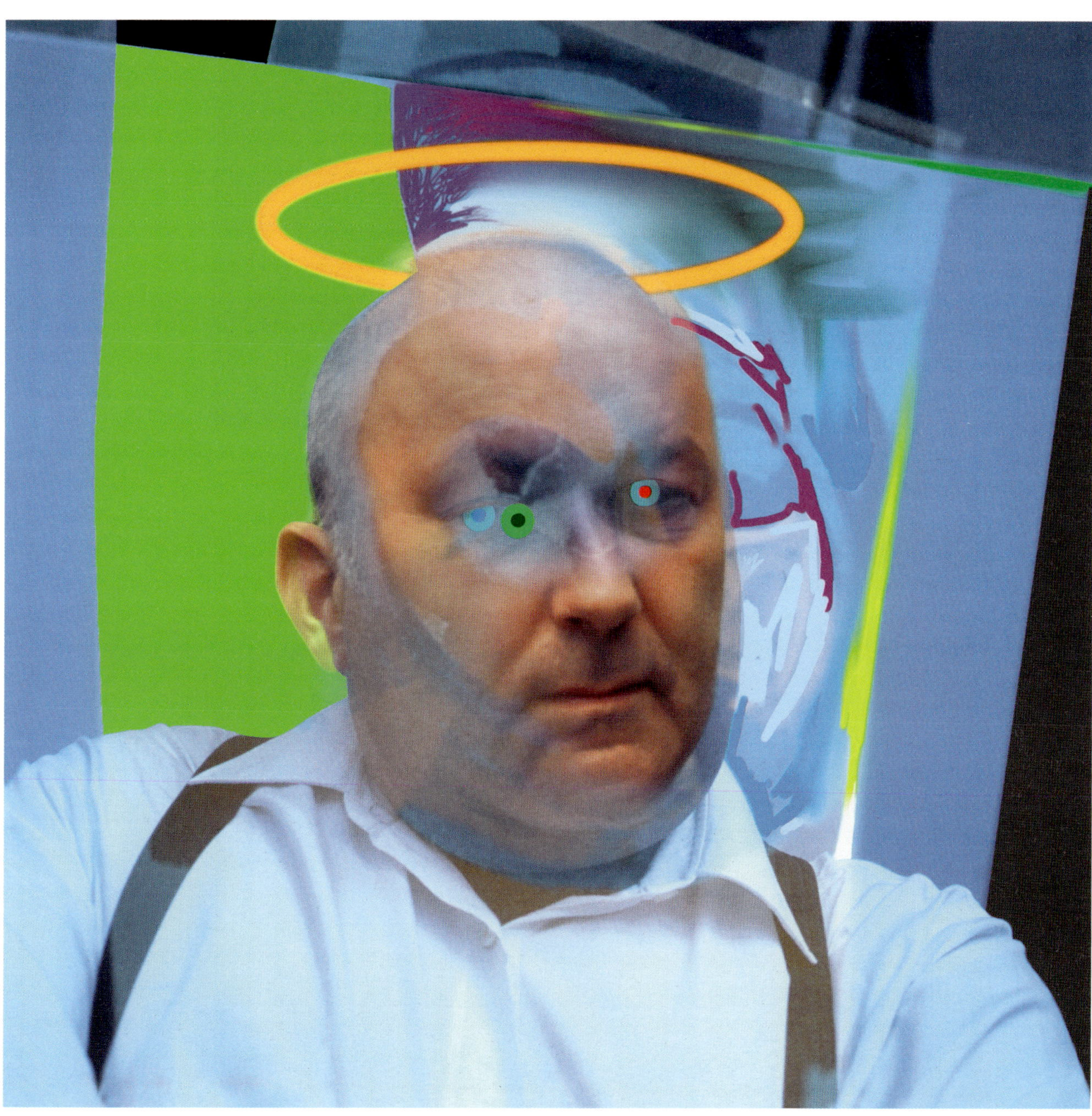

Dieter Roth 1993

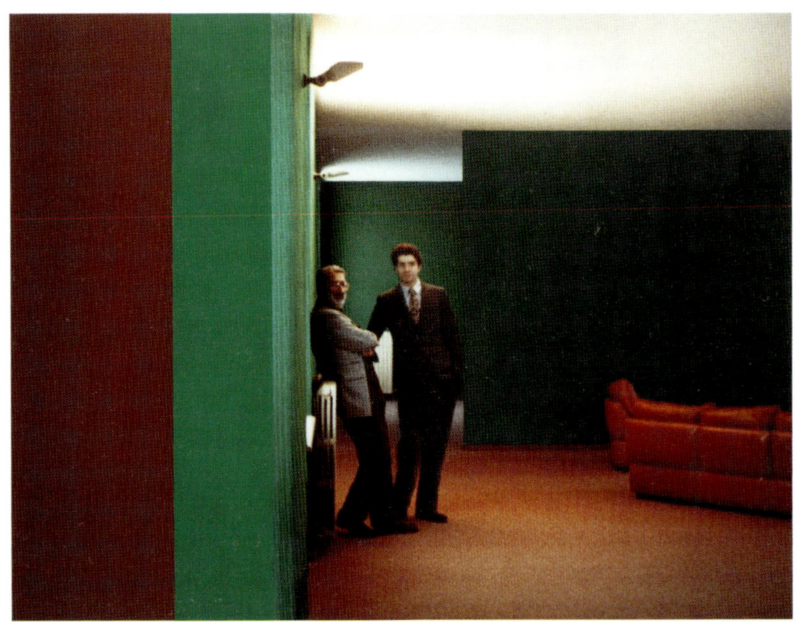

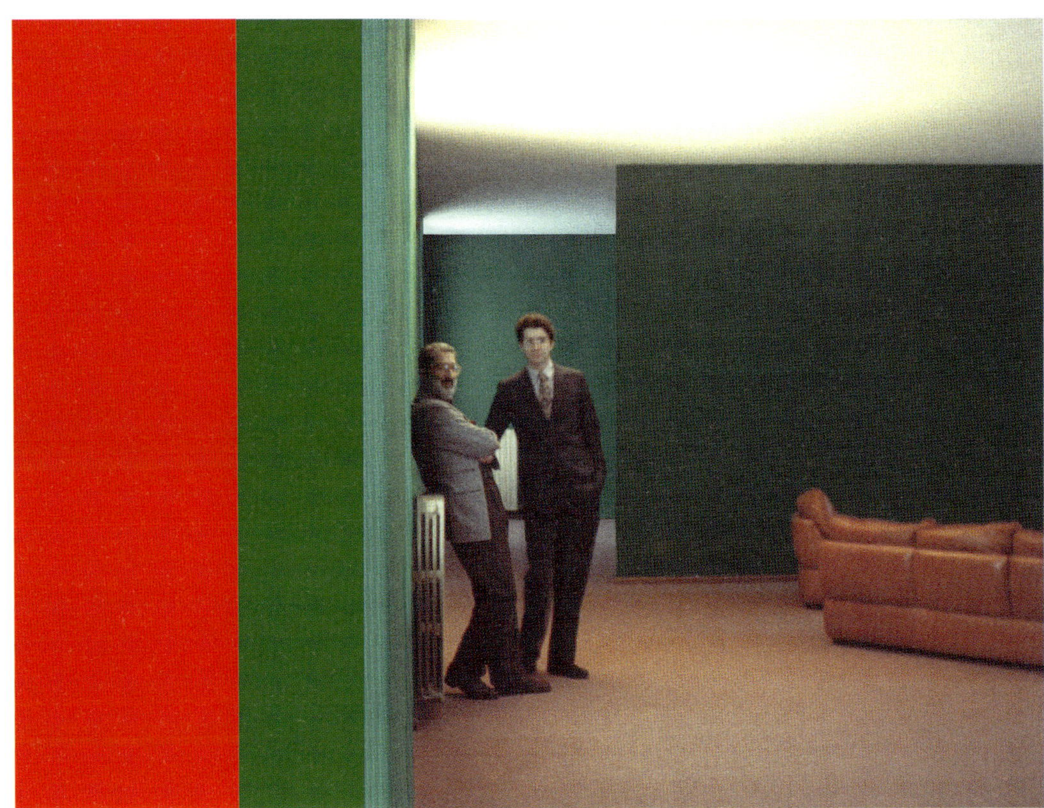

Two gentlemen of Alba 1991

Giorgio Marconi e figlio 1996

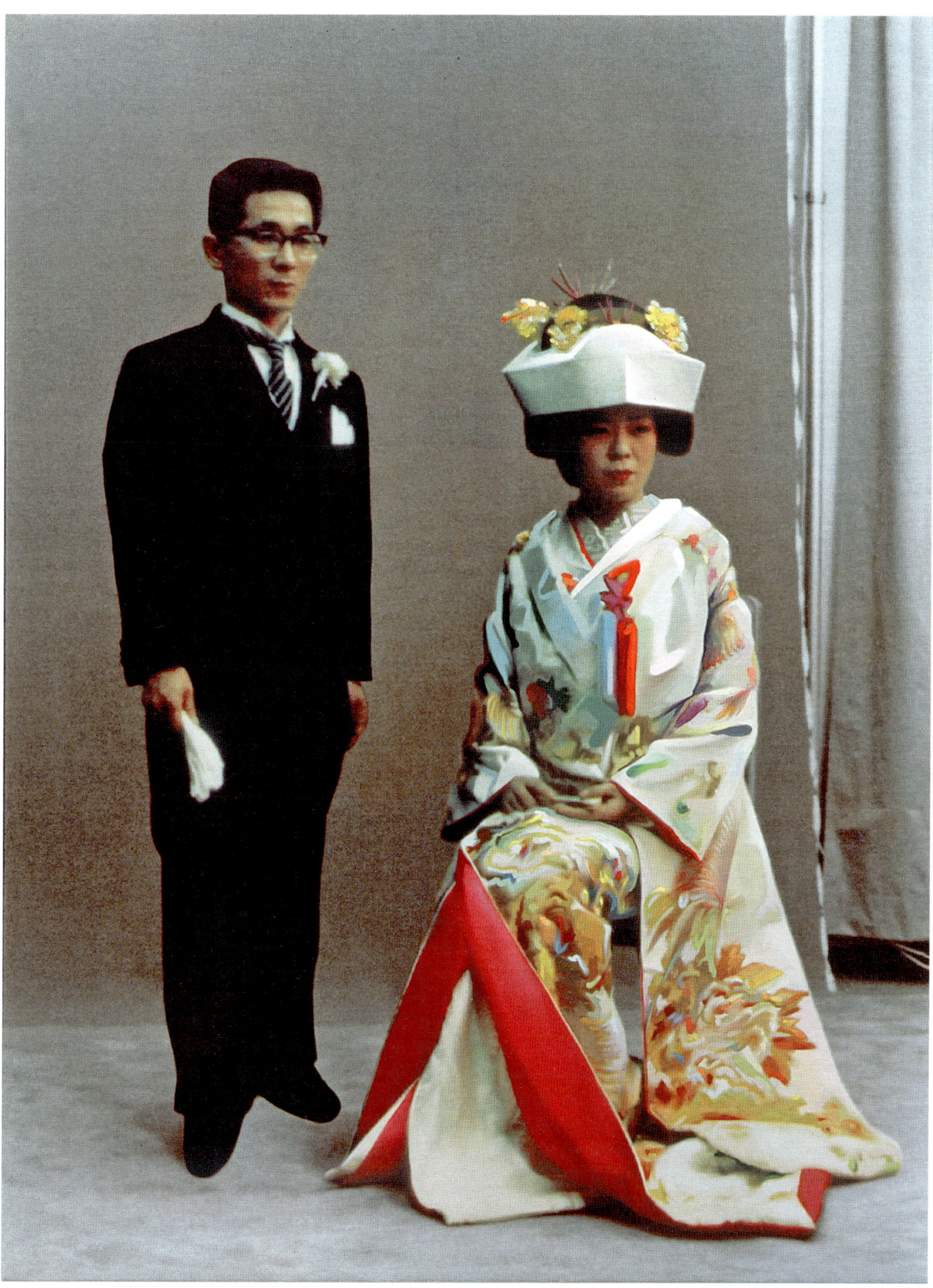

Testament 1993

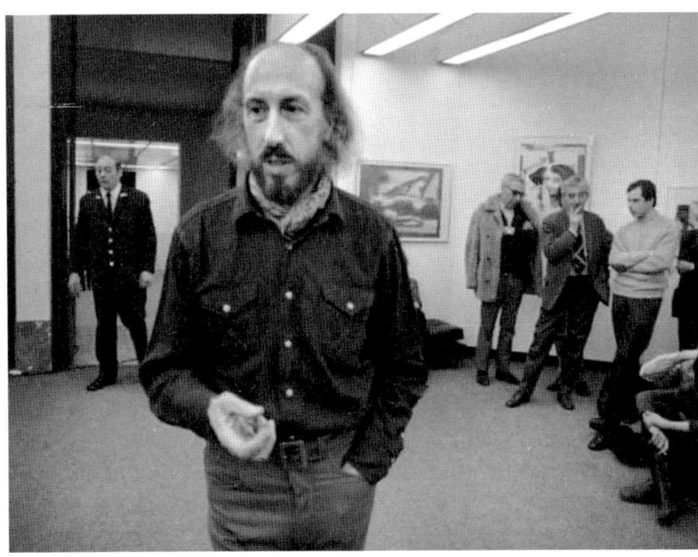

Still from Jef Cornelis' film of Richard Hamilton at the Palais des Beaux-Arts, Brussels 1971

Talk at the Palais des Beaux-Arts, Brussels, 1971

Richard Hamilton with an introduction by Mark Godfrey and annotations by Fanny Singer

During his show "Metamorfose van het object" at the Palais des Beaux-Arts in Brussels in 1971, Hamilton spoke to a group of students from the Fine Arts Academy and was filmed by Jef Cornelis, a documentary filmmaker who had made several television films about artists and exhibitions in Europe. The following transcription, previously unpublished, is an extraordinary summary of his thoughts at this time.

Hamilton begins with a succinct analysis of four categories of painting that he deploys in his work: figuration; diagrammatic representation of information or space; painting which foregrounds the material qualities of paint; and semiotic painting, where a work might include signs or words. Remarkably, Hamilton shows that each kind of painting can be useful (and deployed without parody or quotation) even if he does not subscribe to the belief system around it. He acknowledges the Abstract Expressionist mark for instance, even though he does not find a drip of paint to be "sensuous." Other European artists were beginning to juxtapose different kinds of abstract strokes to represent modernism as an exhausted set of options (for example Sigmar Polke in Moderne Kunst, *1968), but no one else was putting together these four kinds of painting to explore their different functions.*

Hamilton later connects his tendency to make different versions of a work and his scepticism towards signature style. Having embarked on his Polaroid project in part to substantiate these two ideas (various artist-friends were given the camera and instructed to photograph Hamilton as they wished), for reasons he explains, to his surprise he found himself trying to paint a Francis Bacon-style brushstroke. This act seems to anticipate postmodernist appropriation tactics like Sherrie Levine's, but Hamilton describes the motivation in more traditional terms: he was learning a new skill. Hamilton believed that as an artist, he should always be learning ways of making, whether printing processes, computer programmes, or how to paint like Francis Bacon in this particular instance—just as a few years earlier he had asked how to paint onto glass as Duchamp had done. Two very different models of artistic practice merge in his thinking here: the artist as an inquisitive artisan with an expanding skill-set, and the artist as a thinker, investigating and deconstructing conventional ideas of authorship.

A close friend of Duchamp's through the 1960s, Hamilton asked what his legacy might mean to artists of his and later generations. Here, two years after Duchamp's death, Hamilton criticises Conceptual artists whom he thinks read Duchamp the wrong way, and proposes that to take him seriously is to be "iconoclastic in relation to Duchamp." As he mentions, when he gave this talk, Hamilton was beginning work on an "impossible painting"—the Soft pink landscape [p. 230]*—which could seem a good example of what being "iconoclastic in relation to Duchamp" might mean; but in view of his comments here it is interesting to ask whether this sylvan scene could be Hamilton's response to* Étant donnés, *to which he alludes at another point in the talk (he does not connect* Soft pink landscape *to* Étant donnés*).*

Many of the Conceptual artists would have criticised such a work, and painting in general, but at the end of this talk Hamilton comes up with an extraordinary justification of painting through the language of Conceptual art. If anything that documents an artist's

thought is a work of art, then ready-made, a neon text, or photostat of a dictionary definition is no more or less valid an art work than a painting. With razor-like thinking Hamilton cuts through the discourses of the time that would deny works like his own their place among radical practices.

I find that everything I do is concerned with one of four means of representation, that is, concerned either with one way of doing something or with a number of ways superimposed on one another. The first way is probably pure figuration, pure photographic rendering—the kind of traditional way in which people perceive the world and the way they perceive an experience of the world through a two-dimensional surface. A lot of the work that I have done is concerned with photography. Rather than paint it in a laborious kind of way, I say: "All right, I know that we can paint it but the camera can do that kind of job perfectly well." So very often I find myself using the camera at that one level: information about imagery.

Then I find that there's a geometrical approach, a diagrammatic way of providing information or receiving information—so that perspective is sometimes elaborated in a very precise way. Then there are occasions when I remember that paint itself has some quality, that the medium of paint is important; American Abstract Expressionism was concerned almost entirely with that plastic quality of paint.[1] So I put paint in a very direct way onto a photograph or onto a drawing. But I don't think I use it for a sensuous enjoyment of the paint. I'm saying that there is that other response to paint, and if I put it on, on a print or on a painting, I feel that it's a kind of token, it's a representation. It simply signifies that kind of mark is a category: the plastic quality of the paint.

There are also other ways of receiving information. For example, a cross is a mark which has some plastic quality, but it also means something—it has a meaning as a sign: it means "no", so a tick means "yes." I think that signs appear sometimes in my work.[2] Sometimes I'm interested in language expressed in a literary form. So some of these prints have words attached to them, and what I think they're all about, really, are ways of communicating at a visual level. The interest for me in painting is to explore the whole of that territory, rather than to find a style which I can say is my own and to go on working in that vein. In a way, I try to exploit my talents: I think that it's possible to use any kind of technical facility, any skill of handling that I might have received from institutions, even those which have a rather bad reputation. These days no-one has any respect for the Royal Academy in London, but I have a very high regard for the skills it gave me, because I like to think that I can do a certain number of things. I feel I can do what I want to do because I have this technical facility given me by an education in a very stuffy academic art school.[3]

A lot of the work that I do is done in series. That is to say, when I start a painting, I do studies for it; there are occasions when I make several versions of the same subject,

1. Hamilton would have seen the exhibition *Opposing Forces* at the Institute of Contemporary Arts in 1953, which included three Jackson Pollock paintings from 1949. In 1958 the Whitechapel Gallery staged Pollock's first major exhibition, and a selection of works by Willem de Kooning, Jean Dubuffet, Antoni Tàpies, Franz Klein, Jackson Pollock, Mark Rothko and Clyfford Still from the E. J. "Ted" Power collection was exhibited at the ICA. In 1959 *The New American Painting*—an exhibition organised by the Museum of Modern Art, New York, and held at the Tate Gallery—signalled the supremacy of the New York-based art over the School of Paris.
2. Hamilton's discussion of signs suggests a familiarity with the terminology of French structuralist theory. Growing out of the early twentieth-century teachings of the Swiss linguist Ferdinand de Saussure, one of the founding fathers of semiotics, structuralism was adapted and brought to a broader audience by theorists including Claude Lévi-Strauss and Roland Barthes, whose *Mythologies* (1957) sought to examine the "second-order signs" of bourgeois cultural myths.
3. In 1938, Hamilton enrolled as a student of painting at the Royal Academy Schools, where he studied until 1940 (when the college was closed due to the outbreak of World War II). For other details of his training, see Chronology.
4. Hamilton gestures toward his series of collotype studies for the print *Portrait of the artist by Francis Bacon* (1970–71); each of the seven studies was given a different oil paint treatment.

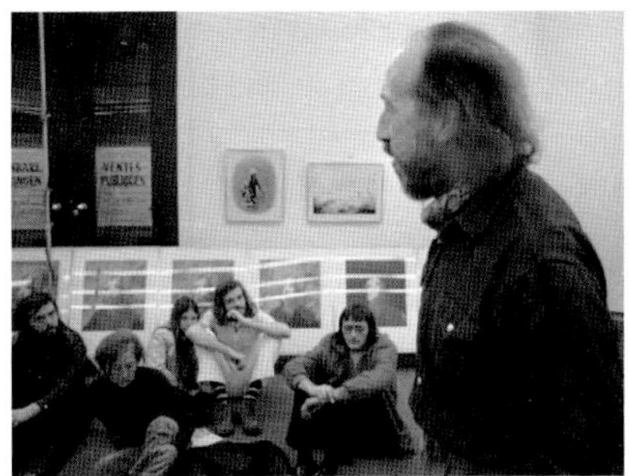

sometimes because I can't decide which would be best. It may be indecision on my part, or it may be a planned programme, but certainly there is always a feeling that if there's one possibility of approaching a work, then there are also others. Why should I say that this one is the right one? I would always hesitate to say "this is good and this is bad." And since I can't say "this is good and this is bad," I have to say, "well, I will do both, or as much as I feel is of interest." In this case, it started with an idea I had about eighteen months ago.[4] Roy Lichtenstein showed me his new Polaroid camera, in his studio, and took a photograph of me.[5] He gave me the photograph. Then somebody else happened to do that same thing: a man in Canada called Iain Baxter, who was an artist I liked very much. So when I got back to London, I bought a Polaroid camera and gave it to artist friends and said: "Take a photograph of me." And I've accumulated now I think about twenty-five or so of these photographs by quite distinguished artists like Claes Oldenburg, Jasper Johns... Each of them I find interesting. I expected that it would prove that the camera was unimportant, but I think this has been disproved, because every photograph is in a way very strongly identified with the artist.

Now, the one that's most strongly identified with the artist is Francis Bacon's photograph.[6] When I gave him the camera, it was as though he'd never held a camera before. He was unsure of which direction to point it in, even! So he took a photograph, and of course, the camera is completely automatic so there's nothing to decide in the way of exposure—it does it all for you. All you have to do is point it and press the button. But since the conditions were rather bad (the lighting conditions were poor, the exposure was very long and so I moved, and Francis Bacon waved the camera), the result was that we had rather a blurred photograph. He said: "That's not very good. It isn't sharp." So we had to try again. And we tried another half-dozen times until he got a photograph that he liked the look of and that he felt was technically alright. But I asked him if I could use them in any way I wanted, and he agreed that "yes, of course, they're yours."

So I took the first one that he had taken and made a collotype.[7] I rearranged the format a little. That's to say, I made it more like a Francis Bacon by placing the image in relation to the rectangle in such a way that it seemed to me to be completely typical of Francis Bacon's composition. Then the Polaroid was reproduced by a process called collotype. Having got the proofs, I began to work on them. I had hoped that Bacon would make some marks on them, and then I would take over and become the printer, and I would print these marks with silkscreen on top. But Francis Bacon was unable to do this—I think he wanted to at first, but he was told by his gallery that this would be bad policy. The Marlborough Gallery didn't approve of his making a print in this way.[8] So he said that it would be better not to. I said: "All right. I'll make the marks myself." I began to make these studies. Because I wasn't Francis Bacon, I couldn't be sure that I would make the right sort of marks on the paper: I had to go very tentatively towards the image.

5. Hamilton visited Lichtenstein in his New York studio in March 1968. Lichtenstein took Hamilton's picture, spurring the latter's *Polaroid Portraits* series. Over the next 33 years Hamilton amassed 128 portraits eventually published in four volumes of 32 photographs each.
6. At Bacon's invitation, Hamilton joined him for lunch at Robert Carrier's eponymous London restaurant on 14 July 1969. Hamilton brought his Polaroid camera along and asked Bacon to take his portrait. Bacon's favourite of the multiple exposures was published in the first volume of *Polaroid Portraits* (1972) and shows Hamilton sitting before a patterned curtain.
7. A collotype is a type of print made by photographically exposing a sheet of light-sensitive gelatin to the original image without using an intervening screen. Unlike halftone letterpress or offset lithography, collotype allows printing in continuous tone without the aid of halftone screen, thus offering photographic accuracy in fully permanent ink.
8. Bacon first showed with Marlborough Gallery, London, in 1960 and remained affiliated with them until his death in 1992. In the 1960s and 1970s Marlborough represented a number of notable artists including Frank Auerbach, Lucian Freud, Barbara Hepworth, R.B. Kitaj, Henry Moore and Victor Pasmore.

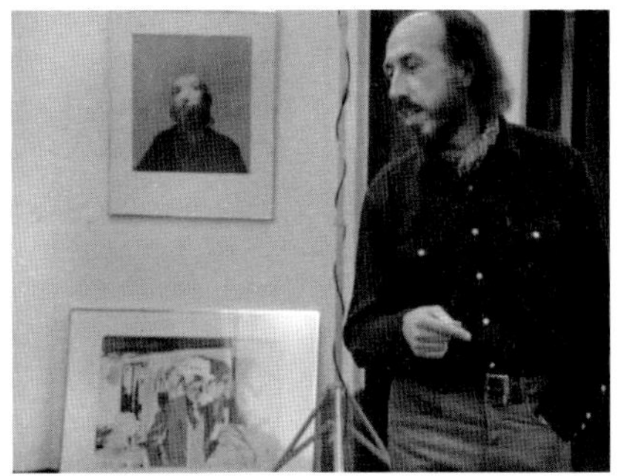

After I'd made two or three, I asked Francis Bacon to come and have dinner. We had dinner and he looked at the studies, and said: "I don't think this mark is very good, and when I paint, I paint in a particular way..." I'd been trying to get certain qualities which I'd got from reproductions of his work; I had his catalogues with me all the time, and I was trying to imitate certain kinds of marks. Sometimes I wasn't successful. So he said: "Well, I do it this way. I take a piece of cloth, a stocking or a piece of jersey, and dab it in the paint and put it on the canvas." So I learned how to do the Francis Bacon marks. And gradually I got to the point where I produced something that I found like Francis Bacon, and reasonably satisfying as something of mine. And I learned a great deal—the interest for me was that I learned so much about Francis Bacon's work in doing this.

For example, I found that it was necessary always to cover the background. The background, which was a brocade curtain in a restaurant, was too complex. Bacon never paints a negative. This is becoming complex, but it's interesting—it's not really about Bacon entirely. But the curious thing about his work, I found, was that he always painted a form; when he made a mark with a brush, it was always a form, never a void. It was never nothing; it was always something. A mark meant something. It was not just space.

When Cézanne painted, any mark meant form, or it meant space, and the two things were completely interchangeable. Every brushstroke was either the space which defined the form, or the form on the other side. The brushstroke can move on either side of this form.[9] This is something very important, and something that I learned at school. I've always thought about colour and any mark that I make as being either one thing or the other, and very often a mark can move along a contour. But Francis Bacon doesn't work like that: he has a blank canvas, which may be coloured all over; then he puts his form onto the space. So the canvas is a well-defined form which he fills with objects, which are the paint. What began to emerge in the Bacon studies was that the whole image was too interrelated, background and form, so I began to find that it was really more like Francis Bacon when the background was simple. This is a long way to arrive at a statement about something as simple as that! Nevertheless it was necessary.

Eventually, Francis Bacon looked at all of the studies and said: "The one that I like is this one." He happened to have on a shirt of exactly this colour, and I think that he thought the marks that I'd made on the other studies were really not very good. They weren't his marks. So this one satisfied him. It was his photograph, it had some of the character of his painting, which was very easily understood. And that was the one that I made into the print. So these are studies for that print, although they're not like the print particularly.

From the time of the cavemen there's been a mythic quality about representation. It's something to do with the gods; it's a magical thing. But at the time that we're speaking of, in the mid-1950s, there was only one kind of painting, and that was concerned with the medium of paint and with a kind of decoration.[10] It was abstract; it was not concerned with myth; it wasn't concerned with a kind of magic that was outside the artist. There was a kind of magic involved, but it was a much more introspective involvement with artistic matters.

9. Here Hamilton gestures to his left arm and the space surrounding it to demonstrate how Cézanne's marks—whether describing void or volume—were transposable.
10. Hamilton is referring again to Abstract Expressionism (see n. 1) and to Clement Greenberg's ideas of medium specificity most famously explained in his 1960 essay "Modernist Painting."
11. Hamilton first met Andy Warhol in 1963 at a party celebrating the opening of the Marcel Duchamp retrospective at the Pasadena Museum, California—for which Hamilton made his first visit to the United States. Warhol was in Los Angles for the opening of his exhibition of *Silver Elvises* at the Ferus Gallery.
12. Hamilton is referring to *Soft pink landscape* (1971–72), a painting conceived alongside *Soft blue landscape* (1976–80). Both depict a wooded landscape, populated by a pair of female figures and a roll of Andrex brand toilet tissue, whose perimeters blur into abstraction.

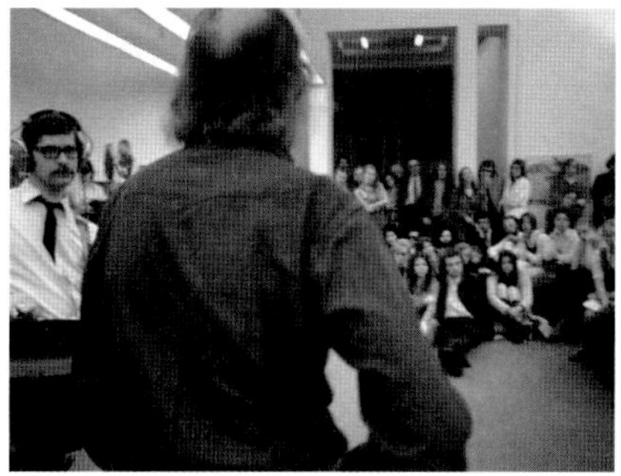

The message and the content of painting were the painting itself, and not the story of the painting or the subject of the painting. So I felt that it was necessary to look at the popular arts very carefully, find out what they did—what the techniques were, the methods, why they had this power—and then say: "Well, if they can, maybe art should be done in this way. Maybe it's possible to produce a painting which has the same qualities." What was difficult about this was my discovering, in looking at the work, that really the difference between fine art and the popular arts as expressed in the magazines and television and all the other mass media techniques was that they were designed for a short period of life, whereas fine art is designed for a long period of life. This was the basic distinction. So I said that fine art can be concerned with everything that the mass media are concerned with—but it can't be transient or short-lived. Because that would make it not fine art. However, after a period of fifteen, nearly twenty years, I find that that was a false assumption. Because Andy Warhol, for example, isn't concerned with timelessness; he is concerned with exactly the same transitory nature of the mass media.[11] Warhol wants to be situated in exactly the same kind of relationship with the public as magazines, television and cinema are.

Now, he wants that, but I think that the work immediately becomes assimilated into the fine art field. You can't say that Warhol's work is ready for the junk-heap because it's ten years old. So he's disproved my basic assumption, and if he's disproved that then I have to assume that I was wrong, and that there are no exceptions. You can't say, at this stage, that art has to be anything! You can't say: "It can't be short-lived." I think it's dangerous to make assumptions. So I wouldn't like to say now that a painting of any kind is impossible. In fact, at the moment I'm engaged on an impossible painting.[12] It's a romantic landscape—it's like Claude or Poussin or Turner. What I'm trying to do is recreate that kind of experience, that visual experience. This whole concept of a soft pink landscape is so nauseating that I have to have some slightly ironic theme also involved, so that I can say that it's slightly funny too, and that makes it acceptable. Also, it is stylistically derived from a particular kind of advertising, for toilet paper in this case. So I can excuse it in many ways. But quite seriously, I'm interested in that kind of problem—the problem of an eighteenth century relationship to the world. I don't think that one has to be modern. Rather, we have to be involved in a particular kind of style: a way of representing in which everything is grist to the mill, all can be used.

We have a false picture of Duchamp as being a man who didn't work, who worked himself out of art.[13] But then after his death, you find that there's a work that he was producing for the last twenty years of his life, an extraordinary work which is very important, and which is also a contradiction in its style with almost everything else that he did.[14] So I feel that Duchamp is iconoclastic towards himself, and that if one is going to follow him, one must also be iconoclastic. But I want to be iconoclastic in relation to Duchamp. I think that what he would like most is for others to position themselves in opposition to him. One should love him, be devoted to every work that he produced, but at the same time not be willing to follow a particular path, that is to say, his every path.

13. Hamilton was first introduced to Marcel Duchamp's work in 1948 when Nigel Henderson invited him to Roland Penrose's personal library in London to see the *Green Box* (1934). Hamilton met Duchamp in 1959, at which point the artists established a close friendship that would endure until Duchamp's death in 1968. In 1966, Hamilton installed the largest European retrospective during Duchamp's lifetime, *The Almost Complete Works of Marcel Duchamp*, at the Tate Gallery, for which he made a sculptural replica of the *Large Glass* (the original being too fragile to travel from Philadelphia).
14. Hamilton learned of the existence of Marcel Duchamp's final work, *Étant donnés: 1. La chute d'eau, 2. Le gaz d'éclairage (Given: 1. The Waterfall, 2. The Illuminating Gas)* (1946–66), from William Copley in early spring of 1969. He visited the Philadelphia Museum of Art to see the work on 17 September that year, accompanied by Rita Donagh and several other friends and colleagues.

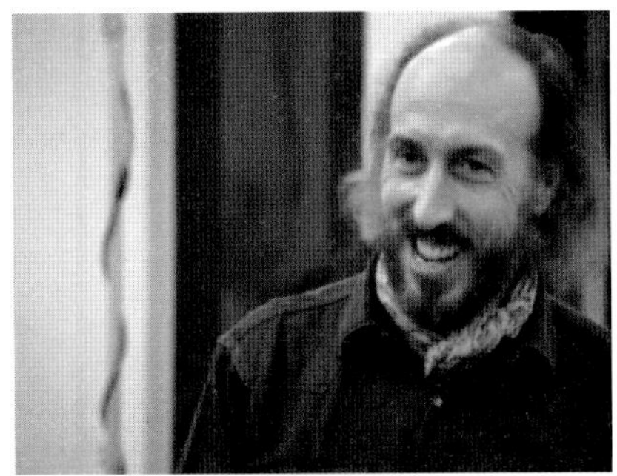

I have very little respect for a lot of work that is done now, for a lot of conceptual work[15] that derives from Duchamp and for a lot of neo-Dada which comes directly from Duchamp, because I think Duchamp would have said that had he done it himself, he too would have been against it. So I do find that very often something I've done is an echo, produces an echo of Duchamp, though I usually realise it afterwards. It's not because I consciously try to make something like Duchamp, but rather that very often I find that something has happened which I remember afterwards: "Oh yes, Duchamp did that in 1913 in *Pharmacy* or some other work."[16]

The reason artists like etching is that it's always better when it's printed.[17] You can make any mark on an etching-plate and discover that a mark which would be ludicrous on paper has quality when it's printed. Other mediums are not like that. Offset litho, for example, can be terrible unless it's handled with sympathy. I like offset litho very much. I don't like lithography from a stone, working on a stone. I like very mechanical techniques, which, because of their mechanical qualities, force one to add the sensual interest. They're much more demanding. A print which is a reproduction by offset lithography of a watercolour or a crayon drawing or the like is sometimes treated as a print nowadays. I think this is an absolute abomination—it's a terrible kind of object to produce. In a way, these Francis Bacon things are much more mechanical, but on the other hand there is a direct involvement with the medium, at a physical level even; I like to be at the printing press, handling every piece of paper every time. There seems always to be a chance of something going wrong, because the controls are so rigid. The need for control is so great that one learns a lot, and that is the reason that the prints have quality, if they have quality.

I'm not at all interested in raising a camera to my eye and taking a photograph. I never do. Well, I very rarely do it. I have cameras, but I never use them to make photographs. I use them as part of the techniques and media of painting.[18] In the first place, I make collage additions to paintings. I've needed something a different size because, say, the object that I wanted to put into the painting was too small, and thought: "Well, the simplest way is to photograph it and enlarge it and stick it on the painting." So I wasn't a photographer. I was simply copying something and putting it onto something else; I was changing the scale. I think most of my use of photography is of that order: to take something that exists, is already made—not a ready-made object but an object somebody else has made from the world around him—and I use it as an object from that world.

A lot of artists now, I think, don't look at the world directly. The paintings up to the end of the nineteenth century were all a direct experience of the world. People looked at the world and they experienced something and they tried to record that experience. But now I think the general experience of the world comes through magazines, through television, through cinema. There are many ways of experiencing the world, but the most important

15. In 1963, in his essay "Concept Art," the young American artist and musician Henry Flynt gave one of the earliest definitions of what would become known as conceptual art, claiming that: "Since 'concepts' are closely bound up with language, concept art is a kind of art of which the material is language." Sol LeWitt published his *Paragraphs on Conceptual Art* in *Artforum* in 1967, followed in 1969 by his *Sentences on Conceptual Art* (which first appeared in *0–9*, New York, and in the inaugural issue of *Art-Language*, London), in which he asserted that "Ideas can be works of art." In the same year, Joseph Kosuth published his manifesto *Art after Philosophy*, which likewise aimed to define conceptual art and in which he suggested that "the 'value' of particular artists after Duchamp can be weighed according to how much they questioned the nature of art."
16. *Pharmacy*, described by Duchamp as a "rectified ready-made," is a commercial chromolithograph of a winter landscape to which he added two sets of three tiny vertical dots in red and green gouache.
17. Hamilton considered himself equally a painter and printmaker. Though his myriad printed works betray a protean attitude toward medium, he frequently engaged in intaglio. The first exhibition of his etchings was mounted at Gimpel Fils, London, in 1950, comprising the suite *Variations on the theme of a Reaper* (1949) executed in the small print studio at Slade run by John Buckland Wright. In 1973, Hamilton would work with the renowned intaglio master printer Aldo Crommelynck on *Picasso's meninas*.

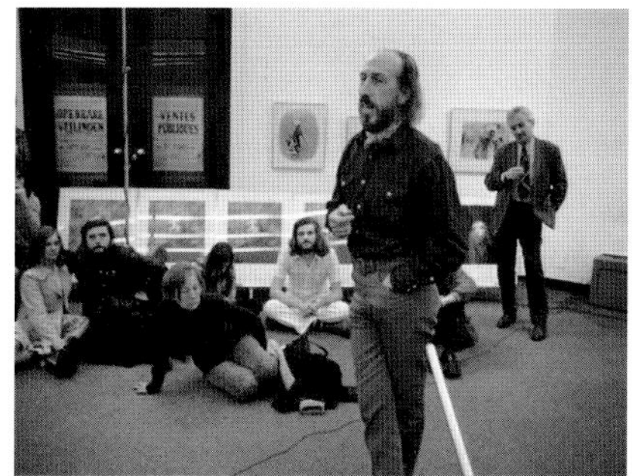

ways now are these secondary ways. The direct way of perceiving the world is of less importance to everybody, and I think that's very significant. These uses of photography are a kind of acceptance of that fact—well, an acceptance of a conclusion that I regard as a fact. I say this is part of the world now; though it has already been reduced to two dimensions on a flat piece of paper—I can use it as if I were using a view out of the window. And I certainly don't feel myself to be stealing something from photographers, nor do I feel myself to be operating in the way that they operate.

There's an exhibition in Nuremberg at the moment and I suppose a lot of conceptual art will be there. The theme of the exhibition, because it's on the occasion of the 500th anniversary of Dürer, is a statement they've taken from Dürer: "What beauty is, I don't know."[19] And so I've tried to think not only what beauty was, but also what art was and is now, at this present time. I decided first of all that a work of art is really no more than evidence that somebody has thought of a work of art. I think Duchamp establishes that the work of art itself is of no importance, because the work of art can change. It changes after its production through, in the first place, decay, and it also changes because the people who look at it change. This is one of the facts that one accepts about a work of art, now that we understand that it isn't a permanent, timeless thing. So that you can say only that the work of art is telling you something about what the artist thought. What is important about the work of art is that it carries some thread, some information, from the mind of the artist. One has to say: "This is what's important—it's what happened in the artist's mind that is important, not what happened on the piece of paper, or the canvas, or the object. This is an intermediary vehicle." I've carried this process further and said that anything that communicates an artist's thoughts is a work of art. It doesn't need even to be made by the artist—it doesn't need to be in any particular style, because you can work in another person's style and it will still be a work of art. You can work ironically or seriously, you can do anything—anything is possible. The only thing that's important is that what is produced is a document which relates to an idea. I ended up by saying that a painting is evidence that an artist has proposed a work of art. And I don't see why a painting isn't just as good evidence that a work of art has been produced as, well, any other kind of activity that artists can engage in.

… Is that enough?

18. In the 1960s, Hamilton kept a Leica camera in his studio that he used to make 35mm slides for lectures. It was mounted on a copying stand and fitted with bellows and a reflex attachment to enable extreme close-ups. He described how he used the camera as a kind of microscope and cropping device: "I became addicted to using it as a microscope to look at details of any printed material around—playing at making compositions." A poster for a Roy Lichtenstein exhibition that Hamilton had visited in New York City in 1963 was subjected to his "microscope": "It was possible to make interesting crops on the already magnified regular field of dots with its intrusion (at that scale) of alien marks." From the negative taken by Hamilton, one of the cropped compositions was made into a two-colour screenprint titled *A little bit of Roy Lichtenstein for…* (1964).
19. Hamilton is paraphrasing a famous line attributed to Dürer: "What beauty is, I know not, though it adheres to many things." This was part of the title of the second Nürnberg Biennale, *Was die Schönheit sei, das weiss ich nicht – Künstler – Theorie – Werk.* Hamilton was supposed to contribute a text titled "Propositions" to the catalogue, but a postal strike in the UK delayed the arrival of his letter and his text was only later published in his *Collected Words.* This text matches some of the ideas expressed in this part of the talk. As 1971 marked the quincentennial of Albrecht Dürer's birth, dozens of exhibitions honouring Dürer were mounted worldwide in that year. In Nuremberg—Dürer's birthplace—multiple shows were on view at the Germanisches Nationalmuseum, including the largest selection of Dürer's work (comprising more than 730 items) to ever have been shown.

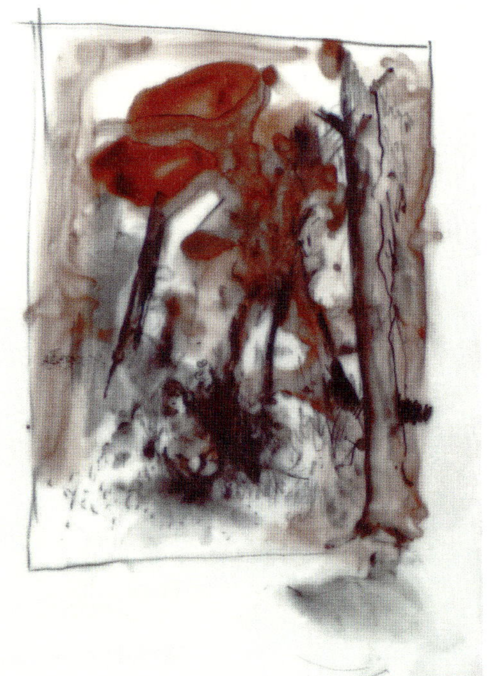

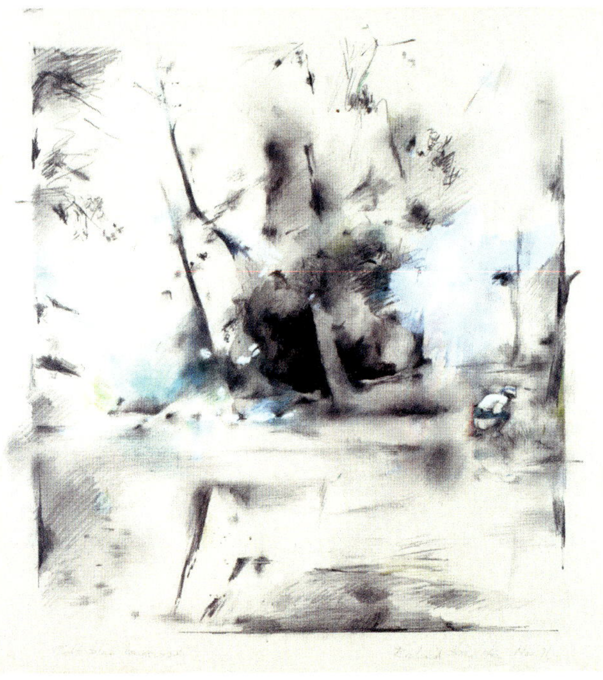

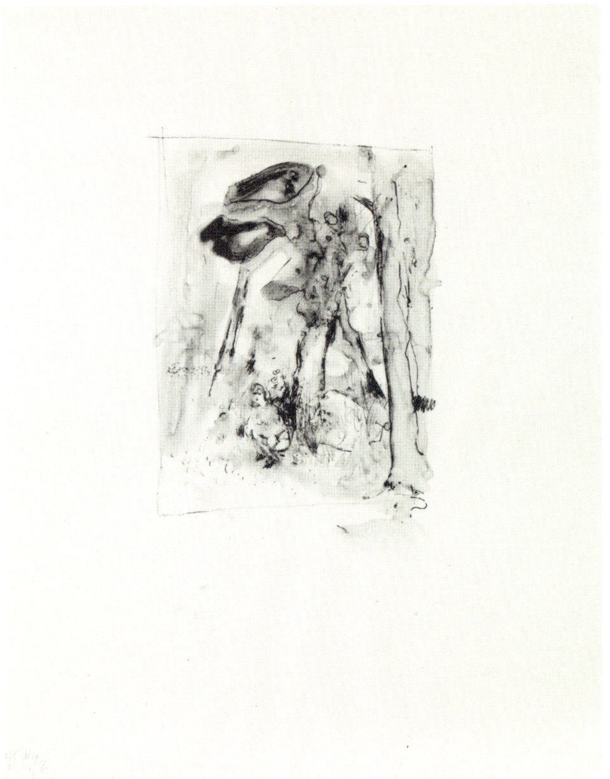

Eine kleine schöne Scheisse für Dieter 1971

Soft blue landscape – study 1971

Eine kleine schöne Scheisse 1971

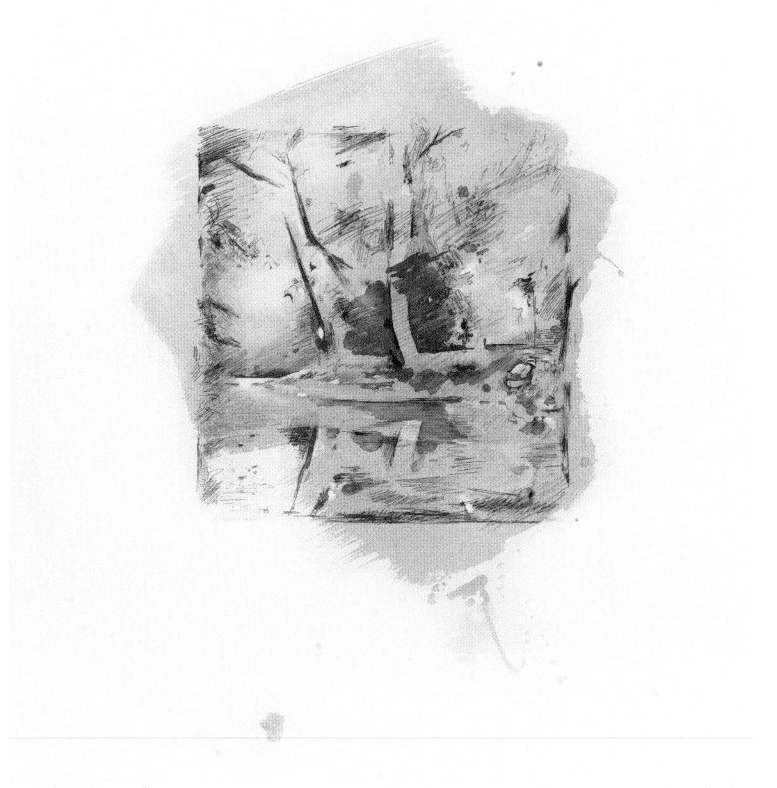

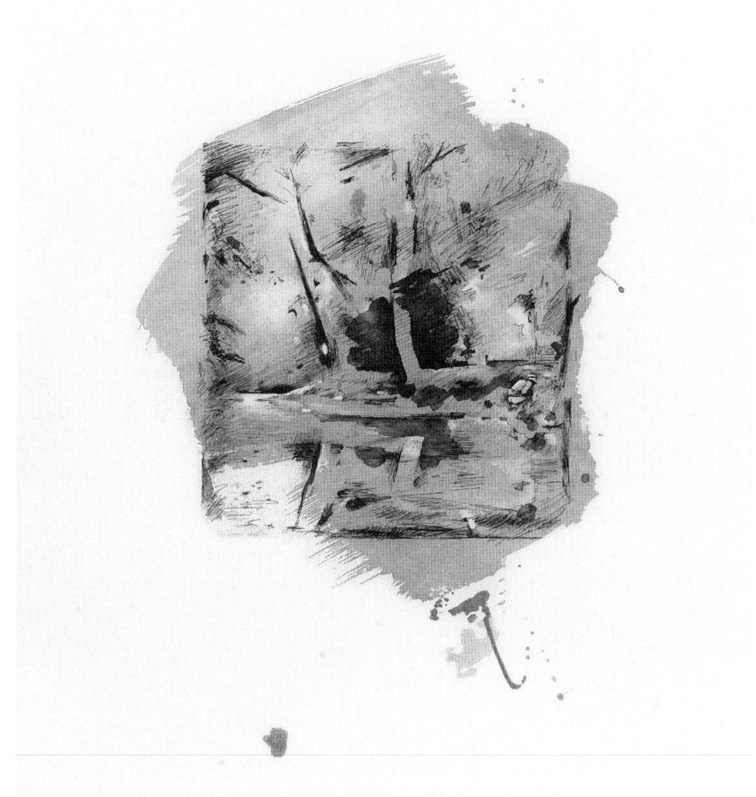

By the soft blue waters of Miers 1972

By the waters of Miers 1972

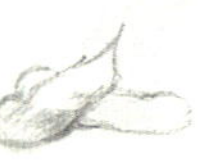

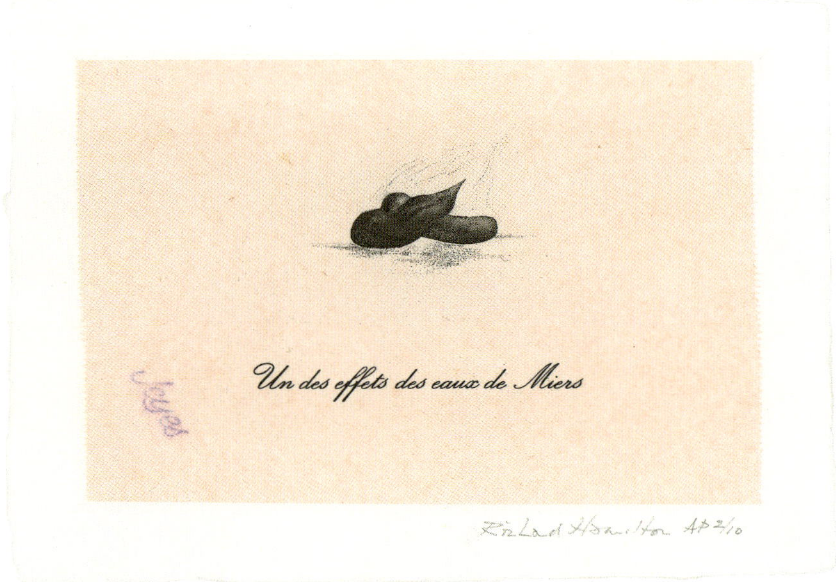

Étude pour les eaux de Miers 1972
Un des effets des eaux de Miers 1973

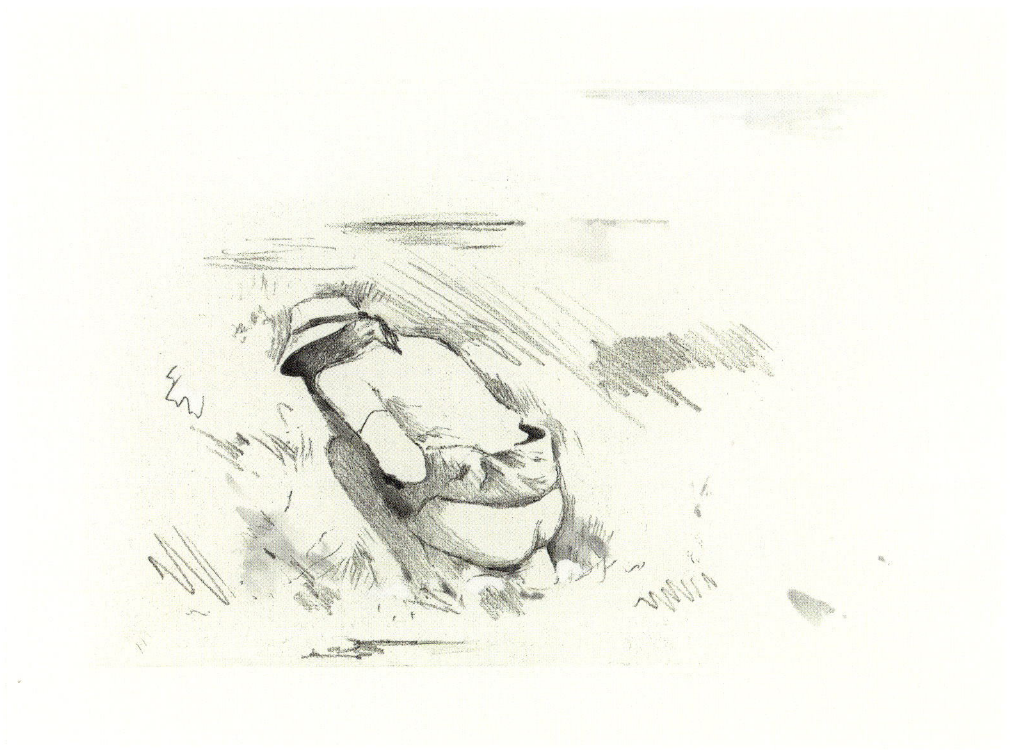

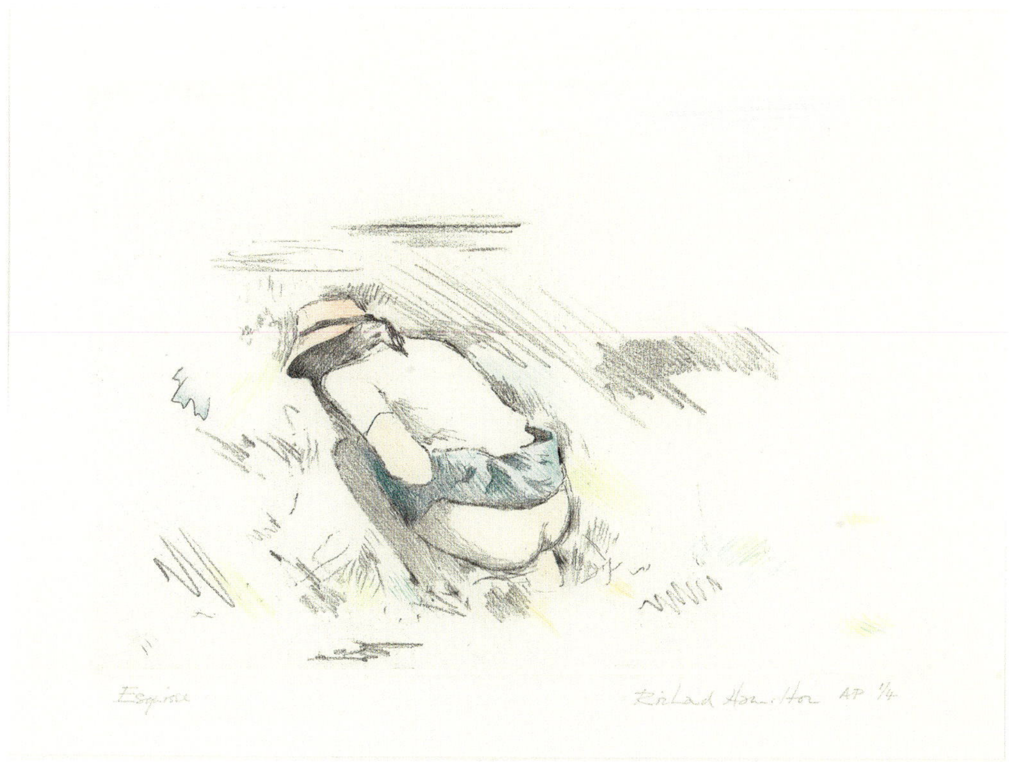

Esquisse – stage proof 1972

Esquisse 1972

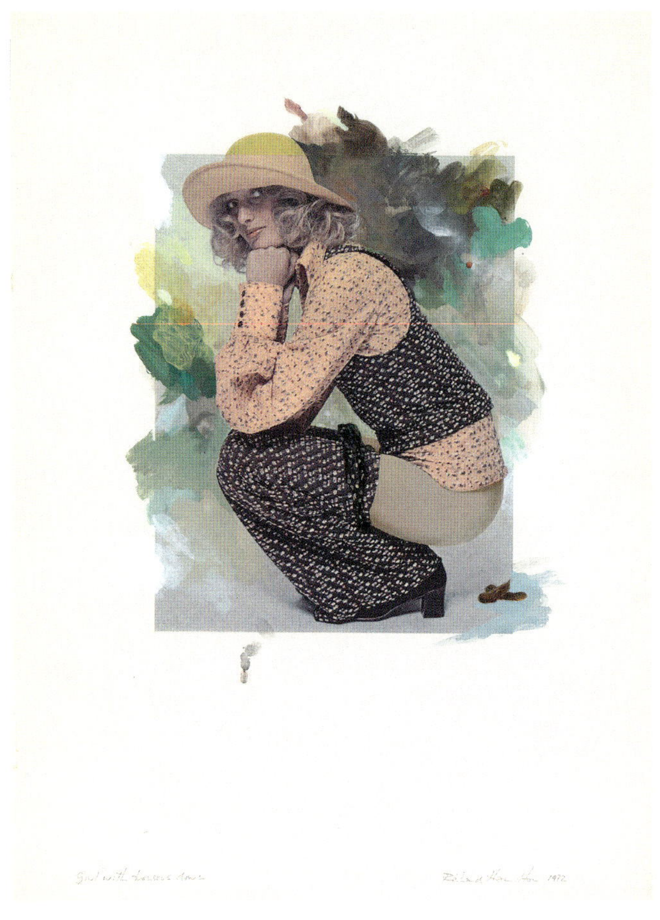

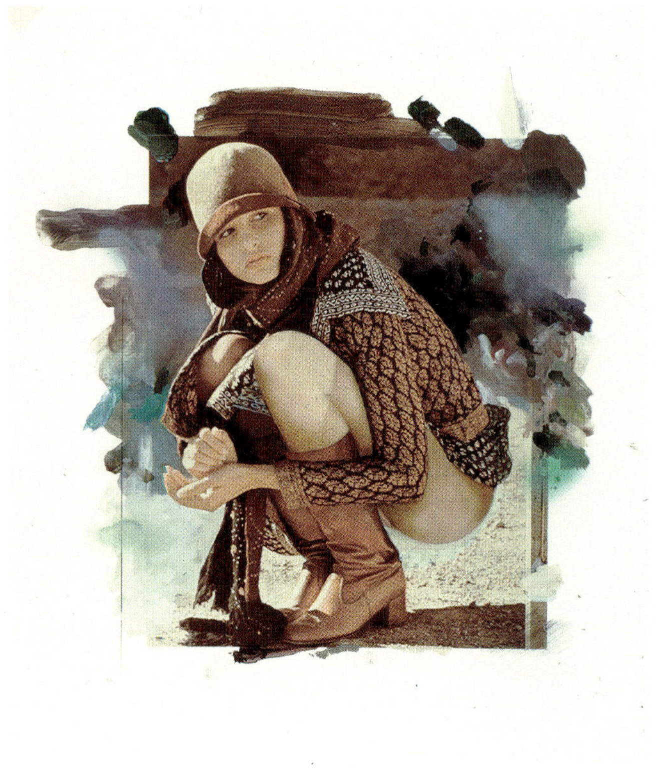

Girl with trousers down 1972

Girl with skirt up 1972

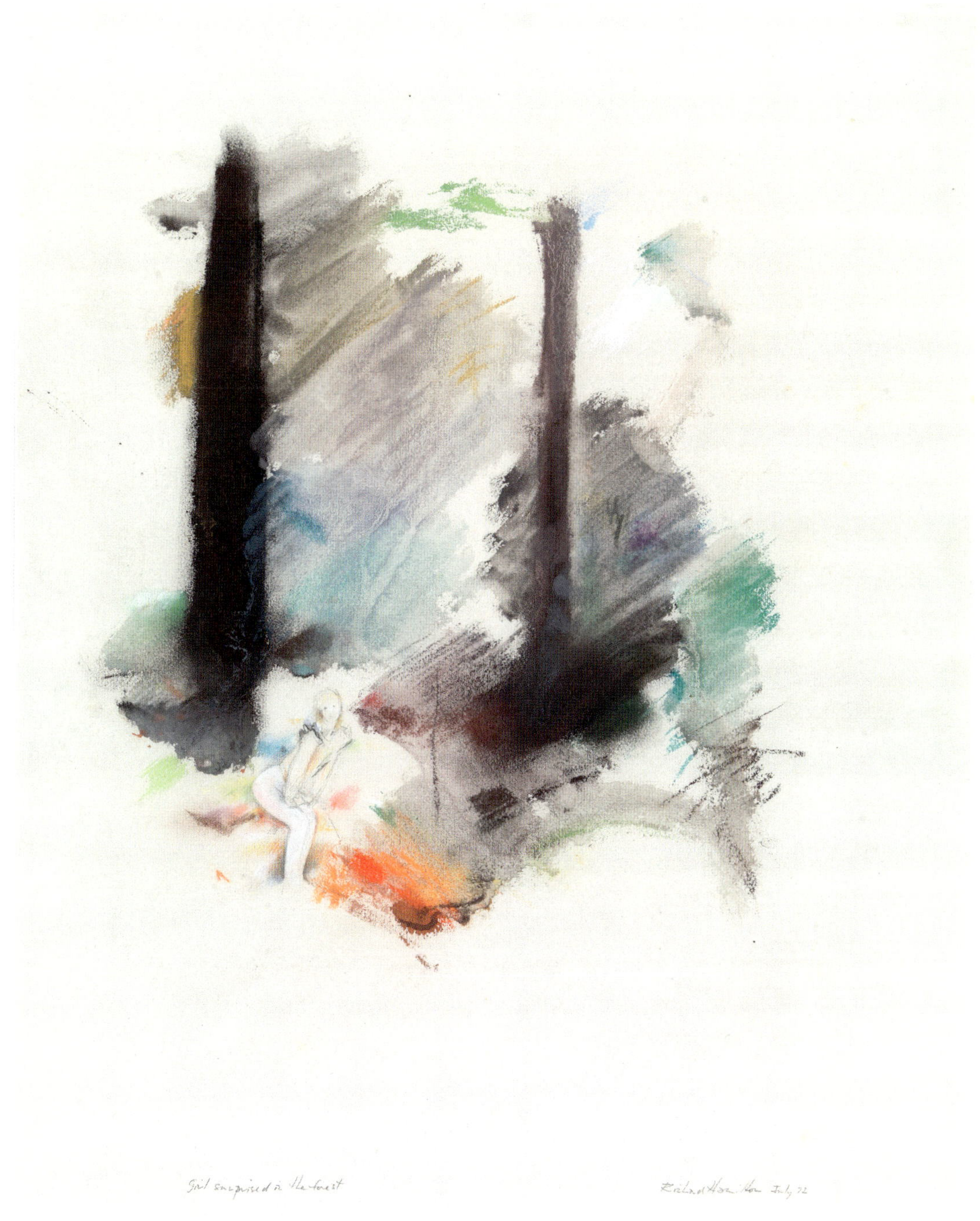

Girl surprised in the forest 1972

SINDACATO NAZIONALE MERCANTI D'ARTE MODERNA

CORSO VENEZIA, 47 20121 MILANO - TELEFONO 77.50

A tutti i Mercanti d'Arte Moderna — 18 dicembre 1972

Loro Sedi

Nel tardo pomeriggio di sabato 16 dicembre 1972 è stata rubata dal salone a pianterreno dello Studio Marconi, Via Tadino 15, Milano, un'opera dell'artista, *Richard Hamilton*.

Descrizione dell'opera:
Si tratta di due normali cartoline di tipo stereoscopico, a colori, rappresentanti in verticale mazzi di fiori con aggiunte a mano dell'artista (nella prima un rotolo di carta igienica Andrex in basso a destra, nella seconda vari tocchi di colore nella parte inferiore).

Originariamente le due cartoline erano montate insieme su un fondo di cartone bianco, entro una cornice di cm. 24 x 33 a filetto di alluminio. Le due cartoline non sono firmate dall'artista.

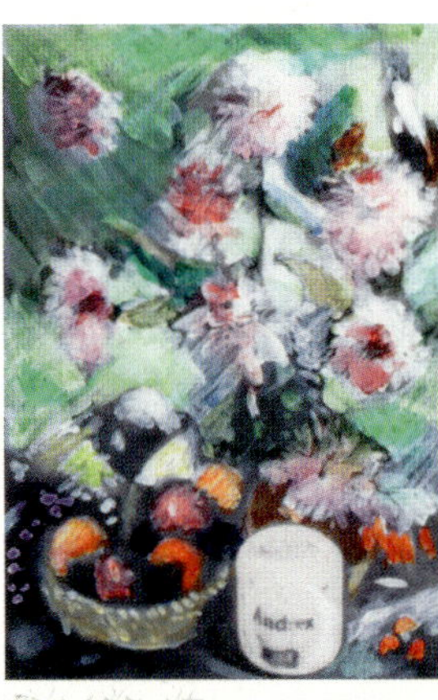

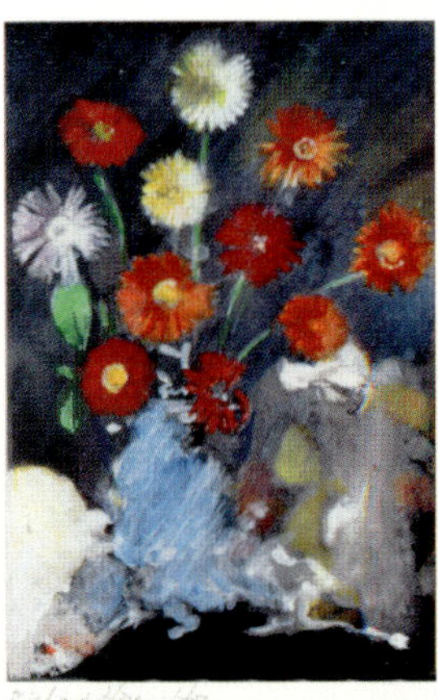

Late in the afternoon of Saturday, 16 December 1972, a work by the English artist, *Richard Hamilton*, was stolen from the ground floor gallery at Studio Marconi, Via Tadino 15, Milano.

Description of the work:
Two ordinary, coloured, stereoscopic, vertical postcards figuring vases of flowers with retouches by hand by the artist (in the lower right hand corner of the first, a roll of Andrex toilet paper, and in the lower half of the second, various patches of colour). Originally, the two postcards were mounted together on white cardboard in an aluminium frame of 24 x 33 cm. Neither of the two postcards are signed by the artist.

Chi fosse a conoscenza della attuale collocazione o ricevesse proposte relative all'acquisto di queste opere è pregato di darne immediata comunicazione agli organi di Polizia e alla Segreteria di questo Sindacato.

La Segreteria

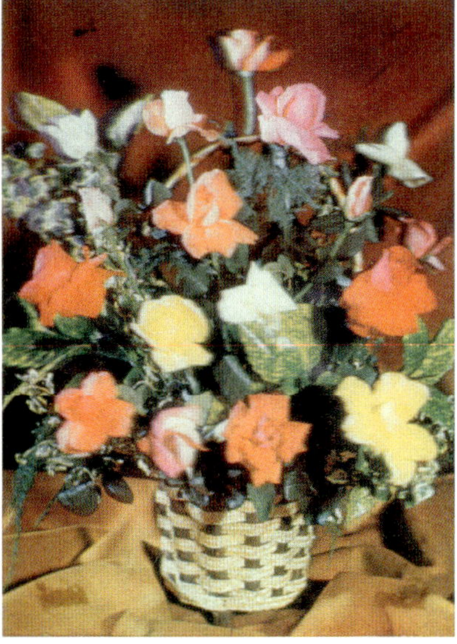

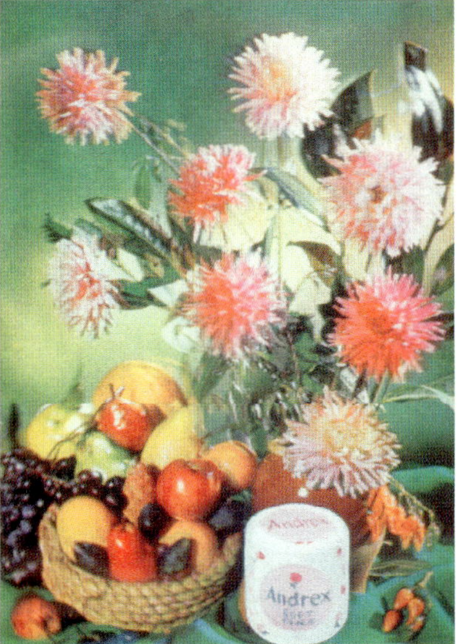

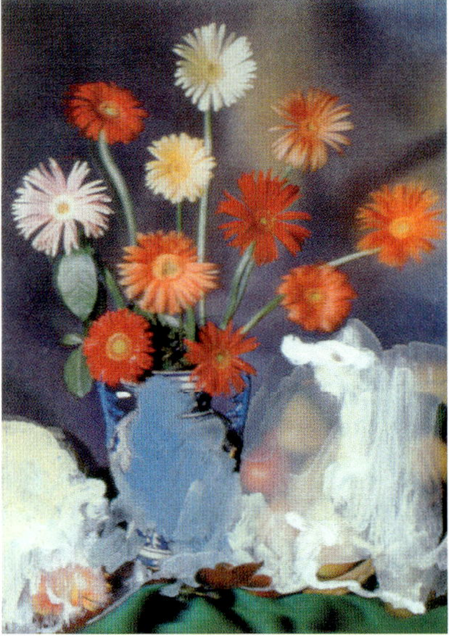

A Tutti Mercanti d'Arte Moderna 1972

Flower-piece postcards a–c 1971

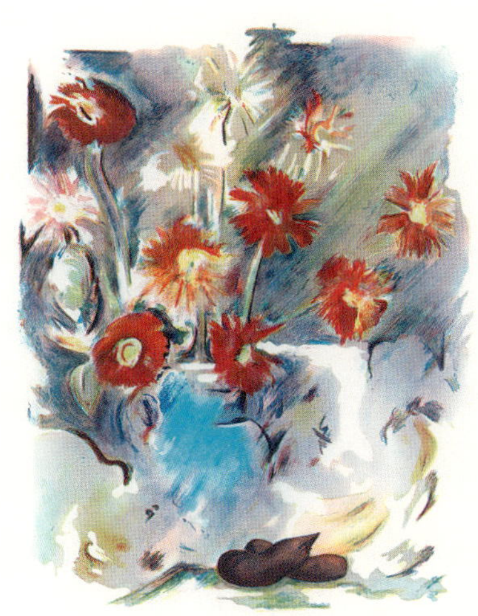

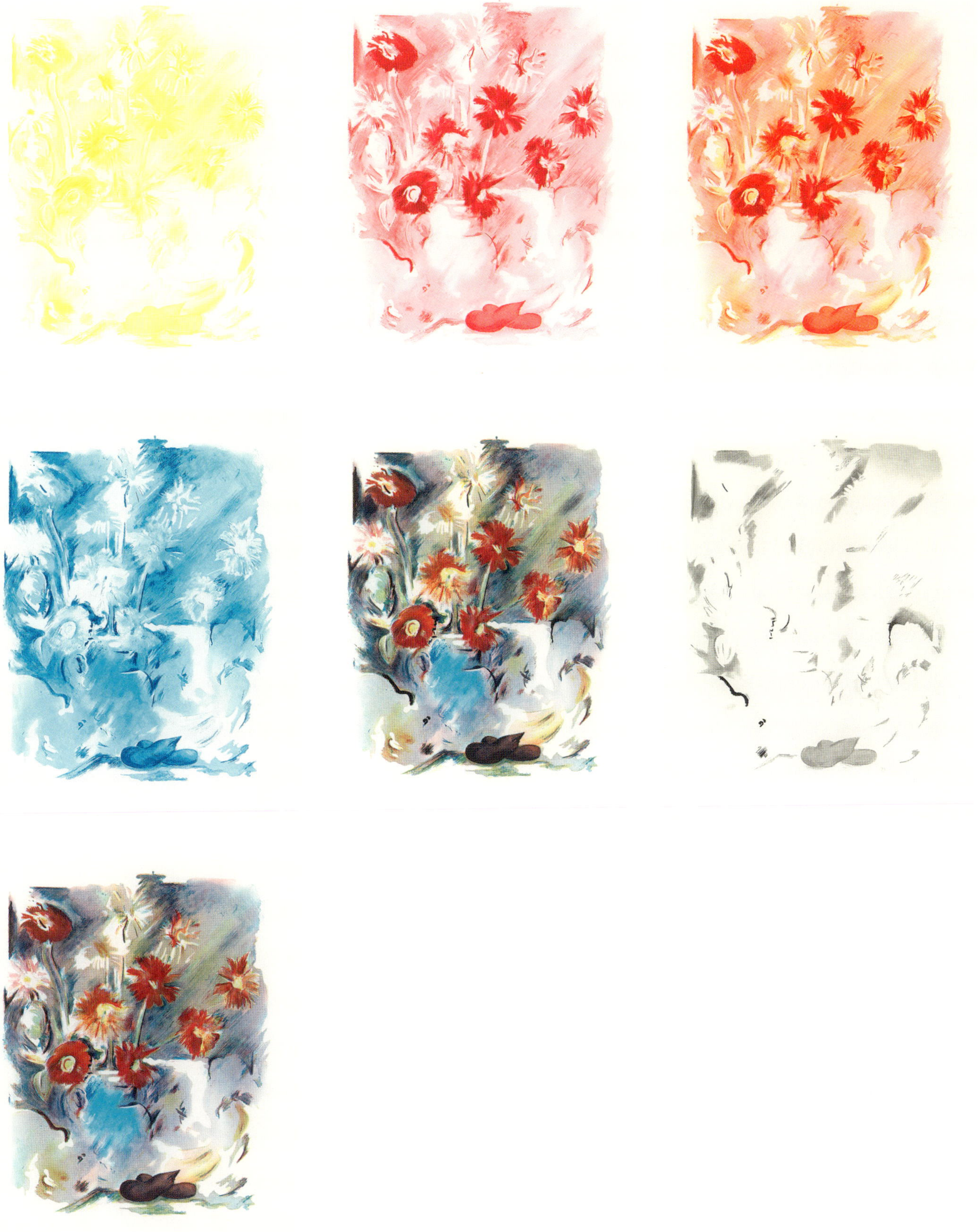

Trichromatic flower-piece progressives 1973–74

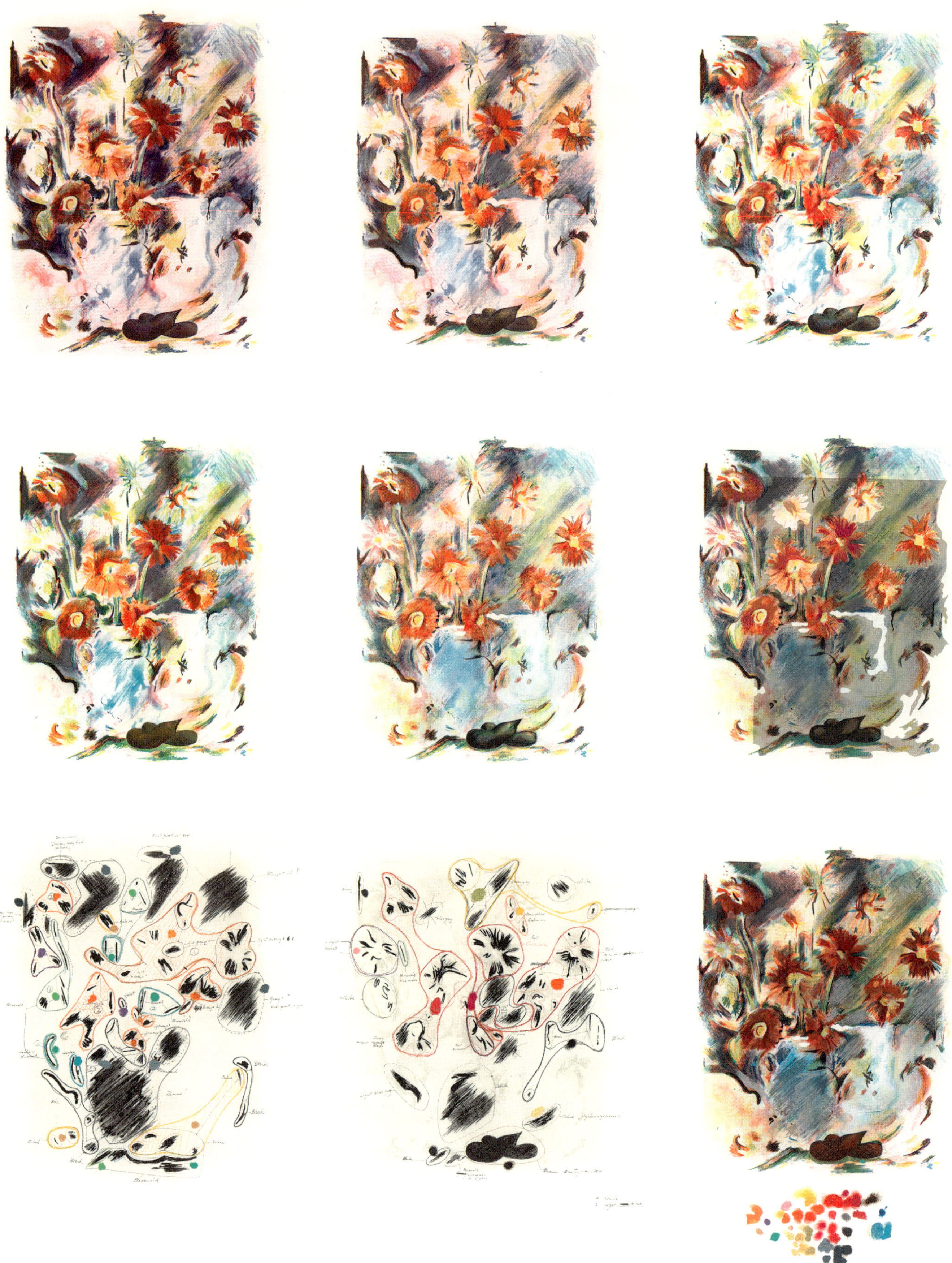

Flower-piece – trial proofs 1973

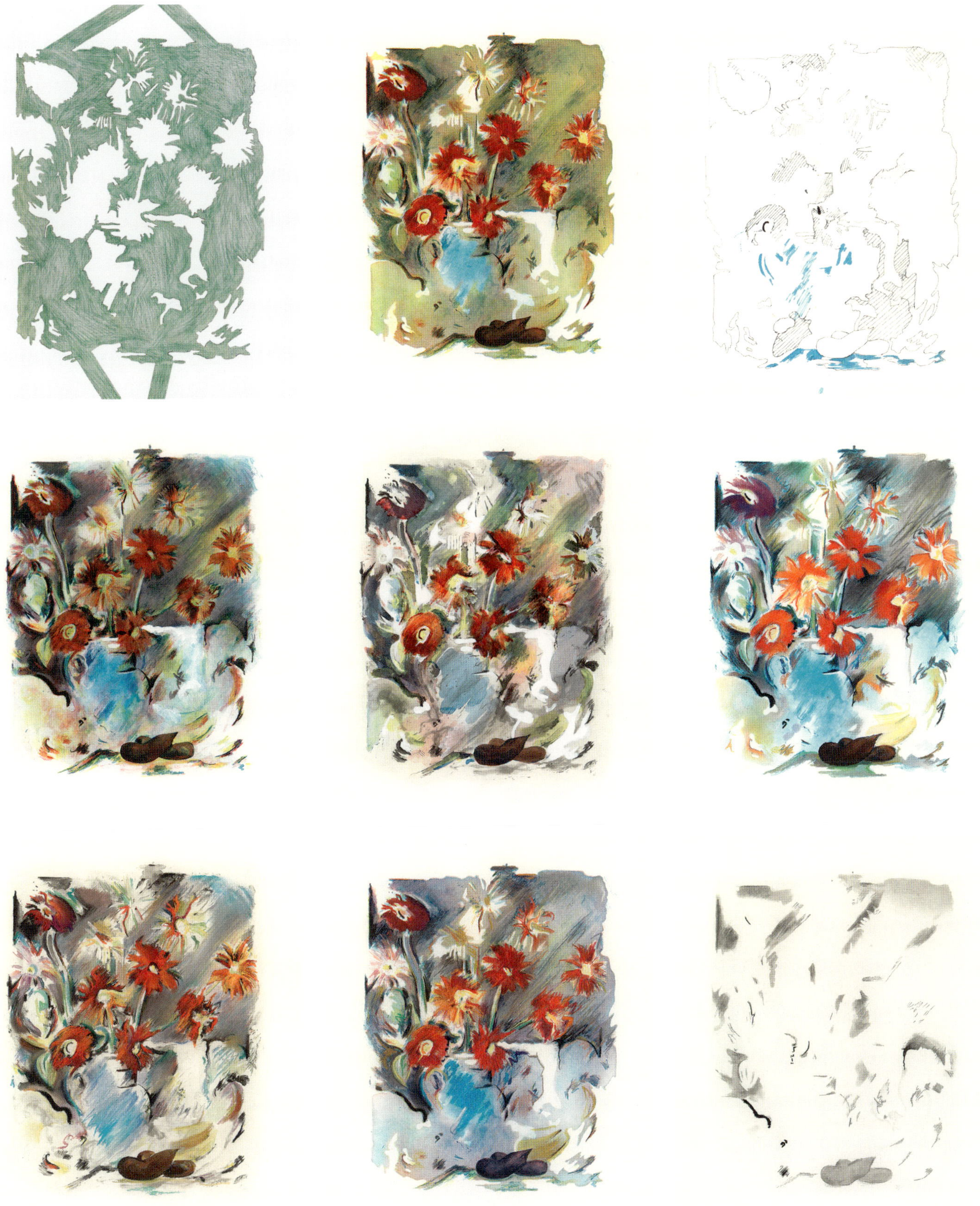

Flower-piece – trial proofs 1973

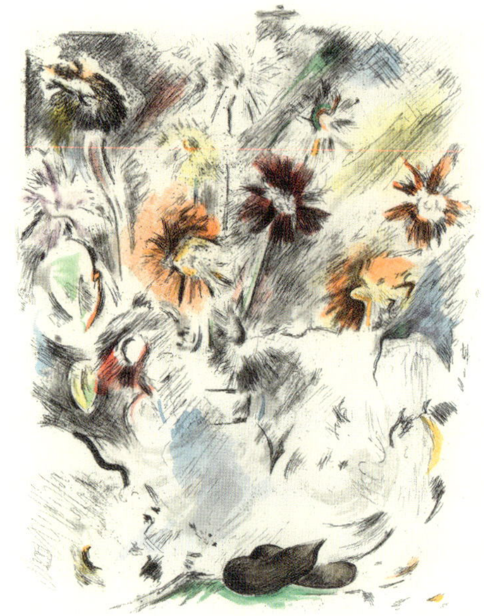

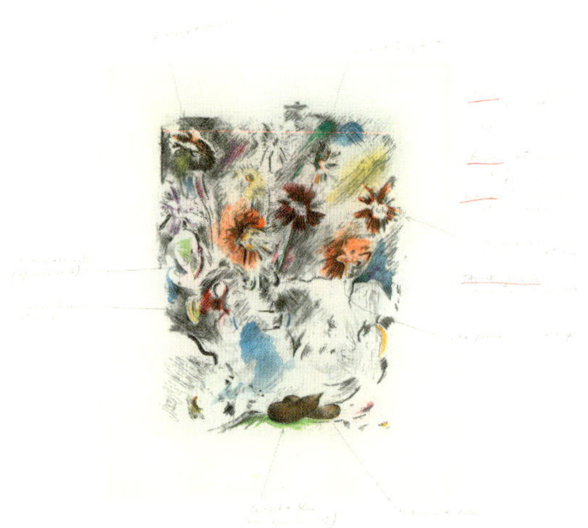

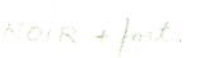

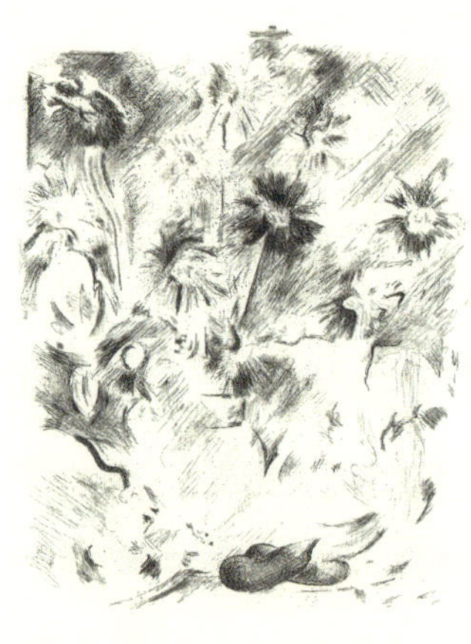

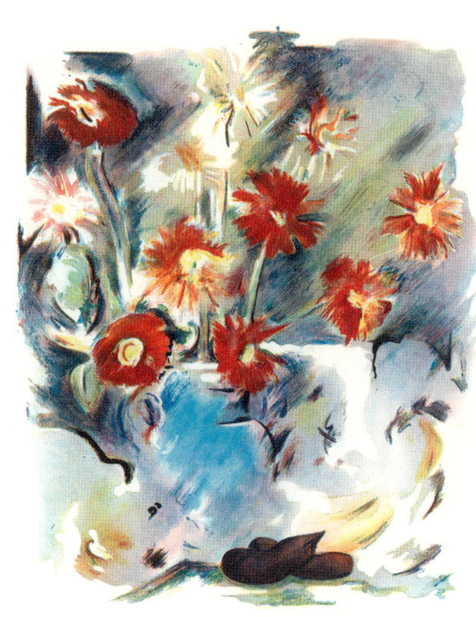

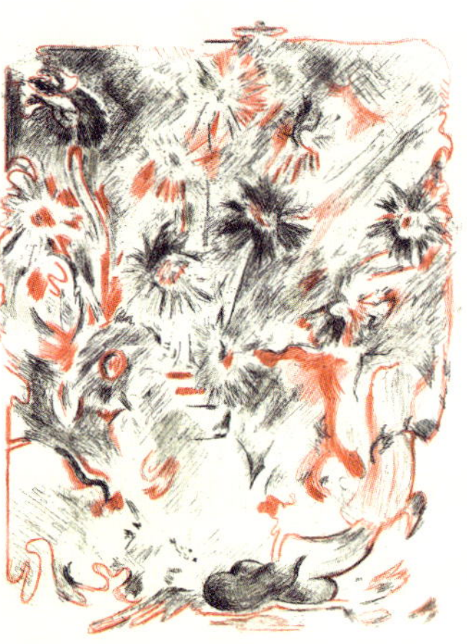

Multi-coloured flower-piece 1974

Multi-coloured flower-piece – proof marked up by Crommelynck with colour instructions for printer 1974

Trichromatic flower-piece progressives 1973–74

Trichromatic flower-piece 1973–74

Multi-coloured flower-piece – progressive 1974

Multi-coloured flower-piece – working proof 1974

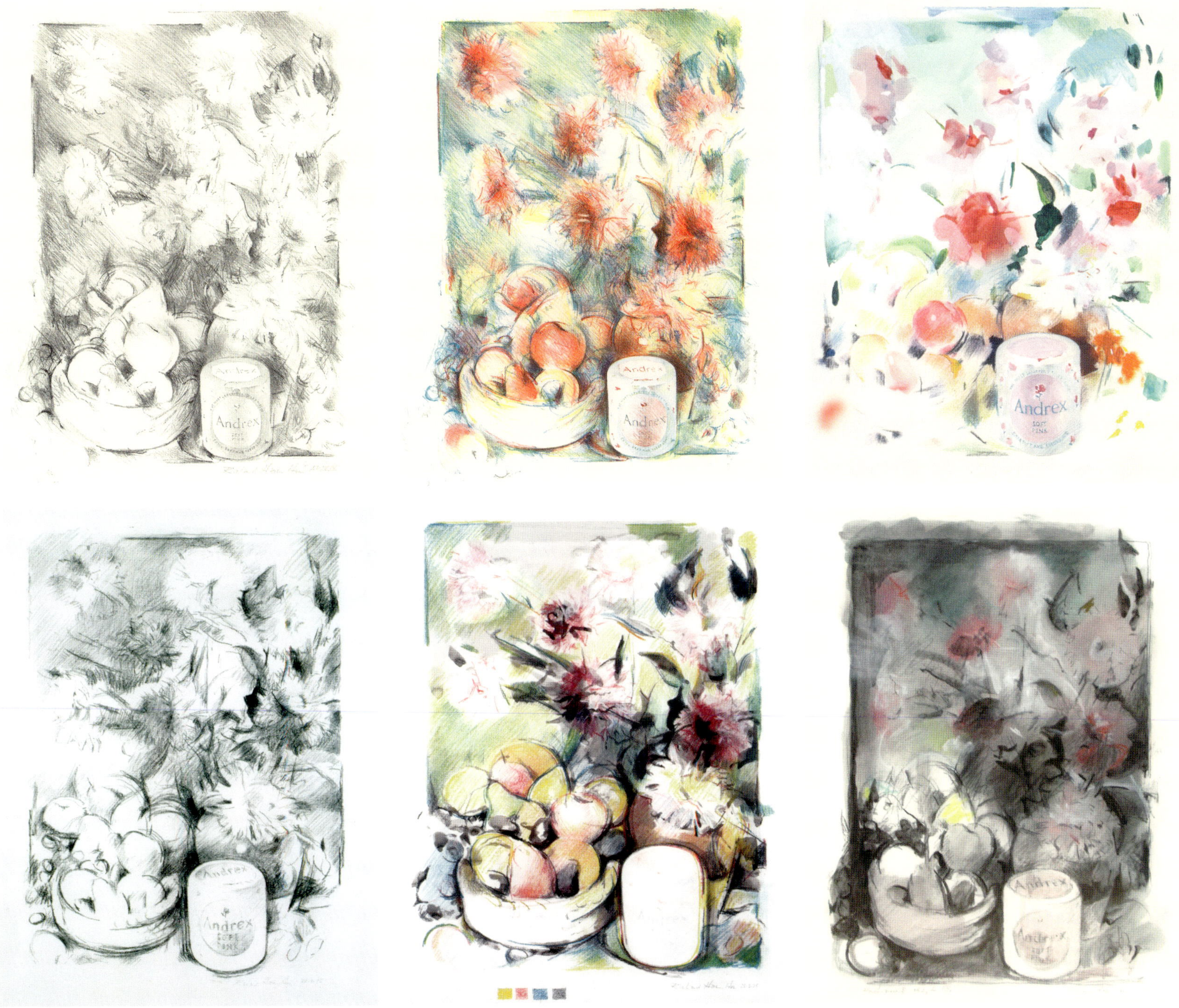

Flower-piece B – cyan separation 1975

Flower-piece B – study for litho 1975

Flower-piece B – crayon study 1975

Flower-piece B – trichromatic study 1975

Flower-piece study (b) 1973

Flower-piece B – study for litho 1975

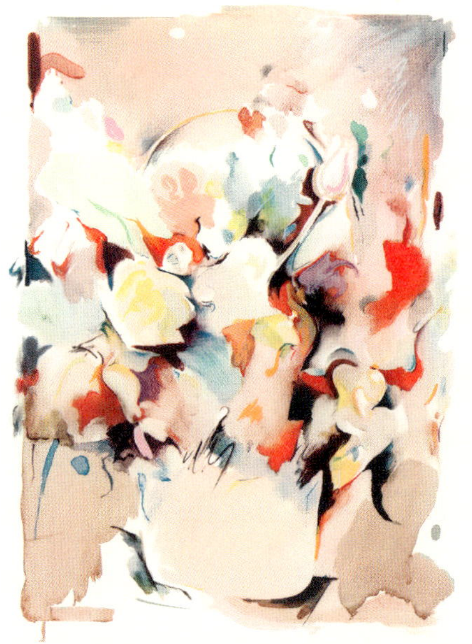

Flower-piece A 1974

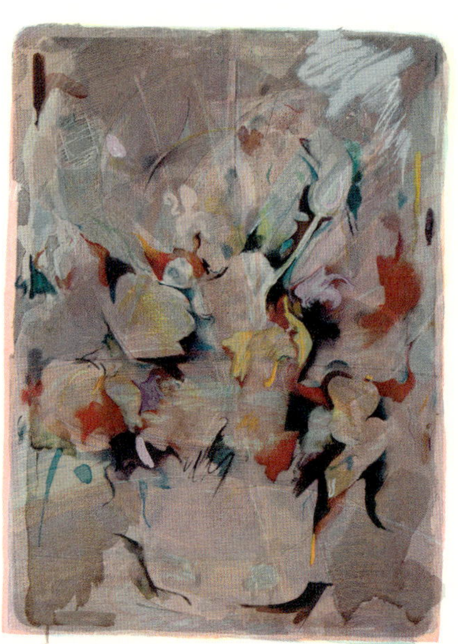

Two flower-pieces
(with Dieter Roth) – stage proof II 1974

Two flower-pieces (with Dieter Roth) 1974

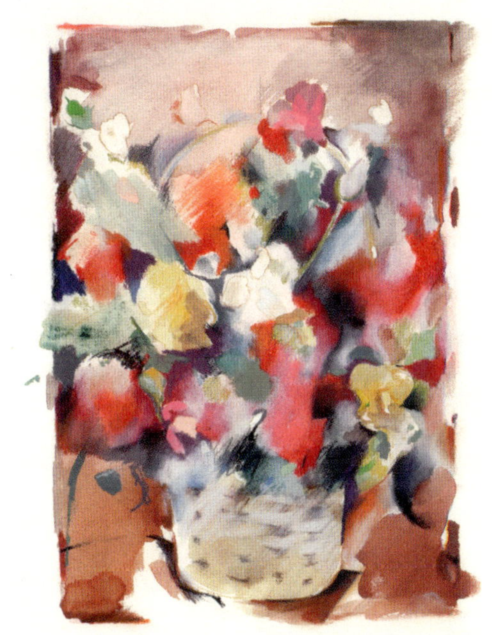

Flower-piece study (a) 1971

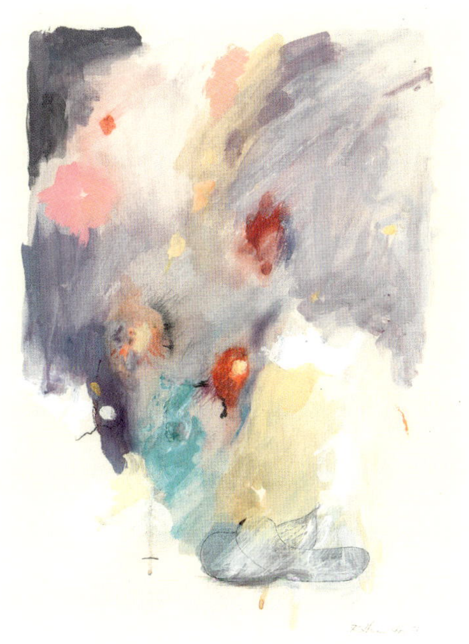

Flower-piece 1971

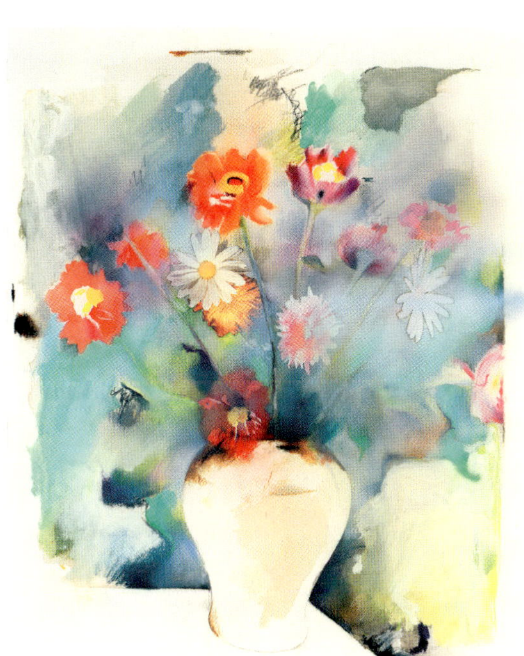

Flower-piece 1971

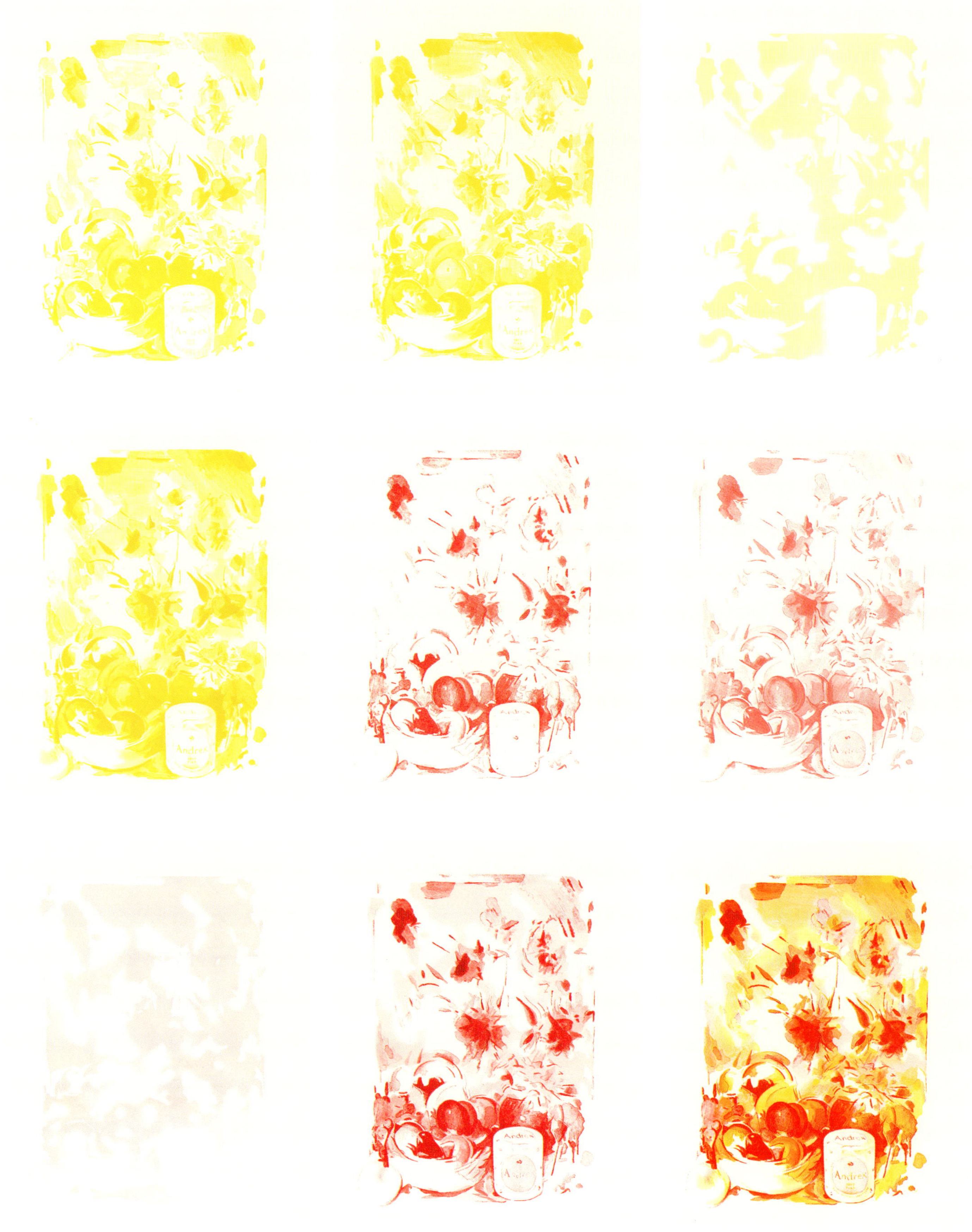

Flower-piece B – 15 progressives 1975

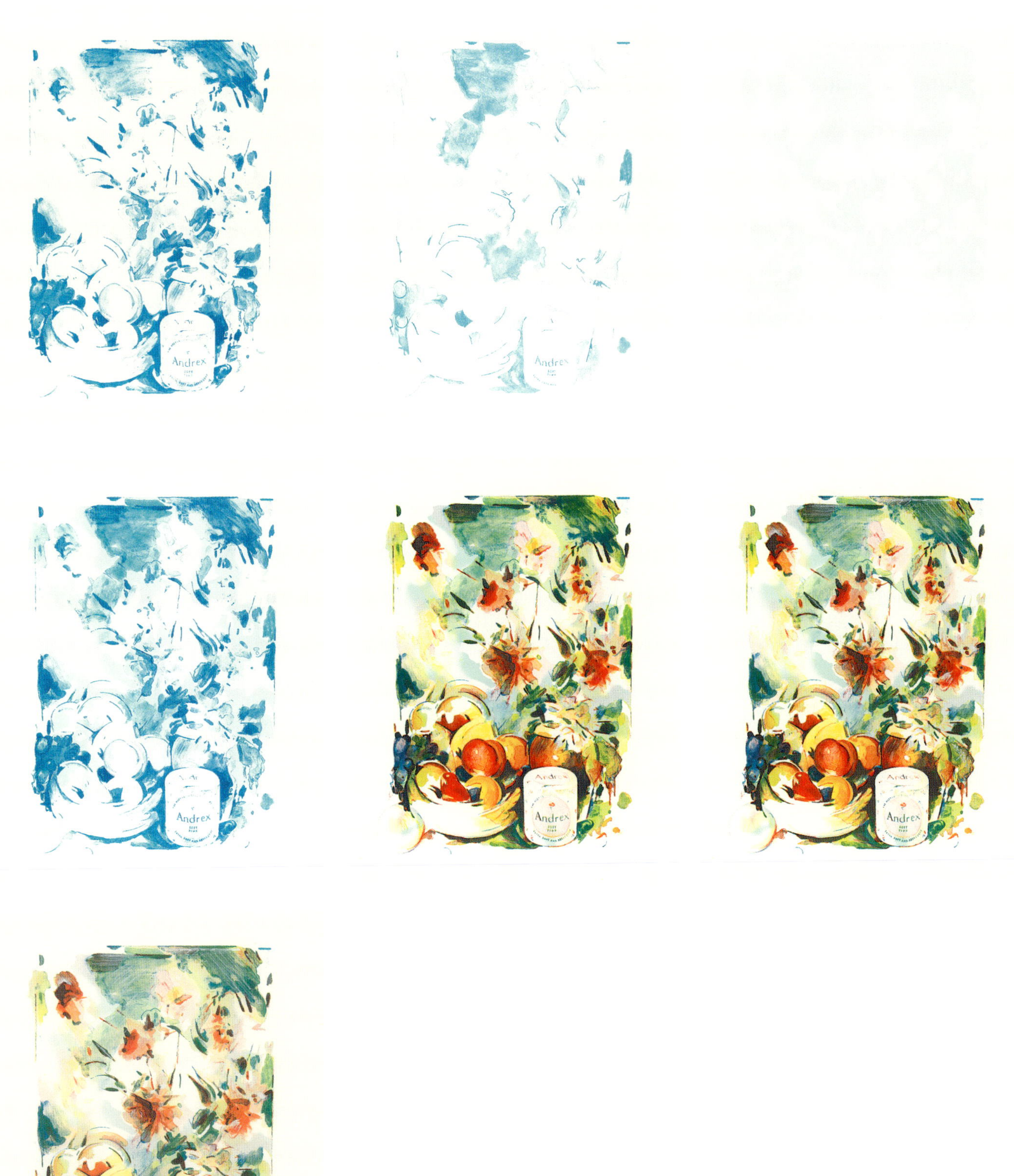

Flower-piece B 1975

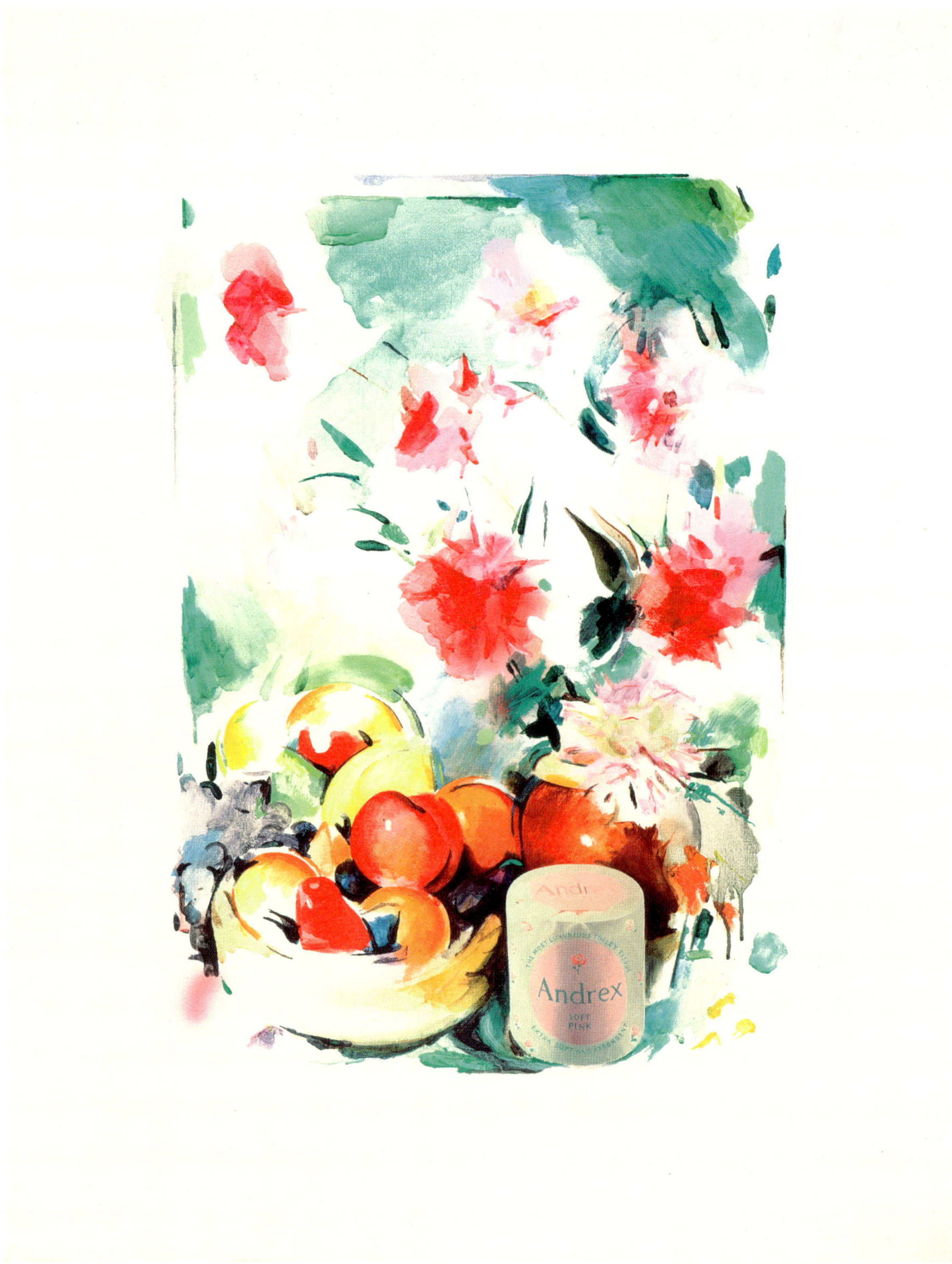

Flower-piece I 1971–74

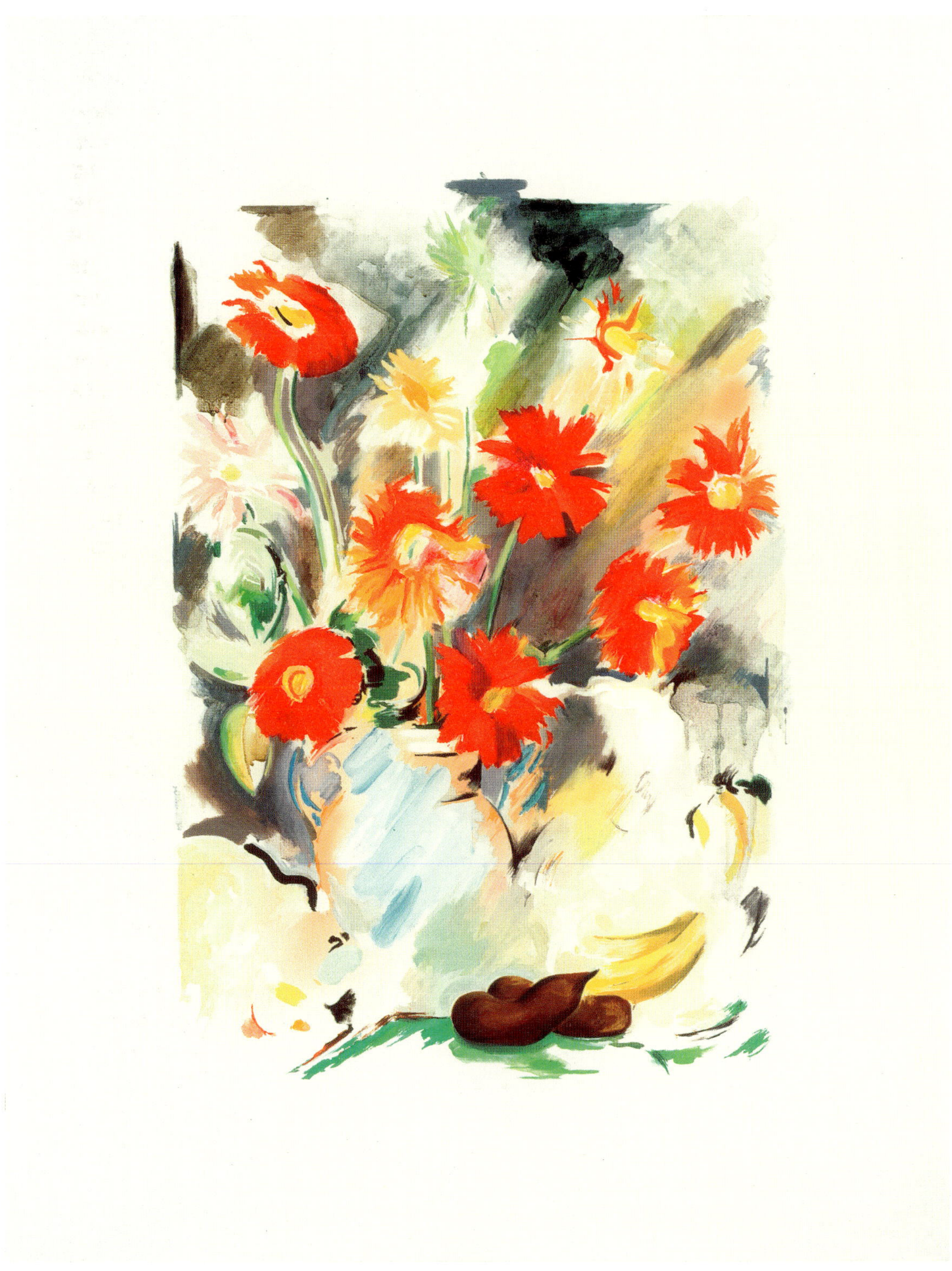

Flower-piece II 1973

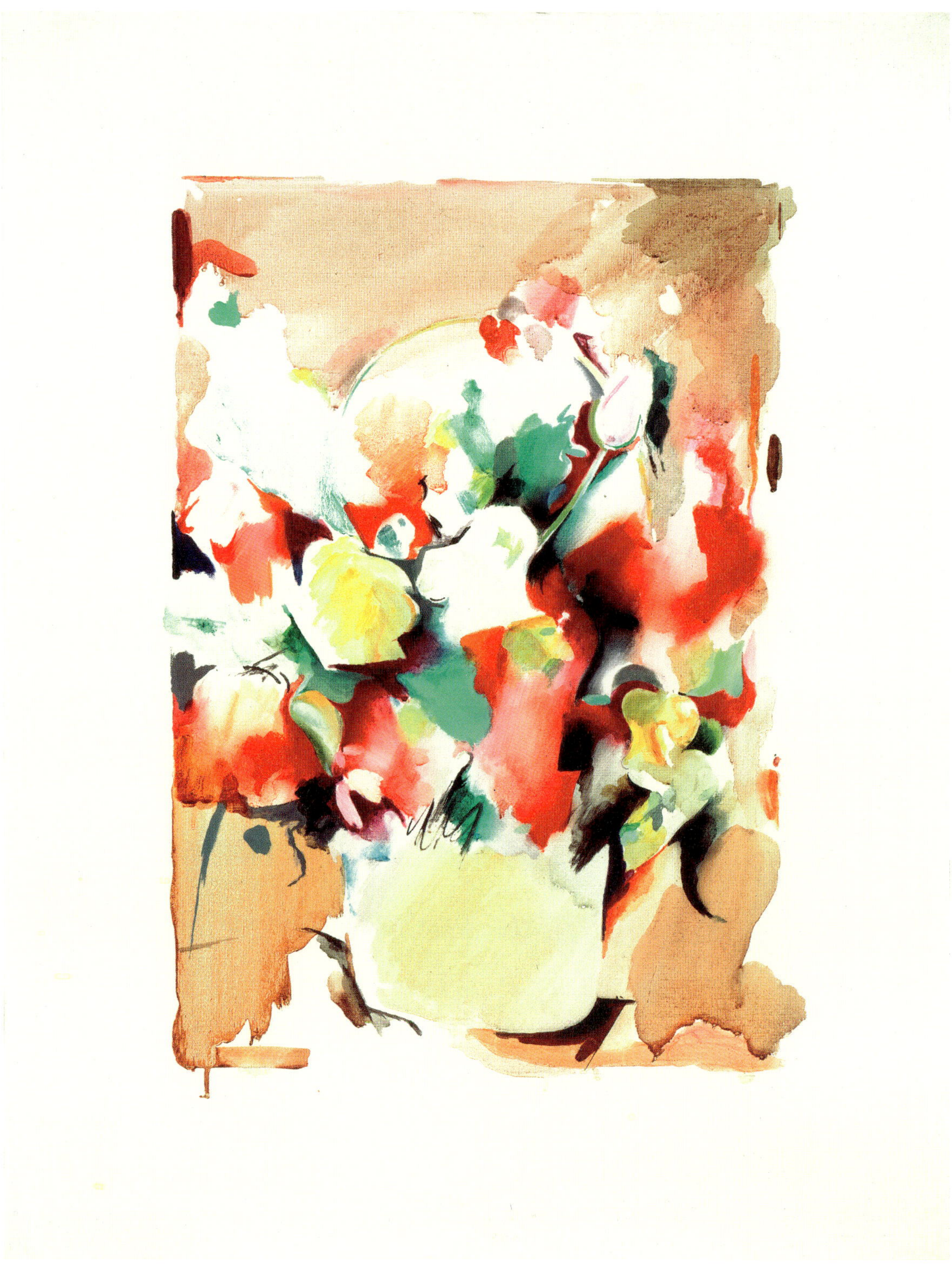

Flower-piece III 1973–74

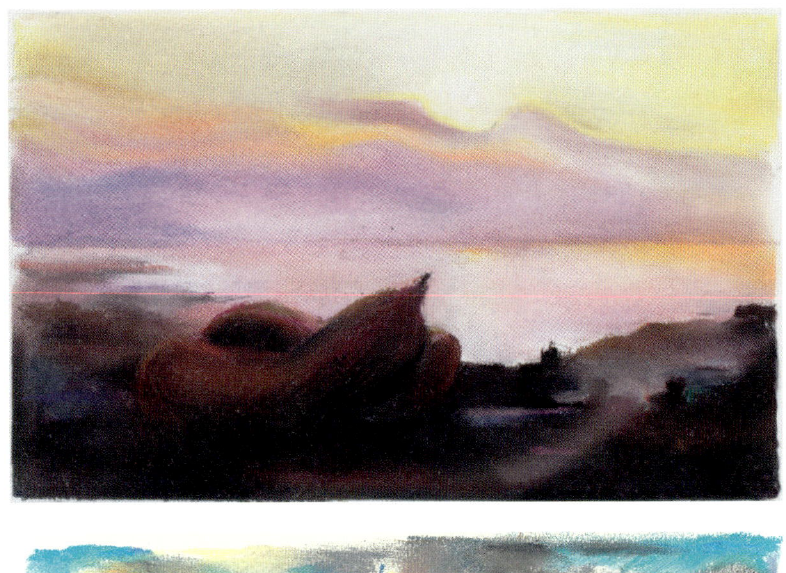

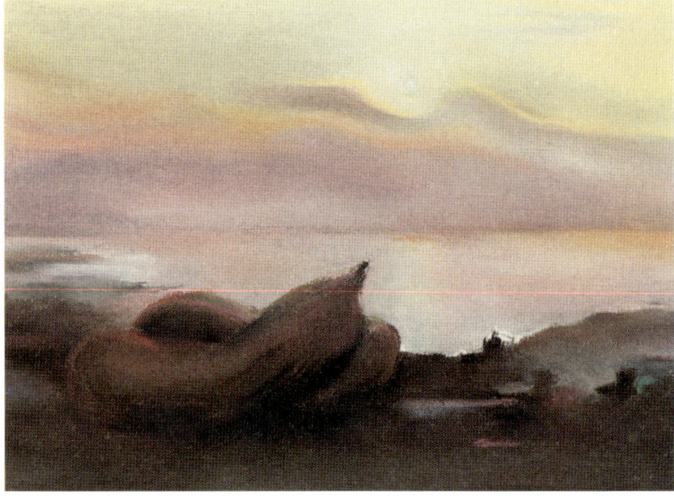

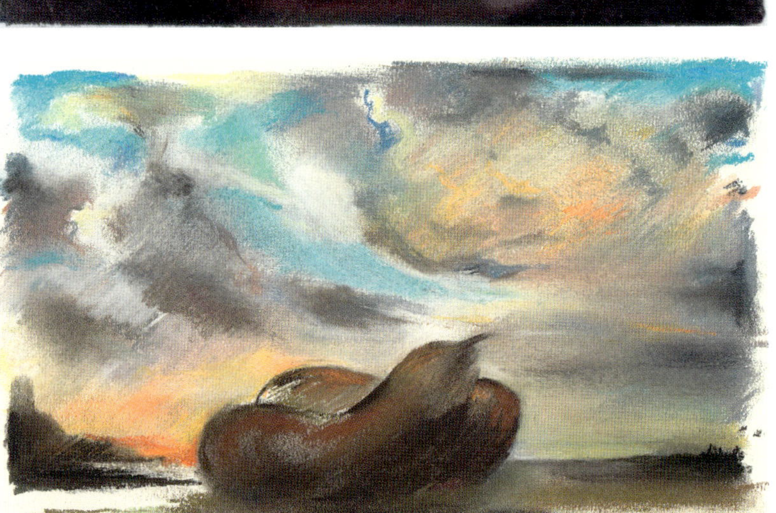

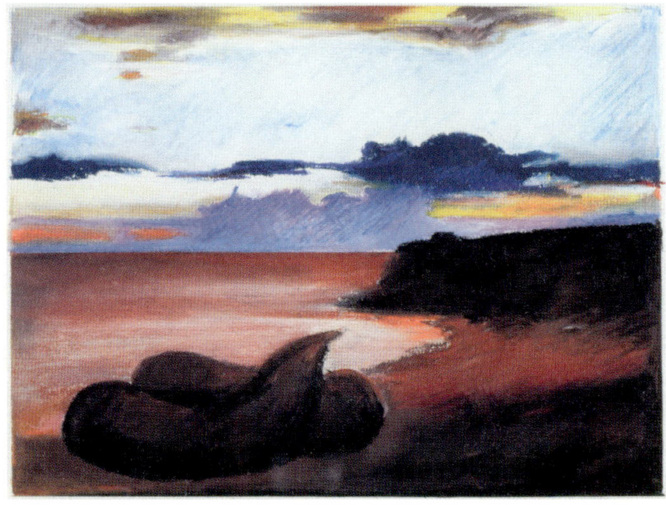

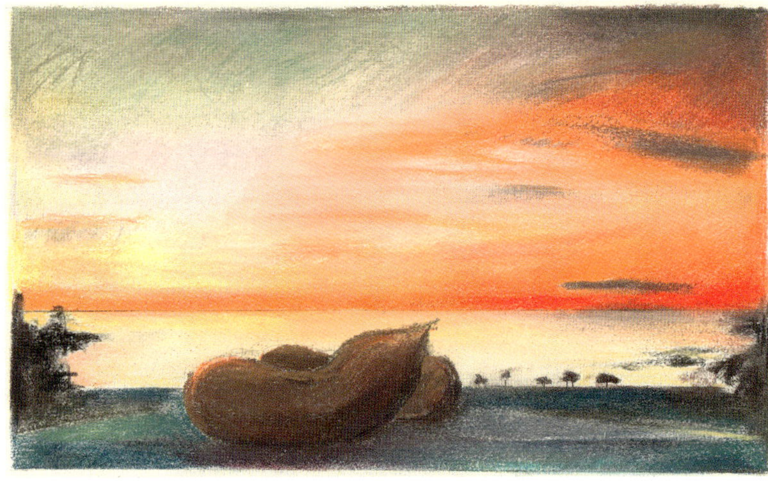

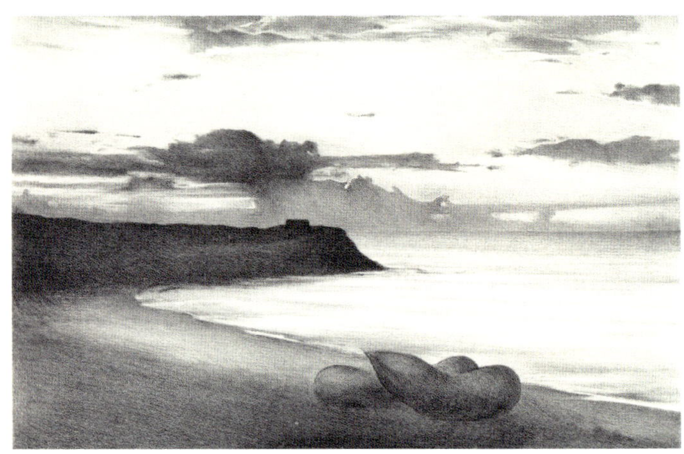

Sunrise 1974
Sunset (a) 1974
Sunset (d) 1974

Sunrise 1975
Sunset (f) 1975
Sunset (f) 1975

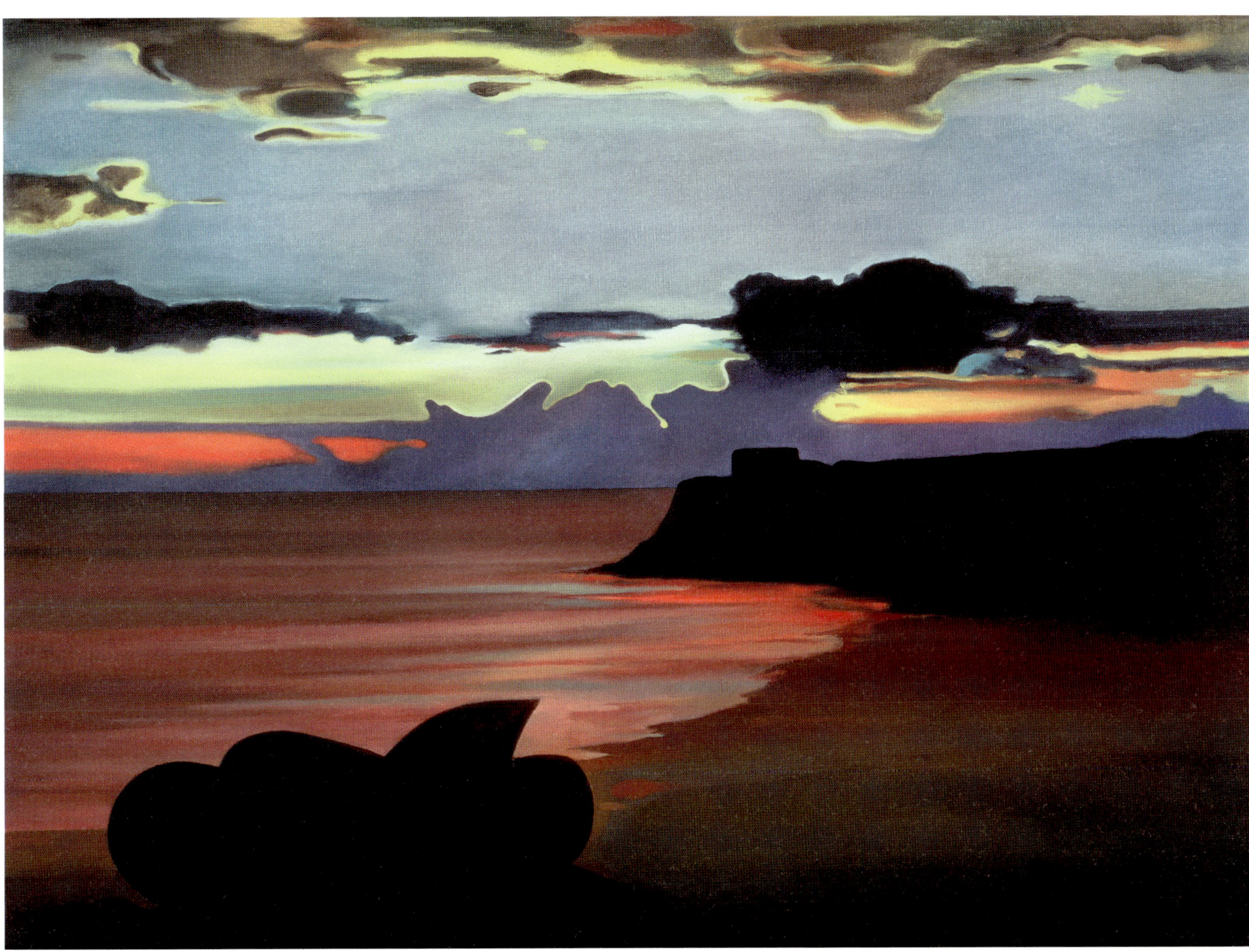

Sunset 1975

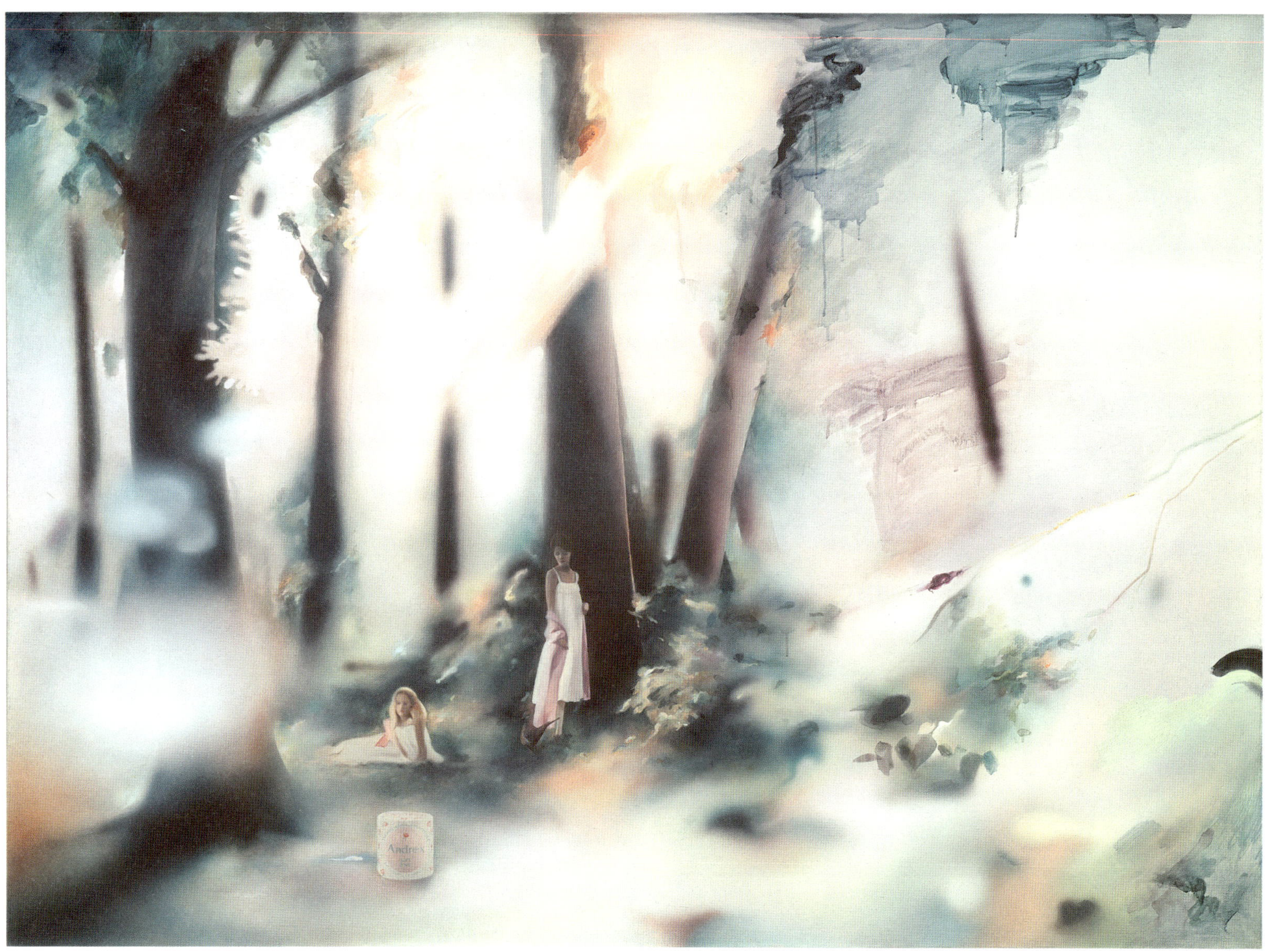

Soft pink landscape 1971–72

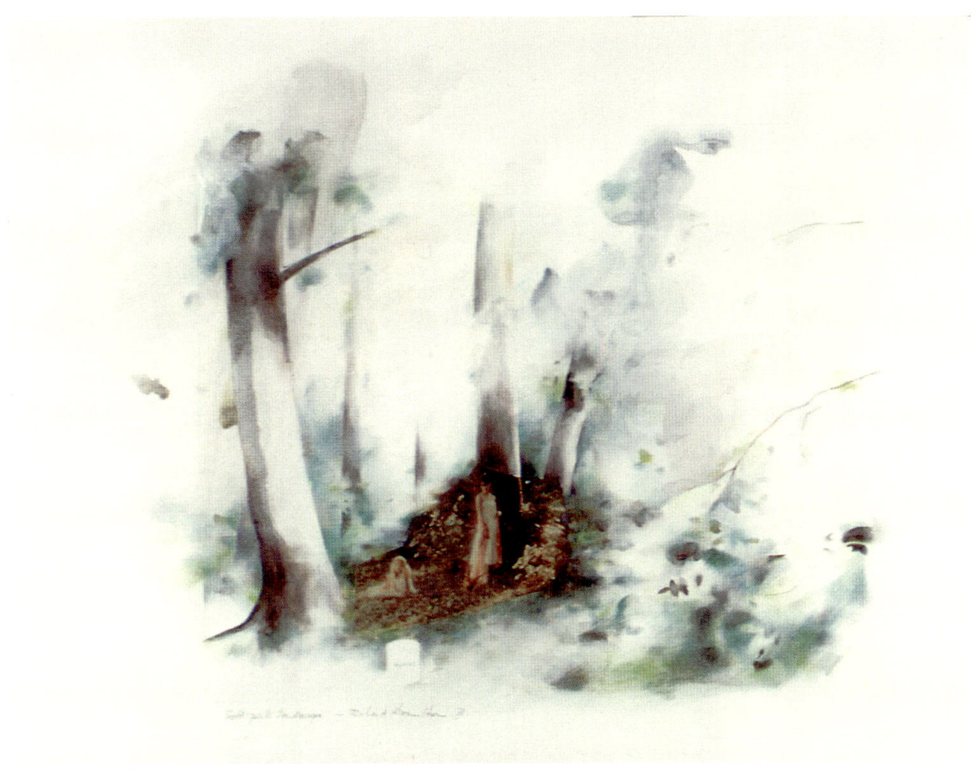

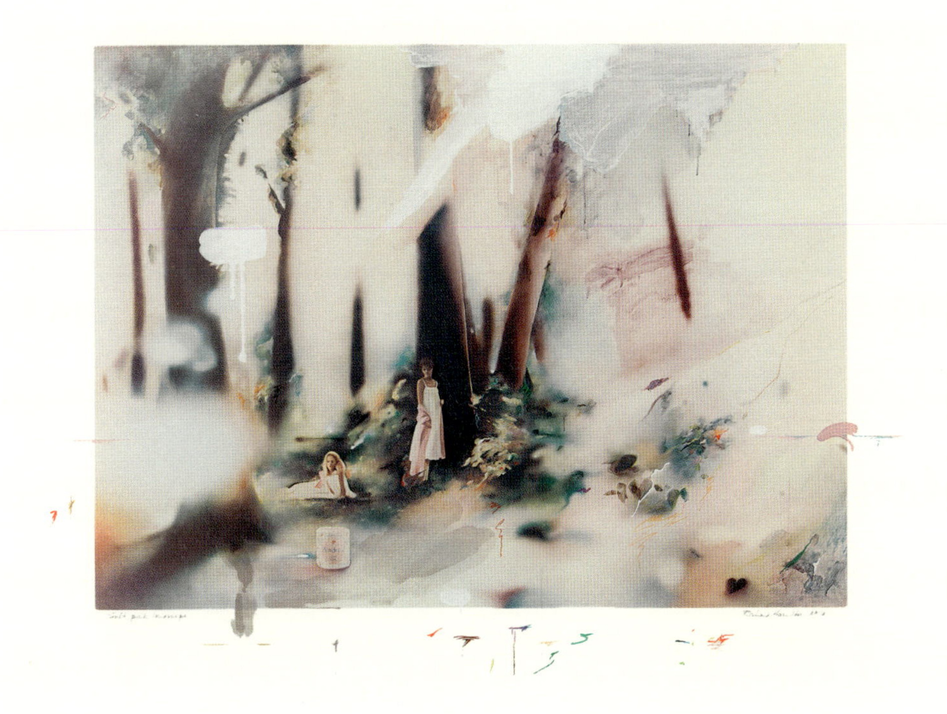

Soft pink landscape – study 1971
Soft pink landscape – collotype 1980

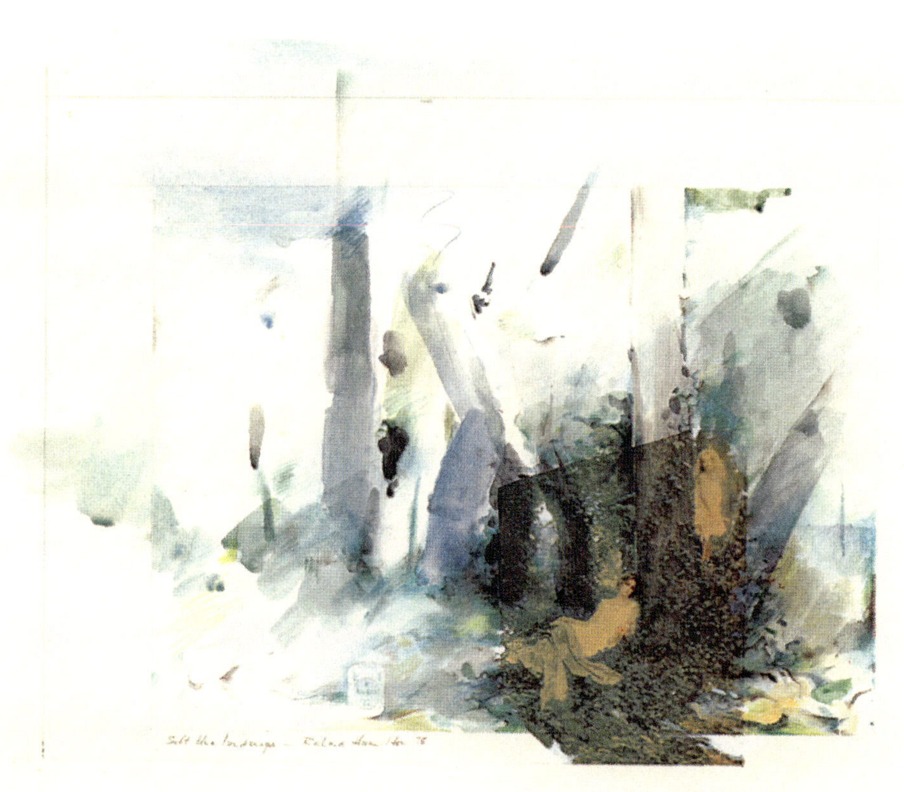

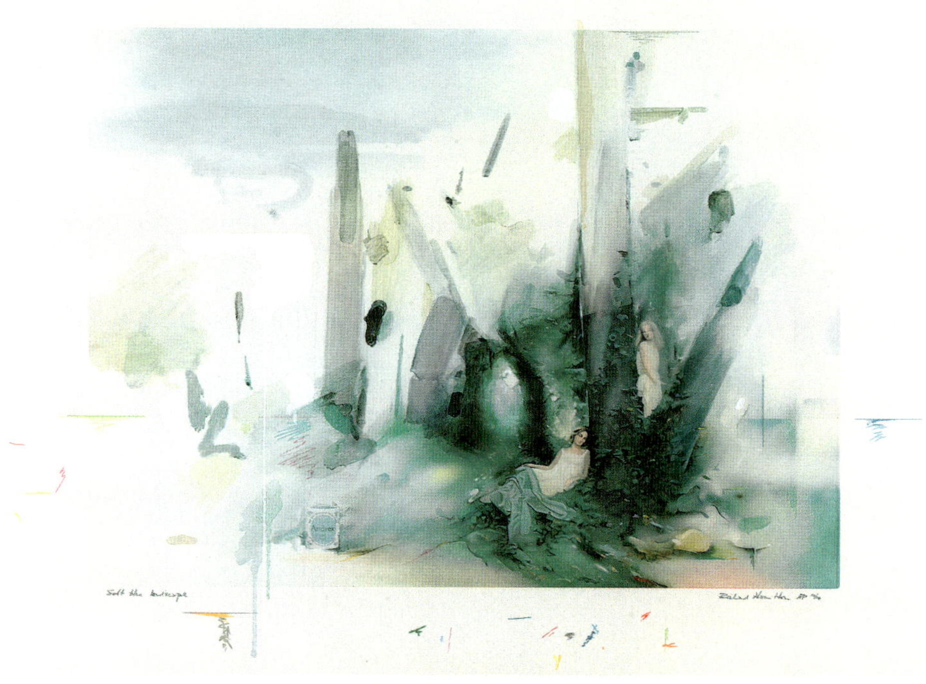

Soft blue landscape – study 1975

Soft blue landscape – collotype 1979

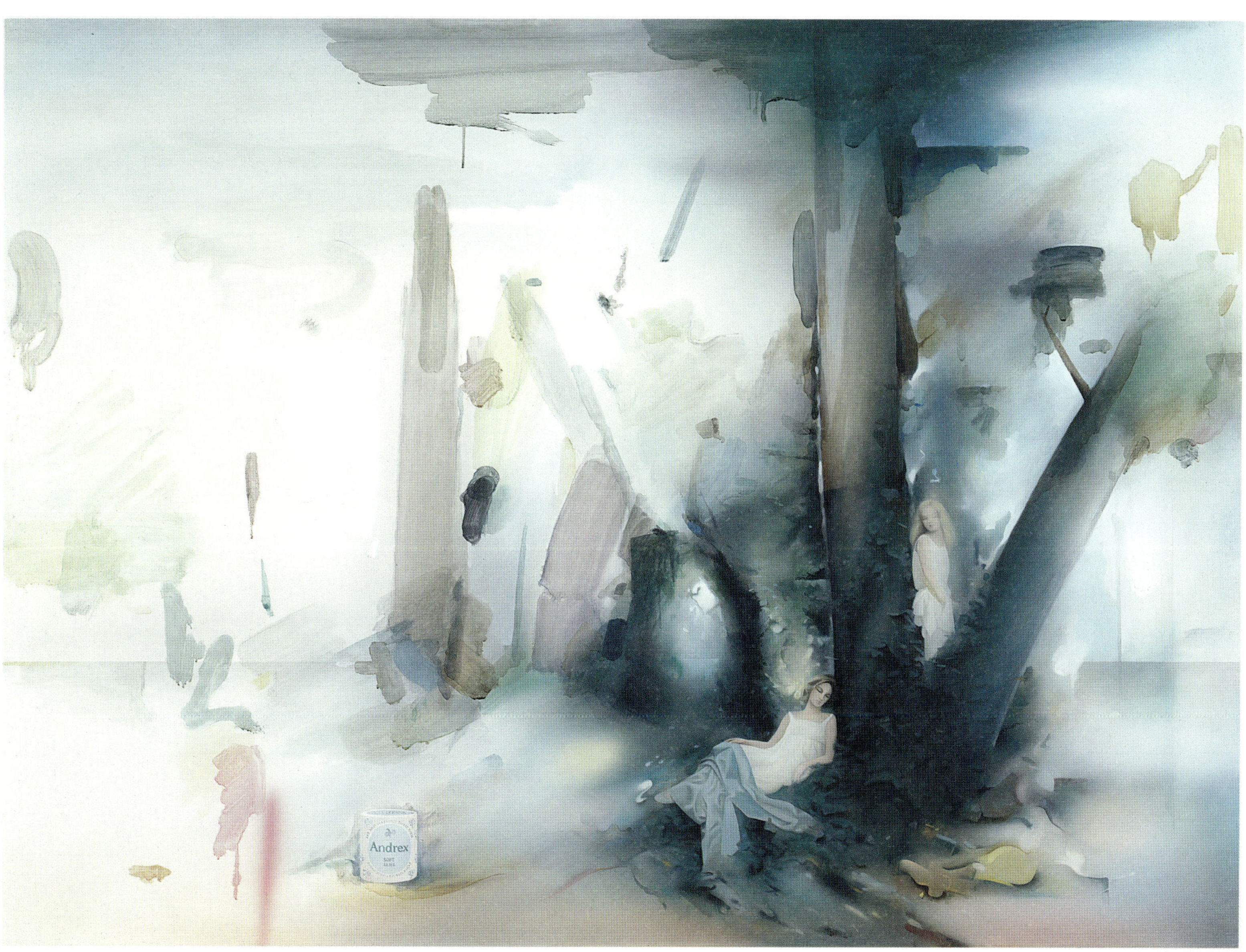

Soft blue landscape 1976–80

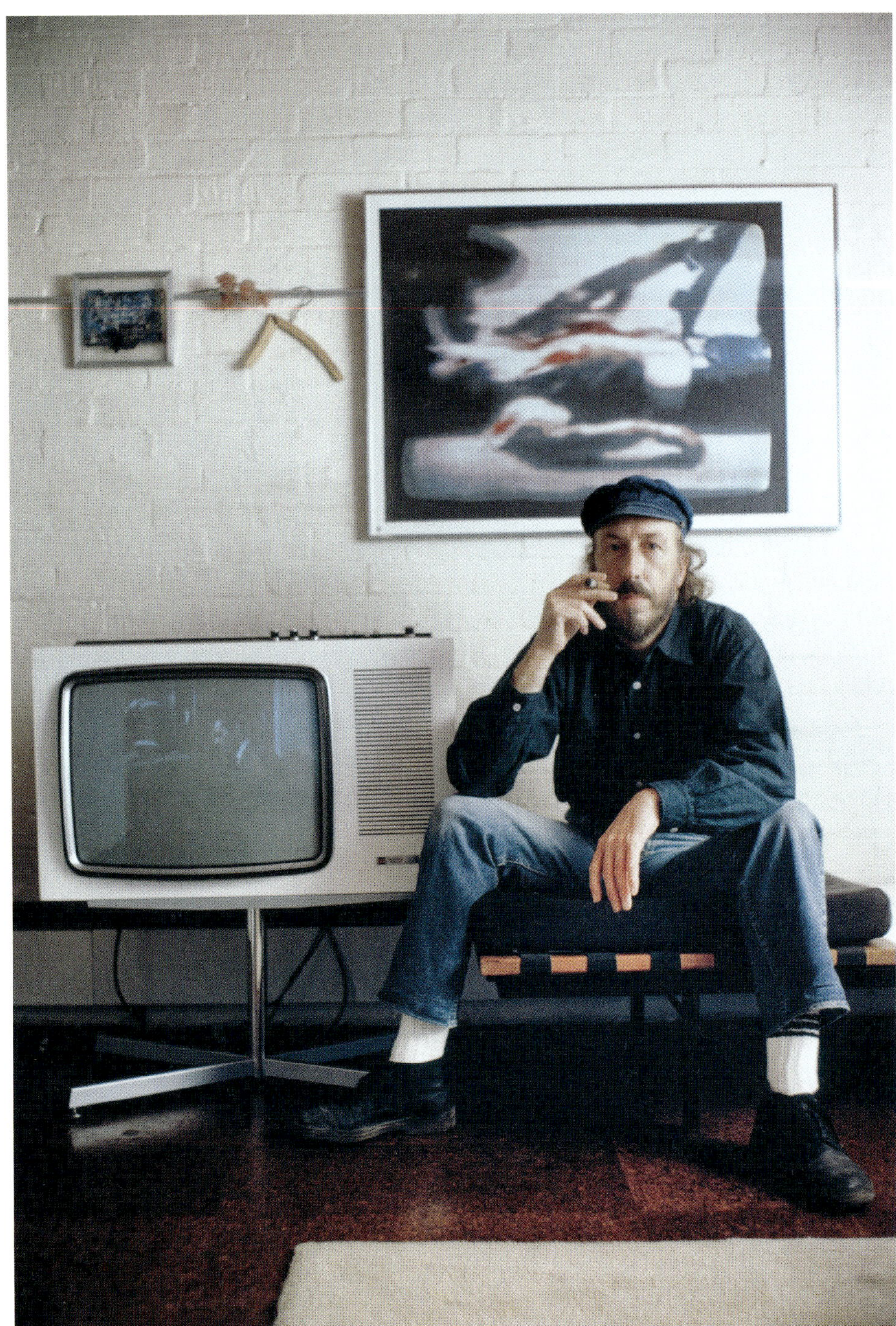

Hamilton with *Kent State* 1970

Television Delivers People

Mark Godfrey

Protest pictures

In the final years of his life, Richard Hamilton prepared a group of exhibitions that brought together works dealing explicitly with political subjects: *Protest Pictures* (Inverleith House, Edinburgh, 2008), *Modern Moral Matters* (Serpentine, London, 2010) and *Civil Rights etc.* (a joint exhibition with Rita Donagh at the Hugh Lane, Dublin, 2011). Hamilton had not always structured his shows in this way: in 1969 he first displayed his *Swingeing London* paintings [pp. 163–67] at Robert Fraser's in London opposite his pictures based on images of seaside bathers, and in 1971 at Marconi in Milan he premiered his set of *Kent State* prints [pp. 252–55] opposite his series *Portrait of the artist by Francis Bacon* [pp. 184–85]. Disgusted by the war on Iraq and the continued Israeli occupation of the Palestinian territories, Hamilton seems to have wanted to foreground this aspect of his output by the late 2000s. He was also interested in the idea of these political works being considered as the antithesis to other aspects of his late production—painting Tony Blair as a devil-cowboy one day, and an Angel and Virgin in a Fra Angelico-inspired loggia the next. Indeed, he saw a "programme of polarity" operating throughout his oeuvre and said working in this way was a lesson learned from Marcel Duchamp, whose "primary philosophical tenet was antithesis."[1] But the decision to cleave the political works away from the rest of his oeuvre has its dangers. It can mean forgetting the connections of such works to other aspects of his practice: producing an overly committed picture of the artist and implying that some works have historical determinants while others are timeless in their concerns, whereas Hamilton was keen to relate each kind of work to historical conditions. He recognised, for instance, that paintings such as *Respective* (1951) [p. 35] connected to research done during World War II about the way pilots saw the landscape while flying, and later, noting how each element of an interior such as *Las meninas* "bears a testimony to Spanish history," implied the same for his own interiors.[2]

This essay will centre on four "political" works that were included in his three late shows, namely *Kent State* (1970), *The citizen* (1982–83), *Treatment room* (1983–84) and *War games* (1992). But instead of grouping them together with other works dealing with political subjects, I want to relate them to other parts of Hamilton's oeuvre and to the broader questions that he put to himself. The route I will take is to examine how this group of four works emerged from two sets of issues Hamilton was addressing by the late 1960s. One dealt with what it meant to make representations of people; the other concerned what to make of a technology that was becoming a ubiquitous feature of the modern interior: television.

People

In a TV programme broadcast in 1987, Hamilton introduced himself by saying: "I'm a figurative artist and that means that I need subject matter, human subject matter, and sometimes human subject matter of a very powerful nature."[3] As we know, Hamilton made a lot more besides figurative paintings, but as a figurative artist, and not one interested in the approach of contemporaries such as Lucian Freud, Hamilton necessarily encountered the problem of where to derive source material from if not from the bodies of models

1. Richard Hamilton, "The Scatological Period," in *Shit and Flowers* (London: Alan Cristea Gallery, 2010), 7.
2. Richard Hamilton, "An Inside View," in *Richard Hamilton: Exteriors, Interiors, Objects, People* (Winterthur: Kunstmuseum Winterthur, 1990), 43.
3. Hamilton speaking about himself on the TV programme *Painting with Light,* 1987.

posing in his studio. Sometimes he spoke about the search for subjects; at other times he claimed to come across compelling images of people by chance. Working from snapshots, publicity photographs, postcards and film stills, he would begin to ask how photography represents people in a world mediated by images and to probe moments of breakdown. He was fascinated by the contact sheets that Marilyn Monroe scratched to erase those photographs that did not come up to her own standards of image-presentation, and also by what happens to an image of a crowd in Trafalgar Square when it is "grossly deteriorated"[4] by enlargement and when the depicted humans become not simply anonymous, but broken shapes. Blowing up a seaside image to make *People* (1965–66) [p. 116], Hamilton would note that at a certain point of enlargement photography ceases to provide information about a scene and instead becomes almost abstract, as a mother and child are turned into amoebic blobs.

Such observations about the limits of photographic representation, I believe, paved the way for related questions about the limits of political representation. How can "the people" be represented?[5] What can an artist do to "represent" those people who do not feel represented by their governments? These were the subjects Hamilton was exploring by 1970, issues that surely were connected to those he addressed back in 1964, when, with his *Portrait of Hugh Gaitskell as a Famous Monster of Filmland* [p. 251], he confronted a leader whom he felt did not represent the views of the British left and their hopes for unilateral nuclear disarmament.

Television

Hamilton's other main concern revolved around the way various media distorted and presented information and images to modern subjects, and how artists, using their own media of painting, printmaking or installation, could reflect on these new forms of delivery. Early in his career Hamilton had been fascinated with the way media extended our reach out to the world beyond our immediate environment, notably in 1955 with his installation *Man, Machine and Motion* [pp. 42–47], featuring photographs taken underwater and in space. His enquiry flipped around the next year in his famous 1956 collage *Just what is it that makes today's homes so different, so appealing?* [p. 49], which dramatised how the world—through media—reached into the postwar domestic interior. This collage marks the first appearance in his work of a technology that had a privileged, if so far rarely acknowledged place in Hamilton's thinking: the television.[6] On its screen, a woman is on the telephone: in other words, on TV one saw another medium, rather than a scene, as if to celebrate that the function of TV was to deliver information.[7]

In the film about his work, which he made with James Scott in 1969, Hamilton zoomed in on this part of the collage, and, with a surtitle reading "Television" remaining on the screen, cut from the collage to his own face speaking on another television [fig. 1]. Like other IG members, Hamilton used to crowd around the black and white TV set that Reyner

4. Richard Hamilton, "Notes on Photographs," in *Collected Words 1954-1982* (London: Thames & Hudson, 1982), 68.
5. As Hal Foster has shown, Warhol also asked himself these questions, and like Hamilton "evoked the mass subject in two opposite ways: through iconic celebrity and abstract anonymity." See the section "Mass Witnessing," in Foster's essay "Death in America," *October* 75 (Winter 1996), 36–59.
6. One exception is David Sylvester, who remarked that Hamilton's "mass imagery does not belong to the billboard, the soup can, the Brillo box, the strip cartoon; it is imagery transmitted through a TV set." See David Sylvester, "Seven Studies for a Picture of Richard Hamilton," in *Richard Hamilton* (London: Anthony d'Offay Gallery, 1991), 9. Lynda Morris also wrote that Hamilton "moved the century-old relationship between painting and photography to one between painting and television." See Lynda Morris, *Pictures of Pictures* (Bristol: Arnolfini; Norwich: Norwich Gallery, 1999), 20.

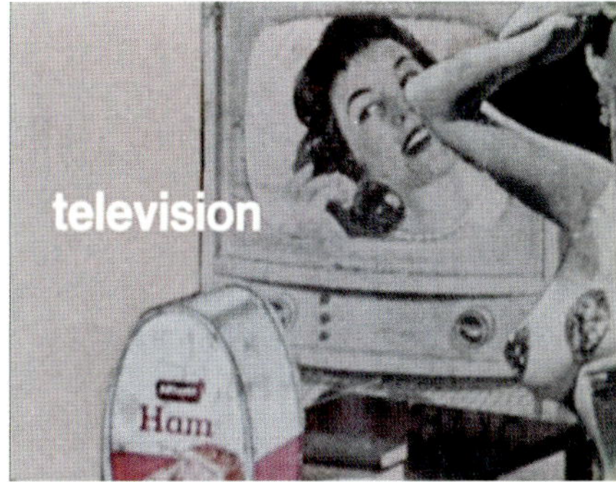

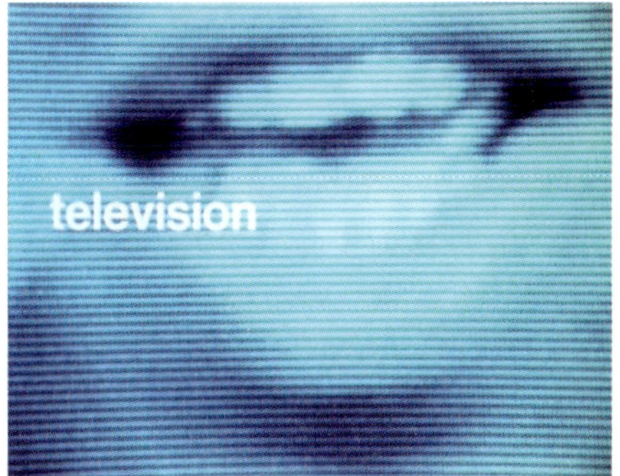

fig. 1
Successive frames in James Scott's film on Hamilton, 1969

Banham brought into the ICA in the early 1950s, and having worked as a designer for Granada Television in 1955, he posed before a TV in a photograph taken of his installation at the Daily Mail's *Ideal Home Exhibition* in 1958. Twenty years later he would include a TV set in his National Gallery show *The Artist's Eye.* He introduced his exhibition of paintings at the Hanover Gallery in 1964 with a preface including the line: "TV is no less legitimate an influence than New York Abstract Expressionism."[8] The Hanover show featured his second piece of work that included a television, the painting *Interior II* (1964) [p. 109]. To the right of the figure of the actress Patricia Knight, Hamilton collaged a Decca TV cut out from an advert, and delicately pasted onto its face the image of what by this moment was *the* most watched TV event in history—the assassination of John F. Kennedy.[9] Television was already delivering people into the interior, bringing catastrophic and violent events of world historical importance into their living rooms, but to what effect? Hamilton would later remark of this work: "It is extraordinary, isn't it, to have the idea that an assassination can happen in real time in your living-room and you might be more interested in something else?"[10]

In *Interior II* Patricia Knight ignores Kennedy's fate, yet in the years after it was made Hamilton could and would not ignore those events that reached into his living room via TV, and indeed went on to make significant works that start from this scenario of TV delivering people. When his thinking about people and about television came together, Hamilton faced new questions: how to represent *the way* television delivers people to the interior? How does television control the people watching it? How can an artist acknowledge the way TV represents and controls people, but at the same time make counter-representations? There were other challenges too, and to appreciate these it is worth pausing to consider some of the ways television was discussed at this historical moment, even though there is no strong reason to believe that Hamilton was familiar with these discussions.

In 1969, Marshall McLuhan claimed that "television is the most significant electric media because it permeates nearly every home in the country, extending the central nervous system of every viewer as it works over and moulds the entire sensorium with the ultimate message."[11] Raymond Williams, writing in 1974, also noted the intrusion of television into the modern interior, relating the rise of television in the postwar period to the "significantly higher investment in the privatised home."[12] Both thinkers, then, like Hamilton, were interested in the impact of television within the modern domestic interior, but they differed when it came to describing how it was consumed. McLuhan wrote evocatively about the TV child: "The war in Vietnam has written its bloody message on his skin; he has witnessed the assassinations and funerals of the nation's leaders; he's been orbited through the TV screen into the astronaut's dance in space…"[13] All three of these subjects can be found in Hamilton's works of this time, but it is Williams' account of TV reception that is more significant if we want to understand the challenges Hamilton faced when it came to making works based on television images. Williams argued that the television viewer does not so much consume individual stories or events, but that "in all developed broadcasting systems the characteristic

7. Hamilton took the television from an advert for Stromberg-Carlson sets published in *Life* magazine in January 1955. The image of the woman on the phone appeared in the advert, but was excised and then pasted back by Hamilton. This supports my claim that Hamilton was interested in this figure as a recursive image of media. See John-Paul Stonard, "Pop in the Age of Boom: Richard Hamilton's *Just what is it that makes today's homes so different, so appealing?," The Burlington Magazine* 149 (September 2007), 616.
8. Richard Hamilton, "Introduction," in *Paintings etc. '56–64* (London: Hanover Gallery, 1964), n. p.
9. Close examination of *Interior II* reveals that the Kennedy image has been collaged onto the Decca television set.
10. Graham Heathcote, "British Pop Artist Explains his Art," *The Fort Scott Tribune,* 22 July 1992, B3.
11. "Playboy Interview: Marshall McLuhan," *Playboy* magazine (March 1969).
12. Raymond Williams, *Television: Technology and Cultural Form,* 2nd ed. (London: Routledge, 1990), 23.
13. McLuhan, *Playboy* magazine.
14. Williams, *Television,* 86.

organisation, and therefore the characteristic experience, is one of sequence or flow."[14] "It is evident," he continued, "that what is now called 'an evening's viewing' is in some ways planned, by providers and then by viewers, *as a whole;* that it is in any event planned in discernible sequences which in this sense override particular programme units."[15] If TV broadcasts were planned and consumed as flows, then Hamilton would face a particular problem: how to wrest single images from the flow?

Stuart Hall's "Encoding and Decoding in the Television Discourse," first published in 1973 and reworked in 1980, was another landmark text on this subject. Hall made the simple point that "a 'raw' historical event cannot, *in that form,* be transmitted by a television newscast. Events can only be signified within the aural-visual forms of the televisual discourse. In the moment when a historical event passes under the sign of discourse, it is subject to all the complex formal 'rules' by which language signifies."[16] Taking this into account, Hamilton's task—in confronting and transforming television images—would be to think through the discursive forms of television, the "encodings" at work in television, as much as the "stories" that television produces from raw events. Hall's essay ended with three ideas about reception. It was possible, Hall wrote, for a viewer to "understand both the literal and connotative inflection given by a discourse but to decode the message in a *globally* contrary way." Hall called this an "oppositional" reception, concluding that "one of the most significant political moments is the point when events which are normally signified and decoded in a negotiated way begin to be given an oppositional reading."[17] In transforming television images, could Hamilton also provide an oppositional reading?

Finally, Mary Ann Doane's "Information, Crisis, Catastrophe," written in the late 1980s, helps us to better understand the challenges faced by Hamilton. Starting by showing how "the temporal dimension of television would seem to be that of an insistent *present-ness*—a *This-is-going-on* rather than a *That has been,* a celebration of the instantaneous,"[18] she argued that "television news provide[s] a seemingly endless stream of information, each bit (as it were) self-destructing in order to make room for the next,"[19] and then claimed that "television has been conceptualised as the annihilation of memory, and consequently of history, in its continual stress upon the *nowness* of its own discourse."[20] How could Hamilton oppose this aspect of the discourse, creating mnemonic art works from an experience of a technology whose function had been seen to destroy the mnemonic?

With these ideas in mind it is evident that even though television delivered people to this "figurative artist" searching for subject matter, as an artist also concerned with mediation, Hamilton could never simply use television images to make figurative works: Hamilton would need to reflect on the role of the television in the interior, on the transformations of images through delivery, on the discourses of television and the different temporal registers and mnemonic capacities of television and his art works, and with these considerations in mind I will now turn to *Kent State.*

15. Ibid., 93.
16. Stuart Hall, "Encoding/Decoding," in Stuart Hall, Dorothy Hobson, Andrew Lowe and Paul Willis (eds.), *Culture, Media, Language: Working Papers in Cultural Studies, 1972-79* (Birmingham: Centre for Contemporary Cultural Studies, 1980), 108
17. Ibid., 116.
18. Mary Ann Doane, "Information, Crisis, Catastrophe," in Patricia Mellencamp (ed.), *Logics of Television* (Bloomington: Indiana University Press, 1990), 222.

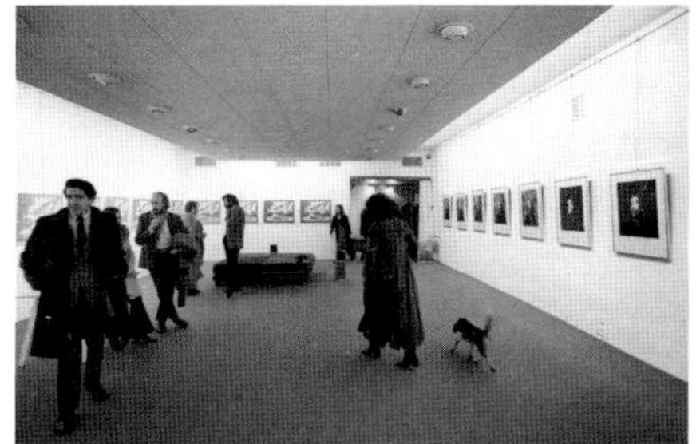

fig. 2
Exhibition at Studio Marconi, Milan, 1971

Kent State

The genesis of *Kent State* [p. 252] was explained by Hamilton in his *Collected Words:* he had been approached by a Munich print dealer, Dorothea Leonhart, who wanted to work with him to make a very large edition screen print of excellent technical quality. Hamilton had just bought a colour television and felt that "there might be a subject staring me in the face from the TV screen," so he "set up a camera in front of the TV for a week."[21] He photographed a number of entertainment shows, sports programmes and news items, and in the course of all this, on 4 May 1970, he watched and photographed the "shooting of students by National Guardsmen at Kent State University. This tragic event produced the most powerful images that emerged from the camera, yet I felt a reluctance to use any of them. It was too terrible an incident in American history to submit to arty treatment. Yet here it was in my hand, by chance… It seemed right that art could keep the shame in our minds."[22]

Hamilton selected a single photograph of a student lying prone on the ground, his right arm stretched out by his side: this was Dean Kahler, who was not one of the four killed, but who suffered spinal injuries in the shootings. He had photographed more dramatic images of crowds of students and of a young woman screaming but this close-up image had a tragic calm about it, and might have brought to mind iconic paintings such as Holbein's *The Body of the Dead Christ in the Tomb* (1521–22). From this photograph of his television screen, Hamilton set to work to make his print, but within some months presented the resulting works in two distinct ways. First, in September 1970 in Ottawa in a survey of his prints, Hamilton showed the single final screen print made from fifteen layers of pigment; soon afterwards, for a show of recent work at Studio Marconi in Milan in January 1971 [fig. 2], he showed fifteen individual stage proofs for *Kent State* in a long row from the faintest to the penultimate stage (more recently he tended to show twelve of the fifteen in a grid of three rows [pp. 254–55]).

Writing about his work on *Swingeing London* (1968–69)—the last work before *Kent State* to take on a polemical newsworthy subject—Hamilton remarked that "the sense of outrage subsided into quiet deliberations on the technical requirements of the expression of that anger."[23] One can imagine a similar process at work in the months he produced *Kent State,* when, having recognised that he could not do anything concrete and immediate to help the students, Hamilton determined to devote his energy to making this print as carefully as he could. Indeed, he undertook a monumental amount of work to make the print, with each of the 5000 sheets silkscreened fifteen times. There would have been many mistakes and a lot of waiting while ink dried between silk-screening sessions. All this time and labour was being devoted to crafting and disseminating a picture that would keep alive an image of an atrocity that television producers were content to flash before their audiences and then replace with the next news item.

But Hamilton's work is more than just a commemoration of Kahler's fate. In composing the print, Hamilton was careful to position the neat rectangle, which signals the edges of the

19. Ibid., 224.
20. Ibid., 227.
21. Hamilton, *Collected Words,* 94.
22. Ibid.
23. Ibid., 104.

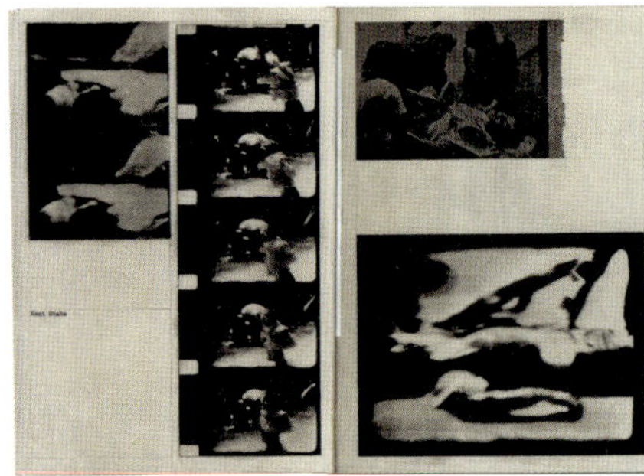

fig. 3
Pamphlet for Studio Marconi, Milan, 1971, showing images from various sources of the Kent State shootings

television set, off-centre on the white sheet of paper. Within this black rectangle nests the curved rectangle of the TV screen. This means Kahler's image is framed three times (and four times if we count the actual metal frame encasing the paper when the print is displayed), and this framing serves to emphasise that this is not just a print of an image captured on TV, but a work about the mediation of this image by television. This mediation (rather than Vietnam or Cambodia) is also the subject of a double-page spread of images in the small pamphlet published by Marconi to accompany the stage proofs: the spread included the source photograph for his print, a photograph torn out of a newspaper and a strip of images printed from a film reel [fig. 3]. These were all images of the Kent State shootings, but each was in a different medium so that the spread foregrounded the array of media as much as the content of the images.

Mediation was also the focus of a text Hamilton composed for the Ottawa and Marconi catalogues. Without making any reference to the Vietnam War, the escalation of military activity in Cambodia, the student protests or the injuries suffered by Kahler, Hamilton's text described the transfer of information from the Ohio campus to the headquarters of an American news agency to the BBC in London to his living room, and then from there to the place where the print was made. As the image of the student travelled this journey in space, so its form transformed at each stage: from an image poorly captured on cine-camera film to electric signals to magnetic tape to a picture on a television screen, and then from the photograph of that screen to the different screens used to make the eventual print.[24] Hamilton's text is startlingly cold—he later called it "remorseless" and "menacing."[25] What it captures is the indifference of media to its content, and the underlying meaning seems to be that although Hamilton's project was to recreate the image of a shot-down student, television media works in a very different way, usually to desensitise us to its content. That is why it has become so easy to consume images of faraway wars and, unlike Kahler, to do nothing.

When we think about the row or grid of prints, and ask what it meant for Hamilton to present the work in this way, we see, once again, that he was torn between the desire to commemorate his subject and the need to reflect on the problems of television reporting, transmission and consumption. Presenting the stage proofs for *Kent State* was another way for Hamilton to draw his viewer's thoughts to the analogous prior stages of the image's mediation, but it was also a means by which Hamilton could focus his viewers even more intensely on this image as they followed the row or grid and watched its gradual appearance. Slowing down their gaze, making them look at a single image again and again, Hamilton found another way to resist the logic of television and its insistence on the speedily changing image. Yet as the colours built up, the presentation also brought a kind of promise of development and in this respect its structure differs from Warhol's grids of silkscreened images, where there is often a degree of deterioration over the grid. The promise was that eventually the image would cohere and that the student's features would finally sharpen. Yet this promise is not fulfilled: reaching the final print we realise the image is still blotchy and indistinct. Colours appear like smudges not properly attached to the body, we can't

24. "A cine-camera films an event on a university campus in Ohio, USA… The film is processed and put into the hands of an American TV network… which transforms the images into electric signals later beamed at an antenna on a satellite orbiting the earth… Later the message is re-transmitted as part of a BBC news broadcast to be detected by a TV receiver." See Richard Hamilton, "Kent State," in *Richard Hamilton: Prints* (Ottawa: National Gallery of Canada, 1970), 14–15.
25. Hamilton, *Collected Words,* 94.
26. Richard Hamilton as quoted in "Colour Television: Seven Singular Choices," *Radio Times,* 12 November 1970.
27. Hamilton, *Richard Hamilton: Prints,* 14–15.
28. Rita Donagh and Richard Hamilton, *A Cellular Maze* (Derry: Orchard Gallery, 1983), n. p.

quite make out what is happening above the torso and the pixelated grid of the television screen is still dominant. Hamilton remarked that when he first saw the image on television, there had been "different kinds of distortion in the image."[26] Rather than resolving this, in the last print he confronted the distortion and loss of information involved in television transmission, and more painfully, acknowledged that making a print of a televisual image can only exacerbate this loss.

With this in mind, it is worth turning to the last lines of Hamilton's text where he switches from cold technical description to an enigmatic epigram. "Fifteen layers of pigment," he wrote, "a tragic chorus monotonously chanting an oft repeated story. In one eye and out the other."[27] If each layer of the print—or indeed each stage print—is imagined as a part of a chorus, their chant is tragic not only because it concerns the story of a wounded student. It is tragic because the print can only point to the way television works: to put images before viewers' eyes momentarily and imperfectly so they grow adept at forgetting them.

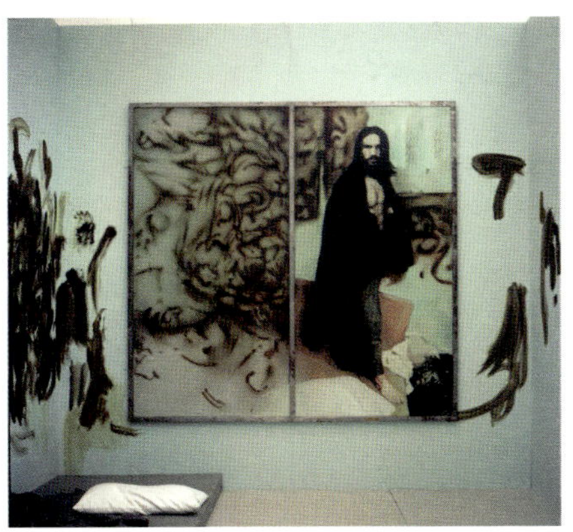

fig. 4
The citizen installed in *A Cellular Maze,* Orchard Gallery, Derry, 1983

The citizen

Some ten years after he worked on the *Kent State* prints, Hamilton had another powerful encounter with a television image: "By chance in 1980," he wrote, "I was struck by a scene in a TV documentary about republican prisoners in the H-blocks… What we had heard of the blanket protest, mainly through the propaganda agencies of Sinn Fein, could not prepare us for the startling photographic documentation on TV."[28] Following this second, unplanned-for delivery into his interior, this time of an upsetting image of a figure refusing to be represented by the government of his country, Hamilton went on to paint *The citizen* [p. 256]. It was completed in 1983, and shown that year first at the Guggenheim in New York and next at the Orchard Gallery in Derry, alongside Rita Donagh's series of paintings and drawings of "the Maze Prison, formerly Long Kesh."[29] Hamilton presented the painting in a mocked-cell, daubing the walls around it with smears of brown paint [fig. 4]. They named the exhibition *A Cellular Maze,* accompanying it with a publication typeset like a seventeenth-century political pamphlet for which each wrote a text [fig. 5]. Donagh had been examining civil war tracts, and she admired the pamphlets published in Derry addressing the Troubles and questions of colonialism and language by writers associated with the Field Day Theatre Company including Seamus Heaney, Tom Paulin and Seamus Deane.[30] Hamilton's painting is usually discussed alongside two subsequent works, *The subject* (completed in 1990 and first shown at the Carnegie International, Pittsburgh, in 1991) [p. 257] and *The state* (completed in 1992 and premiered in Hamilton's British Pavilion at the Venice Biennial in 1993) [p. 258].[31] In respect for the fact that it existed outside this triptych structure for the first years of its existence, here I will consider *The citizen* on its own.

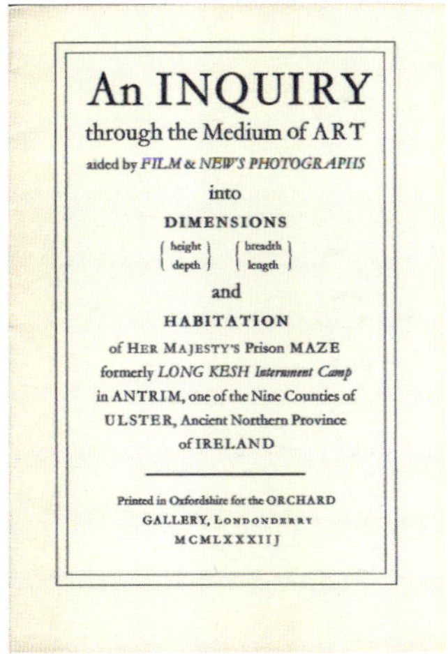

An INQUIRY
through the Medium of ART
aided by *FILM & NEW'S PHOTOGRAPHS*
into
DIMENSIONS
(height / depth) (breadth / length)
and
HABITATION
of HER MAJESTY'S Prison MAZE
formerly *LONG KESH Internment Camp*
in ANTRIM, one of the Nine Counties of
ULSTER, Ancient Northern Province
of IRELAND

Printed in Oxfordshire for the ORCHARD
GALLERY, LONDONDERRY
MCMLXXXIIJ

fig. 5
Frontispiece for the pamphlet for *A Cellular Maze*

29. Hamilton used the title *The citizen* to refer to the prisoners' desire to be citizens of a united Ireland rather than subjects of the British Queen, but as Richard Morphet wrote in the 1992 Tate catalogue, the title had other resonances. "The title is taken from the 'Cyclops' episode of *Ulysses,* in which Bloom, Joyce's hero, comes into conflict with a pugnacious Fenian bar-fly known to all as 'citizen'. The citizen is associated by Joyce with an heroic Irish chieftan, Finn MacCool, as well as with the giant Polyphemus of Homer's *Odyssey.*" See Richard Morphet (ed.), *Richard Hamilton* (London: Tate Gallery, 1992), 177. Hamilton went on to make a drawing and print titled *Finn MacCool* [fig. 6] in 1983–84 based on a photograph of Raymond Pius McCartney, another of the IRA prisoners in Long Kesh.
30. Rita Donagh in conversation with the author, February 2013.
31. *The subject* also had its origins in television but in a very different way: Hamilton was invited to take part in a BBC series where artists were given the chance to work with a computer painting programme, and decided to take the opportunity to make a pendant painting for *The citizen.* He hoped to show how both the IRA and the Orangeman were trapped and for that reason he repeated the prisoner's cell window above the Orangeman's shoulder. Curiously, he also repeated the swirls of paint that appear on the floor of the Long Kesh cell above the Orangeman's hand.

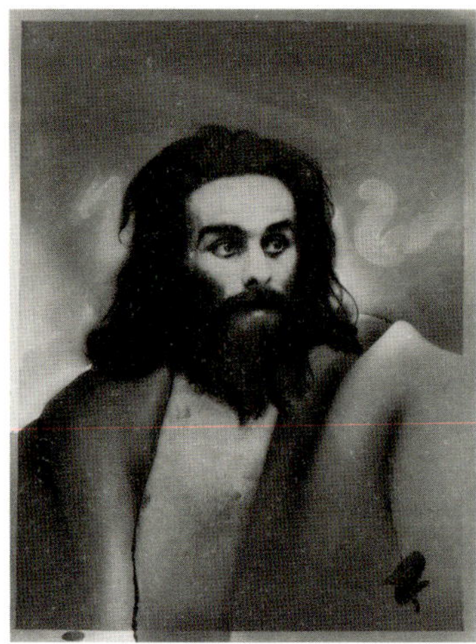

fig. 6
Finn MacCool, 1983
Photo-etching, aquatint and engraving on paper

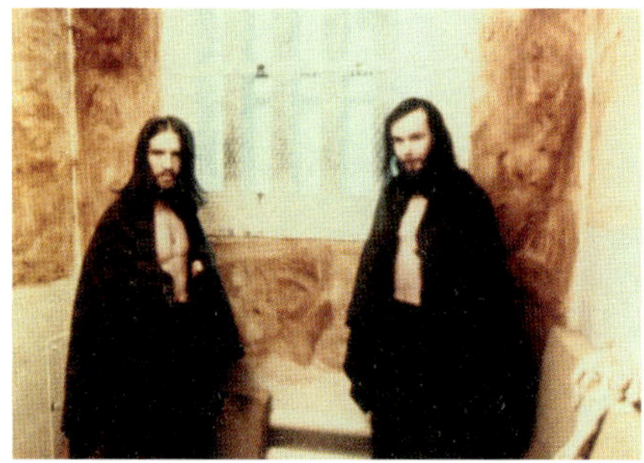

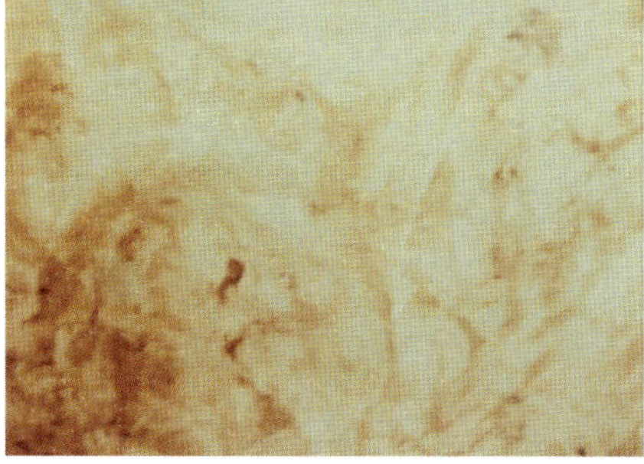

fig. 7
Stills from Robin Denselow's Newsnight report on the Maze prison, 27 October 1980

Opening his text in *A Cellular Maze,* which he designed, Hamilton stated that "a major function of art has been to reflect contemporary appearances."[32] This might seem a curious introduction to *The citizen* yet the word "appearances" foregrounds that, once again, Hamilton's concern was with what was happening in the H-blocks and especially with how these events were appearing through the media. Before coming to the painting, it is therefore worth thinking about the television shows Hamilton watched and the circumstances of their broadcasts. These programmes appeared at a time when there was extremely limited television reporting of IRA prisoners in the UK, and indeed frequent censorship of any productions possibly sympathetic to their actions. As Liz Curtis noted in her 1984 study *Ireland: The Propaganda War. The British Media and the "Battle for Hearts and Minds,"* the prisoner protests had begun in 1976 and it was not until March 1979 that journalists were allowed in. "Even then, only a small group was let in, and they were not permitted to speak to protesting prisoners."[33] For their part, the IRA could not be viewed simply as passive players in this media war, simple victims of censorship: when, finally, cameras did get into the prison, it was clear to Hamilton that by covering their cells with excrement, the prisoners had been aiming to create "newsworthy"[34] images. He later commented that "these people in prison saw this as a way of presenting themselves to a wider public and they enjoyed the opportunity of having a TV camera going into their cells to see them in this condition. That was why they were doing it—to present themselves to a public—to make the public aware of their condition. It's the creation of an icon."[35]

Hamilton's painting was based on stills taken in a report by Robin Denselow on the BBC programme Newsnight.[36] Denselow began with footage of the prison exterior, and moved inside to pictures of political graffiti scratched into corridor walls demanding "POW status." Prison workers in protective outfits are seen next, hosing excrement off cell walls. The camera then enters a cell to reveal two prisoners standing and facing forwards, surrounded by walls smeared with their excrement; because of the cramped conditions and the lack of a wide-angle lens, the cameraman cannot get a full picture of the men's bodies, nor their environment, so he swivels away from their faces towards the walls, points the lens towards a corner of the floor, then back to their faces and then down to their feet, and then up to the ceiling [fig. 7]. Finally (and in a scene prefiguring Steve McQueen's chilling corridor sequence in *Hunger* [2008]), the cameraman walks up a corridor as prisoners bang on their cell doors. Over these scenes Denselow reports that "the smell is indescribable. These are the first pictures to be taken of the protestors. They have been living in these quite unbelievable conditions for two years and seven months… These two are not among the seven who are going on hunger strike but looking at the conditions in which the protestors have chosen to live for so long, one can only conclude that if those on hunger strike decide it should be to the death, then to the death it will be."[37]

32. Donagh and Hamilton, *A Cellular Maze,* n. p.
33. Liz Curtis, *Ireland: The Propaganda War* (London: Pluto Press, 1984), 258.
34. Donagh and Hamilton, *A Cellular Maze,* n. p.
35. Hamilton speaking about *The citizen* on the TV programme *Painting with Light,* 1987.
36. Denselow's report is at the time of writing (January 2013) available on the Newsnight website. The transcription of his voiceover is from this site. Granada Television's *World in Action* was actually the first to present images of the cells, but they were not used by Hamilton.
37. http://www.bbc.co.uk/programmes/p00lx397.
38. Thatcher herself objected to BBC coverage of the IRA, saying that "newspaper and television coverage can give the convicted criminals on hunger strike the myth of martyrdom they crave, but the true martyrs are the victims of terrorism." See Curtis, *Ireland: The Propaganda War,* 205.
39. Donagh and Hamilton, *A Cellular Maze,* n. p.
40. *The citizen* was first illustrated in the catalogue *Acquisition Priorities: Aspects of Postwar Painting in Europe* (New York: Solomon R. Guggenheim Museum, 1983), and in this publication the frame appears unrusted and without the attached title.

Hamilton worked on *The citizen* between 1980 and 1983—a period during which Denselow's prophecies would be realised, with Bobby Sands dying in May 1981, and while the debate raged in the UK on whether images of funerals should be screened on TV.[38] As with *Kent State,* one of Hamilton's ambitions was to devote his artistic labour to making a painting that could serve as a powerful and lasting tribute to a figure of resistance. *The citizen* had to acknowledge how the prisoners presented themselves for television, but also had to prolong their image beyond the duration allotted by a television establishment anxious to keep such pictures off-screen. Hamilton's compositional choices followed from this need to make the painting as iconic and as affecting as possible for the eventual viewer: first he selected Hugh Rooney, the prisoner who reminded him more of paintings of Christ. ("An oft declared British view of the IRA as thugs and hooligans did not match the materialisation of Christian martyrdom so profoundly contained on film."[39]) He had to collage two stills from the TV footage to assemble Rooney's upper and lower halves in order to create a full-length picture of his body. By isolating Rooney from his compatriot, Hamilton also presented him as a lonelier figure, denied of any community. (He also silenced Rooney, who was heard to speak to fellow prisoners in the Newsnight footage.) Perhaps in recognition of the fact that he was working with TV images where Rooney's image had appeared as a grid of RGB pixels, Hamilton chose to paint the skin on his face and feet in unblended patches of colour. The prisoner's body appears somewhat mediated; however, by painting Rooney life-size, Hamilton set up a direct, one-on-one confrontation between viewer and depicted figure, and he showed Rooney's foot stretching out as if stepping into the viewer's space.

Behind and to the side of the figure of the citizen Hamilton painted the cell window, the ragged foam mattress, a filthy floor and the excrement-covered walls, but then set to work to complement this with a second panel of the same size. Showing only swirls of excrement on the cell walls, this panel was joined to the other half in a specially constructed steel frame, with a strip of metal keeping both halves apart. (This frame was later treated with acid to create rusty patches, giving the impression that the excrement was finding its way into the real space of display.[40]) The left panel has sometimes been seen as an abstract counterpart to the figurative right panel,[41] but there is far more to it than that. Indeed, I would argue that it is through the left part of the painting that Hamilton's most radical ideas are made manifest.

In thinking about this left panel, it might be helpful to remember that in the years prior to *The citizen,* Hamilton had himself been painting turds sitting on romantic beaches (*Sunset,* 1975 [p. 229]) and underneath bunches of flowers; in some of these works, watery brown paint resembles smears of excrement (*Flower-piece III,* 1973–74 [p. 227]). Prepared by this scatological turn in his own work, Hamilton, in the face of his own "vehement rejection" of "each new IRA assault" (his words from the pamphlet) seems to have identified with the IRA prisoners as fellow artists.[42] "Each cell is marked with the graphic personality of its inhabitants," he wrote, "the walls look different because the pigment, of their own creation,

41. "In continuance of Hamilton's interest in figuration/abstraction, the subject provided an opportunity to present this interdependence in stark conjunction." See Morphet (ed.), "The citizen," in *Richard Hamilton,* 177.
42. Hamilton's work is sometimes compared to Gerhard Richter's 1989 series *October 18, 1977,* which includes paintings of prisoners in cells. The fact that Hamilton identified with the IRA prisoners connects to an argument recently made by Kaja Silverman about Richter, who has written that when he saw the photographs of the RAF members, he "was able to recognise the analogies linking *him* to the terrorists and to the police." See Kaja Silverman, *Flesh of My Flesh* (Palo Alto: Stanford University Press, 2009), 14.
43. Ellmann was interested in the "comms" that the prisoners scrawled on tiny pieces of paper and passed to each other, and the way these written texts expanded as their bodies dwindled. "Letters actually take the place of food, because they occupy the thresholds of digestion—mouth, foreskin, anus—where love has pitched his mansion too, as Yeats might say." See Maud Ellmann, *The Hunger Artists: Starving, Writing & Imprisonment* (London: Virago Press, 1993), 83. The "comms" were also the subject of two works by the Derry-based artist Locky Morris, shown at the Cornerhouse in Manchester and at the Orchard Gallery in Derry in 1992 and 1994 respectively.

is deployed in varying ways." Hamilton also associated the "wall paintings of Long Kesh" with "the megalithic spirals of New Grange" and the "Gaelic convolutions of the book of Kells." Though other people later described the hunger strikers as artists (Maud Ellmann, in her 1993 book *The Hunger Artists*[43]), this was a massive projection on Hamilton's behalf and not one substantiated by the footage where the shit seems to cover the walls more evenly and randomly, or at least not in spirals. Nonetheless, this was how Hamilton chose to represent the excrement, and it is also noteworthy how carefully Hamilton painted the "wall paintings" on his left panel. He used a variety of tones, colours and brushes to depict the swirls and curves of excrement, painting delicately and quite thinly. Whereas others before him, Cy Twombly in particular, had applied "turd-like scatological magmas of brown paint" to canvas in order to debase their paintings,[44] Hamilton painted excrement like ornamental patterns to elevate and associate the prisoners' daubings with ancient Irish art forms.

The left panel, as a consequence, invites viewers to find dignity and beauty in abject bodily waste, and by extension in the prisoners' acts of resistance. But more than that, it creates a different kind of *space* to the confined space depicted on the right. Rather than showing the wall as a wall, reaching to the ceiling or with its lower limit meeting the floor, Hamilton got rid of any spatial indicators in the left panel. Whereas viewers, given the life-size scale of the figure, are easily able to orient themselves in relation to the scale of the depicted scene on the right, they are unable to when looking to the left. Because of this the left side becomes a free space, the very opposite to the confined space of the prison. It is a space for imagination, a space for a citizen, not a subject. All of which is to say that Hamilton turned the shit-covered walls of a prison not only into Irish art, but into a space of liberation.

Treatment room

One year after completing *The citizen,* Hamilton accepted an invitation to take part in Michael Regan's Arts Council exhibition titled *Four Rooms.* It had been turned down by several venues when Liberty's of London offered to stage it, much to Hamilton's approval, and he set about making a work that marks another kind of reflection on television, *Treatment room* [pp. 260–61]. This was his first installation for almost thirty years, and in a text composed for the small catalogue accompanying *Four Rooms,* Hamilton contrasted *Treatment room* with his early exhibition installations and representations of the postwar interior. Looking back to *This is Tomorrow* (Whitechapel Art Gallery, London, 1956) and the collage *Just what is it…,* Hamilton recalled that "the course we seemed to be taking was towards a rosy future, and our changing world was embraced with a confident, starry eyed, Utopianism." Now, however, having worked on a very different interior in 1983—*The citizen's* prison cell—"a complete polarity becomes evident between the brash expectations of the fifties and the present consciousness of depression." It was this consciousness that led him to create an interior "inspired by the bleak, disinterested, seedily clinical style of the establishment institution."[45] And, whereas a jukebox had played rock in the *Fun house* (1956) and a television set had seemed a joyous presence in the interior of *Just what is it…*, now a television would signal a very different reality.

44. This is Yve-Alain Bois describing Twombly's *Untitled* (1961). See Yve-Alain Bois, "Der liebe Gott steckt im Detail: Reading Twombly," in *Abstraction, Gesture, Ecriture: Paintings from the Daros Collection* (Zurich: Scalo, 1999), 78. See also the section about the 1961 paintings in Richard Leeman, "Blood and Shit," in Cy *Twombly* (London: Thames and Hudson, 2005), 129.
45. Richard Hamilton, "Rooms," in *Four Rooms* (London: Arts Council of Great Britain, 1984).

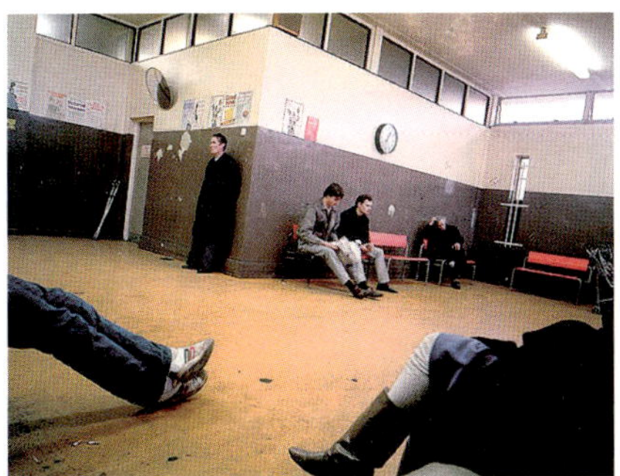

fig. 8
Paul Graham,
Waiting Room, Poplar DHSS, East London, 1985
Chromogenic colour print
The Museum of Modern Art, New York

Treatment room comprised an interior constructed to recall an NHS waiting room or a DHSS Labour Exchange, its walls painted with a dark green band below and a pale green-cream above (Paul Graham's now famous photographs of job centres, *Beyond Caring,* also made in 1984, show these exact same colours) [fig. 8]. Within the room there is a sink, a bucket and a slab-bed with a rough blanket slumped across it. To the side of the bed is an angled partition wall: the imagined operator would stand behind this, viewing the imagined patient through a reinforced glass window. The operator has a control panel that Hamilton took from a Bosch oven, a move that suggests to me another contrast with his earlier works: whereas Hamilton had celebrated the Braun toasters and portable grills in the 1960s, now German electrical products were being used as if to cook a patient. Suspended over the bed was a television monitor, and on that monitor, continuously and in silence, footage played of Margaret Thatcher, taken from the final party political broadcast of the 1983 election campaign.

In his text for *Four Rooms* Hamilton gave two different suggestions about the role of the television in the installation. He wrote that in the kind of room on which *Treatment room* is based, "surveillance is prevalent; one way mirrors and closed circuit video security systems are the ubiquitous overseers of public spaces."[46] One purpose of the TV is thus to draw the viewer's thoughts to this new use of monitors in a society of surveillance. A second role of the TV is that it makes us think that the imagined patients have to watch Thatcher while they wait for their medical treatment. Hamilton concluded his text by asking: "Is the vision of Mrs Thatcher patronising a victim of the Health Service part of the future we once thought so bright?" Thinking about these two roles, Hal Foster has written that "*Treatment room* thus combines two regimes of surveillance and spectacle and, in doing so, suggests that they are not as exclusive as Foucault and Debord might have thought."[47] Without contesting this conclusion, I would argue that there is a third suggestion at play in the installation, namely that Thatcher's image is itself the treatment being administered to the patient (not unlike the images which are screened to Alex in *A Clockwork Orange* [1971]).[48] Understanding the installation this way, it becomes imperative to ask why Hamilton chose this particular footage of the then Prime Minister, and indeed why the monitor is silent.

Thatcher's final party political broadcast before the 1983 election was screened on 7 June, when it was evident that the Conservative Party was sweeping towards re-election "to the strains of Elgar," as *The Guardian* put it.[49] Because victory was assured and only the ballots of a few floating voters were at stake, Thatcher did not need to remind viewers of her "successes" in the Falklands and elsewhere. Instead, her campaign consultant, Gordon Reece, sought to create "a soft, image-setting reminder of her leadership … You have to create an impression and a mood," he told the *New York Times.*[50] In the TV broadcast he directed, Thatcher is set in an interior which is the very antithesis of the futuristic ones Hamilton had celebrated in the 1950s and 1960s: she appears in a wooden armchair, flanked by eighteenth-century antique desks, a lamp and two vases of chrysanthemums, with a gilt-framed darkened painting, a bookshelf and a plush velvet curtain behind her: it was this "establishment" interior that was being projected into the clinical institutional

46. Ibid.
47. Hal Foster, "Citizen Hamilton," in *Richard Hamilton: Protest Pictures* (Edinburgh: Inverleith House, 2008), 11.
48. This comparison has also been made by Hans Ulrich Obrist and Julia Peyton-Jones in their foreword to the catalogue *Richard Hamilton: Modern Moral Matters* (London: Serpentine Gallery, 2010), 7.
49. "A Last Look at the Election", *The Guardian,* 8 June 1983, 14.
50. Gordon Reece as quoted in R. W. Apple Jr., "Tory Campaign: Shrewd and Brutal," *The New York Times,* 8 June 1983.

interior of the *Treatment room.* As she speaks, Thatcher is immobile, her hands clasped on her lap. The camera holds still, zooms in slightly, then holds again, and her voice is just as stable: Reece had worked specifically to eliminate her higher and sharper notes and had perfected her mellifluous tone by 1983. The Conservative slogan was "Britain's on the right track. Don't turn back," and it was this message of stability that was powerfully created by every element of the broadcast.

Hamilton, with his canny understanding of changes in media conventions, his appreciation of what Stuart Hall had called the "encoding" of TV, must have recognised that the significance of the 1983 election broadcast was precisely *not* to do with the words Thatcher uttered. Instead this was the first general election when "impression and mood" counted more than policy, and when British politicians (years after their American counterparts) were turning to design consultants to mould their TV image. This was a frightening turn, but it is precisely because of this that Hamilton would have chosen to use this particular footage of Thatcher in the installation. It might seem that he muted Thatcher to dis-empower her; I would argue the very opposite—by silencing the monitor he invited viewers to share his understanding that this broadcast was operating on the level of image and mood and that it did not matter whether her words could actually be heard. The treatment in *Treatment room* is subjection to this new form of image politics, and the final horror of the piece is that this footage intrudes in a space recalling the public institutions that Thatcher did so much to dismantle.

War games

Hamilton had seen Deal Kahler, Hugh Rooney and Margaret Thatcher while watching TV and though he might have been shocked and angered by their appearances, he had been fascinated nonetheless that television had managed to bring these people into his home. *War games* [p. 262], his last television-themed work, is the only one to depict the context of his domestic interior, yet in this piece, people are absent. It is characteristic of Hamilton's intelligence that he realised that this absence of people was one of the defining characteristics of the media coverage of the 1992 Gulf War.

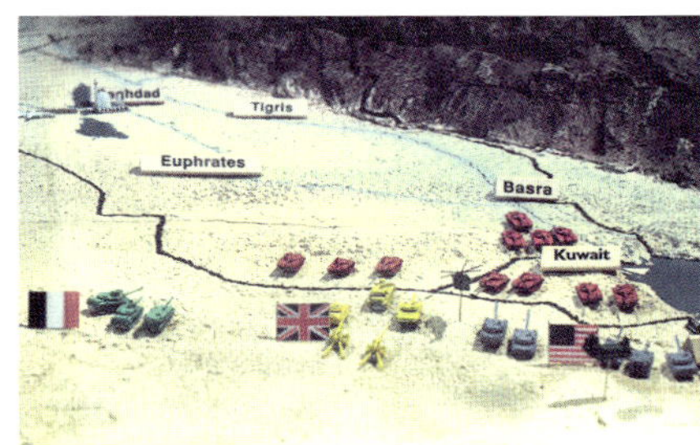

fig. 9
Photograph of the "sandpit" used on Newsnight by Hamilton, 1992

The work shows a large TV monitor on a cabinet above a video player, a row of cassettes and a folded newspaper whose headline reads "The Mother of Battles." The TV screen presents an image based on the Newsnight reporting of the war: a model of the Gulf that the presenter Peter Snow christened the "sandpit" [fig. 9]. It shows the sea, the desert and a ridge of mountains, a landscape populated by warships, ranks of different coloured tanks and a few flags. To make the work Hamilton photographed his living room and printed the image on canvas using a Scanachrome machine. The image was rendered as a series of horizontal lines on the canvas, resembling scan lines on a TV monitor. To create a kind of paradox that draws attention to the mediated nature of the entire image (the screen, the newspaper and, indeed, the whole photographed and printed interior), Hamilton next hand-painted the area of the television screen—the only part of the actual scene where such scan lines would have been visible. Finally, below the TV he added a line of dripping blood.

The work might seem more direct in its address than the others I have discussed, but Hamilton was equally astute in recognising that what was at stake in 1992 was not just another war, but a new moment in media history. Hamilton accused television itself of having a guilty role in the war. Jean Baudrillard, writing the same year Hamilton made the painting, agreed that "the media promote the war, the war promotes the media, and advertising competes with the war … In this forum of war which is the Gulf, everything is hidden: only TV functions as a medium without a message, giving at last the image of pure television."[51] Richard Morphet, introducing *War games* when it was first shown in Hamilton's 1992 Tate retrospective, referred to the technophilia that characterised much TV reporting: "The television screen often showed the participating generals delivering their press conferences with the aid of monitors, so that video replays were replayed on countless television tubes throughout the world: the television set itself was the image on our screens."[52] At the other end of the spectrum to these spectacular presentations of missile hits was a kind of reporting that infantilised the subject. Hamilton must have been appalled by Newsnight's decision to represent the war with a sandpit and toy tanks, and to underline his distaste he played his own games, mimicking this infantilising by painting the television in a particularly naïve way. Each tank and battleship is painted as a ten-year-old boy might paint a model airplane.[53]

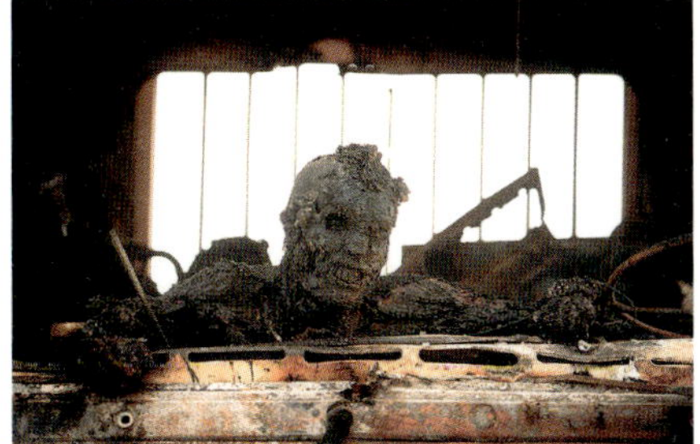

fig. 10
Iraqi Soldier, Nasiriyah, March 1991
© Kenneth Jarecke/Contact Press Images

But it was not only the method of reporting that Hamilton targeted in *War games:* he also recognised that the press conferences and sandpits failed—or chose not—to show the violent deaths of Iraqi soldiers. The blood "oozing out from under the screen"[54] was a reminder of the people kept off-screen, and it is interesting that Hamilton appropriated the devices of macabre and of horror films for this purpose, for others at the time were also realising that this turn to the macabre was the necessary means to represent deaths that the media repressed: Jeff Wall's work *Dead Troops Talk* (albeit concerned with the Soviet invasion of Afghanistan) also dates from 1992, and in their attempts to think about the Gulf War in the UK, other cultural figures in Britain also used horror-film tactics. In "A Cold Coming," commissioned by and published in *The Guardian* in 1991, the poet Tony Harrison took the most famous press photograph of the "road to Basra," an image showing the corpse of a driver hunched over his car windscreen [fig. 10], and imagined the "charred Iraqi" speaking to him like the waking dead, bitterly complaining that unlike his American counterparts, he had not been able to store his sperm before he went off to war.

> "Don't look away! I know it's hard
> to keep regarding one so charred,
> so disfigured by unfriendly fire
> and think it once burned with desire."[55]

51. Jean Baudrillard, *The Gulf War Did Not Take Place* (Bloomington: Indiana University Press; Sydney: Power Publications, 1995), 31–63.
52. Morphet (ed.), *Richard Hamilton,* 185.
53. Baudrillard, for his part, was similarly disgusted by Peter Snow's French counterparts: "By the force of the media," he wrote, "this war liberates an exponential mass of stupidity, not the particular stupidity of war, which is considerable, but the professional and functional stupidity of those who pontificate in perpetual commentary on the event: all the Bouvards and Pécuchets for hire, the would-be raiders of the lost image, the CNN types and all the master singers of strategy and information who make us experience the emptiness of television as never before." See Steve Redhead (ed.), *The Jean Baudrillard Reader* (Edinburgh: Edinburgh University Press; New York: Columbia University Press, 2008), 116.
54. David Mellor quoting Hamilton in "The Pleasures and Sorrows of Modernity: Vision, Space and the Social Body in Richard Hamilton," in *Richard Hamilton,* 38.
55. Tony Harrison, "A Cold Coming," in *The Gaze of the Gorgon* (Newcastle: Bloodaxe Books, 1992), 51.

After television

Richard Hamilton's career—from the 1940s to 2011—spanned the life of television. He died just as television did, or at least television as he represented it. TV is no longer the privileged medium bringing news into the domestic interior, since we now consume moving-image news on iPads, smartphones and laptops, and we do this whenever and wherever we please. Other artists today are working on these new forms of news-delivery, no one more pertinently than Thomas Hirschhorn, whose recent videos show these devices with fingers swiping through images taken in the aftermath of suicide bombings and other explosions—exactly the images news agencies censor. In Hamilton's era, many artists working alongside him made television their explicit subject. This was a career-long pursuit for Hamilton's friend Nam June Paik; others worked only occasionally on TV, including Richard Serra, whose title for his sharp analysis of the workings of American commercial television, *Television Delivers People* (1973), I have borrowed here.[56] Other than in *Treatment room,* Hamilton did not work with monitors, but it is evident that perhaps because he worked outside of television and "video art," he was able to think about television and its ways of presenting (or repressing) information and of controlling subjects with particular acuity.

Hamilton made several other works in the last twenty years of his life dealing with urgent political subjects, such as his portrait of Tony Blair (*Shock and Awe,* 2007–8 [p. 263]), a painting of Mordechai Vanunu (*Unorthodox rendition,* 2009–10 [p. 265]) and a pair of maps presenting the situation in Israel/Palestine (*Maps of Palestine,* 2009–10 [p. 264]). Though the Blair portrait, composed on a computer, to a certain extent evokes the online distribution of news images, Hamilton never seems to have been as interested in the circumstances of an event's mediation as he was in the four works discussed here. However, for all his attention to mediation, for all the acuteness with which he identified changes in TV conventions, it should be clear that his primary motivation was always to make lasting art works to stand alongside others from the history of art. While he was fascinated to discover in 1990 (on TV, of course) that an image of *The citizen* eventually made its way onto the walls of Long Kesh where IRA prisoners appropriated it to commemorate the 1970s protests,[57] he also imagined the painting elsewhere. *The Saensbury Wing* (1999–2000 [p. 296]) is a small picture, an exquisite rendering of Venturi and Scott Brown's Sainsbury Wing of the National Gallery, London, in the manner of the Dutch master Pieter Saenredam (hence the punning title). In it we see the long view towards where Cima da Conegliano's altarpiece *The Incredulity of Saint Thomas* (c. 1502–4) has been displayed, but its place has been taken by *The citizen.* What would it mean, Hamilton asks, for the prisoner's image to have migrated from Long Kesh to his TV at home to a canvas and then for the painting to stand in this new interior, the National Gallery? For a once-ephemeral image to find a lasting home where, as Hamilton wrote of the Gallery's Van Eyck's *Arnolfini Portrait* (1434), it might "move its audience with profound simplicity"[58] yet without its urgency ever diminishing.

56. In *Television Delivers People,* a text scrolls down the screen to the accompaniment of a Muzak soundtrack. The text concerns the function of television in the American commercial context, Serra's argument being that television delivers people to advertisers.
57. In 1990, Hamilton watched a TV programme that included an interview with Raymond Pius McCartney, on whom he had based *Finn MacCool.* McCartney was interviewed in prison, and Hamilton noticed that on his cell walls he had pasted an image of his painting. "It seems that things had come full circle when a painting of an image derived from a TV presentation of the dirty protests period of the 'H' blocks becomes an icon in the very same cells when the cameras return years later to show the calm that resulted from acceptance of the hunger strikers' demands." Hamilton in correspondence with Stephen Snoddy, 13 December 1991, quoted in Stephen Snoddy, "'Yes'... & No ...," in Morphet (ed.), *Richard Hamilton,* 56.
58. Hamilton, *Collected Words,* 264.

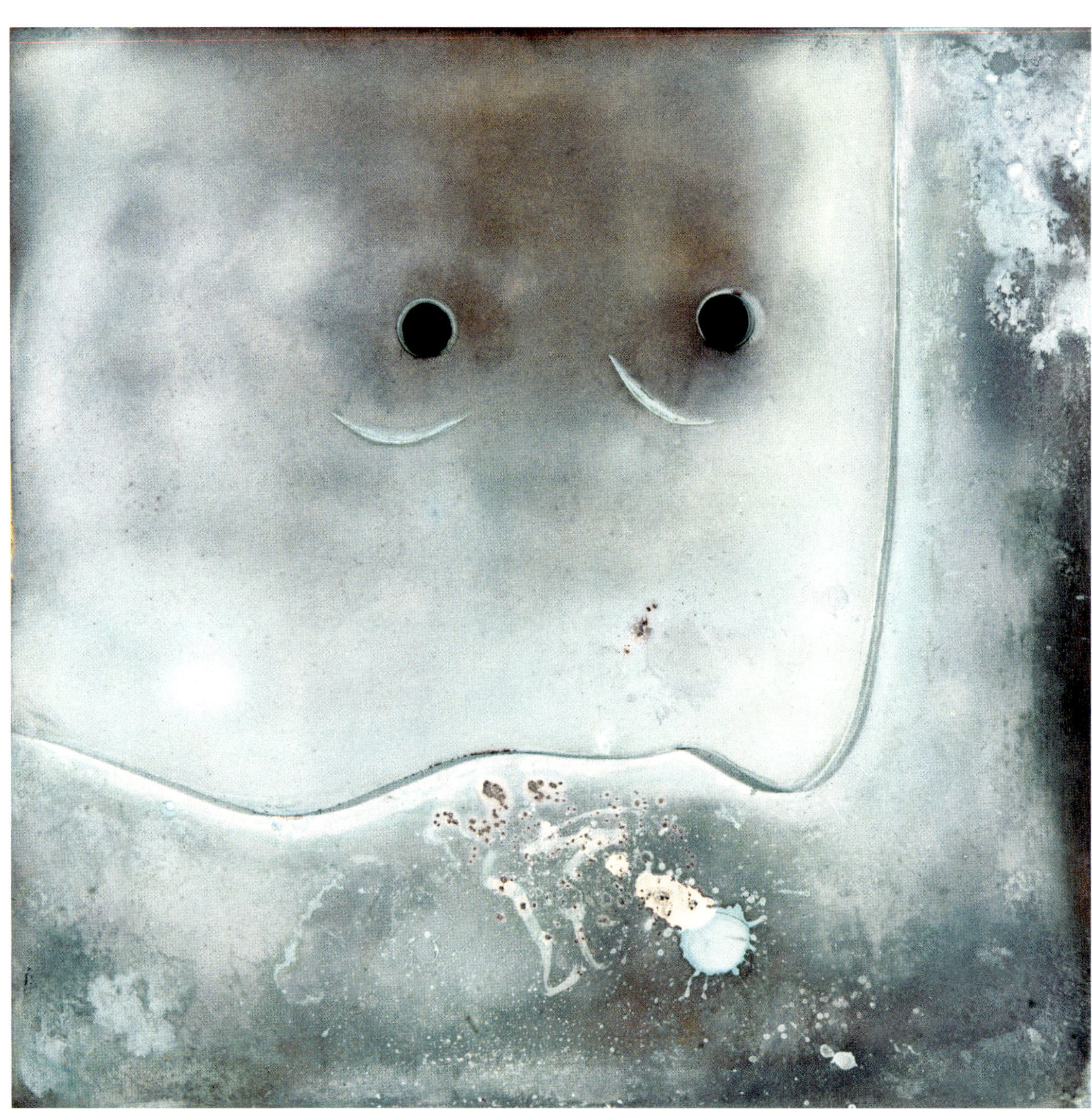

Study for "Portrait of Hugh Gaitskell as a Famous Monster of Filmland" 1963–70

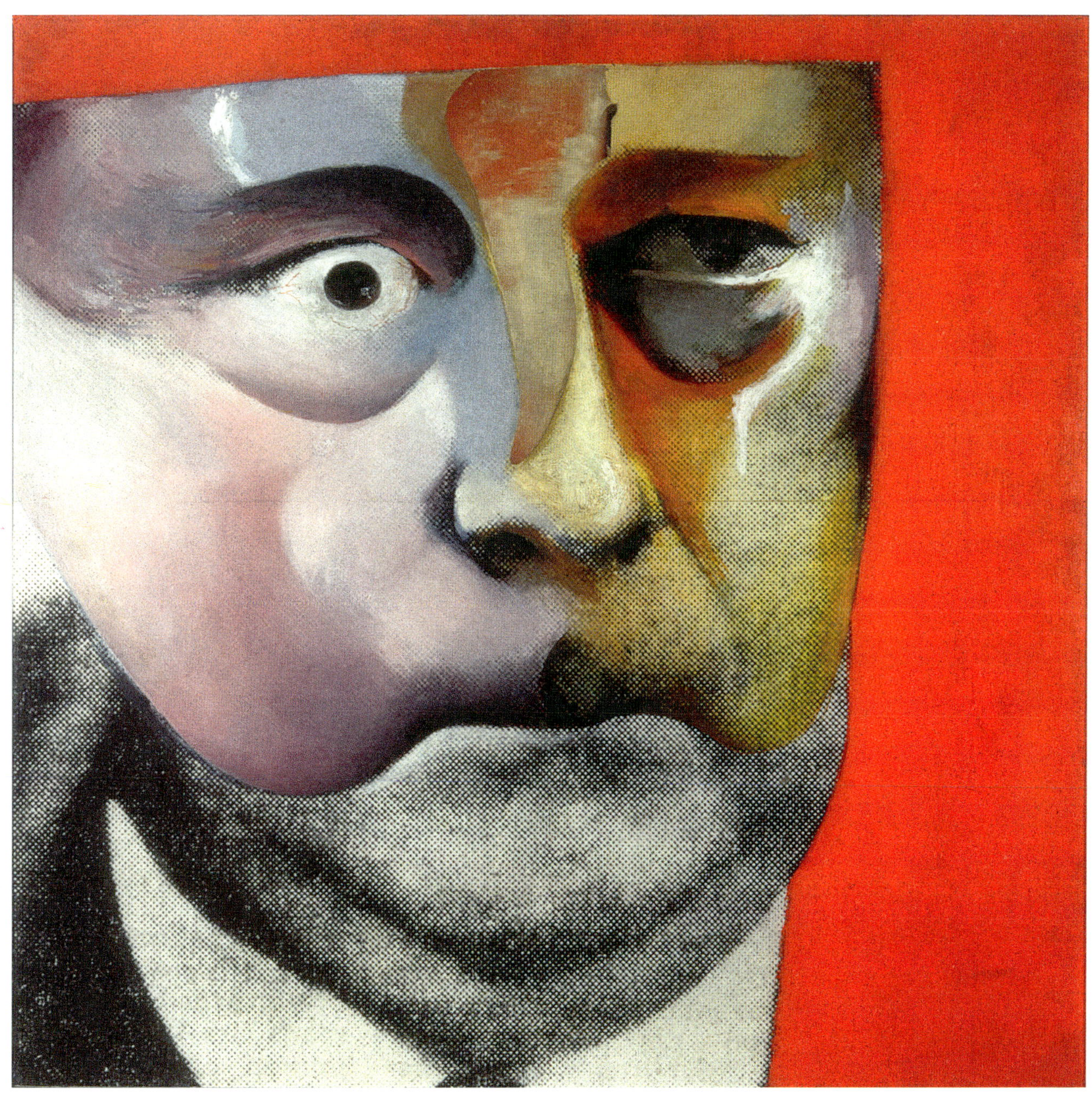

Portrait of Hugh Gaitskell as a Famous Monster of Filmland 1964

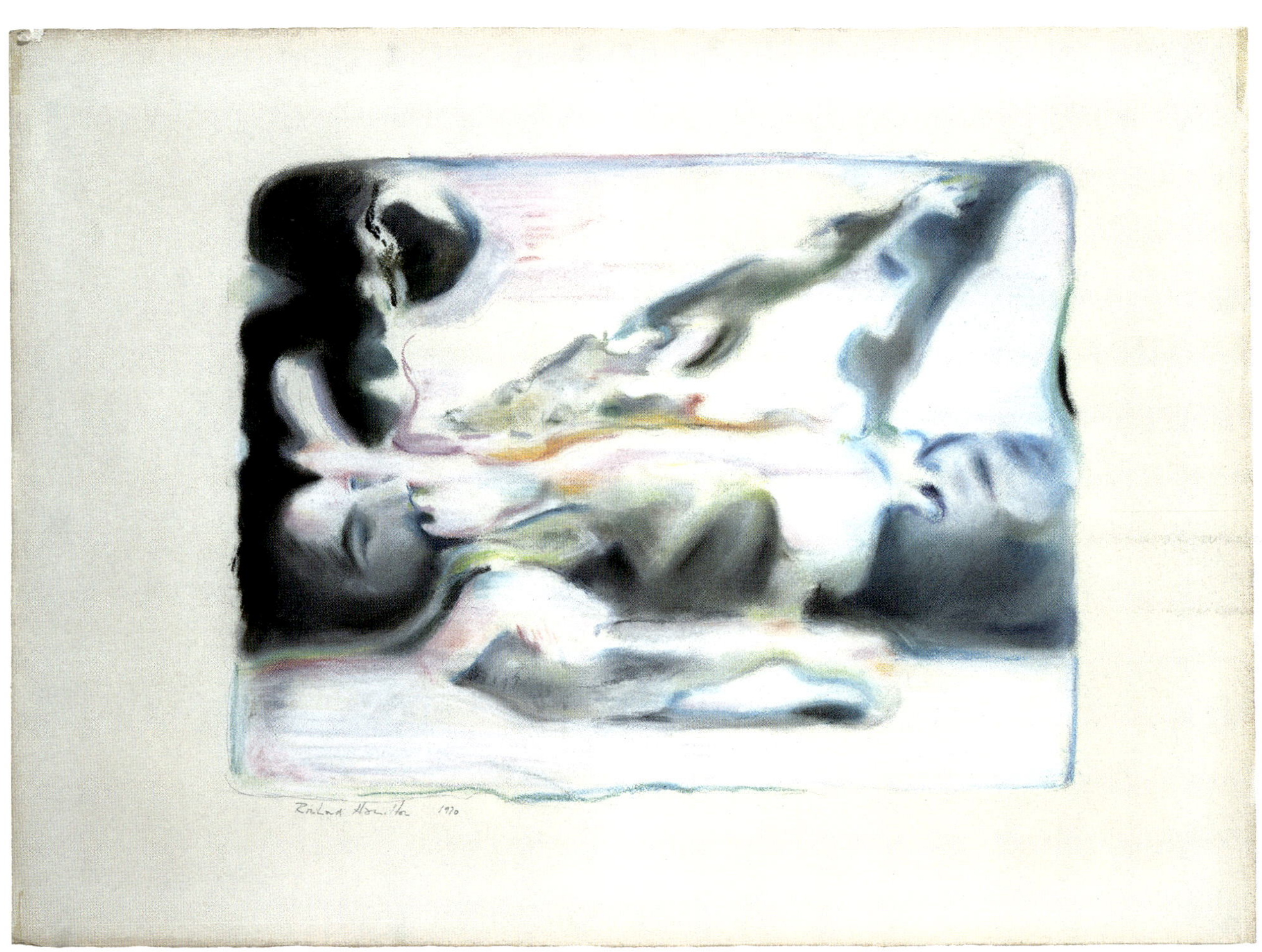

Kent State 1970

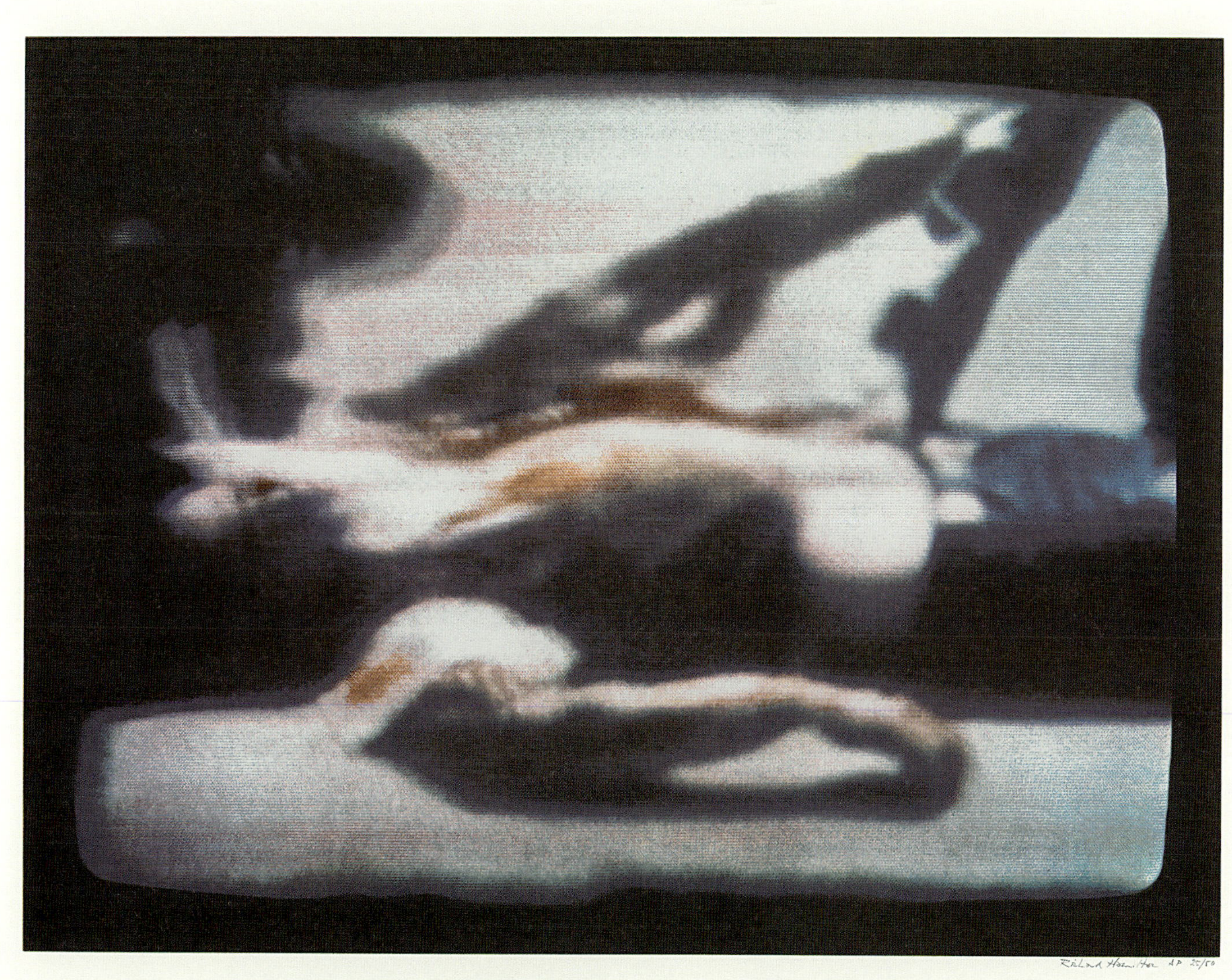

Kent State – screen print 1970

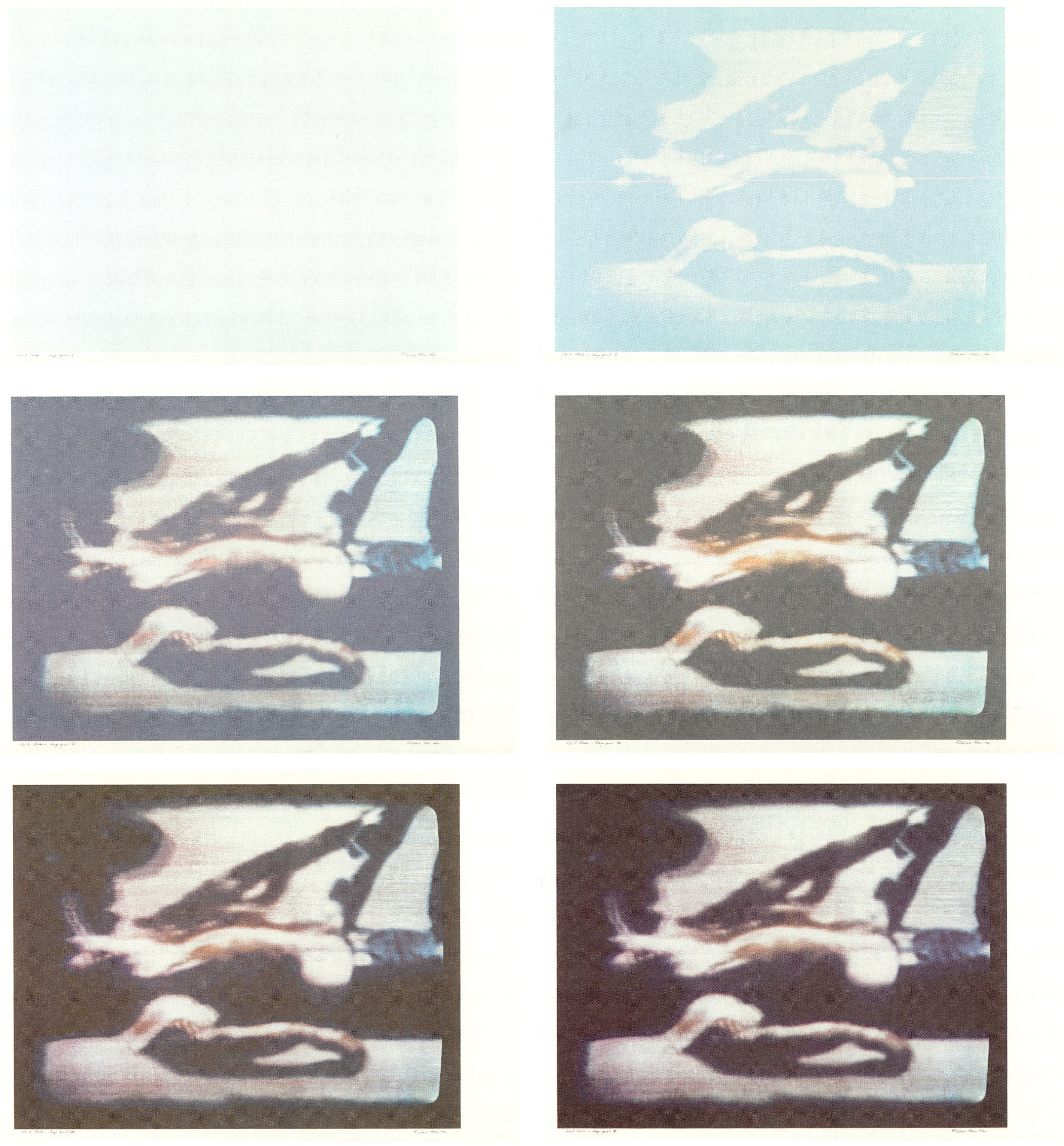

Kent State – stage proofs 1970

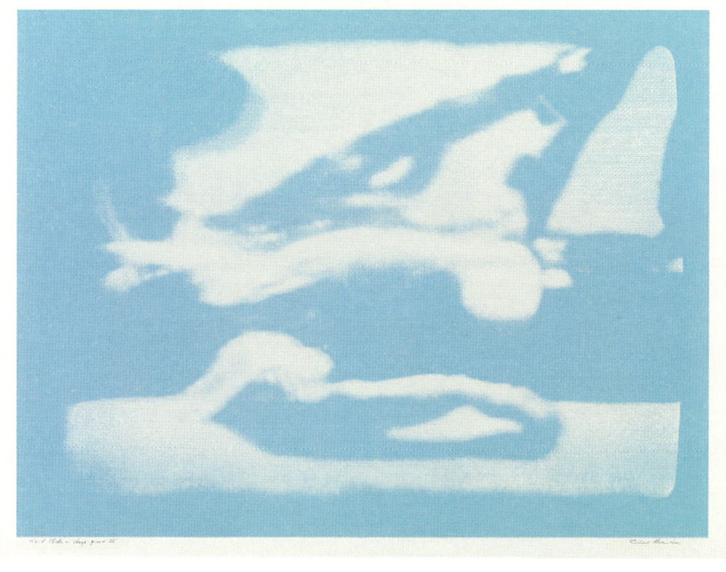

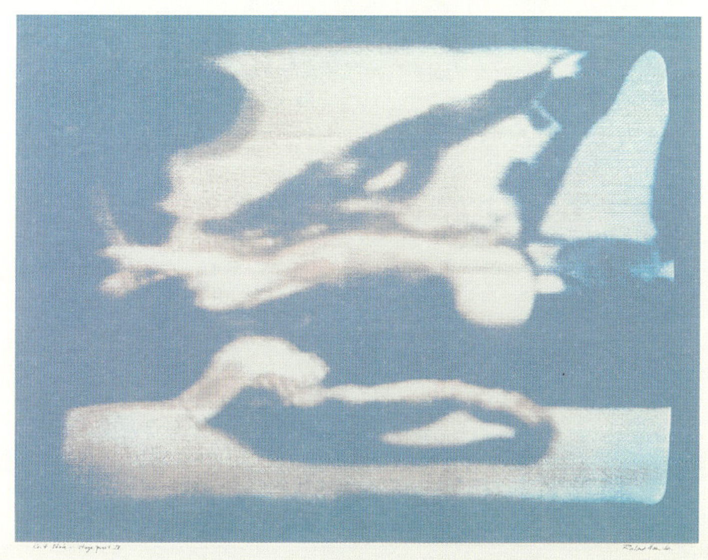

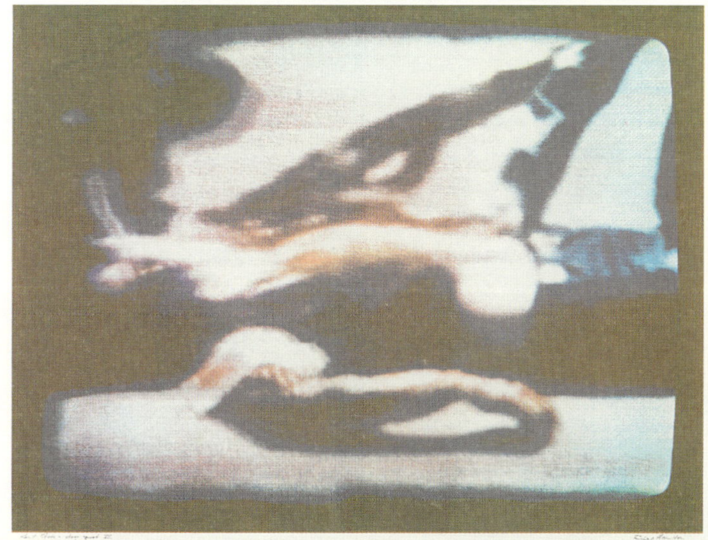

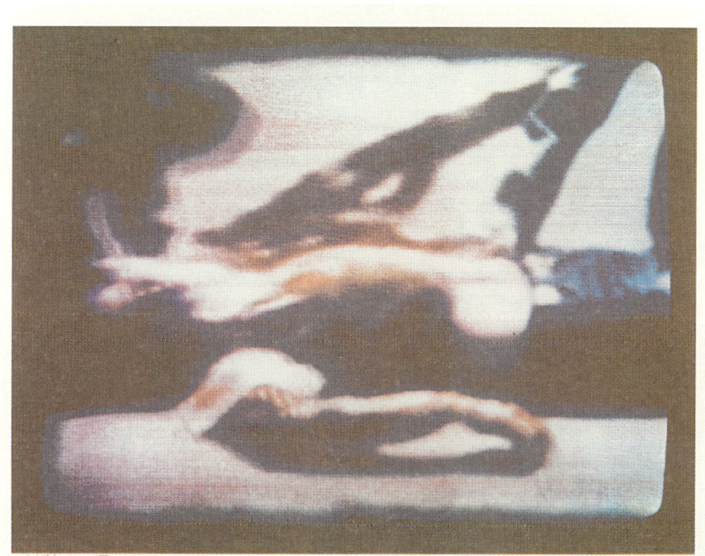

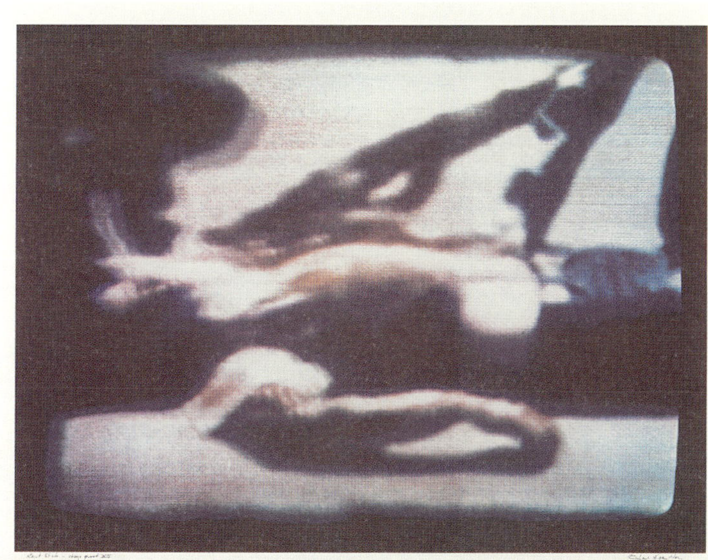

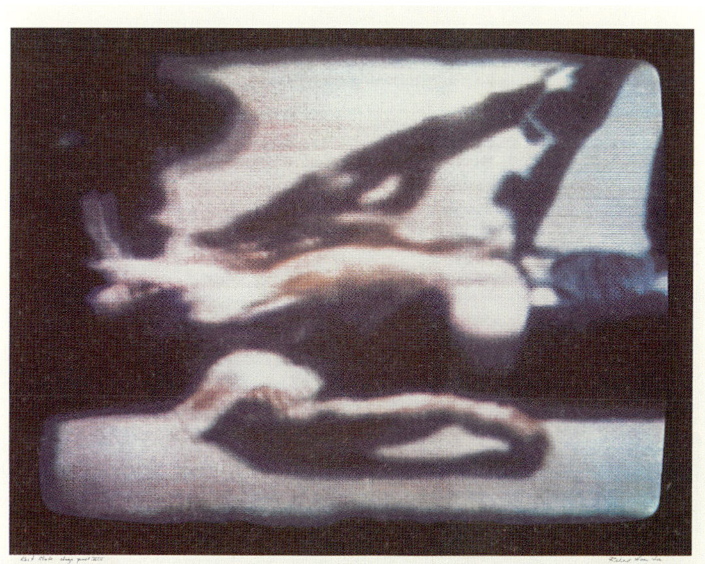

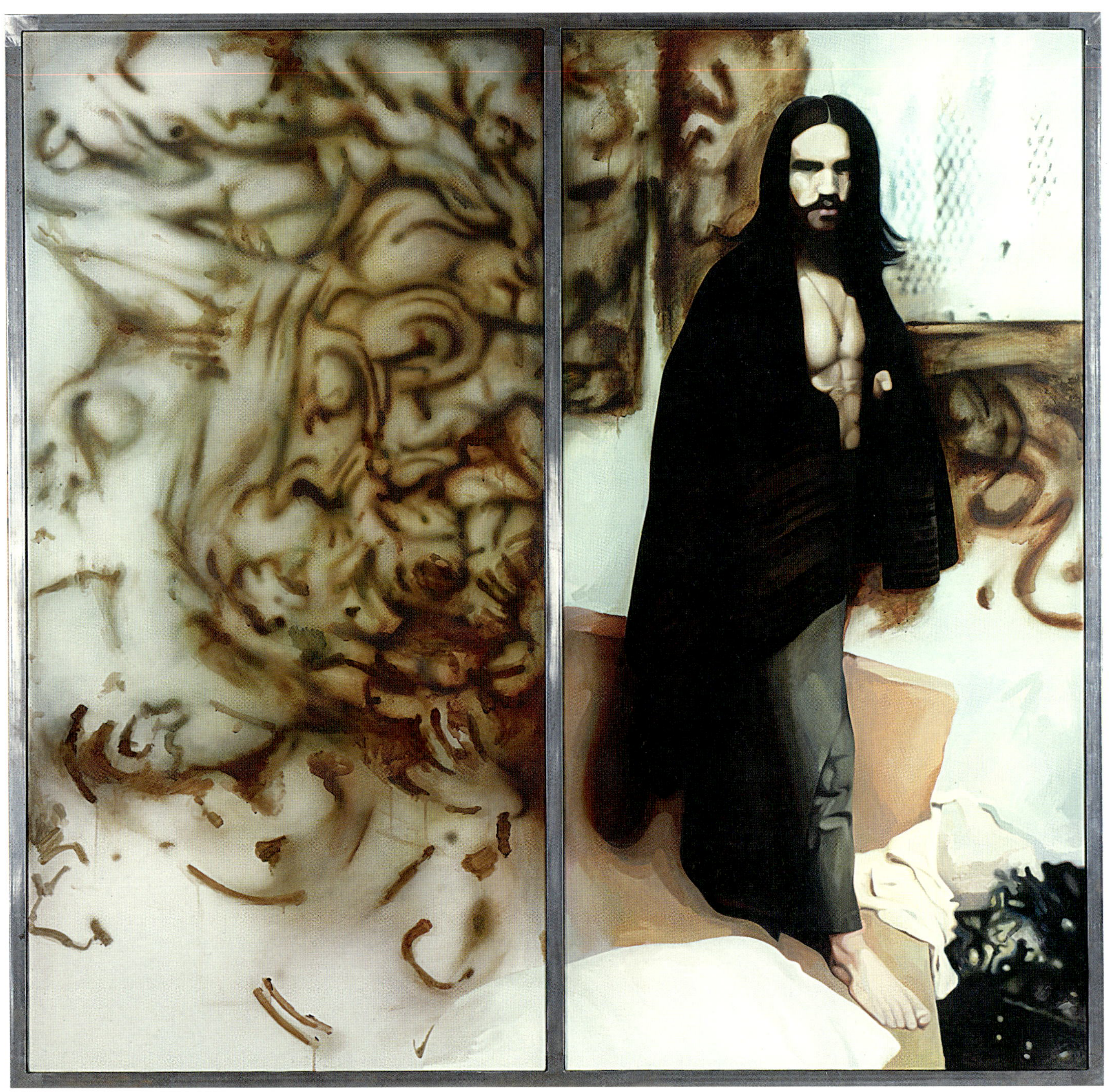

The citizen 1982–83

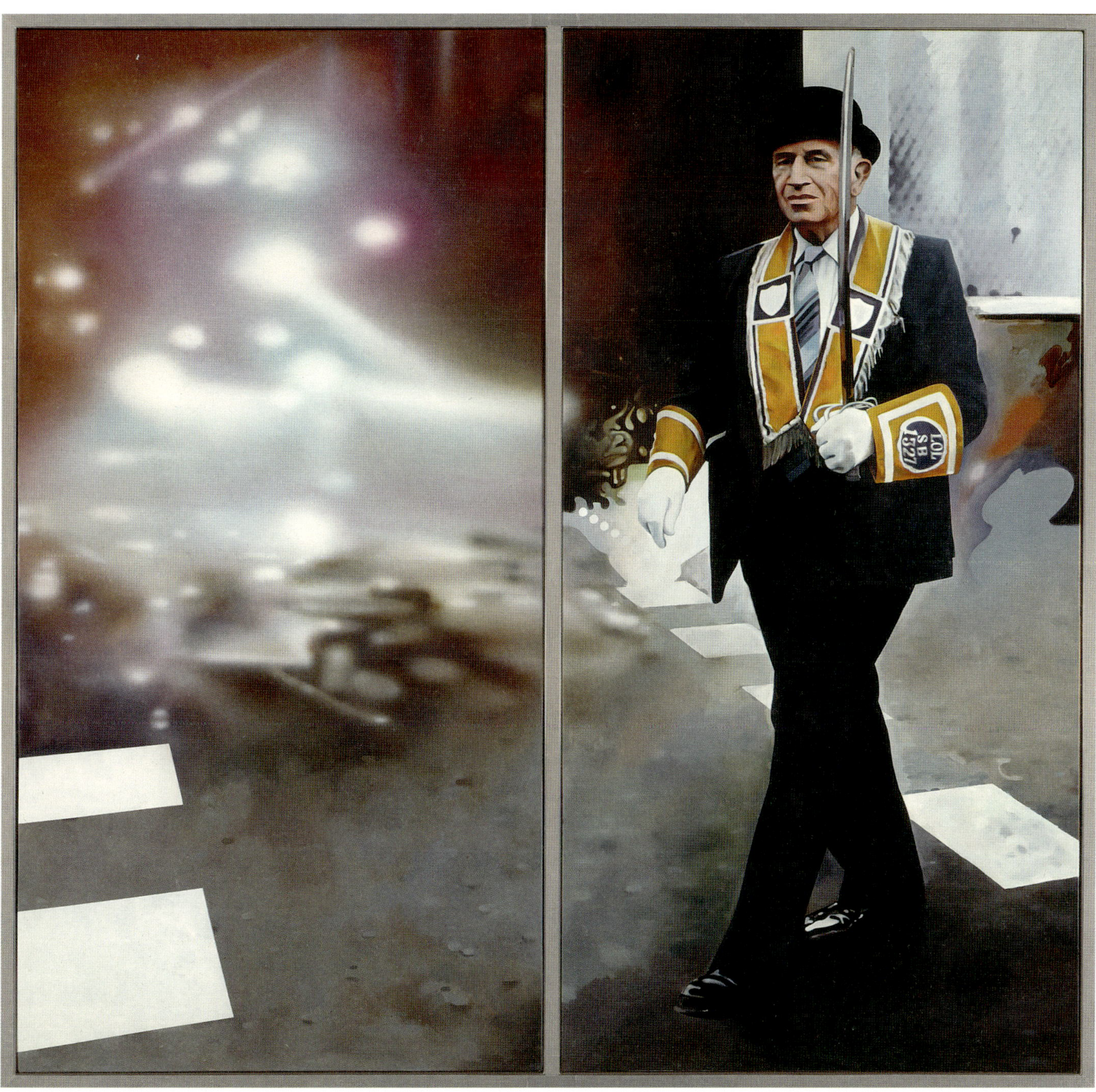

The subject 1988–90

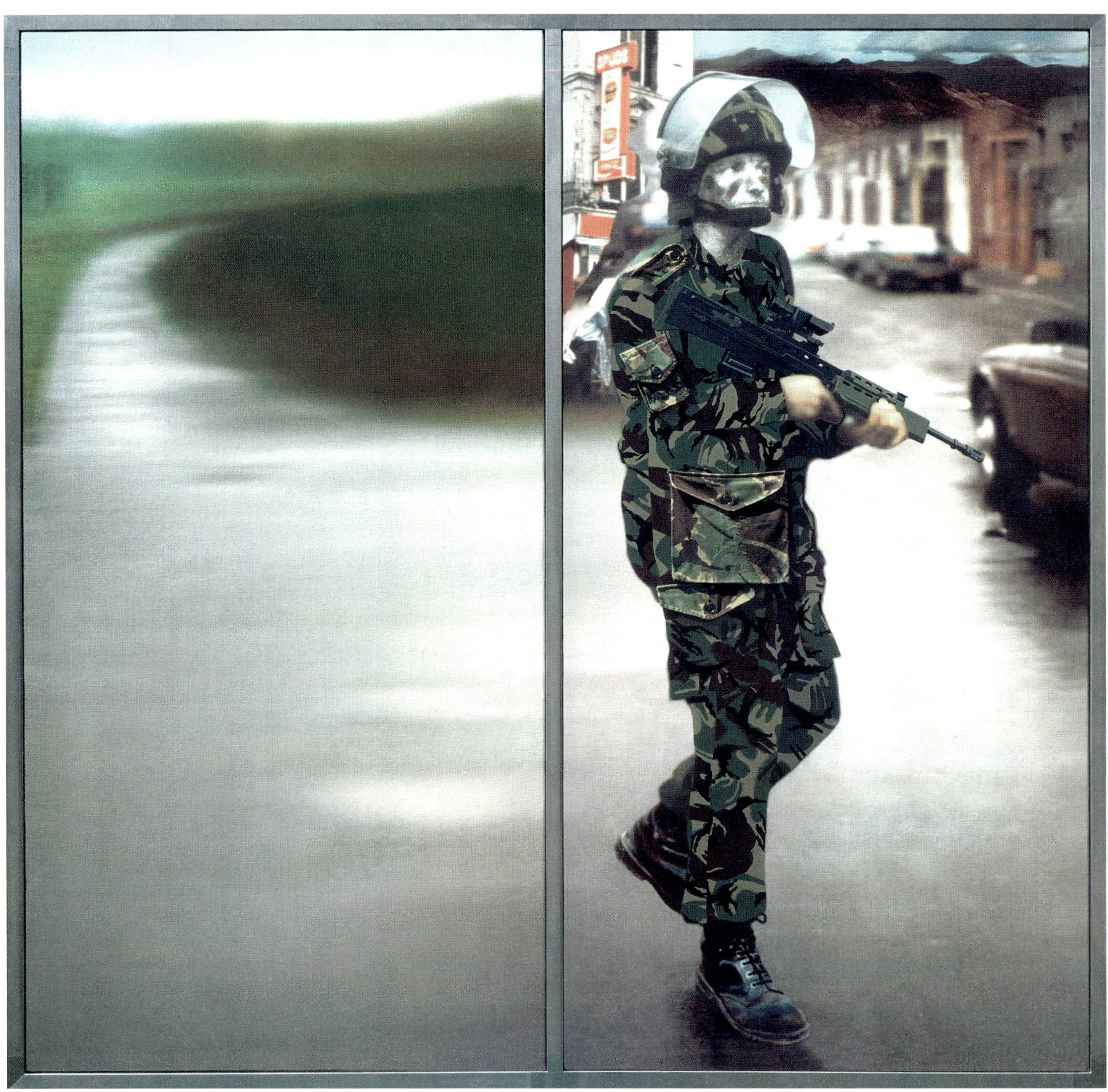

The state 1993

Treatment room (installation) 1983–84

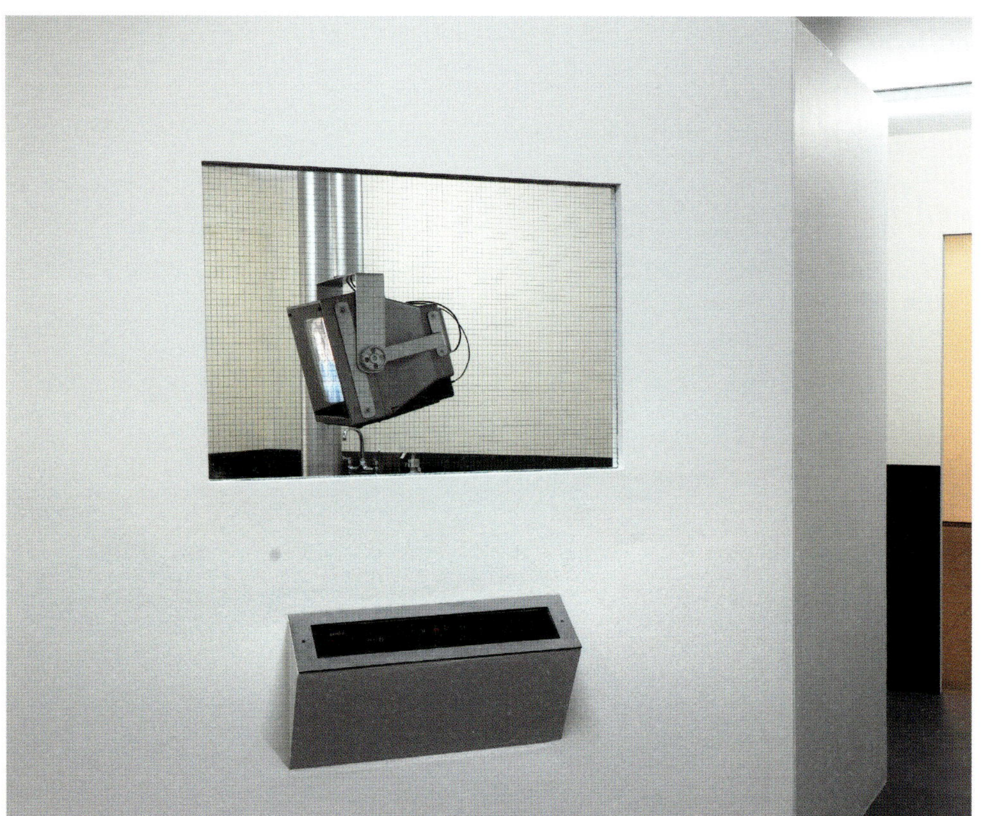

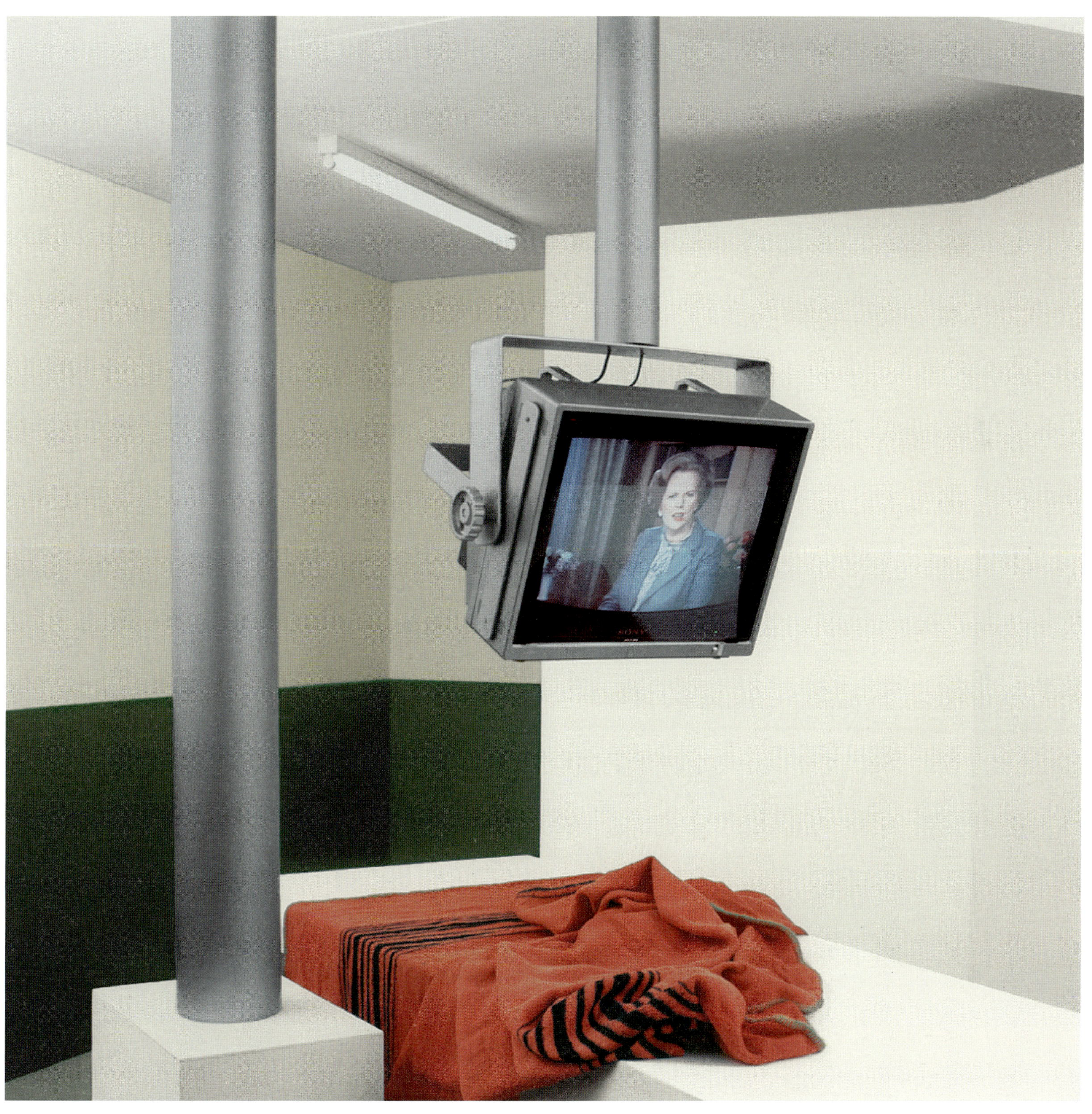

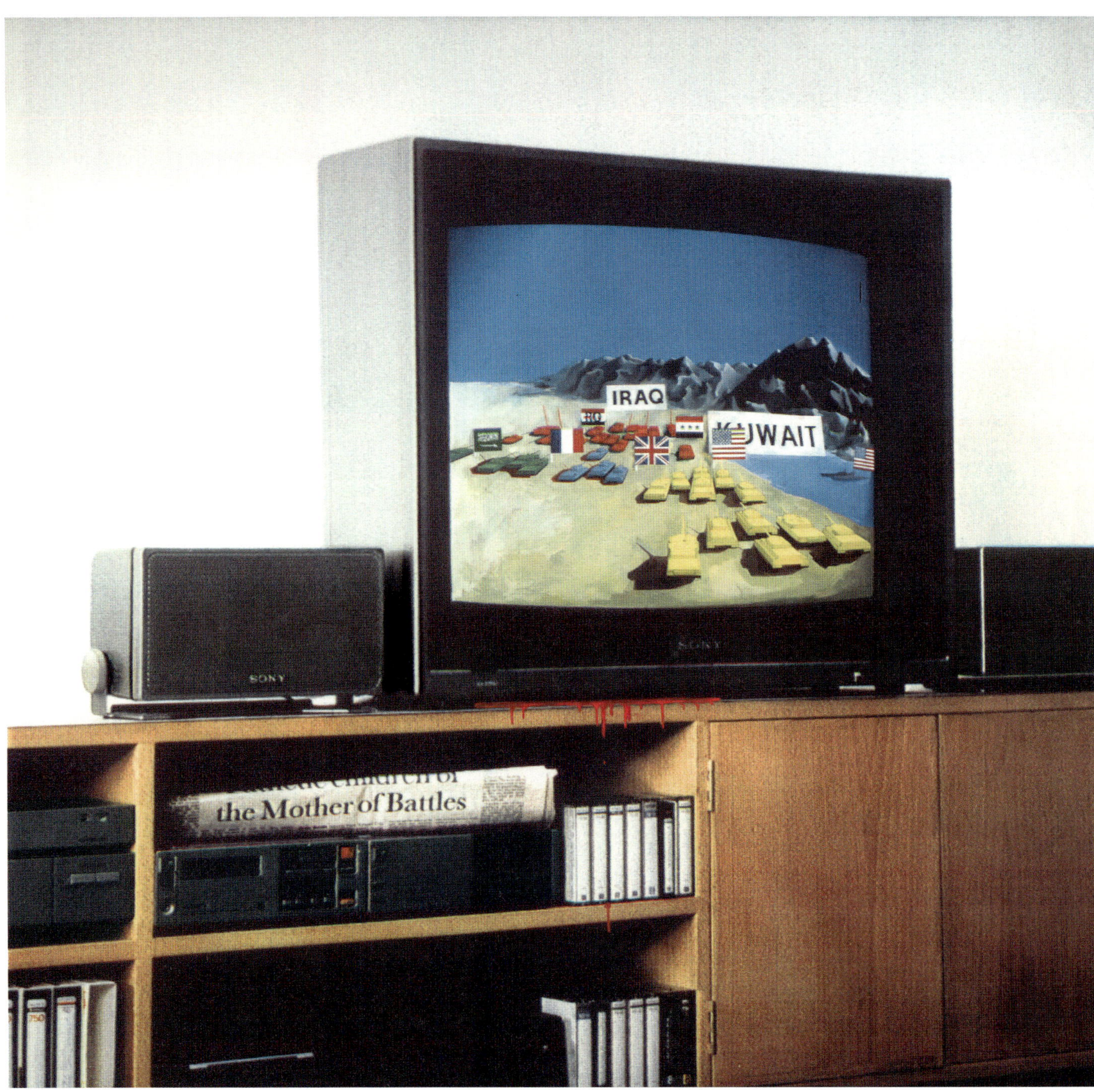

War games 1991–92

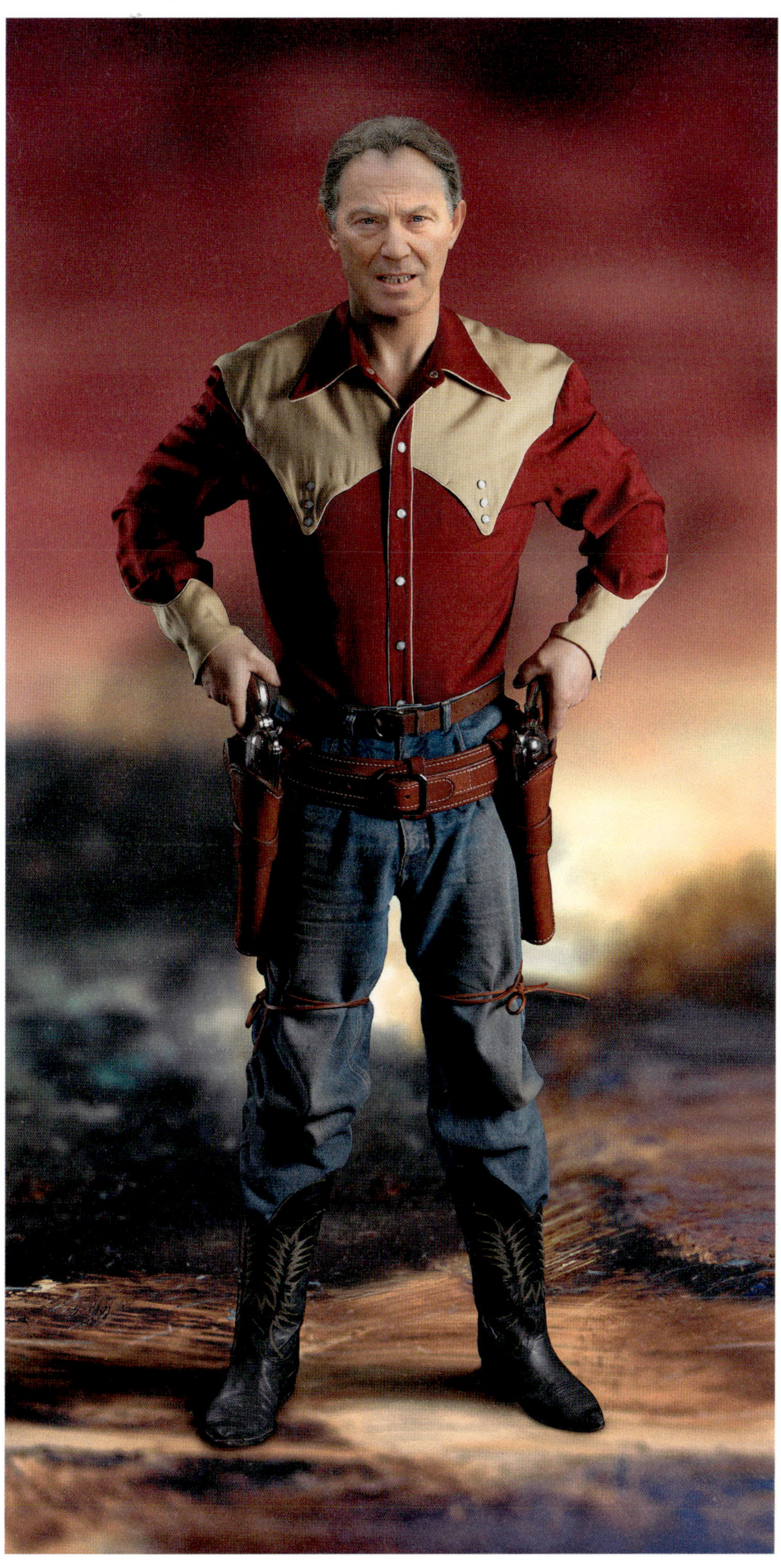

Shock and Awe 2010

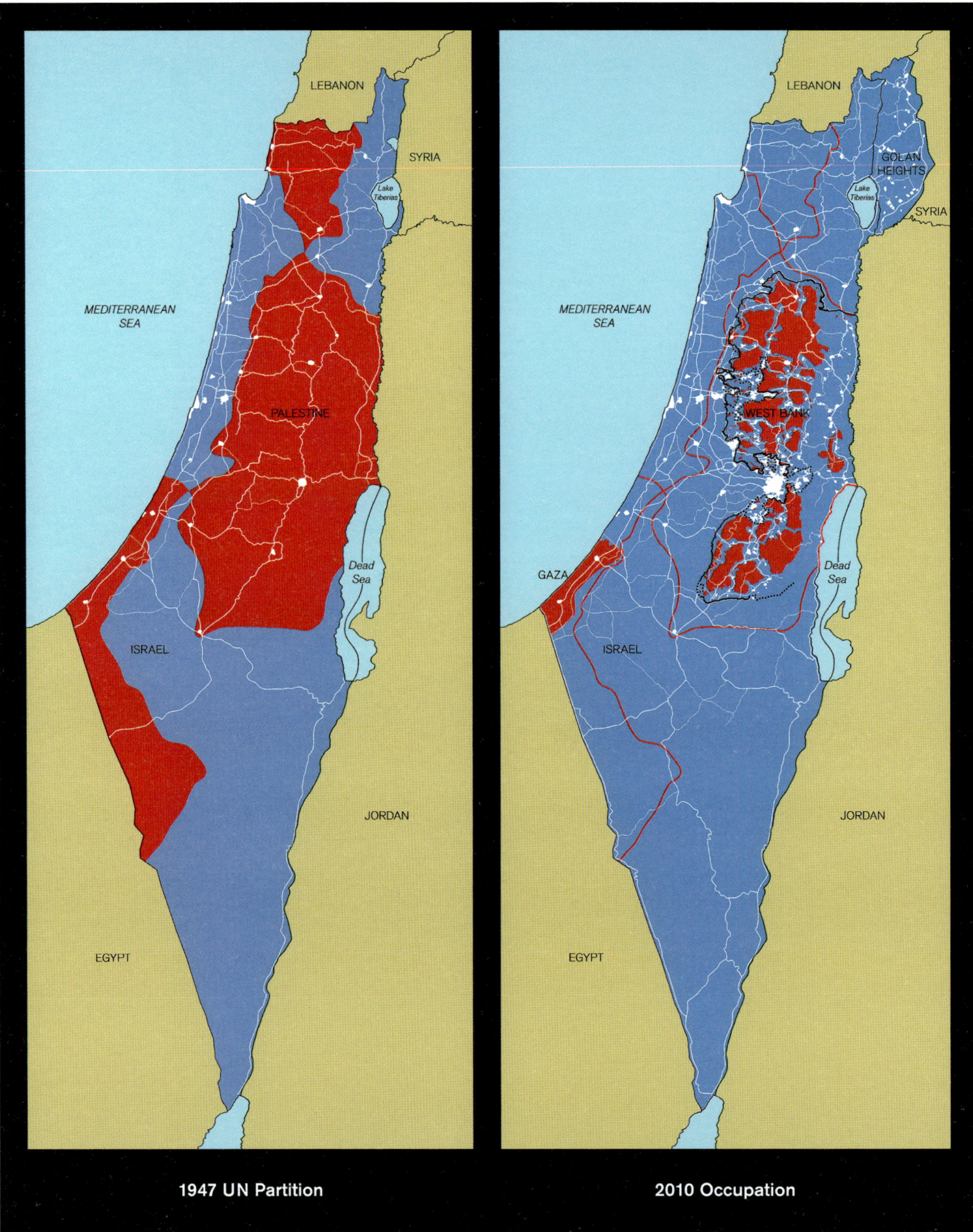

Maps of Palestine 2009

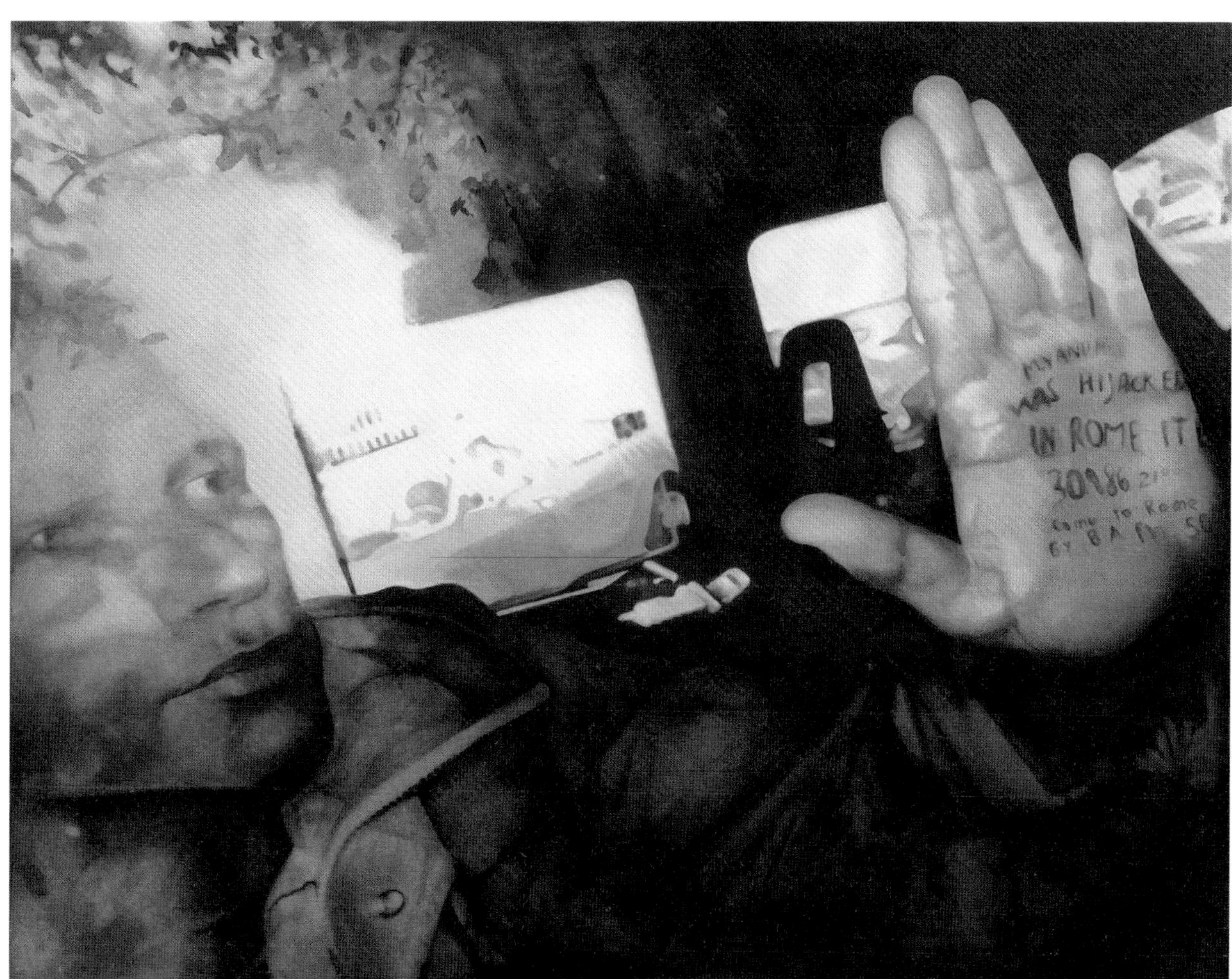

Unorthodox rendition 2009–10

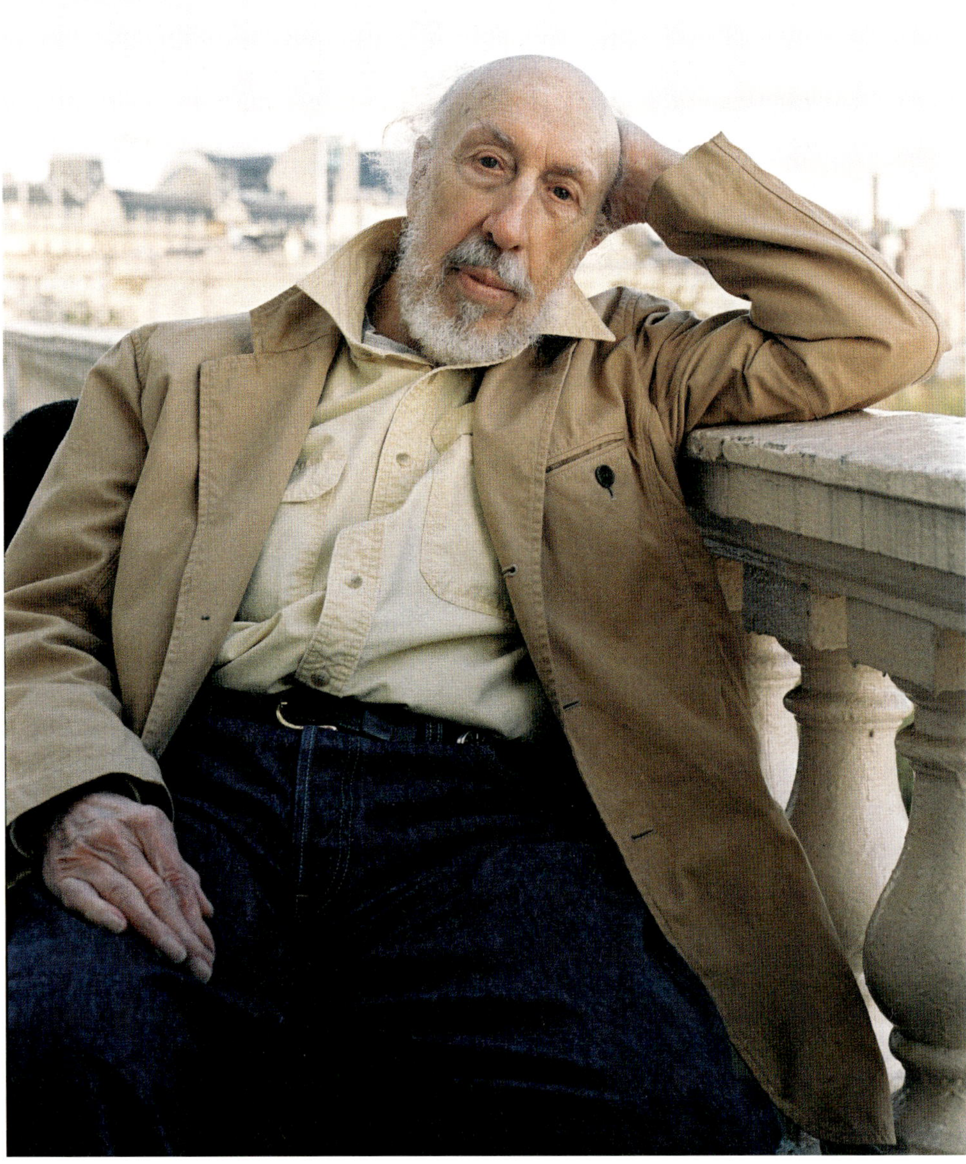

Wolfgang Tillmans, *Richard Hamilton* 2005

Richard Hamilton's "Late" Work

Fanny Singer

Lateness is being at the end, fully conscious, full of memory, and also very (even preternaturally) aware of the present.[1]
Edward Said

The paintings and prints that Richard Hamilton produced during the last twenty-five years of his life have received little critical attention. They have never been the subject of a dedicated scholarly publication, and there have been few exhibitions focused predominantly on this period. The most comprehensive of these was the National Gallery's *Richard Hamilton: The Late Works,* which opened in October 2012, a year after the artist's death at the age of eighty-nine. Though the nineteen works presented there clearly intersected with certain motifs previously explored by Hamilton, such as Renaissance perspective and the domestic interior (as in *Lobby,* 1988–89 [p. 284]), they also marked a crucial departure; all but two of the works were made using digital technologies at some or all stages of the creative process.

In an unusual manoeuvre for a living artist, it was Hamilton himself who chose to title the exhibition *The Late Works.* Though this designation originated with Hamilton, the idea of "late work," more generally, raises several issues, not least in its tacit assumption that the last works are always shaped by an artist's acute awareness of mortality. This was, of course, Hamilton's intention: both to acknowledge the very real possibility that he would not live long enough to see the exhibition, and to play on the double meaning of "late" as both an art-historical term and a synonym for "dead." But the conventional notion of "late work" also amused Hamilton because it was suggestive of the future view of a critic or art historian reflecting on the "late work" (as a typology) of a famous artist. In other words, his deployment of the term "late" anticipated the inclination to bracket diverse pieces as a coherent body of work, not to mention the arrival of essays like this one.

Hamilton's pre-emptive attempt to discourage, or even mock, this tendency, constitutes a playful kind of self-historicising. It is also characteristically paradoxical—that is, his designation of two decades' worth of works as "late" both insists on and undermines their separateness from the rest of his oeuvre. Indeed, it is precisely because of this conflict that these works reflect some of the qualities that Edward Said famously attributed to a "late style": intransigence, contradiction and difficulty (characteristics that for Hamilton are not exclusive to the late works, but are—I would argue—most concentrated there). Building on a close reading of Theodor W. Adorno's writings on Beethoven, Said went on to identify in late work an inclination toward "tamper[ing] irrevocably with the possibility of closure."[2] Even as Hamilton insisted on a certain kind of closure, he was meddling with the conventional sense of lateness. The works he chose to bracket must therefore be regarded as in some sense distinct from the works that preceded them, despite their evolution from those same works.

1. Edward Said, *On Late Style: Music and Literature against the Grain* (New York: Vintage, 2007), 16.
2. Ibid., 7

The language of computers

Hamilton's fascination with machines and technology dates back to World War II, when he was employed first by the Royal Engineers and then at Electric and Musical Industries. However, it was a decade later, during his time as a member of the Independent Group (IG), that he first began to imagine that computers might hold promise for the "fine" arts. In 1954, Hamilton read Claude Shannon's 1948 essay "A Mathematical Theory of Communication," which was assigned by the critic and curator Lawrence Alloway to the members of the IG. The article theorised that all manner of content—sounds, words, images, information—could be transmitted down a wire as a binary series of ones and zeros. According to Hamilton's later account, it "revealed the mind-blowing notion that electrical currents switching on and off could articulate everything—the digital era was born."[3]

Though Hamilton had used a computer to aid in the construction and printing of *Five Tyres remoulded* in 1971 [p. 159], it was only in the 1980s that he began to feel that such a machine might be useful in creating other work. As early as 1985, in reference to his commitment to emerging computer technologies, Hamilton noted: "Having reached a certain age it seemed that unless I came to grips with another language immediately I would remain monolingual for the rest of my days. I decided that it would be of more practical use to be able to communicate with a computer rather than non-English-speaking people."[4]

Despite his devotion to learning the "language of computers," it was only in 1987, with his participation in a six-part BBC series called *Painting with Light,* that he realised the potential of employing a computer in the manipulation of images.[5] For the programme, six artists collaborated with a technician on the creation of an artwork using a Quantel Paintbox. Launched in Britain in 1981, this computer possessed a revolutionary interface that allowed the user to "draw" and "paint" on a cathode ray tube as freely as on canvas. In his segment on *Painting with Light,* Hamilton produced an image that became the foundation for both the print *The Apprentice Boy* (1988) [fig. 1] and the painting *The subject* (1988–90) [p. 257].

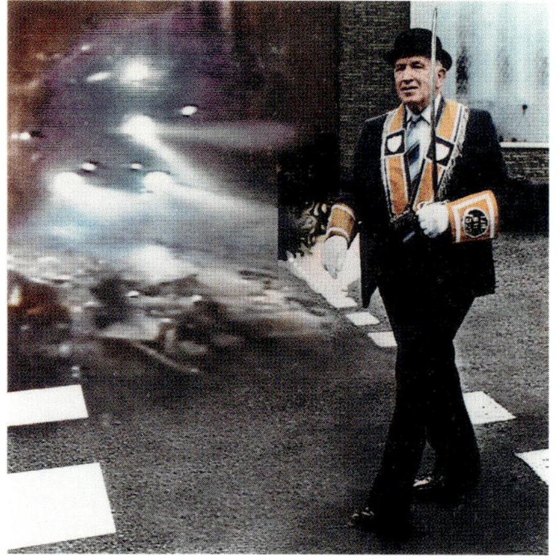

fig. 1
The Apprentice Boy, 1988
Dye transfer

Hamilton quickly identified the Paintbox's potential for integrating diverse source materials into a single plane, allowing him to make truly seamless versions of the multimedia collages he had experimented with throughout his career. He had long felt that that which distinguished the greatest printmakers was their success in "translating between media, making plausible a semblance of marks which should only be expected from hand application."[6] The Paintbox revealed itself to be an ideal tool for translation. Indeed, following his experience on *Painting with Light,* he insisted that "all the prints and paintings I made subsequently utilised, in a variety of ways, digital image-processing equipment."[7] The experience of operating the machine prompted Hamilton to purchase one in 1992, which he used for the rest of the decade.

Five years after *Painting with Light,* Hamilton was again invited to appear on television with his Paintbox. For a segment of the BBC's popular science programme Q.E.D. he created an update of his 1956 collage *Just what is it that makes today's homes so different,*

3. Richard Hamilton, *Painting by Numbers* (London: Alan Cristea Gallery, 2006), 6.
4. Richard Hamilton, from a note written for *Gran Bazaar,* 1985, quoted in Richard Hamilton, *Interactions: Marcel Duchamp, Francis Bacon, Sherril F. Martin, Dieter Roth, Lux Corporation, Ohio Scientific* (Stockholm: Thorden Wetterling Galleries, 1987), 19.
5. The documentary was directed by David Goldsmith and produced by Griffin Productions for the BBC, London, in 1987. The other artists featured in the multi-part series were Howard Hodgkin, Jennifer Bartlett, Larry Rivers, Sidney Nolan and David Hockney.

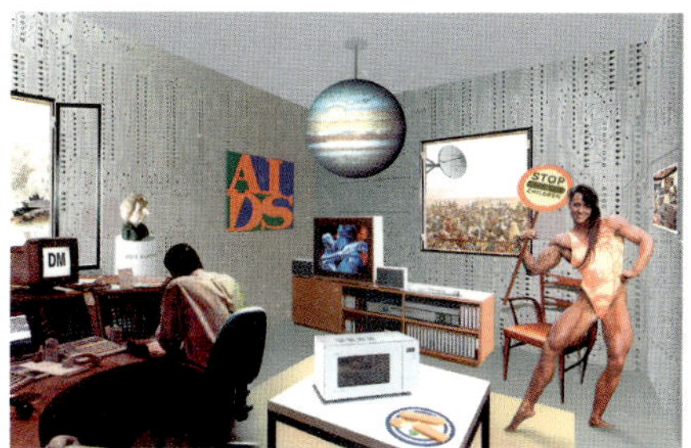

fig. 2
Just what is it that makes today's homes so different?, 1992
Laser jet print

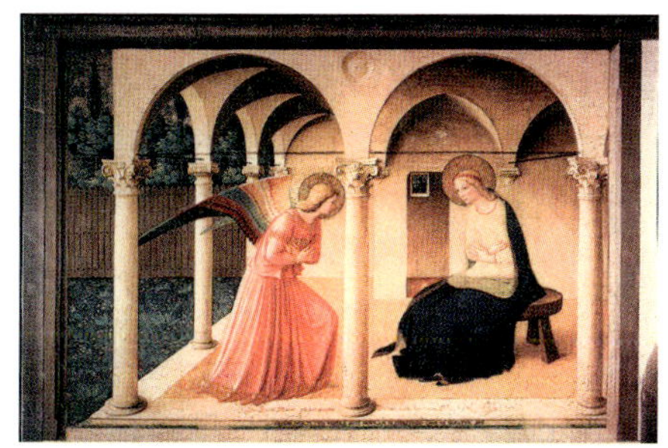

fig. 3
Fra Angelico,
Annunciation, c. 1440
Fresco
Convento di San Marco, Florence

so appealing? [p. 49], making the whole of his creative process transparent to viewers. That Hamilton elected to rework his best-known image forty years on and in the context of a TV show illustrates the publicness of his engagement with computers at this late stage of his career. He was a self-conscious advocate for this emergent technology, and the reworked image likewise speaks of his keen awareness of the cultural zeitgeist. This new work, which has the shorter title *Just what is it that makes today's homes so different?* [fig. 2] (the premillennial home is apparently no longer "so appealing"), teems with objects heralding the arrival of the digital age: walls are fashioned from scanned circuit boards; a television monitor displays a frame from the 1992 film *The Lawnmower Man,* in which two characters are joined in "virtual reality" coitus; a man sits at a computer connected to global financial markets; a satellite is affixed to the house's exterior; a microwave replaces the vacuum cleaner of the 1956 version as a paragon of domestic convenience. The print shows the extent to which Hamilton had become engaged with the notion of the digital interior—that is, not only is it an interior furnished with the late-capitalist emblems of the digital era, but one conceived entirely through digital means.

Hamilton's 2005–7 work, *The Passage of the Angel to the Virgin,* made exactly twenty years after he first used the Paintbox, is emblematic of how the computer shifted his practice into new territory—a place in which the sacred commingles with the secular. *The Passage of the Angel to the Virgin,* the title of which puns on Marcel Duchamp's *The Passage from Virgin to Bride* (1912), was a work Hamilton referred to as a "digital painting" (that is, made without his typical intervention of oil paint at some stage).[8] Closely quoting Fra Angelico's famous San Marco *Annunciation* fresco (c. 1440) [fig. 3], its "Angel" and "Virgin" are presented as naked women situated in the uncanny hyper-reality of a digitally-rendered landscape. This digital painting exactly reproduced (or rebuilt) the architecture depicted in Fra Angelico's fresco by translating the improbable set of rules and vanishing points of the original into the computer language of a 3D rendering programme called LightWave—all without ever using a scanned or collaged image of his source, as he might have done previously. *The Passage of the Angel to the Virgin*'s touchless, even achieropoetic quality becomes inextricably bound up with the subject of the divine.

Hamilton always challenged himself to work in opposition—even to be "iconoclastic towards himself," as he remarked of his mentor Marcel Duchamp.[9] The digital works of Hamilton's later years see him meeting this challenge. This is not to say that his embrace of digital technologies represents a moment of rupture: many affinities and subjects persisted, from collage and photography to interiors and perspective. But an undeniable shift did occur: nude "angels" began to occupy the spaces of digitally constructed architecture, while sleek, unyielding surfaces replaced the handmade finish of earlier work. And yet, Hamilton did not intend for his increasingly frequent use of recognisably Judeo-Christian motifs to substantiate, or defer to, any given belief system (to which he in fact did not subscribe). His somewhat idiosyncratic aim was to achieve a kind of secular numinosity through technical fluency and layered narrative. In works such as *The Passage of the Angel to the Virgin,*

6. Richard Hamilton, *Richard Hamilton Prints: A Complete Catalogue of Graphic Works, 1939–83* (London, Stuttgart: Edition Hansjörg Mayer in collaboration with Waddington Graphics, 1984), 12.
7. Hamilton, *Painting by Numbers,* 7.
8. Though "painting" is Hamilton's term, used in conversation with the author in 2007, it is listed as a "digital montage" (distinct from other pieces described as "inkjet prints") in the catalogue for *A Host of Angels,* an exhibition held at the Palazzetto Tito as a contribution of Fondazione Bevilacqua La Masa to the Venice Biennale in 2007.
9. Richard Hamilton speaking on the occasion of his exhibition *Métamorphose de l'Objet* at the Palais des Beaux-Arts, Brussels, in 1971. Filmed by Jef Cornelis, Dutch/English, 36:30 minutes, broadcast on the Flemish television network VRT on 24 April 1971.

Hamilton encouraged an analogy between the theme of Annunciation (that is, the moment of Mary's superphysical impregnation by God) and digital creation (an artwork created without physical touch): the medium and the message became one.

The digital interior

In 1984, Hamilton took part in a group exhibition titled *Four Rooms,* for which he created the installation *Treatment room* (1983–84) [pp. 260–61], a critique of Margaret Thatcher's then-current assault on the National Health Service. On the occasion, he published a text regarding his long-standing interest in interiors:

> Since 1956, the date of the *This is Tomorrow* exhibition, I have found myself returning persistently to the subject of architectural interiors. The interest has been expressed in three ways: (a) devising dwelling spaces of the kind I like to live in, (b) making exhibition installations; these do not impose the functional constraints of a domestic environment—nor inhibit, because of their temporary nature, a more dynamic, insistent claim on consciousness; (c) representing interiors in paintings and prints, wherein even the limitation of structural plausibility is removed. My third category, the portrayal of rooms on paper or canvas (together with that other strange and important conditional case: the representation of interior spaces on the cinema or TV screen) overlaps both (a) and (b). As a painter, I find this pictorial rendering the most fascinating of all for (c) offers the possibility of sub-encounters, two-dimensional simulations of interiors within the three-dimensional envelope of an actual interior.[10]

Hamilton's reference to "the possibility of sub-encounters, two-dimensional simulations of interiors within the three-dimensional envelope of an actual interior" anticipates the avenues that would open up through his creative engagement with the computer. The notion of a digital interior—a fictive space that exists only in the digital cosmos—was expanded when Hamilton participated in the group exhibition *Five Rooms* at the Anthony d'Offay Gallery, London, in 1995. Having been allocated a room with seven walls on which to hang works, he created a series of works he called *Seven rooms* (1995) [fig. 4] which represents seven distinct spaces in Northend, Hamilton's home in Oxfordshire.[11]

For *Seven rooms,* Hamilton chose to develop ideas earlier worked through in *Langan's,* an "analogue" painting from 1976 [p. 280]. Commissioned for Peter Langan's London restaurant, this piece began with a black and white photograph of the brasserie taken during construction, over which Hamilton painted a photo-realistic table setting. The finished picture was to be installed on the wall it depicted, so that the distinctive pattern of the wall-covering would be echoed within the smaller dimensions of the painting. When the restaurant managers covered over the patterned panel, the painting lost its primary referent and Hamilton insisted on its removal. Each painting in the *Seven rooms* series was

10. Richard Hamilton, quoted in the exhibition catalogue *Four Rooms: Howard Hodgkin, Marc Camille Chaimowicz, Richard Hamilton, Anthony Caro* (London: Arts Council of Great Britain, 1984), n. p.
11. The one exception is *Ghosts of Ufa,* which does not take a room in Hamilton's house as a subject, but rather is a painted version of a print he had created for a show in Bremen in 1994. Though the painting shares its site-specific "white cube" frame with the six other paintings in the d'Offay show, the core of the composition does not depict an interior space resembling those shown in the other works in the suite.

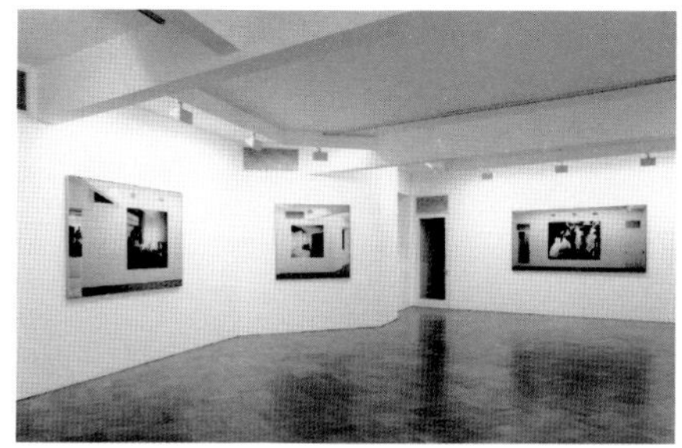

fig. 4
Seven rooms, Anthony d'Offay Gallery, 1995

governed by a similar investment in site-specificity [fig. 4]. The "frame" of gallery space represented in each painting is the common denominator, the tether to the environment that bore each panel. Within this "frame" is an image that seems to be a photo-realistic painting but is in fact a digitally manipulated photograph (with some painted elements) of a room in Northend (for which each work is respectively named: *Kitchen, Bathroom, Passage, Dining room, Bedroom, Dining room/kitchen*). These images of Northend's interior were never independently realised photographic works and were therefore never physically hung in the d'Offay gallery: *Seven rooms* presents a purely speculative idea of how such an installation might have looked.

To make these works, Hamilton took photographs of each wall of the gallery, and then digitally transposed each image of the Northend rooms onto the wall he had selected for it. Each room-within-a-room piece was printed onto canvas (touched with oil paint or left alone) and installed on its corresponding gallery wall in the *Five Rooms* exhibition, thus doubly framing each image within the envelope of the "white cube."[12] With this nesting configuration, Hamilton produced works that represented the very space that anchored them institutionally: a digitally achieved *mise en abyme*. And yet, his commitment to site-specificity—in this case the space of a commercial art gallery—was not working from the principles of institutional critique (i.e. revealing the ideological construction of an exhibiting institution). Rather, it constituted an exploration of the dynamics of space itself, a consideration of the extent to which an illusion of reality could be retained despite a reorganisation of its elements. When the paintings were re-installed at the Catherine David-curated documenta X in 1997, Hamilton insisted on the total reconstruction of the d'Offay interior, fearing a loss of the paintings' spatial dynamism. Though much could be read into Hamilton's overlaying of a commercial space onto an institution such as documenta, the most important transaction took place *within* each work, where he negotiated the plausible assembly of environments at once real and virtual.

Hamilton argued that the question "In which way does this differ from a photograph?" is central to the works that grew from his site-referential series: "The task of recreating a photograph (for example, the background of [his digital print] *The annunciation*) in such a way that it is more like a photograph than the lens-generated original is interesting, even to the extent that its lack of flaws is what differentiates the simulation from the photograph."[13] The original photograph of the d'Offay gallery included in *An annunciation (a)* (1994–2004) [p. 295] (as well as in the closely related print, *The annunciation,* 2005) underwent a computerised transformation that changed everything—and yet seemingly nothing. Hamilton laboriously deconstructed, and then reconstructed, the interior space of the gallery in *The annunciation;* nine state proofs were made during the manipulation of the walls alone[14] [fig. 5]. First, Hamilton used what he referred to as Adobe Illustrator's "vocabulary of vector description" to adjust the quality of the spotlighting and subtly alter the gradation of the walls, to render it, in his words, "reminiscent of an early Renaissance perspectival space."[15] In *An annunciation (a),* each component of the original photograph—excepting the grate, light

12. The term "white cube" owes its historicization to Brian O'Doherty, who wrote a series of essays published in *Artforum* in 1976, later gathered in his book *Inside the White Cube.*
13. Hamilton, *Painting by Numbers,* 5.
14. Ibid., 51. A "state proof" refers to a print pulled from an in-progress plate; Hamilton uses the term to mean a print-out of a computer file as it appeared on his screen.
15. Ibid., 53.

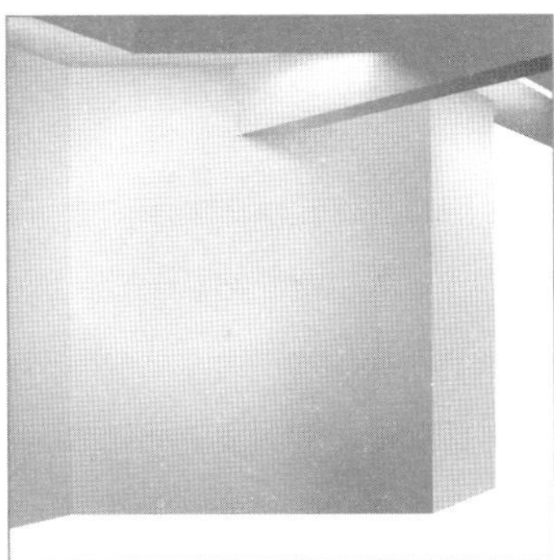

fixture, floor and window—was modified in isolation, before being brought back together to form an eerily perfect whole.

Throughout his engagement with digital media, Hamilton referred repeatedly to the problem of "resolution." This was initially optical, then subsequently thematic. He described resolution as "the fineness of detail that can be distinguished in an image."[16] What he identified as the "resolution problem," then, was that the available technologies could not concentrate enough dots in a square inch for an image to conceal its digital nature. As Hamilton evolved his practice and embraced the limits of the technologies at hand (specifically digital media's inability to achieve the sensuous quality of paint for which he had earlier yearned), examining this tension would ultimately underpin all of his digitally rendered works.[17] His increasing investment in the idea of a uniquely digital facture took his work into the airless purlieus of hyper-reality, an ineluctable consequence of the refinement of digital printing. Even as early as 1998 Hamilton had envisioned the computer-crafted future of virtual reality:

> It is now possible for computers to provide a visual experience of a three-dimensional kind in real time—they can create a virtual reality analogous to our perception of the real world (assuming that there is such a thing as the real world). Understandably, resolution is somewhat limited at the moment ... But it won't be many years before the experience will be something like real life ... I begin to wonder if the virtual world will simply be an identical replacement of our biological world ...[18]

A Host of Angels

In the work that follows *Seven rooms,* three major concerns enter Hamilton's practice. We see the re-engagement with Marcel Duchamp; the introduction of the human figure; and the emergence of Renaissance-era iconography connected to the Annunciation. All of this occurs as Hamilton is increasingly questioning the coming together or pulling apart of analogue and digital media, of painting and printmaking.

Hamilton was first introduced to Duchamp's work in 1948 when Nigel Henderson, a fellow student at the Slade School of Fine Art, brought him by Roland Penrose's personal library to see the *Green Box* (1934). Nearly ten years later, he was invited by Duchamp to work with the art historian George Heard Hamilton on the production of an English version of the *Green Box* notes; this three-year project concluded with the book's publication in 1960. In advance of the 1966 Tate Gallery retrospective, *The Almost Complete Works of Marcel Duchamp,* which Hamilton curated, he embarked on the creation of an exact replica—sanctioned by Duchamp—of the *La Mariée mise à nu par ses célibataires, même* (*The Bride Stripped Bare by her Bachelors, Even*, 1915–23[p. 157]), often known as the *Large Glass,* a two-year process that brought him into a position of unparalleled intimacy

16. Ibid.
17. Invited to deliver the William Townsend Memorial Lecture at University College, London, in 1991, Hamilton gave a paper titled "The Hard Copy Problem" in which he said: "I have yet to be persuaded that it will, some day, be possible to build a computer dedicated to image processing that can equal the brain of Velázquez or to construct a printer that can output hard copy to equal the sensory experience of his great painting *Las meninas.*" A version updated in 1998 is reprinted in Etienne Lullin, *Richard Hamilton: Prints and Multiples 1939–2002* (Winterthur: Kunstmuseum/Richter Verlag Düsseldorf; New Haven, CT: Yale Center for British Art, 2003), 279.
18. From Hamilton's lecture, "The Hard Copy Problem."

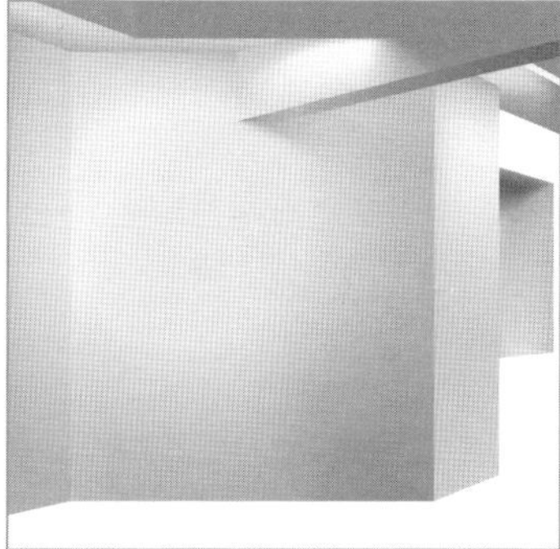

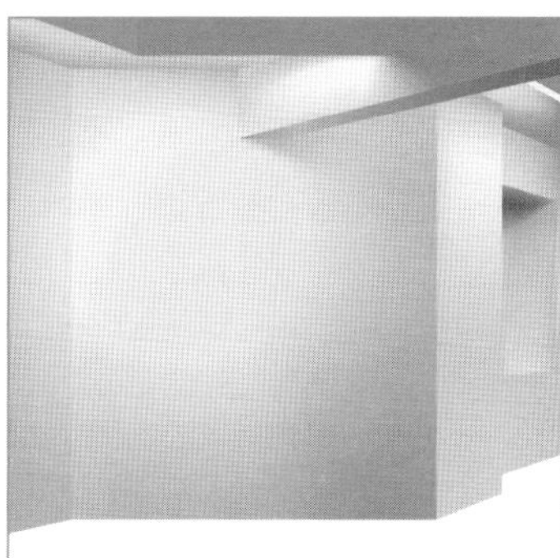

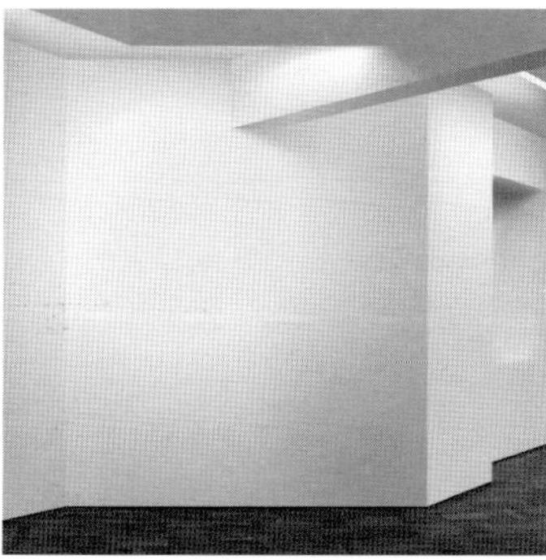

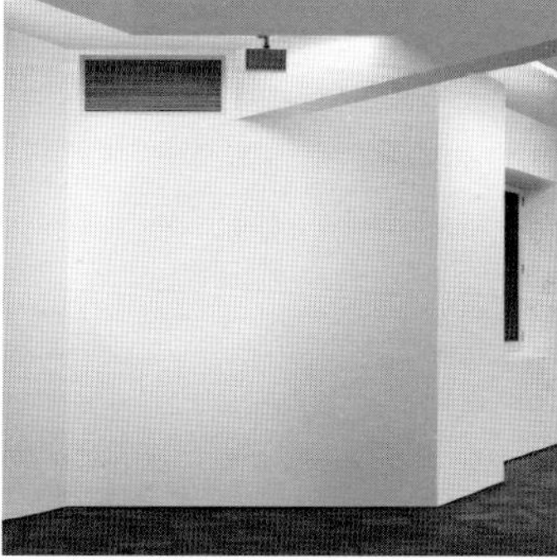

fig. 5
Nine stage proofs for the wall for *The annunciation,* 2005

with the work born of the *Green Box* (Duchamp saw the sculptural work as a reification of the reams of notes contained in the *Box*). Hamilton's complex and allusive relationship to Duchamp is evident throughout his oeuvre, but it was never more prominent than in his late work. The first of Hamilton's digital works to make this engagement explicit is the painting *The passage of the bride* [p. 297]—a titular allusion to Duchamp's 1912 canvas, *The Passage from Virgin to Bride*—which nimbly responds to the open-ended conditions of Duchamp's *Large Glass.*

The lower section of the *Large Glass,* described by Duchamp as "La Machine Célibataire" (Bachelor Machine), is contained within *The passage of the bride,* in the form of a framed and glazed drawing hanging on the wall of a corridor in Hamilton's home. This drawing, one of Hamilton's many studies for his reconstruction of Duchamp's *Large Glass,* is a full-size perspective rendering of the lower part of the *Glass.* The original source photograph of the corridor showed what appeared to be a vacant frame as the glaring southern light drowned out its delicate graphite lines. Hamilton's solution was to add an overlay of a transparency from a colour photograph of the lower half of his reconstructed *Large Glass,* explaining that "because the intention was to replace the drawing with the reconstruction, it was necessary to give the illusion that the new image was under the surface of the reflecting glass."[19] He carefully selected a degree of transparency that would impart the inserted image with a ghosted quality, thus effectively giving the impression that the *Glass* is beneath glass—an improbable, impossible act of layering.

Duchamp's *Large Glass* imagines a domain in which all human interactions are mediated by technology (a future that was, incidentally, depicted in part in Hamilton's beloved *Blade Runner,* 1982). The body, as such, would be rendered extraneous, elevated via technology to a supernal realm. Duchamp's copious notes for the *Large Glass* divulge his sustained interest in this abstract space, for him best represented by the fourth dimension (and a grasping for an elusive "realness" analogous with Hamilton's deployment of the computer in his quest to visualise a virtually rendered reality). The mirror was, for Duchamp, a conceptually fecund object, a possible window to the fourth dimension, a notion that Hamilton honoured by conflating the *Large Glass* with both a mirror and a window in his own painting. Hamilton replaces Duchamp's mechanomorphic "Bride" with a recognisably human form, positioned in an act of congress at once salacious and chaste with her "Bachelors" (who retain their Duchampian silhouette). This woman appears in the glass pane without her corporeal self doubling in the "real" environment depicted, though she had in fact originated there prior to her digital displacement.[20]

A later work titled *Descending nude* (2006) [p. 300] comprises a very literal engagement with Duchamp's famous Eadweard Muybridge-inspired painting of a figure in motion, *Nude Descending a Staircase, No. 2* (1912). *Descending nude* also recalls Hamilton's nudes from the 1950s, such as *re Nude* (1954) [fig. 6], in which figuration and abstraction meet in a jumble of marks intended to create a sense of spectator movement toward and away from an object.[21] In *Descending nude,* Hamilton eschews the Duchamp-

19. Richard Hamilton, *Site-referential Paintings* (San Francisco: San Francisco Museum of Modern Art; London: Anthony d'Offay Gallery, 1996), 20.
20. Richard Hamilton, *Richard Hamilton: New Technology and Printmaking* (London: Alan Cristea Gallery, 1998), 35.
21. Hamilton's works in this vein were in part triggered by his interest in Eadweard Muybridge's photographs of animal and human locomotion (1887); a drawing, *After Muybridge* (1953), and a print, *Man walking (after Muybridge)* (1953), make this source plain.

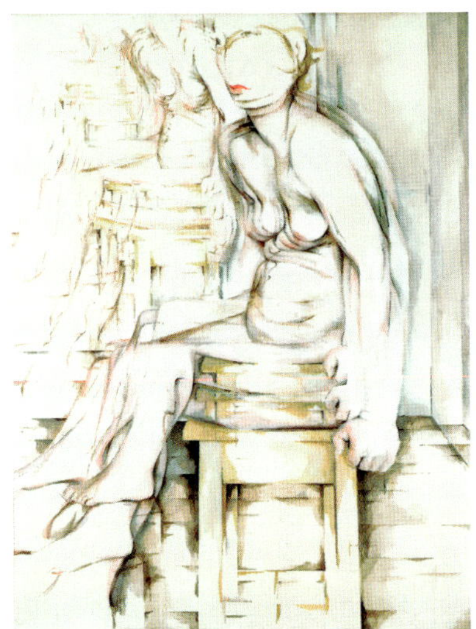

fig. 6
Re-nude, 1954
Oil on panel
Moderna Museet, Stockholm

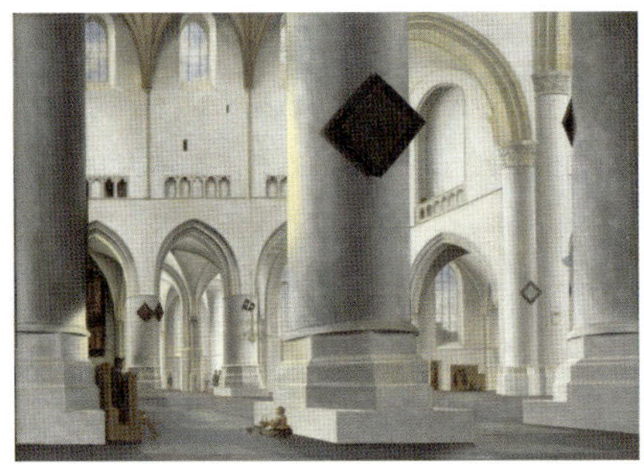

fig. 7
Pieter Jansz Saenredam,
The Interior of the Grote Kerk at Haarlem,
1636–37
Oil on oak
National Gallery, London. Salting Bequest, 1910

inspired composite appearance of the earlier figurative work in favour of the unnerving hyper-clarity of the digital medium. Here again, as in *The passage of the bride,* a nude is trapped within the virtual space of the mirror, only this time she also stands outside the frame, firmly grounded in "real space" as she regards her other selves (as Hamilton himself did in the lenticular self-portrait *Palindrome,* 1974) [p. 14], in a fractured progression through what Duchamp would have appreciated as fourth dimensional.

The model from *The passage of the bride,* in a kind of "mirrorical return," wanders into Hamilton's cavernous rendering of the National Gallery's Sainsbury Wing in his painting *The Saensbury Wing* (1999–2000) [p. 296].[22] This work was created for the exhibition *Encounters: New Art from Old,* for which twenty-four artists were asked to respond to a work of their choice from the National Gallery collection. Hamilton selected Pieter Jansz Saenredam's *The Interior of the Grote Kerk at Haarlem* (1636–37) [fig. 7] and set about finding an interior that could provide the subject from which to generate his own piece. The museum's then-recent Robert Venturi-designed wing, named for the donors who funded its construction, provided the type of environment Hamilton had envisioned and explains the punning portmanteau of a title given to the resulting work.

For *The Saensbury Wing,* Hamilton began by scanning a photograph he had taken of the Sainsbury galleries. From there, he manipulated the angle of view and the internal spatial dynamics of the vista, and worked with a CAD 2D/3D programme for architect-engineers called MicroStation at the Richard Rogers Partnership to create a three-dimensional computer model of the space. He then tackled lighting effects, using LightWave to colour and texture a computer visualisation of what "his" final gallery would look like.[23] The more Hamilton began to tinker with the scanned image, the more the peculiarities of the original architecture vexed him; he therefore aimed to "correct" what he saw as flaws in the architectural design—broadening Venturi's openings, flattening his semi-circular arches, blasting through his low ceilings and aerating the more distant rooms.[24] Hamilton's divergence from his original intent to follow Saenredam's stringent mathematical programme reveals a slackened interest in constructing a "real" space. His tweaks to the exhibition setting in fact recall the *Seven rooms* series: *The Saensbury Wing* also has a deceptively straightforward relationship to site—this time with the added complication of Hamilton having rendered the work's environmental referent utterly fictive. Ultimately, *The Saensbury Wing* departs altogether from the actual space of the National Gallery. In his final version, following a series of states, Hamilton achieved a kind of super-reality in which female "angels" stroll naked through the museum and the role of Jesus Christ is assumed by the messianic figure of an IRA prisoner "on the blanket," drawn from Hamilton's earlier work *The citizen* (1982–83).[25]

Unlike the *Seven rooms* series that served as their inspiration, the paintings *An annunciation (a)* (1994–2004) [p. 295], *An annunciation (b) v2* (2005), *Bathroom – fig. 1 II* (2004) and *Bathroom – fig. 2 II* (2005–6) all contain a figure, generally a naked woman. This was Hamilton's gesture toward populating these interiors, giving them a "token life-force" as he had done with his 1956 collage *Just what is it…* about which he later noted: "my 'home'

22. *A mirrorical return,* the title of a digital print version of *The passage of the bride,* is Hamilton's own translation of "Renvoie Mirrorique," a phrase used in reference to the "Oculist charts" in Duchamp's *Green Box* notes. The use of the phrase refers to the fact that the model from the earlier painting returns, in mirrored orientation, to Hamilton's work a year later, finding herself the subject of a new composition.
23. Richard Morphet, *Encounters: New Art from Old* (London: The National Gallery, 2000), 145–46.
24. Ibid., 145.
25. In *The Saensbury Wing,* Hamilton replaced the altarpiece that hangs at the culmination of the hall—Giovanni Battista Cima da Conegliano's *The Incredulity of Saint Thomas* (c. 1502–4)—with his own painting, *The citizen* (1982–83).

would have been incomplete without its token life-force so Adam and Eve struck a pose along with the rest of the gadgetry."[26] In Hamilton's later digital interiors, "Adam" is usurped by a lone female figure, a "nude angel."

Hamilton began using the term "nude angels" to collectively describe the subjects of the works he had in mind for an unrealised exhibition at the San Marco convent in Florence, home to Fra Angelico's *Annunciation* fresco.[27] He later applied the phrase to the majority of the figures featured in *A Host of Angels,* an exhibition held at the Palazzetto Tito as a contribution of Fondazione Bevilacqua La Masa to the Venice Biennale in 2007, named after his habit of calling these unclad models—and the occasional close friend—his "angels." Hamilton conceded that "some theologians would argue that angels are male, but I lean to [John] Milton's view that they are pure spirits without substance or gender. Since pure spirits without substance are difficult to configure, the female form is my preferred option."[28] This statement legitimated his depiction of Archangel Gabriel as a naked woman in *The Passage of the Angel to the Virgin,* and yet it also indicates that, in Hamilton's rather esoteric thinking, the immaterial and divine are somehow analogous to the digital.

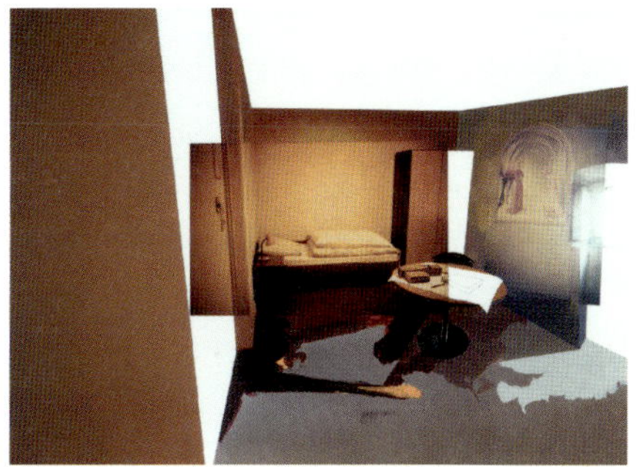

fig. 8
Grove of Academus, 1979
Collage and acrylic on panel
Private collection

Many of Hamilton's nude models did indeed take on a semi-sacred role, especially when inserted into works inspired by Fra Angelico's San Marco *Annunciation;* he described his own print, *The annunciation,* as a "direct response" to the fresco.[29] Hamilton had been drawn to the San Marco *Annunciations* since he first encountered them thirty years beforehand, and had included a representation of one as early as 1979 in his painting-collage *Grove of Academus* [fig. 8]. The Annunciation image appealed to Hamilton on an aesthetic level but equally for its wider cultural ubiquity as one of the most frequently visualised stories in Western history. In the digital age, as Hamilton recognised, the image gains its aura not—as Walter Benjamin famously argued—from its singularity or location, but rather from the velocity and frequency with which it is circulated.[30] In creating a version of a scene that had already spawned millions of copies and iterations, Hamilton sought to dispassionately engage an unavoidable reality, the very fact of image transmission.

In 1972, Marshall McLuhan's collaborator Edmund Carpenter observed that "electricity has made angels of us all."[31] Hamilton's substitution of a piece of modern technology for the Angel is indeed evocative of the melting of information into the ethereal sphere (of radio, of telecommunications and, most critically, of the Internet). That the Virgin is receiving the news of her fate via modern technology makes this piece a sequel of sorts to *Just what is it that makes today's homes so different, so appealing?,* in that the housewife pictured in the earlier collage is liberated by the addition of a few extra feet of cord to her new vacuum cleaner. Here, however, Hamilton's twenty-first-century Virgin reposes, receiving the Word wirelessly.

Hamilton's *The Passage of the Angel to the Virgin,* the only of his versions of the Annunciation to exactly replicate the composition of the Fra Angelico fresco, is likewise the first fully digital work that Hamilton referred to as a "painting." Unlike the inkjet print *The annunciation,* in which Hamilton painted with oils at various stages before its final digital printing, *The Passage of the Angel to the Virgin* was made entirely with photographic and

26. Richard Hamilton, *Exteriors, Interiors, Objects, People* [exh. cat. Winterthur, Kunstmuseum, 1990] (Stuttgart; London: Editions Hansjörg Mayer, 1990), 44.
27. Hamilton, *Painting by Numbers*, 53.
28. Richard Hamilton and Angela Vettese, *Richard Hamilton: A Host of Angels* (Venice 2007), n. p.
29. Hamilton, *Painting by Numbers,* 53.
30. For more on how the speed of travel of an image has replaced the emphasis on its aura, see David Joselit, *After Art* (Princeton, NJ: Princeton University Press, 2012), 8.
31. Edmund Carpenter, *Oh, What a Blow That Phantom Gave Me!* (New York: Bantam, 1972), 3.

digitally rendered imagery; no section was touched by his brush. With the virtual sublimation of the analogue photograph (now replaced by a version both composed and printed digitally and frequently manipulated beforehand), I implored Hamilton to outline the distinction between photograph, print and painting, which are so fused (and confused) in his practice. He recalled the widely quoted response to the announcement of photography's discovery in 1839, often misattributed to Paul Delaroche: "From today painting is dead." After a brief pause, Hamilton said, "Maybe now it's photography that is dead."[32]

The "last" work

Hamilton's final project, completed days before his death, began in 2010 as an invitation to respond to Honoré de Balzac's short story *Le Chef-d'oeuvre inconnu* (*The Unknown Masterpiece*, 1832).[33] *Untitled* (which has previously been referred to in print as *Balzac (a) + (b) + (c)* and *Le chef-d'oeuvre inconnu—a painting in three parts*) [pp. 302–4] comprises three stretched canvases. The panel on the left represents Hamilton's initial conception: a digital collage of his source materials, embellished with preliminary digital marks. The central panel is the digital sketch that would have served as the underpainting for the oil painting Hamilton intended to make. The right canvas is a digital approximation of how an oil painting might have looked.

In Balzac's tale, set in Paris in 1612, a young unknown painter named Nicolas Poussin pays a visit to the studio of the established painter Porbus, where he meets the old master Frenhofer. The latter laments his inability to finish a portrait titled *La Belle Noiseuse.* Eager to be of assistance, Poussin offers his lover Gilette as a new model and her beauty inspires Frenhofer to quickly complete his painting. Poussin and Porbus are subsequently invited to Frenhofer's studio where they regard the anticipated masterpiece. All that is visible, however, is a perfectly rendered foot, the lone figurative detail visible amid the maelstrom of marks that make up the canvas's totality. To their eyes, the work is nothing but "a mass of strange lines forming a wall of paint"; Frenhofer mysteriously dies in a studio fire the following day.[34] *The Unknown Masterpiece* is often seen as prefiguring the invention of abstraction in Western modernism, published some eighty years before the first experiments of Kasimir Malevich and Wassily Kandinsky. In that it describes a vexed, misunderstood masterpiece, it is that much more compelling that Hamilton's unfinished final work should be an illustration of its failed reception.

Frenhofer's destroyed masterpiece had a special resonance for several real-life artists. Paul Cézanne identified himself as a Frenhofer figure, while Pablo Picasso illustrated the story for Ambroise Vollard, and eventually moved into the Paris studio where Balzac's tale is set. That Hamilton's work includes the self-portrait images of artists including Nicolas Poussin, Gustave Courbet and Titian (an echo of whose famous *Venus of Urbino,* 1583, can also be found in the pose of Hamilton's nude) suggests a self-conscious insertion of himself into a genealogy of masters. And yet, a void lies at the heart of this work: the conspicuous

32. In conversation with the artist, 21 May 2007.
33. See Michael Bracewell, "An Introduction to Richard Hamilton's *Balzac (a) + (b) + (c),*" in Christopher Riopelle and Michael Bracewell, *Richard Hamilton: The Late Works* (London: The National Gallery, 2012), 32. Though John-Paul Stonard referred to the Balzac work as "unfinished" in his article "Image Resolution" in *Artforum* (March 2013, p. 137), Hamilton himself insisted that the work was finished, even in its tripartite configuration. Two days prior to his death, during a visit with Vicente Todolí to discuss the retrospective exhibition, he made it clear that he had found a solution to the work (email correspondance with Vicente Todolí, August 2013).
34. Honoré de Balzac, *The Unknown Masterpiece,* trans. Richard Howard (New York: The New York Review of Books, 2001), xxiv.

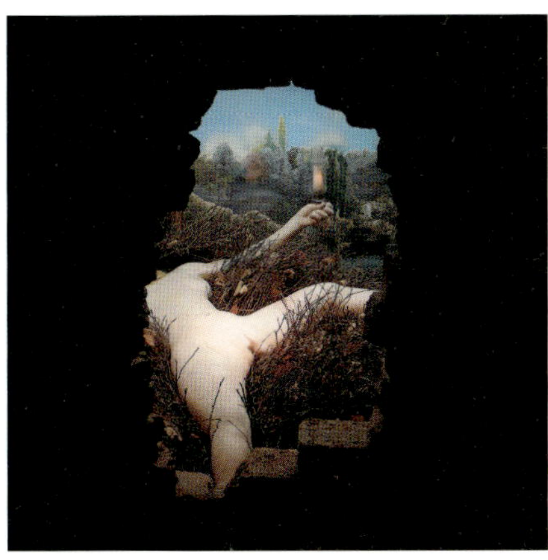

fig. 9
Marcel Duchamp. *Étant donnés: 1. La chute d'eau, 2. Le gaz d'éclairage,* 1946–66
Mixed media assemblage
Philadelphia Museum of Art

absence of Hamilton himself. Michael Bracewell stops short of describing the H-frame easel as metonymic for "Hamilton"—the signature with which Hamilton re-branded a number of consumer objects, from a Braun toaster to a Ricard ashtray—but he nonetheless describes the easel as deriving "from Hamilton's own studio."[35] Regardless of whether the easel can be interpreted as a spectre of the late artist, the space between the backgrounded figures is indeed a potent one. Bracewell sees the empty easel positioned there as "slightly threatening … and sinister, as the empty cross of its frame appears to confront the viewer."[36] More telling still is the fact that the easel is the sole compositional element that Hamilton did not borrow from history; it comes not just from recent times but from Hamilton's immediate surroundings—it is emphatically his.[37] Indeed, a portrait of Hamilton from 1978, in which his limbs are entwined with those of his easel, seems almost to presage its reappearance in *Untitled*. The photograph embedded in the third volume of *Polaroid Portraits* was taken by the Swedish artist Carl Fredrik Reuterswärd, and shows Hamilton standing behind his H-frame easel, one arm slung around its central crux while his chin virtually rests on a horizontal support. As though contending for the role of subject, they seem almost yoked together. In *Untitled*, the central shaft of the easel strongly bisects the composition while simultaneously receding into the background, seeming to bleed into the contours of the two figures who flank it.

Another striking aspect of the *Balzac* work is that it provides the first meaningful representation, in Hamilton's oeuvre, of a studio. Though there had been instances of an overt consciousness of artistic activity (as in *Instant painting,* 1980), the space of the studio had never before been so explicitly articulated. Intriguingly, the only two earlier incidences in which an artist appears in a studio-like room both portray Picasso: *Picasso's meninas* (1973), in which Hamilton's portrait of Picasso replaces Velázquez at the easel in his painting *Las meninas* (1656); and *Picasso au château* (1978–79), an acrylic painting with a collage of Picasso seated in an ornate hall in which several of his paintings are also displayed, two of which are propped on an easel. Hamilton first saw *Guernica* (1937) in London in 1938 and described himself as being "awestruck" by Picasso's large wartime canvases, exhibited at the Victoria and Albert Museum in 1945. Picasso—considered a heretic by Hamilton's professors at the Royal Academy—remained, even as Hamilton surpassed his influences, an immovable figure and point of reference.

And yet even in this final work Hamilton could not relinquish his debt to the other great iconoclast of the twentieth century, Duchamp—specifically to his *Bride Stripped Bare…* The nude in the foreground of Hamilton's image is, figuratively, stripped by the trio of "bachelors" who regard her. That Hamilton chose to include Courbet in this grouping is a possible allusion to his *L'Origine du monde* (1866), a still-shocking painting widely believed to have influenced the posture and positioning of the spread-legged mannequin of Duchamp's *Étant donnés: 1. La chute d'eau, 2. Le gaz d'éclairage (Given: 1. The Waterfall, 2. The Illuminating Gas)* (1946–66) [fig. 9], a tableau-like scene permanently installed behind a door at the

35. Bracewell, *Richard Hamilton: The Late Works*, 34.
36. Ibid., 31.
37. This proposition disregards the small practical edits Hamilton made to his borrowed imagery, for example Titian's and Courbet's hands, which were photographed from a model in Hamilton's studio and Photoshopped onto the appropriate figures.

Philadelphia Museum of Art. *Étant donnés* was Duchamp's final work, constructed in secret over the course of two decades; even Hamilton, close as he was to Duchamp, did not know of or see the work until 1969, a year after Duchamp's death.

Hamilton said of his *Balzac* project: "This is my *Étant donnés.*"[38] This assertion suggests an acute awareness of the work's position in his oeuvre—in line with the self-conscious decision to call his late work "late"—but also of the common thematic strands. For example, like *Étant donnés,* the *Balzac* works are concerned with the historicization of the male gaze, through an implicit catalogue of the mode of representing (or rendering) a female nude: from the High Renaissance to the dawn of photography (the female model here is from Louis-Camille d'Olivier's 1855 photo *Nu allongé etude no. 531*) to the early twenty-first century, when Hamilton has reanimated her through Bézier curves—parametric guides used in computer graphics to render smooth and infinitely scalable forms.

The question of "resolution" thus remained central to Hamilton's late work, as the creative process necessitated the constant translation of visual information: from painted stroke to parametric curve, from photographic emulsion to pixels (in turn, subject to the disfiguration of dots per inch). In achieving seamlessness at turns, the appearance of the digital works plays on the tension of disguising their origins. Hamilton's unflagging commitment to a computer to produce these pieces was in itself an indicator of these qualities, in that few (if any) artists of his stature were then using computers in such a way. But Hamilton never sought comfortable transactions, nor did he aim to fit snugly in amongst his peers—he was less inclined than ever to do so during the final twenty-five years of his career. Hamilton's late works continually interrogate the limits of resolution and the complexity of digital space, as well as his career-long engagement with the influence of Duchamp. Moreover, they deliberately problematise the very meaning of "late."

38. Quoted in Christopher Riopelle, "An Irresistible Invitation: Richard Hamilton at the National Gallery," in *Richard Hamilton: The Late Works,* 16.

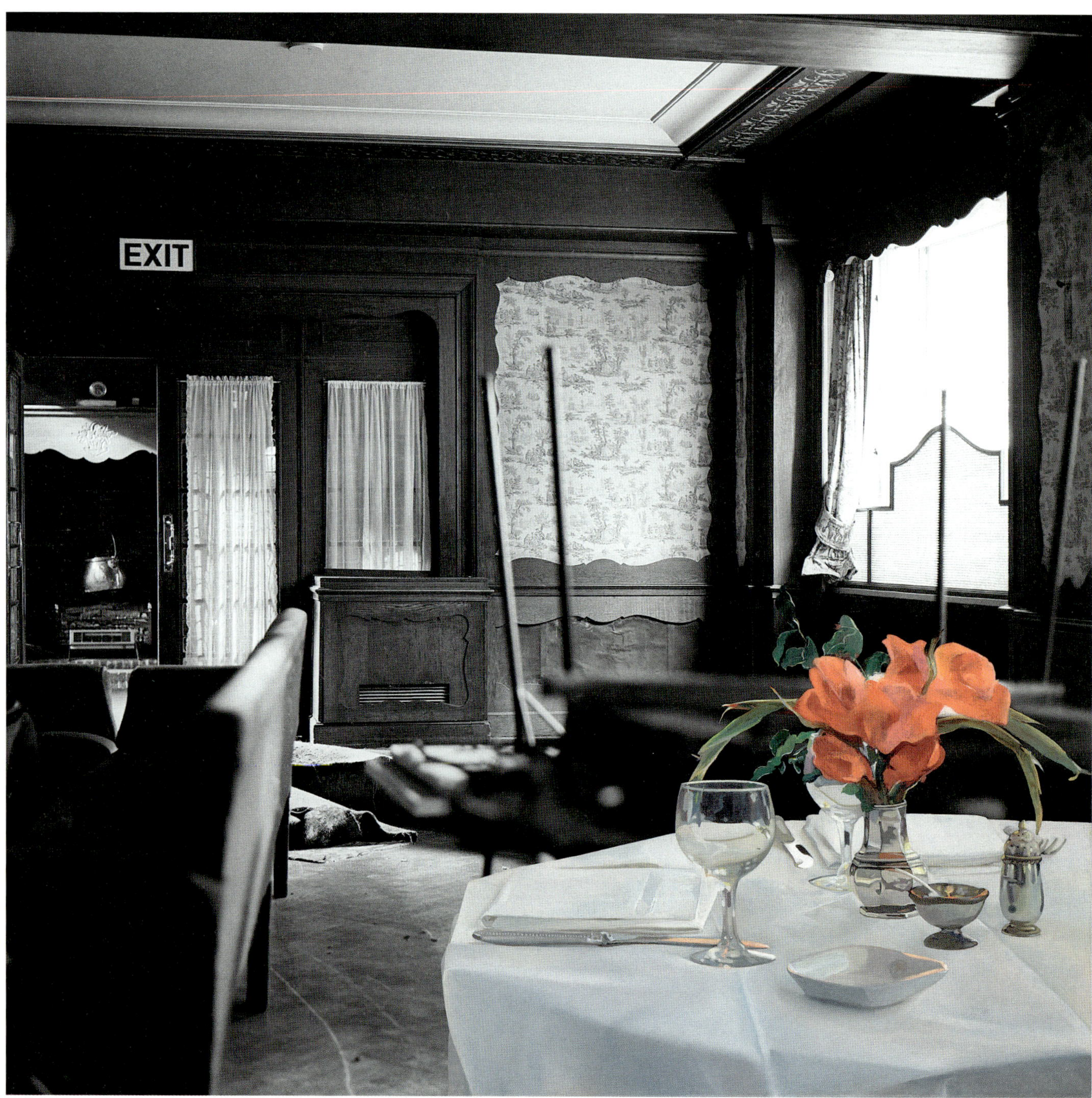

Langan's 1976

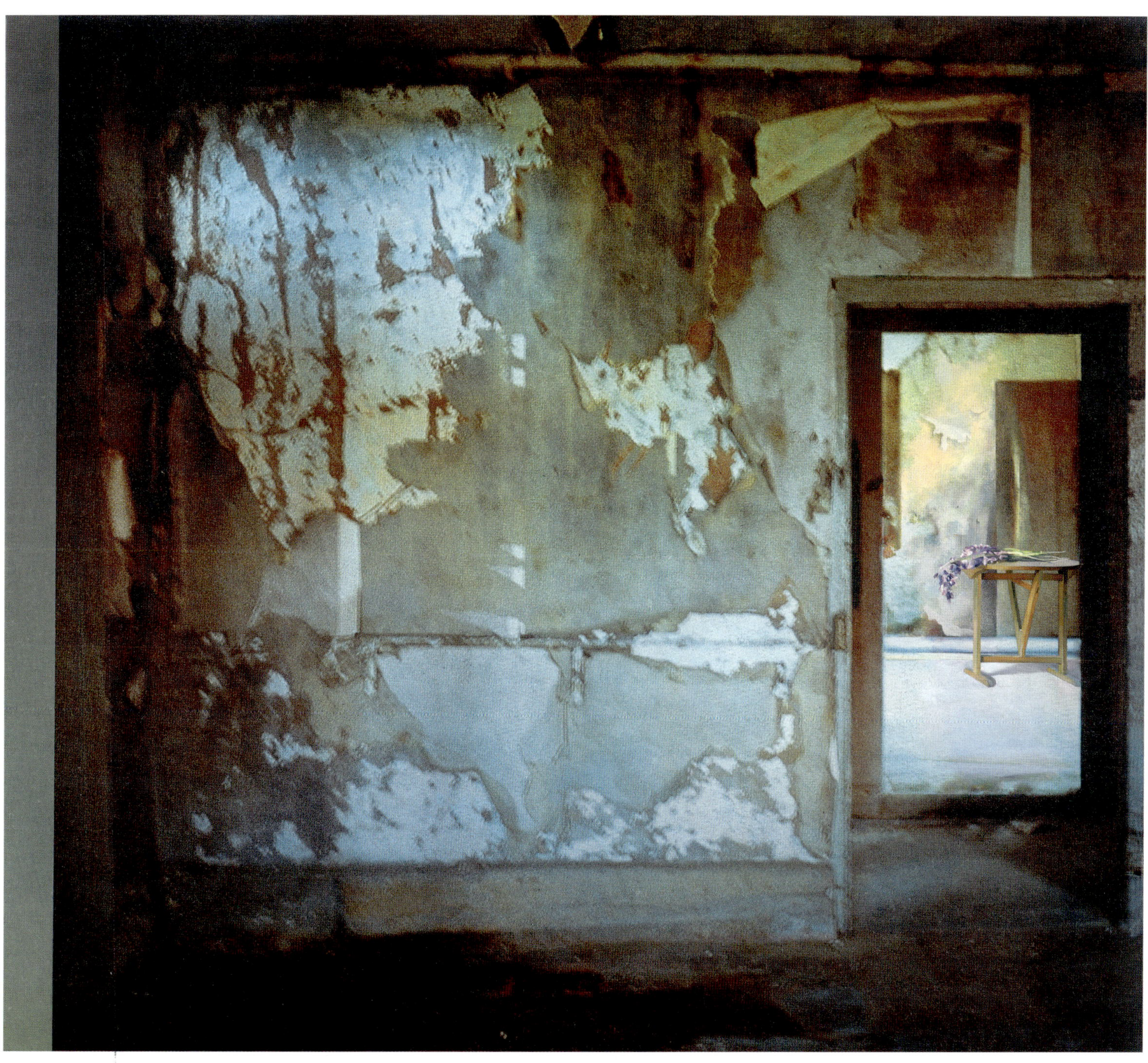

Northend II 1991

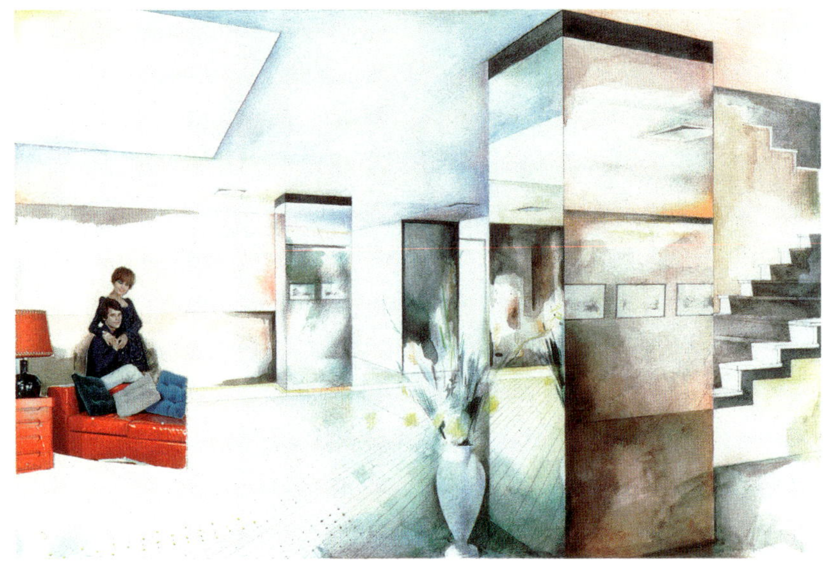

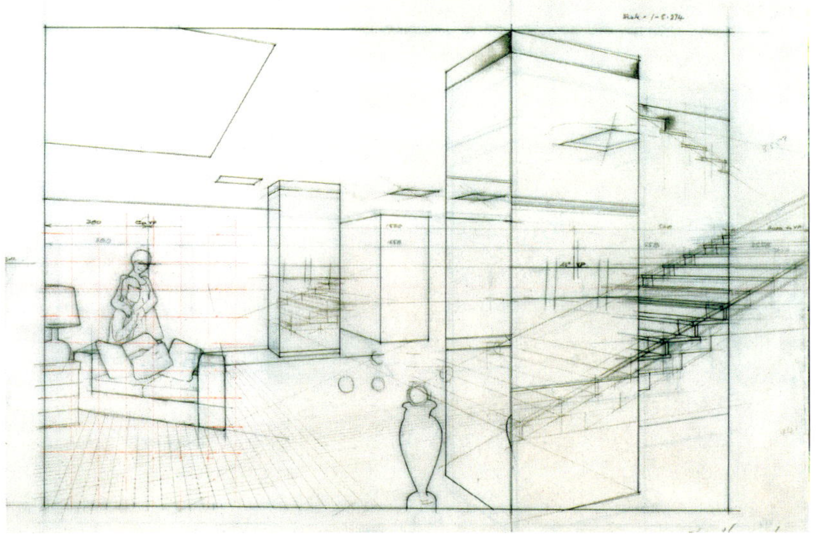

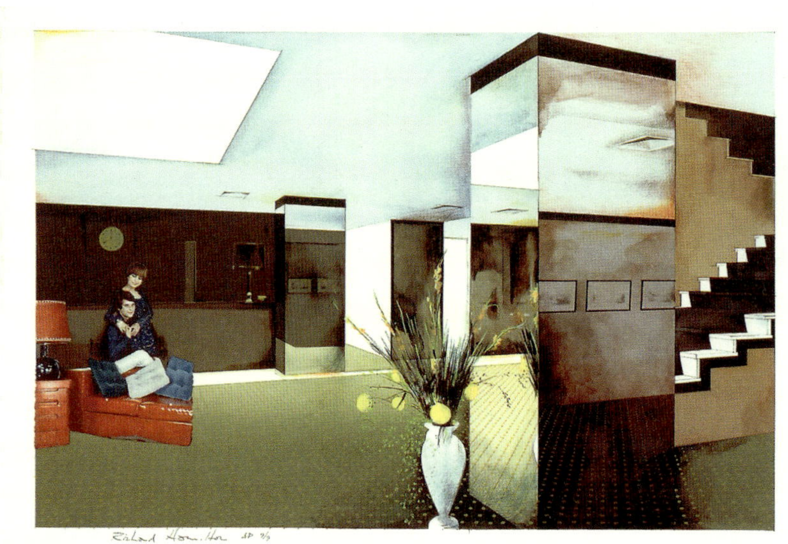

Europhotel-Berlin 1974–75

Lobby – working drawings 1984

Lobby 1984

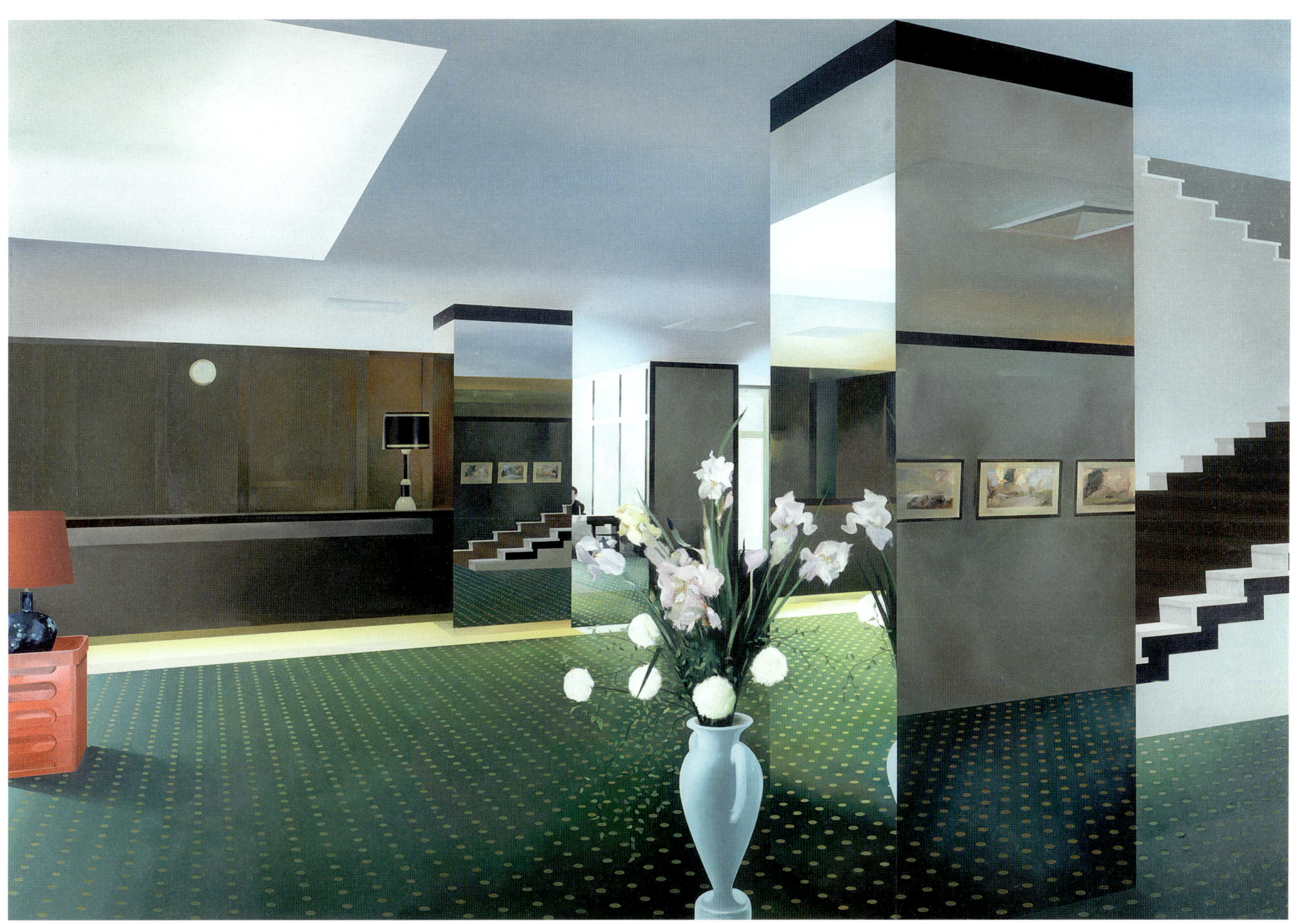

Lobby 1985–87

Lobby (installation) 1988

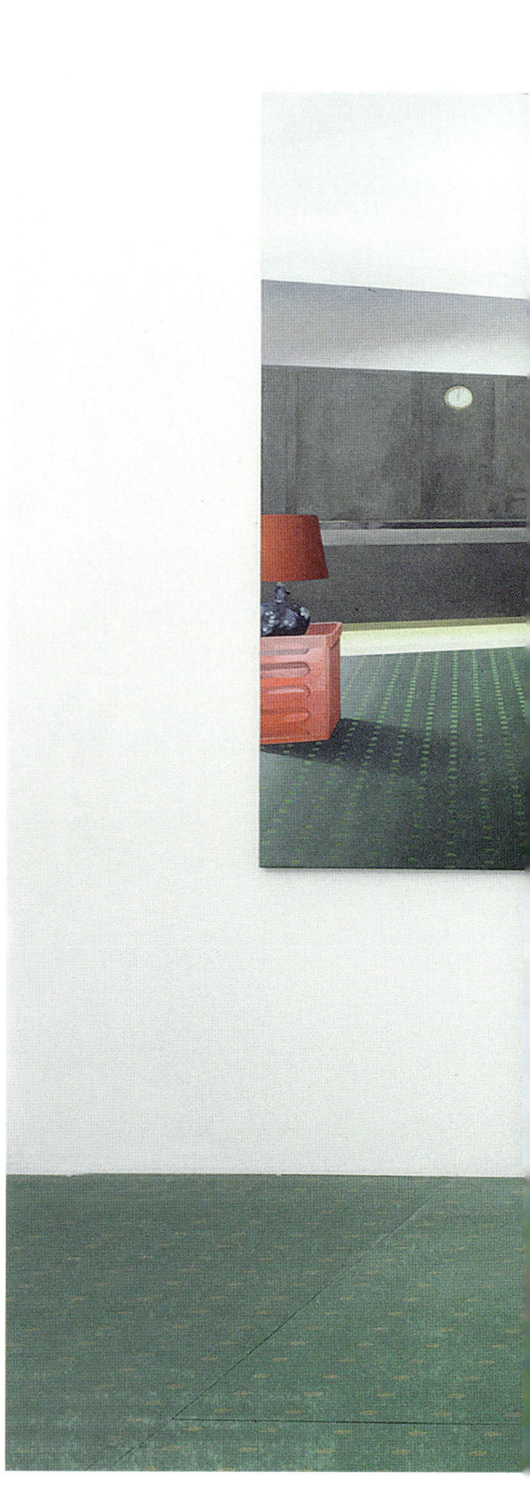

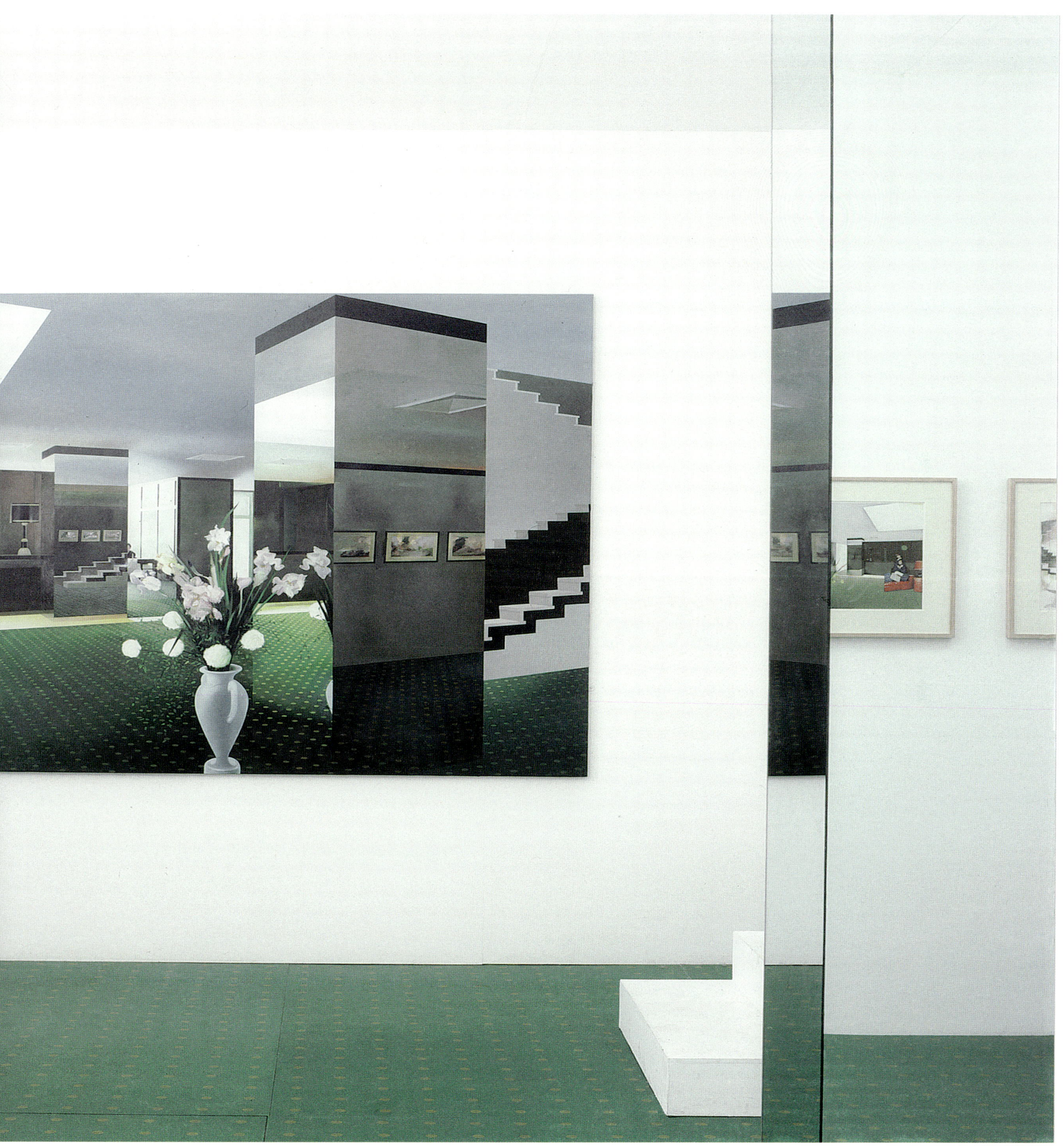

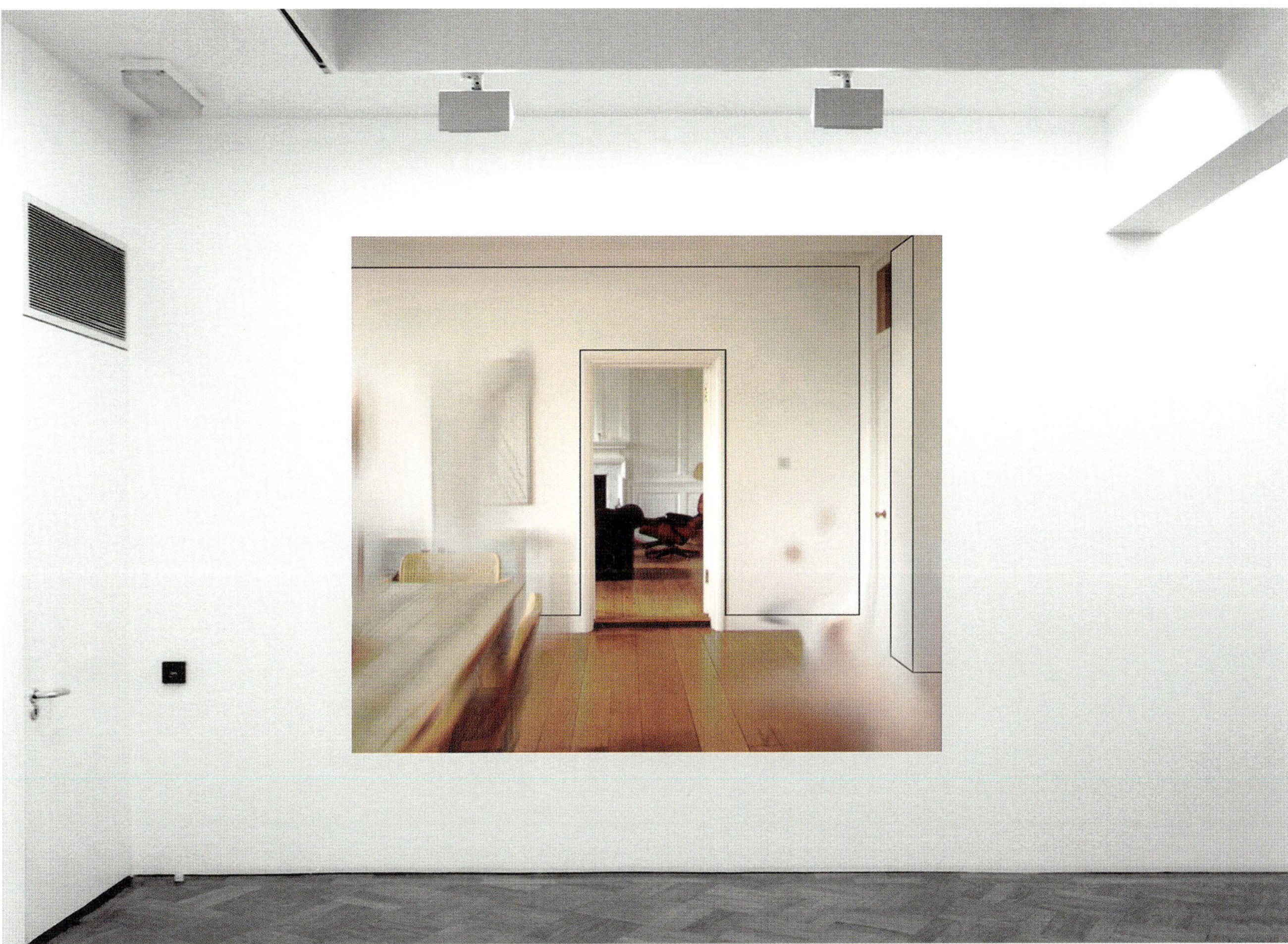

Dining room 1994–95

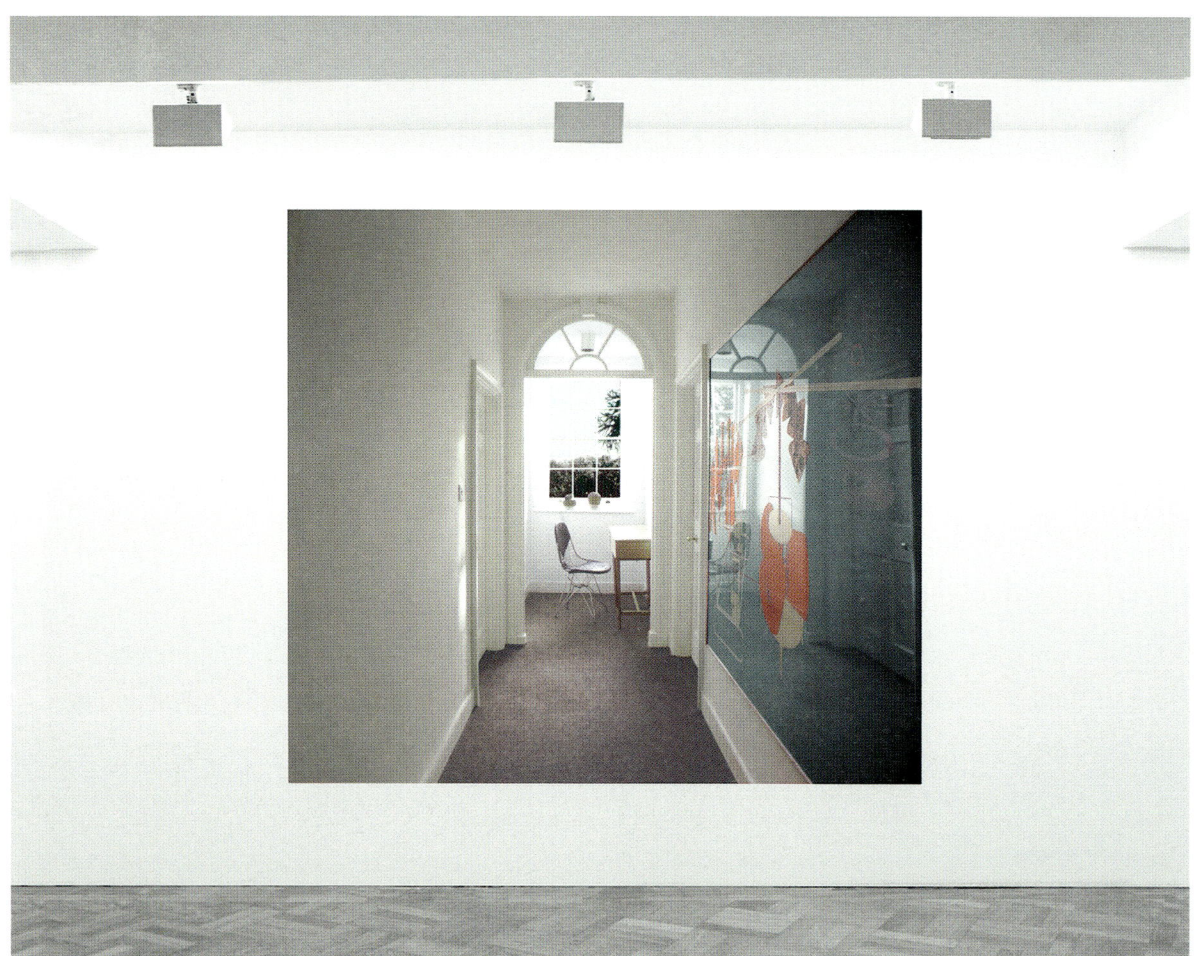

Passage 1994–95

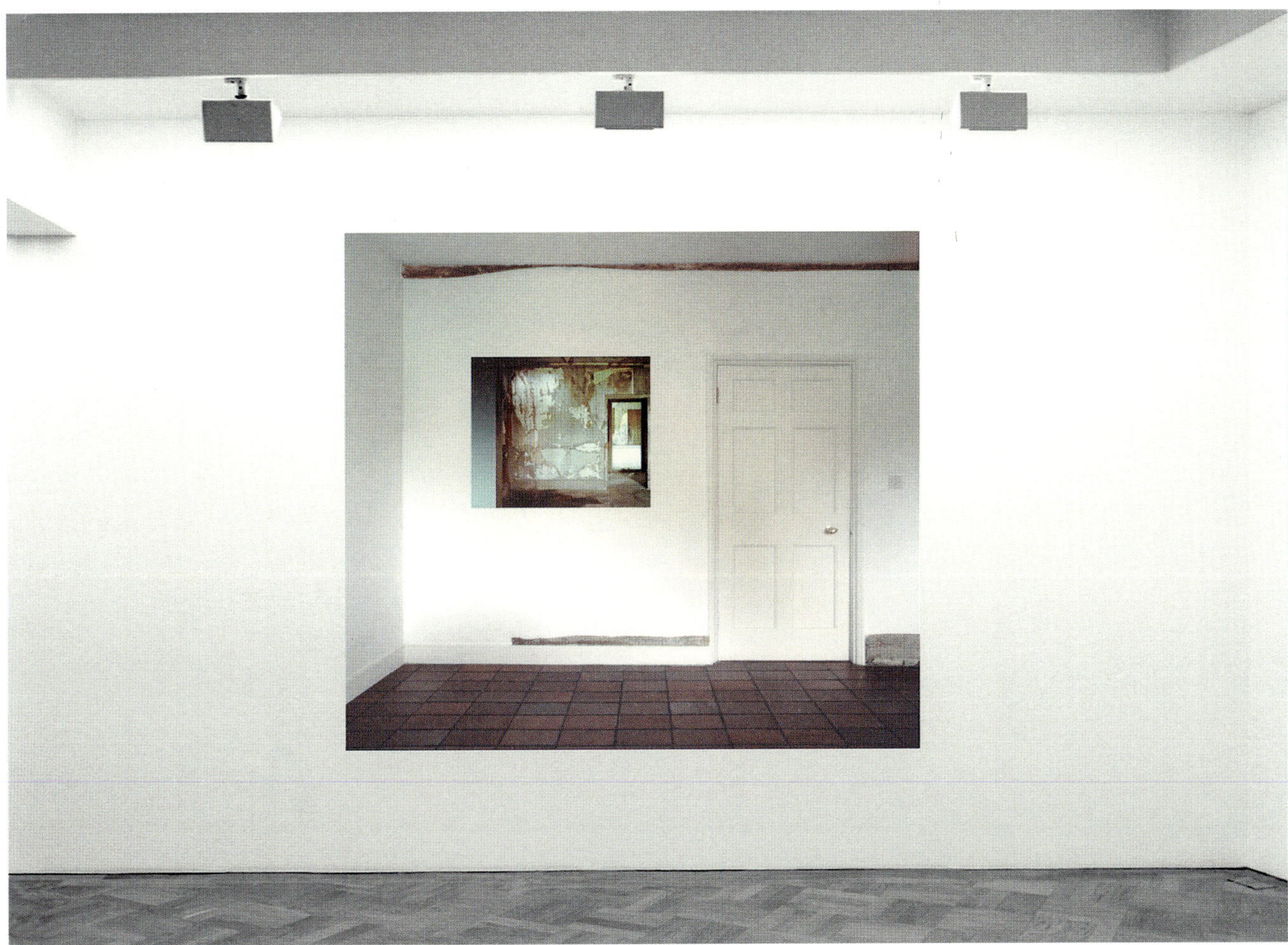

Kitchen 1994–95

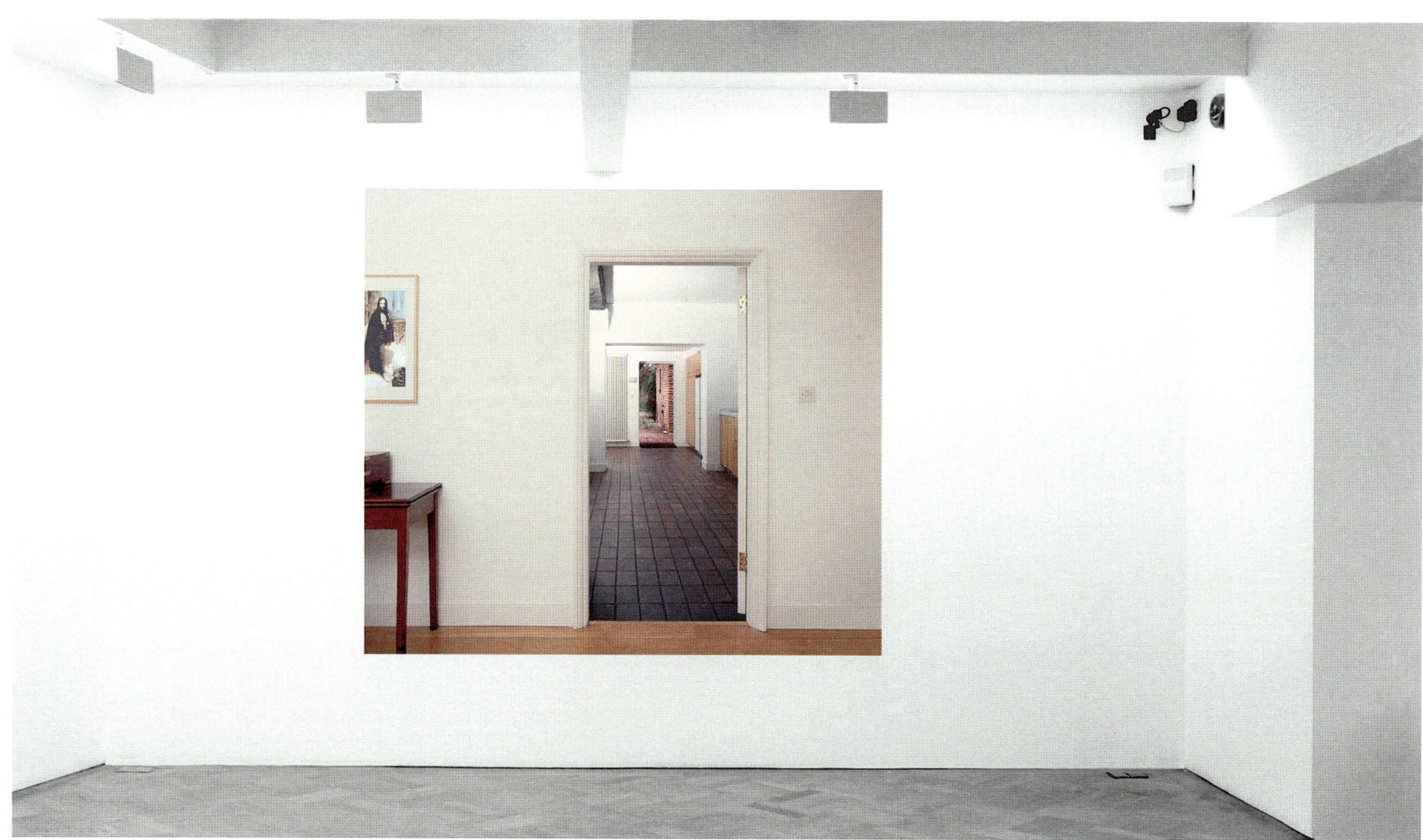

Dining room/kitchen 1994–95

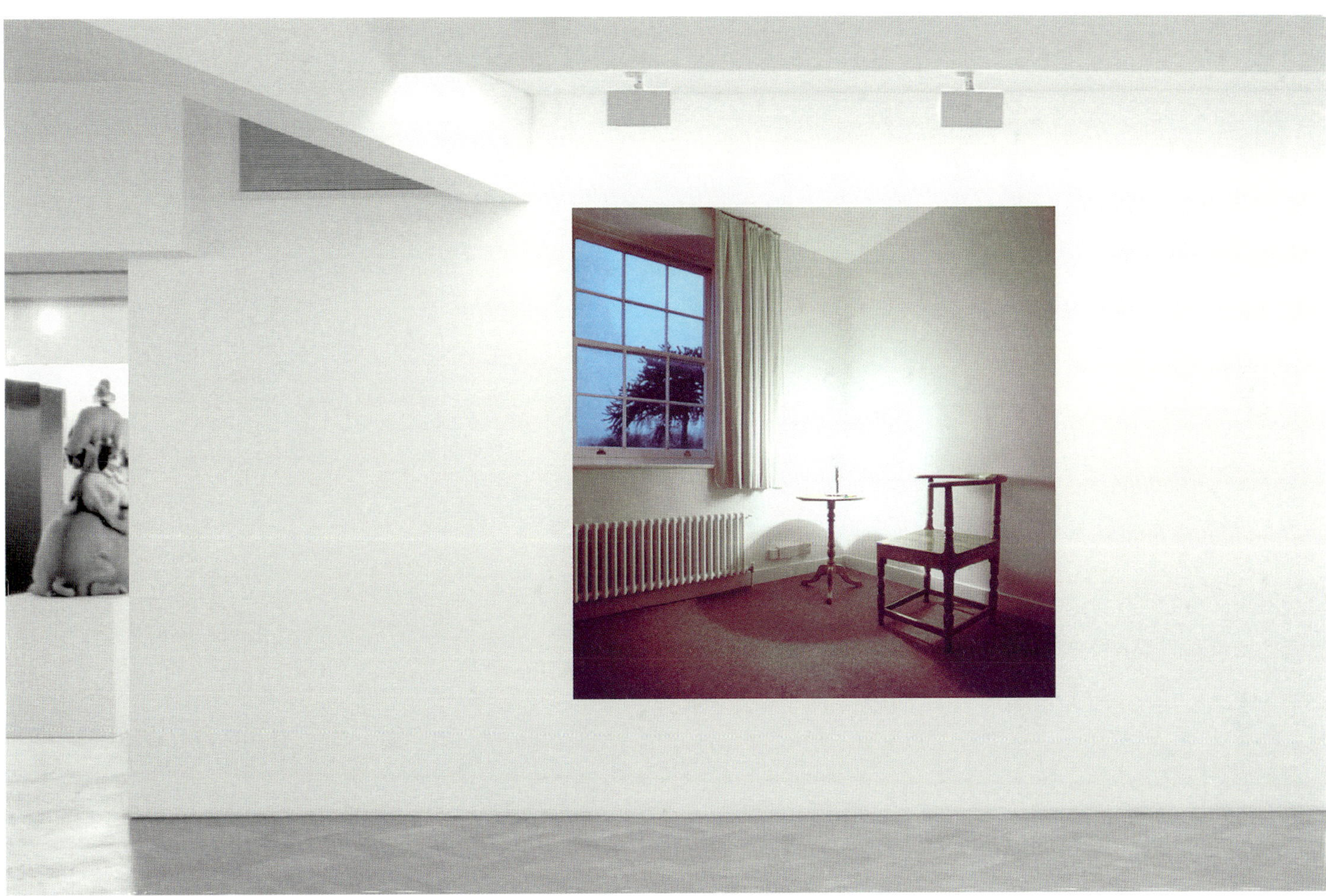

Bedroom 1994-95

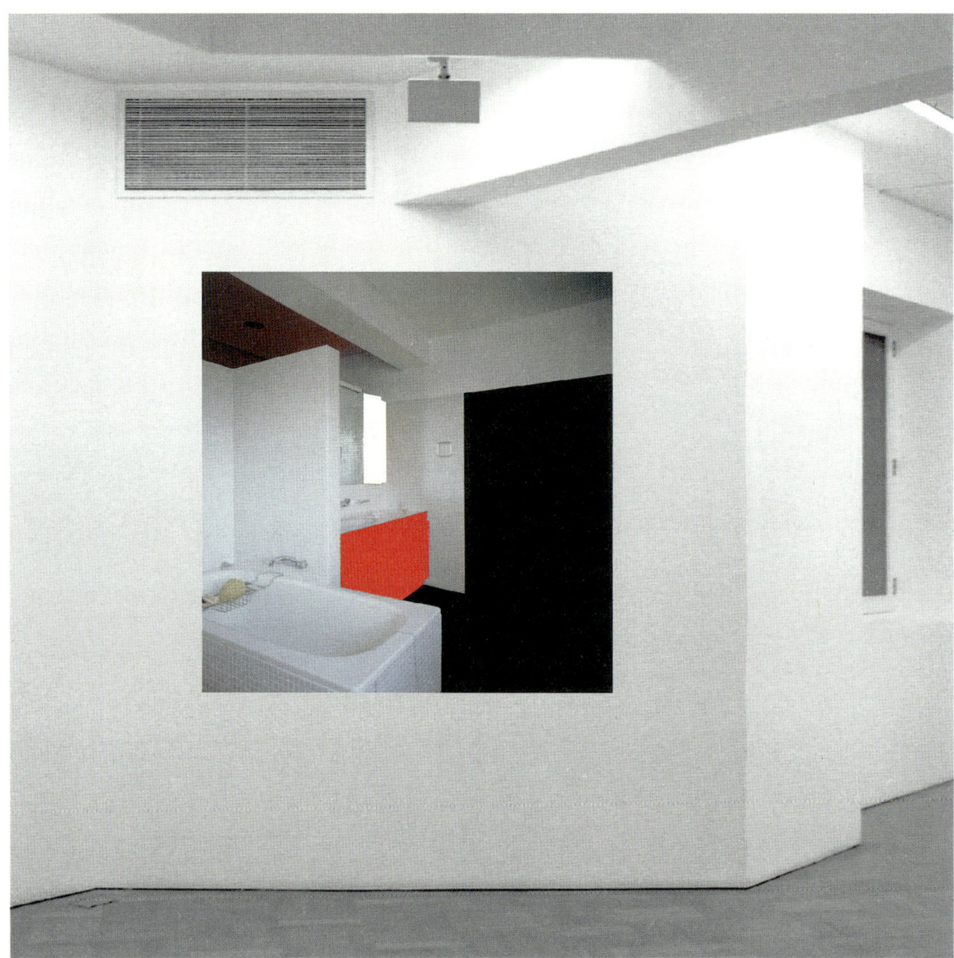

Bathroom 1994–95

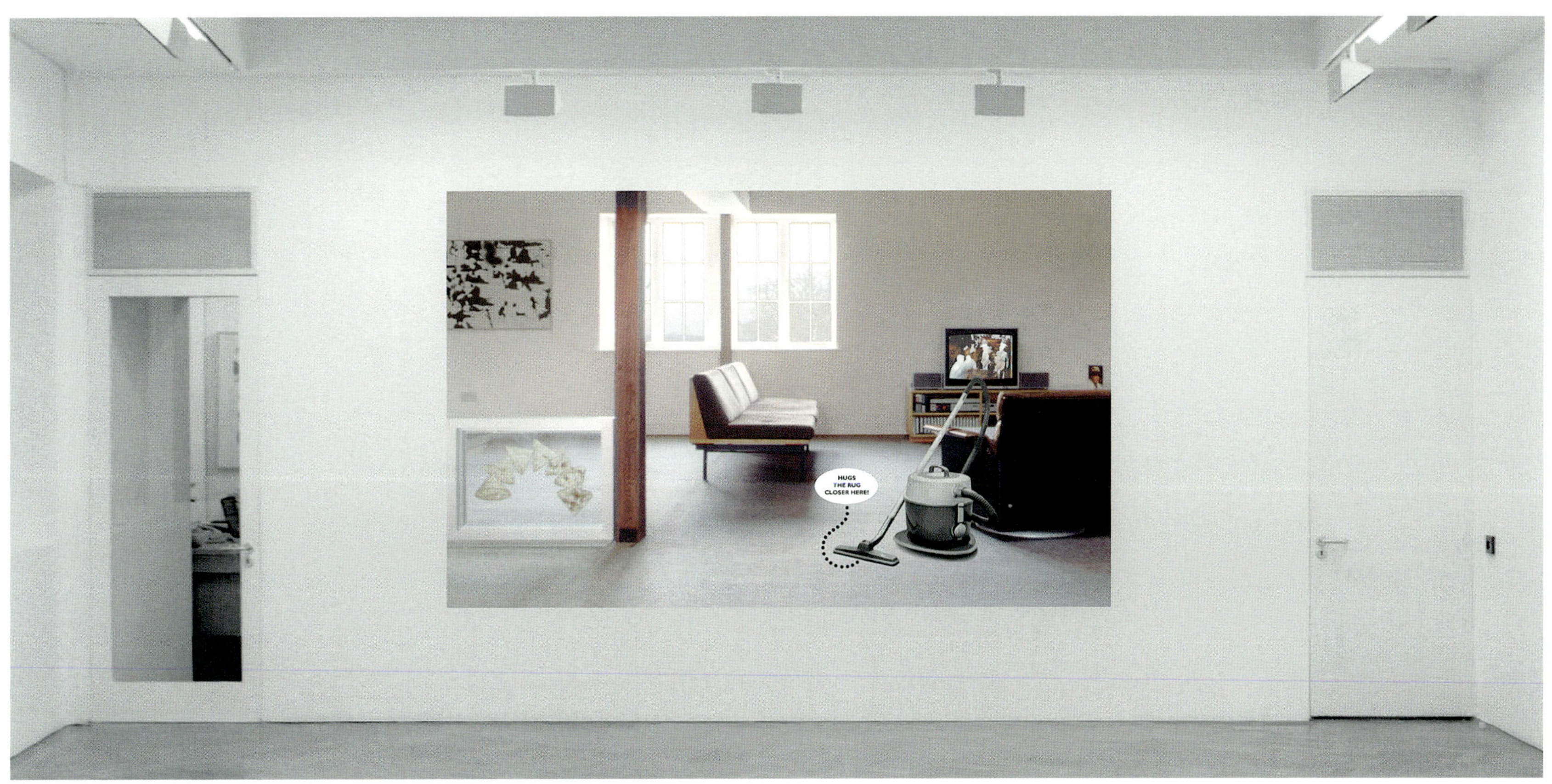

Attic 1995-96

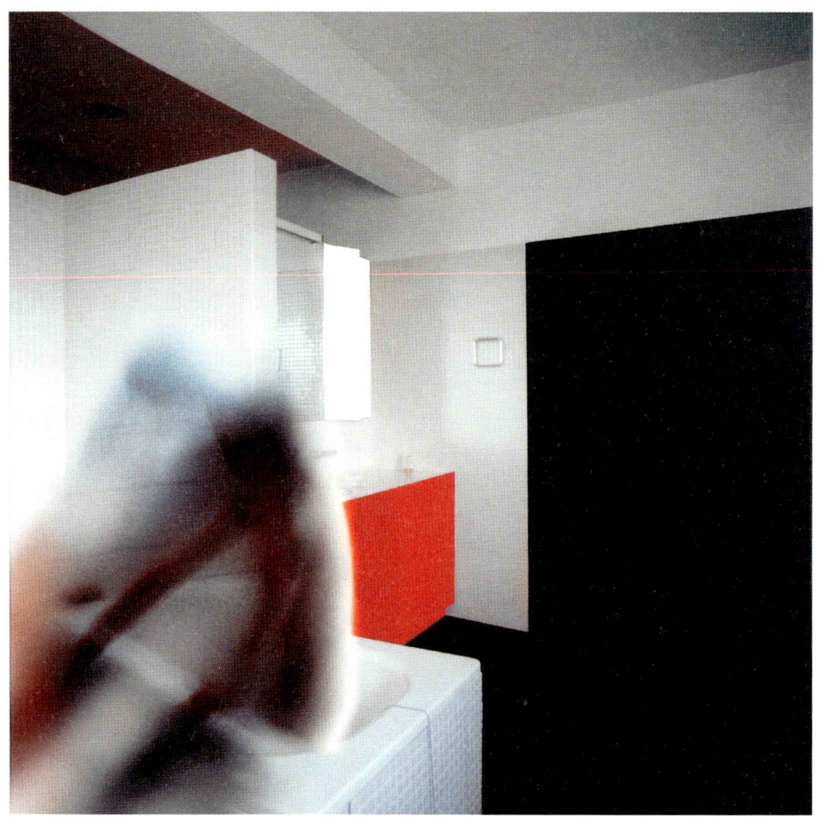

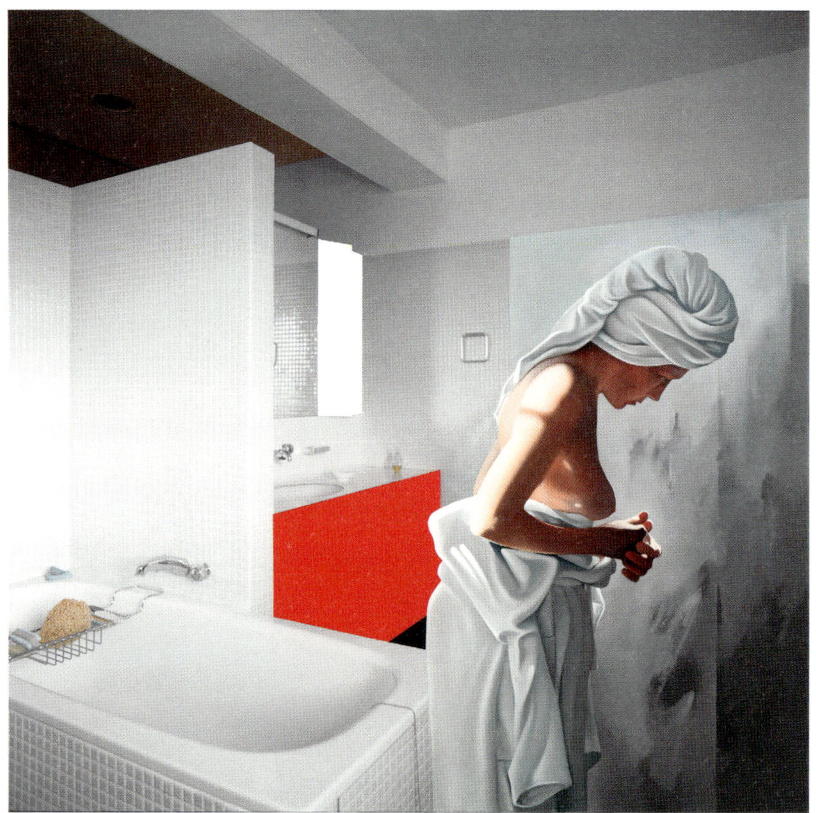

Bathroom fig. 1 II 1997–2004

Bathroom fig. 2 II 2005–6

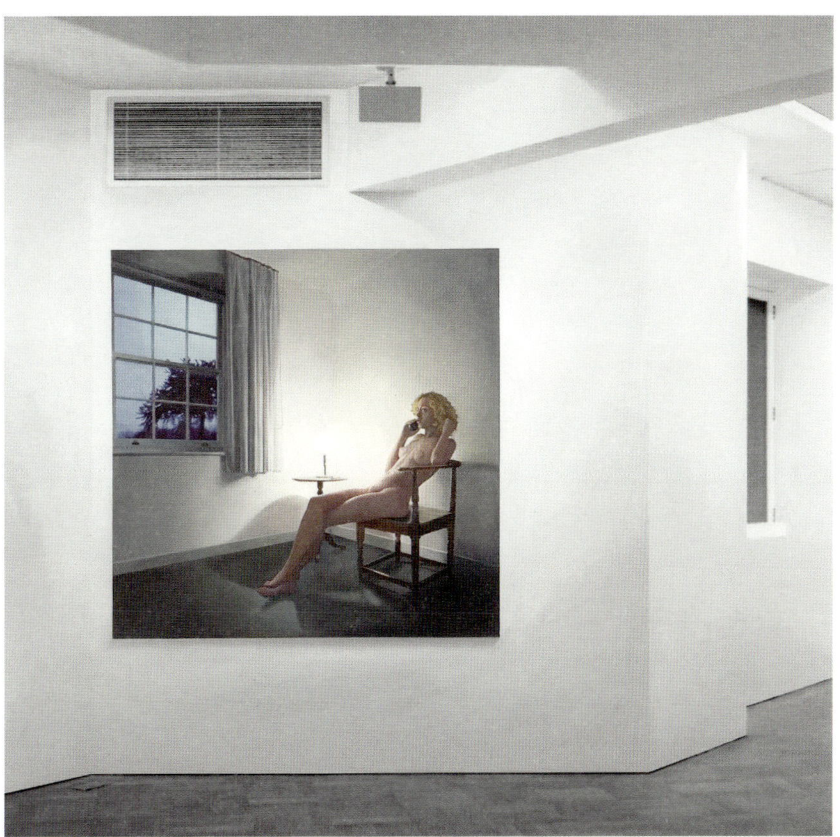

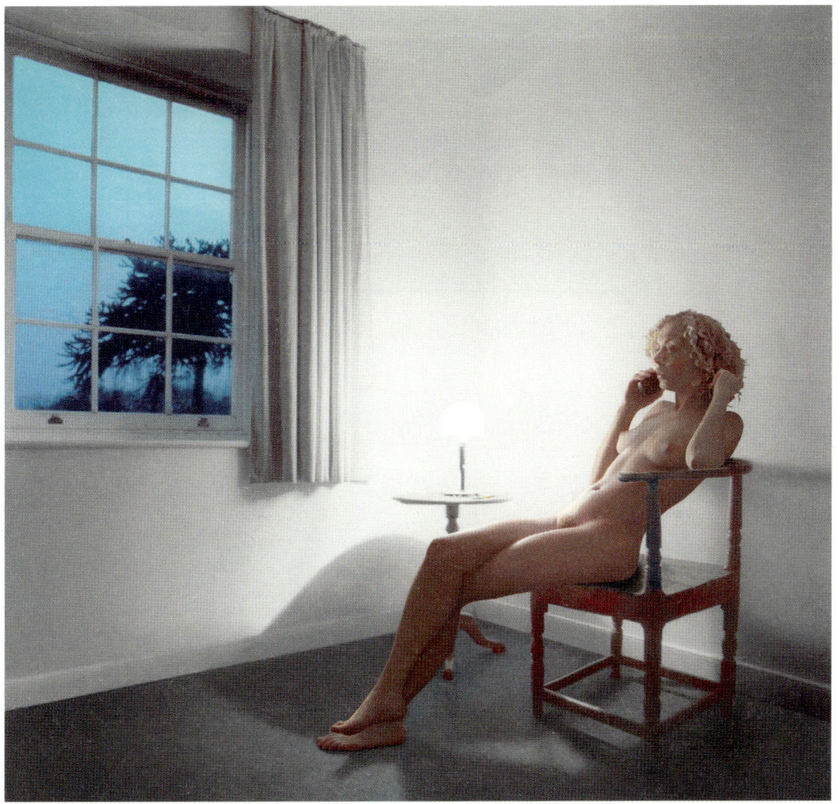

An annunciation (a) 1994–2004

An annunciation (b) 2005–6

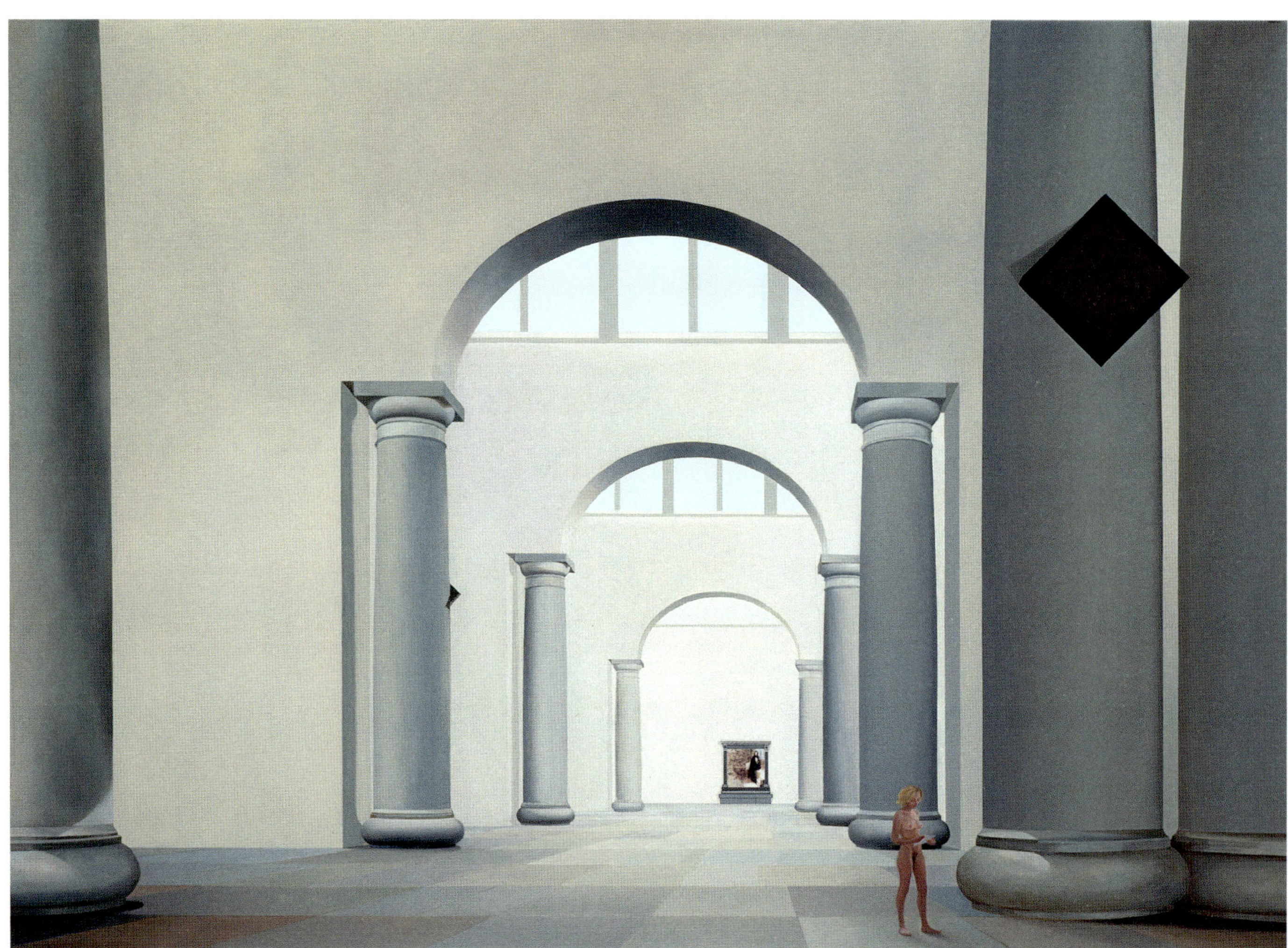

The Saensbury Wing 1999–2000

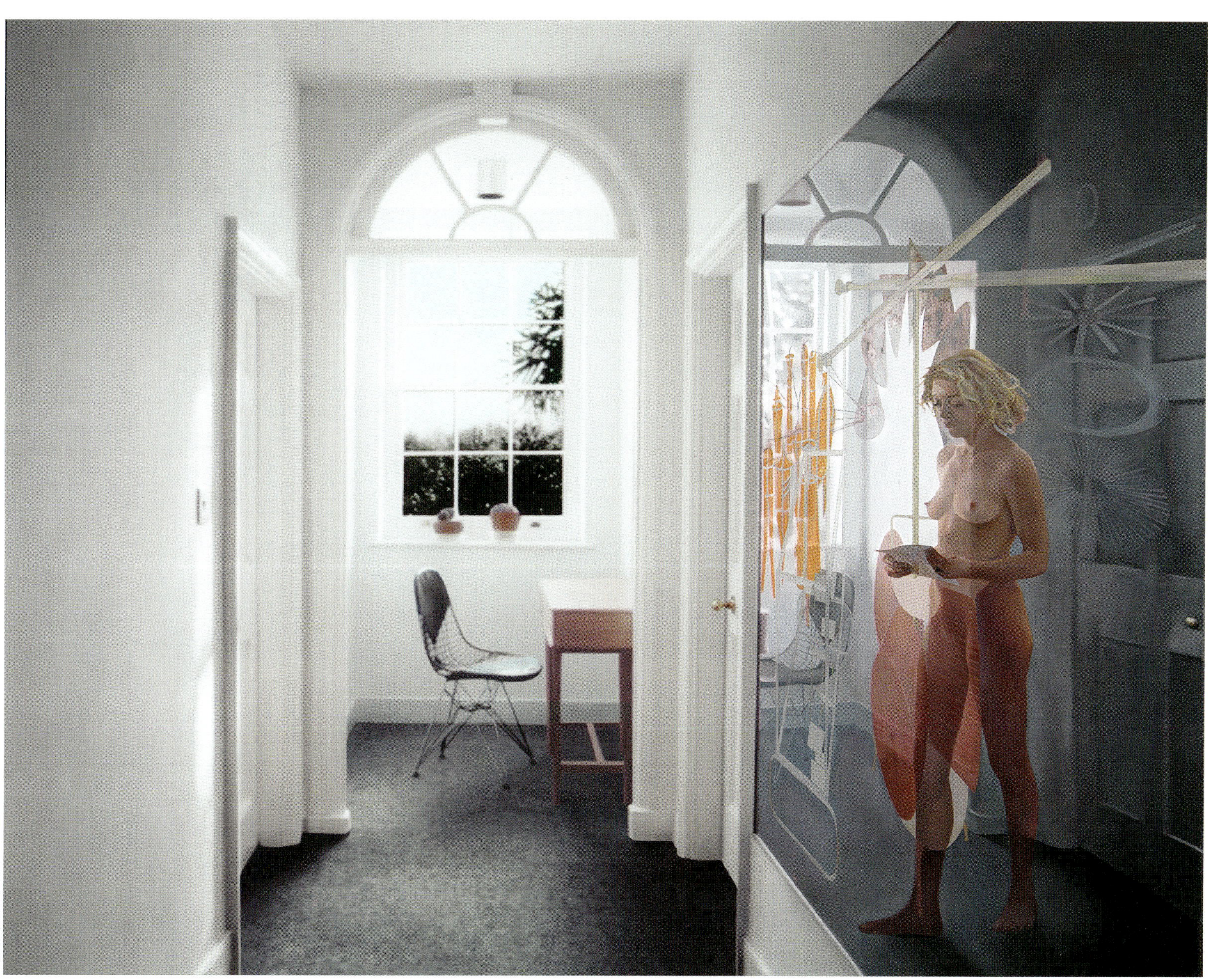

The passage of the bride 2004

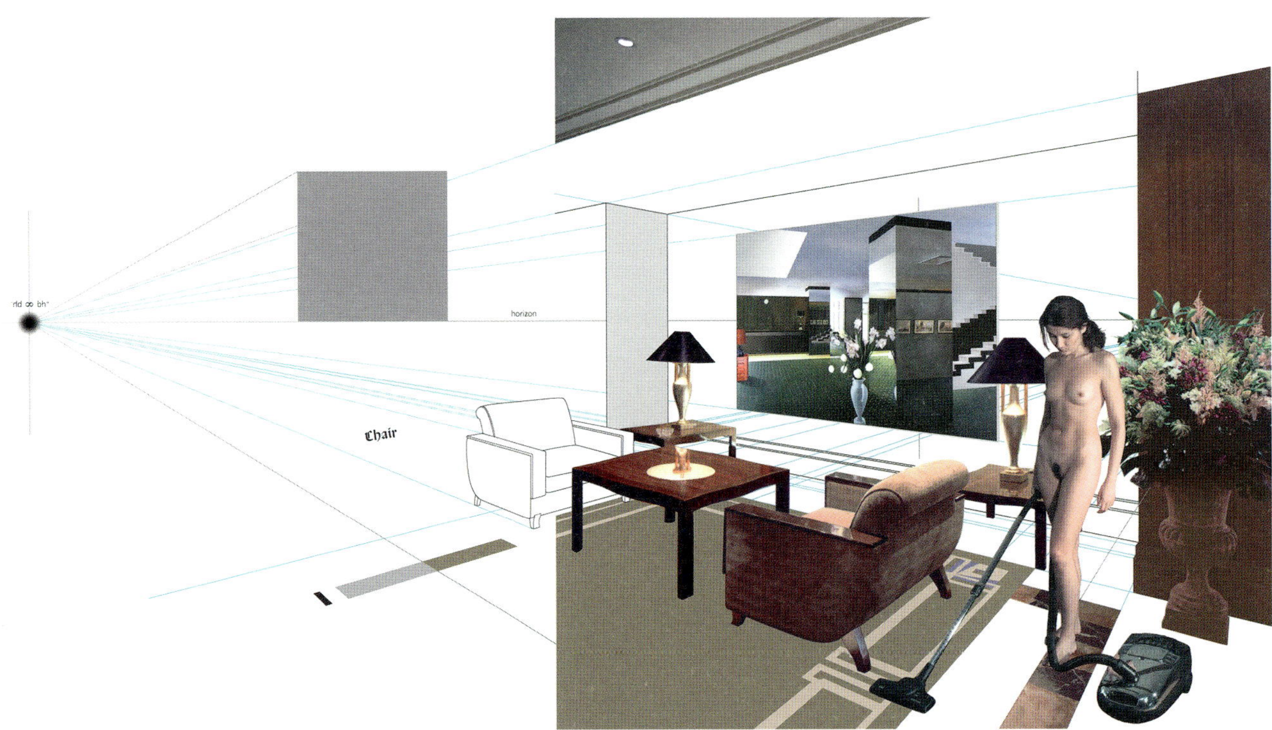

Chiara & chair 2004

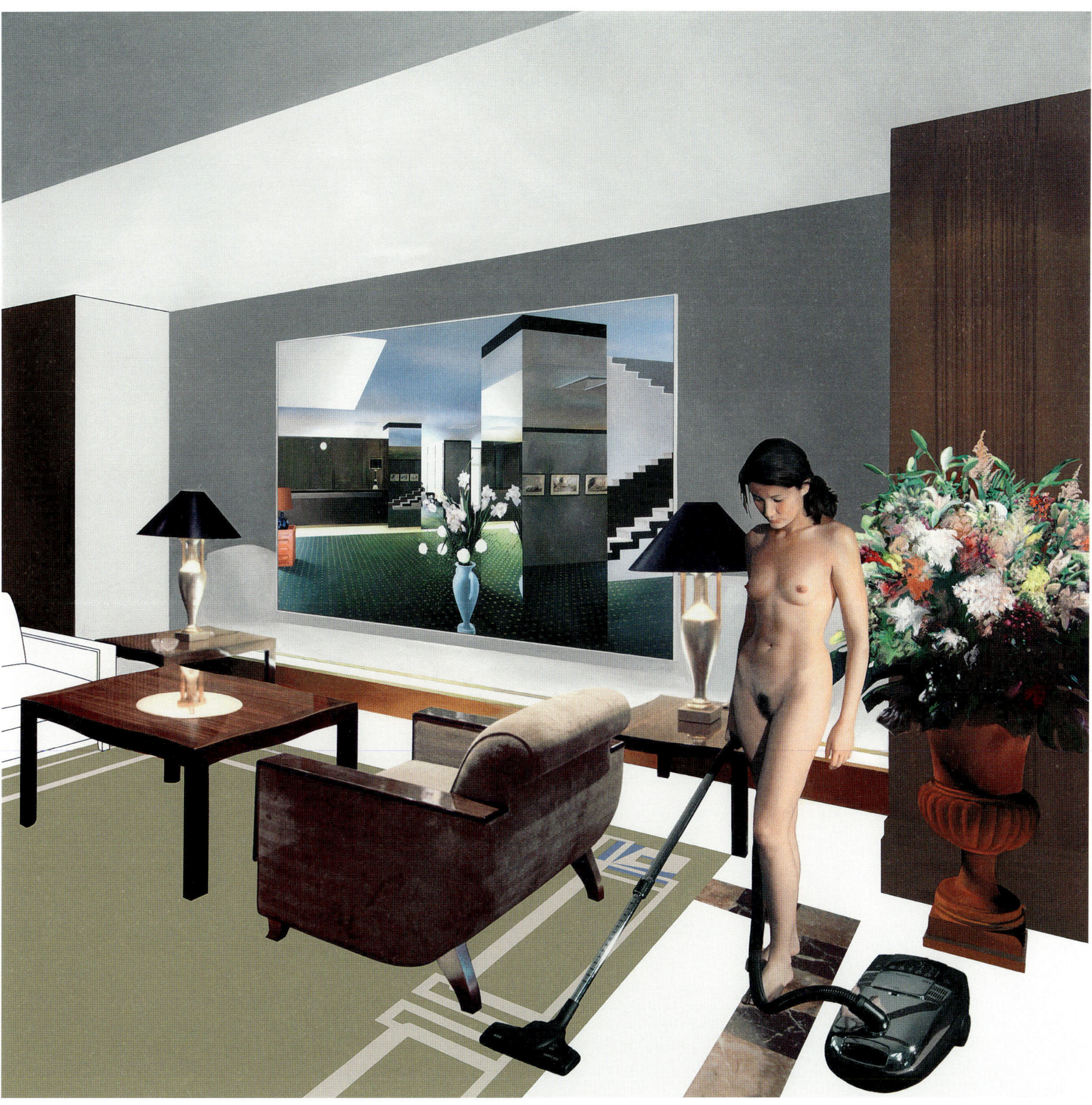

Hotel du Rhône 2005

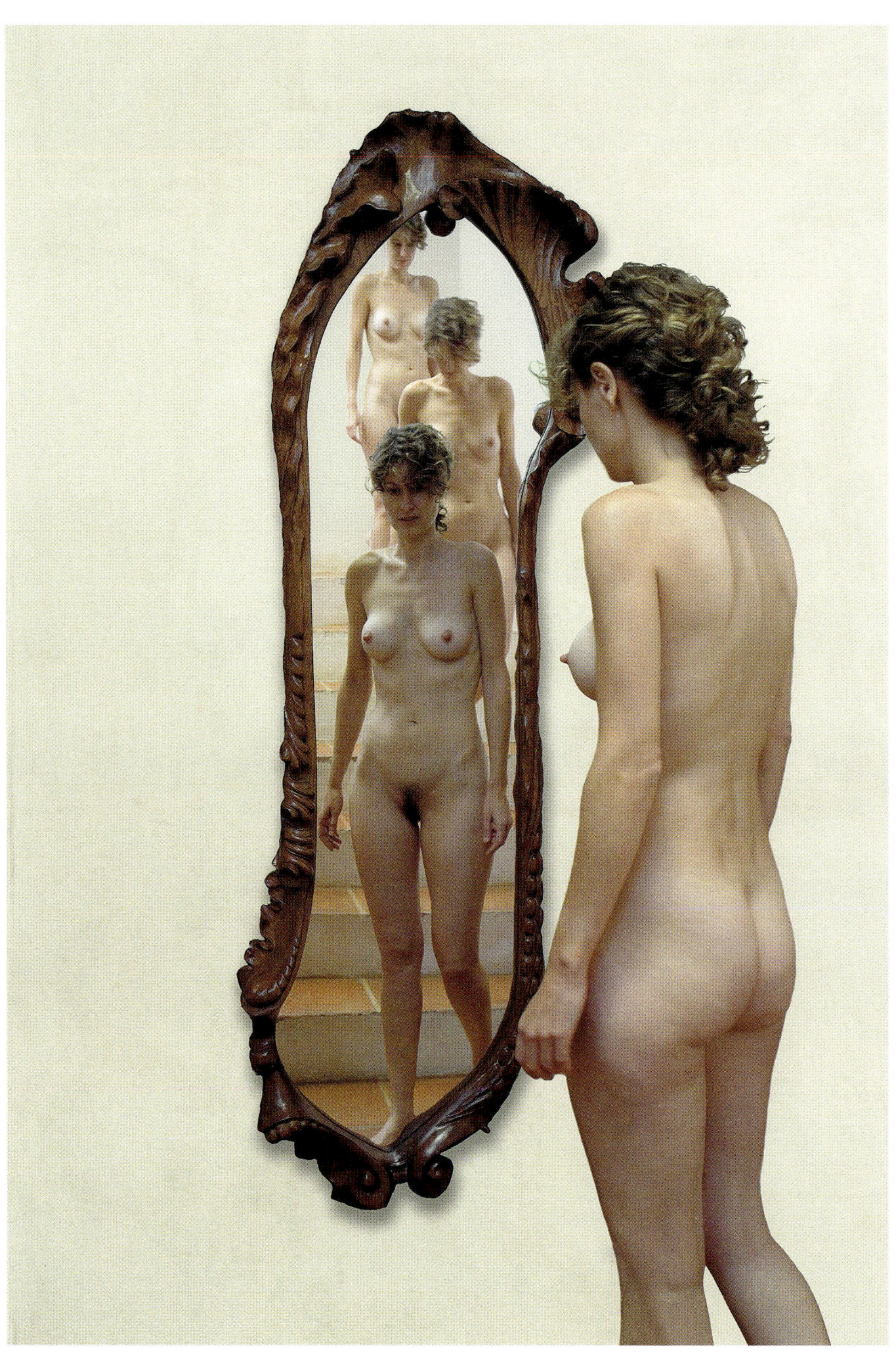

Descending nude 2006

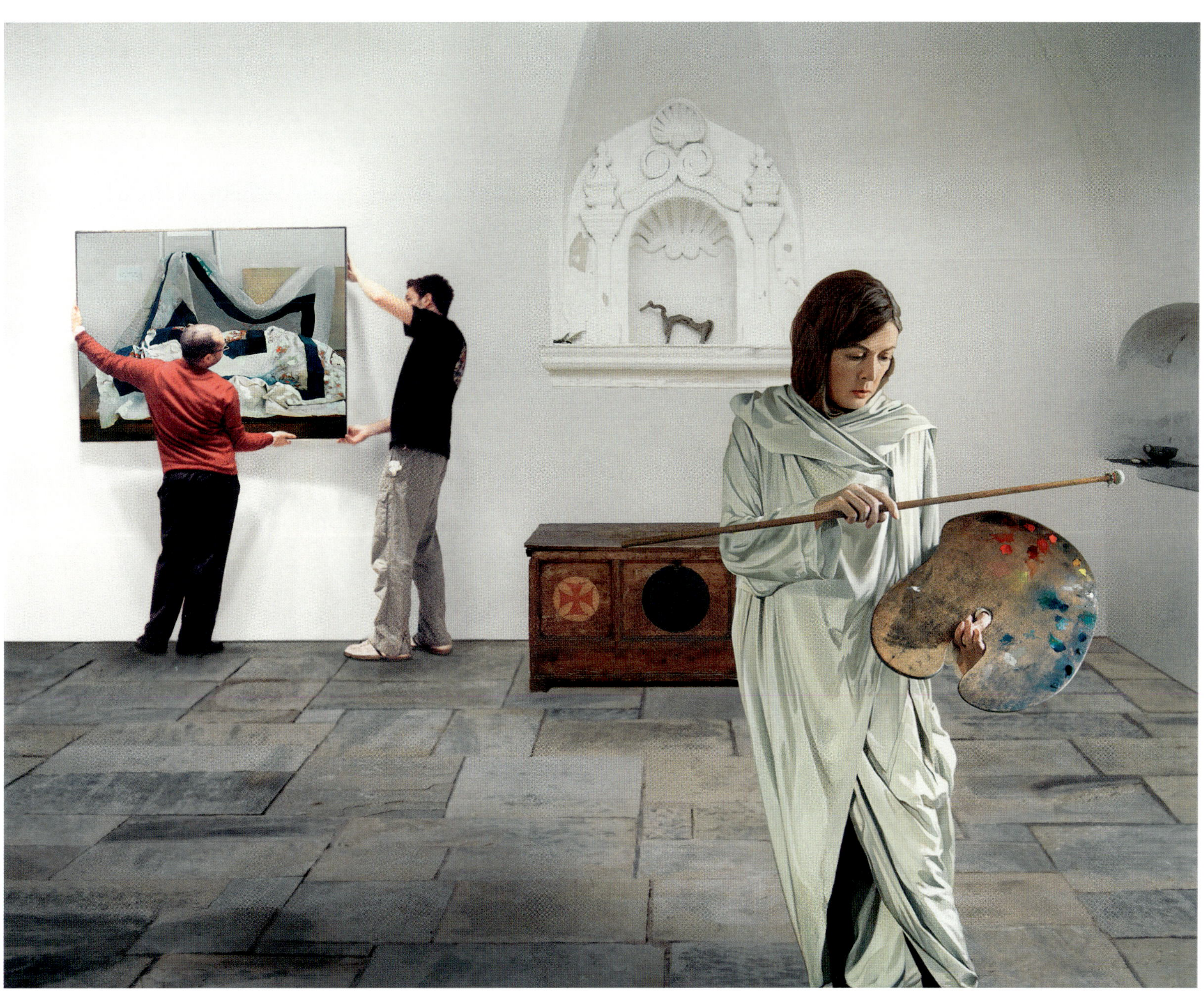

Portrait of a woman as an artist 2007

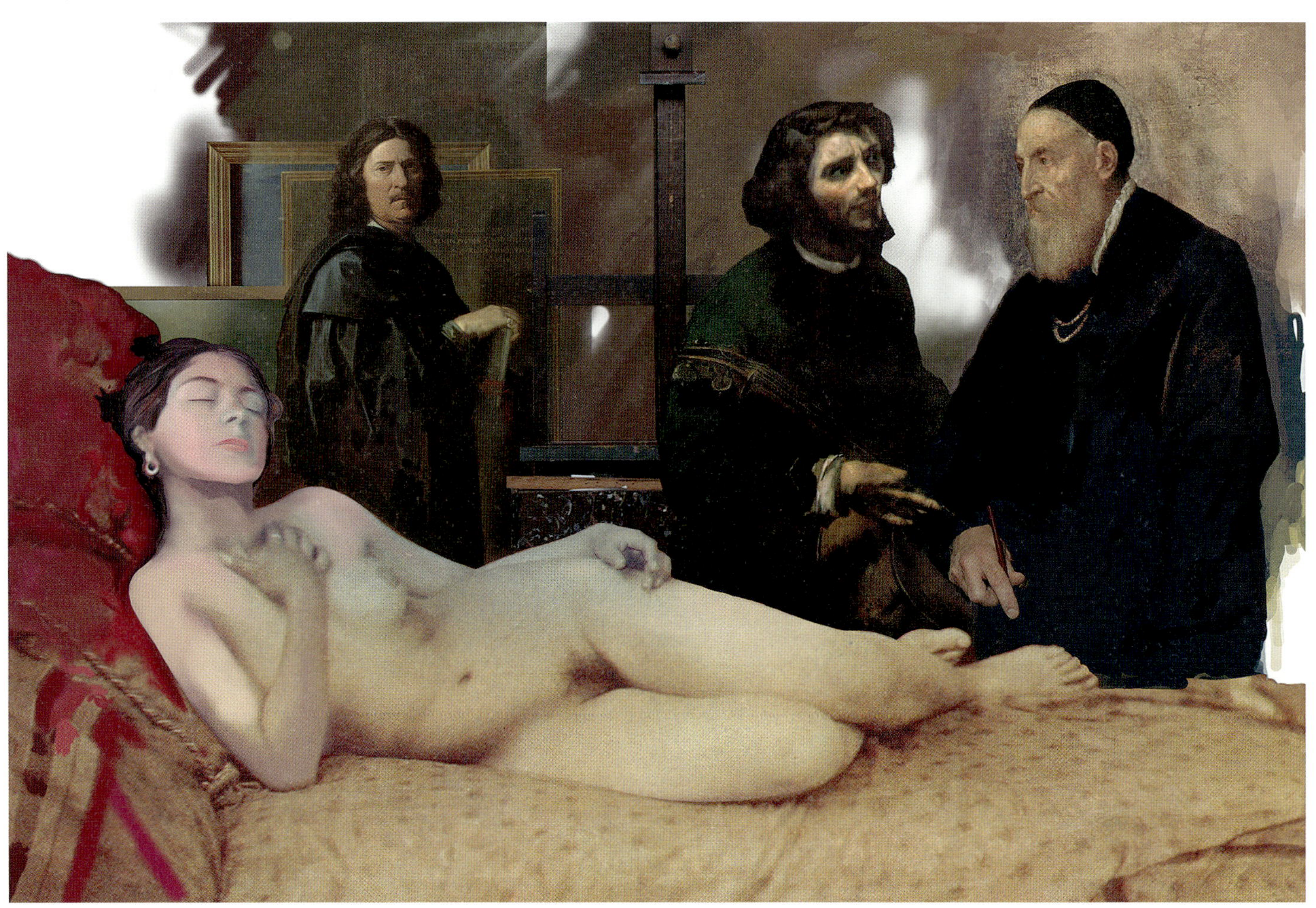

untitled 2011

Chronology

by Fanny Singer

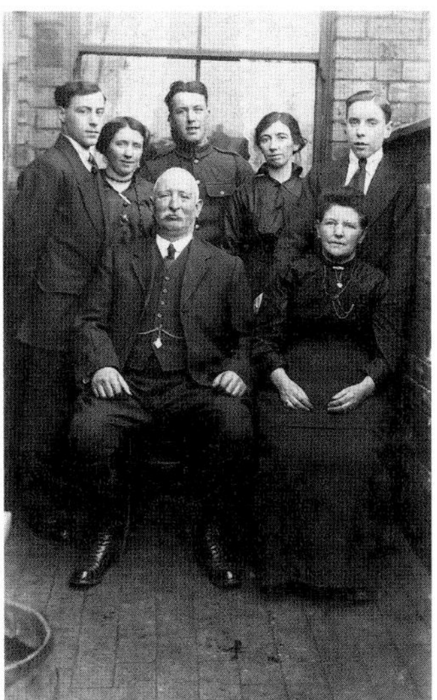

Hamilton's father Peter (back row, third from left) in military uniform, surrounded by family, c. 1913

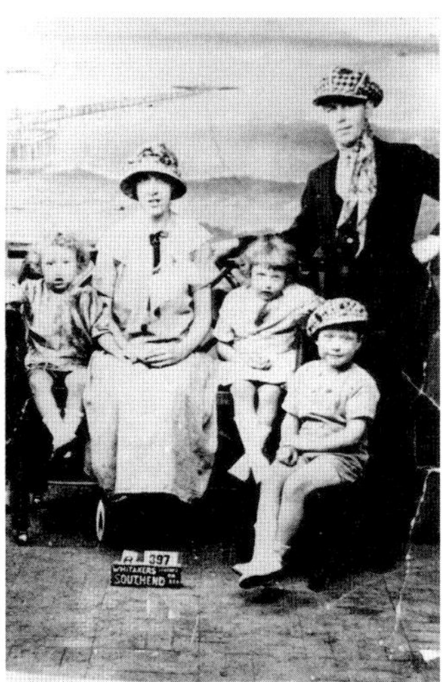

Hamilton family portrait (from left: Richard, Constance, Stella, Peter and Peter), c. 1925

1922–28

Born Richard William Hamilton on 24 February 1922 in a council flat on Bell Street, Marylebone, London. The third child of Constance Elizabeth (née Ellerbeck) and Albert William Hamilton (known as Peter), had two older siblings: a half brother, Peter, and a sister, Stella. His father, who had worked in the mines on leaving school, then in the army—stationed in Ireland and later, from 1914–18, in the trenches of the Somme—earned a living driving a delivery van for Maconochie Brothers. He went on to deliver cars for a company specialising in luxury sports brands such as Alvis and Jaguar, and he sometimes took Hamilton along for a ride.

1929

The family moved home regularly, from Marylebone to Camden Town, then to Belgravia and finally to Pimlico. Hamilton attended primary school nearby at St Peter's in Eaton Square.

1934

Won first prize in an exhibition of children's art held in the Victoria Tower Gardens adjacent to the Houses of Parliament. Though still enrolled in elementary school and unable to officially register, was given permission by his teacher, Mr Smith, to attend adult education evening classes in art at the London County Council in Southwark and Millbank (until 1936).

1935

Interviewed by Sir Walter Russell, Keeper of the Royal Academy Schools, at the recommendation of Sir Guy Dawber, former President of the Royal Institute of British Architects. Dawber had noticed Hamilton's draughtsmanship the previous year at the children's drawing competition. Russell advised him to apply for a studentship at the Royal Academy Schools when he turned 16.

1936

Finished elementary school and worked for a year as an office junior in the advertising department of an electrical engineering firm, Drake & Gorham. Continued evening classes in art both at Westminster School of Art, Vincent Square, and at St Martin's School of Art, where his teachers included Mark Gertler, best known for *Merry-Go-Round* (1916), Bernard Meninsky and William Roberts. The International Surrealist Exhibition opened in the New Burlington Galleries (June–July), including six works by Man Ray, whose Rayographic technique had impressed Hamilton. A sketchbook from this period comprises tourist views of London, including a picture of Covent Garden that shows a burgeoning interest in perspective.

1937

He passed on his way to work, the Reimann School and Studios of industrial and commercial art on Regency Street, still under construction. Reimann, a Bauhaus-influenced design school, was newly arrived from Berlin. Employed there in a junior role and permitted to draw in the life class in his spare time. Refugees from Germany included Heinz Loew and Herr Flachslander. Also working there were the Welsh artists Richard Huws, William Matvyn Wright and Merlyn Evans, whose work was included in the International Surrealist Exhibition.

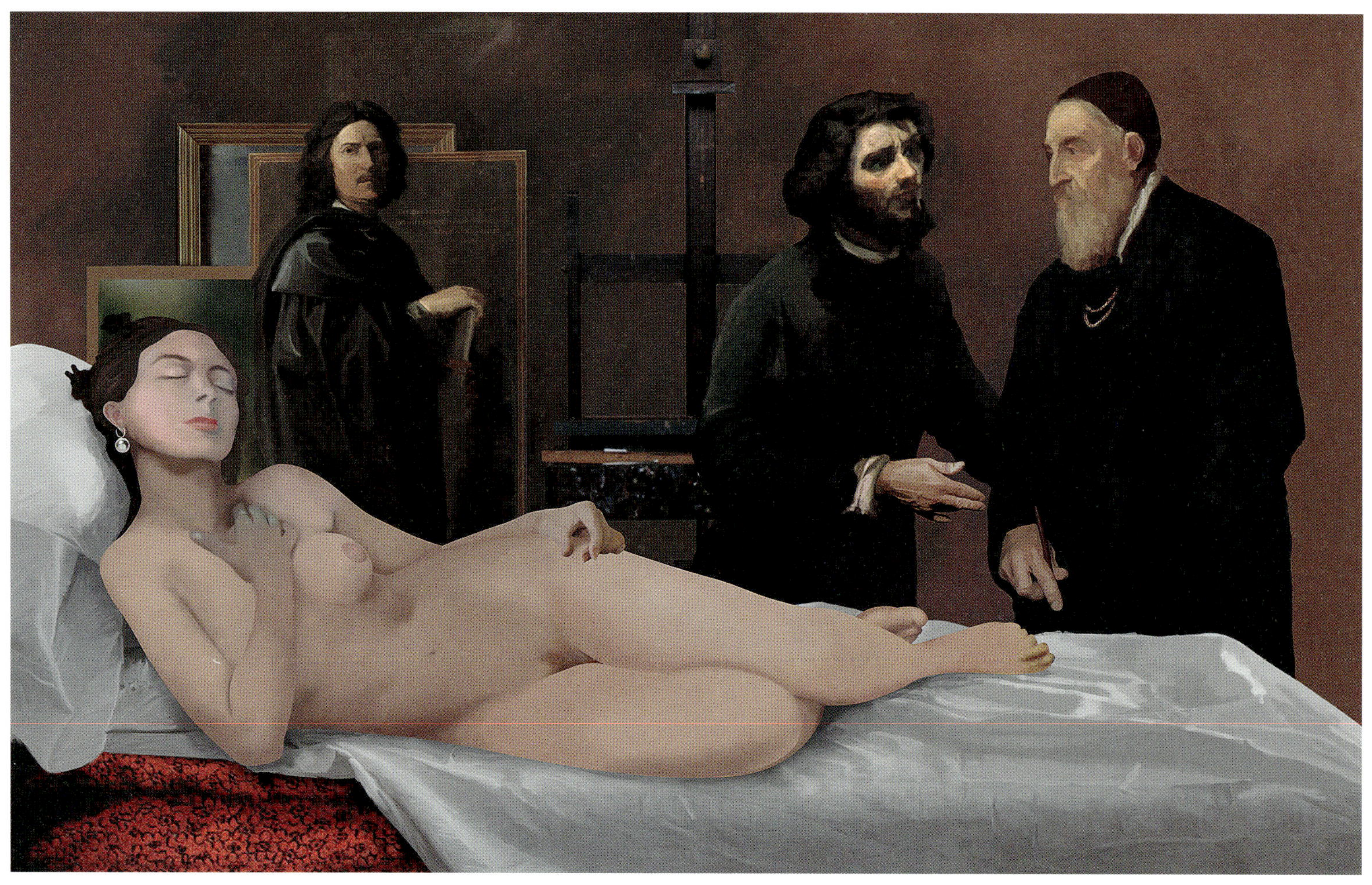

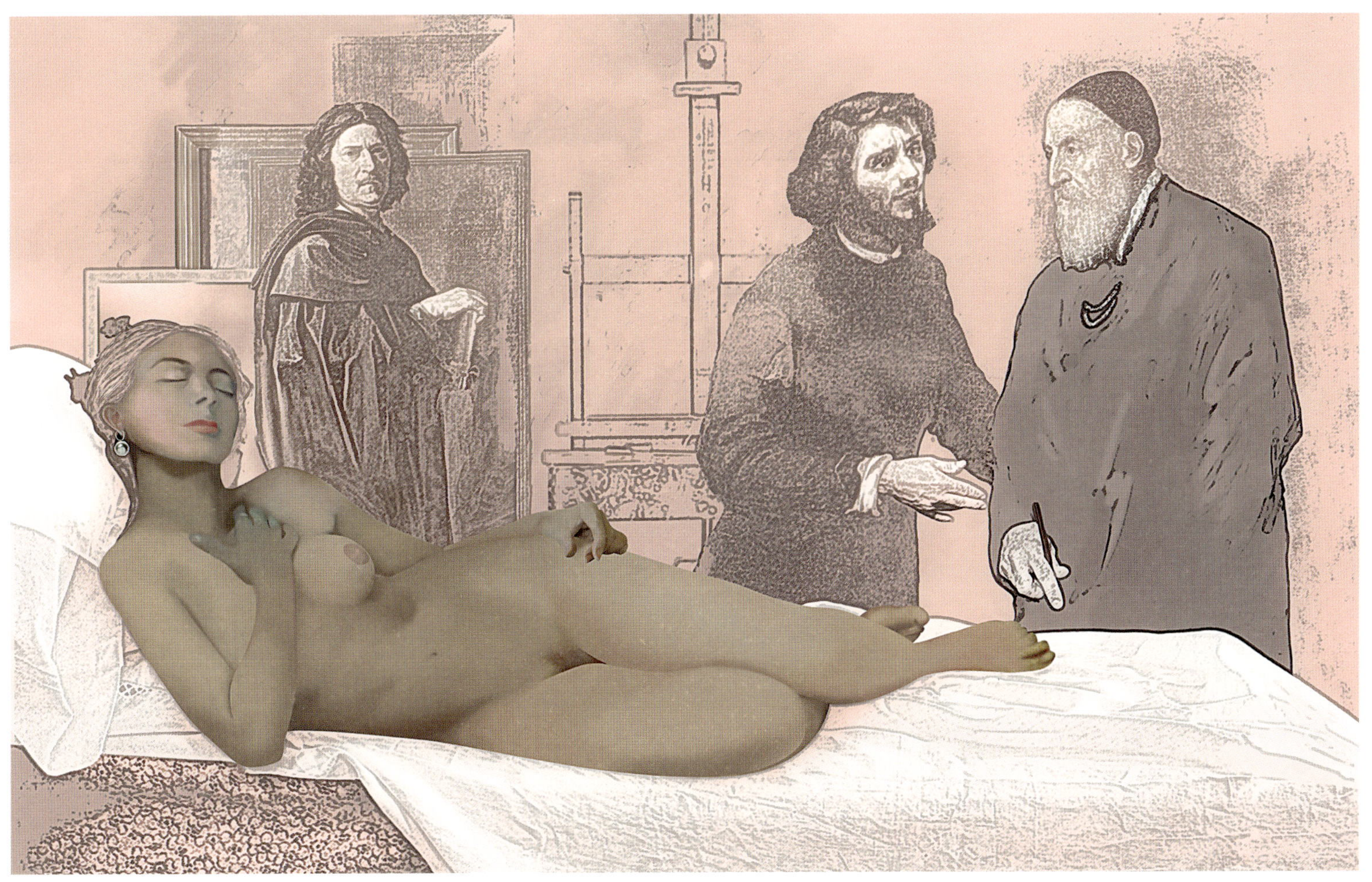

Chronology

by Fanny Singer

1922–28

Born Richard William Hamilton on 24 February 1922 in a council flat on Bell Street, Marylebone, London. The third child of Constance Elizabeth (née Ellerbeck) and Albert William Hamilton (known as Peter), had two older siblings: a half brother, Peter, and a sister, Stella. His father, who had worked in the mines on leaving school, then in the army—stationed in Ireland and later, from 1914–18, in the trenches of the Somme—earned a living driving a delivery van for Maconochie Brothers. He went on to deliver cars for a company specialising in luxury sports brands such as Alvis and Jaguar, and he sometimes took Hamilton along for a ride.

1929

The family moved home regularly, from Marylebone to Camden Town, then to Belgravia and finally to Pimlico. Hamilton attended primary school nearby at St Peter's in Eaton Square.

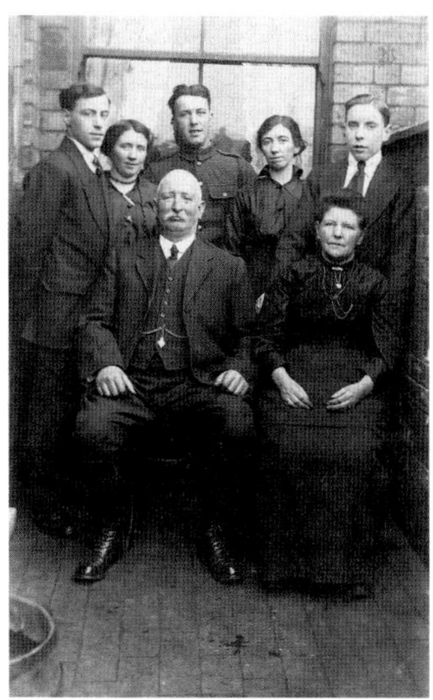

Hamilton's father Peter (back row, third from left) in military uniform, surrounded by family, c. 1913

1934

Won first prize in an exhibition of children's art held in the Victoria Tower Gardens adjacent to the Houses of Parliament. Though still enrolled in elementary school and unable to officially register, was given permission by his teacher, Mr Smith, to attend adult education evening classes in art at the London County Council in Southwark and Millbank (until 1936).

1935

Interviewed by Sir Walter Russell, Keeper of the Royal Academy Schools, at the recommendation of Sir Guy Dawber, former President of the Royal Institute of British Architects. Dawber had noticed Hamilton's draughtsmanship the previous year at the children's drawing competition. Russell advised him to apply for a studentship at the Royal Academy Schools when he turned 16.

1936

Finished elementary school and worked for a year as an office junior in the advertising department of an electrical engineering firm, Drake & Gorham. Continued evening classes in art both at Westminster School of Art, Vincent Square, and at St Martin's School of Art, where his teachers included Mark Gertler, best known for *Merry-Go-Round* (1916), Bernard Meninsky and William Roberts. The International Surrealist Exhibition opened in the New Burlington Galleries (June–July), including six works by Man Ray, whose Rayographic technique had impressed Hamilton. A sketchbook from this period comprises tourist views of London, including a picture of Covent Garden that shows a burgeoning interest in perspective.

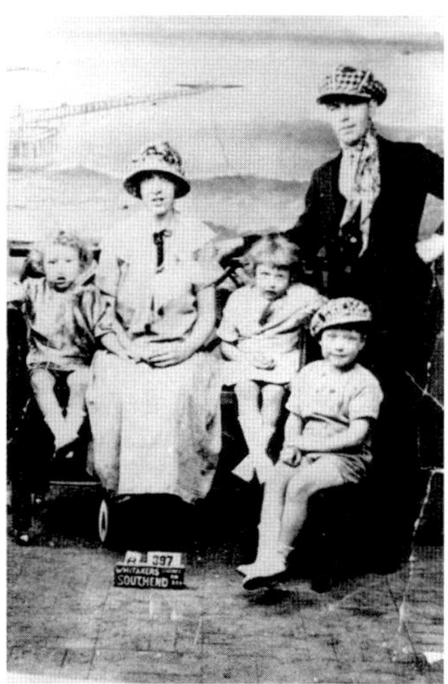

Hamilton family portrait (from left: Richard, Constance, Stella, Peter and Peter), c. 1925

1937

He passed on his way to work, the Reimann School and Studios of industrial and commercial art on Regency Street, still under construction. Reimann, a Bauhaus-influenced design school, was newly arrived from Berlin. Employed there in a junior role and permitted to draw in the life class in his spare time. Refugees from Germany included Heinz Loew and Herr Flachslander. Also working there were the Welsh artists Richard Huws, William Matvyn Wright and Merlyn Evans, whose work was included in the International Surrealist Exhibition.

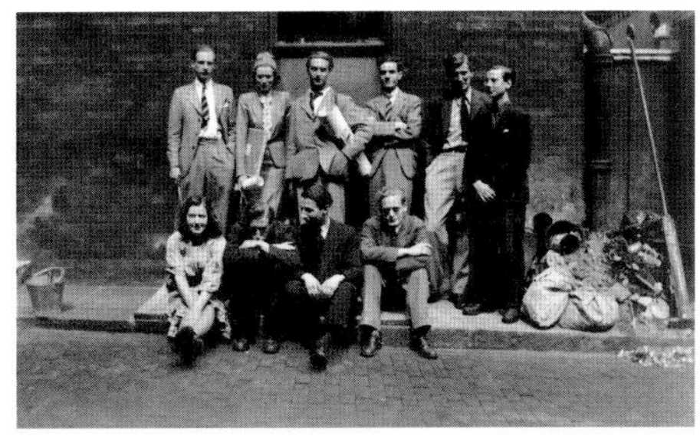

Hamilton (front row, second from left) with a group of students at the Royal Academy Schools, 1940

The instructor in stage dress design, Professor Haas-Heye, also a refugee, became a mentor and gave Hamilton a shilling to see Pablo Picasso's *Guernica* (1937) on show in London.

First forays into printmaking: prints made by scratching an image onto a celluloid sheet and passing the inked celluloid through his mother's laundry mangle as a make-shift press.

1938

Enrolled as a student of painting at the Royal Academy Schools (to 1940). Teachers included F. Ernest Jackson, Sir Walter Russell and Walter Bayes, the latter of whom gave a series of 12 lectures on perspective from which Hamilton claimed that "every little bit of information stayed in my head for the rest of my life." Hamilton copied various paintings in the National Gallery, including Zanobi Strozzi's *Annunciation* (c. 1440–45). Attended evening classes in etching and lithography at the Central School for Arts and Crafts, where he made print copies from Old Masters at the National Gallery.

First attended avant-garde theatre and dance performances. Saw *The Impact of Machines* (July) at the London Gallery in Cork Street, which Belgian Surrealist E.L.T. Mesens co-directed with Roland Penrose. The exhibition strongly anticipated several concerns of the Independent Group and Hamilton's exhibition *Man, Machine and Motion* (1955). In late September, *Guernica* was exhibited at the Whitechapel Art Gallery and the New Burlington Art Gallery in London, along with 67 preparatory sketches.

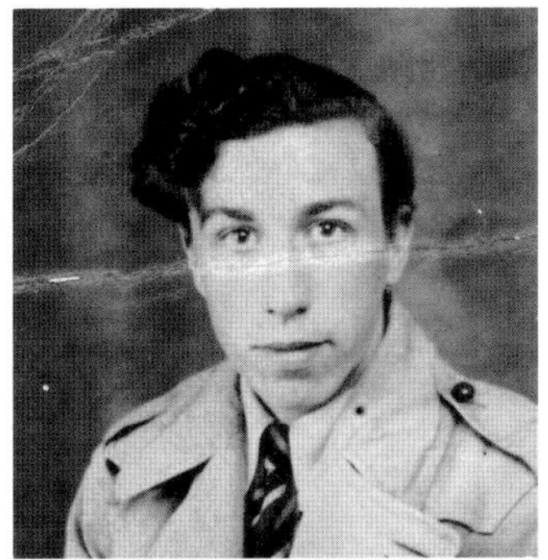

Hamilton in uniform, c. 1940

1939

Travelled to France for the summer vacation with friends from the Royal Academy Schools. After a few days his friends dispersed leaving him on his own to survive on what remained of his scant savings. He returned to London in time to hear Prime Minister Neville Chamberlain's declaration of war on Germany on 3 September.

1940

Too young to join the army when the Royal Academy Schools closed, Hamilton was sent to a Labour Exchange. Having only an arts education was initially deemed problematic, but his drawing skills redeemed him; he spent nine months in a Government Training Centre learning engineering draughtsmanship. For the remainder of the war he was in "reserved occupation" in London.

1941

Employed as a jig and tool draughtsman at Design Unit Group (to 1942), an engineering design office. Also employed at EMI (Electric & Musical Industries, formerly His Master's Voice) in Hayes, West London (1942–45), where he developed an interest in hi-fi equipment and began accumulating the components to build a stereo at home during the blackouts. Rented a flat in Newman Street, Soho. Drank at The Wheatsheaf and The Fitzroy Tavern with the Welsh artist and writer Nina Hamnett, the Welsh poet Dylan Thomas and the Tamil poet Tambimuttu, among others. First met the curator and critic David Sylvester. Met Inge Osterly, who—together with her son Stanislas—sat for portraits. Began to visit the American Embassy's library to peruse American lifestyle magazines including *Life, Look, Playboy* and *Good Housekeeping*.

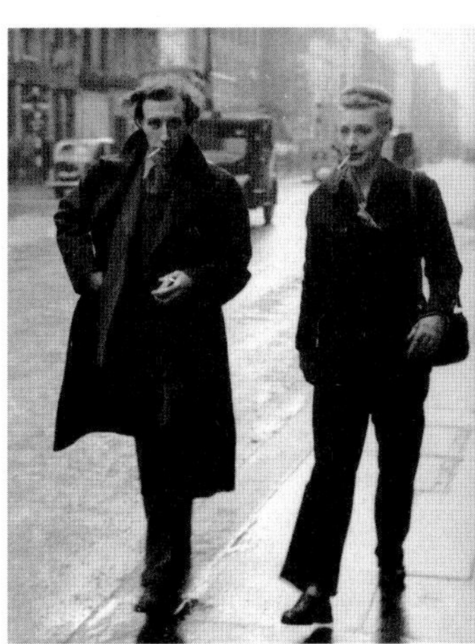

Hamilton with Inge Osterly, London, c. 1941

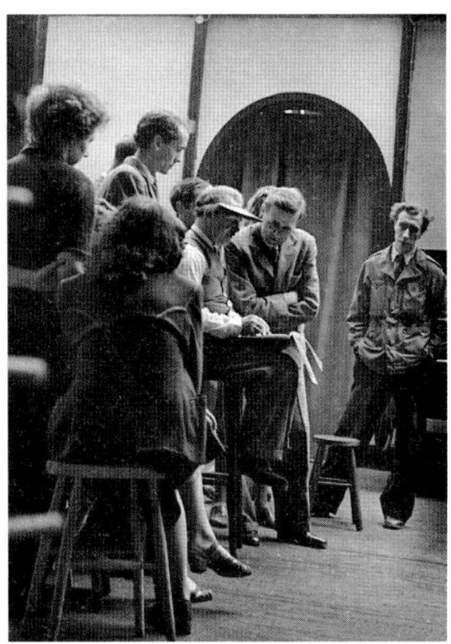

Hamilton (far right) with a group surrounding André Lhote at the Anglo-French Art Centre, St John's Wood, London, 1946

1942

Moved to Paddington where he remained through the Blitz. Organised a music club at EMI for weekly lunchtime concerts of recorded music from the HMV archives.

1943

Involved with acoustical engineers, as amateur enthusiasts, in the design of moving-coil pick-ups and horn speakers. Attended the first and many subsequent meetings of the Society for the Promotion of New Music.

1944

At EMI, met his future wife, a research assistant in the chemistry laboratory named Terry O'Reilly. Also at EMI, participated in the design team for the manufacture of the first British transistors (to 1945). Around this time, had his interest in printmaking stimulated by displays of French artists' books, including publications by Vollard, in the foyer of the National Gallery.

1945

Saw an exhibition of Matisse's and Picasso's large wartime canvases at the Victoria and Albert Museum. Attended numerous concerts at Wigmore Hall and elsewhere, especially those organised by the French Institute.

1946

In January, applied to the Hardship Tribunal and was permitted to return to the newly reopened Royal Academy Schools, whose new president, Alfred Munnings, an established sporting artist, was opposed to the concept of "Modern Art"; new teachers included Philip Connard and Walter Thomas Monnington. In July, expelled for "not profiting from the instruction given in the Painting School," resulting in re-conscription. Despite protestations, consigned to an additional 18 months of military service in the Royal Engineers in Aldershot. Immersed himself in the English classics from the regimental library, from Chaucer to Hardy, and treasured a personal two-volume Odyssey Press edition of James Joyce's *Ulysses* (1922).

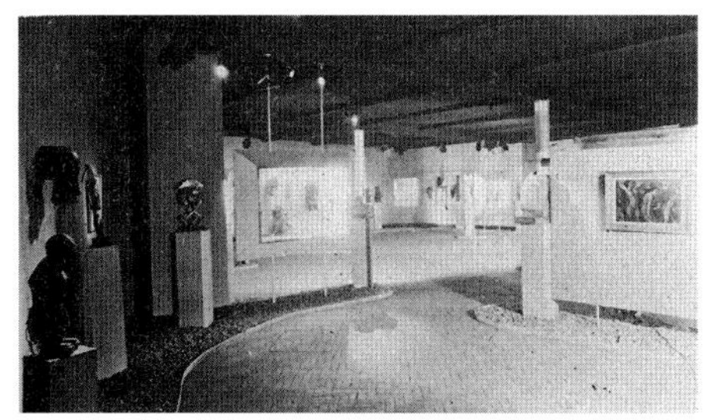

40,000 Years of Modern Art: A Comparison of Primitive and Modern, ICA, London, 1948

Peter Gregory, E.L.T. Mesens, Roland Penrose, Herbert Read, Geoffrey Grigson and Peter Watson founded the Institute of Contemporary Arts (ICA) with the intention of creating a space for modernist debate outside the parameters of the Royal Academy and the Tate Gallery. Their first two exhibitions, *40 Years of Modern Art* (1948) and *40,000 Years of Modern Art* (1948–49) held at Academy Hall on Oxford Street, London, were formative, radical shows whose success enabled the organisation to obtain a permanent space on the upper floor of 17–18 Dover Street.

1947

Began a series of studies for illustrations to *Ulysses* (by the end of 1949, he had finished 29 studies). Completed an Army Education Corps Instructors course and a camouflage course, in which he made models of landscapes from an aerial viewpoint. In September, married Terry O'Reilly, whom the architectural critic Reyner Banham would later describe as the "help-meet and domestic Muse of Richard."

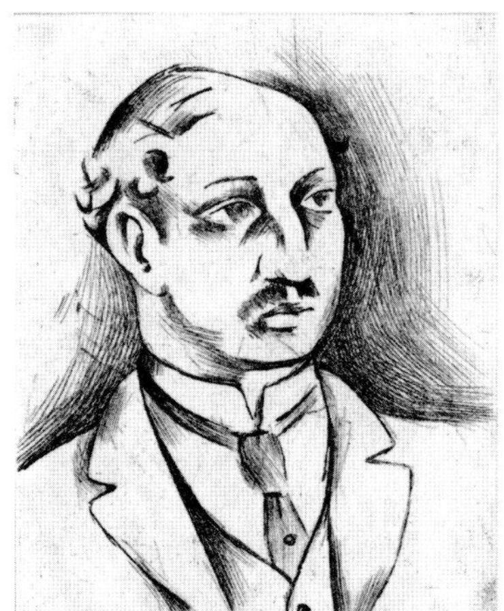

Hamilton's drawing from his series of illustrations of James Joyce's *Ulysses*

GEZA SZOBEL

SUZANNE &
PIERRE FREMONT

RICHARD HAMILTON

GIMPEL FILS

50 SOUTH MOLTON STREET, W.1

MAY 3720 FEBRUARY 1950

Catalogue for *Variations on the theme of a Reaper*, Gimpel Fils, London, 1950 (courtesy Gimpel Fils)

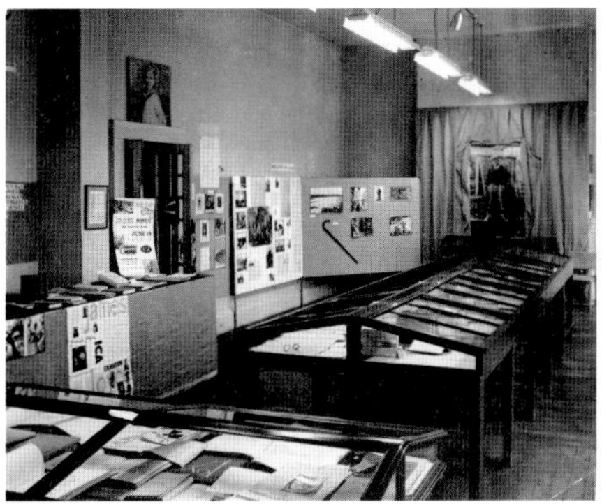

Installation of *James Joyce: His Life and Work*, with Hamilton's poster design for the exhibition visible affixed to a display case, ICA, London, 1950

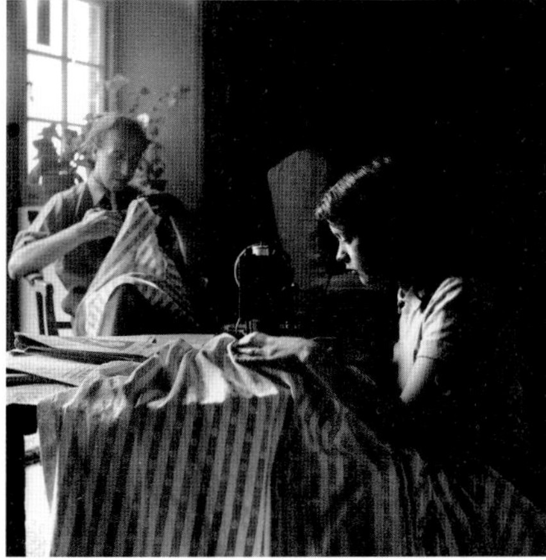

Hamilton and Terry at Lee Miller and Roland Penrose's Farley House Farm estate in Sussex, 1950
(Courtesy Lee Miller Archive)

1948

First met Nigel Henderson, a veteran of the Royal Air Force and student at the Slade School of Fine Art. Hamilton was interviewed at the Slade by William Coldstream and enrolled there to study painting (to 1951), focusing his energies on life drawing and etching (teachers included the illustrator and peintre-graveur John Buckland Wright). Henderson was well connected in the London art world; he introduced Hamilton to fellow students Eduardo Paolozzi and William Turnbull, as well as to the writings of D'Arcy Wentworth Thompson, whose book on morphology, *On Growth and Form* (1917), inspired Hamilton's first major installation, *Growth and Form*, as part of the Festival of Britain (1951). Of his friendship with Henderson, Hamilton would later say, "If I only got that from the Slade—that companionship with Henderson—it is enough for a lifetime. He was an incredible person." Henderson introduced him to Marcel Duchamp's *Green Box* (1934) in Roland Penrose's library. Penrose later endorsed Hamilton's exhibition on the subject of growth and form at the ICA.

1949

Married, unemployed and without funds, the couple was obliged to live in a room in Hamilton's parents' council flat. Thanks to his experience at Reimann Studios, found work making models for industrial and government exhibitions. Daughter Dominica (Dominy) was born on 22 November.

Used sketches made from Siegfried Giedion's 1948 book *Mechanization Takes Command* for a series of etchings, *Variations on the theme of a Reaper*, executed in the small print studio at Slade run by John Buckland Wright. The series, comprising various depictions of farm equipment, equally reflected the variety of perspectives of the subject and the array of techniques used to create the prints. Fernand Léger visited the Slade and held an individual crit with Hamilton; Léger admired these works.

Absorbed the Hollywood aesthetic of the period by virtue of frequenting the cinema three times a week. Invited by the art director of *Vogue* magazine to join a new scheme to find young artists for commissions to illustrate their pages, he attended weekly studio sessions for fashion artists. After some months of involvement, his work was ultimately dismissed by the editor as interesting but "a little arty" for *Vogue*.

1950

Visited Paolozzi in Paris, who took him to Alberto Giacometti's studio. Paolozzi also introduced him to an American friend, Bob Rose, who organised a trip to the South of France; travelled to Chartres and to the Dordogne region to seek out the cave art near Lascaux. While on the beach in Cerbère, met by chance the playwright Benn Levy and his wife Constance Cummings, with whom he formed an enduring friendship.

Exhibited his etchings, *Variations on the theme of a Reaper* (1949), at Gimpel Fils, London (February). Purchasers included Roland Penrose, the orientalist Arthur Waley and the artist Lynn Chadwick.

Conceived and designed his forthcoming *Growth and Form* exhibition, which was initially proposed as a collaboration with Paolozzi and Henderson, but both artists declined after early conversations. First met Peter Watson, backer and art editor of the literary magazine *Horizon*, and Sonia Orwell (née Brownell), second wife of George Orwell.

Bernard Gheerbrant, founder of La Hune bookshop in Paris, organised the exhibition *James Joyce: His Life and Work* at the ICA (June–July). Hamilton helped install the exhibition

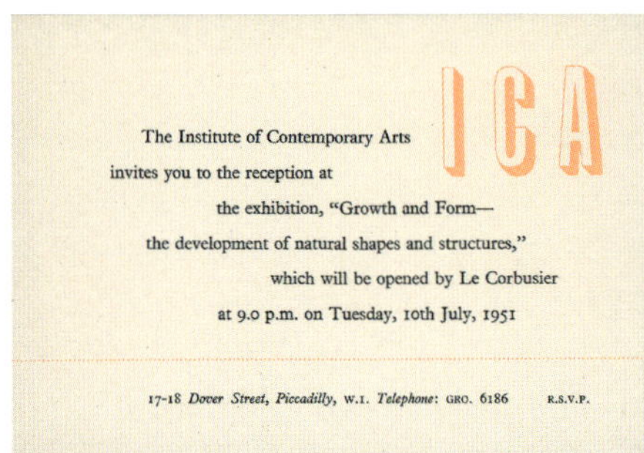

ICA

The Institute of Contemporary Arts
invites you to the reception at
the exhibition, "Growth and Form—
the development of natural shapes and structures,"
which will be opened by Le Corbusier
at 9.0 p.m. on Tuesday, 10th July, 1951

17-18 Dover Street, Piccadilly, W.1. *Telephone*: GRO. 6186 R.S.V.P.

Invitation card to *Growth and Form*, ICA, London, 1951

and design the catalogue—a folded poster, representing his first attempt at typography—and was thus exposed to other artists' illustrations of *Ulysses*, including those of Henri Matisse and Frank Budgen. Gheerbrant added a selection of Hamilton's *Ulysses* illustrations to the show, marking their first display. Became friends with the typographer Anthony Froshaug and the artist Gordon House.

1951

Peter Gregory, an early patron/founder of the ICA and Managing Director of Lund Humphries, introduced Hamilton to T. S. Eliot at Faber & Faber, with whom he discussed publishing an illustrated *Ulysses*. Eliot, however, felt it would be too difficult to reset the manuscript for a limited edition. With Terry, made models from Royal Ordinance maps of Stevenage, Basildon and other towns for friend Ronald Avery, who had a contract for work in the architectural section of the Festival of Britain. Coinciding with this Festival, *Growth and Form* was opened by Le Corbusier, who endorsed the show enthusiastically on the BBC. A book of essays by scientists edited by Lancelot Law Whyte was published to accompany the exhibition.

First met the French modernist painter Jean Hélion and the architectural critic and historian Peter Reyner Banham, whom Hamilton would later describe as "the first person who ever understood my work."

With savings of £800 from model-making and exhibition installation, took out a mortgage for a parcel of land on Hurst Avenue in Highgate, overlooking a playing field, and collaborated with Elidir Davies on the design of a house in which he lived from 1952. With Terry, visited Lee Miller and Roland Penrose at Farley Farm House in East Sussex. Penrose bought Hamilton a share in the Wine Society.

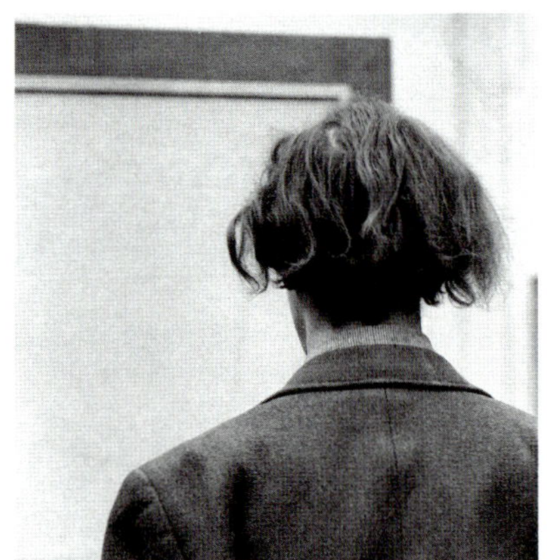

Hamilton standing before a Kasimir Malevich painting in *Twentieth Century Masterpieces*, Tate Gallery, London, 1952

1952

With the expiration of his student grant and only infrequent work model-making, interviewed with William Johnstone for a job at the Central School of Arts and Crafts, London, where attitudes were warming to the Bauhaus approach. As an instructor of Basic Design, taught ideas elaborated from *Growth and Form* to students in the craft departments. Participated in the ICA's exhibition *Young Painters* at the Dover street space.

Dorothy Morland, director of the ICA from 1951, with Richard Lannoy, a photographer and gallery assistant, sent invitations to members of the ICA to precipitate the organisation of a discussion group there. Hamilton subsequently became a founding member of the Independent Group at the ICA (formerly the Young Independent Group), alongside Reyner Banham (convenor) and John McHale, Toni del Renzio, Eduardo Paolozzi, William Turnbull, Nigel Henderson, Colin St John Wilson, James Stirling, Theo Crosby, Alison and Peter Smithson and Magda and Frank Cordell. In April, Paolozzi gave the inaugural lecture, for which he used an epidiascope to project images from his collages of science fiction, advertisements and popular literature sources across the walls.

During this time, Hamilton supplemented his income by manufacturing lampshades for the high-end craft shop, Primavera, which held regular exhibitions of contemporary and traditional craft from Britain and abroad. Visited the exhibition *Twentieth Century Masterpieces* at the Tate Gallery (July–August), where he saw Kasimir Malevich's *White on White* (1918) and Marcel Duchamp's *The Bride* (1912), marking the first time Hamilton encountered a painting by Duchamp in person.

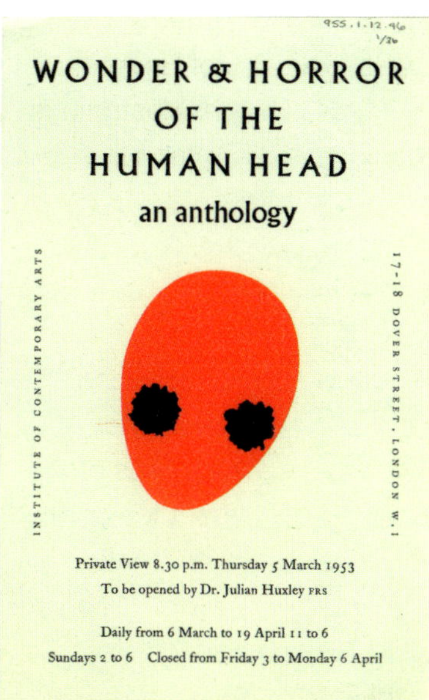

Invitation for *Wonder and Horror of the Human Head*, ICA, London, 1953

1953

At the recommendation of Hugh Casson, Director of Architecture for the Festival of Britain, was interviewed by Lawrence Gowing, head of the Fine Art Department, King's College, University of Durham (later University of Newcastle upon Tyne). Appointed Lecturer in Design, initially teaching the fundamentals of design to first-year students; later the "basic course" with Victor Pasmore (to 1966). With the help of a student, Arthur Pulford, began research on devices designed to extend man's mobility and capabilities. Also restored the disused printmaking facilities at Newcastle, instituted evening classes, and began making etchings.

Remained a London resident rather than move his family to Newcastle, commuting weekly for the next 13 years. Began to work in his *Trainsition* series (1954) to develop a perspective system to describe a moving spectator, partly influenced by his train journeys between London and Newcastle.

With wife Terry, installed *Wonder and Horror of the Human Head* at the ICA, comprising material collected by Roland Penrose and Lee Miller (March–April). Paolozzi, Henderson and the Smithsons collaborated on an exhibition at the ICA titled *Parallel of Life and Art* (September–October). Contributed a session on "New Sources of Form" to the "Aesthetic Problems of Contemporary Art" lecture series at the ICA (November).

1954

During regular meetings with the Independent Group, discussed emergent theories of cybernetics. In Newcastle upon Tyne, took on the role of organising and installing, with students, exhibitions in the Fine Art Department's Hatton Gallery. Designed catalogues and posters, and produced them using the resources of the University print shop.

1955

Exhibited *Paintings 1951–55* at Erica Brausen's Hanover Gallery, London (January), where the work of René Magritte, Francis Bacon, Alberto Giacometti, Henry Moor, Man Ray and Graham Sutherland was also shown. Though reviewed favourably by Alloway and Banham and discussed by the IG at the ICA, the show was a commercial failure. Among the few purchasers were Benn Levy and his wife Constance Cummings, with whom Hamilton had developed a friendship during his trip to France in 1950.

Conceived and designed *Man, Machine and Motion*, an installation of photographs laminated onto plastic sheets (made by the plastic division of the nearby Thomas de la Rue factory), then fitted into a steel armature. The photographs represented the categories "Aquatic", "Terrestrial", "Aerial" and "Interplanetary." It was installed at the Hatton Gallery (May) and the ICA (July).

Worked for Sidney Bernstein as a consultant designer for Granada Television before the company began transmissions.

Son Roderic was born.

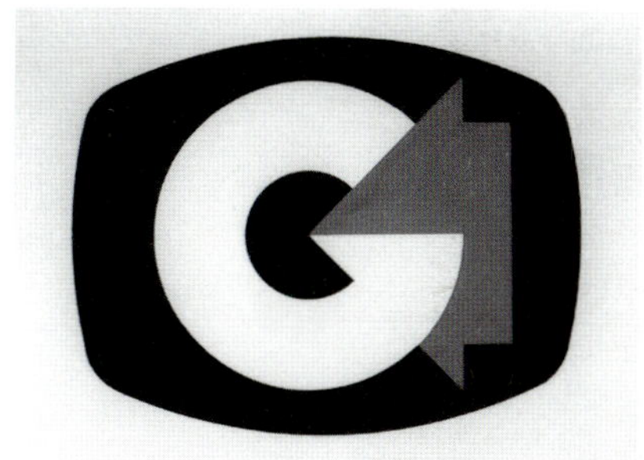

Hamilton's design for the Granada Television logo, c. 1956

1956

Alison and Peter Smithson designed the *House of the Future* for the *Daily Mail Ideal Home* Exhibition, in which actors costumed as a "family from the future" performed a daily routine for the visitors to the show.

The young architect Theo Crosby curated *This is Tomorrow*, a seminal exhibition at the Whitechapel Gallery, London (August–September), for which 36 practitioners were grouped

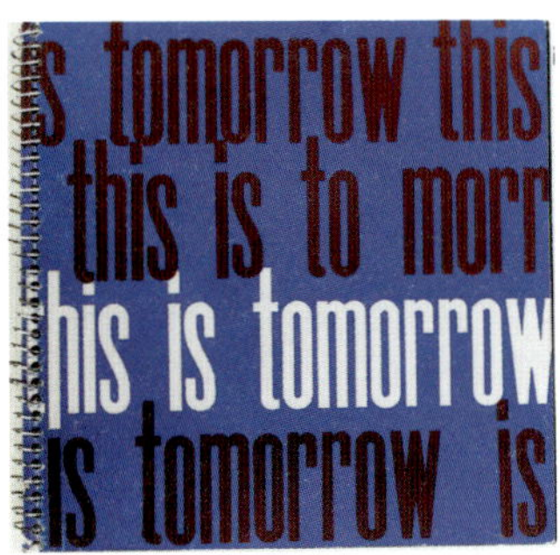

Catalogue for *This is Tomorrow*,
Whitechapel Gallery, London, 1956

into teams of three. Hamilton worked with artist John McHale and architect John Voelcker on an environment treating both the nature of perception and the proliferation of popular imagery in society. With Magda Cordell and Terry as "picture researchers" Hamilton made a collage for the publication according to a pre-assembled list of components: "Space; Man; Woman; Humanity; History; Food; Cars; Domestic Appliances; Cinema; Newspaper; TV; Telephone; Comics; Tape Recording." Titled *Just what is it that makes today's homes so different, so appealing?*, the collage was used in the catalogue and as a black & white poster for the show.

An exhibition highlighting American Abstract Expressionism, titled *Modern Art in the United States: A Selection from the Collection of the Museum of Modern Art, New York*, was displayed at the Tate.

In Newcastle's Fine Art Department, met frequently with a fellow lecturer and friend, the French-speaking art historian George Knox, to translate Duchamp's *Green Box* notes, as Hamilton was monolingual. Lectured at the ICA on Duchamp's *Large Glass* (1915–23) (which he would later reconstruct for the Tate Gallery) and its relationship to the *Green Box* notes using his own diagram of the artwork. Wrote to Duchamp enclosing a copy of this diagram with a request for corrections or confirmations. On the recommendation of David Sylvester, worked as a designer for *Encounter* magazine. Concurrently, worked as a consultant designer for Churchill Gear Machines, Blaydon on Tyne, south of Newcastle upon Tyne (to 1962).

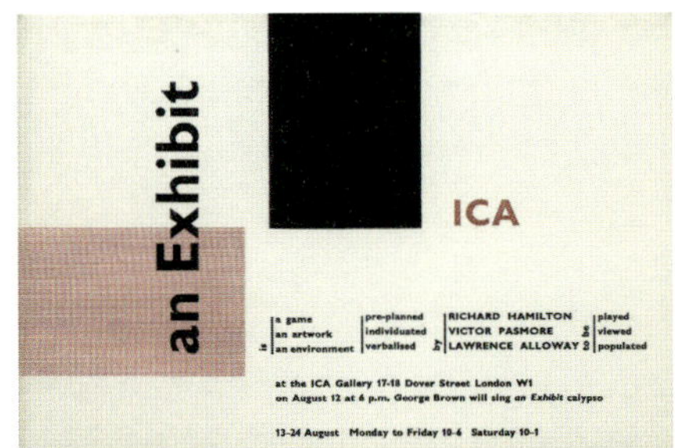

Invitation card to *an Exhibit*,
ICA, London, 1957

1957

Sent a letter to the Smithsons proposing an exhibition based on the principles presented in his newly composed "Pop art" credo:

Pop Art is:
Popular (designed for a mass audience)
Transient (short-term solution)
Expendable (easily forgotten)
Low cost
Mass produced
Young (aimed at youth)
Witty
Sexy
Gimmicky
Glamorous
Big business.

Began work on *Hommage à Chrysler Corp.*, which aimed to examine his own proposition. In May, received a reply from Duchamp to his letter from the previous year, inviting him to collaborate with George Heard Hamilton, Professor in the History of Art at Yale University, on a complete English version of the *Green Box* notes.

Along with Alloway and Pasmore, Hamilton conceived and designed *an Exhibit*, installed at the Hatton Gallery, Newcastle upon Tyne (June), and in revised form at the ICA (13–24 August).

At the invitation of Hugh Casson, began teaching Interior Design one day a week at the Royal College of Art (to 1961). Listened to lectures by the radical architect and theorist Buckminster Fuller. First met Richard Smith and Peter Blake.

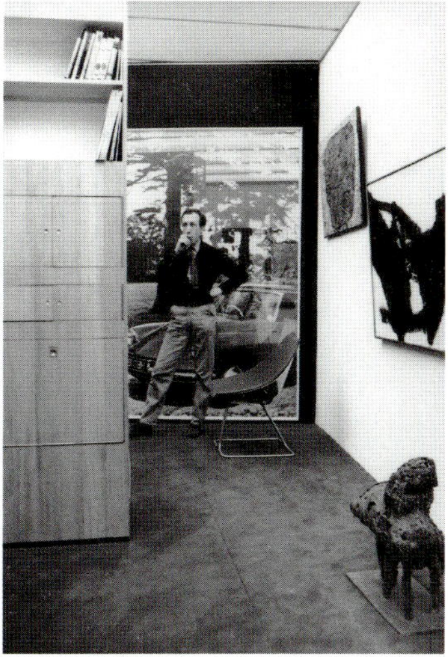

Hamilton in his "Gallery for a Collector of Brutalist ad Taschite Art" at the *Ideal Home Exhibition*, Olympia, London, 1958

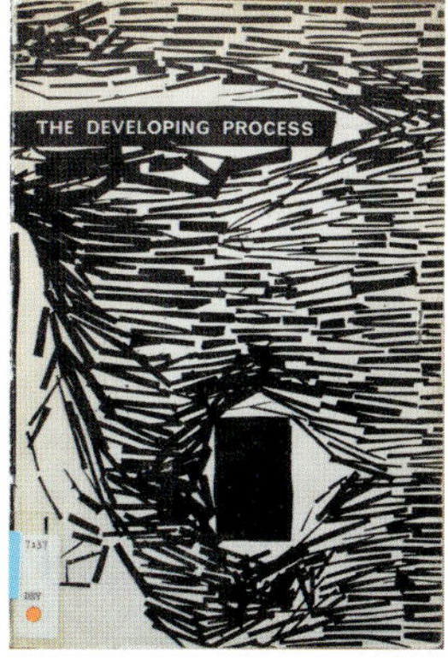

Catalogue for *The Developing Process,* ICA, London, 1959

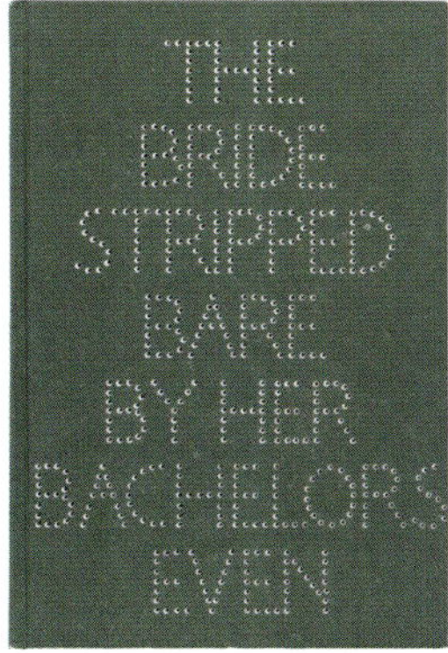

The Bride Stripped Bare by her Bachelors Even, A Typographical Version by Richard Hamilton of Marcel Duchamp's Green Box, translated by George Heard Hamilton, 1960

1958

Corresponded regularly with Duchamp on the *Green Box* project. Hugh Casson enlisted him to design a display at the *Ideal Home Exhibition*, Olympia, in West London, for which he created *Gallery for a Collector of Brutalist and Tachiste Art* (March), near an Edwardian-style display by Cecil Beaton. A central living unit he designed (dubbed the "Bachelor Column") and chairs (made from a design by Harley Earl) were then moved to Hamilton's home in Highgate. A selection of works by Willem de Kooning, Jean Dubuffet, Antoni Tàpies, Franz Klein, Jackson Pollock, Mark Rothko and Clyfford Still from the E. J. "Ted" Power collection were exhibited at the ICA, London (March).

Took part in the Campaign for Nuclear Disarmament (CND) protest march to Aldermaston, alongside 9,000 fellow marchers making their way to Falson Field, opposite the Atomic Weapons Research Establishment. Hamilton carried with him a life-size image of Marilyn Monroe from Billy Wilder's 1955 film *The Seven Year Itch*; the cut-out had been used in Hamilton's collaborative exhibition installation for *This is Tomorrow* in 1956.

Argentine artist and designer Tomás Maldonado invited Hamilton and Terry to visit the Hochschule für Gestaltung (HfG), Ulm, where they stayed in one of the apartments designed by Max Bill for tutors and guests. Subsequently Hamilton regularly received the HfG's quarterly publication, *Ulm*, which along with Braun product leaflets were inspirational source material. Kenneth Rowntree took over Lawrence Gowing's professorship at Newcastle. Hamilton regularly visited the playwright and Labour MP Benn Levy and his family at his Walter Gropius-designed London home, where he met refugees from the Hollywood of the McCarthy era as well as Labour MPs Aneurin Bevan, Jennie Lee and Michael Foot.

1959

With Kenneth Rowntree in charge at Newcastle, Pasmore as Head of Painting (moving increasingly toward abstraction) was given the freedom to develop a new first year basic course with Hamilton. The foundation of the teaching programme was their shared experience at the Central School in 1952.

Together with Pasmore, Hamilton installed a free-standing version of *an Exhibit* called *Exhibit 2*, combining the three-dimensional frame system from *Man, Machine and Motion* with the panels of Perspex from *an Exhibit* (Hatton Gallery).

Spent months visiting film production companies and researching film aspect ratios and film, lens and audio innovations for a lecture on technological developments in the entertainment industry, "Glorious Technicolor, Breathtaking Cinemascope and Stereophonic Sound," delivered at Newcastle, the ICA, Cambridge and the Royal College; demonstrated the Polaroid camera to each audience by taking a photograph of it. Also lectured on "The Design Image of the Fifties."

An exhibition held at the ICA, titled *The Developing Process*, brought together the teaching work of the staff at Newcastle upon Tyne and Leeds College of Art, with an illustrated catalogue expressing the views of the teachers (published by Hamilton at the Department of Fine Art).

After three years of correspondence, first met Duchamp at a dinner arranged by William and Noma Copley at their home in Longpont-sur-Orge, outside Paris. Other guests included Jean and Eva Tinguely and Man and Julia Ray. Published an illustrated essay on the challenges of translating Duchamp's notes into type in *Uppercase 2*; interviewed Duchamp for the BBC Third Programme; and visited Duchamp at Neuilly.

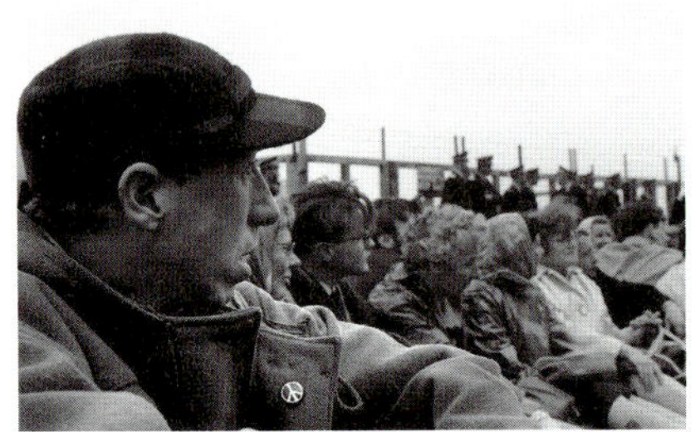

Hamilton at a CND Polaris Protest at Holy Loch, Scotland, 1961

1960

Received the William and Noma Copley award, which paid for the printing costs of a "typographic" version of Duchamp's *Green Box*, a project that had consumed the previous three years. The book was published by Lund Humphries in an edition of 1,000 copies and reviewed by Jasper Johns.

Beginning of Hamilton's lifelong friendship with Dieter Roth, via correspondence, following an introduction from Daniel Spoerri and Jean Tinguely after installing the *Edition MAT* exhibition in Newcastle (to which Roth contributed work).

In October, Hugh Gaitskell, Leader of the Labour Party, delivered a speech against unilateral nuclear disarmament at the Labour Party Conference that divided the party and alienated its neutralist, pacifist members.

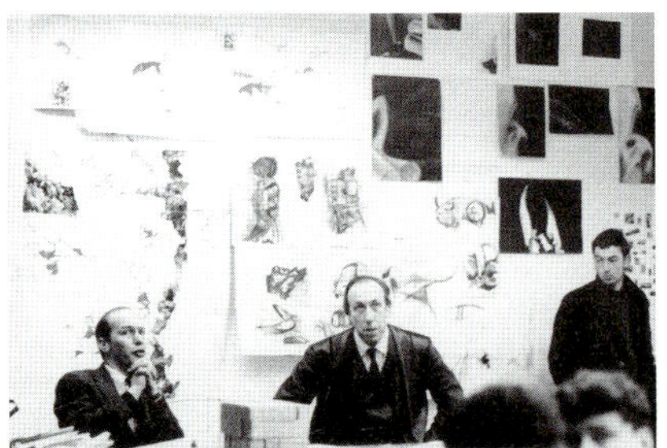

Hamilton with Richard Smith (left) teaching the Newcastle foundation course, c. 1962

1961

On 20 January, President John F. Kennedy's inaugural address included the exhortation "Together let us explore the stars..." which inspired Hamilton's series of paintings *Towards a definitive statement on the coming trends in menswear and accessories* (1962–63).

Invited by the students of the Royal College of Art Painting School to participate in a "crit" of their production, marking his first exposure to the work of RCA "Pop Art" students; awarded a prize to David Hockney, with R.B. Kitaj as the runner-up. Met Cedric Price and continued correspondence with Dieter Roth. Edited a series of monographs at the William and Noma Copley Foundation (to 1965), the first of which was dedicated to Hans Bellmer, and wrote an article, "The books of Diter Rot," [sic] for *Typographica*.

Participated in a CND Polaris Protest at Holy Loch and was imprisoned alongside many fellow protesters.

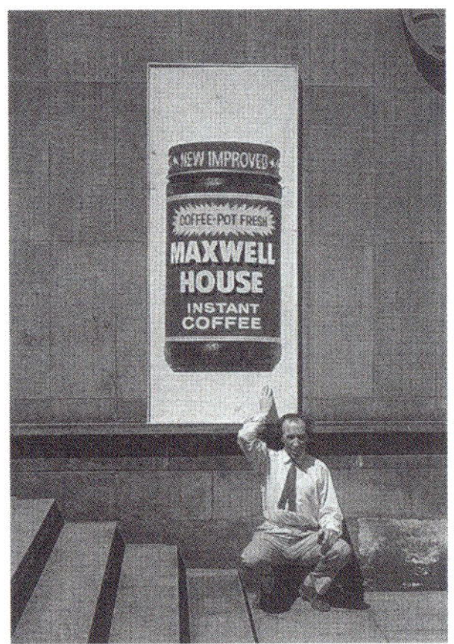

Hamilton with Mark Lancaster's *Maxwell House*, Newcastle, 1962

1962

Interviewed Duchamp for BBC TV's Monitor programme. At the first group exhibition of "Pop" paintings at the Arthur Jeffress Gallery on Davies Street, *New Approaches to the Figure*, exhibited *Pin-up* (1961) alongside works by Peter Blake, David Hockney and R.B. Kitaj. First met Emmett Williams, Robert Filliou, Ben Vautier and other Fluxus members at the *Festival of Misfits* exhibition at Gallery One, London, and at the ICA.

In November, Hamilton's wife Terry died in a car accident; Banham later recollected that she had been "among other things, protest-oriented, but one of the beautiful, electric protestors, not one of the drips; and she summed up (for me) one of the crises of our time: how to reconcile unavoidable admiration for the immense competence, resourcefulness and creative power of American commercial design with the equally unavoidable disgust at the system that was producing it?" (Banham, "Representations in Protest," *Arts in Society*). Hamilton asked Terry's mother to move in to the Highgate House to help care for his and Terry's children, 13-year-old Dominy and 7 ½-year-old Roderic.

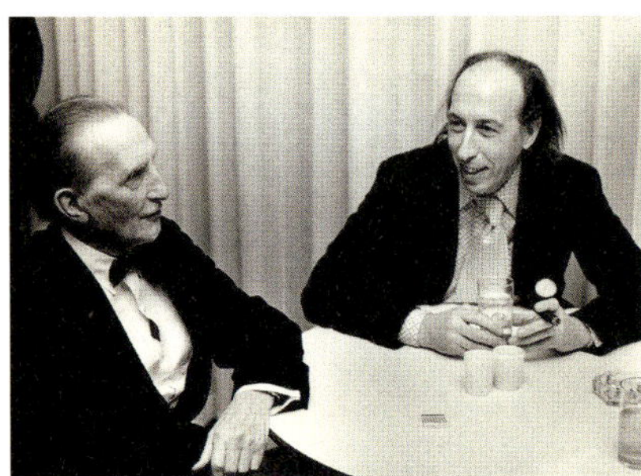

Hamilton with Marcel Duchamp at the Museum of Modern Art, New York, 1963 (courtesy George Cserna)

1963

Invited by the Duchamps to Cadaqués, a Spanish coastal town favoured by artists including Salvador Dalí, Joan Miró and Pablo Picasso.

Made his first visit to the United States, where he was met at the New York airport by the Copleys. While there, saw the *Large Glass* in person at the Philadelphia Museum of Art and lectured on Duchamp's piece at the Guggenheim Museum, New York; Yale University,

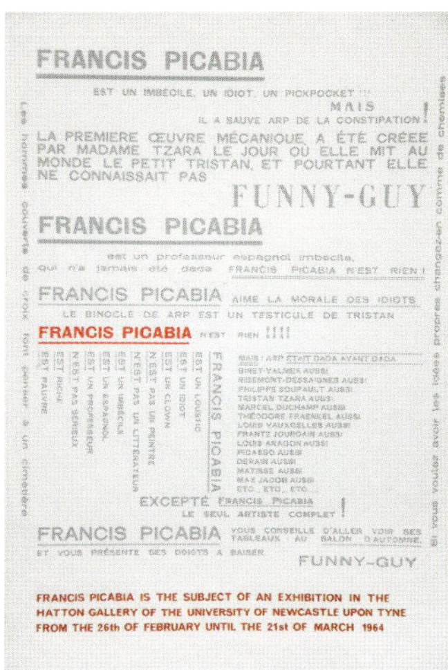

Poster for the Francis Picabia exhibition organised by Hamilton at the Hatton Gallery, Newcastle upon Tyne, 1964

New Haven; Boston and Pasadena. With Lawrence Alloway, visited Richard Artschwager's studio; and with the Duchamps, travelled from New York to Los Angeles to attend the Duchamp retrospective at the Pasadena Museum, California (October–November), at the invitation of Walter Hopps, the exhibition's organiser. Hopps was the former director of the Ferus Gallery, Los Angeles, where Hamilton saw Andy Warhol's series of *Silver Elvises* (September–October). Met Warhol at the Duchamp party in Pasadena; Claes Oldenburg at his exhibition at the Dwan Gallery, Los Angeles; and other Ferus Gallery artists Larry Bell, Billy Al Bengston, Joe Goode, Robert Irwin and Alison Knowles. Made a weekend outing to Las Vegas with the Duchamps and party, and spent a day with Joseph Cornell in Utopia. With Irving Blum, Hopps' successor at the Ferus Gallery, visited Pacific Ocean Park (known by locals as "P.O.P.") and wandered into a novelty shop where he purchased a button—pointed out to him by Blum—that read "SLIP IT TO ME." His visit to the US showed him that his "enterprise, that of expressing the interests of a consumer society in fine art terms, was a named movement—Pop Art. This, with its masters and camp followers, was a band wagon which had overrun me; I picked myself up and prepared to jump on it" (*Collected Words*, p. 55).

With the encouragement of Gordon House, made his first screenprints with Chris Prater. Began work on *Five Tyres*, a complex drawing in single-point perspective, but abandoned it. During this time, frequented the Morden Tower in Newcastle, where Tom Pickard conducted poetry readings by Basil Bunting, Allen Ginsberg, Lawrence Ferlinghetti and Robert Creeley, among others.

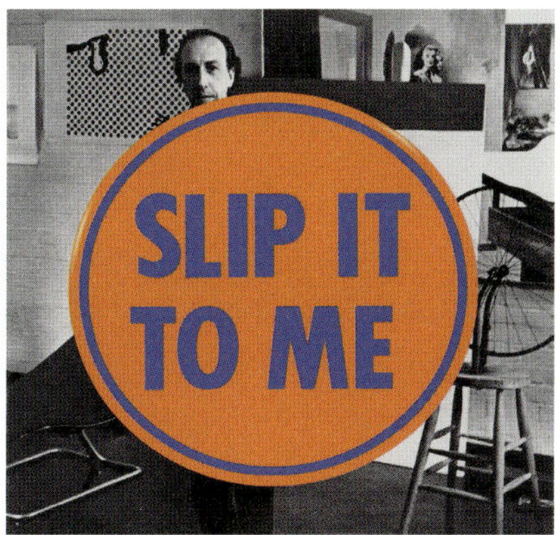

Catalogue for *Paintings etc. '56–64* at the Hanover Gallery, London, 1964

At the invitation of Gordon House, designer of *Living Arts*, shot the magazine's cover as a "self-portrait montage" helped by the American stylist Betsy Scherman. Hamilton posed in full American football regalia alongside a 1963 Ford Thunderbird coupe, a lingerie-clad model, a Mercury space capsule replica (from the stores of the Shepperton Film Studios), a Hoover Constellation vacuum (first seen in the *Just what is it…* collage) and other symbolic objects, while Robert Freeman (photographer of four Beatles albums) shot exposures from above at a construction site near the future site of Tate Modern.

After seeing his contribution to *Living Arts*, influential art collector E. J. "Ted" Power, whom Hamilton had known for many years, purchased *Hommage à Chrysler Corp.* (1957) from him directly. When asked why he had only then decided to purchase a work, he said that until reading the text Hamilton wrote for the magazine he "didn't know [Hamilton] was serious" (Letter from Hamilton to the Tate Gallery, 3 July 1996).

1964

Together with Ronald Hunt, organised the first Francis Picabia retrospective in the UK at the Hatton Gallery (March). Hamilton's *Portrait of Hugh Gaitskell as a Famous Monster of Filmland* (1963) was exhibited at the ICA (a year after Gaitskell's death)—a painting described in the accompanying catalogue as an "example of violence as a weapon." Hanover Gallery hung *Paintings etc. '56–64.* Ed Ganz, a Californian collector, bought Hamilton's 1956 *Just what is it…* collage. The show was well received and some paintings sold—including the Tate Gallery purchase of *Towards a definitive statement on the coming trends in menswear and accessories (a) "Together let us explore the stars"* (1962)—though too few to allow Hamilton to leave his teaching post.

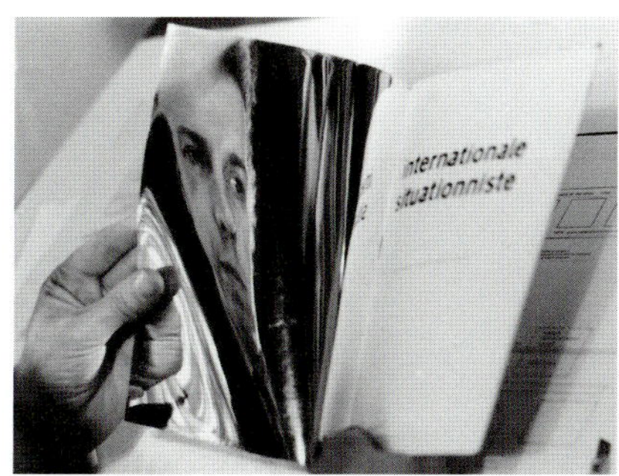

Hamilton reflected in a sheet inserted into the journal *internationale situationniste*, early 1960s

Bryan Ferry, future lead singer of UK chart-topping glam band Roxy Music, enrolled at Newcastle University and began taking Hamilton's course in Fine Art. With another student, Mark Lancaster, Hamilton investigated the condition of Kurt Schwitters' *Merzbarn* (1947–48)

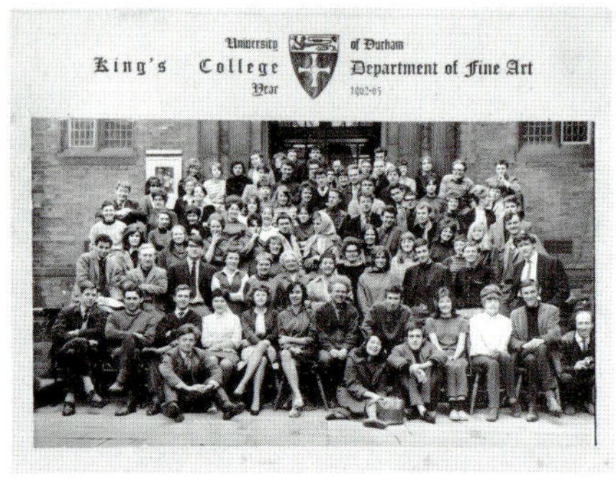

Hamilton (bottom right) in the end of year photograph of the Fine Art Department of King's College, University of Newcastle upon Tyne, 1962–65 (courtesy Derek Morris)

in Elterwater, the Lake District, at the behest of the Arts Council of Great Britain. After a tour led by the barn's owner, Harry Pierce, Hamilton recommended extensive protective measures and on-site restoration under the stewardship of the Arts Council, but this was deemed impossible.

Made *Epiphany*, an enlarged reproduction of the lapel badge purchased during his trip to the US. He found its message, "SLIP IT TO ME," to be emblematic of the "audacity and wit" of American art at the time. Its title likewise referenced James Joyce's definition of an epiphany: "The soul of the commonest object, the structure of which is so adjusted, seems to us radiant. The object achieves its epiphany" (James Joyce, *Stephen Hero*, Chapter XXV). Also began to experiment with extreme photographic close-up. Made *Desk*, his first experimentation with the language of de Stijl. Worked with Nancy Thomas on BBC TV's Monitor profile on the Swiss kinetic artist Jean Tinguely. Met the Swiss artist Dieter Roth in person and through him the Korean-American video art pioneer Nam June Paik.

Asked by the Arts Council of Great Britain to join its Art panel, Hamilton suggested a Marcel Duchamp retrospective at the Tate Gallery and was asked by the Council to organise it. Agitated for the ICA to commission artists, chiefly from within the Institute, to make screenprints with Chris Prater at Kelpra Studio. Each of the 24 artists—including Patrick Caulfield, Bridget Riley, Howard Hodgkin and David Hockney—produced a single print in an edition of 40; these were subsequently shown at the ICA gallery (November).

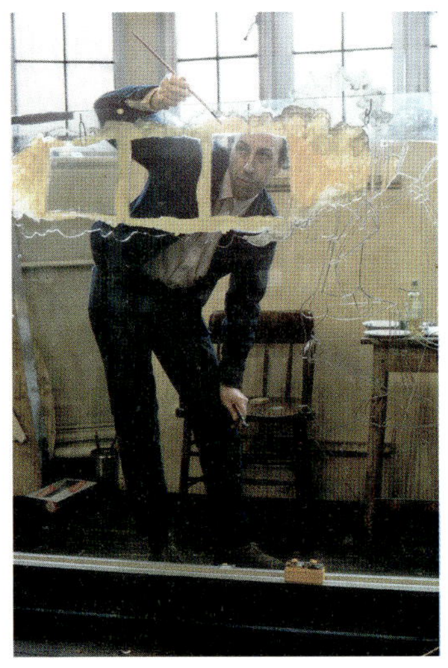

Hamilton working on his reconstruction of the *Large Glass*, 1965

1965

Further deterioration of Kurt Schwitters' *Merzbarn* necessitated its move from the Cylinder Estate in Elterwater, for which Newcastle University allocated funds at Hamilton's urging. Students including Mark Lancaster, Tim Head and Fred Brookes assisted in the careful mapping and documentation of the piece prior to its removal.

Began reconstruction of Duchamp's *Large Glass* and of the studies made between 1912 and 1915. Designed the first edition of *The Spoils* for Basil Bunting, and edited Eduardo Paolozzi's *Kex* and the Dieter Roth *Copley Book* for the William and Noma Copley Foundation. First met Jasper Johns, John Cage, Merce Cunningham and Jim Dine.

1966

Finished a reconstruction, sanctioned by Duchamp, of the *Large Glass*, which he presented, along with its studies, at the Hatton Gallery in Newcastle. Wrote notes for the catalogue, designed by Gordon House, and installed *The Almost Complete Works of Marcel Duchamp* at the Tate Gallery (June–July), the largest European retrospective during Duchamp's lifetime.

First solo exhibition at Robert Fraser Gallery, London (October), showing his *Guggenheim reliefs and studies* (paintings sold to Peter Ludwig and to the Solomon R. Guggenheim Museum, New York, which purchased three versions: *Black and White, Black* and *Spectrum*). Quit full-time teaching to concentrate on his own work. Students had included Roy Ascott, Stephen Buckley, Tony Carter, Nick de Ville, Rita Donagh, Bryan Ferry, Noel Forster, Tim Head, Adrian Henri, Mark Lancaster, Mali Morris, Matt Rugg, Ian Stephenson, John A. Walker, John Walters and Mary Webb.

Attended the "Destruction in Art Symposium," where he met Fluxus- and Actionism-affiliated artists including Gustav Metzger, Wolf Vostell, Hermann Nitsch and Yoko Ono, as well as John Lennon.

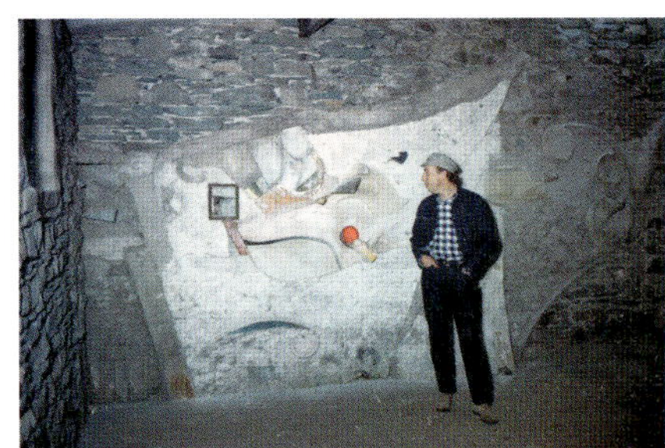

Hamilton in Kurt Schwitters' *Merzbarn*, 1966

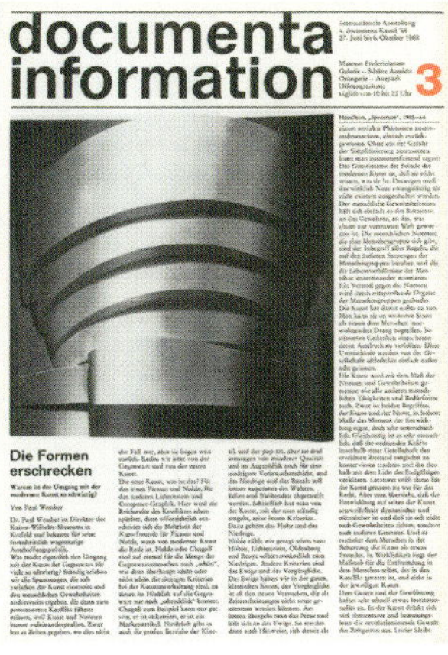
documenta information 3

Die Formen erschrecken

Hamilton's work illustrated in a newspaper published for documenta IV, 1968

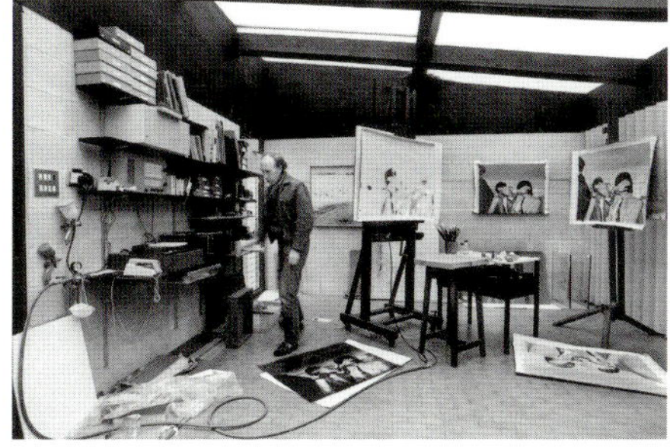
Hamilton in his studio in Highgate, London surrounded by versions of *Swingeing London*, 1968

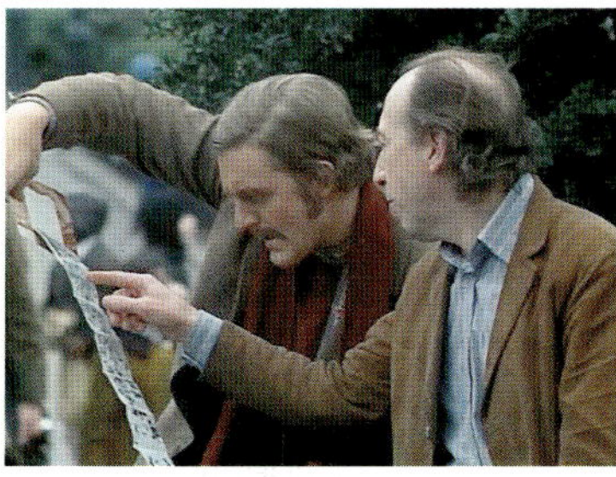
Hamilton in a cameo role as a "Pop Artist" in Brian De Palma's film *Greetings*, 1968 (courtesy Brian De Palma and West End Films)

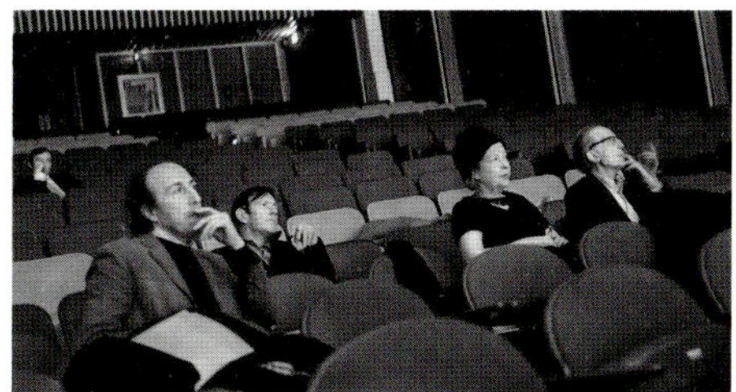
Jasper Johns, Hamilton, John Cage, Teeny and Marcel Duchamp at a dress rehearsal of Merce Cunningham's "Walkaround Time," Buffalo, New York, 1968 (courtesy James Klosty)

Schwitters' *Merzbarn* arrived in Newcastle and was installed in the Department of Fine Art by the head of Art History, Ralph Holland. Fred Brookes continued conservation and reconstruction efforts once the piece was installed in the Hatton Gallery.

With Marcel Duchamp's *Chocolate Grinder No. 2* (1915) in mind, Hamilton began *Toaster* (1966–67, reconstructed 1969), featuring an image of a Braun toaster designed in 1963 remade with acrylic components arranged on a blurred photographic background.

1967

First exhibition of drawings and prints in Germany at Galerie Ricke, Kassel (March); first show of paintings in New York at Galerie Alexandre Iolas (May).

In June, Robert Fraser, in whose gallery Hamilton had exhibited the previous year, was arrested for drug possession along with Rolling Stones members Mick Jagger and Keith Richards at Richards' home in Sussex. Hamilton conceived and organised a group exhibition of gallery artists and other prominent London artists called *Tribute to Robert Fraser* (August), mounted in "support for Fraser's plight" while the gallery director was imprisoned.

First exhibition in Italy at Studio Marconi (November). First screenprint with Domberger, Stuttgart. Met the pioneering political artist John Heartfield. Exhibited *My Marilyn (paste-up)* (1964), alongside works by artists including Richard Avedon, Willem de Kooning, Claes Oldenburg, Robert Rauschenberg, James Rosenquist and Andy Warhol in a group show, *Homage to Marilyn*, at the Sidney Janis Gallery, New York (December).

1968

Visited Roy Lichtenstein in his New York studio (March) and had his portrait taken by him. This spurred his *Polaroid Portraits* series, for which Hamilton offered an artist friend or acquaintance a Polaroid camera with the request, "take a photograph of me." Over the next 33 years he amassed 128 portraits, published in four volumes. With Jasper Johns, John Cage, Marcel and Teeny Duchamp travelled to Buffalo, New York, to see Merce Cunningham's "Walkaround Time" whose set design—supervised by Johns—was based on the *Large Glass*. Designed the cover sleeve for The Beatles' self-titled album, popularly known as "The White Album." The band agreed to leave the cover blank at Hamilton's insistence; the album came with a fold-out poster—also designed by Hamilton—that featured candid snapshots of the four musicians, presented as a mock small press publication in a "limited edition" of 5,000,000.

Showed in *documenta IV*, Kassel, Germany, where he exhibited some of the *Towards a definitive statement* series, three *Guggenheims* and *I'm dreaming of a white Christmas* (1967–68). In Kassel, first met the Belgian artist and poet Marcel Broodthaers. Made a print edition of *The critic laughs*, whose proceeds benefited documenta. Worked in Milan with various printers and made etchings at Grafica Uno. First collaboration with Dieter Roth. Visited Joseph Beuys in Düsseldorf after seeing his exhibition at the Van Abbemuseum in Eindhoven, the Netherlands.

Completed a multiple of Marcel Duchamp's *Oculist witnesses*. Was working on *Picturegram*, a painting from a photograph of Guillaume Apollinaire's original manuscript, when a telegram arrived from Teeny Duchamp informing him of Marcel Duchamp's death on 2 October.

Visited Canada as a juror for the exhibition *Canadian Artists '68*, where he met Greg Curnoe, Iain Baxter and the members of the artist collective General Idea, founded that year in Montreal.

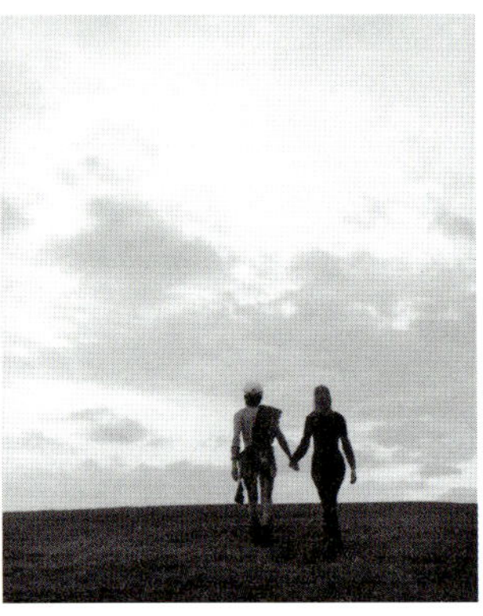

Location shot for James Scott's *Hamilton* film for Maya Productions, 1969

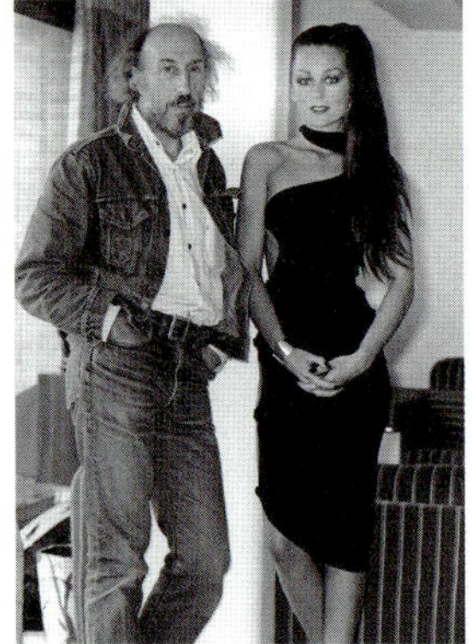

Hamilton with Lorraine Chase, the model for his "commercial" for *The critic laughs*, 1969

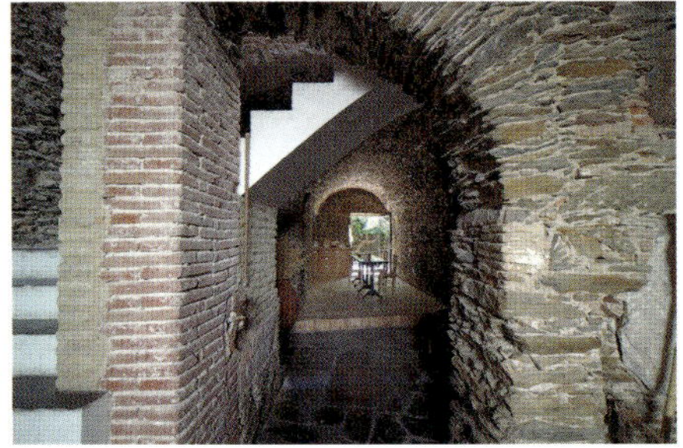

Interior of Hamilton's house in Cadaqués, Spain, 1970

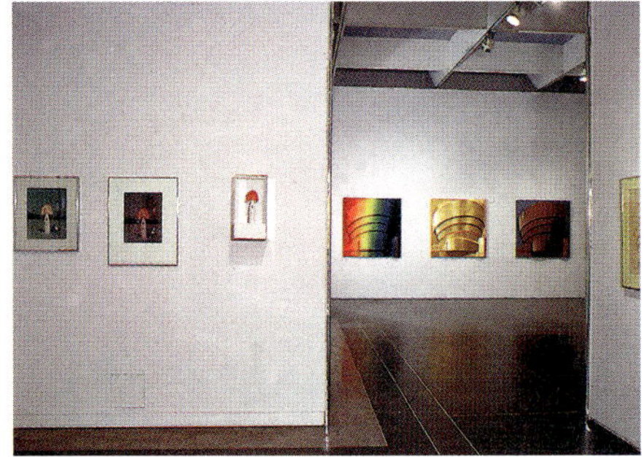

Retrospective at Tate Gallery, London, 1970

Began *Swingeing London 67*, a series of paintings and prints based on a newspaper photograph of the Rolling Stones frontman Mick Jagger handcuffed to Hamilton's art dealer Robert Fraser; the two were seen through the frame of a prison van window en route to Chichester Magistrates Court to address charges of illegal drug possession. Each painting in the series explored a different painterly style and treatment of materials, using everything from oil to enamel paint, half-tone screenprinting, relief and collage.

Had a cameo role as a "Pop Artist" in Brian De Palma's *Greetings*, Robert De Niro's first feature film. Saw *Cybernetic Serendipity* at the ICA's new location on The Mall (August–October), a groundbreaking exhibition curated by Jasia Reichardt that gathered over 325 participants from technical, commercial and fine art backgrounds to mount a display of computer-assisted artwork.

1969

The Arts Council commissioned director James Scott to make a film about Hamilton; titled *Richard Hamilton*, this collaboration between Scott and Hamilton was screened at the ICA. The film included Hamilton's commercial for *The critic laughs.*

Awarded joint first prize (with Mary Martin) in the John Moores Painting Prize, Liverpool. Made his first dye-transfer print with Creative Colour, Hamburg. Attended Gilbert and George's "living sculpture" performance *Underneath the Arches* in Cable Street, London. In June, exhibited his *Swingeing London* series at the Robert Fraser Gallery, London, in what was to be the gallery's second to last show before its closure (*Swingeing London 67 (f)* was purchased by the Tate Gallery).

In early spring Hamilton had learned of the existence of Marcel Duchamp's final work, *Étant donnés*, from William Copley. He attended the inauguration at the Philadelphia Museum of Art on 17 September with Rita Donagh and many other artists.

Participated in *Art by Telephone*, an exhibition of conceptual art at the Chicago Museum of Contemporary Art inspired by László Moholy-Nagy's *Telephone paintings* (1922) (October); 37 artists—including Richard Artschwager, John Baldessari, Mel Bochner, James Lee Byars, Hans Haacke, Sol LeWitt, Robert Morris, Bruce Nauman, Claes Oldenburg, Richard Serra, Robert Smithson and Wolf Vostell—were asked to dictate the terms of an artwork over the telephone, to be created on-site by a third party. Hamilton's work, *Chicago project I*, was executed by Ed Paschke, a young American artist.

Hamilton bought a derelict house in Cadaqués, Spain, and began the process of restoration.

1970

Awarded the Talens Prize International by a jury of Dutch museum directors. An Arts Council retrospective of his work, curated by Richard Morphet, was mounted at the Tate Gallery (March–April). Hamilton was involved in the exhibition design, which included, among other details, the installation of metallic edges for the walls on which some works were displayed. The show subsequently travelled to the Stedelijk van Abbemuseum, Eindhoven (May), and the Kunsthalle, Bern (July).

First screenprint with Dieter Dietz, Lengmoos, Germany, on the subject of the shooting of students by National Guardsmen at Kent State University, Ohio: *Kent State* (edition of 5,000). First collotype with Heinz Haffner, Stuttgart, Germany.

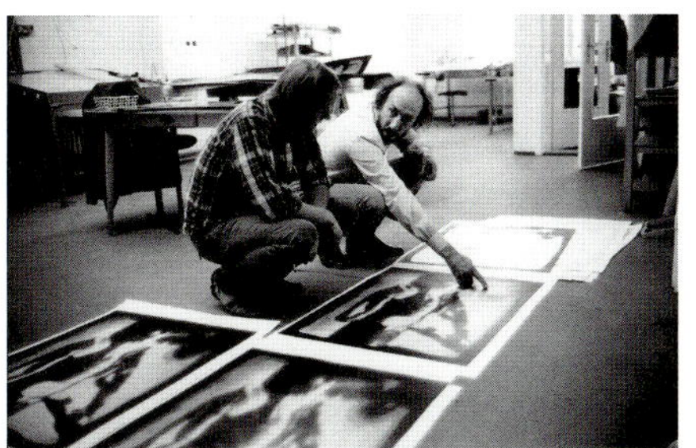

Hamilton working on *Kent State* with Dieter Dietz at Dietz Offizin, Lengmoos, Germany, 1970

1971

Gave Clive Barker a painting to be cremated for a sculpture in which the remains would be placed in an urn (Joe Tilson and David Hockney also contributed works for this series). Took part in the exhibition *Metamorphose de l'Objet* at the Palais des Beaux-Arts, Brussels, where he was filmed in conversation about his work for a documentary by the art filmmaker Jef Cornelis (broadcast on the Flemish television network VRT on 24 April).

Made *The critic laughs* (1971–72), which began as a ready-made of a set of novelty sugar teeth affixed to a Braun electric toothbrush. The title refers to Jasper Johns' sculpture, *The Critic Smiles* (1969). When the teeth deteriorated, Hamilton invited the Fluxus artist Hans Sohm to recreate a version using dental plastic, and engaged a commercial manufacturer to produce a small edition multiple for the Réne Block gallery in Berlin. Began *Soft pink landscape*; completed the edition of Marcel Duchamp's *Sieves*; and returned to the *Five Tyres* subject, using computer programming to solve the perspective problem through a collaboration with the Massachusetts Institute of Technology and with Sherril Martin, manager of computer animation at the nearby Kaye Instruments, Inc.

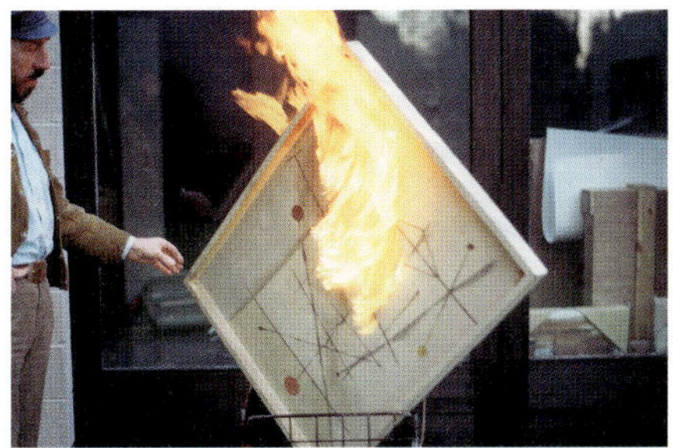

Hamilton cremating one of his own paintings for the artist Clive Barker's *Urn*, 1971

While in the US, invited by Barbara Rose to participate in a Marcel Duchamp symposium at the University of California, Irvine, and taught at the University of Wisconsin, Madison, for one semester. Designed an adjustable jointing device for the mitres of canvas stretchers and applied for a provisional patent.

1972

Made *Release*, a print variation of *Swingeing London 67*, for Release, an organisation providing legal support for people accused of infringement of drug laws. Shows this year included *Prints, Multiples and Drawings* at the Whitworth Art Gallery, Manchester (January); *Five Tyres remoulded* at Nigel Greenwood, London (May); *Kent State* and *Release Progressives* at the ICA, London (June); *Hamilton* paintings and prints at Studio Marconi, Milan; and *Grafik und multiple objekte* at Ulmer Museum, Ulm (December).

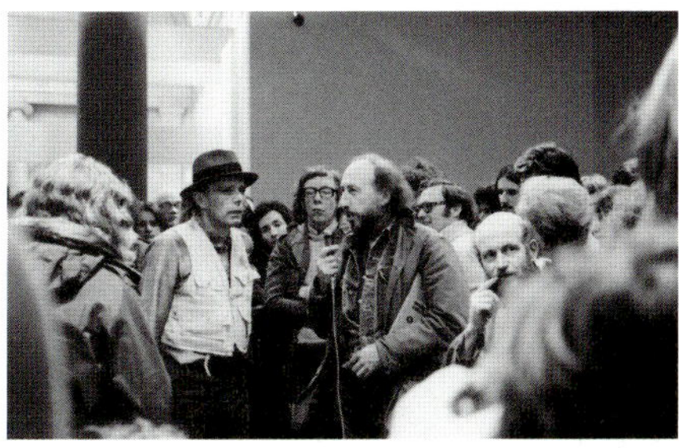

Joseph Beuys, Hamilton and Gustav Metzger in discussion at the Tate Gallery, London, 1972

1973

For a publication of 60 prints by different artists intended as a homage to Pablo Picasso on his 90th birthday in 1971, made *Picasso's meninas*, his first with Picasso's etcher, Aldo Crommelynck. Also began *Trichromatic flower-piece* with Crommelynck in his Paris atelier as an experiment in colour-separated printing with hand-etched plates (until 1974). Through Crommelynck met Catherine Deneuve, Marcello Mastroianni and Jacqueline Picasso and was reacquainted with Sonia Orwell. Upon seeing Hamilton's print proofs, Orwell remarked: "You know, Richard, life's not all shit and flowers" (Quoted in Hamilton, *Shit and Flowers*, p. 13).

Visited the US, where there was a painting retrospective of his work at the Solomon R. Guggenheim Museum, New York (September), and a print retrospective at the Davison Art Center, Middletown, Connecticut (September–November). While there, attended the opening of the Marcel Duchamp retrospective at the Philadelphia Museum of Art.

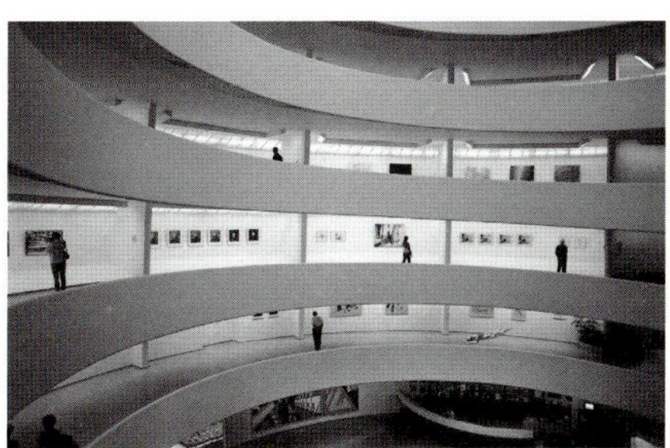

Retrospective at the Solomon R. Guggenheim Museum, New York, 1973 (courtesy of the Guggenheim)

1974

Made a postcard based on *Chicago project* in homage to John Cage. Visited Japan for the first time in March to discuss *Lux 50 – functioning prototype* (a production amplifier given a "Pop sculptural treatment"), a commission by Lux Corporation, manufacturers of HiFi amplifiers, to make a work of art to celebrate the founding of the company. First exhibition

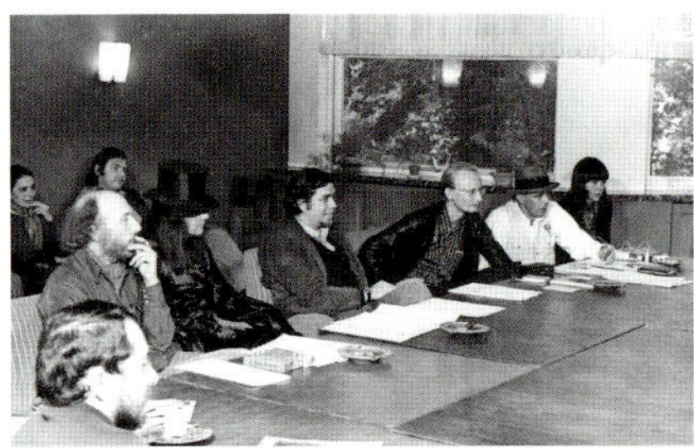

Hamilton with James Lee Byars and Joseph Beuys at a conference at the Tate Gallery, London, 1974

of his work in Spain, at Galeria Cadaqués (July). Stayed briefly in Berlin under the DAAD scheme. Met the artists James Lee Byars and Mario Merz. Published the *Trichromatic flower-piece progressives portfolio* (1973–74), comprising seven "states" of the etching, accompanied by an introductory text by the Belgian poet and artist Marcel Broodthaers who, on leaving Germany, moved with his family to North London, near to where Hamilton lived.

1975

Made four lithographs with Kenneth Tyler at Tyler Graphics in New York, and experimented further with the possibilities of manual colour separation and trichromatic registration. At the invitation of Vinçon, a famous Barcelona design shop and gallery, made variations on the "Ricard" branded carafe, sign and ashtray by adding an "h" after the "c" to spell "Richard"; these were exhibited at Franco Bombelli's Galeria Cadaqués (August) in an installation mounted for one day only.

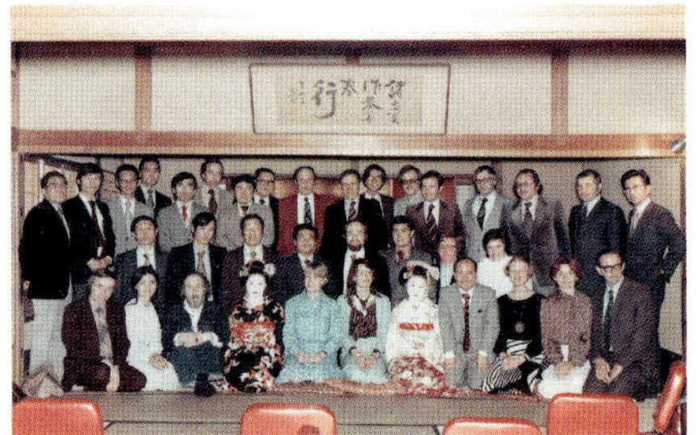

Hamilton (first row, third from left) visiting the Lux Corporation headquarters, Japan, 1974

1976

"Collaborations" made with Dieter Roth in Cadaqués, Spain. Bought a derelict farm complex in Oxfordshire and began the process of restoration and adaptation. Both Cedric Price and Frank Newby came to look at the project. Hamilton employed architect Stephen Mullin, as he had done when he built a studio at Hurst Avenue in the 1960s. Mullin worked for Price from 1964–70.

1977

"INTERFACEs" begun with Dieter Roth in Cadaqués, Spain, and completed in London. Exhibited *Release* stage proofs and related work at the Tate Gallery (August). Bryan Ferry, lead singer of Roxy Music, released the hit single *This is Tomorrow*, a tribute to Hamilton. Ferry, who frequently credited his former teacher's inspiration, would later reminisce that "[Hamilton] once remarked that I was his 'greatest creation'—which I find hard to believe" (*The Observer*, 19 April 2009).

Moved to Oxfordshire in December.

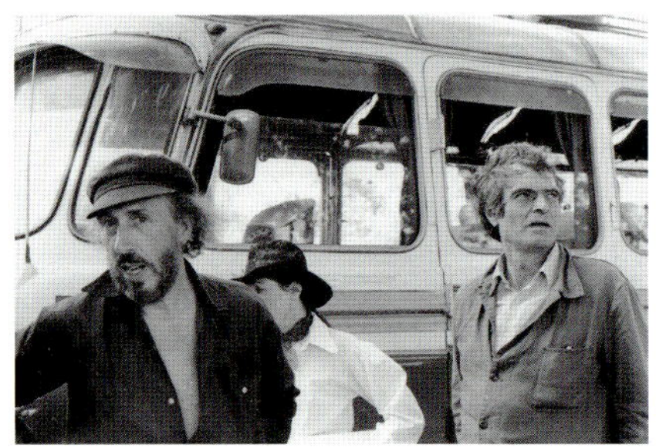

Hamilton with Marcel Broodthaers, c. 1974 (courtesy Maria Gilissen)

1978

Invited by the National Gallery, London, to participate in *The Artist's Eye* (July–August), for which he selected paintings from the collection and installed them alongside furniture from his home (including an ironing board, a working television set and chairs by Marcel Breuer and Charles and Ray Eames).

American artist Hannah Wilke produced *I Object, Memoirs of a Sugargiver* (1977–78). Hamilton took the photographs for the diptych, in which Wilke appeared nude on the rocks near the beach in Cadaqués, Spain, echoing the pose of the mannequin in *Étant donnés*.

1979

First experiments with photogravure. Exhibited *Shit and Flowers* at the Galeria Cadaqués, Spain (July). Appeared in the documentary film *Fathers of Pop (The Independent Group)*, by Reyner Banham and Julian Cooper (commissioned by the Arts Council of Great Britain).

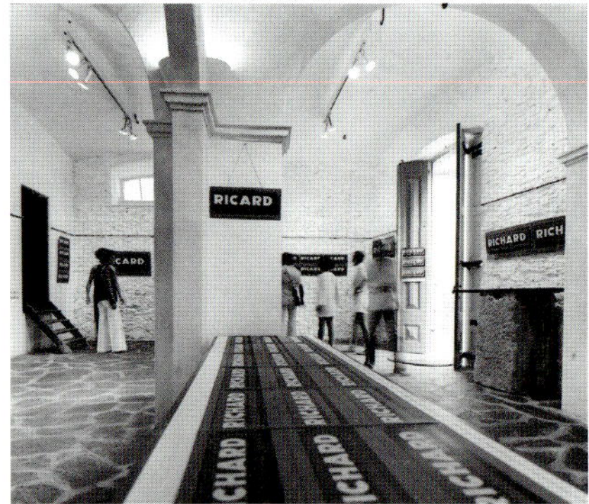

Installation of the exhibition *Ricard* at Franco Bombelli's Galeria Cadaqués, Spain, 1975 (courtesy of F. Catalá Roca)

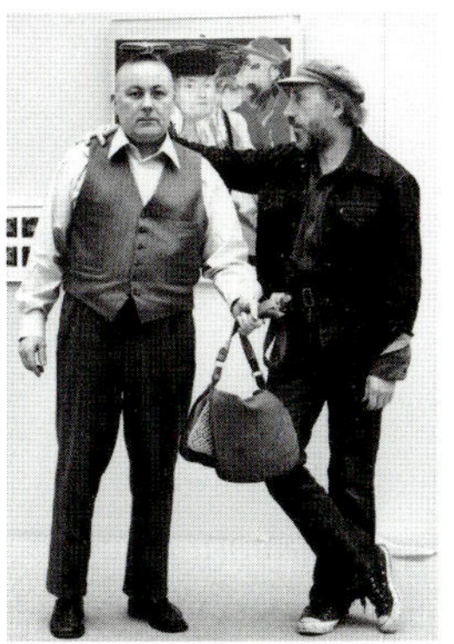
Hamilton with Dieter Roth, 1977

1980

First use of a large-format Polaroid camera in Amsterdam to make an edition of *Instant painting*. The television commercial of *The critic laughs* was included in Robert Hughes' BBC series on art since 1880, *The Shock of the New*. At a lunch in New York hosted by Jasper Johns, was teased by Bridget Riley for his habitual plagiarism; failing to recall any appropriations of Op-Art, he was informed that the Andrex advertisement he had used in *Soft pink landscape* (1971–72) had been conceived by Riley during her tenure at the J Walter Thompson advertising agency. Was invited to open a major exhibition of the work of Dieter Rams, *Design: Dieter Rams & Berlin*, at the Internationales Design Zentrum, Berlin.

1981

In Paris, with Aldo Crommelynck, made *In Horne's house* in honour of the James Joyce centenary. Resumed activity on the *Ulysses* series of illustrations and began a series of photographic self-portraits, made through a pane of glass marked with oil paint. Bought a small, inch-thick Epson HX-20 computer with the dimensions of a sheet of A4 paper with a miniature monitor, a built-in mini-cassette tape drive for the programmes and a tiny built-in printer.

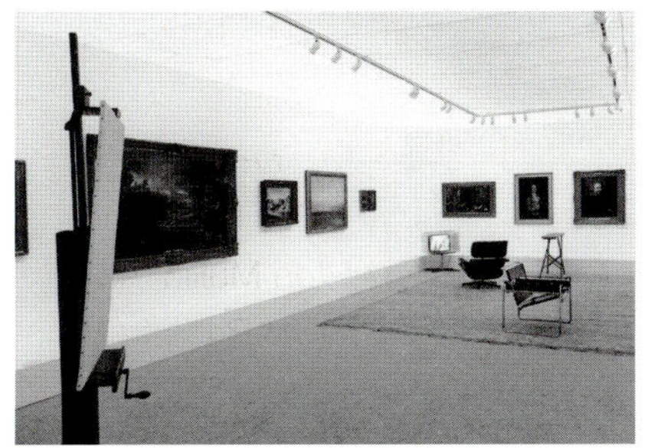
Installation of the exhibition *The Artist's Eye*, curated by Hamilton at The National Gallery, London, 1978

1982

Designed and published *Collected Words*, a work that brought together the full range of Hamilton's writings and lectures in a single illustrated volume. Was represented in the group exhibition *'60 '80: Attitudes/Concepts/Images* at the Stedelijk Museum, Amsterdam (April).

1983

First exhibition of *The citizen* at the Solomon R. Guggenheim Museum, New York, in *Aspects of Postwar Paintings in Europe* (May). From New York it travelled to the Orchard Gallery, Derry, to join Rita Donagh's exhibition *A Cellular Maze: Image and Process*, a retrospective of the graphic works at the Tate Gallery (December). Won the World Print Council Award.

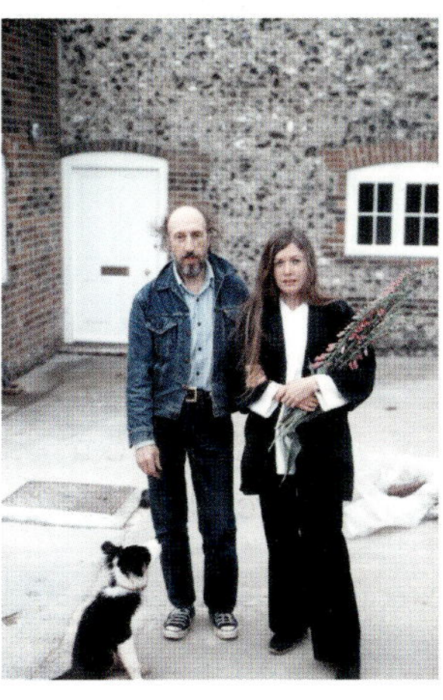
Hamilton and Rita Donagh at Northend, 1978 (courtesy Greg Curnoe)

1984

First exhibition in Sweden. Acquired an Altos 586 computer and learned UNIX, a programming language which he mastered and adapted to his own needs. Asked to design the OHIO Scientific computer for a Swedish computer company, Isotron, he proposed a set of stacked boxes with separate functions. Participated in *Four Rooms*, an Arts Council touring exhibition curated by Michael Regan. The show opened at Liberty's, London, where Hamilton installed *Treatment room*, a pointed critique of Margaret Thatcher's cuts to public funding, with an emphasis on the National Health Service. The other three artists were Anthony Caro, Marc Camille Chaimowicz and Howard Hodgkin. The exhibition *A Cellular Maze* at the ICA (May) with Rita Donagh presented *The citizen* for the first time in London.

1986

First print with Kurt Zein in Vienna. First display of the *OHIO prototype* computer at Riverside Studios, London.

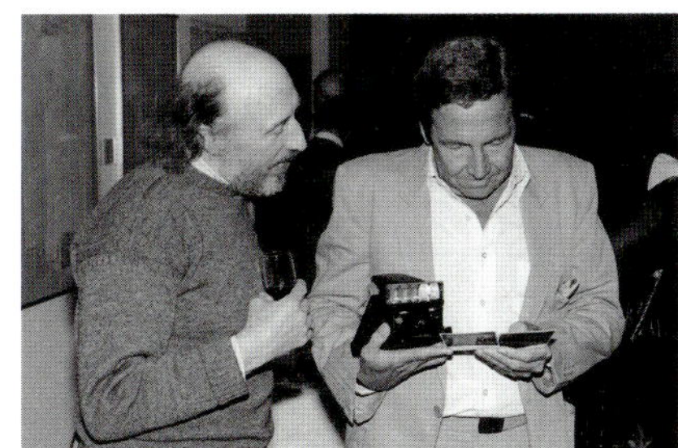
Hamilton with Robert Rauschenberg, 1981

1987

Participated in a series of TV programmes titled *Painting with Light*, made for the BBC by Griffin Production, in which six artists were invited to work with a trained computer operator

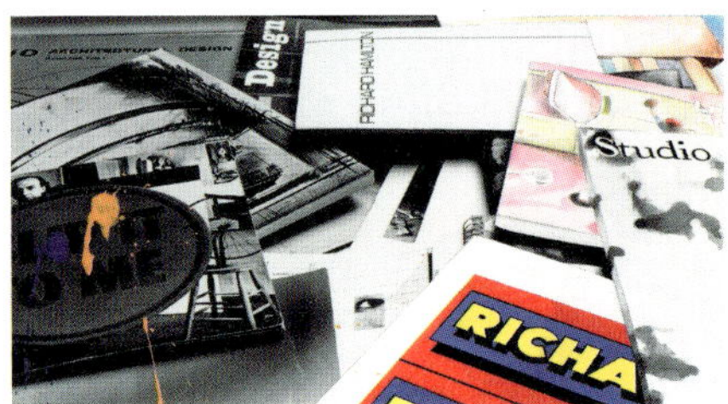

Jacket design for Hamilton's book *Collected Words*, 1982

on a Quantel Paintbox computer. Hamilton tackled a subject meant to complement his painting *The citizen* by using the Paintbox's state-of-the-art "collaging" technology to make a work portraying an Orange parade in the north of Ireland. A reconstruction of the *This is Tomorrow* "Fun house" was installed at the Clocktower, New York.

1988

Treatment room was re-exhibited, along with three other room installations representing "office," "hotel" and "prison," in *Richard Hamilton: Installations* at the Fruitmarket Gallery, Edinburgh (March–May), curated by Mark Francis. Reworked the Orangeman painting on a Quantel Graphic Paintbox, at a higher resolution, as a study for *The subject* (1988–90).

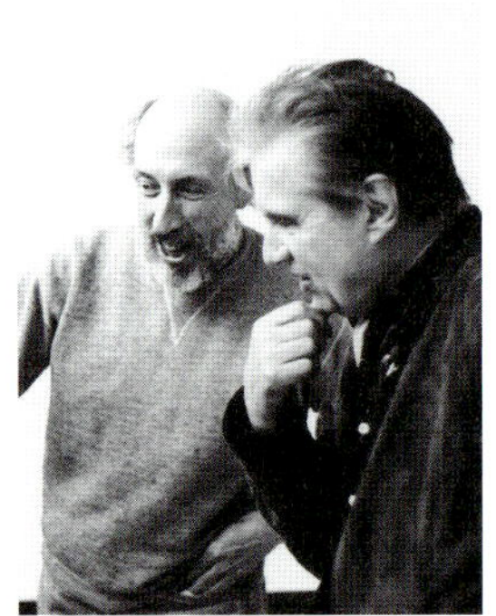

Hamilton with Francis Bacon, 1983 (courtesy Barry Joule)

1989

Ingvar Larsson, head of research at DIAB, a computer engineering and manufacturing firm, revived Hamilton's design project for the computer company Isotron (acquired by DIAB). Hamilton's *Diab DS-101* computer, based on the OHIO concept, was completed and exhibited at the Moderna Museet, Stockholm; Hamilton referred to this machine as his "dream computer." Exhibited *Image & Process* and *Lobby* at the XX Bienal Internacional, Sao Paulo (October).

1990

Reconstructed a version of *an Exhibit* (1957) for the exhibition *The Independent Group: Postwar Britain and the Aesthetics of Plenty* which opened at the ICA (February–April) and toured to IVAM in Valencia, Spain (May–September); MoCA, Los Angeles (November–January, 1991); University Art Museum, U.C. Berkeley (February–April, 1991); and the Hood Museum, Dartmouth College, Hanover, New Hampshire (June–August, 1991).

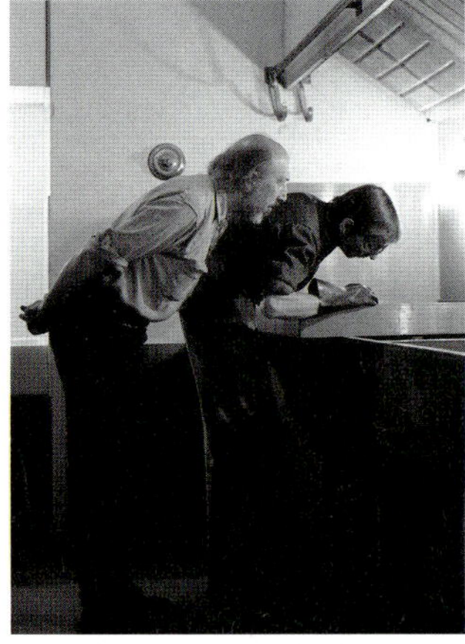

Hamilton working with Aldo Crommelynck, Paris, 1985

1991

Delivered the William Townsend Memorial Lecture at University College London on "The Hard Copy Problem," which dealt with the proliferating technology of the computer and the questions it raises for artists as regards the resolution and durability of an image.

Married Rita Donagh in July.

1992

The Tate Gallery retrospective (June) toured to the Irish Museum of Modern Art (October). Bryan Ferry's TV documentary *This is Tomorrow*, featuring juxtapositions of Pop Art and pop music of his own and Hamilton's, was aired on 20 June on Channel 4.

1993

Commissioned by Andrea Rose, Brendan Griggs and Gill Hedley, Hamilton represented Great Britain at the Venice Biennale and was awarded the Golden Lion for Painting.

Invited by the BBC to participate in a series of half-hour programmes entitled *Q.E.D.* In his slot, titled "Art and Chips," Hamilton demonstrated an artist's use of a computer to generate art: recreated the experience of making his 1956 collage *Just what is it…* in a manner appropriate to the 1990s, replete with objects heralding the arrival of the Digital Age. Produced the resulting print, *Just what is it that makes today's homes so different?*, in an edition of 5000 with fifty artist's proofs and invited viewers to write a postcard to the BBC to receive a free copy.

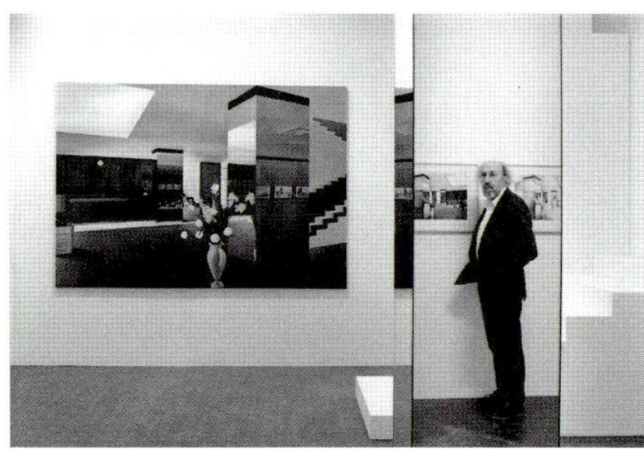

Hamilton in his *Lobby* installation at the Fruitmarket Gallery, Edinburgh, 1988

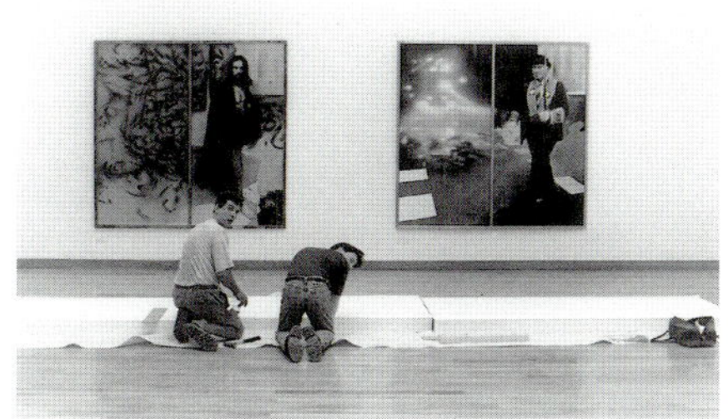

Hamilton's installation in the British Pavilion at the Venice Biennale, 1993 (courtesy William Feaver)

1995

Exhibited *Seven rooms,* a series of seven digitally-manipulated paintings, in a group show titled *Five Rooms* at the Anthony d'Offay Gallery, London.

1996

Exhibited the *Seven rooms* paintings in a show titled *Site-Referential Paintings* at the San Francisco Museum of Modern Art (February). Represented in *Face à l'Histoire 1933–1996* at the Centre George Pompidou, Paris (December). The Museum of Modern Art, New York, acquired *Pin-up* (1961).

1997

Awarded the Arnold Bode Prize at documenta X, Kassel (curated by Catherine David), where he showed the site-specific *Seven rooms* paintings (1995) installed in a re-creation of the Anthony d'Offay Gallery interior, alongside the "typosophic pavilion" created with Ecke Bonk. Daughter Dominy died in December.

1998

The *New Technology in Print* exhibition at Alan Cristea, London, gave a first look at Hamilton's foray into digital media with a focus on his continued engagement with printmaking. A major exhibition of prints, *Subject to an Impression*, opened at the Kunsthalle, Bremen.

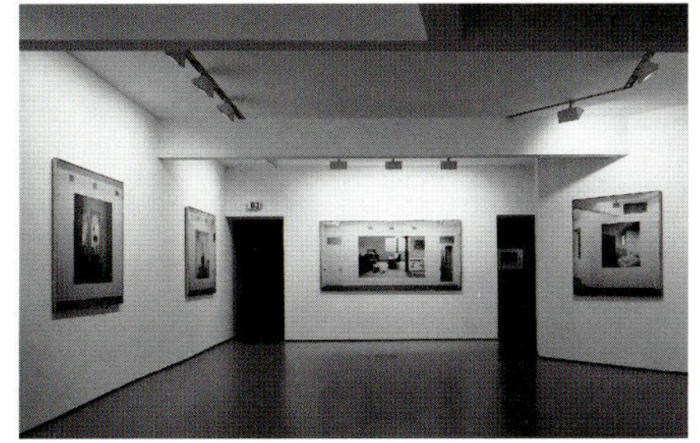

Installation view of the restaging of Hamilton's *Seven rooms* exhibition at documenta X, Kassel, 1997

1999

Made a Member of the Order of the Companions of Honour (December). Exhibited in the Ljubljana Trienalle, Slovenia. Published *Marcel Duchamp: à l'infinitif*, a "typotranslation" of Duchamp's "White Box Notes" in collaboration with Ecke Bonk and Jackie Matisse Monnier.

2000

Exhibited *Vier Räume* (Four Rooms) at the Museum Fridericianum, Kassel (December). Exhibited works, including *Lobby* (1985–87), in the group show *Suite Substitute IV: Beautiful Strangers* at the Hotel du Rhône, Geneva (June–July). A photograph of the installation became the basis of the digital print *Chiara & chair* (2004).

2001

Exhibited *Imaging James Joyce's Ulysses*, more than 100 drawings, etchings and prints made from the 1940s onwards to illustrate James Joyce's novel *Ulysses* (1922), at the Cankarjev dom gallery, Ljubljana (June), which travelled to the Kunsthalle Tubingen, Germany (October).

2002

The British Museum exhibited *Imaging James Joyce's Ulysses* (February); in the catalogue, Hamilton said of Joyce and Marcel Duchamp: "Their genius pervades my life." Exhibited the print retrospective *Prints and Multiples 1939–2002* at the Kunstmuseum Winterthur, Switzerland (the home of Hamilton's complete print collection).

Typo/Typography of Marcel Duchamp's Large Glass shown in the exhibition *retinal. optical.visual.conceptual* curated by Ecke Bonk and Sarat Maharaj at the Museum Boijmans Van Beuningen, Rotterdam.

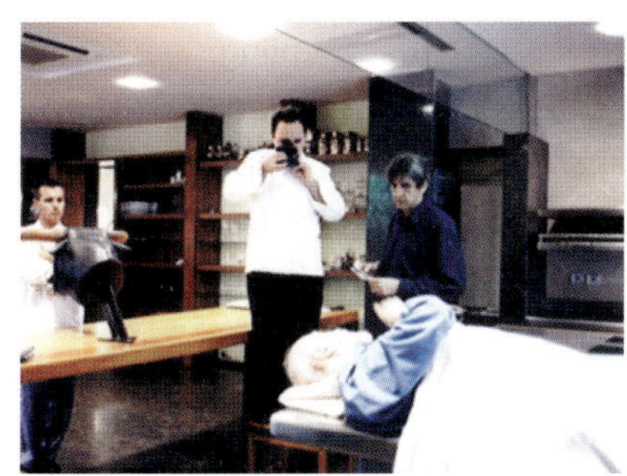

Chef Ferran Adrià photographing Hamilton in the kitchen of his restaurant elBulli, Roses, Spain, 1999

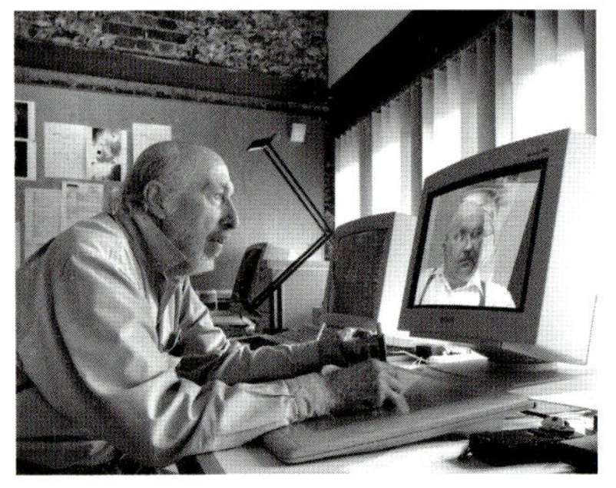

Hamilton working on his portrait of *Dieter Roth* on his Paintbox computer, Northend, 1998

2003

The Museum of Contemporary Art in Barcelona (MACBA), Spain, staged a retrospective of his work (March–June), for which Hamilton designed the catalogue. The Retrospective then travelled to the Ludwig Museum, Cologne (June). Exhibited *Typo/Topography of Marcel Duchamp's Large Glass*, *The heaventree of stars* (1998) and *studies for heaventree* (shown on his Diab DS-101 computer) in *Days Like These* (February–May), the Tate Triennial jointly curated by Jonathan Watkins and Judith Nesbitt.

2004

Exhibited *Prints and Multiples 1939–2002* at the Yale Center for British Art, New Haven (February).

2006

Awarded the Max Beckmann Prize for Painting. Exhibited *Products* at the CQL Design Centre, Shanghai (September). Prior to that, the exhibition *Painting by Numbers* at Alan Cristea Gallery, London (May–June), comprised a range of Hamilton's digital works (from between 1992 and 2005) made using either Quantel Printbox or Apple Macintosh computers.

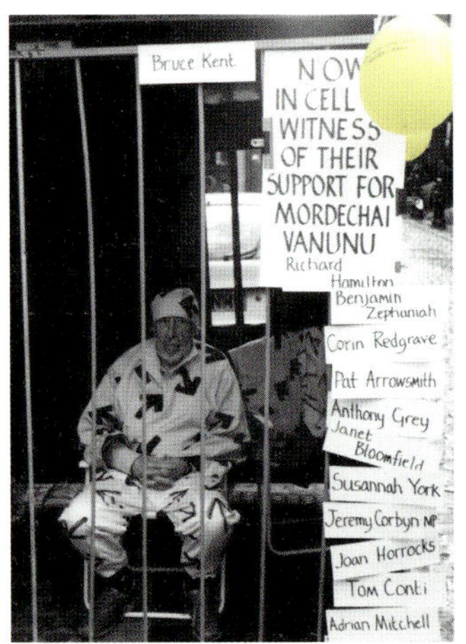

Campaign to Free Vanunu
12-hour vigil, outside Israeli embassy, London, 30th September 2001
24 celebrities participated
Photograph by Ernest Rodker

2007

Exhibited *A Host of Angels* at the Palazzetto Tito, Venice, as a contribution of the Fondazione Bevilacqua La Masa to the 52nd Venice Biennale. One of the paintings was inspired by Fra Angelico's San Marco *Annunciation* (c. 1440); the installation of rooms included furniture and appliances from Hamilton's home that appear in the images.

2008

Awarded the Praemium Imperiale prize for painting by the imperial family of Japan on behalf of the Japan Art Association.

Collaborated with the UWE Centre for Fine Print Research on the creation of *The Hutton Award*, a commission from the British Art Medal Trust to make a medal of dishonour to be included in an exhibition at the British Museum. The medal, created with 3D modelling and printing, depicted former Prime Minister Tony Blair (who resigned in 2007) on one face and Alastair Campbell (Blair's one-time Director of Communications and Strategy) on the other.

Exhibited *Virtual Spaces* at the Kunsthalle Bielefeld, Germany (May), and *Protest Pictures* at Inverleith House, Edinburgh (August).

2009

Exhibited *Toaster deluxe* (2008), a series of 14 unique digital and relief prints at the Gagosian Gallery, London (April). These pieces reprised an image Hamilton had been working with intermittently from the mid-1960s: a Braun toaster remodelled into an eponymously branded art object. With Vicente Todolí, edited and collaborated with the designer Fernando Gutiérrez on *Food for Thought: Thought for Food*, a book exploring the gastronomic creativity of elBulli, inspired by Chef Ferran Adrià's controversial participation in documenta XII.

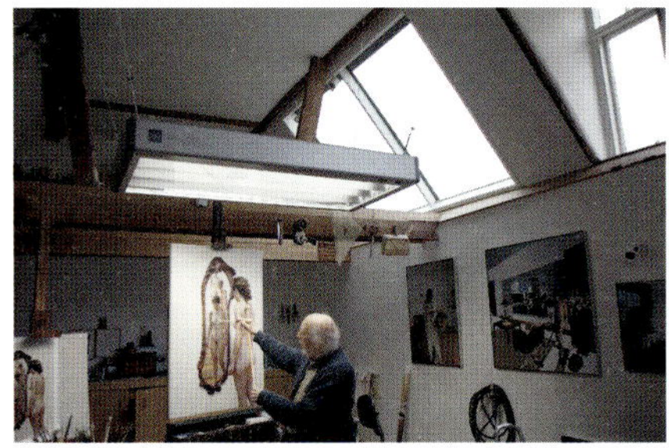

Hamilton working on *Descending nude* in his Northend studio, 2006

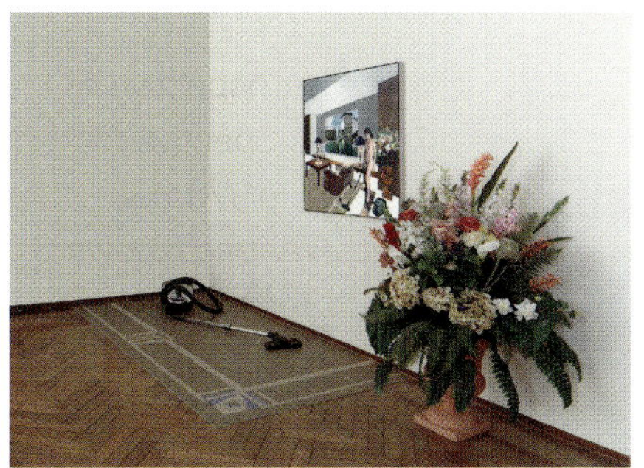

Installation of the exhibition *A Host of Angels* at the Fondazione Bevilacqua La Masa, Palazzetto Tito, Venice, 2007

2010

Exhibited his *Picasso's meninas* at the Museo Nacional del Prado, Madrid, alongside Francisco de Goya's and Pablo Picasso's versions of Diego Velázquez's *Las meninas* (March). The solo show titled *Modern Moral Matters* that opened at the Serpentine Gallery, London (March), brought together Hamilton's major political works, including a new work titled *Unorthodox rendition*, a portrait of Mordechai Vanunu, the Israeli nuclear technician who was kidnapped in 1986 after telling the world that Israel had a nuclear weapons programme. Exhibited *Shit and Flowers* at the Alan Cristea Gallery, London (May), comprising prints and paintings from Hamilton's 1970s "scatological period." Exhibited *The Hutton Award* in a group exhibition, *Medals of Dishonour*, at the British Museum, London (June).

2011

Ferran Adrià closed elBulli in July, having requested that Hamilton symbolically lock the doors of the restaurant after the final meal; Hamilton, seriously ill, could not attend the last supper.

an Exhibit (1957) was installed as part of *Modern British Sculpture*, Royal Academy of Arts, London (January–April), alongside a reconstruction of the small stone barn that housed Kurt Schwitters' unfinished *Merzbarn* (1947–48).

Civil Rights etc. opened at the Hugh Lane Gallery, Dublin (September–January 2012) in which Rita Donagh's paintings were hung alongside Hamilton's work from the earlier *Modern Moral Matters* exhibition.

Hamilton died on 13 September.

2012

Richard Hamilton: The Late Works opened at The National Gallery, London (October).

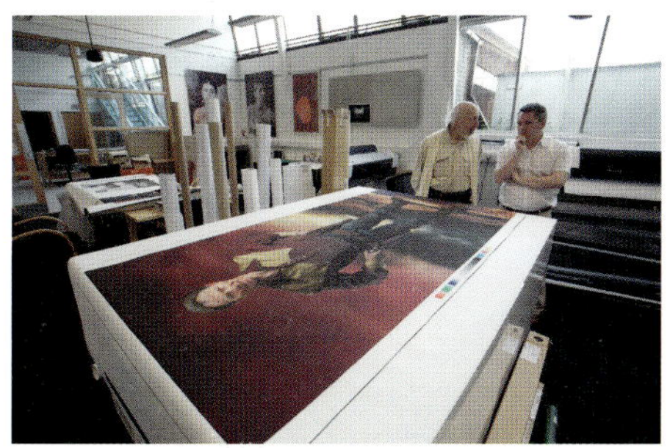

Hamilton with Professor Steve Hoskins working on *Shock and Awe* at the Centre for Fine Print Research at the University of the West of England, Bristol, 2009 (courtesy Paul Laidler)

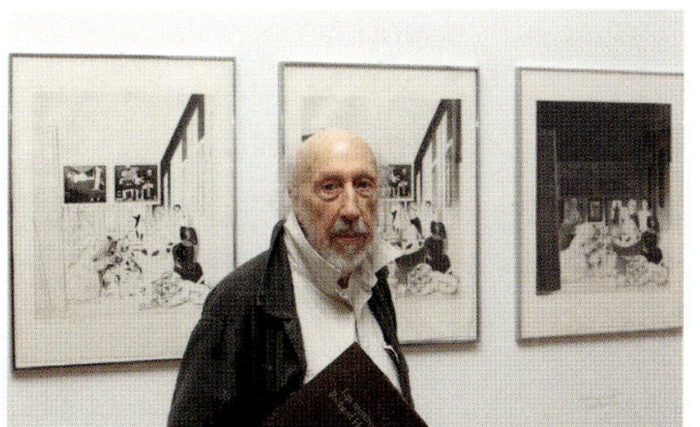

Hamilton at his exhibition *Las meninas de Richard Hamilton* at the Prado, Madrid, 2010

List of Works

* *Works only on show at the Museo Nacional Centro de Arte Reina Sofía*

** *Works only on show at Tate Modern*

Reaper (a)
1949
Hard-ground etching
17.3 x 24.7 cm (plate);
28.7 x 32.7 cm (sheet)
Private collection

Reaper (b)
1949
Drypoint and roulette
16.2 x 23.6 cm (plate);
23 x 29 cm (sheet)
Private collection

Reaper (c)
1949
Hard-ground etching
and dry stipple
20 x 24.7 cm (plate);
27.1 x 35.9 cm (sheet)
Private collection

Reaper (d)
1949
Drypoint and roulette
17 x 27.2 cm (plate);
27.6 x 41.4 cm (sheet)
Private collection* /
Tate: Purchased 1982**

Reaper (e)
1949
Hard-ground etching and roulette
17.5 x 22.3 cm (plate);
23 x 29 cm (sheet)
Private collection* /
Tate: Purchased 1982**

Reaper (f)
1949
Drypoint, roulette and punches
16.5 x 22.3 cm (plate);
23.7 x 28.3 cm (sheet)
Private collection

Reaper (g)
1949
Hard-ground etching
22.4 x 32.3 cm (plate);
28 x 38.2 cm (sheet)
Private collection* /
Tate: Purchased 1982**

Reaper (h)
1949
Drypoint and roulette
17.5 x 25 cm (plate);
28.6 x 35.3 cm (sheet)
Private collection* /
Tate: Purchased 1982**

Reaper (i)
1949
Lift-ground and aquatint
19.8 x 27.6 cm (plate);
27.2 x 35.9 cm (sheet)
Private collection* /
Tate: Purchased 1982**

Reaper (j)
1949
Hard-ground etching and roulette
9.9 x 22.1 cm (plate);
24.6 x 35.7 cm (sheet)
Private collection* /
Tate: Purchased 1982**

Reaper (k)
1949
Engraving, roulette and drypoint
17.5 x 19.8 cm (plate);
28.1 x 38.6 cm (sheet)
Private collection

Reaper (l)
1949
Engraving, aquatint and drypoint
16.3 x 24.3 cm (plate);
37.3 x 45 cm (sheet)
Private collection

Reaper (m)
1949
Drypoint and roulette
12 x 15 cm (plate);
25.3 x 30.3 cm (sheet)
Private collection

Reaper (n)
1949
Hard-ground etching and
traces of etched roulette
20 x 27.3 cm (plate);
27 x 36 cm (sheet)
Kunstmuseum Winterthur.
Donated by Dr Frank and
Wiltraud Rentsch, 2003

Reaper (o)
1949
Lift-ground aquatint
19.7 x 14.8 cm (plate);
29.7 x 27.2 cm (sheet)
Private collection

Reaper (o)
1949
Lift-ground and colour
aquatint from three plates
19.7 x 14.8 cm (plate);
29.7 x 27.2 cm (sheet)
Private collection

Reaper (p)
1949
Drypoint and roulette
17.9 x 17.2 cm (plate);
39.4 x 28.3 cm (sheet)
Private collection

Chromatic spiral
1950
Oil on panel
53.5 x 47 cm
Tate: Presented
anonymously 1998

Induction study II*
1950
Ink, wash and gouache on paper
25 x 33.6 cm
Private collection

Microcosmos; plant cycle – study
1950
Ink and wash on paper
23.9 x 25.3 cm
Private collection

Growth and Form
1951 ICA, London,
reconstructed in 2014
Installation

Heteromorphism study*
1951
Ink and wash on paper
24 x 20.4 cm
Private collection

Particular system
1951
Oil on canvas
101.5 x 127 cm
Private collection

Respective
1951
Oil on hardboard
91.5 x 122 cm
Pallant House Gallery,
Chichester, UK (Wilson Loan 2006)

Self-portrait b
1951
Hard and soft-ground etching,
engraving, drypoint, aquatint
and punch
30 x 20 cm
Private collection* /
Tate: Purchased 1982**

Self-portrait – study*
1951
Ink wash on paper
24 x 20.5 cm
Victoria and Albert Museum,
London. Given by the Artist

d'Orientation
1952
Oil on hardboard
117 x 160 cm
Private collection

Sketch for "Ex-Position"*
1952–53
Gouache, watercolour, pencil
and ink on paper
35.5 x 30.1 cm
Colección Malla i Figueras

Out and up
1953
Ink and watercolour on paper
34.3 x 48.6 cm
Tate: Accepted by HM Government
in lieu of tax and allocated to the
Tate Gallery 1992

Sketch for "Super-Ex-Position" I*
1953
Ink and watercolour on paper
laid on board by the artist
19.05 x 25.4 cm
Private collection, United Kingdom.
Courtesy of Simon Lee Gallery

Drawing for "Trainsition"*
1954
Pencil, ink and watercolour
on paper
23 x 37 cm
Private collection

Trainsition III
1954
Oil on panel
76 x 56 cm
Private collection

Trainsition IIII
1954
Oil on panel
91.5 x 122 cm
Tate: Purchased 1970

Man, Machine and Motion
Hatton Gallery, Newcastle upon
Tyne; and ICA, London, 1955,
reconstructed by The New Museum
for the exhibition "Ghosts in the
Machine" curated by Massimiliano
Gioni and Gary Carrion-Murayari,
New York,
2012 Installation

See, hear, smell, touch
1956
Collage
21 x 22.1 cm
Museum Ludwig, Cologne/
Donation Ludwig
[Work not in the exhibition]

Just what is it that makes today's homes so different, so appealing?
1956, reconstructed in 1992
Cibachrome
Collage
26 x 25 cm
Private collection

This is Tomorrow
Group 2 installation
With John Voelcker
and John McHale
1956, reconstructed in 1987
Mixed media
415 x 600 x 300 cm
IVAM, Institut Valencià d'Art
Modern, Generalitat.
Gift of the artist

an Exhibit
With Victor Pasmore
and Lawrence Alloway
1957 Hatton Gallery, Newcastle
upon Tyne; and ICA, London,
reconstructed in 2014
Installation

Study for "Hommage à Chrysler Corp."
1957
Ink, gouache and collage on paper
34.5 x 21.5 cm
Private collection

Hommage à Chrysler Corp. (a)
1957
Lithograph with pastel, gouache
and collage on newsprint
35.5 x 49.5 cm
Private collection

Hommage à Chrysler Corp.
1957
Oil, metal foil and collage on panel
122 x 81 cm
Tate: Purchased with assistance
from the Art Fund and the Friends
of the Tate Gallery 1995

Study for "Hers is a lush situation"
1957
Ink, crayon, watercolour, gouache,
and metal foil on paper
23 x 37 cm
Private collection

Hommage à Chrysler Corp.
1958
Collage and ink
47 x 37 cm
Private collection

Hers is a lush situation, etching
1958
Hard-ground etching, blind
embossed, coloured crayon
with collage
17.2 x 25 cm (plate);
27.5 x 40.2 cm (sheet)
Private collection

Hers is a lush situation
1958
Oil, cellulose, metal foil
and collage on panel
81 x 122 cm
Pallant House Gallery, Chichester,
UK (Wilson Gift through The Art
Fund 2006)

Toastuum
1958
Ink, watercolour, aerosol paint,
and collage on paper
44 x 38 cm
Private collection

$he
1958–61
Oil, cellulose and collage on panel
122 x 81 cm
Tate: Purchased 1970

The bride stripped bare by her bachelors, even
1960
Documentation and book about
"The Bride Stripped Bare by her
Bachelors, Even"
A4-sized box and papers
Private collection

Pin-up
1961
Oil, cellulose and collage on paper
122 x 81 cm
The Museum of Modern Art,
New York. Enid A. Haupt Fund
and an anonymous fund, 1996

Glorious Techniculture
1961–64
Oil and collage on asbestos panel
122.9 x 122.9 cm
The Museum of Modern Art,
New York. Enid A. Haupt Fund
and The Sidney and Harriet Janis
Collection (by exchange), 1999

AAH!*
1962
Oil on panel
81 x 122 cm
Hessisches Landesmuseum
Darmstadt

Towards a definitive statement on the coming trends in menswear and accessories (a) sketch II
1962
Gouache, metal foil and
collage on paper
25.5 x 35.5 cm
Collection Amy Gold
and Brett Gorvy

Towards a definitive statement on the coming trends in menswear and accessories (a) "Together let us explore the stars"
1962
Oil and collage on panel
61 x 81 cm
Tate: Purchased 1964

Towards a definitive statement on the coming trends in menswear and accessories (b)
1962
Oil and collage on panel
67.5 x 87.3 cm
Private collection

Towards a definitive statement on the coming trends in menswear and accessories (b) sketch
1962
Gouache and collage on paper
25.5 x 35.5 cm
[Work not in the exhibition]

Towards a definitive statement on the coming trends in menswear and accessories (c) Adonis in Y-fronts
1962
Oil and collage on panel
61 x 81.3 cm
The Art Institute of Chicago.
Restricted gift of Muriel Newman
in honour of Emese and James N.
Wood; Walter Aitken Endowment

Towards a definitive statement on the coming trends in menswear and accessories (d)**
1963
81 x 122 cm
Oil, collage, perspex relief on panel
Museum Ludwig, Cologne/
Donation Ludwig

Study for "Portrait of Hugh Gaitskell as a Famous Monster of Filmland"**
1963–70
Copper on aluminium relief
and collage on motorised disc
45.5 x 45.5 cm
Private collection

Portrait of Hugh Gaitskell as a Famous Monster of Filmland
1964
Oil and collage on photograph
on panel
61 x 61 cm
Arts Council Collection,
Southbank Centre, London

A little bit of Roy Lichtenstein for...**
1964
Screen print on paper
51.1 x 69.2 cm
Tate: Presented by Rose and
Chris Prater through the Institute
of Contemporary Prints 1975
[P04249]

Epiphany
1964
Cellulose on panel
122 cm diameter
Private collection

Five Tyres abandoned**
1964
Screen print on paper
44.8 x 74.9 cm
Tate: Presented by Rose and
Chris Prater through the Institute
of Contemporary Prints 1975

Interior I
1964
Oil and collage on panel with
inlaid mirror
122 x 162 cm
Kunsthaus Zürich, Legat Erna
und Curt Burgauer

Interior II
1964
Oil, cellulose, collage and
metal relief on panel
122 x 162.5 cm
Tate: Purchased 1967

Interior study (b)
1964
Collage, oil, pastel and
gouache on paper
38 x 51 cm
Private collection, London

Interior study (c)
1964
Collage, oil and pastel on paper
38 x 51 cm
Pallant House Gallery, Chichester,
UK (Wilson Loan 2006)

Magic Carpets
1964
Collage on printed
perspective grid
38 x 49.5 cm
Private collection

Desk
1964
Oil and collage on
photograph on panel
62.5 x 89 cm
Scottish National Gallery
of Modern Art, Edinburgh

My Marilyn (paste-up)
1964
Oil on photograph
51 x 62 cm
Museum Ludwig, Cologne/
Donation Ludwig

My Marilyn
1965
Oil, collage and photograph
on panel
102.5 x 122 cm
Collection Ludwig, Ludwig Forum für
Internationale Kunst, Aachen

Marcel Duchamp
**La Mariée mise à nu par
ses célibataires, même****
[The Bride Stripped Bare by her
Bachelors, Even (The Large Glass)]
1915–23, reconstruction by
Richard Hamilton 1965–66,
lower panel remade 1985
Oil, lead, dust and varnish on glass
277.5 x 175.9 cm
Tate: Presented by William N. Copley
through the American Federation of
Arts 1975
[T02011]

Marcel Duchamp
Nine malic moulds
1914–15, reconstruction
by Richard Hamilton 1965
Oil and lead on glass
113.7 x 30.6 x 76.1 cm
Private collection

Marcel Duchamp
**Glider containing a water mill
(in neighbouring metals)**
1913–15, reconstruction by
Richard Hamilton 1966
Oil and lead wire and
tin sheet on glass
147 x 79 cm
Private collection

Oculist witnesses – study
1965
Ink on tracing paper
59 x 48.2 cm
Private collection

Still-life
1965
Photograph with sprayed
photo tints
89.5 x 91 cm
Museum Ludwig, Cologne /
Donation Ludwig

Still-life – study
1965
Collage
20.5 x 20.5 cm
Private collection

Trafalgar Square study*
1965
Oil and acrylic on panel
40.5 x 61 cm
Private collection, courtesy
Fondazione Marconi, Milan

Whitley Bay
1965
Oil and photograph on panel
81 x 122 cm
Birmingham Museums Trust

People
1965–66
Oil and cellulose on photo
on panel
81 x 122 cm
Private collection

**The Solomon R. Guggenheim –
architect's visual***
1965
Pastel and gouache
51 x 58.5 cm
The Museum of Modern Art,
New York. Gift of Charles B.
Benenson, 1967

**The Solomon R. Guggenheim
(Black)**
1965–66
Fibreglass and cellulose
122 x 122 x 19 cm
Solomon R. Guggenheim Museum,
New York

**The Solomon R. Guggenheim
(Black and White)**
1965–66
Fibreglass and cellulose
122 x 122 x 19 cm
Solomon R. Guggenheim Museum,
New York

**The Solomon R. Guggenheim
(Gold)**
1965–66
Fibreglass, cellulose and gold leaf
122 x 122 x 20.5 cm
Louisiana Museum of Modern Art,
Humlebæk, Denmark.
Long-term loan: Museumsfonden
of 7 December 1966

**The Solomon R. Guggenheim
(Metalflake)**
1965–66
Fibreglass, acrylic and metalflake
122 x 122 x 18 cm
Private collection

**The Solomon R. Guggenheim
(Neapolitan)**
1965–66
Fibreglass and cellulose
122 x 122 x 18 cm
Tate: Purchased 1970

**The Solomon R. Guggenheim
(Spectrum)**
1965–66
Fibreglass and cellulose
121.9 x 121.9 x 20.3 cm
Solomon R. Guggenheim Museum,
New York

Trafalgar Square
1965–67
Oil on photograph on panel
81 x 122 cm
Museum Ludwig, Cologne /
Donation Ludwig

Bathers I
1966–67
Mixed media on
photo-sensitized fabric
84 x 117 cm
Museum Ludwig, Cologne /
Donation Ludwig

Toaster
1966–67
Chromed steel and Perspex
on colour photograph
81 x 81 cm
Private collection

Bathers II*
1967
Oil and colour
photo-sensitized fabric
76 x 114.5 cm
Private collection

**I'm dreaming of a white
Christmas – sketch***
1967
Watercolour, gouache, crayon
and pencil
69 x 101 cm
Museum Ludwig, Cologne /
Donation Ludwig

**I'm dreaming of a white
Christmas – study**
1967
Lithograph and gouache
71 x 91.5 cm
Private collection
[Work not in the exhibition]

Toaster – lithograph
1967
Offset lithograph in 4 colours,
screen printed from 4 stencils,
and collaged with metalized
polyester
58.4 x 58.4 cm (plate);
89 x 63.5 cm (sheet)
Private collection

**I'm dreaming of a white
Christmas**
1967–68
Oil on canvas
106.5 x 160 cm
Museum Ludwig, Cologne /
Donation Ludwig

Richard Hamilton
(in collaboration with Dieter Roth)
Bei uns*
1968–69
Acrylic, collage, cellulose
and gouache on photo
53.5 x 79 cm
Dieter Roth Foundation, Hamburg.
C/ Dieter Roth Estate / courtesy
Hauser & Wirth

Oculist witnesses
With Marcel Duchamp
1968
Mirror silver in laminated glass
51 x 63.5 cm
Private collection

Richard Hamilton
(in collaboration with Dieter Roth)
People/Popel*
1968
Acrylic, collage, cellulose
and gouache on photo
53.5 x 79 cm
Colección Malla i Figueras

People multiple (1/1)
1968
Photographs on board
or aluminium
44 x 69 cm
Kunstmuseum Winterthur.
Donated by Dr Frank and
Wiltraud Rentsch, 2002

The critic laughs
1968
Photo-offset lithograph,
laminated screen print
22 x 9 x 5 cm
Private collection

Swingeing London 67 – sketch
1968
Pencil, pastel, watercolour,
and metalized acetate on paper
33 x 48 cm
Arts Council Collection, London
[Work not in the exhibition]

Swingeing London 67 – poster
1968
Photo-offset lithograph
69 x 47 cm (plate);
70.5 x 50.0 cm (sheet)
Private collection* / Tate: Presented by Rita Donagh 1978**

Swingeing London 67 – screen print
1968
Relief, screen print on oil on photograph on hardboard
58.5 x 79 x 7.5 cm
Pallant House Gallery, Chichester, UK (Wilson Gift through The Art Fund 2006)

Swingeing London 67 – working drawing*
1968
Ink and gouache on photo
40.5 x 51 cm
Private collection

Swingeing London 67 (a)
1968–69
Oil on canvas and screen print
67 x 85 cm
Private collection

Swingeing London 67 (b)
1968–69
Oil on canvas and screen print
67 x 85 cm
Museum Ludwig, Cologne / Donation Ludwig

Swingeing London 67 (c)
1968–69
Silkscreen ink on synthetic polymer paint on canvas
67 x 85 cm
The Museum of Modern Art, New York. Donald L. Bryant Jr., Douglas S. Cramer, Ronald S. Lauder, and John Angelo Funds, 2002

Swingeing London 67 (d)
1968–69
Oil on canvas and screen print
67 x 85 cm
Private collection
[Work not in the exhibition]

Swingeing London 67 (e)
1968–69
Enamel on canvas and screen print
67 x 85 cm
Private collection

Swingeing London 67 (f)
1968–69
Screen print on canvas, acrylic and collage
67 x 85 cm
Tate: Purchased 1969

Swingeing London 67
1969
Screen print and pastel on paper
71 x 88 cm
Private collection
[Work not in the exhibition]

The Beatles
1968
Cover design
31 x 32 x 0.7 cm
Private collection

The Beatles
1968
Collage
90.2 x 60 cm
Private collection

Polaroid Portraits
1968–2001
128 polaroid photographs
17.7 x 12.7 cm each
Private collection

People again
1969
Crayon, gouache and collage on photo
31 x 51 cm
Private collection
[Work not in the exhibition]

Richard Hamilton
(in collaboration with Dieter Roth)
Bei ihr*
1969
Dye transfer with acrylic
38.7 x 54.1 (plate);
48.8 x 64.1 (sheet)
Colección Malla i Figueras

Fashion-plate study (a) self-portrait
1969
Collage, enamel and cosmetics on paper
70 x 50 cm
Private collection

Fashion-plate (cosmetic study II)
1969
Collage, enamel, acrylic and cosmetics on lithographed paper
100 x 70 cm
Private collection

Fashion-plate (cosmetic study III)
1969
Collage, enamel, acrylic and cosmetics on lithographed paper
100 x 70 cm
Private collection

Fashion-plate (cosmetic study V)
1969
Collage, acrylic and cosmetics on lithographed paper
100 x 70 cm
Private collection

Fashion-plate (cosmetic study VI)
1969
Collage, enamel and cosmetics on lithographed paper
100 x 70 cm
Francesca and Massimo Valsecchi

Fashion-plate (cosmetic study VII)
1969
Collage, pastel, acrylic and cosmetics on lithographed paper
100 x 70 cm
Private collection

Fashion-plate (cosmetic study VIII)
1969
Collage, enamel, acrylic and pastel on lithographed paper
100 x 70 cm
Francesca and Massimo Valsecchi

Toaster study I
1969
Letrafilm on colour photograph
38.7 x 20.7 cm
Private collection

Kent State
1970
Pastel on paper
56.5 x 76.2 cm
Private collection, courtesy Fondazione Marconi, Milan

Kent State – screen print
1970
Screen print from 13 stencils
67.3 x 87 cm (plate);
73 x 102.2 cm (sheet)
Private collection* /
Tate: Purchased 1984**

Kent State – stage proofs
1970
12 screen prints
67.3 x 87 cm (plate);
73 x 102.2 cm (sheet)
Private collection

Portrait of the artist by Francis Bacon – study I
1970
Oil on collotype
82 x 69 cm
Karin und Uwe Hollweg Stiftung, Bremen

Portrait of the artist by Francis Bacon – study II
1970
Oil on collotype
82 x 69 cm
Karin und Uwe Hollweg Stiftung, Bremen

Portrait of the artist by Francis Bacon – study III
1970
Oil on collotype
82 x 69 cm
Karin und Uwe Hollweg Stiftung, Bremen

Portrait of the artist by Francis Bacon – study IV
1970
Oil on collotype
82 x 69 cm
Karin und Uwe Hollweg Stiftung, Bremen

Portrait of the artist by Francis Bacon – study V
1970
Oil on collotype
82 x 69 cm
Karin und Uwe Hollweg Stiftung, Bremen

Portrait of the artist by Francis Bacon – study VI
1970
Oil on collotype
82 x 69 cm
IVAM, Institut Valencià d'Art Modern, Generalitat

Eine kleine schöne Scheisse*
1971
Gouache and graphite pencil on tracing paper
30.6 x 23.8 cm
Colección MACBA. Fundación MACBA. Familia Bombelli Deposit

Eine kleine schöne Scheisse für Dieter*
1971
Collotype
22 x 15 cm (plate);
45 x 35 cm (sheet)
Private collection

Flower-piece*
1971
Pencil and acrylic on paper
75.7 x 56 cm
Private collection

Flower-piece*
1971
Pencil, conte crayon, collage, pastel, watercolour and acrylic
76.2 x 56 cm
Private collection

Flower-piece postcards a–c*
1971
Acrylic on 3D postcards
14.5 x 10.2 cm
Colección MACBA. Fundación MACBA. Familia Bombelli Deposit

Flower-piece study (a)*
1971
Pastel, watercolour and gouache
53.5 x 40.5 cm
Colección Malla i Figueras

Five Tyres remoulded (portfolio)
1971
Relief cast in white silicone elastomer, 7 screen prints in black on Mylar, and 1 sheet of text in 5-colour collotype
60 x 85 cm
Private collection* /
Tate: Presented by the Contemporary Art Society 1975**

I'm dreaming of a black Christmas
1971
Screen print on collotype with collage
50.8 x 76.1 cm (plate);
74.7 x 100 cm (sheet)
Private collection* /
Tate: Purchased 2013**

Sieves
With Marcel Duchamp
1971
Screen print in laminated glass
48.5 x 61 x 1 cm
Museo Nacional Centro de Arte Reina Sofía, Madrid

The critic laughs – case
1971
Ink, Ben Day tints, and metalized acetate on Mylar
46 x 65.5 cm
IVAM, Institut Valencià d'Art Modern, Generalitat

Soft blue landscape – study*
1971
Collage, coloured pencils and watercolour on paper
37 x 34 cm
Colección MACBA. Fundación MACBA. Familia Bombelli Deposit

Soft pink landscape – study*
1971
Collage, coloured pencils and watercolour on paper
56 x 75.5 cm
Colección MACBA. Fundación MACBA. Depósito Familia Bombelli

Soft pink landscape
1971–72
Oil on canvas
123.5 x 164.3 cm
Ludwig Museum – Museum of Contemporary Art, Budapest

The critic laughs
1971–72
Electric toothbrush with teeth, case and instruction book
Case: 27 x 11 x 6.5 cm
Private collection

Flower-piece I
1971–74
Oil on canvas
95 x 72 cm
Private collection

A Tutti Mercanti d'Arte Moderna*
1972
Acrylic and newsprint on paper
30.8 x 21.7 cm
Colección MACBA. Fundación MACBA. Familia Bombelli Deposit

By the soft blue waters of Miers*
1972
Drypoint, aquatint, hard- and soft-ground etching, hand-coloured with watercolour and gouache
64 x 57.3 cm (plate);
85.2 x 68.9 cm (sheet)
Private collection

By the waters of Miers*
1972
Drypoint, aquatint, hard- and soft-ground etching
64 x 57.3 cm (plate);
90.1 x 69.1 cm (sheet)
Private collection

Esquisse*
1972
Soft-ground etching, watercolour touched by the artist
19 x 27.2 cm (plate);
36 x 45 cm (sheet)
Private collection

Esquisse – stage proof*
1972
Soft-ground etching
19 x 27.2 cm (plate);
36 x 45 cm (sheet)
Private collection

Étude pour les eaux de Miers*
1972
Pencil and graphite on paper
18 x 28 cm
Colección MACBA. Fundación MACBA. Familia Bombelli Deposit

Girl surprised in the forest*
1972
Pastel and watercolour on paper
59 x 47 cm
Private collection

Girl with skirt up
1972
Collage, pencil, acrylic and oil on printed paper
56 x 40.5 cm
Private collection

Girl with trousers down
1972
Collage, acrylic and oil
56 x 40.1 cm
Private collection

Polaroid Portraits, vol. 1
1972
Edition Hansjörg Mayer. Stuttgart, London and Reykjavik
Book
16.5 x 12.5 x 1 cm
Private collection

The critic laughs – illustration
1972
Letraset on photo on board
21.6 x 19.7 cm /
16 x 16.2 cm (paper)
IVAM, Institut Valencià d'Art Modern, Generalitat

Trade mark
1972
Ink and pencil on board
22 x 41 cm
IVAM, Institut Valencià d'Art Modern, Generalitat

Flower-piece II
1973
Oil on canvas
95 x 72 cm
Private collection

Flower-piece – black plate study*
1973
Ink wash on Mylar
54 x 38 cm
Private collection

Flower-piece – mask*
1973
Mylar
62.3 x 32.8 cm
Private collection

Flower-piece study (b)*
1973
Coloured pencils and acrylic on paper
58.5 x 46 cm
Colección MACBA. Fundación MACBA. Familia Bombelli Deposit

Flower-piece study (c)*
1973
Pastels and acrylic on paper
58.5 x 46 cm
Colección MACBA. Fundación MACBA. Familia Bombelli Deposit

Flower-piece – trial proof*
1973
First trial proof with normal etching inks
65 x 50 cm
Private collection

Flower-piece – trial proof*
1973
Proof with pastel additions
65 x 50 cm
Private collection

Flower-piece – trial proof*
1973
Proof with process inks
65 x 50 cm
Private collection

Flower-piece – trial proof*
1973
Proof with pastel additions
65 x 50 cm
Private collection

Flower-piece – trial proof*
1973
Proof
65 x 50 cm
Private collection

Flower-piece – trial proof*
1973
Proof with letrafilm mask
65 x 50 cm
Private collection

Flower-piece – trial proof*
1973
Colour etching with list of inks
65 x 50 cm
Private collection

Flower-piece – trial proof*
1973
Colour etching with list of inks
65 x 50 cm
Private collection

Flower-piece – trial proof*
1973
Colour etching with trials of inks
65 x 50 cm
Private collection

Flower-piece – trial proof*
1973
Proof
65 x 50 cm
Private collection

Flower-piece – trial proof*
1973
Proof with pastel and acrylic
65 x 50 cm
Private collection

Flower-piece – trial proof*
1973
Magenta printed black with yellow, red and blue acrylic
65 x 50 cm
Private collection

Flower-piece – trial proof*
1973
Blue proof with pastel
65 x 50 cm
Private collection

Flower-piece – trial proof*
1973
Proof in black with pastel
65 x 50 cm
Private collection

Flower-piece – trial proof*
1973
Colour etching with pastel
65 x 50 cm
Private collection

Flower-piece – working drawing*
1973
Mylar
56.5 x 39 cm
Private collection

Un des effets des eaux de Miers
1973
Stipple etching and aquatint, printed Chine collé with Jeyes Bonco toilet paper
11.3 x 17.5 cm (plate);
15 x 20.9 cm (sheet)
Private collection

Flower-piece III
1973–74
Oil on canvas
95 x 72 cm
Private collection

Trichromatic flower-piece*
1973–74
Colour aquatint in 3 colours and black from 4 plates
42.4 x 33 cm (plate);
65.2 x 50.5 cm (sheet)
Private collection

Trichromatic flower-piece progressives
1973–74
7 colour etchings in portfolio
Portfolio: 65 x 50 cm
Museo Nacional Centro de Arte Reina Sofía, Madrid

Flower-piece A*
1974
Collotype and screen print
45.5 x 30 cm (plate);
65.5 x 50 cm (sheet)
Private collection

Multi-coloured flower-piece*
1974
Colour etching
30 x 24 cm (plate);
50.5 x 41.5 cm (sheet)
Private collection

Multi-coloured flower-piece – proof marked up by Crommelynck with colour instructions for printer*
1974
Etching and aquatint
48.7 x 41.2 cm
Private collection

Multi-coloured flower-piece – progressive*
1974
Hard-ground etching
30 x 24 cm (plate);
50.5 x 41.5 cm (sheet)
Private collection

Multi-coloured flower-piece – progressive*
1974
Coloured aquatint from 3 plates
30 x 24 cm (plate);
50.5 x 41.5 cm (sheet)
Private collection

Multi-coloured flower-piece – working proof*
1974
Black and white print with coloured pencil
30 x 24 cm (plate);
40.7 x 26 cm (sheet)
Private collection

Palindrome
1974
Lenticular acrylic, laminated on collotype in 5 colours
60.9 x 45.7 cm
Private collection* /
Tate: Presented by Tate Members 2010**

Sunrise*
1974
Pastel on paper
31 x 40 cm
Colección MACBA. Fundación MACBA. Familia Bombelli Deposit

Sunset (a)
1974
Pastel on paper
31 x 40 cm
Private collection

Sunset (d)
1974
Pastel on paper
31 x 41 cm
Private collection

Sunset (e)
1974
Pastel on paper
31 x 42 cm
Private collection

Richard Hamilton
(in collaboration with Dieter Roth)
Two flower-pieces*
1974
Collotype, screen print and collage
65 x 50 cm
Private collection

Europhotel-Berlin
1974–75
Coloured pencils, collage and watercolour on paper
46 x 58.5 cm
Private collection

Flower-piece B*
1975
Lithograph in 3 colours and white, from 6 stones and 4 plates
42 x 31 cm (plate);
65 x 50 cm (sheet)
Private collection

Flower-piece B – 15 progressives*
1975
Lithographs from 6 stones and 4 plates
42 x 31 cm (plate);
65 x 50 cm (sheet)
Private collection

Flower-piece B – crayon study*
1975
Lithograph in 4 colours from 4 stones
42 x 31 cm (plate);
65 x 50 cm (sheet)
Private collection

Flower-piece B – cyan separation*
1975
Lithograph
42 x 31 cm (plate);
65 x 50 cm (sheet)
Private collection

Flower-piece B – study for litho*
1975
Conte and wash on paper
58.5 x 46 cm
Private collection

Flower-piece B – study for litho*
1975
Pencil on paper
57 x 45 cm
Colección MACBA. Fundación MACBA. Familia Bombelli Deposit

Flower-piece B – trial proof*
1975
Lithograph and pastel
65 x 50 cm
Col.lecció Olor Visual, Barcelona

Flower-piece B – trichromatic study*
1975
Coloured pencils and wash on paper
58.5 x 46 cm
Colección MACBA. Fundación MACBA. Familia Bombelli Deposit

Soft blue landscape – study*
1975
Watercolour, colour pencils and collage
56 x 76 cm
Colección Malla i Figueras

Soft blue landscape – study*
1975
Collage, coloured pencils and watercolour on paper
56 x 76 cm
Colección MACBA. Fundación MACBA. Familia Bombelli Deposit

Sunrise
1975
Collotype
17.3 x 23.3 cm (plate);
33.1 x 40 cm (sheet)
Private collection

Sunset
1975
Oil on canvas
61 x 81 cm
Private collection

Sunset (f)
1975
Lithograph from 1 stone in 2 colours
23.9 x 35.9 cm (plate);
42 x 53.8 cm (sheet)
Private collection* /
Tate: Presented by Tyler Graphics Ltd in honour of Pat Gilmour, Tate Print Department 1974–77, 2004**

Sunset (f)*
1975
Pastel on paper
31 x 40 cm
Colección Malla i Figueras

Sunset (i)
1975
Pastel on paper
31 x 43 cm
Private collection

Sign
1975
Vitreous enamel on steel
34.7 x 70 cm
Private collection

Advertisement
1975
Screen print from 5 stencils
55 x 42 cm (plate);
64 x 49.1 cm (sheet)
Private collection

Langan's
1976
Oil on photograph on cloth
92 x 92 cm
Private collection

Soft blue landscape
1976–80
Oil on canvas
122 x 162.5 cm
Private collection

Carafe
1978
Enamel paint on glass
9 x 20 x 6 cm
Private collection

Polaroid Portraits, vol. 2
1978
Edition Hansjörg Mayer.
Stuttgart, London and Reykjavik
Book
16.5 x 12.5 x 1 cm
Private collection

Ashtray
1979
Enamel paint on yellow glass
3.4 x 15.5 x 13.5 cm
Private collection

Lux 50 – functioning prototype
1979
Aluminium support, cellulose
and anodised aluminium
100 x 100 cm
Private collection

Soft blue landscape*
1979
Collotype in 7 colours and
screen print from approximately
10 stencils in 40 colours
61.4 x 85 cm (plate);
72.5 x 91.8 cm (sheet)
Private collection

Soft pink landscape
1980
Collotype in 7 colours and
screen print from approximately
10 stencils in 35 colours
59.3 x 82 cm (plate);
72.8 x 91.6 cm (sheet)
Private collection*

Soft pink landscape – printers proof*
1980
Collotype
52.5 x 70 cm (plate);
73 x 91.8 cm (sheet)
Private collection

Soft pink landscape – study II*
1980
Hand-retouched and
airbrushed collotype
52.5 x 70 cm (plate);
73 x 91.8 cm (sheet)
Private collection

Polaroid Portraits, vol. 3
1982
Edition Hansjörg Mayer. Stuttgart,
London and Reykjavik
Book
16.5 x 12.5 x 1 cm. Two copies
Private collection

Self-portrait (1965)**
1982
Collotype and screen print
on paper
38.4 x 30 cm
Tate: Presented by
Tate Members 2010
[P79805]

The citizen
1982–83
Oil on canvas (2 canvases)
200 x 100 cm each
Tate: Purchased 1985

Finn MacCool**
1983
Photo-etching, aquatint
and engraving on paper
53.5 x 39.8 cm
Tate: Purchased 1991
[P77492]

Treatment room**
1983–84
Installation
275 x 550 x 550 cm
Arts Council Collection.
The South Bank Centre, London

Lobby
1984
Collotype in 6 colours
33 x 48 cm (plate);
43 x 50.3 cm (sheet)
Private collection* /
Tate: Presented by
Tate Members 2009**

Lobby – working drawings
1984
Pencil and red ink on
Mylar film (4 sheets)
42 x 60 cm each
Private collection

Lobby
1985–87
Oil on canvas
175 x 250 cm
Private collection

Lobby
1988
Installation
310 x 550 x 550 cm
Private collection

The subject
1988–90
Oil on canvas (2 canvases)
200 x 100 cm each
Tate: Purchased 1993

Self-portrait 12.7.80 a
1990
Oil on cibachrome on canvas
75 x 75 cm
Karin und Uwe Hollweg Stiftung,
Bremen

Self-portrait 13.7.80 a
1990
Oil on cibachrome on canvas
75.4 x 75.6 cm
IVAM, Institut Valencià d'Art Modern,
Generalitat

Self-portrait 04.3.81 b
1990
Oil on cibachrome on canvas
75 x 75 cm
Private collection

Self-portrait 05.3.81 a
1990
Oil on cibachrome on canvas
75 x 75 cm
Private collection

Self-portrait 05.3.81 c
1990
Oil on cibachrome on canvas
75 x 75 cm
Karin und Uwe Hollweg Stiftung,
Bremen

Northend II*
1991
Oil on cibachrome on canvas
99.3 x 108.7 cm
Private collection

Two gentlemen of Alba
1991
Oil on cibachrome
100 x 78 cm
Private collection, courtesy
Fondazione Marconi, Milan

War games**
1991–92
Oil paint on Scanachrome
on canvas
200 x 200 cm
San Francisco Museum of Modern
Art. Gift of Vicki and Kent Logan

Dieter Roth
1993
Humbrol enamel on
cibachrome on canvas
75 x 75 cm
Private collection

Testament*
1993
Oil on cibachrome on canvas
82 x 60 cm
British Council Collection

The state
1993
Humbrol enamel and cloth
on cibachrome on canvas
(2 canvases)
200 x 100 cm each
Tate: Purchased 1993

Derek Jarman
1994
Oil and enamel on cibachrome
on canvas
75 x 75 cm
Private collection

Bathroom
1994–95
Cibachrome and oil on canvas
122 x 122 cm
Private collection

Bedroom
1994–95
Cibachrome and oil on canvas
122 x 178 cm
Hessisches Landesmuseum
Darmstadt
[Work not in the exhibition]

Dining room
1994–95
Cibachrome on canvas
122 x 162 cm
Leeum, Samsung Museum of Art

Dining room/kitchen
1994–95
Cibachrome on canvas
122 x 203 cm
Leeum, Samsung Museum of Art

Kitchen
1994–95
Cibachrome on canvas
122 x 162 cm
Private collection

Passage*
1994–95
Cibachrome on canvas
121 x 147.5 cm
Museumslandschaft Hessen
Kassel, Neue Galerie, Städtischer
Kunstbesitz (municipal art collection)

An annunciation (a)
1994–2004
Oil on cibachrome on canvas
119.5 x 119.5 cm
Private collection

Attic
1995–96
Cibachrome on canvas
122 x 244 cm
Philadelphia Museum of Art:
Purchased with funds contributed
by the Committee on Twentieth-
Century Art, with additional funds
contributed by Mr. and Mrs. Keith L.
Sachs, The Dietrich Foundation, and
Marion Boulton Stroud, 1997
[Work not in the exhibition]

Giorgio Marconi e figlio*
1996
Cibachrome and oil on canvas
120 x 160 cm
Private collection

À l'infinitif
1999
Documentation and book about
"The Bride Stripped Bare by her
Bachelors, Even"
Private collection

Bathroom - fig.2 II
2005-6
Oil on Fuji/Océ LightJet on canvas
100 x 100 cm
Private collection

The Saensbury Wing
1999–2000
Oil on canvas
59.7 x 82 cm
Private collection

Polaroid Portraits, vol. 4
2001
Edition Hansjörg Mayer.
Stuttgart, London and Reykjavik
Book
16.5 x 12.5 x 1 cm. Two copies
Private collection

Table with ashtray
2002
Slate, oak, brass and glass
130 x 60 x 33 cm
Private collection

Bathroom - fig.1 II
1997–2004
Cibachrome on canvas
50 x 50 cm
Private collection

Chiara & chair
2004
Inkjet digital print
60.7 x 89.2 cm (plate);
73.2 x 107.5 cm (sheet)
Private collection* /
Tate: Purchased 2004**

The passage of the bride
2004
Oil on cibachrome on canvas
102 x 127 cm
Private collection

Hotel du Rhône
2005
Oil on Fuji/Océ LightJet on canvas
100 x 100 cm
Private collection

An annunciation (b)
2005–6
Oil on canvas
56.5 x 55.5 cm
Private collection

Descending nude*
2006
Oil on Fuji/Océ Lightjet on canvas
110 x 73 cm
Private collection

Portrait of a woman as an artist
2007
Oil on Fuji/Océ LightJet on canvas
100 x 123 cm
Private collection

Toaster deluxe 1
2008
Inkjet, stainless steel, polycarbonate on Somerset velvet for Epson paper 505 gsm, GM WaterWhite Museum glass, tulip wood, brass, expanded neoprene, polyethylene
88.5 x 73.3 x 3 cm
Alan Cristea

Toaster deluxe 2*
2008
Inkjet, stainless steel, polycarbonate on Somerset velvet for Epson paper 505 gsm, GM WaterWhite Museum glass, tulip wood, brass, expanded neoprene, polyethylene
88.5 x 73.3 x 3 cm
Katherine and Keith Sachs

Toaster deluxe 5
2008
Inkjet, stainless steel, polycarbonate on Somerset velvet for Epson paper 505 gsm, GM WaterWhite Museum glass, tulip wood, brass, expanded neoprene, polyethylene
88.5 x 73.3 x 3 cm
Private collection

Toaster deluxe 6*
2008
Inkjet, stainless steel, polycarbonate on Somerset velvet for Epson paper 505 gsm, GM WaterWhite Museum glass, tulip wood, brass, expanded neoprene, polyethylene
88.5 x 73.3 x 3 cm
Private collection

Toaster deluxe 7
2008
Inkjet, stainless steel, polycarbonate on Somerset velvet for Epson paper 505 gsm, GM WaterWhite Museum Glass, tulip wood, brass, expanded neoprene, polyethylene
88.5 x 73.3 x 3 cm
Private collection

Toaster deluxe 8
2008
Inkjet, stainless steel, polycarbonate on Somerset velvet for Epson paper 505 gsm, GM WaterWhite Museum glass, tulip wood, brass, expanded neoprene, polyethylene
88.5 x 73.3 x 3 cm
Frank and Lorna Dunphy collection

Toaster deluxe 9*
2008
Inkjet, stainless steel, polycarbonate on Somerset velvet for Epson paper 505 gsm, GM WaterWhite Museum glass, tulip wood, brass, expanded neoprene, polyethylene
88.5 x 73.3 x 3 cm
Private collection

Toaster deluxe 10
2008
Inkjet, stainless steel, polycarbonate on Somerset velvet for Epson paper 505 gsm, GM WaterWhite Museum glass, tulip wood, brass, expanded neoprene, polyethylene
88.5 x 73.3 x 3 cm
Private collection, London

Toaster deluxe AP 1*
2008
Inkjet, stainless steel, polycarbonate on Somerset velvet for Epson paper 505 gsm, GM WaterWhite Museum glass, tulip wood, brass, expanded neoprene, polyethylene
88.5 x 73.3 x 3 cm
Private collection

Toaster deluxe AP 2*
2008
Inkjet, stainless steel, polycarbonate on Somerset velvet for Epson paper 505 gsm, GM WaterWhite Museum glass, tulip wood, brass, expanded neoprene, polyethylene
88.5 x 73.3 x 3 cm
Private collection

Toaster deluxe deconstructed
2008
Inkjet, stainless steel, polycarbonate on Somerset velvet for Epson paper 505 gsm, GM WaterWhite Museum glass, tulip wood, brass, expanded neoprene, polyethylene
88.5 x 73.3 x 3 cm
Private collection

Maps of Palestine**
2009
EFI VUTEK inkjet solvent print on canvas
200 x 175 cm
Private collection

Unorthodox rendition
2009–10
Oil on canvas
75 x 95 cm
Private collection

Shock and Awe
2010
Hewlett-Packard inkjet print on HP Premium canvas
200 x 100 cm
Private collection

untitled
2011
Epson inkjet on Hewlett-Packard Resolution canvas
Three parts, each 112 x 176
Private collection

Bibliography

1. Writings by the artist

See also all other sections.

"5 Tyres remoulded." *Studio International* 183, no. 945 (1972), 276–77. Reprinted in *Collected Words.*

A Cellular Maze. Derry: Orchard Gallery, 1983. Texts by Rita Donagh and Richard Hamilton.

"A Wholemeal Loaf for Joseph." In *Ohne die Rose tun wir's nicht: für Joseph Beuys*, 148–49. Heidleberg: Edition Staeck, 1986.

"About Art Teaching, Basically." *Motif* 8 (Winter 1961), 17–23. Reprinted in *Collected Words*.

"An Exposition of $he." *Architectural Design* 32, no. 10 (October 1962), 485–86. Reprinted in *Collected Words*.

"Anteckner am fotographie." *Konstmagasinet* (Malmo), no. 12–13 (September 1991), 20–23. Swedish translation of "Photography and Painting."

Ark 34 (Summer 1963), 4, 14–16, 24–26, 34–38.

"Art and Design." In *Popular Culture and Personal Responsibility*, 135–56. Conference lecture (26–28 October 1960). London: National Union of Teachers, 1961. Reprinted in *Collected Words*.

"Artificial Obsolescence." *Product Design Engineering* (January 1963). Reprinted in *Collected Words*.

Carnegie International 1991. Pittsburgh: The Carnegie Museum of Art, 1991. Includes statement by Hamilton.

Collaborations of Ch. Rotham. Stuttgart: Edition Hansjörg Mayer; Cadaqués: Galería Cadaqués, 1977. Texts and play *Die Grosse Bockwurst* by Dieter Roth and/or Richard Hamilton.

Collected Words 1953–1982. London: Thames & Hudson, 1982. Compilation of writings by Hamilton.

"Colour Television: Seven Singular Choices." *Radio Times*, 12 November 1970.

Contemporary British Artists with Photographs by Walia. New York: St Martin's Press, 1979.

Copley Book. Chicago: William and Noma Copley Foundation, 1965. Introduction by Hamilton.

"Der Widerstand von Long Kesh." *du*, no. 513 (November 1983), 32–35. German translation of *A Cellular Maze*.

"Diagrammar." In *The Developing Process* [exh. cat.], 19–26. Newcastle upon Tyne: University of Durham, 1959. Reprinted in *Collected Words.*

"Dieter Roth: 1930–1998." Recollections by Richard Hamilton, Maja Oeri, Paul McCarthy, Emmett Williams, Patrick Frey, Dieter Schwarz, Corinne Diserens, Gary Garrels, and Harald Szeemann. *Artforum* 37, no. 2 (1998), 90–101.

"Duchamp." *Art International* 7, no. 10 (January 1964), 22–28. Reprinted in *Collected Words*.

"Endangered Species." *The Tamarind Papers* 13 (1990), 34.

"First Year Studies at Newcastle." *Times Educational Supplement*, 1960. Reprinted in *Collected Words*.

"FoB+10." *Design*, no. 149 (May 1961), 40–51. Reprinted in *Collected Words*.

"For the Finest Art, Try Pop." *Gazette*, no. 1 (1961). Reprinted in *Collected Words*.

Four Rooms. London: Arts Council of Great Britain, March 1984. Includes text by Hamilton.

"Glorious Technicolor, Breathtaking CinemaScope and Stereophonic Sound." 1959 lecture on technical innovations in the entertainment industries, first published in *Collected Words.*

"Hamilton's Plaint." *Art Monthly*, no. 49 (September 1981).

"Hommage à Chrysler Corp." *Architectural Design* 28, no. 3 (March 1958), 120–21. Reprinted in *Collected Words*.

In Horne's House. London: Waddington Graphics, 1982. Reprinted in *Collected Words*.

INTERFACEs. 2 vols. Basel: Roth's Verlag, 1988.

"Interfaces." *Sondern* (Zurich), no. 4 (1979), 154–68.

"John Latham." In *John Latham: Early Works 1954–1972*, 7–16. London: Lisson Gallery, 1987.

Kex. Chicago: William and Noma Copley Foundation, 1966. A collection of Eduardo Paolozzi's scrapbook pages edited into a continuous text by Hamilton.

Le Grand Déchiffreur: Richard Hamilton sur Marcel Duchamp. Zurich: JRP/Ringier, 2009. Collected interviews and correspondence between Marcel Duchamp and Richard Hamilton.

"Letter." *Art Monthly* (March 1977).

"Letter." *Catalyst*, January 1971, 78.

"Letters." *Aspects*, no. 11 (Summer 1980).

"Magical Myth for Our Time." *Sunday Times* (London), 22 February 1970, 51. Reprinted in *Collected Words*.

"Making their Mark." *The Independent*, 17 December 1991.

Marcel Duchamp. À l'Infinitif / In the Infinitive. A typotranslation by Richard Hamilton and Ecke Bonk of Marcel Duchamp's *The White Box*, translated from the French by Jackie Matisse, Richard Hamilton and Ecke Bonk. Northend: The typosophic society, 1999.

"NOT SEEN and/or LESS SEEN of/by MARCEL DUCHAMP/RROSE SELAVY 1904–64." Introduction and notes in *The Mary and William Sisler Collection Catalog.* New York: Cordier & Ekstrom, 1965.

"Persuading Image." *Design*, no. 134 (February 1960), 28–32. Published version of lecture, "The Designed Image of the Fifties." Reprinted in *Collected Words.*

"Photography and Painting." *Studio International* 177, no. 909 (March 1969), 120–25. Partly reprinted in *Collected Words.*

Polaroid Portraits, vol. 1. Stuttgart; London; Reykjavik: Edition Hansjörg Mayer, 1972. Polaroid photographs of Hamilton by 32 artists.

Polaroid Portraits, vol. 2. Stuttgart; London; Reykjavik: Edition Hansjörg Mayer, 1977. Polaroid photographs of Hamilton by 32 artists.

Polaroid Portraits, vol. 3. Stuttgart; London; Reykjavik: Edition Hansjörg Mayer, 1983. Polaroid photographs of Hamilton by 32 artists.

Polaroid Portraits, vol. 4. Stuttgart; London; Reykjavik: Edition Hansjörg Mayer, 2002. Polaroid photographs of Hamilton by 32 artists.

"Portrait of Hugh Gaitskell as a Famous Monster of Filmland." 1964, first published in *Collected Words*.

"Propositions." *Catalyst* (May 1971), 20. Reprinted in Collected Words.

"Recollections of Joseph Beuys." *Art Monthly*, no. 94 (March 1986), 10–11.

Richard Hamilton: Proposiciones. Barcelona: MACBA / UAB-Universitat Autònoma de Barcelona, 2010.

"Roll of Honour: Marcel Broodthaers." *Art Monthly*, no. 1 (October 1976), 3.

"Roy Lichtenstein." *Studio International* 175, no. 896 (January 1968), 20–24. Reprinted in *Collected Words*.

"Statement by the Artist." In *Twentieth Century Artists on Art*, ed. Dore Ashton, 143–44. New York: Pantheon, 1985.

"Statement on 'Glorious Techniculture'." *Architectural Design* 21, no. 11 (November 1961), 497.

The Almost Complete Works of Marcel Duchamp. London: The Arts Council of Great Britain, 1966. Introduction and catalogue notes by Hamilton.

The Artist's Eye. London: National Gallery, 1978. Catalogue introduction. Reprinted in *Collected Words*.

"The Books of Diter Rot." *Sondern* (Zurich), no. 2 (1977). Updated text of *Typographica* (1961). German translation. Reprinted in *Collected Words*.

"The Books of Diter Rot." *Typographica*, no. 3 (June 1961), 21–40. Reprinted in *Collected Words*.

The Bride Stripped Bare by her Bachelors, Even. London: Lund Humphries, 1960. Typographic version by Richard Hamilton of Marcel Duchamp's *Green Box*, translated by George Heard Hamilton. Reprinted in *Collected Words*.

The Bride Stripped Bare by her Bachelors Even Again. Newcastle upon Tyne: Department of Fine Art, University of Newcastle upon Tyne, 1966. Reprinted in *Collected Words*.

The Expendable Ikon: Works by John McHale, 45, 47. Buffalo, NY: Albright-Knox Art Gallery, 1984.

"The Large Glass." In *Marcel Duchamp 1887–1968*, ed. Anne d'Harnoncourt and Kynaston McShine, 57–67. New York: Museum of Modern Art, 1973. First publication of Hamilton's "Large Glass" lecture. Reprinted in *Collected Words*.

"The Little World of Dieter Roth." *Sondern* (Zurich), no. 3 (1978), 34–57.

"The Ship on the Wall." *Lovely Jobly* 11, no. 111 (1991), 22.

The Transmogrification of Bloom. London: Waddington Graphics, 1986.

"The Visual Arts under Attack." *The Guardian*, 21 November 1991.

"Thesen." In *Kunst Praxis Heute: Eine Dokumentation der aktuellen Ästhetik*, 25. Cologne: DuMont, 1972. Includes German translation of "Propositions."

"Towards a Typographic Rendering of the *Green Box*." In *Uppercase* 2, ed. Theo Crosby et al. London: Whitefriars, 1959. Reprinted in *Collected Words*.

"U-L-M Spells H.f.G." *The Architect's Journal* 128, no. 3307 (17 July 1958), 73, 75. Reprinted in *Collected Words*.

"Ulm." *Design*, no. 126 (June 1959), 53–57. Reprinted in *Collected Words*.

"Urbane Image." *Living Arts 2* (June 1963), 44–59. Reprinted in *Collected Words*.

"Urbanismer." *Konstrevy*, no. 3 (Stockholm, 1967). Swedish translation of "Urbane Image" by Leif Nylen.

"When the Fan Hits the XXXX." *Art Monthly*, no. 51 (November 1981), 25–26.

"Work in Progress." *Chroniques de l'Art Vivant*, no. 29 (April 1972), 10–11. Includes French translation of "Propositions."

2. Printed interviews with the artist

Amaya, Mario. "Son of the Bride Stripped Bare." *Art and Artists* 1, no. 4 (July 1966), 22–28.

Buck, Louisa. "Pop Art and After." *The Independent Review*, 21 January 2003, 12–13.

Cork, Richard. "Richard Hamilton Interviewed by Richard Cork." In *Pop Art*, Art & Design Profiles, ed. Andreas C. Papadakis, 26–33. London: St Martin's Press, 1992.

Craig-Martin, Michael. "Richard Hamilton in Conversation with Michael Craig-Martin." In *Talking Art I (ICA Documents 12)*, ed. Adrian Searle, 73–74. London: Institute of Contemporary Arts, 1993.

Glazebrook, Elizabeth. "Slick it to me: Polaroid Portraits, Vol. I." *Studio International* 184, no. 949 (November 1972), 198–200.

Graham-Dixon, Andrew. "That Was Then." *The Independent*, 13 August 1991.

Hall, James. "The Apollo Portrait: Richard Hamilton." *Apollo* 131, no. 336 (February 1990), 101–4.

Hare, Bill, and Andrew Patrizio. "Hamilton's Progress." *Alba*, no. 9 (August 1988), 40–43.

Jones, Jonathan. "You too can have a mind like this." *The Guardian*, 18 May 2000, 12–13. www.theguardian.com/culture/2000/may/18/artsfeatures6.

Lischka, Gerhard Johan. "Das Sofortbild Polaroid." *der Löwe* (October 1977), 12–16.

"Richard Hamilton." *der Löwe*, Eine Kulturephilosophische Zeitschrift, no. 5 (July 1975), 9.

Obrist, Hans Ulrich. "Hans Ulrich Obrist interview: Richard Hamilton." *Domus*, no. 871 (June 2004), 80–83.

—. "Hans Ulrich Obrist interview: Richard Hamilton (part 2)." *Domus*, no. 872 (July–August 2004), 96–99.

Safran, Yehuda. "The Godfather of Pop." *Domus*, no. 837 (May 2001), 132–35.

Scanlan, Patricia. "HAIKU-OHIO." *Lovely Jobly* 11, no. 11 (1991), 45.

"The Distant Involvement of Richard Hamilton." *Vanguard* 7, no. 6 (October 1978), 12–14.

Vivian, Valerio. "Colloquio con Richard Hamilton." *Arte in* 3, no. 6 (Winter 1990), 45–46.

Watkins, Jonathan. "Richard Hamilton: My Love of Art Came from Museums." *Art International* (Paris), no. 10 (Spring 1990), 51–52.

Watkins, Jonathan. "The Reconstruction of Duchamp's Large Glass." *Art Monthly,* no. 136 (May 1990), 3–5.

Willing, Victor. "What Kind of Art Education?" *Studio International* 172, no. 881 (September 1966), 132–33.

Zänker, Jürgen."Pop-Dialog." *Kunstforum*, no. 111 (January–February 1991), 110–17.

3. Films, audio tapes, radio and television programmes

Broadcast items are included whether or not a transcript or recording exists.

A Tear is Better than a Bad Word, BBC Radio Three, 14 July 1974. Dieter Roth interviewed by Hamilton.

Art-Anti-Art, BBC Third Programme, 13 November 1959. Interview with Marcel Duchamp.

Artists as Consumers: The Splendid Bargain, BBC Third Programme, 11 March 1960. Discussion between Lawrence Alloway, Basil Taylor, Richard Hamilton and Eduardo Paolozzi in the "Art-Anti-Art" series.

Artists Talking. Richard Hamilton – 1: Paths of Parody and Pastiche, Lecon Arts, 1989. Tape/slide conversation with Sarat Maharaj.

Artists Talking. Richard Hamilton – 2: Coolness or Satire?, Lecon Arts, 1989. Tape/slide conversation with Sarat Maharaj.

Audio Arts, vol. 2, no. 4, 1976. Marcel Duchamp's 1959 BBC interviews with George Heard Hamilton and Richard Hamilton.

Audio Arts, vol. 6, no. 1, side 1, 1983. Interview by Michael Compton recorded at the ICA, London, on 4 November 1982 to mark the publication of *Collected Words*.

Audio Arts, vol. 9, no. 2, Autumn 1988. Tape recording of Roy Lichtenstein and Richard Hamilton in conversation with Marco Livingstone, discussion at the Museum of Modern Art, Oxford.

BBC Third Programme, 11 March 1961. Discussion.

Beyond Time, feature documentary on the life of William Turnbull, including interview segments with Richard Hamilton, Alex Turnbull (dir.), 2011.

Canciones de Cadaqués, Edition Hansjörg Mayer and Galerie Cadaqués, July 1976. Double album of EP records by Dieter Roth and Richard Hamilton, with sleeve photographs by Rita Donagh.

Collaborations Readings, Audio Arts, London, 1978. Tape recordings of readings from *Collaborations* by Dieter Roth, Richard Hamilton and Duncan Smith.

Comment, BBC Third Programme, 19 January 1961.

Conversation with Christopher Finch and James Scott, Maya Film Productions, London, 1968. Unpublished pre-edited transcript of tape made for James Scott film.

Conversations with Artists: Epiphanies, BBC Radio Three, 4 April 1985. Conversation with Richard Cork.

Den som gapar..., SRT Kanal 1 TV, Stockholm, 8 March 1992. Interview on the crash in the art market.

Fathers of Pop (The Independent Group), The Arts Council of Great Britain, London, 1979. Film (40 min) by Reyner Banham and Julian Cooper.

Filmed conversation between Richard Hamilton and curator Manuela Mena on the occasion of his exhibition *Las Meninas de Richard Hamilton* at the Prado Museum, May 2010.

Interview by Nigel Finch, February 1977. Interview with Dieter Roth and Richard Hamilton.

Kaleidoscope, BBC Radio Four, 9 April 1973. Interview on Picasso.

Kaleidoscope, BBC Radio Four, 6 March 1980. Talk about Hamilton's exhibitions at Anthony d'Offay Gallery and Waddington Gallery, London.

Kaleidoscope, BBC Radio Four, 6 February 1981. Review of the Jasper Johns exhibition.

Kaleidoscope, BBC Radio Four, 11 November 1982. Interview by Paul Vaughan to mark the publication of *Collected Words*.

Kaleidoscope, BBC Radio Four, 30 March 1984. Interview on exhibition at the Museum of Modern Art, Oxford.

Late Show, BBC 2, 20 February 1990. On the occasion of the *Independent Group* exhibition.

Late Show Special, BBC 2, 6 September 1991. Discussion with Andrew Graham-Dixon on the occasion of the *Pop Art* exhibition at the Royal Academy, London.

Looking into Paintings: Episode 1: Meanings – or How Art Doesn't Imitate Life, Malachite Productions for Channel 4, London, 13 November 1985. Interview by Alistair Smith about *The citizen*.

Moving From Chaos to Form, BBC Radio Three, 21 June 1972. Joseph Beuys interviewed by Hamilton.

New Comment, BBC Third Programme, 18 November 1964. Interview by Andrew Forge produced by Leonie Cohn. Broadcast in part on 18 November 1964, on "New Comment"; in full on 5 April 1965.

Painting with Light, Griffin Film Productions, London, 1987. One of a series of six television programmes of artists working on the Quantel Paintbox.

Perspective, in *Camera*, BBC Radio Three, 30 April 1971. Interview with John Donat.

Richard Hamilton, Maya Film Productions, London, 1969. Film (25 min) directed by James Scott, made for the Arts Council of Great Britain.

Richard Hamilton, 15 mei–28 juni 1970, Brussels. Hamilton speaking on the occasion of an exhibition at the Palais des Beaux-Arts, Brussels, during his *Metamorphose de l'Objet* exhibition, 1971. Filmed by Jef Cornelis. Dutch/ English, 36:30 min.

Richard Hamilton lecture at the Victoria & Albert Museum, 9 March 2010, on the occasion of his *Modern Moral Matters* exhibition at the Serpentine Gallery, 3 March–25 April 2010.

Shock of the New, BBC 2 Television, 1980. "Commercial" by Hamilton for *The critic laughs*, included in Robert Hughes' art series for television.

Talking Art: Richard Hamilton, 14 February 1990. In conversation with Michael Craig-Martin on the occasion of the *Independent Group* exhibition at the ICA, London.

The Arts This Week, BBC Third Programme, 18 March 1970.

The Independent Group: The Impact of American Pop Culture in the Fifties, The Open University, 1975. Talk by Hamilton. First broadcast by BBC Radio for the A351 course, "Modern Art from 1848 to the Present Day."

The Obsessive Image, BBC Third Programme, 15 May 1968. Discussion with Christopher Finch, Anne Seymour and Allan Jones, produced by Leonie Cohn. Recorded 3 May 1968.

Third Ear, BBC Radio Three, 28 March 1988. Interview by Julian Spalding.

This is Tomorrow, BBC Third Programme, 17 August 1956.

Unpublished video footage of an interview conducted in 2010 by Alex Turnbull for his feature documentary, *Beyond Time* (2011), William Turnbull Studio Archive.

4. One-man and two-man exhibition catalogues (in chronological order)

Variations on the Theme of a Reaper. London: Gimpel Fils, 1950. Single-page list of exhibits.

Growth and Form. London: Institute of Contemporary Arts, 1951.

Man, Machine and Motion. Newcastle upon Tyne: University of Durham, 1955.

Richard Hamilton: Paintings 1951–55. London: Hanover Gallery, 1955. Single-page handlist.

an Exhibit, ed. Lawrence Alloway. Newcastle upon Tyne: Hatton Gallery, 1957.

Paintings, etc. '56–64. London: Hanover Gallery, 1964.

The Solomon R. Guggenheim: Six Fibreglass Reliefs. London: Robert Fraser Gallery, 1966. Poster and two foolscap sheets.

Paintings 1964–1967. New York: Alexandre Iolas Gallery, 1967.

Richard Hamilton: Collagen, Zeichnungen und Seriegraphien. Kassel: Galerie Ricke, 1967. Folded card.

Richard Hamilton: dipinti e disegni 1957–1968. Milan: Studio Marconi, 1968. Folded 12-page sheet with Italian translation of "Urbane Image" by Daniela Palazzoli.

Bilder + Zeichnungen sowie das graphische Gesamtwerk. Hamburg: Galerie Neuendorf, 1969. With phonetic German translation of "Urbane Image" by Dieter Roth.

Cosmetic Studies. Milan: Studio Marconi, 1969. Folded card.

Richard Hamilton: Graphic Work since 1963. Stuttgart: Württembergischer Kunstverein, 1969. Folded card with German text.

Richard Hamilton: Swingeing London 67, People, Graphics 1963–68. London: Robert Fraser Gallery, 1969. Four-page handlist.

Richard Hamilton. London: Tate Gallery, 1970.

Richard Hamilton: Prints. Ottawa: National Gallery of Canada, 1970. Separate French language version.

Edizioni Recenti – Recent Editions. Milan: Studio Marconi, 1971.

Richard Hamilton. Berlin: Galerie René Block, 1971. With German translation.

Richard Hamilton: Prints and Multiples. Amsterdam: Stedelijk Museum, 1971. With Dutch translation.

Hamilton. Milan: Studio Marconi, 1972. With Italian translation.

Richard Hamilton: Prints, Multiples and Drawings. Manchester: Whitworth Art Gallery, 1972.

Kent State. Berlin: Galerie René Block, 1973.

Richard Hamilton. New York: Solomon R. Guggenheim Museum, 1973.

The Prints of Richard Hamilton. Middletown: Davison Art Center, Wesleyan University, 1973.

Richard Hamilton. Berlin: Nationalgalerie, 1974. Extended German edition of Guggenheim catalogue.

Richard Hamilton: Das Graphische Werk. Frankfurt: Galerie Meyer-Ellinger, 1974.

Richard Hamilton Graphics. Edinburgh: Scottish Arts Council, 1974.

Obra Gráfica y Múltiples 1964–74. Barcelona: Galería Eude, 1975.

Paintings, Pastels, Prints. London: Serpentine Gallery, 1975.

Richard Hamilton. Gerona: La Fontana d'Or, 1976. Folded card, six A4 pages.

Richard Hamilton: Schilderijen, Pastels en Grafiek. Amsterdam: Stedelijk Museum, 1976. With Dutch translation.

Collaborations of Ch. Rotham / Richard Hamilton and/or Dieter Roth. Stuttgart: Edition Hansjörg Mayer; Cadaqués: Galería Cadaqués, 1977.

Drawings and Graphics: Richard Hamilton. Grenoble: Musée–Place de Verdun, 1977. French translation of John Russell's text for the Guggenheim catalogue.

Release: Stage Proofs and Related Works 1968–9 and 1972. London: Tate Gallery, 1977.

INTERFACEs: Artists Statements September 1977–February 1978. Manchester: Whitworth Art Gallery, University of Manchester, 1978. Catalogue/poster folded sheet.

INTERFACEs: Dieter Roth and Richard Hamilton [exh. cat. Waddington and Tooth Galleries II, London, February–March 1978]. Folded card, 9 pages.

Richard Hamilton Graphics. Vancouver: Vancouver Art Gallery, 1978.

Richard Hamilton: Studies – Studien 1937–1977. Bielefeld: Kunsthalle Bielefeld, 1978.

INTERFACEs von Richard Hamilton und Dieter Roth [exh. cat. Kunsthalle Bielefeld, May–July 1979], by Erich Franz. Bielefeld: Kunsthalle Bielefeld, 1979.

A Cellular Maze [exh. cat. Orchard Gallery, Derry, August 1983], by Rita Donagh and Richard Hamilton. Derry: Orchard Gallery, 1983.

Interiors 1964–79. London: Waddington Galleries, 1980.

Richard Hamilton: Drawings, Prints and Paintings 1941–55. London: Anthony d'Offay Gallery, 1980.

Richard Hamilton: Kent State 1970, 63–66. Amsterdam: Stedelijk Museum, 1981.

Image and Process. Hasselt: Provinciaal Museum, 1982. Broadsheet with Dutch text.

Richard Hamilton: Image and Process. Stuttgart: Edition Hansjörg Mayer in association with Tate Gallery, 1983.

Prints 1939–83. Stuttgart: Edition Hansjörg Mayer in association with Waddington Graphics, 1984.

Richard Hamilton: Grafik 1953–81. Stockholm: Nationalmuseum, 1984.

Interactions. Stockholm: Thorden Wetterling Galleries, 1987.

Richard Hamilton: Installations. Edinburgh: Fruitmarket Gallery, 1988.

Richard Hamilton: Work in Progress on Illustrations for James Joyce's Ulysses. Derry: Orchard Gallery, 1988.

Richard Hamilton: teknologi < idé> konstverk. Stockholm: Moderna Museet, 1989.

Exteriors, Interiors, Objects, People. Winterthur: Kunstmuseum Winterthur, 1990.

Richard Hamilton. London: Anthony d'Offay Gallery, 1991.

Prints: Graphic Works Continued 1984–91. Stuttgart: Edition Hansjörg Mayer in association with Waddington Graphics, 1992.

Richard Hamilton. London: Tate Gallery, 1992.

Richard Hamilton: XLV Biennale di Venezia, British Pavilion, Venice, 13 June–10 October 1993. London: The British Council, 1993.

Richard Hamilton: Site-referential Paintings. San Francisco: San Francisco Museum of Modern Art, 1996. Catalogue published in conjunction with a "New Work" exhibition organised by the San Francisco Museum of Modern Art (London: Crawford Digital Colour, 1996).

New Technology and Printmaking. London: Edition Hansjörg Mayer in association with Alan Cristea Gallery, 1998.

Richard Hamilton: Subject to an Impression. Bremen: Kunsthalle Bremen, 1998.

Tuppence Coloured. London: Edition Hansjörg Mayer in association with Alan Cristea Gallery, 2001.

Richard Hamilton: Imaging Ulysses. London: British Museum, 2002.

Collaborations: Relations – Confrontations/Dieter Roth/ Richard Hamilton. Stuttgart: Edition Hansjörg Mayer; Porto: Fundaçao de Serralves, 2003.

Richard Hamilton: Prints and Multiples 1939–2002. Winterthur: Kunstmuseum Winterthur; Dusseldorf: Richter Verlag, 2003.

Richard Hamilton: Products™. London: Gagosian Gallery, 2003.

Richard Hamilton: Retrospective: Paintings and Drawings 1937 to 2002. Barcelona: Museu d'Art Contemporani de Barcelona, 2003.

Richard Hamilton: Selected Works. Chichester: Pallant House Gallery, 2005.

Painting by Numbers. London: Edition Hansjörg Mayer, 2006.

Richard Hamilton. London: Dickinson, 2006.

A Host of Angels. Venice: Fondazione Bevilacqua La Masa, 2007.

Richard Hamilton: Protest Pictures 1963–2008. Edinburgh: Inverleith House, Royal Botanic Garden; London: Gagosian Gallery, 2008.

Virtuelle Räume. London: Edition Hansjörg Mayer in association with Kunsthalle Bielefeld, 2008.

Modern Moral Matters. Cologne: Walther König, 2010.

Richard Hamilton: Shit and Flowers. London: Alan Cristea Gallery, 2010.

Civil Rights etc. Rita Donagh and Richard Hamilton [exh. cat. Dublin City Gallery The Hugh Lane, Dublin, September 2011–January 2012], by Michael Bracewell, Declan McGonagle and Barbara Dawson. Dublin: Dublin City Gallery The Hugh Lane, 2011.

Richard Hamilton: The Late Works. London: National Gallery, 2012.

5. Selected group exhibition catalogues (in chronological order)

This is Tomorrow [exh. cat. Whitechapel Art Gallery, London, August–September 1956], ed. Theo Crosby. London: Whitechapel Art Gallery, 1956.

Nieuwe Realisten [exh. cat. Haags Gemeentemuseum, The Hague, June–August 1964], ed. W. Jos de Gruyter. The Hague: Haags Gemeentemuseum, 1964. Catalogue issued as a newspaper.

The 1964 Pittsburgh International: Exhibition of Contemporary Painting and Sculpture [exh. cat. Carnegie Museum of Art, Pittsburgh, October 1964–January 1965], foreword Gustave von Groschwitz. Pittsburgh: Carnegie Museum of Art, 1964.

European Drawings [exh. cat.], ed. Lawrence Alloway. New York: The Solomon R. Guggenheim Foundation, 1966.

Robert Fraser Gallery, London [exh. cat. Studio Marconi, Milan, June 1966]. Milan: Studio Marconi, 1966.

Drawing towards Painting 2 [exh. cat. Arts Council Gallery, London, April–May 1967]. London: Arts Council, 1967.

Ars multiplicata. Cologne: Wallraf-Richartz-Museum, 1968.

documenta IV [exh. cat. documenta, Kassel, June–October 1968]. Kassel: Druck + Verlag, 1968.

Pop Art Redefined [exh. cat. Hayward Gallery, London, July–September 1969], ed. John Russell and Suzi Gablik. London: Thames & Hudson, 1969.

Kelpra Prints [exh. cat. Hayward Gallery, London, June–July 1970]. London: Arts Council of Great Britain, 1970.

Métamorphose de l'objet: art et anti-art 1910–1970 [exh. cat. Palais des Beaux-Arts, Brussels, April–June 1970]. Brussels: La Connaissance, 1970.

British Painting and Sculpture 1960–1970: An Exhibition Organised by the Tate Gallery and the British Council, London [exh. cat. National Gallery of Art, Washington DC, November 1970–January 1971], ed. Edward Lucie-Smith. London: Tate Gallery and the British Council, 1971.

Graphik der Welt: Internationale Druckgraphik der letzten 25 Jahre [Graphics of the World: International Printed Graphics of the Last 25 Years, exh. cat. Kunsthalle Nürnberg, Nuremberg, August–November 1971], by Wolf Stubbe. St Gallen: Erker Verlag, 1971.

Combattimento per un'immagine: fotografi e pittori [Fighting for a Picture: Photographers and Painters, exh. cat. Il Museo Civico di Torino, Turin, March–April 1973], by Daniela Palazzoli and Luigi Carluccio. Turin: Associazione Amici Torinesi dell'arte contemporanea, 1973.

Grafische Techniken [Graphic Techniques, exh. cat. Neuer Berliner Kunstverein, Berlin, February–March 1973]. Berlin: Neuer Berliner Kunstverein, 1973.

Arte inglese oggi 1960–76 [British Art Today 1960–76, exh. cat. Palazzo Reale, Milan, February–May 1976]. British Council exhibition. Milan: Electa, 1976.

Pop Art in England: Beginnings of a New Figuration 1947–63 [exh. cat. Kunstverein Hamburg, February–March 1976], ed. Uwe M. Schneede and Frank Whitford. Hamburg: Kunstverein Hamburg, 1976.

The Human Clay: An Exhibition Selected by R.B. Kitaj [exh. cat. Hayward Gallery, London, August 1976]. London: Arts Council of Great Britain, 1976.

documenta VI [exh. cat. documenta, Kassel, June–October 1977]. Kassel: Paul Dierichs, 1977.

Englische Kunst der Gegenwart [Contemporary British Art, exh. cat. Künstlerhaus Palais Thurn und Taxis, Bregenz, July–October 1977], intro. Norbert Lynton. Bregenz: Verein Bregenzer Kunstausstellungen, 1977.

Malerei und Photographie im Dialog von 1840 bis heute [Painting and Photography in Dialogue from 1840 until Today, exh. cat. Kunsthaus Zürich, May–July 1977], curated by Erika Billeter. Bern: Benteli, 1977.

A Treasury of Modern Drawings: The Joan and Lester Avnet Collection [exh. cat. Museum of Modern Art, New York, April–July 1978], by William S. Lieberman. New York: Museum of Modern Art, 1978.

The Mechanised Image: An Historical Perspective on 20th Century Prints [exh. cat. Portsmouth Museum and Art Gallery, Portsmouth, 1978], by Pat Gilmour. London: Arts Council of Great Britain, 1978.

Nachbilder: vom Nutzen und Nachteil des Zitierens für die Kunst [Copies: The Uses and Disadvantages of Quoting in Art, exh. cat. Kunstverein, Hannover, June–July 1979]. Hannover: Kunstverein, 1979.

Für Augen und Ohren [For Eyes and Ears, exh. cat. Akademie der Künste, Berlin, January–March 1980], ed. René Block. Berlin: Akademie der Künste, 1980.

Instantanés [Instantaneous, exh. cat. Centre Georges Pompidou, Paris, May–July 1980], ed. Alain Sayag. Paris: Centre Georges Pompidou, 1980.

Kelpra Studio: The Rose and Chris Prater Gift [exh. cat. Tate Gallery, London, July–August 1980], intro. Pat Gilmour. London: Tate Gallery, 1980.

Printed Art: A View of Two Decades [exh. cat. Museum of Modern Art, New York, February–April 1980], ed. Riva Castleman. New York: Museum of Modern Art, 1980.

British Artists in Berlin: Two Decades of the DAAD's Artists-in-Berlin-Programme [exh. cat. Goethe Institute, London, October–November 1981], preface Wieland Schmied. London: Goethe Institute, 1981.

Druckgraphik Wandlungen eines Mediums seit 1945 [Printed Graphics: Transformations of a Medium since 1945, exh. cat. Kupferstichkabinett, Nationalgalerie, Berlin, June–August 1981], ed. Alexander Dückers. Berlin: Reiter-Druck, 1981.

Instant fotografie [Instant Photography, exh. cat. Stedelijk Museum, Amsterdam, December 1981–January 1982], ed. Els Barents. Amsterdam: Stedelijk Museum, 1981.

Momentbild: *Kunstlerphotographie* [exh. cat. Kestner-Gesellschaft, Hannover, March–April 1982], ed. Carl Haenlein. Hannover: Kestner-Gesellschaft, 1981.

Westkunst: Zeitgenössische Kunst seit 1939 [Western Art: Contemporary Art since 1939, exh. cat. Rheinhallen, Cologne, May–August 1981], ed. Laszlo Glozer. Cologne: DuMont, 1981.

'60–'80 Attitudes / Concepts / Images: Een keuze uit twintig jaar beeldende kunst / A Selection from Twenty Years of Visual Arts [exh. cat. Stedelijk Museum, Amsterdam, April–July 1982], ed. Ad Petersen and Karei Schampers. Amterdam: Stedelijk Museum, 1982.

Art contre / against Apartheid [exh. cat. Fondation Nationale des Arts Graphiques et Plastiques, Paris, November–December 1983]. Paris: Artists du monde contre l'apartheid, 1983.

Aspects of British Art from the Solomon R. Guggenheim Collection [Solomon R. Guggenheim Museum, New York, March–May 1983], by Lisa Dennison. New York: Solomon R. Guggenheim Museum, 1983.

Contemporary Masters: The World Print Awards [exh. cat. Museum of Modern Art, San Francisco, September 1983]. San Francisco: San Francisco Museum of Modern Art and World Print Council, 1983.

Photography in Contemporary Art [exh. cat. National Museum of Modern Art, Tokyo, October–December 1983], ed. Hisae Fujii. Tokyo: National Museum of Modern Art, 1983.

Artistic Collaboration in the Twentieth Century [exh. cat. Hirshhorn Museum, Washington DC, June–August 1984], ed. Cynthia Jaffee McCabe. Washington DC: The Smithsonian Institution Press, 1984.

Four Rooms, an Arts Council Touring Exhibition Devised by Howard Hodgkin [exh. cat. Liberty's, London, February–March 1984]. London: Arts Council of Great Britain, 1984.

The Hard-Won Image: Traditional Method and Subject in Recent British Art [exh. cat. Tate Gallery, London, July–September 1984], ed. Richard Morphet. London: Tate Gallery, 1984.

Pop Art 1955–70 [exh. cat. touring exhibition in Australia, organised by the International Council of the Museum of Modern Art, New York], ed. Henry Geldzahler. Sydney: International Cultural Corporation of Australia, 1985.

Antidotes to Madness? Richard Hamilton, Nam June Paik, Ree Morton, Hannah Collins and Piotr Sobieralski [exh. cat. Riverside Studios, London, April 1986], by Maureen O. Paley. Folded card. London: Riverside Studios, London, 1986.

Beuys zu Ehren [Hommage to Beuys, exh. cat. Städtische Galerie im Lenbachhaus, Munich, July–November 1986], ed. Armin Zweite: Munich: Städtische Galerie im Lenbachhaus, 1986.

Falls the Shadow: Recent British and European Art: 1986 Hayward Annual [exh. cat. Hayward Gallery, London, April–June 1986]. London: Arts Council of Great Britain, 1986.

Studies of the Nude [exh. cat. Marlborough Fine Art, London, March–May 1986], intro. William Packer. London: Marlborough Fine Art, 1986.

Aldo Crommelynck [exh. cat. Waddington Graphics, London, March–April 1987], ed. Pat Gilmour. London: Waddington Galleries, 1987.

Pop Art: USA – UK [exh. cat. Odakyu Grand Gallery, Tokyo, July–August 1987, travelled to Daimaru Museum, Osaka, September 1987; Funabashi Seibu Museum of Art, Funabashi, October–November 1987; and Sogo Museum of Art, Yokohama, November–December 1987], by Lawrence Alloway, Marco Livingstone et al. Tokyo [?]: Pop Art: USA – UK Catalogue Committee, 1987.

The International Art Show for the End of World Hunger [exh. cat. touring exhibition organised by the Minnesota Museum of Art, 1987–90], by Patterson Sims et al. New York: Artists to End Hunger, 1987.

This is Tomorrow Today: The Independent Group and British Pop Art [exh. cat. Institute for Art and Urban Resources, New York, October–December 1988], by Brian Wallis, Lawrence Alloway et al. New York: P.S.1, Institute for Art and Urban Resources, 1987.

Richard Hamilton and Tom Phillips: A Question of Style [exh. cat. Australian National Gallery, Canberra, March–June 1988], intro. Pat Gilmour. Canberra: Australian National Gallery, 1988.

Zurück zur Natur, aber wie? Kunst der letzten 20 Jahre [Back to Nature, but How? Art from the Last 20 Years, exh. cat. Städtische Galerie im Prinz-Max-Palais, Karlsruhe, April–July 1988], ed. Helga Walther-Dressler and Erika Rödiger-Dirof. Karlsruhe: Selbstverlag, 1988.

20a Bienal Internacional de Sao Paulo [exh. cat. Bienal de Sao Paulo, October–December 1989]. Sao Paulo: Fundação Bienal de São Paulo, 1989; also four-page brochure on Hamilton with essay by Richard S. Field in artist catalogue folder in British section.

Blasphemies, Ecstasies, Cries [exh. cat. Serpentine Gallery, London, January–February 1989, travelled to Norwich School of Art Gallery, Norwich, April–May 1989, and Mostyn Gallery, Llandudno, June–July 1989], ed. Andrew Brighton. London: Serpentine Gallery, 1989.

Glasgow's Great British Art Exhibition [exh. cat. Glasgow Museums and Art Galleries, March–May 1990], ed. Julian Spalding. Glasgow: McLellan Galleries, 1990.

High & Low: Modern Art and Popular Culture [exh. cat. Museum of Modern Art, New York, October 1990–January 1991], by Kirk Varnedoe and Adam Gopnik. New York: Museum of Modern Art, 1990.

The Independent Group: Postwar Britain and the Aesthetics of Plenty [exh. cat. ICA, London, February–April 1990, travelled to the IVAM, Valencia, May–September 1990; the Museum of Contemporary Art, Los Angeles, November 1990–January 1991; University Art Museum, University of California at Berkeley, February–April 1991; and Hood Museum of Art, Dartmouth College, Hanover, New Hampshire, June–August 1991], ed. David Robbins. Cambridge, MA; London: MIT Press, 1990.

The Readymade Boomerang: Certain Relations in 20th Century Art, 8th Biennale of Sydney [exh. cat. Art Gallery of New South Wales, Sydney, April–June 1990], intro. René Block. Sydney: Biennale of Sydney, 1990.

Pop Art [exh. cat. Royal Academy of Arts, London, September–December 1991, travelled to Museum Ludwig, Cologne, January–April 1992, and Centro de Arte Reina Sofía, Madrid, June–September 1992]. London: Royal Academy of Arts, 1991.

Carnegie International 1991 [exh. cat. The Carnegie Museum of Art, Pittsburgh, October 1991–February 1992]. Pittsburgh: The Carnegie Museum of Art; New York: Rizzoli, 1992.

documenta X: Short Guide / Kurztührer [exh. cat. documenta, Kassel, June–September 1997]. Ostfildern-Ruit: Hatje Cantz, 1997.

Computers & Printmaking: An Exhibition Featuring Work from a Joint Research Project at Camberwell College of Arts and Chelsea College of Art and Design, The London Institute, The Integration of Computers within Fine Art Practice [exh. cat. Birmingham Museums and Art Gallery, September–December 1999]. Birmingham: Birmingham Museums and Art Gallery, 1999.

Modern British Art at Pallant House Gallery [exh. cat. Pallant House, Chichester], by Stefan van Raay, Guy Frances et al. London: Scala, 1999.

A Survey of Photomechanical Prints [exh. cat. University of the West of England, Bristol, October 2000], ed. Carinna Parraman, Paul Thirkell et al. Bristol: Impact Press, 2000.

Encounters: New Art from the Old [exh. cat. National Gallery, London, June–September 2000], ed. Richard Morphet. London: National Gallery, 2000.

PhotoGraphics [exh. cat. Alan Cristea Gallery, London, April–May 2000], ed. Marco Livingstone. London: Alan Cristea Gallery, 2000.

Happiness: A Survival Guide for Art + Life, Mori Art Museum [exh. cat. Mori Art Museum, Tokyo, October 2003–January 2004], ed. David Elliott. Tokyo: Mori Art Museum, 2003.

Prints: Cecil Higgins Art Gallery [exh. cat. Cecil Higgins Art Gallery & Museum, Bedford, 2004]. Bedford: Trustees of the Cecil Higgins Art Gallery, 2004.

British Pop [exh. cat. Museo de Bellas Artes de Bilbao, October 2005–February 2006], ed. Marco Livingstone. Bilbao: Museo de Bellas Artes, 2005.

Covering the Real: Art and the Press Picture, from Warhol to Tillmans [exh. cat. Kunstmuseum Basel, April–August 2005], ed. Hartwig Fischer. Basel: Kunstmuseum Basel, 2005.

Drawing from the Modern 2: 1945–1975 [exh. cat. the Museum of Modern Art, New York, March–August 2005], ed. Gary Garrels. New York: Museum of Modern Art, 2005.

Print Matters: The Kenneth E. Tyler Gift [exh. cat. Tate Modern, London, November 2004–March 2005], ed. Sean Rainbird, 46–47. London: Tate Publishing, 2005.

Self Portrait: Renaissance to Contemporary [exh. cat. National Portrait Gallery, London, October 2005– January 2006, and Art Gallery of New South Wales, Sydney, February–March 2006], ed. Anthony Bond and Joanna Woodall, 196–97. London: National Portrait Gallery, 2005.

The Undiscovered Country [exh. cat. Hammer Museum, Los Angeles, October 2004–January 2005], ed. Russell Ferguson. Los Angeles: Hammer Museum, 2005.

Eye on Europe: Prints, Books and Multiples / 1960 to Now [exh. cat. Museum of Modern Art, New York, October 2006–January 2007], by Wendy Weitman and Deborah Wye. New York: Museum of Modern Art, 2006.

Galeria Cadaqués: Obres de la Col. lecció Bombelli [exh. cat. MACBA, Museu d'Art Contemporani de Barcelona, September–November 2006], ed. Roland Groenenboom. Barcelona: MACBA, 2006.

Instalaciones y Nuevos Medios en la Coleccion del IVAM: Espacio, Tiempo, Espectador [exh. cat. Institute Valencia d'Art Modern, Valencia, September 2006–February 2007], by Francisco Camps, Consuelo Ciscar et al. Valencia: IVAM, 2006.

L'Action restreinte: l'art moderne selon Mallarmé [exh. cat. Musée des Beaux-Arts, Nantes, April–July 2005], by Corinne Diserens, Jean-François Chevrier et al., 271, 273–74. Nantes: Musée des Beaux-Arts de Nantes, 2006.

Making History: Art and Documentary in Britain from 1929 to Now [exh. cat. Tate Liverpool, February–April 2006], by David Campany, Lynda Morris et al. London: Tate Publising, 2006.

Visions & Re-Visions on the Boulevard of Broken Dreams [exh. cat. Kunstverein Bremen, June–August 2006], ed. Wolfgang Hainke. Bremen: H & H Schierbrok Edition, Kunstverein Bremen, 2006.

British Vision: Observation and Imagination in British Art 1750–1950 [exh. cat. Museum voor Schone Kunsten, Ghent, October 2007–January 2008], ed. Robert Hoozee. Brussels: Mercatorfonds; Ghent: Museum voor Schone Kunsten, 2007.

Peter Saville: Estate 1–127 [exh. cat. Migros Museum für Gegenwartskunst, Zurich, November 2005–January 2006], ed. Heike Munder. Zurich: JRP|Ringier; Les Presses du réel, 2007.

Pop Art Portraits [exh. cat. National Portrait Gallery, October 2007–January 2008, travelled to Staatsgalerie, Stuttgart, February–June 2008], ed. Paul Moorhouse. London: National Portrait Gallery; New Haven, CT: Yale University Press, 2007.

The Painting of Modern Life [exh. cat. Hayward Gallery, London, October–December 2007, and Museum of Contemporary Art, Castello di Rivoli, Turin, February–May 2008], ed. Ralph Rugoff. London: Hayward Publishing, 2007.

Pop Art Is.... London: Gagosian Gallery, 2007.

Entre Chien et Loup [exh. cat. Kent Gallery, New York, September–October 2008], ed. Douglas Walla. New York, Kent Gallery, 2008.

Interieur Exterieur: Living in Art, from Romantic Interior Painting to the Home Design of the Future [exh. cat. Kunstmuseum Wolfsburg, November 2008–April 2009], ed. Marcus Brüderlin and Annelie Lütgens. Ostfildern-Ruit: Hatje Cantz, 2008.

This is Tomorrow [exh. cat. archive exhibition catalogue (1956), Whitechapel Art Gallery, London, September 2010–March 2011] (facsimile edition). London: Whitechapel Gallery, 2010.

Art et science-fiction: la Ballard Connection [exh. cat. Musée d'art moderne et contemporain, Geneva, 2011], ed. Valérié Mavridorakis. Geneva: Musée d'art moderne et contemporain de Genève, 2011.

The Mystery of Appearance: Conversations Between Ten British Post-War Painters [exh. cat. Haunch of Venison, London, December 2011–February 2012], ed. Catherine Lampert. London: Haunch of Venison, 2011.

Glam! The Performance of Style [exh. cat. Tate Liverpool, February–May 2013], ed. Darren Pih, 109–21: "Richard Hamilton: Art, Style, Personae and New Aesthetics," by Michael Bracewell. London: Tate Publishing, 2013.

Pop Art Design [exh. cat. Vitra Design Museum, Weil am Rhein, October 2012–February 2013, travelled to Louisiana Museum of Modern Art, Humlebæk, February–June 2013, and the Barbican Museum, London, October 2013–February 2014), ed. Mateo Kries and Mathias Schwartz-Clauss. Weil am Rhein: Vitra Museum; DAP, 2013.

6. Monographs and sections of books

Alloway, Lawrence. "The Development of British Pop." In *Pop Art*, ed. Lucy Lippard, 26–68. London: Thames & Hudson, 1966.

Amaya, Mario. *Pop Art ... and After.* New York: Viking, 1965.

—. *Pop as Art: A Survey of the New Super Realism*, 31–42. New York; London: Studio Vista, 1965.

Art Now, vol. 5: *Man-Made Nature*. Tokyo: Kodansha, 1971.

Aubry, Brigitte. *Richard Hamilton: Peintres des apparences contemporaines (1950–2007)*. Dijon: Les Presses du réel, 2009.

Aynsley, Jeremy, and Harriet Atkinson (eds.). *The Banham Lectures: Essays on Designing the Future*. London: Berg, 2009.

Bezzola, Tobia, and Franziska Lentzsch (eds.). *Europop*, 103–17. Zurich: Kunsthaus Zürich; Cologne: DuMont, 2008.

Bickers, Patricia, and Andrew Wilson (eds.). *Talking Art: Interviews with Artists Since 1976*, 340–45. London: Ridinghouse, 2006.

Bonk, Ecke, Hans Belting, Richard Hamilton et al. *Monte Carlo Method: A Typosophic Manual. Ecke Bonk: Typosophes sans frontières*. Munich: Schirmer Mosel, 2007.

Bracewell, Michael. *Re-make, Re-model: Art, Pop, Fashion and the Making of Roxy Music, 1953–1972*. London: Faber & Faber, 2007.

Brauer, David E. *Pop Art: US/UK Connections, 1956–1966*. Houston: The Menil Collection; Ostfildern-Ruit: Hatje Cantz, 2001.

Brown, Paul, Charlie Gere at al. (eds.). *White Heat Cold Logic: British Computer Art 1960–1980*. Cambridge, MA: The MIT Press, 2008.

Castleman, Riva. *Modern Prints since 1942*, 138–41, 165. London: Barrie and Jenkins, 1973.

Coldwell, Paul, and Barbara Rauch (eds.). *The Personalised Surface: New Approaches to Digital Printmaking*. London: FADE, Fine Art Digital Environment and University of the Arts London, 1996.

Compton, Michael. *Pop Art,* 56–61. London: Hamlyn, 1970.

—. "Pop Art in Britain." In *Pop Art*, ed. Andreas C. Papadakis, 63–73. London: Art & Design, 1992.

Cooke, Lynne. "The Independent Group: British and American Pop, a 'Palimpcestuous' Legacy." In *Modern Art and Popular Culture*. New York: Museum of Modern Art, 1990. Published in conjunction with the exhibition *High & Low*.

Coutts-Smith, Kenneth. *The Dream of Icarus: Art and Society in the Twentieth Century*, 178–80. London: Hutchinson, 1970.

Crispolti, Enrico. *La Pop Art*. Milan: Fabbri, 1966.

Crow, Thomas. *The Rise of the Sixties: American and European Art in the Era of Dissent*. London: Laurence King; New Haven, CT: Yale University Press, 2004 (first published London: Weidenfeld and Nicholson; New York: Harry N Abrams, 1996).

D'Harnoncourt, Anne, and Kynaston McShine (eds.). *Marcel Duchamp*. New York: Museum of Modern Art; Philadelphia: Philadelphia Museum of Art; Munich: Prestel, 1974.

"Eduardo Paolozzi." In *Contemporary Sculpture: Arts Yearbook 8*, 160–63. New York: Arts Digest, 1965. Interview by Hamilton.

Endicott Barnett, Vivian. *100 Works by Modern Masters from the Guggenheim Museum*, 139 and covers. New York: Harry N Abrams, 1984.

Finch, Christopher. *Image as Language: Aspects of British Art 1950–68*, 19–35. Harmondsworth: Penguin, 1969.

—. *Pop Art: Object and Image*. London: Studio Vista, 1968.

Foster, Hal. "Homo Imago" and "Richard Hamilton, or the Tabular Image." In *The First Pop Age: Painting and Subjectivity in the Art of Hamilton, Lichtenstein, Warhol, Richter, and Ruscha*, 1–16, 17–61. Princeton; Oxford: Princeton University Press, 2011.

Foster, Hal (ed.). *Richard Hamilton (October Files, no. 10)*. Cambridge, MA; London: The MIT Press, 2010.

Foster, Hal, and Mark Francis. *Pop*. 21–25. London: Phaidon, 2005.

Foster, Hal, Rosalind Krauss, Yve-Alain Bois, and Benjamin H.D. Buchloh. *Art Since 1900: Modernism, Antimodernism and Postmodernism*, 385–89. 2 vols. London: Thames & Hudson, 2004.

"From Painters, a Different Tack for Photographers." In *Frontiers of Photography*. New York: Time-Life Books, 1972.

Fuller, Peter. "The Hard-Won Image." In *Images of God: The Consolations of Lost Illusions*, 98–108. London: Chatto and Windus, 1985.

Guadagnini, Walter (ed.). *Pop Art 1956–1968*, 126–39. Milan: Silvana, 2007.

Gualdoni, Flaminio. *Richard Hamilton: una collezione '60/'70*. Milan: Studio Marconi, November 1990.

Handbuch Museum Ludwig: Kunst des 20. Jahrhunderts. Cologne: Museum Ludwig, 1979.

Jacob, Wenzel J. *Die Entwicklung der Pop Art in England*. Frankfurt: Peter Lang, 1986. PhD thesis.

Kellein, Thomas (ed.). *1968. Die Große Unschuld*. Cologne: DuMont, 2009.

Leach-Ruhl, Dawn. *Richard Hamilton: The Beginnings of his Art*. Frankfurt; Berlin: Peter Lang, 1993. Translation by Eileen Martin.

—. *Studien zu Richard W. Hamilton: Das Frühwerk*. Ann Arbor: UMI, 8718894, 1986. Dissertation, Ruhr-University, 1986.

Livingstone, Marco. *Pop Art: A Continuing History*. London: Thames & Hudson, 1990.

Maharaj, Sarat. *The Dialectic of Modernism and Mass Culture: A Study of Pop Art in Britain with Special Reference to Richard Hamilton's and Eduardo Paolozzi's Work (1935–85)*. Reading: University of Reading, 1985. Unpublished PhD thesis.

Mason, Catherine. *A Computer in the Art Room: The Origins of British Computer Arts 1950–80*. Hindrigham: JJG Publishing, 2008.

Massey, Anne. *The Independent Group: Modernism & Mass Culture in Britain 1945–1959*. Manchester: Manchester University Press, 1995.

Melly, George. *Revolt into Style: The Pop Arts in Britain*. London: Allan Lane, The Penguin Press, 1970.

Mirrors of the Mind. Portfolio of prints. New York: Multiples Inc. and Castelli Graphics, 1975.

Miyakawa, Atsushi. *About Quotation Continued*, 65–79. Alice in Mirrortown Series, No. 5, 1969.

Mortimer, Elizabeth. "Richard Hamilton." In *The Swindon Collection of Twentieth Century British Art*, 60–62. Swindon: Thamesdown Borough Council, 1991.

Obrist, Hans Ulrich. *Conversations, Volume 1*. Paris: Manuella, 2008.

—. *Formulas for Now*. London: Thames & Hudson, 2008.

Osterwold, Tilman. *Pop Art*. 210–17. Cologne: Taschen, 1989.

Richard Hamilton: Prints 1939–83. Vol. 1 of Print Catalogue Raisonné. London: Edition Hansjörg Mayer in association with Waddington Graphics, 1984.

Richard Hamilton: Prints 1984–91. Vol. 2 of Print Catalogue Raisonné. London: Edition Hansjörg Mayer in association with Waddington Graphics, 1992.

Richer, Francesca, and Matthew Rosenzweig (eds.). *No. 1: First Works by 362 Artists*, 166. New York: DAP Distributed Art Publishers, 2005.

Robertson, Bryan, John Russell, and Lord Snowdon. *Private View: The Lively World of British Art*, 258–59. London: Nelson, 1965.

Ruhrberg, Karl. "Zwischen Faszination und Kritik." In *Kunst im 20. Jahrhundert – Auswahlkatalog*, 230–32. Cologne: Das Museum Ludwig, 1986.

Russell, John, and Suzi Gablik. *Pop Art Redefined*, 73–76, 88–91. London: Thames & Hudson, 1969.

Shaw, Jeffrey, and Peter Weibel (eds.). *Future Cinema: The Cinematic Imaginary after Film*, 88–95. Karlsruhe: ZKM | Center for Art and Media Karlsruhe; Cambridge, MA; London: MIT Press, 2003.

Scharf, Aaron. "Art and Photography Today." In *Art and Photography*, 249–51. London: Allen Lane, The Penguin Press, 1968.

Schwarz, Dieter. *Kunstmuseum Wintertur*. Zurich: Swiss Institute for Art Research, 2007.

"Statements by the Artist." In *Towards Another Picture: An Anthology of Writings by Artists Working in Britain 1945–1977*, ed. Andrew Brighton and Lynda Morris, 24, 78–79, 122, 148–49. Nottingham: Midland Group Nottingham, 1977.

Taylor, Michael R. Marcel Duchamp: *Étant donnés – Manual of Instructions*. New Haven, CT: Yale University Press, 2009.

"The Pop Art Symposium: General Discussion." In *Pop Art*, ed. Andreas C. Papadakis, 48–61. London: Art & Design, 1992.

The Tate Gallery Report 1964–65, 38–39. London: Tate Gallery – HMSO, 1966.

The Tate Gallery Report 1967–68, 60–61. London: Tate Gallery, 1968.

The Tate Gallery Report 1968–70, 84–87. London: Tate Gallery, 1970.

The Tate Gallery Report 1970–72, 114–19. London: Tate Gallery, 1972.

The Tate Gallery 1980–82: Illustrated Catalogue of Acquisitions, 252–53. London: Tate Gallery, 1984.

The Tate Gallery 1982–84: Illustrated Catalogue of Acquisitions, 401–5. London: Tate Gallery, 1986.

The Tate Gallery 1984–86: Illustrated Catalogue of Acquisitions, 371–75. London: Tate Gallery, 1988.

Thistlewood, David. *A Continuing Process: The New Creativity in British Art Education 1955–65*. London: Institute of Contemporary Arts, 1981.

Tono, Yoshiaki. "Richard Hamilton." In *Chatting with Artists*, 249–65. Tokyo: Iwanami, 1982.

Vaizey, Marina. *The Artist as Photographer*, 123–25. London: Sidgwick & Jackson, 1982.

Van Deren, Coke. *The Painter and the Photograph: from Delacroix to Warhol*, 247–49, 314–15. Albuquerque: University of New Mexico Press, 1972.

Wilson, Andrew. *Richard Hamilton: Swingeing London 67 (f)*. London: Afterall Books, 2011.

Wilson, Simon. *Tate Gallery: An Illustrated Companion*, 240. 2nd ed., revised and expanded. London: Tate Gallery, 1991.

Woods, Gerald, Philip Thompson, and John Williams. *Art without Boundaries 1950–70*, 128–29. London: Thames & Hudson, 1972.

Wyver, John. *Vision on: Film, Television and the Arts in Britain*, 103–6. New York: Wallflower – Columbia University Press, 2007.

7. Articles in periodicals and newspapers

Alloway, Lawrence. "Artists as Consumers." *Image*, no. 3 (February 1961), 14–19.

—. "Art News from London: All over the Place." *ARTnews* 54, no. 3 (May 1955), 11, 65.

—. "Pop Art since 1949." *The Listener* 67, no. 1761 (27 December 1962), 1085–87.

—. "Pop Art: The Words." *Auction 1*, no. 4 (February 1968), 7–9 (reprinted in *Topics in American Art since 1945*, 119–22. New York: Norton, 1975).

—. "Popular Culture and Pop Art." *Studio International* 178, no. 913 (July–August 1969), 16–21.

—. "Re vision." *Art News and Review* 6, no. 26 (22 January 1955), 5.

—. "This is Tomorrow." *ARTnews* 55, no. 5 (September 1956), 64.

Almansi, Guido. "Humour o tragedia nella provocazione pop?" *Arte* (Milan) 215 (February 1991), 66–69.

—. "Watteau escrementizio." *Nuovi Argomenti*, no. 2 (1976), 191–94.

Arts Magazine 41, no. 8 (Summer 1967), 58. Review of exhibition, Alexandre Iolas Gallery, New York.

Aubry, Brigitte. "Le mariage du pinceau et de la lentille: le peinture hybride de Richard Hamilton." *Études Photographiques*, no. 11 (May 2002), 125–39.

—. "Produire une ambivalence: la résolution du conflit abstraction/figuration dans les 'Irish Paintings' (1983–1993) de Richard Hamilton." *Art Présence*, no. 53 (January–March 2005), 2–13.

Azizov, Zeigam. "Richard Hamilton: From Pop Art to Computer Projections." *Omnibus/documenta X*, hors série (October 1997), 13.

Banham, Reyner. "Ideal Interiors." *Architectural Review*, no. 734 (March 1958), 207–8.

—. "Man, Machine & Motion." *Architectural Review* 118, no. 703 (July 1955), 51–53.

—. "Persuading Image: A Symposium." *Design*, no. 138 (June 1960), 54–57.

—. "Representations in Protest." *New Society*, 8 May 1969, 717–18.

—. "This Is Tomorrow." *October*, no. 136 (Spring 2011), 32–34.

—. "This is Tomorrow Exhibit." *Architectural Review* 120, no. 716 (September 1956), 186–88.

—. "Vision in Motion." *Art*, 5 January 1955, 3.

—. "Work in Progress." *Architectural Review* 140, no. 833 (July 1966), 61–62. Review of exhibition, Robert Fraser Gallery, London.

Baro, Gene. "Hamilton's Guggenheim." *Art & Artists* 1, no. 8 (November 1966), 28–31.

Beechey, James. "Art and the 1960s. London and Birmingham." *The Burlington Magazine* 146, no. 1219 (October 2004), 700–2.

Behrman, Pryle. "Print Polymath." *Printmaking Today* 11, no. 2 (Summer 2002), 4–5.

Bekker, Pieter. "Richard Hamilton." *James Joyce Broadsheet*, no. 61 (February 2002), 3.

Bell, Julian. "A Rapturous Spooky Dream." *The New York Review of Books* 57, no. 13 (19 August 2010), 14.

Bell, Tiffany. *Arts Magazine* 52, no. 6 (February 1978), 33. Review of *INTERFACEs* exhibition, Carl Solway Gallery, New York.

Bergob, Christiane. "Letter from London." *Kunstforum International*, no. 71–72 (April–May 1984), 312–14. Review of *Four Rooms* exhibition at Liberty's, London.

Bevan, Roger. "Just what is it that makes Richard Hamilton so different, so appealing?" *The Art Newspaper* (June 1992), 10.

—. "Richard Hamilton: Image and Process." *Print Quarterly* 1, no. 2 (June 1984), 138–42.

Birnbaum, Daniel. "Richard Hamilton." *Artforum* 41, no. 9 (May 2003), 76.

—. "Richard Hamilton, Museum Ludwig Cologne." *Artforum* 42, no. 4 (December 2003), 141.

Blok, Cor. "Richard Hamilton: Towards a Definitive Statement?" *Museumjournaal* 15, no. 4 (September 1970), 170–75, 223.

Bohrer, Karl Heinz. "Vergiftete Visionen vom Schönen." *Frankfurter Allgemeine Zeitung*, 3 November 1975.

Bracewell, Michael. "Physics can be so Aesthetic." *The Independent on Sunday*, 12 October 2003, 8.

—. "Richard Hamilton: Toaster Deluxe." *Art Monthly*, no. 327 (June 2009), 27–28.

—. "The Thrill of it All." *Frieze*, no. 79 (November–December 2003), 78–81.

—. "This Was Tomorrow." *The Independent*, 23 May 2006, 14–15.

Brett, Guy. "Putting on the Style." *The Times*, 14 March 1970.

Brighton, Andrew. "Hamilton, IG, Mythmaking & Photography." *Creative Camera* (London), no. 303 (May 1990), 28–30.

Buck, Louisa. "Entrevista con Richard Hamilton." *Arte y Parte* 43 (February–March 2003), 19–27.

Büsser, Martin. "Pin-up à la Cézanne." *Konkret: Politik & Kultur* (September 2003), 60–61.

Burn Guy. "Crónica de Londres." *Goya*, no. 98 (September 1970), 104–6.

—. "Richard Hamilton Interiors '64–'69." *Arts Review* 32, no. 6 (28 March 1980), 155.

Burr, James. "The First 'Pop' Painter." *Apollo 91*, no. 97 (March 1970), 238.

Causey, Andrew. "A Question of Identity." *Illustrated London News*, 4 April 1970, 27.

Caves, Richard E. "Collected Words, 1953–1982." *Print Collector's Newsletter* (March–April 1983).

—. "Richard Hamilton: Prints 1939–83; Image and Process." *Print Collector's Newsletter* 15, no. 6 (January–February 1985), 221–23.

Cohen, David. "Richard Hamilton: A Knowing Consumer." *Modern Painters* 5, no. 2 (Summer 1992), 36–38.

Coleman, Roger. "Will Success Spoil Industrial Design?" *Architecture and Building* (August 1959), 296–97.

Collins, James. "Richard Hamilton: The Two Culture Theory." *Artforum* 12, no. 4 (December 1973), 58–60.

Cooke, Lynne. "Dread and Desire." *Art International* 5 (Winter 1988), 73–74.

—. "Richard Hamilton." *Parkett* 25 (September 1990), 114–20.

—. "Richard Hamilton, Pop Pioneer and Technophile." *Tile Journal of Art* (New York) 4, no. 3 (March 1991), 10.

Coppel, Stephen. "Richard Hamilton's Ulysses Etchings: an Examination of Work in Progress." *Print Quarterly* 6, no. 1 (March 1989), 10–42.

Cork, Richard. "Nomads Cross the Wasteland." *The Times*, London, 16 June 1993.

—. "Our (Old) Man in Venice." *The Times*, London, 23 July 1992.

—. "POP: Yesterday's Rebels, Today's Old Masters." *Telegraph Magazine, The Daily Telegraph*, 11 May 1991, 30–45.

Craig-Martin, Michael. "Details, Close-ups and Surfaces." *Modern Painters* 15, no. 1 (Spring 2002), 36.

Crosby, Theo. "This is Tomorrow." *Architectural Design* 26, no. 9 (September 1956), 302–4.

—. "This is Tomorrow." *Architectural Design* 26, no. 10 (October 1956), 334–36.

Crow, Thomas. "The Absconded Subject of Pop." *RES: Anthropology and Aesthetics*, no. 55/56 (Spring–Autumn 2009), 5–20.

Danneff, Tiffany. "Hunting Down the Pop Archetypes." *The Sunday Telegraph*, 23 June 1991.

Davenport-Hines, Richard. "Everyday Epics." *Times Literary Supplement*, 10 July 1992.

Del Renzio, Toni. "Richard Hamilton." *Art Monthly* (London), no. 159 (September 1992), 455.

—. "Style, Technique and Iconography." *Art and Artists* 2, no. 4 (11 July 1976), 34–39.

Denvir, Bernard. "Exhibition at the Tate." *Arts International*, no. 14 (May 1970).

DeShong, Andrew. "Will the Real Richard Hamilton Please Stand Up?" *Artweek* 5, no. 35 (19 October 1974), 1, 16.

Dimitrijevic, Nena. "Richard Hamilton: Image and Process." *Flash Art* 116 (March 1984), 42.

Dixon, Stephen, and Michael McNay. "Bone of Contention." *The Guardian*, 16 December 1976.

Dupuis-Panther, Ferdinand. "Richard Hamilton – Introspective." *Schwarzaufweiss*, 23 September 2003.

Ehrlich, Richard. "Artist's Eye." *Art and Artists* 13, no. 4 (August 1978), 40–41.

Ellis, Charlotte. "Four Rooms." *Architectural Review* 175, no. 1046 (April 1984), 62–63.

Falconer, Morgan. "Never Too Old for the Joy of Techs." *Times 2*, 23 May 2006, 20. www.thetimes.co.uk/tto/arts/article2408825.ece.

Feaver, William. "Living it up at Hotel Limbo." *The Observer*, 7 July 1991, 52.

—. "Paint Teaser of Pop." *The Observer*, June 1992.

Ferry, Bryan. "Still the Top of the Pops." *The Independent on Sunday*, 23 June 1991, 24.

Field, Richard S. "Hamilton." *Print Quarterly* 22, no. 3 (September 2005), 348–51.

Field, Simon. "Objects More or Less." *Art and Artists* 4, no. 1 (April 1969), 57–58.

Finch, Christopher. "A Fine Pop Art Continuum." *New Worlds* 51, no. 176 (October 1967), 15–19.

—. "Richard Hamilton." *Art International* 10, no. 8 (October 1966), 16–23.

—. "Richard Hamilton at the Tate." *Arts Magazine* (New York) 44, no. 6 (April 1970), 49–50.

Fischer, Alfred M. "Richard Hamilton Introspektive." *Vernissage Rheinland* 3 (2003), 15–19.

Flemming, Hanns Theodor. *Das Kunstwerk* 23, no. 3–4 (December 1969), 56, 81.

Forge, Andrew. "In Duchamp's Footsteps." *Studio International* 171, no. 878 (June 1966), 248–51.

Foster, Hal. "Arqueología de una cultura." *La Vanguardia, Culturas*, 19 March 2003.

—. "At Inverleith House." *London Review of Books* 30, no. 16 (14 August 2008), 37.

—. "At the Hayward." *London Review of Books* 29, no. 21 (November 2007), 16.

—. "Citizen Hamilton." *Artforum* 46, no. 10 (Summer 2008), 397–403.

—. "Just What Was It...?." *Artforum* 50, no. 5 (January 2012), 187.

—. "On Richard Hamilton." *London Review of Books* 33, no. 19 (6 October 2011), 37.

—. "On the First Pop Age." *New Left Review*, no. 19 (January–February 2003), 93–112.

—. "Pop Eye." *London Review of Books* 24, no. 16 (22 August 2002), 6–7.

Francis, Mark. "Richard Hamilton: London and Dublin." *The Burlington Magazine* 134, no. 1074 (September 1992), 616–18.

Frank, Peter. "Richard Hamilton at the Guggenheim." *Art in America* 62, no. 1 (January–February 1974), 97–99.

Fuller, Peter. "Close-Up." *Harpers Bazaar* (February 1970), 17.

—. "Richard Hamilton." *Aspects*, no. 10 (Spring 1980).

—. "Richard Hamilton: The Tate Gallery." *Connoisseur* 173, no. 697 (March 1970), 196.

—. "The Necessity of Art Education." *Art Monthly*, no. 47 (June 1981), 27–29. This article resulted in a lengthy correspondence between Fuller and Hamilton, published in subsequent issues of *Art Monthly*, nos. 49, 50, 51 and 53.

Gilmour, Pat. "Richard Hamilton: Graphic Retrospective." *Art Monthly* 82 (December 1984), 16–17.

—. "Richard Hamilton: Painter of Prints and Printer of Paintings." *Arts Review* 22, no. 5 (14 March 1970), 137.

—. "Symbiotic Exploitation or Collaboration: Dine and Hamilton with Crommelynck." *Print Collector's Newsletter* XV, no. 6 (January–February 1986), 194–98.

—. "The Art Films of James Scott." *Art and Artists*, no. 4 (March 1970), 16–19.

Glozer, Laszlo. "Staedische Galerie im Lenbachhaus." *Pantheon*, no. 32 (July 1974), 312–13.

—. "Tod am Bildschirm oder: Die Kunst und die Medien." *Frankfurter Allgemeine Zeitung*, 30 December 1970 (reprinted in *Kunstkritiken*, Frankfurt, 1974).

Godfrey, Tony. "Days like These; This was Tomorrow. London; Roche Court, Salisbury." *The Burlington Magazine* 145, no. 1202 (May 2003), 381–83.

Graham-Dixon, Andrew. "Popping On." *The Independent Magazine*, no. 145 (15 June 1991), 56–60.

—. "Richard Hamilton: Father of Pop." *ARTnews* 90, no. 2 (February 1991), 102–7.

Greenwood, Michael. "British Painting '74." *Artscanada* 32, no. 1, issue no. 196/7 (March 1975), 29–34.

Grieve, Alastair. "'This Is Tomorrow': A Remarkable Exhibition Born from Contention." *The Burlington Magazine* 136, no. 1093 (April 1994), 225–32.

Guasch, Anna Maria. "Qué es lo que hace a Richard Hamilton tan diferente?" *Arte* (2003), 24–25.

Halasz, Piri. "A Devastating Elegance: Richard Hamilton, Master of English Pop Art." *ARTnews* 72, no. 9 (November 1973), 86–87.

Hall, James. "The Apollo Portrait: Richard Hamilton." *Apollo* 131, no. 336 (February 1990), 101–4.

Harrod, Tanya. *Art International* XXVI, no. 2 (April–June 1983), 77–78. Review of *Collected Words*.

Hawcroft, Francis W. "Prints, Multiples and Drawings by Richard Hamilton." *Connoisseur* 179, no. 720 (February 1972), 151.

Hensher, Philip. "Bigger Than Marilyn or The Beatles." *The Mail on Sunday*, 25 November 2007, 11.

Herchenröder, Christian. "Bilder mit Abgrund." *Handelsblatt*, 18 July 2003.

Highmore, Ben. "Richard Hamilton at the Ideal Home Exhibition of 1958: Gallery for a Collector of Brutalist and Tachiste Art." *Art History* 30, issue 5 (November 2007), 712–37.

—. "Rough Poetry: 'Patio and Pavilion' Revisited." *Oxford Art Journal* 29, no. 2 (2006), 269, 271–90.

Hirsch, Faye. "Prints: Hamilton's Multiplex." *Art in America* 92, no.8 (September 2004), 48–53.

Holden, Christopher, and Roy Perry. "The Reconstruction of the Lower Panel of Duchamp/Hamilton's 'Large Glass'." *Conservator* 2 (1987), 3–13.

Iglesias del Marquet, Josep. "Una historia del pop-art." *Goya*, no. 140–41 (September 1977), 153–54.

Ishizaki, Kouichirou, Ben Yama, and Ichiou Haryu. "Richard Hamilton." *Hangwa Geijutsu* 52 (1986), 59–83.

Januszczak, Waldemar. "Popastic!" *The Sunday Times Magazine*, 19 January 2003, 14–15. www.thesundaytimes.co.uk/sto/culture/article215277.ece.

Johns, Jasper. "Duchamp," *Scrap*, no. 2 (23 December 1960), 4.

Jouffroy, Alain. "Art de demi brume à Londres." *L'Oeil*, no. 149 (May 1967), 84.

—. "L'Actualism." *Connaissance des Arts*, no. 186 (18 August 1967), 42–49.

Kaizen, William R. "Richard Hamilton's Tabular Image." *October* 94 (Autumn 2000), 113–28.

Katz, Jonathan D. "Dada's Mama: Richard Hamilton's Queer Pop." *Art History* 35, issue 2 (April 2012), 336–53.

Kaye, Caroline. *Art Monthly*, no. 151 (November 1991), 29. A response to Frank Whitford's review of d'Offay exhibition.

Kenedy, R. C. "Richard Hamilton." *Art International* XIV, no. 3 (March 1970), 45–53, 57.

—. "Richard Hamilton Visited." *Art and Artists* 4, no. 12 (March 1970), 20–23.

Kent, Sarah. "Turd Man." *Time Out*, no. 1090 (10 July 1991), 47.

Kliemann, Thomas. "Schöner wohnen mit dem Lollypop." *General-Anzeiger*, 16 July 2003.

Koldehoff, Stefan. "Ich soll der Vater der Pop-Art sein? Eher bin ich der Grossvater!" *Monopol* 4 (2007), 60–63.

Kudielka, Robert. "Tate Gallery London." *Das Kunstwerk* (Stuttgart) 23, no. 9–10 (June 1970), 44–45.

Kuspit, Donald B. "Richard Hamilton at Cowles." *Art in America* 68, no. 10 (December 1980), 153–54.

Kustow, Michael. "Richard Hamilton à la Tate Gallery." *Opus International*, no. 18 (June 1970), 49–53.

Leach-Ruhl, Dawn. "Das imaginaire Museum der Gegenwart XIV – Richard Hamilton 'Lux 50'." *Das Kunstwerk* I–XLII (Stuttgart, March 1989), 63–64.

—. "The Chronology of Richard Hamilton's Reaper Series." *Print Quarterly* V, no. 1 (March 1988), 66–71.

Lewis, Adrian. "British Avant-Garde Painting 1945–1956: Part III." *Artscribe International*, no. 36 (August 1982), 14–27.

—. "Collected Words by Richard Hamilton." *Artscribe International* 39 (February 1983), 63–66.

Lewison, Jeremy. "1991 Carnegie International, Pittsburgh." *The Burlington Magazine* 134, no. 1067 (February 1992), 146–47.

Livingstone, Marco. "Anthony d'Offay Gallery: Richard Hamilton." *The Burlington Magazine* 113, no. 1062 (September 1991), 635–36.

—. "L'héritage du pop art anglais leurres: voir double." *Art Press* 160 (July–August 1991), 18–25.

Lord, Barry. *Artscanada* 26, no. 1, Art Gallery of Ontario (February 1969), 27–28.

Loring, John. "Not Just so Many Marvellously Right Images." *The Print Collector's Newsletter* IV, no. 5 (November–December 1973), 98–100.

Lubbock, Tom. "Richard Hamilton: Altered Images." *The Independent*, 2 March 2010. www.independent.co.uk/arts-entertainment/art/features/richard-hamilton-altered-images-1914214.html.

Lynton, Norbert. "Art out of News." *The Guardian*, 25 April 1969, 10.

—. "London Letter: Hamilton." *Art International* 8, no. 10 (December 1964), 43.

—. "The Pop of Pop." *The Guardian*, 12 March 1970, 10.

Mahony, Robert. *Arts Magazine* 64, no. 7 (February 1990), 102–3. Review of exhibition, Paul Kasmin Gallery, New York.

Martens, Jutta. "Keine Angst vor dem Glanz der Reklame." *Art* (Hamburg, Gruner + Jahr) 11 (November 1990), 138–39.

Martin, Richard. "A Past as Palpable as the Present: Image and History in the Art of Richard Hamilton." *Arts Magazine* 60, no. 2 (October 1985), 80–83.

—. "Richard Hamilton." *Arts Magazine* 55, no. 2 (October 1980), 8.

Massey, Anne. "The Independent Group, London, ICA." *The Burlington Magazine* 132, no. 1045 (April 1990), 284–85.

McAvera, Brian. "Richard Hamilton, Ulysses and the Flaxman Factor." *Art Monthly* 19, no. 124 (March 1989), 19–21.

McCarthy, David. "Pop Redux." *Art Journal* 60, no. 4 (Winter 2001), 107–9.

McCorquodale, Charles. *Art International* 19, no. 10 (December 1975), 25. Review of exhibition, Serpentine Gallery, London.

McKenzie, Suzie. "In with the ART CROWD." *Radio Times* (20–26 June 1992), 25–26.

McNay, Anna. "Richard Hamilton: The Late Works." *Studio International* (1 September 2013), www.studiointernational.com/index.php/richard-hamilton-the-late-works.

McNay, Michael. "Big Daddy of Pop." *The Guardian*, 25 July 1966, 7.

—. "Painters Talking – I: Richard Hamilton." *The New Review* 2, no. 16 (July 1975), 21–28.

Melville, Robert. "One-Man Show at the Hanover." *Architectural Review* 137, no. 816 (February 1965), 141–42.

—. "The Power of the Word." *New Statesman*, 20 March 1970, 420–21.

Moffat, Isabelle. "'A Horror of Abstract Thought': Postwar Britain and Hamilton's *Growth and Form* Exhibition." *October* 94, The Independent Group (Autumn 2000), 89–112.

Moraes, Angelica. "Festa para as olhos." *Veja* (Sao Paulo, 18 October 1989), 150–54.

Morphet, Richard. "Richard Hamilton's 'Interior II'." *The Burlington Magazine* 110, no. 781 (April 1968), 219–20.

[Morphet, Richard]. *Studio International* 172, no. 884 (December 1966), p. i. Advertisement for Peter Stuyvesant Foundation Collection.

Moure, Gloria. "Entrevista a Richard Hamilton." *Cimali*, no. 11/12 (October 1981)

Mullaly, Terence. "Father of British Pop Art." *Daily Telegraph*, 21 March 1970.

Mullins, Edwin. "Father of Pop Art." *Daily Telegraph* Magazine, 13 March 1970, 45–48.

Muñoz, Jorge. "Richard Hamilton: el padre del Pop español." *Inversión y Capital*, no. 458 (28 March 2003), 66–67.

Murphy, Gavin. "'Hey, That's Interesting!': Richard Hamilton's *Finn MacCool*." *The Irish Review*, no. 39 (Winter 2008), 101–15.

Myers, Terry. *Flash Art*, no. 150 (January–February 1990), 132. Review of exhibition, Paul Kasmin Gallery, New York.

Nemeczek, Alfred. "Der Pop-Furst mischt sich ein." *Das Kunstmagazin* (Hamburg, Gruner + Jahr) 12 (December 1990), 120–21.

Nicholson, Anne. "Invisibilities in the 'Large Glass'." *The Month* 237, no. 1310 (second new series, vol. 9, no. 2) (November 1976), 383–87.

Nixon, Mignon, Alex Potts, Briony Fer, Antony Hudek, and Julian Stallabrass. "Round Table: Tate Modern." *October*, no. 98 (Fall 2001), 3–25.

Oakes, Philip. "Profits from the Present." *The Sunday Times*, 16 November 1969.

Obrist, Hans Ulrico. "Pop Daddy." *Tate Magazine*, no. 4 (March–April 2003), 60–62.

"Octogenarian Salute" (editorial). *The Burlington Magazine* 144, no. 1189 (April 2002), 203.

Odling-Smee, James. "Richard Hamilton: 'Work in Progress'." *Arts Review* 41, no. 2 (January 1989), 63–64. Review of exhibition of *Ulysses* illustrations at Arts Council of Northern Ireland Gallery, Belfast.

Ohff, Heinz. "Cosmetic Studies." *Das Kunstwerk*, no. 23 (February–March 1970), 76.

—. "Hamilton Ausstellung." *Das Kunstwerk* 23, no. 11–12 (October 1970), 71–72.

—. "Prints, 1939–83." *Das Kunstwerk* 38, no. 4–5 (September 1985), 166–67.

Overy, Paul. "Hamilton's World." *Financial Times*, 25 March 1970.

Palazzoli, Daniela. "Un lecca-lecca per l'arte." *Il Giornale*, 25 November 1990.

—. "Viaggio fuori stagione." *Domus*, no. 516 (November 1972), 52.

Palmer, Frederick. "Painting and Photography: A Love-Hate Affair." *The Artist* 103, no. 4 (April 1988), 21–23.

Perry, Arthur. "Richard Hamilton's Graphics." *Artmagazine* 10, no. 42 (February–March 1979), 37–40.

Phillips, Tom. "Cogent Consumerism." *Times Literary Supplement*, no. 4156 (26 November 1982), 1294.

Pietsch, Hans. "Fantasievoller Stratege des Wandels." *Das Kunstmagazin*, no. 4/03 (2003).

"Pop Daddy." *Vogue* (London) 127, no. 4 (15 March 1970), 90–91.

"Pop-Pionier Hamilton in Hamburg." *Der Spiegel*, no. 50 (8 December 1969), 177–79.

Potts, Alex. "Realism, Brutalism, Pop." *Art History* 35, issue 2 (April 2012), 288–313.

Poynor, Rick. "The Prophet of Pop." *Blueprint*, no. 88 (28 June 1992), 28–29.

Procktor, Patrick. "Techniculture." *New Statesman* 68, no. 1756 (6 November 1964), 710.

Ratcliff, Carter. *Art International* 22, no. 1 (January 1978), 87–88. Review of *INTERFACEs* exhibition, Carl Solway Gallery, New York.

Reichardt, Jasia. "People: Retrospective Exhibition at the Tate Gallery." *Architectural Design*, no. 345 (July 1969).

—. "Pop Art and After." *Art International* 7, no. 2 (25 February 1963), 42–47.

"Richard Hamilton." *Album*, no. 2 (March 1970), 40–42.

"Richard Hamilton." *Mizue*, no. 781 (1970), 65–79. Japanese text.

"Richard Hamilton: est-il le précurseur du pop art?" *Jardin des Arts,* no. 185 (April 1970), 61–65.

"Richard Hamilton: Fashion Plates." *London Magazine*, no. 9 (March 1970), 82–83.

"Richard Hamilton: Methoden zur Rückeroberung der Bildweld für die Kunst." *Künstler – Kritisches Lexikon der Gegenwartskunst* (Munich, 1988), 1–16.

"Richard Hamilton: Notizen zu meiner Arbeit." *Das Kunstwerk*, no. 7 (18 January 1965), 3–4, 13.

Richter, Horst. "Richard Hamilton." *Weltkunst*, 15 September 2003.

Roberts, Keith. "Current and Forthcoming Exhibitions." *The Burlington Magazine* 120, no. 905 (August 1978), 547–48. Review of *The Artist's Eye*.

Robertson, Bryan. "Firing Line." *The Spectator*, 28 October 1966, 18.

—. "The Legacy of Duchamp." *The Spectator*, 14 March 1970.

Rose, Barbara. "The Decline of the West, the Revolt of the Masses." *New York Magazine*, 22 October 1973, 112–13.

Rosenberg, Harold. "Dogma and Talent." *The New Yorker*, 15 October 1973, 115–19.

Russell, John. "A Joyce Devotee Who Saw How Sexy a Car Could Be." *The New York Times*, 27 February 2004, 29. www.nytimes.com/2004/02/27/arts/art-review-a-joyce-devotee-who-saw-how-sexy-a-car-could-be.html.

—. "All Images are Equal." *The Sunday Times*, 15 March 1970.

—. "Art News from London: Richard Hamilton." *ARTnews* 63, no. 9 (January 1965), 49.

—. "London/NYC: The Two-way Traffic." *Art in America* 53, no. 2 (April 1965), 130–31.

—. "Pop Reappraised." *Art in America*, no. 57 (July 1969), 78–88.

—. "Richard Hamilton." *Art in America*, no. 58 (March 1970), 115–19.

Sales, Enric. "Hamilton en el MACBA." *Arte* LXIV, no. 1475 (May 2003), 80.

Schlüter, Ralf. "Bilder zur Zeit." *Das Kunstmagazin* (August 2003).

Schmerler, Sarah. "Portrait of the Artist as Many Men." *Artists* (15–22 August 2002).

Seidel, Martin. "Richard Hamilton – Introspective." *Kunstforum* (August 2003), 346–48.

Shone, Richard. "Pop Art. London, Royal Academy." *The Burlington Magazine* 133, no. 1065 (December 1991), 856–57.

Singer, Fanny. "Richard Hamilton's *Chiara & chair*." *The Burlington Magazine* 154, no. 1315 (October 2012), 701–6.

—. "Richard Hamilton's *The annunciation*." *Print Quarterly* 25, no. 3 (September 2008), 267–77. Reprinted in *Tate Papers*, issue 14 (1 October 2010).

Snoddy, Steven. "'The Citizen' and 'The Subject': Richard Hamilton and Ireland." *Irish Arts Review Yearbook* 9 (1993), 163–66. http://irishartsreview.com/irisartsreviyear/pdf/1993/20492729.pdf.bannered.pdf.

Spalding, Julian. "Collected Words, 1953–82." *The Burlington Magazine* 125, no. 967 (October 1983), 631–32.

Spencer, Catherine. "The Independent Group's 'Anthropology of Ourselves'." *Art History* 35, issue 2 (April 2012), 314–35.

Spencer, Charles. "Richard Hamilton: Painter of 'Being Today'." *Studio International* 168, no. 858 (October 1964), 176–81.

Spens, Michael. "Richard Hamilton: 'Protest pictures'." *Studio International* (29 August 2008), www.studiointernational.com/index.php/richard-hamilton--protest-pictures-/.

Spurrier, Raymond. "A Sign of the Times." *The Artist* 99, no. 2 (February 1984), 16–19.

Stonard, John-Paul. "Image Resolution." *Artforum* 51, no. 7 (March 2013), 137–38.

—. "Pop in the Age of Boom: Richard Hamilton's 'Just what is it that makes today's homes so different, so appealing?'." *The Burlington Magazine* 149, no. 1254 (September 2007), 607–20.

—. "The 52nd Biennale. Venice." *The Burlington Magazine* 149, no. 1253 (August 2007), 576–78.

Sylvester, David. "Art in a Coke Climate." *The Sunday Times Magazine*, 26 January 1964, 17–23.

Tallman, Susan. "Richard Hamilton's Ulysses." *Arts Magazine* 63, no. 1 (September 1988), 23–24.

Tarantino, Michael. "Richard Hamilton." *Artforum* 27, no. 1 (September 1988), 158.

Tatransky, Valentine. "Richard Hamilton." *Art International* XXVI, no. 3 (July–August 1983), 34–38.

"The Bride Stripped Bare by Richard Hamilton, Even." *Tate Art Magazine*, Tate Modern Special, no. 21 (November 2000), 56–59.

Thirkell, Paul. "From the Green Box to Typo/Topography: Duchamp and Hamilton's Dialogue in Print." *Tate Papers*, issue 3 (1 April 2005). www.tate.org.uk/research/publications/tate-papers/green-box-typotopography-duchamp-and-hamiltons-dialogue-print.

Tickner, Lisa, and David Peters Corbett. "Being British and Going… Somewhere." *Art History* 35, issue 2 (April 2012), 206–15.

Tisdall, Caroline. *The Guardian*, 10 October 1975, 8. Review of exhibition at Serpentine Gallery, London.

Tyler, Kim. "Three Films and the Art of Richard Hamilton." *The Art Book* 14, no. 4 (November 2007), 69–71.

Wagner, Anne. "Tomorrow is Here Again." *London Review of Books* 34, no. 19 (11 October 2012), 24–25.

Walker, John A. "Hamilton's Influence." *Art Monthly*, no. 159 (September 1992), 7.

Ward, Ossian. "Richard Hamilton: History Boy." *Time Out*, posted 18 March 2010. www.timeout.com/london/art/richard-hamilton-history-boy.

Watkins, Nicholas. "An Interview with Victor Pasmore." *The Burlington Magazine* 143, no. 1178 (May 2001), 284–89, 288.

Weingart, Brigitte. "This was Tomorrow." *Texte zur Kunst* 13, no. 51 (September 2003), 160–66.

Whitfield, Sarah. "Pop Art and Photography." *The Burlington Magazine* 149, no. 1257 (December 2007), 873–75.

Whitford, Frank. "Les Origines britanniques du Pop Art." *Revue de l'Art*, no. 30 (1975), 77–81, 110–11.

—. "Veneer All Through." *Art Monthly*, no. 149 (September 1991), 3–5.

Winter, Peter. "Die Falltü ist die Botschaft." *Frankfurter Allgemeine Zeitung*, 15 January 1991.

—. "Richard Hamilton: Exteriors, Interiors, Objects, People." *Das Kunstwerk* 44, no. 3 (March 1991), 64–65.

—. "Richard Hamilton: Studien 1937–77." *Pantheon* 36, no. 4 (October 1978), 374–75.

Wood, Jeremy. *Pantheon* 38, no. 3 (July–September 1980), 226. Review of exhibitions, Anthony d'Offay Gallery and Waddington Gallery, London.

Wood, Paul. "Richard Hamilton." *Artscribe International* 72 (November–December 1988), 77–78.

Wullschlager, Jackie. "The Shock of the Ordinary." *The Financial Times*, 13 October 2007, 15. www.ft.com/intl/cms/s/0/ffd64352-7928-11dc-aaf2-0000779fd2ac.html#axzz2iqVrRsqv.

Yeomans, Richard. "Basic Design and the Pedagogy of Richard Hamilton." *Journal of Art and Design Education* 7, no. 2 (1988), 155–73.

Index

A

Adorno, Theodor W. 94 and 267
Adrià, Ferran 11, 193 and 324-326
Allen, Deborah 129
Alloway, Lawrence 54, 56-58, 71-73, 75, 93, 104, 268, 312, 313 and 316
Antonioni, Michelangelo 176
Apollinaire, Guillaume 318
Artschwager, Richard 99, 104, 316 and 319
Ascott, Roy 317
Avedon, Richard 318
Avery, Ronald 67 and 311

B

Bacon, Francis 98, 178, 184, 186, 201-204, 206, 235, 268, 312 and 323
Baghramian, Nairy 134
Baldessari, John 193, 319
Balzac, Honoré de 172 and 276- 278
Banham, Peter Reyner 68-70, 74, 75, 93, 94, 125-129, 237, 309, 311, 312, 315 and 321
Barker, Clive 320
Barnett, Correlli 126
Barthes, Roland 125, 170 and 202
Baudelaire, Charles 169, 175 and 178
Baudrillard, Jean 125 and 247
Bayes, Walter 308
Baxter, Iain 203 and 318
Beaton, Cecil 314
Beethoven, Ludwig van 267
Bell, Larry 187 and 316
Bellmer, Hans 315
Bengston, Billy Al 316
Benjamin, Walter 101, 170, 275
Berlin, Irving 100
Bernal, John Desmond 64
Bernstein, Sidney 312
Beuys, Joseph 187, 318, 320 and 321
Bevan, Aneurin 314
Bill, Max 70, 192 and 314
Blair, Tony 235, 248 and 325
Blake, Peter 129, 192, 313, 315
Blum, Irving 94 and 316
Bochner, Mel 319
Bonk, Ecke 193 and 324
Bracewell, Michael 125, 128, 132, 276 and 277
Braun, Artur 130
Braun, Erwin 130
Brausen, Erica 312
Brecht, Bertolt 94
Breuer, Marcel 321
Bronowski, Jacob 67
Broodthaers, Marcel 95, 188, 318 and 321
Brookes, Fred 317 and 318
Brown, Scott 248
Büchel, Christoph 134
Buckland Wright, John 206 and 310
Buckley, Stephen 191 and 317
Budgen, Frank 311
Bunting, Basil 192, 316 and 317
Byars, James Lee 319 and 321

C

Cage, John 188, 317, 318 and 320
Campbell, Alastair 325
Caro, Anthony 190, 270 and 322
Carpenter, Edmund 275
Carter, Tony 317
Cassatt, Mary 169
Casson, Hugh 312-314
Caulfield, Patrick 317
Cézanne, Paul 96, 98, 131, 204 and 276
Chadwick, Lynn 310
Chaimowicz, Marc Camille 189, 270 and 322
Chamberlain, Neville 308
Chaucer, Geoffrey 309
Clair, René 67
Coldstream, William 310
Conegliano, Cima da 248 and 274
Connard, Philip 309
Cooper, Julian 321
Copley, William 92, 186, 205 and 319
Copley, Noma 314, 315 and 317
Cordell, Frank 311
Cordell, Magda 73 and 313
Cornelis, Jef 12, 200, 201, 269 and 320
Cornell, Joseph 316
Courbet, Gustave 170, 172, 276 and 277
Craig-Martin, Michael 102 and 104
Creeley, Robert 186 and 316
Crosby, Harry Lillis “Bing” 100 and 101
Crosby, Theo 73, 128, 311 and 312
Crommelynck, Aldo 206, 218, 320, 322, 323
Cummings, Constance 310 and 312
Cunningham, Merce 188, 317 and 318
Curnoe, Greg 189, 318 and 322
Curtis, Liz 242

D

Dalí, Salvador 315
David, Catherine 271
Davies, Elidir 311
Dawber, Sir Guy 307
Deane, Seamus 241
Debord, Guy 245
Degas, Edgar 170
Delaroche, Paul 276
Deleuze, Gilles 132
Deneuve, Catherine 320
Denselow, Robin 242 and 243
Dietz, Dieter 319 and 320
Dine, Jim 186 and 317
Doane, Mary Ann 238
D’Olivier, Louis-Camille 278
Donagh, Rita 10-12, 61, 187, 205, 235, 240-242, 301, 317, 319, 322, 323 and 326
Dubuffet, Jean 202 and 314
Duchamp, Marcel 10, 11, 15, 74, 92, 93, 102, 103, 154-157, 204, 205, 235, 268, 269, 272, 277, 310, 311, 314, 315, 317-320, 324 and 325
Duchamp, Teeny 92, 318
Dunne & Raby 134
Dürer, Albrecht 207,

E

Eames, Charles 174 and 321
Eames, Ray 174 and 321
Earl, Harley 314
Elgar, Edward William 245
Eliot , T. S. 311
Evans, Merlyn 307
Eyck, Jan van 177, 178 and 248

F

Ferlinghetti, Lawrence 316
Ferry, Bryan 192, 316, 317, 321 and 323
Filliou, Robert 191 and 315
Flachslander, Herr 307
Foot, Michael 314
Forster, Noel 317
Foster, Hal 11, 12, 102, 103, 169, 177, 236 and 245
Foucault, Michel 245
Fra Angelico 15, 17, 235, 269, 275 and 325
Francis, Mark 12 and 323
Fraser, Robert 100, 132, 235, 317, 318 and 319
Freeman, Robert 316
Freud, Lucian 203 and 235
Fried, Michael 171
Froshaug, Anthony 311
Fuller, Buckminster 189 and 313

G

Gaitskell, Hugh 236, 250, 251, 315 and 316
Genzken, Isa 134
Gertler, Mark 307
Gheerbrant, Bernard 310 and 311
Ghirlandaio, Domenico 100
Giacometti, Alberto 310 and 312
Giedion, Siegfried 63, 64, 68, 70 and 310
Ginsberg, Allen 316
Gonzalez-Foerster, Dominique 134
Goode, Joe 316
Goya, Francisco de 11 and 326
Gowing, Lawrence 70, 312 and 314
Greenwood, Nigel 320
Gregory, Peter 309 and 311
Griggs, Brendan 323
Grigson, Geoffrey 309
Gris, Juan 99
Gropius, Walter 126 and 314
Guggenheim, Solomon R. 105 and 242
Gugelot, Hans 130
Gursky, Andreas 171

H
Haacke, Hans 193 and 319
Haas-Heye, Otto 127 and 308
Haffner, Heinz 319
Hall, Stuart 238 and 246
Hamilton, Albert William 307
Hamilton, Constance Elizabeth 307
Hamilton, Dominica (Dominy) 310
Hamilton, George Heard 272, 313 and 314
Hamilton, Peter 307
Hamilton, Roderic 312 and 315
Hamilton, Stella 307
Hamnett , Nina 308
Hardy, Thomas 309
Harrison, Tony 247
Head, Tim 192 and 317
Heaney, Seamus 241
Heartfield, John 318
Hedley, Gill 12 and 323
Hélion, Jean 311
Henderson, Nigel 61-66, 69, 72, 74, 191, 205, 272 and 310-312
Henri, Adrian 317
Hepworth, Barbara 94 and 203
Hirschhorn, Thomas 248
Höch, Hannah 175
Hockney, David 94, 187, 268, 315, 317 and 320
Hodgkin, Howard 268, 270, 317 and 322
Holbein, Hans 178 and 239
Holland, Ralph 318
Holzer, Jane 130
Hopps, Walter 92, 93 and 316
House, Gordon 311, 316 and 317
Hughes, Robert 322
Humphries, Lund 65, 311 and 315
Hunt, Ronald 316
Huws, Richard 307

I
Irwin, Robert 187 and 316

J
Jackson, F. Ernest 308
Jackson, Jack 127
Jagger, Mick 100,318 and 319
Johns, Jasper 10, 93, 95, 96, 99, 102, 103, 187, 203,315, 317, 318, 320 and 322
Johnstone, William 83 and 311
Joyce, James 10, 16, 17, 62, 97, 241, 309, 310, 317, 322 and 324
Judd, Donald 133

K
Kahler, Dean 239, 240 and 246
Kandinsky, Vasili 276
Kennedy, John F. 130, 174, 237 and 315
Kepes, György 63 and 64
Kitaj, R. B. 187, 203 and 315
Klee, Paul 67
Klein, Franz 202 and 314
Klein, Yves 174,
Kooning, Willem de 175, 202, 314 and 318
Knight, Patricia 100, 173, 174 and 237
Knowles, Alison 316
Knox, George 313
Kroll, Alex 125 and 127
Kruk, Vinca 133

L
Lacey, Bruce 132
Lancaster, Mark 12, 128, 191, 315, 316 and 317
Langan, Peter 270 and 280
Lannoy, Richard 311
Larsson, Ingvar 323
Laurent, Yves Saint 130
Leckey, Mark 134
Le Corbusier (Charles Édouard Jeanneret-Gris) 66, 67, 70, 71, 73, 74 and 311
Lee, Jennie 314
Léger, Fernand 310
Leonhart, Dorothea 239
Levine, Sherrie 201
Levy, Benn 310, 312 and 314
LeWitt, Sol 206 and 319
Lichtenstein, Roy 93, 97, 101, 102, 107, 129, 132, 171, 175, 176, 186, 203, 207 and 318
Lippi, Fra Filippo 17
Loew, Heinz 307
Loewy, Raymond 129
Lohmann, Julia 134
Loren, Sophia 129
Ludwig, Peter 317

M
Maharaj, Sarat 64 and 324
Maldonado, Tomás 314
Malévich, Kazimir 276 and 311
Magritte, René 312
Man Ray (Emanuel Radnitzky) 74, 187, 307 and 312
Manet, Édouard 95, 98, 170, 171, 172, 175 and 177
Margiela, Martin 133
Marten, Helen 134
Martin, Mary 319
Martin, Sherrill 320
Masaccio 178
Massey, Anne 12, 61, 69 and 93
Mastroianni, Marcello 320
Matisse, Henri Émile Benoît 309 and 311
McHale, John 50, 52, 73, 311 and 313
McLuhan, Marshall 177, 237 and 275
McQueen, Steve 242
Meindertsma, Christien 134
Meninsky, Bernard 307
Merz, Mario 192 and 321
Mesens, E. L. T. 64, 308 and 309
Metzger, Gustav 132, 191, 317 and 320
Meyer, E. J. 72
Miller, Lee 64, 310, 311 and 312
Milton, John 275
Miró, Joan 315
Moholy-Nagy, Lászlo 63, 64, 71, 126, 128, 130, 177 and 319
Monnier, Jackie Matisse 324
Monnington, Walter Thomas 309
Monroe, Marilyn 73, 104, 175, 236 and 314
Moore, Henry 94 and 203
Morisot, Berthe 169 and 174
Morland, Dorothy 311
Morphet, Richard 11, 12, 15, 105, 125, 131, 169, 174, 241, 243, 247, 248, 274 and 319
Morris, Mali 317
Morris, Robert 186 and 319
Morris, William 126
Muybridge, Eadweard 171 and 273
Mullin, Stephen 321
Mulvey, Laura 175
Munari, Bruno 128
Munnings, Alfred 309

N
Nauman, Bruce 319
Nesbitt, Judith 325
Newby, Frank 321
Niro, Robert de 319
Nitsch, Hermann 189 and 317

O
Oldenburg, Claes 93, 99, 186, 203, 316, 318 and 319
Ono, Yoko 188 and 317
O'Reilly, Terry 309
Orwell, George 310
Orwell, Sonia 310 and 320

P
Paik, Nam June 189, 248 and 317
Painlevé, Jean 68, 72 and 75
Painlevé, Paul 68, 72 and 75
Palma, Brian de 176, 318 and 319
Paolozzi, Eduardo 69, 129, 310, 311, 312 and 317
Paschke, Ed 319
Pasmore, Victor 12, 54, 56-58, 71, 72, 74, 128, 203 and 312- 314
Paulin, Tom 241
Penrose, Roland 64, 74, 205, 272 and 308-312
Picabia, Francis 316
Picasso, Jacqueline 320
Picasso, Pablo 11, 98, 127, 206, 276, 277, 308, 309, 315, 320 and 326
Pickard, Tom 316
Pierce, Harry 317
Polke, Sigmar 201
Pollock, Jackson 202 and 314
Poussin, Nicolas 172, 205 and 276
Power, E. J. «Ted» 202, 314 and 316
Prater, Chris 316 and 317
Presley, Elvis 94, 95 and 100
Price, Cedric 192, 315 and 321
Pulford, Arthur 312

R
Rams, Dieter 130, 131, 191 and 322
Rauschenberg, Robert 133, 171, 191, 318 and 322
Ray, Julia 314
Read, Herbert 64, 72 and 309
Reece, Gordon 245 and 246
Regan, Michael 322
Reichardt, Jasia 318
Reimann, Albert 127
Reimann, Klara 127
Renzio, Toni del 311
Richards, Keith 318
Riley, Bridget 317 and 322
Roberts, William 307
Rogers, Richard 274
Röntgen, Wilhelm 68
Rooney, Hugh 243 and 246
Rose, Andrea 323
Rose, Barbara 320
Rose, Bob 310
Rosenquist, James 186 and 318
Roth, Dieter 10, 16, 120, 186, 197, 220, 268, 315, 317, 318, 321, 322 and 325
Rothko, Mark 202 and 314
Rowntree, Kenneth 314
Rugg, Matt 317
Ruscone, Francesco Gnecchi 69, 70 and 74
Ruscha, Ed 93- 97, 99, 101, 134, 171 and 188
Ruskin, John 126
Russell, Sir Walter 307 and 308

S
Saenredam, Pieter Jansz 248 and 274
Said, Edward 267
Sands, Bobby 243
Schwitters, Kurt 10, 316, 317, 318 and 326
Scott, James 236, 237 and 319
Serra, Richard 248
Seurat, Georges-Pierre 177
Shannon, Claude 268
Scherman, Betsy 316
Sohm, Hans 320
Smith, Richard 191, 313 and 315
Smithson, Alison 61 and 93
Smithson, Peter 61, 69, 169 and 312
Smithson, Robert 319
Snow, Peter 246 and 247
Spoerri, Daniel 189 and 315
Stapp, Dr. John 70
Stephenson, Ian 317
Still, Clyfford 202 and 314
Stirling, James 311
Stonard, John-Paul 237 and 276
Strozzi, Zanobi 308
Struth, Thomas 171
Sutherland, Graham 312
Sylvester, David 125, 236, 308 and 313

T
Tambimuttu, Meary James Thurairajah 308
Tàpies, Antoni 202 and 314
Taylor, Elizabeth 100
Thatcher, Margaret 170, 242, 245, 246, 270 and 322
Thomas, Dylan 308
Thomas, Nancy 317
Thompson, D'Arcy Wentworth 64, 65, 75, 104 and 310
Thunderbird, Ford 316
Tilson, Joe 186 and 320
Tinguely, Jean 187, 315 and 317
Tinguely, Eva 314
Titian 172, 173 and 276
Todolí, Vicente 10, 11, 13, 276 and 325
Turnbull, William 69, 310 and 311
Turner, William 205
Tyler, Kenneth 321

V
Van Gogh, Vincent 73
Vanunu, Mordechai 248 and 326
Vautier, Ben 193 and 315
Velázquez, Diego 11, 98, 99, 174, 272, 277 and 326
Velden, Daniel van der 133
Venturi, Robert 248 and 274
Vermeer, Johannes 174
Verushka 130
Ville, Nick de 317
Voelcker, John 50, 52, 73 and 313
Vollard, Ambroise 276 and 309
Vostell, Wolf 186, 317 and 319

W
Wagenfeld, Wilhelm 130
Waley, Arthur 310
Walker, John A. 317
Wall, Jeff 171
Walters, John 317
Watkins, Jonathan 325
Watson, Peter 309 and 310
Warhol, Andy 93- 97, 100, 101, 104-106, 129, 171, 175-177, 186, 204, 205, 236, 240, 316 and 318
Webb, Mary 317
Wedgwood, Josiah 126
West, Franz 134
Whyte, Lancelot Law 65, 72 and 311
Wiener, Martin 126
Wilder, Billy 314
Williams, Emmett 187 and 315
Williams, Raymond 237
Wilke, Hannah 191 and 321
Wilson, Colin St John 70 and 311
Wittkower, Rudolf 66
Wright, Frank Lloyd 105 and 106
Wright, William Matvyn 307

Z
Zein, Kurt 322

Illustration Credits

In addition to the lenders who supplied photographs, the publishers are grateful to the following for supply images for reproduction:

© Henderson Estate, p. 66
Courtesy Archivio Fotografico © La Triennale di Milano. Photo Farabola, p. 70
Architectural Press Archive/RIBA Library Photographs Collection, p. 73
Photo: © Alex Delfanne, p. 80
Photography © The Art Institute of Chicago, p. 88
Photo: © Rheinisches Bildarchiv Köln, pp. 89 y 123
© Courtesy of the artist and Gagosian Gallery, pp. 96 and 99
Courtesy Roy Lichtenstein Foundation, p. 97
Courtesy of the artist and Tate, p. 104
Colección Malla i Figueras, © Xavi Busquets, pp. 120 and 221
© Rita Donagh, p. 132
© 2013. The National Gallery, London/Scala, Florence, pp. 185, 188 and 274
Photo: Tony Evans/Timelapse Library Ltd., p. 240
© Paul Graham. Courtesy Pace Gallery and Pace/MacGill Gallery, New York, p. 245
© Kenneth Jarecke/Contact Press Images, p. 247
© Wolfgang Tillmans, courtesy Maureen Paley, London, p. 266
© Philadelphia Museum of Art, p. 277
Courtesy Lee Miller Archive, p. 310 (below)
Courtesy Whitechapel Gallery, p. 312 (below)
Courtesy George Cserna, p. 315
Courtesy Derek Morris, p. 317 (above)
Courtesy Brian De Palma and West End Films, p. 318 (third image)
Courtesy James Klosty, p. 318 (fourth image)
Courtesy of the Guggenheim, New York, p. 320 (fourth image)
Courtesy Maria Gilissen, p. 321 (third image)
Courtesy Greg Curnoe, p. 322 (third image)
Courtesy Barry Joule, p. 323 (third image)
Courtesy William Feaver, p. 324 (above)
Courtesy Paul Laidler, p. 326 (centre)